The Planning and Preparations for the Battle of Kursk

Volume 1

Valeriy Zamulin

Translated and Edited by Stuart Britton

 Helion & Company Limited

Helion & Company Limited
Unit 8 Amherst Business Centre
Budbrooke Road
Warwick
CV34 5WE
England
Tel. 01926 499 619
Email: info@helion.co.uk
Website: www.helion.co.uk
Twitter: @helionbooks
Visit our blog at blog.helion.co.uk

Published by Helion & Company 2021
Designed and typeset by Mary Woolley (www.battlefield-design.co.uk)
Cover designed by Paul Hewitt, Battlefield Design (www.battlefield-design.co.uk)

Text © Valeriy Zamulin 2021. English edition translated and edited by Stuart Britton © Helion & Company 2021
Images © as individually credited
Maps drawn by Barbara Taylor © Barbara Taylor; maps drawn by George Anderson © Helion & Company

Front cover: Field Marshal Erich von Manstein (right) and General Hermann Hoth with a group of 4th Panzer Army headquarters officers discussing the operational situation for the upcoming Kursk offensive zone, June 21, 1943. (Bundesarchiv, Bild 101I-022-2927-26, photo: Heinz Mittelstaedt)

Every reasonable effort has been made to trace copyright holders and to obtain their permission for the use of copyright material. The author and publisher apologize for any errors or omissions in this work, and would be grateful if notified of any corrections that should be incorporated in future reprints or editions of this book.

ISBN 978-1-914059-22-3

British Library Cataloguing-in-Publication Data.
A catalogue record for this book is available from the British Library.

All rights reserved. No part of this publication may be reproduced, stored in a retrieval system, or transmitted, in any form, or by any means, electronic, mechanical, photocopying, recording or otherwise, without the express written consent of Helion & Company Limited.

For details of other military history titles published by Helion & Company Limited contact the above address or visit our website: http://www.helion.co.uk.

We always welcome receiving book proposals from prospective authors.

Contents

List of Maps 4
Table of Acronyms 5

Part I: "'Citadel' … was the final attempt to retain our initiative in the east" 6
Part II: "It would be better if we grind down the enemy on our defenses …" 277

Index 559

List of Maps

In colour section

1. OKH Operational Order No. 6 from 15 April 1943.   II
2. Tomarovka – Iakovlevo – Syrtsevo sector.   III
3. Prokhorovka – Psel River sector.   IV
4. Kursk Bulge Soviet defence plan and German offensive scheme within the framework of Operation Citadel.   V
5. "Vatutin's Plan": 7th Guards Army Voronezh Front defences and anticipated direction of German offensive.   VI
6. Lipovyi Donets – Northern Donets sector.   VII
7. 7th Guards Army main and second line defences, 1 July 1943 (15th Guards Rifle Division and 36th Guards Rifle Division exclusive).   VIII

Table of Acronyms

A – Army
A-AD – Anti-aircraft Division
A-AR – Anti-aircraft Regiment
AOAS – Aerial Observation, Alerting and Signals
AR – Artillery Regiment
ATAR – Anti-tank Artillery Regiment
ATR – Anti-tank Rifle
Bn. – Battalion
CAR – Cannon Artillery Regiment
CC – Cavalry Corps
DATAR – Destroyer Anti-tank Artillery Regiment
G – Guards
HAR – Howitzer Artillery Regiment
Hvy – Heavy
RD – Rifle Division
Recon. Art. Bn. – Reconnaissance Artillery Battalion
SCR – Supreme Command Reserve
Sep. – Separate
TBr. – Tank Brigade
TC – Tank Corps
TR – Tank Regiment

Part I

"'Citadel' ... was the final attempt to retain our initiative in the east"

If you want to learn something from history,
then I will remind you not to underestimate the Russians.

Heinz Guderian[1]

Such was the assessment that one of the plan's inspirers and a key participant, Field Marshal E. von Manstein, gave in his memoirs regarding the Wehrmacht's summer 1943 offensive.[2]

---

1   The former Colonel General of the Wehrmacht, who was the driving force behind the creation of the German panzer forces, made this assertion in a conversation with the British military historian and military theoretician B.H. Liddell Hart after the Second World War. See B. Liddell-Hart, *Po tu storonu kholma* [*On the other side of the hill*] (Moscow: AST, 2014, p. 36. This is the Russian translation of Liddell-Hart's *The German Generals Talk* (1948).

2   Erich von Manstein (real family name Lewinski) (1887-1973), General Field Marshal of the German Army (1942). Von Manstein had the reputation as the Wehrmacht's most gifted military strategist. He was a veteran of the First World War. During the invasion of the Soviet Union in 1941, he commanded Army Group North's LVI Panzer Corps, which operated in the Baltic region. In September 1941 he assumed command of the Eleventh Army that was operating on the Crimean Peninsula. For his capture of Sevastopol on 11 July 1942, he acquired the honorific title of "Field Marshal". Next, the army under the command of von Manstein was transferred to Leningrad with the mission to capture the city but failed in its effort to do so. In November of 1942, he was appointed the commander of Army Group Don, the forces of which in December 1942 unsuccessfully attempted to free Paulus' army that was encircled in Stalingrad. From February 1943 until March 1944, von Manstein commanded Army Group South. In February and March 1943, he conducted the successful counterblow against the forces of the Southwestern and Voronezh Fronts in Ukraine, as a result of which their offensive was not only stopped, but they were forced to yield back a significant amount of already liberated territory, including the major industrial and administrative center of Khar'kov, as well as Belgorod. For this success, von Manstein was awarded the Oak Leaves to the Knight's Cross. In February 1943 he proposed the idea of cutting off the Kursk salient, which later became the basis of Operation Citadel. In the course of the Battle of Kursk, his troops were able to penetrate 35 kilometers into the Voronezh Front's defenses and to reach the outskirts of Prokhorovka Station, where a major battle involving a large number of tanks and self-propelled guns took place, which entered history as the Battle of Prokhorovka. However, he was unable to carry out the offensive's missions, and moreover, after breaking through the first and second defensive belts of the Soviet forces, the threat arose of the encirclement of

The assertion that the Wehrmacht supposedly had the initiative by the start of the Battle of Kursk is unjustified. As a result of the destruction of Paulus' Sixth Army on the Volga and the powerful counteroffensive conducted later, the initiative had gone fully over to the Red Army. Therefore, in the spring of 1943, after the painful setback suffered by the Soviet forces in Ukraine (which had no significant influence on the course of the war), it was only possible to speak of a Wehrmacht attempt to regain the initiative. Other German commanders and military chiefs openly recognized this. For example, Field Marshal E. von Kleist noted, "After the unsuccessful operation in the summer of 1942 and after Weiss' army group was crushed [In January and February 1943], the German Army on the Eastern Front had lost the initiative."[3] General D. von Choltitz, who commanded the 11th Panzer Division prior to the Battle of Kursk, and later the XXXXVIII Panzer Corps, seconded this opinion. In his memoirs, which were published in the West already after the war, he wrote, "In this period [the spring of 1943], the Supreme High Command was fully preoccupied with the preparation for its final major offensive – which as Hitler was hoping – was supposed to return the strategic initiative to us."[4] The desire of the former Commander-in-Chief of Army Group South to give the greatest weight and significance to the results of his "backhand blow" in Ukraine and the recapture of Khar'kov is understandable; the conception and implementation of this operation were brilliant, and earned him deserved laurels, which is precisely why the assessments of the German generals vary so widely.

However, let us return to the main subject of research, and before laying out and analyzing the Wehrmacht's preparations for the Battle of Kursk, it is necessary to describe at least briefly Germany's military and political situation at the end of March 1943, which is to say, at the moment the Soviet-German front became stabilized following the winter campaign.

Approaching the end of the second year of war with the USSR, where did the Third Reich now stand? To put it briefly, the country had entered a stage of deep crisis. The Soviet Union, despite the staggering defeats suffered in the first stage of the war, had withstood the most powerful blows against its armed forces; the Red Army remained intact, and the Soviet military industry had been evacuated to the east, where now by beginning of 1943 its productivity was constantly increasing. The German offensive of 1942 had failed to accomplish its main objectives – the seizure of the oil-rich Caucasus and the isolation of the center of the Soviet Union from its southern regions. On the contrary, its most powerful grouping under the command of General (later Field Marshal) F. Paulus had suffered a stunning defeat; 91,000 military servicemen

---

    his group's forward combat forces. Therefore, on the night of 16-17 July 1943, the Field Marshal was forced to initiate the withdrawal of his forces back to the offensive's start line. In the winter of 1944, he suffered a major defeat at Korsun'-Shevchenkovskii at the hands of the 1st and 2nd Ukrainian Fronts, and a significant portion of his group was encircled and partially destroyed. On 4 January 1944, because of constant disagreements with Hitler, he was withdrawn into command reserve. After the war, he was sentenced to 18 years of imprisonment by a British court for military crimes on the occupied territory of the Soviet Union. He was released in 1953. He provided a description of the planning for Operation Citadel and his participation in it in his memoirs *Poteriannye pobedy* [*Lost Victories*].

3   Khristoforov, V., Makarov, V., and Khavkin, B., "Field Marshal von Kleist in the Lubianka" (No. 5, 2010), p. 94.
4   Choltitz, D., *Soldatskii dolg: Vospominaniia generala vermakhta o voine na zapade i vostoke Evropy, 1939-1945* [*Soldier's duty: Recollections of a Wehrmacht general about the war in the West and East of Europe, 1939-1945*] (Moscow: Tsentrpoligraf, 2015), p. 137.

alone had fallen into captivity, including 24 generals and 2,500 officers. In addition, five German armies had either been fully destroyed or had been rendered combat ineffective, and 22 German divisions had been smashed. The prominent representative of Nazi Germany's political leadership, the Minister of Armaments A. Speer recalled, "We were shaken by the outcome of the Battle of Stalingrad, and we were not even struck so much by the tragic fate of the soldiers of the Sixth Army as by the fact that Hitler, possessing such enormous power, was unable to prevent the catastrophe. After all, prior to this all of the failures had been offset by victories, which caused us to forget immediately about the suffered losses. This was the first time that nothing similar was foreseen."[5]

In reality, all of the results obtained by the summer campaign of 1942 had been erased by the Red Army's counteroffensive. In the course of the fighting of the winter of 1942-1943, its troops, having seized the strategic initiative, hurled the enemy back from the Volga and the foothills of the Caucasus Mountains all the way to the Maloarkhangel'sk – Ryl'sk – Belgorod line and further beyond to the Molochnaia River, having thereby regained a total of 480,000 square kilometers of territory. This is larger than contemporary area of Italy, Austria and Hungary taken together. In separate sectors the advance to the west amounted to up to 700 kilometers. Moreover, the territory that the Wehrmacht surrendered between the Volga and Donets Rivers was not only enormous, but also very important in an economic respect. Since the middle of 1942, the German *Ostheer*'s rear services and Reich Ministries had actively set out to exploit these lands. In addition, at this moment the threat now hung as well over the loss of what German economists and industrial representatives considered to be the most important regions for the Reich's economy, the Donets coal basin and the Nikopol ore mines.

Even more substantial and extremely dangerous were the direct consequences flowing from this military catastrophe for the armed forces of Germany and its allies, the most important of which were the heavy losses in manpower. Over 21 months of the war, the Wehrmacht's strength in personnel on the Eastern Front had fallen dramatically. Between 1 October 1942 and 31 March 1943 alone, its ground forces had lost 1.3 million men dead, missing or sick in the fighting on Soviet territory. At the same time (over this same period), Germany had managed to send only 1.1 million men to the front, just 84percent of the suffered losses.[6] In addition, great damage had been done to its satellites' armies; over this same period, they had lost 800,000 servicemen.[7] As of 1 April 1943, there were 2,732,000 servicemen in the combat formations of Germany's four army groups that were operating in the East.[8] This was substantially less than those who had crossed the border of the Soviet Union back on 22 June 1941 (for further details, see Table 1), yet by now the Soviet-German front ran along a front of 2,100 kilometers.

---

5   Speer, A., *Vospominaniia* [*Memoirs*] (Moscow: Zakharov, 2010), p. 333.
6   *Sovershenno sekretno! Tol'ko dlia komandovaniia: Strategiia fashistskoi Germanii v voine s SSSR. Dokumenty i materialy* [*Totally classified! Only for the command: Strategy of Nazi Germany in the war with the USSR. Documents and materials*] (Moscow: Nauka, 1967), p. 489.
7   Bleier, W., Drexler, K., Förster, H. and Hass, H., *Germaniia vo Vtoroi Mirovoi Voine (1943-1945)* [*Germany in the Second World War (1943-1945)*]; translated from the German by A.I. Dolgorukov, V.A. Artemenko and I.I. Karabutenko (Moscow: Voenizdat, 1971), p. 226.
8   National Archives and Records Administration USA [henceforth NARA US], T.78, R.581, F.000597.

Table 1: The availability of the main types of forces and means in the Wehrmacht troops on the Eastern Front, 1 April 1943[9]

Army Group	Divisions			Men	Tanks		Guns
	Infantry	Panzer	Total	Total	Total	En route	Total
A	8	1	9	321,800	43	35	581
South	26 (4)	13	39	548,000	887	389	928
Center	70 (5)	8	78	1,221,000	396	181	2,732
North	42 (5)	-	42	642,000	10	7	2,119
Total on the Eastern Front	147	22	169	2,732,000	1,336	612	6360

Note: Numbers in parentheses indicate the number of divisions resting and recuperating in reserve.

Equally important as a matter of concern, from the start of 1943, concomitant with the dwindling strength of the German corps and divisions resulting from the heavy losses were the lowering of the quality and training of the soldiers and officers German *Heer*, because those who had done much for the Reich's victories in the first stage of the war were now gone. The problems with manpower were forcing the increased use of recruits of non-German nationality from occupied countries (even with elite SS troops), who were not necessarily burning with the desire to "pull the chestnuts out of the fire" for their subjugators, even though having wound up in the Wehrmacht, they were forced to submit to its regulations. This led to increased tensions within the units and elements, and the dissipation of their combat effectiveness. By the summer of 1943, for example, in some infantry divisions of Army Group South, Germans comprised only 60percent of the ranks; the rest were Slovaks, Czechs, Alsatians, Slovenians, Poles and even Russian prisoners of war. Moreover, the number of the latter was rising so rapidly that already in August 1943, the OKH sent a special order to the troops, which demanded that Russian prisoners did not exceed 15percent of the total manpower in divisions at the front. At the same time, the decline in the individual training of the soldiers and non-commissioned officers, which became noticeable after Stalingrad, increased particularly after the Battle of Kursk, in the course of which a significant portion of the well-trained men who had prior combat experience would be lost as casualties. This became one of the most important outcomes of this major battle and a substantial factor in the successes of the Red Army in the second stage of the war.

The German mobile divisions, which played a key role in the achievement of great victories in the first stage of the war had also incurred very heavy losses in tanks, self-propelled guns and transport vehicles. I will remind the reader that on 22 June 1941, the Wehrmacht crossed the border of the Soviet Union having 19 full-strength panzer divisions, which numbered 3,300 tanks. By 1 April 1943, the panzer forces on the Soviet-German front had a total of 1,336 tanks,

---

9   NARA US, T.78, R.581, F.000597

of which less than half – 612 – were serviceable. Moreover, Army Group South had 66percent of these, because there was very little in the way of free reserves at the time, so in order to conduct the Field Marshal's counterblow in Ukraine, even his group had to scrape together anything that was combat-ready. After the conclusion of this operation, these tanks and self-propelled guns remained with Army Group South for Operation Citadel. In the rest of the army groups, there was very few tanks and self-propelled guns. For example, Army Group Center, which was holding the largest sector of the front that extended for more than 1,100 kilometers, at that moment possessed only 396 tanks, of which just 181 were operational. In the other two army groups, there were practicaliy nor armored vehicles at all: Army Group A had just 43, 35 of which were operational, and Army Group North had just 10 (7 of which were operational)[10]; see Table 1 for more details.

In a report on 9 March 1943, the General Inspector of Panzer Troops Heinz Guderian wrote:

> German panzer divisions were designed to have four tank battalions, with a total strength of roughly 400 tanks per division. If the number of tanks falls appreciably below the 400 mark, then the whole organization (its manpower and vehicle strength) is no longer in true proportion to its potential offensive power. At the moment we unfortunately have no panzer division which, in this sense, can be said to possess complete combat efficiency. Our success in battle this year, and even more so next year, depends on the recreation of that efficiency.[11]

This quote can be illustrated by the information regarding the woeful state of affairs in Army Group South, which I repeat, had the largest tank park at that time. On 1 April 1943, of the 887 tanks in its tank pool, only 386 were serviceable, which is to say less than 44 percent. In the elite SS Panzergrenadier Division *Leibstandarte Adolf Hitler*, which was under Army Group South's command from February 1943, there were only 29 operational tanks (including two Tiger tanks) on 17 March, after the fighting for Khar'kov and its surrounding area subsided.[12] A similar situation existed in the other mobile divisions of Manstein's group as well; their panzer regiments numbered, as a rule, not more than 35 operational combat vehicles.[13]

The large shortage of armored fighting vehicles and the inability of the German industry to satisfy even the day-to-day needs of the troops forced the Wehrmacht high command to reduce these divisions' tables of organization and equipment (TO&E). From 1 January 1943, an ordinary (not SS) full-strength panzer division was supposed to have 107-120 tanks (according to their respective TO&E), instead of the former 200. However, as time would show, already on the eve of the Battle of Kursk, the Germans were unable to achieve even these target numbers, including in Army Group South, which right up to the start of the fighting continued to hold first place among the army groups in the number of armored fighting vehicles. This compulsory

---

10 NARA US, T.78, R.581, F.000597.
11 As cited in Koltunov, G.A. and Solov'ev, B.G., *Kurskaia bitva* [*Battle of Kursk*] (Moscow: Voenizdat, 1970), p. 20. This quote can be found on page 295 of the English translation of Guderian's memoirs, entitled *Panzer Leader* and published by Da Capo Press in 2002.
12 Isaev, A.E., *1943: Ot tragediia Khar'kova do Kurskogo proryva* [*1943: From the tragedy of Khar'kov to the Kursk breakthrough*] (Moscow: Veche, 2008), p. 138.
13 Ibid., p. 139.

measure to reduce the establishment number of tanks reduced the "staying qualities" and "endurance" of the German panzer divisions. In the previous TO&Es for the panzer divisions, there were hidden internal reserves, which a panzer division commander could efficiently use in a complex situation in order to mitigate (to a certain degree) errors in planning the combat operations or reconnaissance, and without the need to appeal to higher command for support. For example, if an enemy attack proved to be stronger than expected or enemy resistance was more stubborn than anticipated. Now the panzer division no longer had such a "cushion", and thus the previously high effectiveness and results were largely a thing of the past, especially against the backdrop of the growing power of the Red Army's forces. Moreover, in early 1943, the Wehrmacht's troops were experiencing a serious deficit in other weapons as well. In separate cases the shortage of them reached up to a third of table strength. For example, in the spring of 1943, Army Group North's Sixteenth Army had a deficit of 18percent of machine guns, 24percent of light mortars, 25percent of carbines, 26percent of heavy field howitzers, and 33percent of heavy infantry guns.[14]

In connection with this, the role of the artillery had substantially grown. By the spring of 1943, it had become the infantry's primary combat strength multiplier, both when holding their lines and when planning an offensive. On 1 April 1943, there were 6,360 artillery pieces in the four army groups on the Eastern Front. At first glance this number is impressive, several times greater than the number of tanks and self-propelled guns, but when compared with the problems standing in front of the Wehrmacht, this was just a pittance. For comparison's sake, by the start of the Battle of Kursk, the Soviet Central Front alone had more artillery than all of the German armies combined in the east.

At the same time, the Wehrmacht had begun to be deprived of one more important advantage it had once held over the Red Army – its much greater mobility, which to a great extent facilitated its successes in the first two years of the war. From the middle of June 1941 up to January 1943 alone, the German *Ostheer* had lost more than 50percent of the nearly 500,000 wheeled motorized vehicles with which its troops had started the war. On the Stalingrad axis between August 1942 and January 1943 alone, approximately 75,000 vehicles had been destroyed or captured by Soviet forces.[15] As a result, the German high command had also been forced to cut the table strength of motorized transport, primarily in the infantry divisions. If in 1941 each infantry division was supposed to have 902 vehicles, then in 1943 – just 834. In practice the situation with equipping these divisions with vehicles even by their reduced TO&Es was just as difficult as with the tanks; even the divisions assigned to the main offensive for 1943 – Operation Citadel – were unable to receive their authorized number of motorized transport vehicles. In the period of preparing for the summer fighting, the share of horses, and even cattle in moving the troops and equipment of the German ground forces and those of their allies had noticeably increased, especially in the divisions surrounding the Kursk salient by the springtime of 1943, since the majority of them had suffered heavy losses in vehicles in the course of the Red Army's successfully conducted Ostrogozhsk – Rossosh and Voronezh – Kastornoe offensives. At this time, even the panzer divisions were facing this particular difficulty, since coming out of

---

14 Bleier et. al., *Germaniia vo Vtoroi Mirovoi Voine*, p. 226.
15 Samsonov, A.M., *Stalingradskaia bitva* [*Battle of Stalingrad*] (Moscow: Nauka, 1983), p. 514.

winter they found they had more horses than vehicles, in part because the animals were better able to handle the springtime muds of 1943.

Thus, the Wehrmacht had a lack of the necessary strength and means in order to create a firm defense of the front that had become temporarily stabilized by the end of March 1943. Their inability to increase them quickly, together with the declining level of combat training of the men, became the primary objective factor that to a great extent determined the offensive nature of its plan for the summer campaign of 1943.

The defeat at Stalingrad was a shock not only for the Reich's leadership and ruling elite; it also greatly shook the faith of the German soldiers, in whom the mindset of a victor had been persistently cultivated and nurtured by Nazi propaganda. General D. von Choltitz, who commanded the XVII Army Corps back then, wrote:

> Each man right up to the junior officer and even the ordinary soldier began to grasp the obvious: It was impossible to conduct the war any longer by such methods. Up until then the German soldier had dutifully complied with his higher command and its plans. He relied on his superiors, had faith in them and believed in their inherent superiority over the adversary. When military fortune betrayed us at Stalingrad, this faith collapsed among a great number of the soldiers and officers of all levels and types of service.[16]

At the same time, the manifestations of decay and the decline in discipline began to spread in Germany's armed forces. On 19 March 1943, the Reich's Minister of Propaganda J. Göbbels wrote in his personal diary: "The road from Rostov to Taganrog is similar to the road of retreat at Dunkers. As is obvious in such "withdrawals", we are losing an enormous number of weapons, and first of all, heavy weapons ... The rear areas in the course of three and a half years of war have turned into zones of corruption."[17] In February, the OKW[18] issued an order regarding "conduct during a retreat", which demanded tenacity of the soldier when holding each clump of ground. Those who failed to carry out orders were subject to be shot.

In the spring of 1943, a directive letter signed by Hitler went out among the troops, which noted the rise of criminality and moral decay among the officers' staff. Here are just a few examples from this document:

> One officer in a series of petitions in order to receive compensation for the damage to a number of bags that happened as the result of incendiary bombs called them

---

16   Choltitz, *Soldatskii dolg*, p. 132.
17   Bleier, et. al., *Germaniia v Vtoroi Mirovoi voine*, p. 230.
18   Germany's armed forces (Wehrmacht) were created on the basis of a law from 16 March 1935 and consisted of the *Heer* (army), *Luftwaffe* (air force) and *Kriegsmarine* (navy). After 1938, following the abolishment of the Ministry of War, an administrative structure, the *Oberkommando der Wehrmacht* (or Supreme High Command of the Armed Forces), which was located in Berlin, stood at the head of them. Although the Germany ground forces were part of the Wehrmacht, between 19 December 1941 and 30 April 1945, they were formally subordinate to Adolf Hitler personally (as the Supreme Commander-in-Chief of the Army) and to his chief of staff, and not subordinate to the OKW. The *Oberkommando des Heeres* (Supreme High Command of the Army) and its headquarters were located in Brandenburg's city of Zossen (in its suburb of Wünsdorf).

"completely destroyed" and received 10,000 Deutsch Marks in return. In reality, these bags contained only lightly damaged, insignificant items.

... An officer – the commandant of a camp in Ukraine – throughout a lengthy period of time despite existing orders arbitrarily released prisoners of war in exchange for bribes. This, evidently, contributed to the partisan movement ….

... One officer repeatedly, in the presence of subordinates, expressed demoralizing views about the army. In addition, he expressed doubt in the prospects of a German victory! Officers and soldiers talked about his statements ...

... One officer on the Eastern Front, using the pretext of illness, declined to participate in an upcoming battle; and managed to obtain a stay in a medical facility and eventual evacuation back to the Fatherland. Upon returning to the front six months later, taking advantage of bad weather, he feigned a fever for several days in order to avoid service in forward positions ...

... One officer, having learned of a pending major attack by the troops under his command, shot himself in the hand in order to be relieved of participation in this attack. He was sentenced to death for self-mutilation ...

... One officer sold a captured typewriter to a different department, claiming it as his own, and received 700 Deutsch Marks for it, which he kept for himself. When an investigation began, he instructed his subordinate to give false testimony to the court. Despite being confined to his quarters, he arrived with travel accessories at the home of an officer of an allied government and began to entreat him for help in fleeing across the border or in hiding him from German military authorities.[19]

The listed crimes were not isolated cases, but examples of a significant number of similar cases. In June 1943, a special court for the Wehrmacht was created under the Reich military tribunal, which received the authority to punish military service personnel with death or lengthy prison sentences for criticizing the military leadership or the Führer himself.

Because of the major setbacks suffered on the Soviet-German front, agitation and unrest increased among the higher German command staff. The situation with Colonel General R. Schmidt, the commander of the Second Panzer Army, the troops of which since the end of March 1943 had been occupying the defenses south and east of Orel, can serve as the clearest example. As has become clear only recently, this military commander played a special role in the process of forming the general plan for Operation Citadel; in essence, it was he who first conceived this idea (I will dwell on this fact below). Hitler held him in high respect at this time and considered him to be an up-and-coming military commander. However, the events of the preceding winter had greatly affected Schmidt. On 15 April 1943, the Gestapo intercepted a letter to Germany, in which he shared unflattering opinions regarding the Reich's military and political leadership. On 12 January 1948, Schmidt gave the following testimony to a NKVD investigator:

During my command of the panzer army, I sent several letters to my brother Hans Schmidt, who lived in Berlin; in these letters I criticized the Supreme High Command,

---

19 TsAMO RF, F.32, Op.11306, D.436, ll. 251-266.

as well as Hitler, Göring, Himmler and others for their inept leadership of military operations, accusing them of their lack of talent, while simultaneously expressing the intention to leave the army under the pretext of illness. The indicated letters were intercepted by a military censor and served as the justification for my arrest with the accusations of expressing vitriol toward Hitler, agitating against the war and having the intention to desert from the army. The Chief Arbiter Zak had me arrested in the city of Orel with the approval of General Field Marshal Keitel.

After being arrested in Orel, I was delivered by airplane to Hitler's headquarters in Rastenburg (East Prussia), where I was subjected to an interrogation by Colonel General Zeitzler – the Chief of the General Staff. After the interrogation, I was taken to Berlin, where for the next several days I was held under home arrest in my apartment; then I was sent to a prison in the Moabit area in Berlin on 1 May 1943. I remained under arrest from 1 May until early July 1943, after which I was freed from prison thanks to a petition for my release in front of Hitler by his adjutant, Lieutenant General Schmundt.[20]

The former panzer army commander can be considered extremely lucky. On 10 July 1943 Schmidt was released from custody, and two months later, on 20 September, having been discharged from the army, he was even given a monthly pension of 1,050 Deutsch Marks.

However, this case was only the "tip" of the iceberg. At this time, there existed a multi-tentacled opposition to Hitler within the herirarchy of the German Army, headed by Colonel General Beck, who was planning to overthrow of the government. A number of highly-posted officers and generals in the Kursk area were involved with this plot, including General H. Lanz, the commander of an army detachment of the same name under the command of Army Group South; his chief of staff General H. Speidel (the future Chief of Staff of Army Detachment Kempf); Army Group Center's chief of operations Colonel von Treskow; the intelligence chief of this same army group Colonel von Hersdorf; and others. Even Army Group Center's commander-in-chief General Field Marshal Günther von Kluge was aware of the plans to do away with Hitler.[21] At the beginning of 1943, the opposition grouping within the *Heer* had become so strong that it undertook two unsuccessful attempts to assassinate Hitler: On 13 March, there was an attempt to blow up the airplane in which Hitler was returning to Berlin from Smolensk (the headquarters of Army Group Center); and in Berlin, there was a plan to assassinate Hitler during his inspection of captured weapons on the holiday Remembrance Day.

The restoration of the Wehrmacht's lost potential demanded the ramped-up work of industry and an influx of cheap labor, but even here serious problems arose. Between 14 and 24 January 1943, a meeting had taken place in the Moroccan city of Casablanca between the United States President F. Roosevelt and the British Prime Minister W. Churchill, which resulted in a number of important decisions with the aim of increasing pressure on Germany, including the increased bombing of its territory in order to inflict damage to its economic potential that would

---

20 Schmundt was later shot after the assassination attempt against Hitler. Schimdt's interrogation by the NKVD is from the Central Archive of Russia's FSB (the later incarnation of the NKVD and KGB) [TsA FSB Rossii], D. N-21139, T.1, l. 57.
21 Berthold, W. *42 pokusheniia na Adol'fa Gitlera* [*42 plots against Adolf Hitler*]; translated from the German by G. Rudogo. (Smolensk: Ruschich, 2003), p. 263 and 266.

be difficult to repair, place psychological pressure on the German people, and thereby achieve Germany's unconditional surrender as soon as possible. Prior to this, only England's Royal Air Force, and sporadically, the air force of the USSR, had conducted raids against Reich territory, but now the United States Air Force would become involved in the air campaign. At the end of January 1943, the Allied command announced that at the given moment, air operations would comprise their main form of conducting war against Germany. They launched air strikes against both industrial targets and the living quarters of cities with the aim of "undermining the morale of the German people to such an extent, that their capability to put up armed resistance will fatally weaken." Three air raids, conducted between 6 March and 4 April 1943 against Germany's largest center of heavy industry and coal mining, the Ruhr region, were particularly powerful and destructive. The Ruhr valley produced 75percent of Germany's coking coal, more than 60percent of Germany's pig iron and steel, and almost 60percent of its high-quality steel alloys. The scale of destruction was colossal. The bombing of the cities was so thorough (so-called "blanket bombings") that post-damage assessment did not count destroyed buildings, but entire hectares of built-up areas that had been turned into ruins. The raids destroyed not less than half of the more than 300 factory buildings of the Krupp industrial concern, more than 350 hectares of Essen's residential areas, and the center of the Ruhr – Westphal industrial area. The Reich capital was no exception; on 2 March Berlin suffered a massive bombing raid of unprecedented size. According to the information of the German Housing Commission, between 1 October 1942 and 30 September 1943, 914,171 apartments in Germany were destroyed by bombing, including 49,303 in Berlin, 178,712 in Dusseldorf, 133,286 in the Essen district, and 242,578 in Hamburg.[22] In the future, bombing missions over the Reich would continue, and their tempo and intensity would only increase. For example, in the course of an air raid by the British Bomber Command, on the night of 23-24 May 1943 2,500 tons of bombs fell on Dortmund, which was a greater tonnage than the Luftwaffe dropped on Great Britain over the entire year of 1943.[23] On 30 May, when bombing Wuppertal, the British for the first time used incendiary bombs, from which 3,500 inhabitants of the city perished.[24]

Such massive air raids substantially slowed the output of important types of military production and the materials for their production, and also complicated the realization of Adolf Hitler's program of panzer production for 1943, which had been worked out by the Ministry of Military Industry after a conference with the Führer on 22 November 1942. This program included specific goals that were also important for the subject of the given research, such as the production of 90 F. Porsche "Tiger (R)" armed with the 88mm gun (the Ferdinand heavy tank destroyer) before 12 May 1943, and the production of new PzKpfw VI Tiger tanks by the Henschel firm at a starting rate of 25 machines per month, which would increase to 50 machines per month by June 1943.[25]

Germany did not have the possibility to offer reliable protection to even strategic targets, not to mention living quarters. It had committed virtually all of the forces of the anti-aircraft artillery and Luftwaffe into the furnace of the fighting in the East. According to German historians, Germany's Luftwaffe lost approximately 7,000 aircraft in the winter of 1942-1943

---

22 Bleier, et. al., *Germaniia vo Vtoroi Mirovoi voine*, p. 224.
23 Toppel, R., *Kursk 1943: Die groste Schlacht der Zweiten Weltkriegs*, 2017, p. 16.
24 Ibid.
25 Klink, E., *Das Gesetz des Handelns. Die Operation "Zitadelle" 1943* (Stuttgart, 1965), p. 44.

on the Eastern Front. On 9 April 1943, the General Inspector of the Luftwaffe E. Milch announced to J. Göbbels that according to cautious estimates, only after November 1943 would it be possible "given a calm situation, to meet the British, and only in the following spring, which is to say, a year from now, pay them back in the same way. ... Prior to this, the British are able, if I understand everything correctly, to turn the majority of the Reich into fragments and ashes."[26] Afterward, the Minister of Propaganda wrote in his diary: "Because of the war in the East, we have been significantly deprived aerial superiority above Europe, and now, at the very least, in this respect we must yield to the mercy of the British."[27]

It should be noted that the air strikes by the Allied air forces not only had direct influence on the course of the war – they were destroying Germany's economic potential – but also an indirect influence. The protocols of interrogations of prisoners and deserters from the Wehrmacht divisions that were located in the area of the Kursk salient, found in the files of the TsAMO RF [Central Archives of the Russian Federation's Ministry of Defense], show that the bombings of the cities had a large and negative impact on the morale of the military servicemen, especially among the rank and file and the non-commissioned commanders.

At the same time, the flow of labor resources from the East began to dwindle, especially of qualified workers, that were so necessary for the industry. This became particularly perceptible already in the autumn of 1942. The Soviet high command had learned not to allow enormous "pockets" like those that had formed in 1941 and early 1942, while a significant portion of the youth and specialists from the occupied countries had already been forcibly taken to Germany; only those who did functional activities in the rear areas of the operational troops remained. According to the evidence of the Reich Minister of Armaments A. Speer, by the start of April 1943, a deficit of 2,100,000 workers existed in all the branches of the economy,[28] and this when Germany throughout the year of 1943 would make use of up to 6,300,000 prisoners of war and foreign workers.[29]

Rather unexpectedly, the thoughts of Hitler and von Manstein on this subject show up in the transcript of the conference in the headquarters of Army Group South on 11 March 1943:

> **The Führer**: The issue of cadres is our most important question and one of the largest problems. The German is the best soldier, best creator and best organizer. The Italian is a good worker, but the Russian works two to three times better than any Italian. Russians are the best workers of all that we have. Each Russian worker that we send for work in Germany is for us a most important source of capital.
>
> **Field Marshal von Manstein**: For all that, this is incorrect – to initiate a hunt for people, take them to Germany, and then treat them badly. It would be much more proper to conduct a voluntary campaign of recruitment here, gather the people into

---

26 Toppel, *Kursk 1943*, p. 16.
27 Bleier, et. al., p. 223.
28 Speer, A., *Vospominaniia* [*Memoirs*] (Moscow: Zakharov, 2010), p. 347. The English-language translation of Speer's memoirs is entitled *Inside the Third Reich: Memoirs (1942-1945)* published by Avon back in 1971.
29 *Velikaia Otechestvennaia voina. Kratkaia istoriia* [*Great Patriotic War. Short history*] (Moscow: Voenizdat, 1965), p. 232.

battalions, treating them well to come to a consensus. This would be a splendid task for the command teams of the Reich's employment service, which are presently practically inactive here.

The Führer: The employment service and its command teams are reviled by all sides. Nevertheless, (turning to Schmundt[30]), we want to return once again to the problem of employing workers here. Of course, it is necessary to treat the Russian workers well. If they receive normal food, have the possibility to write letters home, even they will work contentedly and won't cause any problems.[31]

Even if you don't consider the norms of human morality and legality, which this man, who unleashed a world holocaust, had long ago tossed aside and forgotten, and only rely on a rational underpinning, nevertheless, reading these words, you won't understand: "What was the sense of exterminating hundreds of thousands of Russians through starvation and in the crematoria of death camps, if they were so valuable for the Reich?"

By the start of 1943, the deficit of working hands began to make itself felt now in the occupied areas of the USSR as well. Several factors influenced this. First was the relentless removal of healthy young workers for work in Germany. Second, the natural and significant loss of life because of the hard conditions of life, anti-partisan actions and genocide with respect to separate nationalities was continuing. Third, the population of occupied territories were more actively striving to evade compulsory labor. The flow of young people into the woods to join the partisans was increasing because of the systematic terror and the increasingly successful partisan struggle against the backdrop of major victories by the Red Army. However, the Wehrmacht's losses were rising, and its troops were in need of constant, fresh batches of recruits (or conscripts). This forced Berlin in January 1943 to make the decision to remove all of the exemptions from active duty belonging to Germans employed in military industry, and to direct them into the combat units, while "guest workers from the east" and prisoners were to occupy their vacated positions of employment, but it was also necessary to find this resource. Thus, at the end of 1942, the measures to confiscate food products and to mobilize labor force were strengthened. For example, an order from 25 November 1942 to the operational rear areas of Army Group Center directed with no equivocation that in addition to the "pacification of areas [the anti-partisan struggle], the task of the troops consists in revealing food reserves and harvesting agricultural output, as well as selecting laborers."[32]

The Wehrmacht's major defeats became the catalyst for the development of the partisan movement; from the second half of 1942, its scale in the rear areas began gradually to expand. In addition, Moscow took a number of steps to support and strengthen it. All this led to fact that Hitler at the end of April 1943 had to issue a special "anti-partisan" directive, in which he ordered: "Consider the struggle with banditry [that was the official Nazi Germany reference to partisans] as equally significant to combat operations at the fronts. The operational departments

---

30 Hitler's personal adjutant.
31 Schwarz, E., *Die Stabilisierung der Ostfront nach Stalingrad. Mansteins Gegenschlag zwischen Donez und Dnjepr im Früjahr 1943. Studien und Dokumente zur Geschichte des zweiten Weltkrieges.* Band 17. Muster Schmidt Verlag (Göttingen, 1986), p. 259.
32 Müller, N., *Vermacht i okkupatsiia* [*Wehrmacht and occupation*] (Moscow: Veche, 2010), p. 197.

of the army headquarters and army group headquarters should direct it. This struggle must be conducted systematically."[33]

However, the main problem remained the Red Army, the power of which was increasing, and its high command had plainly mastered the hard lessons of the preceding years of the war. From the beginning of 1943, the already difficult situation on the Soviet-German front began to deteriorate with each passing day. Soviet forces had developed the offensive to the south and southwest, swiftly depriving the Wehrmacht of vast territory and resources, while armed resistance and sabotage on the lines of communication were growing in the rear areas. At this time, in the zones of responsibility of certain army groups, the military authorities began automatically to assign the civilian population to the category of prisoners of war and to drive them away to work for the Germans like unwilling cattle. An order from the headquarters of Army Group Center's Second Panzer Army dated 22 January 1943 to the commandant of one of the rear areas read: "All of the population in the areas subordinate to you that is fit for military service should be gathered into columns under guard for labor use. Establish the same order in local areas of Kastornoe, Tim, Shshigry and the field commandant's office in Kshen'. The collected people ... will receive the same food rations set for prisoners of war. They should as a matter of principle be sought out on location [which is to say, taken from the local population]"[34] It should be noted, however, that such a barbaric way of treating the civilian population was not new for the Wehrmacht; it had been practiced since the first months of the war. The former chief of the NKVD's Fourth Department General P.A. Sudoplatov in his book of memoirs cites an order from the commander of the 40th Infantry Division General L. Rendulic,[35] which stated, "In order to put an end to all the doubts, I am once again ordering: In a compulsory fashion, convert all local residents of military-age into prisoners, and to destroy suspect elements."[36] By the middle of 1943, the situation would reach a critical point. Large areas, occupied by German forces, would be depopulated. In July, now by a special order from the OKH, responsibility for the confiscation of grain was placed upon the command of the army groups and they would be advised to assign combat troops to force the population to do fieldwork. Even so, such measures had begun to be practiced in separate areas even earlier, back in 1942.

Attentively following the situation regarding human resources, the military-political leadership of Germany already in December 1942 came to the conclusion that it could not get by without "turning the screws" in the Reich itself. Indeed, at the start of the following year, it approved a collection of measures regarding the conducting of "total war", in which the mobilization of labor resources would occupy a special role. This was a rather harsh document and it affected each German adult. However, the arguments and intrigues that flared up when preparing it plainly demonstrated that the Party bureaucratic elite was not ready to give up its privileges and accustomed lifestyle. Therefore J. Göbbel's resonating speech on 18 February 1943 that contained a call for "total mobilization", a recognition of the tragic nature of the situation and the increase in the personal contribution of each German with the aim of mobilizing the

---

33 Klink, *Das Gesetz des Handelns. Die Operation "Zitadelle"*, pp. 302-303.
34 Müller, *Vermakht i okkupatsiia*, p. 357.
35 In the period of the Battle of Kursk, Rendulic would be commanding Second Panzer Army's XXXV Infantry Corps of Army Group Center.
36 Sudoplatov, P., *Pobeda v tainoi voine, 1941-1945* [*Victory in the secret war, 1941-1945*] (Moscow: OLMA-PRESS, 2005), p. 251.

country's forces for the further conducting of the war was addressed first of all to Germany's ruling class, a portion of which wanted, as before, to ignore what was happening. Albert Speer recalled:

> A considerably greater stir was created by my demands that the working time of all government officials be extended to match the hours of armaments workers. That alone, in purely arithmetical terms, would have freed some two hundred thousand administrative people for armaments work. ... Even when Goebbels demanded that leading party members forgo their previous almost limitless luxuries, he could change nothing. And Eva Braun, ordinarily so unassuming, had no sooner heard of a proposed ban on permanent waves as well as the end of cosmetic production when she rushed to Hitler in high indignation. Hitler at once showed uncertainty. He advised me that instead of an outright ban I quietly stop production of "hair dyes and other items necessary for beauty culture," as well as "cessation of repairs upon apparatus for producing permanent waves." ... Nevertheless, Goebbel's speech on "total war" was followed up by a gesture which was roundly applauded by public: He had Berlin's luxury restaurants and expensive places of amusement closed. Goering, to be sure, promptly interposed his bulk to protect his favorite restaurant, Horcher's. But when subsequently some demonstrators (set on by Goebbels) appeared at the restaurant and smashed the windows, Goering yielded. The result was a serious rift between him and Goebbels.[37]

The problems listed above at the beginning of 1943 led to a sharp change in the mood of all levels of German society. The illusion fostered by the victories in 1941 and 1942 and reinforced by propaganda began to disappear amongst the citizenry. A fear about the consequences of defeat seized the German people. After a discussion with a representative of his agency with the OKW Colonel Martin, J. Göbbels wrote in his diary, "He announced that the German people no longer believed the information, that we had absolutely lost [their] trust, and that no matter how we tried, there would no longer be any faith in the government."[38] The Reich's security service, attentively tracking the mood of the people in Germany, noted that most noticeable of all were indifference, apathy and fatigue with the war. Together with tragic news from the front and the daily Allied bombing raids to a significant extent the growing problems with food supplies was contributing to this. Back in the summer of 1942, Hitler became indignant when informed that Germans were going hungry at a time when German forces had already captured Ukraine. He then demanded of Gauleiter Fritz Sauckel, who was in charge of forced labor, to do everything possible to extract resources from the seized territories, even if it would prove necessary to "mobilize all the Jews of Europe and organize a living chain to transfer boxes of food."[39] In the 1942-1943 agricultural year, the Germans transported 5 million tonn [metric

---

37 Speer, A. *Vospominaniia* (Moscow: "Zakharov", 2010), pp. 334-337. These words can be found in the English translation of Speer's memoirs entitled *Inside the Third Reich* as published in paperback by Weidenfeld & Sons in 1995 on pages 352-354.
38 As cited by Bleier, et. al., *Germaniia vo vtoroi mirovoi voine*, p. 229.
39 As cited by Platoshkin, N.N. "Obespechenie naseleniia produktami pitaniia v gody Vtoroi mirovoi voiny" ["Securing the population with food products in the years of the Second World war," *Voenno-*

tons] of grain and 8.78 million tonn of meat and fats in exchange for grain from the occupied territories of the USSR, which enabled increased food rations in Germany in October 1942. However, the problem of keeping the population supplied with food could not be achieved even at a minimum. The average German in 1943 received an average of 2,000 calories per day, which was below the standard determined for an adult.[40] The quality of the food products also declined. Potato starch and barley began to be added to white bread; in place of normal beer, a so-called "simple beer" that was much lower in quality began to appear on sale; and canned foods went missing from shops (tin went to the needs of the Wehrmacht), while sweets became a great luxury.

At the end of winter, immediately following the catastrophic events in the Stalingrad area and the Red Army's following general offensive, the situation in North Africa began to become acute. On 18 January 1943, the German troops launched Operation Albot with the aim of reducing the pressure on the front of the Italian troops, in the course of which some of the British and French forces were driven back, but the numerical superiority of the Allies remained just as predominant as before. Therefore, the commander of the German-Italian grouping in Africa Field Marshal Rommel was forced to abandon Tripoli in Libya and fall back to the "Mareth Line", which ran along the border between Libya and Tunisia. This not only marked a substantial deterioration of the situation of the German forces, but also inflicted a painful blow to the interests and prestige of the German ally, Italy, as it meant the complete loss of its colony in Africa.

In early February Rommel launched an attack against the numerically superior American forces in the vicinity of the Kasserine Pass and drove them back. The Allies were forced to abandon the towns of Feriana and Thelepte (approximately 24 kilometers from Kasserine), evacuate a major airfield, and suffered substantial losses in the process. However, the Allies were able to regroup, and American artillery fire and U.S. counterattacks along the Hatab River brought Rommel's offensive to a stop. The pressure on Rommel's forces increased substantially, but Germany was no longer able to reinforce them and keep them supplied with everything necessary. At the beginning of March 1943 the Field Marshal proposed to Hitler to evacuate the troops from the African continent, but the Führer refused and made a switch in command: On 9 March Erwin Rommel was summoned back to Berlin, and Colonel General Hans-Jürgen von Arnim assumed his place as commander of Panzer Army Africa. However, this proved to be of no use; on 20 March the Allies, going on the offensive simultaneously against the Mareth Line from the south and from the Maknassy area in the west, broke through the German line and pursued the retreating German and Italian troops back to the city of Tunis. Von Arnim's grouping was rather large and fought stubbornly, but after these events it became obvious that it was doomed.

The latter months of 1942 and early 1943 struck a crushing blow against the unity of the countries of the Fascist bloc and the positions of those states that were formally observing neutrality, even though they were in reality supporting Germany and its territorial ambitions. Italy was the first link in this chain to begin to weaken. On three occasions, in December 1942 and March and April 1943, Mussolini advised Hitler to conclude a peace with the Soviet

---

istoricheskii zhurnal] (No. 7, 2011), p. 57.
40   Ibid., p. 58.

Union. Finland was proposing the same thing. The ruling circles of Bulgaria, Romania and Hungary through intermediaries began actively to send out feelers with the aim of concluding separate peace agreements with the USA and Great Britain. The dictator of Romania Admiral I. Antonescu openly acknowledged that "after the Battle of Stalingrad, the Fascist state became unstable."[41] The entire month of April 1943 was marked by visits from the heads of Germany's allied states. They all had the same question: What was Hitler thinking by continuing the war? The Führer could only try to calm them and convince them that the situation in the East had stabilized, and soon the Red Army would again be "showing its spine" to the Wehrmacht. However, this was no longer 1941. After the war, Hitler's adjutant Colonel H. von Bulow wrote:

> On the whole, the following can be said about all the visits of this month: all the visitors arrived distrustful and left as just the same, since they all had communications with other countries. From them they were hearing about the continuous advances made by the Americans and Russians, which left no doubt that they would be pursuing major offensive operations in 1943 as well. However, Hitler was still relying on the weakness of the Russians and hoping for Citadel's success.[42]

The German allies were sincerely promising to meet their obligations, but as subsequent events would show (in August 1943 in Bulgaria, then in Hungary), the time of solidarity with the Reich had vanished forever and each was beginning to think about their own place in the post-war world. The previously hesitant Turkey and Japan took a "firmer" stand against the war with the Soviet Union. In early 1943 hostile rhetoric against the USSR began to disappear in the Turkish press. Meanwhile on 6 March 1943 the Japanese ambassador at a meeting in Berlin directly stated to the German government in response to repeated offers to participate in the dismemberment of the Soviet Union that his country was not ready to enter the war against the USSR. It should be emphasized that Hitler knew full well the value of his satellites; on 11 March 1943 at a conference at the headquarters of Army Group South in Zaporozh'e, he declared to his generals, "We can no longer count on our allies. They are costing us too much. We should cold-bloodedly toss them aside from the calculations regarding the further war."[43]

The sharp decline of Germany's standing in the international arena also became prominent evidence of the crisis it now faced. Before the war, it had diplomatic relations with 40 countries, but after the "catastrophe on the Volga", this number plummeted to 22. Simultaneously, the process of the formation of a broad anti-Hitler coalition began to gather strength. From the second half of 1942 and throughout all of 1943, ten countries declared war against Germany, six against Italy, and four against Japan.

If only to judge from Hitler's well-known statements made in the presence of a relatively large audience, then it is clear that he was adequately assessing the situation that had taken shape by this moment. Take, for example, the conference on 10 January 1943, where he openly

---

41 Bleier, et. al., p. 231.
42 Below, H. von, *Ia byl ad'iutankom Gitlera* [*I was Hitler's adjutant*], translated from the German by G. Rudogo (Smolensk: Rusich, 2003), p. 412.
43 Schwarz, E., Die Stabilisierung der Ostfront nach Stalingrad. Mansteins Gegenschlag zwischen Donez und Dnjepr im Frühjahr 1943. Studien und Dokumente zur Geschichte des zweiten Weltkriegs; Band 17 (Munster Schmidt Verlag, Gottingen, 1986), p. 262.

acknowledged that after Stalingrad, "talk was about a struggle for existence, and not about a war for territorial gain", and on 1 February he offered more detail on this thought: "I can say only one thing: the possibility of ending the war in the East by means of an offensive no longer exists."[44] Even so, according to participants at these meetings, Hitler was unable to reconcile himself to the loss of initiative and simply yield it to the Russians. Thus, he decided to impose his will, having decided by springtime to conduct a major offensive with limited objectives.[45] However, this view, which has become relatively widespread in foreign literature, appears to be somewhat superficial. When taking such an important decision, the personal desires of even such a dictator as Adolf Hitler did not have decisive significance; objective factors were paramount. Indeed, the main one was the clear recognition by the Reich's leadership of the obvious fact that the Soviet Union had no intention to conclude peace, while the Allies at Casablanca made it clearly known that they were expecting only Germany's unconditional surrender. In a situation where Stalin had the superiority in forces and resources, and moreover had the support of such great powers as the United States and England, it would be impossible to force the Soviet leader to accept even a temporary truce. Well, of course, after Stalingrad it would also be hard to take seriously, if only out of despair, any thought that it might be possible to maul the Red Army and bleed it white in the near future. However, as we will see below, it was precisely this notion that caught Hitler's attention. As the former commander of Army Group Center's XII Army Corps General of Infantry Karl Tippelskirch later wrote:

> The fighting over the previous year to various degrees clearly showed both the increased flexibility of the Russian command when resolving operational tasks, and just as before the significant tactical superiority of the German troops on the battlefield. If it was no longer possible to count upon the decisive success of an offensive in the East, then the decision to give the war a defensive character suggested itself. The German defenses ran in the depth of enemy territory and had sufficient space in its rear in order to conduct stubborn defensive fighting in those places where it was advantageous to do so, and in other sectors (especially where a breakthrough by Russian forces was threatening), to conduct elastic withdrawals and subsequent sudden counterattacks in order to weaken the offensive power of the Russians and wear them down.[46]

The discussion and development of a general plan for the summer campaign began in Berlin in February 1943. The former chief of staff of Army Group South General T. Busse asserted that at this time, everyone, including Hitler, the OKH, the commanders-in-chief of the army groups and even the army commanders believed that 1943 would be the final year when Germany would be conducting active combat operations with only the Soviet Union. This was a serious threat. They therefore shared Hitler's desire at whatever the cost to regain the initiative on the Eastern Front, with the aim of having a free hand to repel a possible attack in Europe. As E. von Manstein recalled, the only point of contention was over the way to achieve this: to wait for

---

44   Hitlers Legebesprechungen. Die Protokollfragmente seiner militärischen Konferenzen 1942-1945 (Stuttgart, 1962), p. 122.
45   Tippelskirch, K., Istoriia Vtoroi mirovoi voiny [History of the Second World War] (St Petersburg: Poligon, 1994), p. 23.
46   Ibid, p. 24.

a general offensive by the Red Army soon after the end of the muddy season, in order to defeat it while inflicting heavy losses on the attackers, and then go over to the offensive; or to be the first to strike.[47]

The intensive analysis of the operational situation, their own capabilities, and the condition of the Red Army that was conducted in the OKH between February and the beginning of March increasingly led to the conclusion that the Kursk area offered the most favorable conditions for an offensive operation. In the first place, this bulging salient in the lines was disrupting the lines of communications between the two main army groups, Center and South. In the second place, it was looming over their flanks and presented a convenient place for the launching of Soviet offensives. Finally, at the time the military leadership anticipated no other material costs or expenditures of time, other than planning the operation itself and bringing the troops in the area back up to strength (which in fact was necessary to do).

Of the four commanders-in-chief of the army groups on the Eastern Front, it was namely Erich von Manstein and his headquarters of Army Group South that were the first to take active part in the process of discussing the summer campaign. The Field Marshal believed that the Wehrmacht's objective should be the exhaustion of the Red Army's strength in the center and in the southwest by conducting a flexible defense. The difficult situation not only in the entire Wehrmacht, but first of all in its troops, was prompting this idea. By the conclusion of the winter campaign, Army Group South was holding a sector that stretched 650 kilometers with the forces of 24 infantry and 13 panzer and motorized divisions, while having no reserves.[48] E. von Manstein recalled, "This pre-supposed an operational elasticity on our part which would give maximum effect to the still-superior quality of the German command staffs and fighting troops."[49] Back on 3 February 1943, the Field Marshal had sent the Chief of Staff of the OKH Colonel General Zeitzler a report with an analysis of the situation and a note "for a report to the Führer" that proposed conducting a fighting withdrawal of his army group's right flank to the Melitopol – Dnepropetrovsk line and to take up a defense there, while forming an assault group on its left (northern) flank. According to his thinking, the Russians would pursue the retreating forces, but a strong defense along the Dnepr River would pin them in place there, while his grouping on the left flank with a powerful attack to the east would first split the Russian front, and then having pivoted to the southwest in the direction of the coastline of the Sea of Azov, cut the advancing Russians off from their main forces.[50] As a result on this axis the Red Army would suffer substantial losses and the front would become stabilized. In order to implement this plan, in his opinion it was necessary for his troops to abandon the Don basin, replenish them substantially, and keep firm possession of the Orel – Kursk area, or in the extreme case, the Orel – L'vov area. This proposal received thorough elaboration in Berlin. The former operations officer of the Second Army's headquarters Colonel P. von der Gröben observed:

> OKH had initially intended to rout the Soviet forces in the area west of Kursk by having the Second Army and – adjoining it to the south – the Fourth Panzer Army stage a frontal assault. Two decisive factors caused this plan to be discarded. The shortage

---

47 Manstein, *Poteriannye pobedy*, p. 473.
48 Klink, E., *Das Gesetz des Handelns. Die Operation "Zitadelle" 1943* (Stuttgart, 1966), p. 283.
49 Manstein, *Poteriannye pobedy*, p. 512.
50 Toppel, R., Kursk 1943. Die groste Schlacht der Zweiten Weltkriegs (Paderborn, 2017), p. 20.

of rail transportation facilities [in addition to] partisan attacks made it impossible to accomplish the strategic concentration of forces earmarked for such a large-scale offensive in the time allotted. In addition, the onset of the muddy season arrived in late February, earlier than expected, rendering mobile warfare impossible.[51]

Even the recently appointed Chief of Staff of the OKH Colonel General K. Zeitzler was also inclined to a mobile defense for some time. He put forward the idea of strengthening the line of the Western Dvina – Berezina – Dnepr Rivers (the so-called East Wall) and using it as a fulcrum for conducting a mobile defense. According to the recollections of former staff officers of Army Group Center, its commander-in-chief Field Marshal G. von Kluge proposed a similar idea to withdraw his forces from Orel to the Dnepr and Sozh Rivers (to the Kiev – Gomel – Orsha – Nevel line).[52]

However, both von Manstein's proposal of other options, as well as the conducting of a mobile defense already lost their allure in February 1943. On 9 February, the Soviet Briansk Front fully liberated Kursk and continued pushing to the west, and on 3 March the Germans were forced to abandon L'vov as well. In addition, at the same time, Hitler was also categorically against a major offensive. A new plan was already ripening within him, at least in general outlines. He believed that Germany's armed forces were not ready to implement grand operations successfully at that moment like they had conducted in the preceding two years. Instead, he planned to launch strong, brief, preemptive attacks in the areas of possible Soviet offensives, and thereby restrain the Red Army and stabilize the front. He decided that the main instrument for realizing this plan would be panzer formations, which would be equipped with the latest models of tanks and self-propelled guns. On 18 February in the course of a conference at Army Group South headquarters in Zaporozh'e, he announced:

> We cannot conduct large operations this year. I think we can launch only blows that aren't so large. At the beginning of May, we will receive 98 heavy assault guns of the new Porsche design. In addition to them, another 150 new Tigers. We'll also receive another 200 to 250 tanks, plus 50 heavy self-propelled infantry guns, 100 flame throwing tanks and some number of Pz IV tanks. These latest designs are invulnerable. It is impossible to exaggerate their combat strength. The assault guns can destroy any enemy tank from 2000 meters. Given the unprecedented concentration of heavy artillery along with super heavy tanks, at a minimum it should yield a breach in the defenses. After this, a breakthrough should begin. The objective could be, for example, the railroad leading out of Kharkov to the south. If the new heavy tanks initially did not meet the promised expectations south of Lake Ladoga last autumn, then now these childhood illnesses are in the past. These tanks are now the best in the world and invulnerable. It is impossible to compare the 72-tonn Porsche assault guns with anything else. An assembly of 300-400 tanks can make any breakthrough. In May we'll have for this the resurrected divisions of the Sixth Army – the stabilization of the front of course remains a condition. In addition, an operation south of the Neva

51 Newton, *Kurskaia bitva*, p. 135.
52 Ibid., p. 265.

should begin in order to bring the front closer to Leningrad again. Here as well the achievement of the objective depends upon a gigantic concentration of artillery and tanks.[53]

To E. von Manstein's observation that this plan was in principle feasible, but would bring about heavy losses, Hitler curtly replied, "We must achieve our objectives with the superiority of our armaments. We will achieve little with men, because we don't have many, but we can achieve everything with a mass of the best and heavy weapons of war." On 5 March, when discussing the situation at his headquarters in Vinnitsa, the Führer declared that the panzer units on the Eastern Front should be reinforced in the next few weeks so that they would be ready to act right after the end of the muddy season.[54]

However, the key problem for him was the Don basin. E. von Manstein's proposal implied its temporary abandonment, to which Hitler could not agree for a number of substantive reasons, first and foremost, economic ones. On 5 February 1943, he had held a discussion with a representative of the Reich's coal amalgamation and simultaneously the director of the Hermann Göring Works, P. Pläger, who was accompanied by A. Speer. Pläger requested not to yield any of the territory that was presently under the Wehrmacht's control, and first of all the Don basin. In the opinion of the major industrial monopolies, which he was representing, the loss of the rich coal and ore deposits would have tragic consequences for military industry. The Minister of Armaments and War Production was essentially sharing this point of view. At the conference on 18 February mentioned above, Hitler declared:

> We cannot lose the coal basin of Stalino! The loss of this region would mean an irreparable catastrophe for us. What alone is the Zaporozh'e hydroelectrical station worth!? How much would it cost us to bring it back into operation!? Five turbines are working and generating 54,000 kilowatts of power. The loss of Zaporozh'e is irreplaceable. The Russians can once again produce the best steel. The increased production of ammunition, which they can now only scrape together, would be one result. The consequences defy logic. We are losing the basis of our own production program, about which I just spoke. No! There is no other choice than to shift the units from the Taman Peninsula to Army Group South as quickly as possible. Someone must be put in charge of the transportation and he must be given full authority for resolving this problem. … Stalino is worth ten armies! It is impossible to imagine if the Russians increased their coal potential in the Stalino basin. We need this region even if only for the railroads.[55]

He rejected the idea of giving up the Don basin in an even more categorical form in March 1943 at a conference in the headquarters of Army Group South in Zaporozh'e. On that occasion he declared:

---

53 Schwarz, Stabilisierung der Ostfront nach Stalingrad, p. 255.
54 Toppel, Kursk 1943, p. 20.
55 Schwarz, Stabilisierung der Ostfront nach Stalingrad, p. 255.

I've once again diligently assessed the significance of the Donets region for us. The loss of this region would be intolerable for us. One Russian professor explained that the Russians lost 25percent of their production of steel with the abandonment of this region. If we lose this region, then our entire program of the production of tanks and armaments in the current volume would fall to pieces. In addition, it is impossible even to express in words the significance of Nikopol. The loss of Nikopol's magnesium deposits would mean the war's end! However, to this we must add how important the Zaporozh'e hydroelectrical station is for Nikopol and the Donets region.[56]

The second reason involved morale and politics. Hitler believed that it was impossible to keep concealed the construction of large-scale defensive works in the rear. They would quickly become known to the troops and this would negatively affect their fighting spirit and resolve when fighting the Russians.

The third reason was the paucity of resources. At this moment, Germany no longer had the labor force, building materials or transport means for such large-scale defensive fortifications. Moreover, the Wehrmacht lacked the necessary amount of fuel, ammunition and even time in order to conduct a mobile defense on such a large amount of territory.[57] E. von Manstein maintained that at this time, Hitler was mainly concerned about the Red Army's adoption of a strategic defense along the entire front in expectations of a landing by the Allies in Europe. He wrote:

> A strategy of waiting did not exclude the conducting of a series of attacks with small forces in order to preserve their prestige and to prevent the diversion of German forces from the east. For the Germans this would have been most unpleasant, because we, standing inactive on the defense, would then have to conduct a war on two fronts against strong adversaries.[58]

In the beginning of March, Army Group South's counterblow in Ukraine was progressing well and the operational situation on the southwestern portion of the Soviet – German front noticeably improved for the Wehrmacht. However, the spring thaw began earlier than usual, and the roads gradually became virtually impassable. Thus, it was obvious that after achieving the nearest objectives – the capture of Kharkov and, possibly, Belgorod as well – it would be necessary to suspend combat operations and go over to the planning of combat operations once

---

56 Ibid., p. 261.
57 The problem of a fuel shortage in Germany became acute already in 1942. The summertime operation to seize the Caucasus was aimed at resolving it. The Reich's leadership was striving to develop alternative sources of fuel. For example, in that same year of 1942, already 180,000 automobiles in Germany itself and on occupied territories were powered by coal-burning engines. After the failure of the plans to seize Groznyi and Baku, the construction of factories to produce synthetic fuels began, as well as the repurposing of alcohol plants, in occupied countries as well, to produce an ethyl alcohol that could power automobile and airplane engines. For example, in 1943, such factories were operating in Chernigov, Dnepropetrovsk, Gomel and Suma Oblasts (*Voenno-istoricheskii zhurnal* [No. 5, 2003], p. 48). The problem with ammunition supplies also began to increase noticeably by the middle of September 1943 and was rather acute in the course of Operation Zitadelle.
58 Manstein, *Poteriannye pobedy*, p. 512.

fine weather arrived and the soil dried. On 8 March, E. von Manstein for the first time in a report to Hitler proposed to conduct an offensive once the ground hardened. It was to target the capture of Kursk as the ultimate objective, as well as the area to the south and southwest of that city. In his opinion, to achieve this would require the inclusion in the offensive of Army Group South and a portion of Army Group Center, but with the Second Army, not Model's Ninth Army. The Second Army's defensive front at this time ran along the nose of the salient and extended to the northwest. Thus, Field Marshal von Manstein's initial idea consisted in cutting off not the entire bulge, but only its southern half. The question arises: Just when and by whom was the idea put forth that became the basis of Operation Citadel's plan – the liquidation of the entire salient? Until recently, both Russian and foreign historiography held the persistent opinion that von Manstein was also the one who formulated this plan and presented it to Hitler. However, in 2017, this prevailing opinion was refuted by the German historian R. Töppel on the basis of archival documents. He managed not only to establish the author's identity, but also the precise date and the circumstances of its origination.

On 10 March 1943, G. von Kluge held a telephone conversation with the commander of the Second Panzer Army, which was subordinate to Army Group Center and was holding a sector south of Orel, Colonel General R. Schmidt. The essence of the discussion consisted of the fact that at that time a substantial breach had formed between the right flank of the Second Panzer Army and the left flank of the Second Army, through which troops of the Soviet Central Front had reached the Desna River. The Field Marshal ordered General Schmidt to close the breach with a strong attack, and to accomplish this before the onset of the muddy season. To assist him, G. von Kluge was ready to include the Ninth Army, which had just withdrawn from the Rzhev salient. He was planning that Model's divisions, having deployed south of Orel, would launch an attack toward Kursk, thereby covering the left flank of the Second Panzer Army's assault grouping while pinning down the forces of the Central Front and partially those of the Briansk Front, which might hinder Schmidt's forces from carrying out the plan.

After the telephone conversation ended, the commander of the Second Panzer Army immediately prepared a report to Field Marshal von Manstein, in which he laid out his opinion on this matter. The document stated that his army was now only with great effort restraining the Soviet forces that were lunging toward Briansk. It would be able to hold its positions securely only if the forces of the Ninth Army were committed, which also applied to the order to launch an attack to close the flanks with the Second Army. However, it would be impossible to carry out this operation prior to the onset of the muddy season, although, in the general's opinion, it should not be conducted at all in order not to disperse strength. Subsequently Schmidt proposed a more cardinal solution to the problem than the one the Field Marshal had offered wrote R. Töppel:

> Schmidt suggested that it would be more sensible "to create a more powerful operational group for an attack out of the area south of Orel in the direction of Kursk in cooperation with a different group, advancing out of the Kharkov area to the north." This plan precisely reflects the plan of Operation Citadel. Therefore, it was namely General Schmidt who was the author of the operation's plan. This is confirmed by von Kluge's reaction as well. Late on the evening of 10 March, he called Schmidt and declared that "it should be said that there is something sensible in your train of thought." Still, the Ninth Army would nevertheless be shifted, von Kluge added, but without haste …

On the next day, 11 March 1943 Hitler once again visited the headquarters of Army Group South in Zaporozh'e. Von Manstein, using the occasion, again expressed the desire to eliminate the bulge in the front around Kursk before the onset of the muddy season. To this Hitler retorted, "The bulge is not going anywhere," but added that "the possibilities for launching small attacking blows would be lost." Large operations, Hitler maintained, should be ruled out in the near future. "By means of continuing attacks, we should keep the initiative and keep the correlation of losses, if possible, to 1 to 10. We must periodically inflict losses on the Russian, relying on divisions to a lesser extent and more on contemporary effective weapons. But then we should stop and defend." Manstein was not convinced that this idea was correct. On this day he made an entry in his personal diary about Hitler and the situation of affairs: "Basically there is no clarity in our own intentions. We are standing on different levels. I – on an operational level, and he – on a level of materials and figures. As a consequence of this, we'll never come to a result.

At this time Hitler had no clear idea about where precisely it was necessary to conduct an offensive operation in the spring. ... Two days later, on 13 March, he finally received a final nudge toward reaching a decision, during a visit to Army Group Center's headquarters in Smolensk. In addition to Hitler, Zeitzler and von Kluge, the army commanders took part, and among them in fact was Colonel General Schmidt, who now had the possibility of laying out his plan for an offensive to Hitler personally. Hitler, obviously, was impressed, and on this same day he issued Operational Order No. 5. In this fashion, the plan for Citadel, which foresaw the formation of pincers around Kursk, came to light. Its "father" was Rudolph Schmidt, and its godfathers were Hitler and von Kluge. ... On 15 March Göbbel's noted in his diary: "The Führer has completed his trip to the Central Front. He found excellent circumstances here. He characterized the situation in the center very positively. In fact, Hitler was left with the very best impressions of the leadership."[59]

The cornerstone of the intent behind Order No. 5 was the Wehrmacht's regaining of the initiative and, as a consequence, the imposition of its will on the Red Army:

> The Russians after the conclusion of winter and the springtime muddy season ... will resume the offensive. Therefore, our task ... is to preempt them as far as possible with an offensive in separate places with the aim of imposing our will, if only on one sector of the front. ... On the remaining sectors of the front, the task amounts to bleeding the attacking enemy white. Here we should in advance create an especially strong defense by means of using heavy weapons, improving positions in an engineering respect, deploying minefields in necessary sectors, setting up strongpoints in the rear, creating mobile reserves, etc.[60]

Although there was already no talk about a victorious conclusion to the war, even so, Germany's leadership was plainly overestimating its possibilities and underestimating the growing potential

---

59 Töppel, *Kursk 1943*, p. 22, 23.
60 Parotkin (ed.), *Kurskaia bitva* [*Battle of Kursk*] (Moscow: Nauka, 1970), p. 505.

of the Soviet Union. In the order, three of the four army groups on the Eastern Front were assigned to conduct offensive operations simultaneously with deep objectives. Army Group North was supposed to prepare for the capture of Leningrad, which had already been heroically defended for one and a half years. Army Groups Center and South were to conduct even larger combat operations. They had the objective of encircling and destroying a million-man grouping of the Central and Voronezh Fronts that were holding the Kursk salient. G. von Kluge received the order "… to take steps to improve further the situation between the Second Army and the Second Panzer Army; to continue to improve the defensive positions with artificial obstacles and fortifications and to reinforce them with anti-tank means …. In addition, it was necessary to create an assault grouping and to use it for an offensive in cooperation with the troops of Army Group South's northern wing." In order to create this grouping, it was planned to withdraw "the troops of the Fourth and Ninth Armies from the Viaz'ma area to a shorter line of defense (to the 'Buffalo' position)."

The left-hand, northern pincer that was supposed to close near Kursk was to be formed from the troops of Army Group Center, while its southern counterpart was to be created from the troops of Army Group South. In the document E. von Manstein was instructed to begin the creation of a panzer army in the Belgorod area (on the basis of the Fourth Panzer Army that was already located there), which already by the middle of April was to be ready for an offensive from the south and added "The objective of this offensive consists in the destruction of the enemy's 2nd Army opposite the Second Army by an attack out of the Kharkov area to the north in conjunction with the assault grouping of the Second Army."

Only Army Group A was supposed to remain on the defensive and "as soon as the weather became suitable, to conduct the designated shortening of the front of the Kuban bridgehead with the aim of freeing forces for Army Group South." However, this portion of the plan already on 28 March underwent cardinal changes – Hitler decided to retain the Novorossiisk area with the forces of Army Group A.[61] Thus, E. von Manstein received only two of the approximately 10 divisions that he was supposed to receive under the original plan. The lack of infantry divisions for the operation became the first major problem that acutely arose before the Wehrmacht command already in the stage of planning for the offensive toward Kursk, and it was unable to resolve this problem right up until the beginning of July 1943 and the start of Operation Citadel. Therefore, the document gave the OKH a main assignment – to bring up the forces in the East back to an acceptable strength: "… in the first place, replenish the divisions designated for offensive operations with personnel and equipment, give them rest and increase the level of their combat training, and also strengthen and fortify the sectors of the front, where purely defensive operations are contemplated on our part."

Initially, there was no clear understanding of how events would develop in case of a successful link up of the forces of the two army groups in the area of Kursk as a result of the concentric attack. Later, now in the stage of the practical discussion of the Citadel plan, it is known that E. von Manstein was counting upon pivoting his main forces into the rear of the Southwestern Front (the Donets front for the Germans). However, the generals and field marshals that were close to the OKW and OKH were inclined to continue the offensive toward the northeast,

---

61 Kriegstagebuch der Ia der Heeresgruppe Don/Süd, März bis Juli 1943. BArch-MA. RH 19 VI/45. Bl. 13.

in order to cut Moscow off from the southern areas of the country. At the very least, Field Marshal W. Keitel in his testimony at his interrogation during the Nuremburg trials named just this axis as the main one, though he also emphasized that these proposals "were expressed in the vaguest form."[62]

E. von Manstein and the headquarters of his army group also shared the idea put forth by R. Schmidt and embodied in Order No. 5 but believed that in order to achieve the maximum advantages from it, the offensive should be launched as soon as possible, at the very least by the end of March, which is to say, before the start of the muddy season. However, this calculation proved to be too optimistic, since the spring thaws of 1943 began earlier than usual. Nevertheless, Hitler liked the idea of launching two concentric attacks toward Kursk so much that as we will see further, even though the time for implementing it was missed, he refused to abandon this plan and made it the basis of the primary operation of the summer campaign of 1943.

The commander-in-chief of Army Group South Field Marshal von Manstein later recalled the atmosphere in which this plan was born:

> Now they are saying that the thought of a stalemate in the East was a dream, already in 1943. We will not now speak to whether or not this was actually so. We, the soldiers, could not judge whether or not the possibility of achieving an agreement with the Soviet Union existed from the political point of view in the spring of 1943. ... However, the command of Army Group "Don" (which was re-named back then to Army Group South) was convinced that from a military standpoint – given proper operational leadership – such a stalemate result in the East was possible to achieve [Emphasis the author's]. After all, the path from Stalingrad to the Donets required great sacrifices by the enemy. No matter how dearly Stalingrad cost us, according to reliable calculations by the OKH, the enemy from the start of the war had lost 11,000,000 men. Eventually, the Russians' offensive strength must run out! That in any case is how we viewed the military situation in the East in our headquarters at that time.[63]

Reading these lines, it is impossible not to notice the unrealistic tone that permeates them. Yet this was written by a military commander who had passed through more than one military campaign in this war! They also betray how the political leadership of Germany was "storming" at this time against the forthcoming "requisitions".

It should be noted that the idea of achieving the ultimate exhaustion of the Red Army's strength in the near future and thereby the collapse of the Soviet people's resistance was rather widespread in the political and military circles of the Reich in early 1943. This is not only evident from the transcript of Hitler's conference in Zaporozh'e and the memoirs of E. von Manstein cited above, but also, for example, from the record of the conversations between the Italian State Secretary Bastianini and Germany's Minister of Foreign Affairs J. von Ribbentrop on 8 April 1943:

---

62 *Voenno-istoricheskii zhurnal*, No. 7 (1963), p. 103.
63 Manstein, *Poteriannye pobedy*, pp. 510-511. [Translator's note: I could not find this passage in the edited English-language version of von Manstein's memoirs, so this translation from the Russian, despite the risk of imprecision, is my own.]

The Reich Minister of Foreign Affairs referred to the testimony of a Russian commander of a reserve army who'd been captured; according to information for August [1942], he provided the following figures for total losses: 11.3 million killed, wounded or taken prisoner. Today it is possible to consider that the Russians have lost a minimum of 14,000,000. Out of the 190,000,000 people living in the Bolshevik empire, 70,000,000 live in oblasts now occupied by Germany. There remains another 120,000,000, 14,000,000 of which have been wiped off the ledger. Since 10percent of a country's total population can be taken as the military potential for any population, of these 120,000,000 Russia still has 12,000,000 soldiers under its command. In general, and on the whole, the strength of the Russian people has already significantly weakened after the fighting we've conducted. Even the major Russian attack across the Don shows this. The Russians, unfortunately, managed to complete a breakthrough in the sector held by Germany's allies, as the result of which the Sixth Army was encircled in Stalingrad. The sudden diminution in the Russians' penetrating power over the recent weeks proves that the strength of the Russian people is on the verge of running out.

By the way, it is interesting: If previously it was thought that the Russians would experience difficulties with equipment and ammunition, while at the same time having a surplus of manpower, then now the situation is completely opposite: the difficulties with combat materiel are insignificant, yet now they have a shortage of combat-capable men. On the extended front of struggle from Finland to the Black Sea, the Russians have committed 630 different combat formations into battle. The divisions and brigades on average number 4,000 to 5,000 men, excluding the rear services. All are pointing to great difficulties with procuring enlistments. If Germany would launch new attacks against the Russians, they [the Russians] would increasingly find themselves on the path to the exhaustion of their strength. How far such matters might go in this year, he [Ribbentrop], naturally could not say, since this is purely a military question. However, by year's end the majority of the existing formations today will again be destroyed. If you consider the fact that even now the Russians are calling up 15- and 16-year-olds, while soldiers from elderly contingents are being encountered at the front, then it is fully possible to say: This systematic destruction of the Russian army will lead to the fact that the Russians will draw their last breath one splendid day.

...

The main thing in this war consists in destroying the entire Red Army with repeated attacks, while not penetrating deeply into Russian hinterland. Already now, as mentioned above, 14,000,000 Russians have been wiped from the ledger. Someday the density of population in Russia will become so small, that it will no longer be able to present any threat. Then that moment will arrive, when it will be possible to transfer not 20 divisions to the West for use, but 80 to 100 divisions. The war will be won at that moment when Germany will be able to pounce upon the remaining enemies, which will no longer be able to present any problem.[64]

64 G. Jacobsen, *1939-1945. Vtoraia mirovaia voina. Khronika i dokumenty* [*1939-1945: Second World War. Chronicle and documents*] (Moscow: Mysl', 1995), p. 210. This is the Russian translation of the German *1939-1945 der Zweite Weltkrieg in Chronik und Dokumenten* (Beschreibung). There is no existing

The presented excerpt is in fact Hitler's own thoughts in elaborated form, which over a month before he had expressed at the conference in Zaporozh'e on 11 March, in which he declared: "The Russian total losses up to today correspond to 11 million men including invalids and so forth. Our own losses in Russia are placed at 430,000 – not including Stalingrad. At such a correlation of losses, an end must all the same arrive at some point."[65]

However, not all the key figures of the Wehrmacht were sharing the idea back then of seizing the initiative in the East by means of conducting a relatively large offensive operation. Rather quickly, two centers of gravity of opposing views formed regarding this idea, namely the OKW and OKH, which even before this were competing for Hitler's attention. At this time, an unofficial division of responsibilities existed between them. The OKW was occupied primarily with the Western theater of operations and Africa. At its helm was the headquarters of the OKW's operational leadership headed by General of Artillery A. Jodl. Yet everything that touched upon the Soviet-German front was the responsibility of the German *Heer* and its headquarters headed by Colonel General K. Zeitzler. So, in the first stage of planning the 1943 summer campaign, these two centers of force would use the question of an offensive for bolstering their own positions and recruiting supporters around their rival positions. As we will see ahead, Zeitzler as the Chief of Staff of the OKH would become both a "point of attraction" for adherents of active operations in the East and an inexhaustible advocate, who throughout the spring and beginning of summer would advance not only the idea of a major offensive in the area of the Kursk salient, but precisely Operation Citadel in the form in which it would be implemented, which is to say in the form of two concentric attacks directed to meet in an area east of Kursk. In addition, it should be emphasized that at both this time and throughout the entire period of preparing for the attack toward Kursk, the Führer plainly favored Colonel-General Zeitzler and paid heed to his advice. Indeed, this did not remain unnoticed in his immediate circle. In his diary entry from 9 March 1943, J. Goebbels particularly remarked that Hitler "continues to be very well satisfied with Zeitzler, who is at present his most effective assistant in the conduct of the eastern campaign."[66]

A. Jodl and his supporters were categorically opposed to a major offensive on the Eastern Front. They argued that it was very dangerous to expend the Reich's last reserves in face of the growing problems in the Mediterranean Sea and the overall threat of an amphibious landing by British and American troops in Europe.

As the British historian R. Cross observes, K. Zeitzler was very dissatisfied over the fact that he had essentially been walled off from taking part in commanding the forces in the West, so at any opportunity he inserted sticks into the spokes of the OKW's wheels during its attempts to interfere with matters on the Eastern Front. The Colonel General parried these objections by A. Jodl with the explanation that the forces in the East had become so depleted that they were unable to hold the front without active combat operations, and the analysis of the entire line of the Soviet-German front, which extended 2,520 km from north to south, showed that the most advantageous conditions for on offensive had formed precisely in the area of the Kursk salient. According to his calculations, just 11-12 panzer divisions, supported by infantry, could

---

English translation of this book, so again, this is my translation from the Russian version of a German book.
65 Schwarz, *Die Stabilisierung der Ostfront nach Stalingrad*, p. 262.
66 Goebbels, *The Goebbels Diaries* (The Fireside Press, 1948), p. 322.

guarantee success. On the other hand, Wehrmacht passivity worked in favor of the Red Army, which was gathering strength. The Wehrmacht Major General D. von Choltitz wrote:

> Suspicion toward the General Staff and the fear that it was concentrating too much authority prompted Hitler to create a system of separate responsibilities according to the principle of "divide et impera" ["divide and conquer"]. Therefore, the military organs of command frequently found themselves forced literally to struggle against different organizations of the Reich. At this time, whereas the Chief of the OKH remained responsible for operations only on the Eastern Front, the Supreme Command of the Wehrmacht (OKW), the responsibilities of which, in principle, should have consisted in directing and coordinating the activities of all three major types of armed forces (infantry, air force and navy), was responsible only for operations in the West. Thereby Hitler himself took full control over military operations. It seems excessive for me to say that such a concentration of authority in the hands of one man would have exceeded the physical and mental strength of even a Moltke or von Schlieffen.
>
> The Main Command of the General Staff no longer existed. Its functions had been split up, a consequence of which a definite rivalry arose between the Supreme Command of the Armed Forces (OKW) and the Supreme Command of the Army (OKH). Directed by the justified, but unilateral interests of their respective staff, they both competed for each and every division; I can even say, they fought over every new tank or machine gun that emerged from a factory.[67]

Nevertheless, this does not mean that when taking the decisions regarding major military questions, the Führer ignored the opinions of his generals, and the argument that began in spring over whether it was better to take the initiative and attack in the East or to go over to the defensive shouldn't be viewed only as interdepartmental. Already in March 1943, Hitler brought into his orbit a number of authoritative figures, including for example Colonel General H. Guderian.[68] These men took part in the discussion only with the aim of opening Hitler's

---

67 Choltitz, D. von, *Soldatskii dolg: Vospominaniia generala vermakhta o voine na zapade i vostoke Evropy, 1939-1945* [*Soldier's duty: Recollections of a Wehrmacht general about the war in the west and east of Europe, 1939-1945*]. Translated from the German by V.E. Klimanov (Moscow: Tsentrpoligraf, 2015), p. 147.
68 Guderian, Heinz Wilhelm (1888-1954), Colonel General of the Wehrmacht (1940). In military service from 1907 and a veteran of the First World War. One of the founders of the German armored forces. On 26 August 1939 he assumed command of the XIX Motorized Corps, which took part in the conquest of Poland. A participant in the campaign in France. In November 1940, he became the commander of Panzergruppe 2, which on 22 June 1941 invaded the Soviet Union. It launched an attack in the Minsk – Smolensk direction, then took part in the encirclement of Soviet forces in the Kiev area and the capture of Orel, but it was halted in front of Tula and forced to retreat. On 17 July 1941 Guderian was awarded the Knight's Cross with Oak Leaves. On 26 December 1941 because of conflicts with the commander-in-chief of Army Group Center, Guderian was sent into the reserve pool of commanders, and from 16 November 1942 he was located in the III Army Corps' Department of Replenishments in Berlin. After the Stalingrad disaster, on 28 February 1943 he was appointed Inspector General of Armored Troops. Guderian persistently and continually argued against conducting Operation Citadel. In particular, at the well-known conference on 4 May 1943, in the presence of Hitler he sharply criticized this plan and particularly stressed that this offensive would once and for all sap the armored troops and the entire Wehrmacht of their remaining strength.

eyes to the major objective problems that would arise in the event of the operation's failure. Incidentally, I will point out the important detail that "Fast Heinz" was appointed to the post of Inspector General of Armored Troops on 28 February 1943 after a lengthy fall from grace, which is to say at the moment when the planning for the summer campaign began, and this clearly testifies to the great hopes that Hitler was placing on this type of troops.

Intelligence information plainly shows that the situation in the East, and primarily in the area of the Kursk bulge, was fundamentally and rapidly changing not in Germany's favor, even as von Manstein's "backhand blow" in Ukraine was successfully unfolding. A summary from the Intelligence Department of the OKH on 2 March 1943 stated:

> According to certain recent ... reports, it is not excluded that the enemy has recognized that the preparation for a German offensive is underway ..., initially, he will wait and continuously strengthen his defenses in the effort to achieve his own offensive objectives only once our forces have exhausted themselves. ... The replenishment of his forces is growing constantly and ever increasing their combat strength. The enemy is continuously shifting new forces into the depth of his dispositions opposite the northern flank of Army Group South and the southern face of Army Group Center. Thus, it should be considered that the enemy in anticipation of the German offensive will augment the number of troops and increase their defensive capabilities, which are already on a high level.[69]

However, each side contrived to use information of this type in order to bolster their respective positions. A. Jodl – as confirmation of the fact that the success of the planned offensive was already now in doubt, and yet the preparation for it would unquestionably demand more time, while for example E. von Manstein and K. Zeitzler on the contrary kept insisting that the operation be launched as soon as possible, while the Russian troops still had not yet finished their defensive preparations.

However, let us return to Order No. 5. The withdrawal of Army Group Center's forces from the Viaz'ma salient had begun to be prepared back in the middle of winter. This was a compulsory step and at first had no direct connection with the planning of the summer campaign. On 17 January 1943 troops of the Kalinin Front had taken Velikie Liuki by storm. Therefore, the threat had arisen of the encirclement of Colonel General W. Model's Ninth Army and a portion of Colonel General G. Heinrici's Fourth Army in the Rzhev salient (an area west of Belyi – north

---

Between 10 and 14 July 1943, he journeyed to the Eastern Front in order to inspect first Army Group South, and then Army Group Center. As a result of this trip, a report was prepared that analyzed the effectiveness of the new armored fighting vehicles: the Panther tanks and the Ferdinand self-propelled guns. The document rightly acknowledged that their significance before the Battle of Kursk had been exaggerated by Berlin. These new tanks and tank destroyers could not decisively affect the outcome of the battle, since they were not ready for combat use, and there was too few of them. In July 1944 Guderian became the Chief of Staff of the OKH, but on 28 March 1945 he was sent into retirement after the next conflict with Hitler. On 10 May 1945 he was captured by US forces and was jailed up until June 1948, when he was released.

69 *Sovershenno sekretno! Tol'ko dlia komandovaniia! Strategiia fashistkoi Germanii v voine protiv SSSR: Dokumenty i materialy* [*Totally secret! Only for the command! The strategy of fascist Germany in the war against the USSR: Documents and materials*] (Moscow: Voenizdat, 1967), p. 495.

and east of Rzhev – west of Iukhnov – east of Spas-Demiansk), which was situated at the boundary between two Soviet fronts, the Kalinin Front (on the left) and the Western Front (on the right). It had formed as a result of the Red Army's unsuccessful strategic operation, which was conducted between 8 January and 20 April 1942. Despite a series of major assaults by Soviet troops, undertaken afterward, the Germans were still continuing to hold their lines here throughout the year. According to the uniform opinion of historians, the merits in this belonged to the Ninth Army and personally to its commander, W. Model.

On 25 January 1943, a meeting took place between G. von Kluge and Hitler in the latter's headquarters. After a report on the situation, the Field Marshal received a directive to begin shortening the front lines in the sector of the Ninth and Fourth Armies that very day. The Führer agreed to abandon this triangular 160-km salient intruding into the Red Army's defenses, in order to free up forces to assist Army Group Don, which at that time was under heavy pressure from Soviet forces.[70]

In the course of the meeting, Hitler also confirmed the new combat composition of Army Group Center, which at that time was holding a front that extended for approximately 1,500 km. From 1 January 1943, it was due to have 74 divisions under 18 panzer and army corps headquarters.[71] In their turn, they constituted five armies (the Second, Fourth and Ninth Armies and the Second and Third Panzer Armies).

On 4 February, W. Model through Operational Order No. 800/43 formed a special staff to direct the operation to withdraw the forces to a new line, which received the code name "Buffalo".[72] In order to set up the new positions, all of the army's pioneer and construction units (approximately 30,000 men), as well as prisoners, were made directly subordinate to the army's senior engineer. Thanks to this, the main work was completed within a short period of time, and by the end of this month, a new main line of battle running from Dukhovshchina through Dorogobuzh to Spas-Demiansk, which stretched for around 100 km, was ready to accept troops.[73] The stockpiles of fuel, ammunition, equipment and gear were evacuated by rail in February, and the withdrawal of the army's combat units took place between 1 and 30 March, though in fact the stabilization of the front along the Buffalo line took place already on 22 March. As a result, by the end of March 1943 the defenses of Army Group Center were reduced by 200 km and now extended for approximately 1,250 km.[74]

It should be emphasized that the simultaneous withdrawal of the forces of two armies (one army headquarters, four corps, 21 divisions, including five panzer and motorized divisions, for a total of 324,924 soldiers and officers)[75] was conducted in a relatively organized and stealthy

---

70   Rass, Kristoff, *Chelovecheskii material: Nemetskie soldaty na Vostochnom fronte* [*Human material: German soldiers on the Eastern Front*] (Moscow: Veche, 2013), p. 394.
71   Some of these divisions were considered reserve divisions and were directly subordinate to the army headquarters and army group headquarters.
72   Newton, S., *Pozharnik Gitlera* [*Hitler's fireman*] (Moscow: AST MOSKVA – Khranitel', 2007), p. 257. This is the Russian translation of the author's *Hitler's Commander: Field Marshal Walther Model – Hitler's Favorite General* (Da Capo Press, 2009).
73   Haupt, W., *Srazheniia gruppy armii "Tsentr"* [*Battles of Army Group Center*] (Moscow: Iauza. EKSMO, 2006), p. 227. This is the same book by Werner Haupt published under the title *Army Group Center: The Wehrmacht in Russia, 1941-1945* and published in 1997 by Schiffer Publishing Ltd.
74   Rass, *Chelovecheskii material*, p. 394.
75   Newton, *Pozharnik Gitlera*, p. 256.

manner. The Soviet side was unable to disrupt it or to inflict substantial damage to Model's and Heinrici's forces as they pulled back. This was due as well to subjective reasons. The first information about the enemy's withdrawal from the salient did not arrive at the headquarters of the Western Front until 18 February, five days after this fact had been discovered by the Kalinin Front's intelligence. However, the commander of the 30th Army Lieutenant General V.Ia. Kolpachki tarried with the issuing an order to begin the pursuit; it was dispatched to the troops only on the afternoon of 2 March, at a time when the enemy's main forces had already left Rzhev and even the screening units were prepared to abandon the city. Moscow also failed to react in time; the Stavka's Directive No. 30062 regarding a more energetic pursuit of the enemy by the Kalinin and Western Fronts was signed only at 1715 on 2 March.[76]

The liquidation of the Rzhev salient was beneficial for the Soviet side as well. It also enabled it to withdraw substantial forces into the reserve – two full armies, the 22nd and 41st Armies. In addition, the Germans were compelled to abandon a rather large amount of railroad stock and tanks. According to Soviet data, on 3 March, 35 steam engines, 1,200 railcars and 112 tanks were captured in Rzhev, while 60 steam engines, 500 railcars and more than 80 tanks and 70 guns were seized and destroyed in Viaz'ma on 12 March.[77]

Nevertheless, this German withdrawal was unquestionably a substantial success, one most important for Berlin, which inspired a certain amount of confidence that the ripening plan for a major offensive in the Kursk area would prove to be successful. For Hitler, the withdrawal of the main forces of von Kluge's Army Group Center from the Rzhev salient without large losses, and the storming of Khar'kov by von Manstein's troops that began on 11 March 1943, gave a large nudge to the signing of Order No. 5. After all, there was now no need to shift impressive forces to the south, as had been planned. Thanks to the successful regrouping of the Ninth and Fourth Armies, the process of creating one of the two assault groups in the area of the Kursk bulge began, the formation of which was mentioned in the order. It is hard not to agree with the American scholar Steve Newton, who observes, "The forces freed by Operation Buffalo, in combination with the divisions transferred to Russia from France during the past two months, in large measure compensated for the loss of the Sixth Army at Stalingrad and made it possible (for the final time during the war) for Hitler and the OKH to contemplate a choice between retaking the initiative with an offensive or awaiting the next Soviet attack with a substantial reserve to thwart it."[78]

However, the key words from the cited passage are "in large measure". According to a formal calculation, then 22 divisions of the Germans or their allies were in fact destroyed on the Volga, whereas if you add together the divisions of the Ninth Army and the single SS corps that arrived from France, this yields 24 divisions. However, in addition to the II SS Panzer Corps, Army Group South received a number of other divisions from Europe. The main point is that according to German data, the Wehrmacht had been deprived of more than 800,000 men alone, as well as a significant amount of armaments. The chief of the OKW's Defense Economy

---

76 *Russkii arkhiv. Velikaia Otechestvennaia voina. Stavka Verkhovnogo Komandovaniia. Dokumenty i materialy 1943* [*Russian archive. Great Patriotic War. Headquarters of the Supreme High Command. Documents and materials*] T. 16 (5-3) (Moscow: TERRA, 1999), p. 87.
77 *Istoriia Velikoi Otechestvennoi voiny Sovetskogo Soiuza 1941-1945* [*History of the Great Patriotic War of the Soviet Union, 1941-1945*] T. 6 (Moscow: Voenizdat, 1974), p. 84.
78 Newton, *Pozharnik Gitlera*, p. 260.

and Armament Office General G. Thomas maintained that the loss in equipment was sufficient to equip 45 divisions with all types of weapons, and equaled the total losses over the entire preceding period of fighting on the Soviet-German front. The decrease in tanks and automobiles was comparable to their output by the Reich's industry over six months of operation; in artillery – over three months of operation; and in infantry weapons and mortars – over two months of operation.[79] This factor became the most important cause for Operation Citadel's failure. Having managed at first glance to gather, through the straightening of the front and the transfer a significant portion of their reserves to the East, a seemingly impressive number of divisions to the groupings at Kursk, Germany's leadership would prove unable not only to supply the troops with everything necessary to meet the offensive's assigned objectives but was even unable to bring them back up to authorized strength.

However, let us return to the events of the end of March 1943. At this moment, E. von Manstein and W. Model[80] were indisputably at the center of Berlin's attention. To a significant degree, owing to their efforts and skill, the Wehrmacht was gradually beginning to emerge from the series of defeats that had fallen upon the Germans like a tidal wave since the autumn of 1942. However, according to a shared opinion of both the participants in those events and historians, Hitler was unquestionably more favorably inclined to the commander of the Ninth Army; in contrast, whereas Model was not much loved in the highest echelons of Germany's officer corps, von Manstein enjoyed great respect.[81] Guderian recalled:

79 *Istoriia Btoroi mirovoi voiny 1939-1945*, p. 84.
80 Model, Otto Mortiz Walter (1891-1945), Wehrmacht General-Field Marshal (1944). In military service from 1909 and a veteran of the First World War. From 1919 he was serving with the General Staff. In October 1938, Model became the chief of staff of the IV Army Corps. He was located in this post at the start of the Second World War and took part in the occupation of Poland. A year later he was appointed chief of staff of the Sixteenth Army, which took part in the conquest of France. From November 1940, he served as the commander of the 3rd Panzer Division, and on 22 June 1941 his division crossed the Soviet border as part of General H. Guderian's Panzergruppe 2. In January 1942 he took command of the Ninth Army, at the head of which he defended the Rzhev salient for more than a year. In March 1943 in connection with the overall sharply deteriorating situation on the Soviet-German front, Model withdrew his forces to the area south of Orel, where they took up a defense opposite the Soviet Central Front. In the course of preparing for Operation Citadel, Hitler made him responsible for conducting it on the northern face of the Kursk bulge (Army Group Center's sector). On 5 July 1943, four of his panzer and army corps attacked the positions of three armies of the Central Front. However, Berlin's calculations that the defense of the Soviet troops would collapse after the first powerful blow proved unjustified. Model's troops engaged in three major fights – along the Ol'khovatka and Maloarkhangel'sk directions, and for Ponyri Station, in which they suffered heavy losses. However, they were unable to make a significant advance and were forced to fall back to their line of departure. This became Model's first major setback over the war years. Immediately after the failure of Citadel, Model was made responsible at first for the defense of the entire Orel bulge, and then the evacuation from it. At the conclusive stage of the war in 1944 and 1945, Model commanded the troops of several army groups. On 17 April 1945, he was awarded the Knight's Cross with Diamonds, Oak Leaves and Swords. Later that same month, after the encirclement and destruction of his troops in the Ruhr pocket, he committed suicide. Model was a dedicated Nazi. Numerous facts of the atrocities perpetrated by the Ninth Army under his command in the Rzhev area were documented by Soviet investigators and presented at the Nuremburg trials.
81 Barnett, C. et al., *Voennaia elita Reikha* [*Reich's military elite*], translated from the English by A. Fel'dsherov and O. Razumovsky (Smolensk: Ruchich, 1999), p. 429. This is the Russian translation of the book *Hitler's Generals* by Correlli Barnett (ed.) and published by Grove Press in 2003.

> I once again realized what a pity it was that Hitler could not tolerate the presence of so capable and soldierly person as Manstein in his environment ... Manstein [was] a man of most distinguished military talents, a product of the German General Staff Corps, with a sensible, cool understanding, who was our finest operational brain. Later, when I was entrusted with the duties of Chief of the Army General Staff, I frequently proposed to Hitler that Manstein be appointed chief of the OKW in place of Keitel, but always in vain. It is true that Keitel made life easy for Hitler; he sought to anticipate and fulfill Hitler's every wish before it had even been uttered. Manstein was not so comfortable a man to deal with; he formed his opinions and spoke them aloud.[82]

The Commander-in-Chief of Army Group South also thought rather highly of his former subordinate Model. As the American scholar Carlo D'Este maintains, he praised Model's defensive tactics, but disdained him as a Nazi.[83] In his book of memoirs, E. von Manstein noted the Führer's special favor for the commander of the Ninth Army:

> Colonel-General Model ... enjoyed Hitler's special trust after he had distinguished himself with his distinctive energy and resolve in the 1941 and 1942 campaigns, first as the commander of a panzer corps, and then as commander of the Ninth Army during the heavy defensive fighting of Army Group Center.
> I knew Model well from the time when he had served in my 8th Department of the General Staff; he was monitoring the development of equipment and evaluating it from the point of view of the requirements placed upon it by the General Staff. He was very useful in this role, acting like a pike in a pond full of carps from the departments of the various ministries. Later he served as the chief of staff of the Sixteenth Army in Army Group A, where in turn I was the chief of staff of the army group, and he took part in the preparation of the campaign in the West.
> Model was undoubtedly a very capable staff officer. He had a clear mind and the ability to assess a situation rapidly. ... His unique quality was his uncommon energy, which sometimes even bordered on folly. He combined this quality of his with confidence and the ability to express his opinion firmly. By nature, he was an optimist, who refused to acknowledge difficulties. These traits, his enormous energy and, finally, his desire to achieve good personal relationships with the regime's main actors ... impressed Hitler ... With respect to the regime, he was disposed less critically than the overwhelming number of higher military leaders. However, Model must never be assigned to those few soldiers, who were always obedient to Hitler.[84]

To the above it should be added that in the spring of 1943, Model's efforts received high marks. Back in December 1942, Colonel General Model became a candidate for the post of commander-in-chief of an army group, and in early April 1943 he was sent on assignment to Army Group South to serve as the temporarily acting commander-in-chief in place of E. von Manstein, who

---

82 Guderian, *Vospominaniia soldata*, p. 333.
83 See Barnett, *Voennaia elita Reikha*, p. 429.
84 Manstein, *Poteriannye pobedy*, pp. 525-526. Again, this particular passage does not exist in the abridged English version of the Field Marshal's memoirs, so this is my own translation.

because of health problems had received a leave of absence and had traveled to Berlin. On 3 April 1943, Hitler awarded Model the Knight's Cross with Oak Leaves and Swords. Thus, the decision to put him in charge of conducting the offensive toward Kursk from the north instead of von Kluge, even though Model commanded the subordinate Ninth Army, did not surprise anyone. Even so, this did not add any warmth to their personal relationship, which was already strained even before this.

According to Army Group Center's chief of transportation Colonel H. Teske, on 7 March 1943 the first official order regarding Operation Citadel arrived: promptly to begin sending ten divisions of the Ninth Army from the areas of Smolensk, El'nia and Iartsevo to the area south of Orel.[85] However, this order shouldn't be connected only with the preparation of the offensive toward Kursk; it predated Order No. 5, but in essence went along the same channel of its demands. The main reason for the hasty assembly of Model's army in the Orel salient was the offensive by the Briansk and Central Fronts that was already underway at this time, with the aim of stopping it. Thus, Berlin was planning at first to thwart the plans of the Soviet side and to stabilize the front in this sector, and only later decide how to conduct a summer campaign – whether to go over to the defensive or to begin to prepare its own offensive operation.

Relying on the information from the Ninth Army's journal of combat operations, its headquarters outlined the first stage of planning the offensive toward Kursk in the period between 26 March and 12 April 1943. The date determined for the final assembly of the troops (X-Day) was set for 21 April.[86] The offensive was planned to begin on 25 April. By this moment the divisions assigned for it were to have moved into their jumping-off positions, having taken up a combat formation arranged in a single echelon. Operational Order No. 2916/43 from 24 March, issued by Army Group Center's Operations Department, set these dates and gave the first concrete assignments to the army for the preparation of the operation, which later acquired the code name "Citadel".

On this same day, 24 March, G. von Kluge sent a telegram to Berlin, in which in general outlines he laid out the steps to carry out Order No. 5, and presented the scheme for the forthcoming offensive by his forces. Judging from the document, the army group's command faced two main tasks at this moment: Completing the formation of the assault wedge, which was to be based on the Ninth Army, and putting the divisions that had been transferred to it in shape for an offensive. The documents of its headquarters noted, "The high trust shown the army has inspired enthusiasm and pride in us."[87] The task standing in front of Model was quite complex: under the conditions of the muddy season that had started, to shift several divisions stealthily to the southern portion of the Orel bulge (to the rear of the Second Army), where the network of dirt roads had quite literally dissolved into mud, and ready them to conduct a large operation within an extremely compressed time schedule. Already in mid-April, the Ninth Army was to take over the Second Army's sector of the front,[88] which had been marked as the line of departure for its assault grouping. The main objective of the offensive and the areas for launching the main and secondary attacks had been determined back in March, and

---

85 Newton, *Kurskaia bitva: nemetskii vzgliad*, p. 265.
86 NARA US, T.312, R.317, F.7886035.
87 NARA US, T.312, R.317, F.7886029.
88 Until the beginning of April 1943, troops of the Second Panzer Army had been defending this sector, at which point it had been taken over by the Second Army.

fundamentally wouldn't change until mid-May, as was the case for Army Group South as well. The Ninth Army's journal of combat operations observed:

> In our operation, which was supposed to begin around 1 May, we were to achieve a major breakthrough and launch an attack along converging directions in order to link up with Army Group South's panzer army. The Ninth Army, in the area south of Orel, was to encircle and destroy the enemy located there. The tasks for accomplishing this goal: to assemble the forces of three panzer corps in a narrow sector of the front, and to launch an attack along the Orel – Fatezh – Kursk road, as well as along the railroad to the east of it. Simultaneously with the offensive, it was also to form a strong defensive front to the east.[89]

At the end of March W. Model received a leave of absence until mid-April and together with his chief of operations Colonel H. von Treskow departed for Germany. Therefore the entire responsibility for this complex and large-scale work lay on his staff, which from 1 March had been headed by Colonel H. von Elverfeldt.[90] He had replaced Lieutenant General H. Krebs, who had become the chief of staff of Army Group Center.[91] On 31 March he arrived in Orel

---

89 NARA US, T.312, R.317, F.7886029.
90 Harald Freiherr von Elverfeldt, born on 5 February 1902 in Hildesheim. On 22 March 1918 he became a cadet, and he acquired his first officer's rank of lieutenant on 24 November 1919. He served in the army of the Weimar Republic in infantry units and as a staff officer. By the start of the Second World War, Elverfeldt was serving in the rank of major as the chief of operations of the 3rd Light Division, and on 16 October 1939, he was appointed as chief of operations to the 8th Panzer Division. Between February 1940 and 31 January 1941, Lieutenant Colonel von Elverfeldt served as chief of operations of the XV Army Corps. In this post he took part in the conquest of France and Belgium, for which he was awarded the Iron Cross 1st Class. On 15 March 1941, he became the chief of staff of the LVI Panzer Corps, with which he took part in the invasion of the Soviet Union. On 1 March 1942, he received promotion to the rank of colonel, and on 16 March 1942 Elverfeldt was decorated with the German Cross in Gold. From mid-January 1943, he was transferred into the reserve. From 30 January to 1 October 1943, he was the Ninth Army's chief of staff. On 1 September 1943, he rose to the rank of major general. From 1 November 1943 he served as the Seventeenth Army's chief of staff, before once again being transferred into the reserve, but on 15 February 1944 he took charge of a course for higher officers of combined-arms units. On 16 September 1944 he took command of the 9th Panzer Division. He received the Knight's Cross on 9 December 1944. That month, he was wounded during an Allied air raid and evacuated to a hospital, but already on 1 January 1945 he returned to assume command of the 9th Panzer Division. He was killed in action in Cologne on 6 March 1945 during street fighting. Elverfeldt was posthumously promoted to lieutenant general and awarded the Knight's Cross with Oak Leaves.
91 Hans Krebs, born on 4 March 1898 in Helmstädt. A veteran of the First World War, he was awarded the Iron Cross 2nd Class. After serving in the army of the Weimar Republic, on 6 October 1937 he was transferred to the OKH. On 15 December 1939 Lieutenant Colonel H. Krebs was appointed chief of staff to the VII Army Corps, with which he took part in the invasion of France. From July 1940 he was the first assistant to the German military attaché in Moscow. On 1 October 1940, Krebs was promoted to the rank of colonel. After the start of the war with the Soviet Union, Krebs was in the reserve, but on 14 January 1942 he returned to the army and was appointed as the Ninth Army's chief of staff. On 1 February 1942, Krebs was promoted to the rank of major general. On 30 January 1943, he was withdrawn into the Führer's reserve, but on 1 March 1943 he assumed the post of Army Group Center's chief of staff. On 1 April 1943 Krebs became a lieutenant general. From 5 September 1944

together with a small group of the army's intelligence and logistics officers, as well as several officers of the Operations Department. In order to facilitate the establishment of cooperation within the operational group, Elverfeldt was temporarily housed in the same building with the headquarters of the Second Panzer Army, which was located in the southern portion of the city, but a week later, on 5 April, the operational group of officers moved to Kishkino (6 km northwest of Orel), where in order to camouflage it, their offices were set up in a hospital building.

By this time, the beginning of April, the Ninth Army included three panzer corps (the XXXXI, XXXXVI and XXXXVII) and two army corps (XX and XXIII), all of which were eventually to be fully activated for the operation, but at various stages of it. The panzer corps – from the first day; the XXIII Army Corps – after the penetration of the tactical zone of defenses (from out the second echelon); and the XX Army Corps – in the culminating stage, in the course of a pinning attack on the Ninth Army's right flank. The five corps comprised a total of 19 divisions that had been transferred to Model, or 25.7percent of those belonging to Army Group Center. However, it was planned to use only 12 of them for the attack: six panzer divisions (the 2nd, 4th, 9th, 12th, 18th and 20th Panzer Divisions), one motorized division (the 10th Panzergrenadier Division), one assault division (the 78th Sturm Division), and four infantry divisions (the 7th, 86th, 258th and 292nd Infantry Divisions), which amounted to 63percent of the total belonging to the Ninth Army or 16.2percent of the total belonging to Army Group Center. The plan included the use of seven infantry divisions (the 45th, 72nd, 102nd, 137th, 216th, 251st and 383rd Infantry Divisions) in order to hold the rest of the line (taken over from the Second Army). In addition, W. Model was assigned supplementary assets: three battalions of assault guns, 13 heavy artillery battalions, seven army pioneer battalions, 11 construction battalions, 10 bridging columns, and a number of other specialized units.

For purposes of concealment, the main forces of the Ninth Army were assembled in the vicinity of Smolensk until mid-April. With the aim of saving time and transportation, as well as because of the danger that the Russians would be first to go on the offensive, it was decided to reject the withdrawal of the army's shock forces to an area well behind the front lines and to conduct all the steps to increase their combat readiness in place, which is to say, in the second echelon. The army command exerted every effort to complete the assembly of the troops and the replenishment of the divisions with personnel and equipment by 21 April. However, the conditions of the weather and the roads did not facilitate this – the muddy season had started and the rivers were in flood. In certain divisions holding inactive sectors (the 6th and 72nd Infantry Divisions), the unscheduled measures connected to bringing them back up to strength were postponed, so as not to fritter away the available means, but instead to direct them into the assault grouping, in which nearly all the divisions were rather weak numerically. In the first place, the 4th, 9th, 12th, 18th and 20th Panzer Divisions and the 7th and 86th Infantry Divisions were to pulled back first into the second echelon for replenishment and refitting.

However, from the outset the leadership of Army Group Center regarded the start date set by Berlin, 21 April, rather skeptically. Its headquarters believed that Model's Ninth Army would

he served as chief of staff of Army Group "B". On 20 February 1945, Krebs was bestowed the Oak Leaves to the Knight's Cross, and on 17 February 1945 he became the OKH deputy chief of staff. In mid-March during an Allied air raid on Zossen, he received a light wound. Krebs became the OKH chief of staff on 29 March 1945 but shot himself in Berlin on 1 May 1945.

be able to move into its jumping-off positions in readiness to carry out its given missions no sooner than 1 May. In a report from 24 March 1943, it offered the following proposals for the conducting of the offensive:

a) Several days prior to X-Day or on X-Day, launch an attack with the XXXXI Panzer Corps given a strong concentration of our forces in the southeastern direction, in order to fix the enemy troops in this sector and to secure our flanks in an operational sense;
b) On X-Day launch an attack with the XXXXVI and XXXXVII Panzer Corps simultaneously with the offensive of the southern grouping, advancing in deep combat formations along the axis of the highway leading to Fatezh and the railroad leading to Kursk;
c) Depending on the development of the enemy's situation, on X-Day or somewhat later, the Ninth Army launches an attack with its western flank, and the Second Army with its northern flank and center, with their forces gathered into a shock fist with the aim of pinning down the enemy troops;
d) Subsequently introduce a strong reserve group (the XXIII Army Corps, if possible, consisting of three infantry divisions) that is located at readiness, with the aim of reinforcing the main attack or reaching the eastern sector of the front that has been recaptured from the enemy ....
IV. After completing the operation and the emergence on a new, shorter line east of Kursk, the Ninth Army headquarters with the bulk of its assault forces can be used to carry out a different assignment. In this case it would be useful to reestablish the former boundary line between the Second Army and Second Panzer Army.[92]

Further on in the document, an optimistic version of future events is examined – a Red Army withdrawal. "In the event that the enemy withdraws," wrote G. von Kluge, "an advance may begin earlier, immediately after the end of the muddy season. In order to make the shock army sufficiently strong, it will be necessary to take a risk by transferring troops to it by means of reducing the army group's reserves, since in reserve there remains only the 8th Panzer Division – behind the northern flank; the 36th Infantry Division – northeast of Smolensk; the seriously weakened 5th Panzer Division – behind the Second Panzer Army's northern flank; and the weak 87th Infantry Division, which after a short rest will be moved up to take over the front held by the 3rd Panzer Division (on the northern flank of the Luftwaffe field corps)."[93]

In essence, this document presents the first concrete, detailed draft of a plan for a German offensive toward Kursk from the north. In the future its points would be repeatedly reworked, and the force grouping involved in implementing it would also change. Berlin's gradual recognition of the large forces possessed by the Red Army and search for the bits and pieces that could be gathered for such a grandiose undertaking by Germany would become the reason for these changes, but about this later. For now, I only want to point out one important detail – the modest reserves of Army Group Center. After all, this was only one of the two army groups

---

92 Klink, *Das Gesetz des Handelns. Die Operation "Zitadelle"*, pp. 284-286.
93 Ibid.

upon which fate had fallen to conduct the entire summer campaign in the East, and it had only four divisions in reserve, including two that were openly acknowledged as weak! Later, in May and June, G. von Kluge would receive replenishments in both personnel and equipment, but not a single fresh division would arrive to reinforce his army group. Hitler simply did not have them! Thus, in order to reinforce the Ninth Army, Field Marshal von Kluge would use the only possibility that remained for him – a regrouping within his own army group, which inevitably led to weakening its defenses elsewhere. However, he simply had no other way out, and the Fourth Army would turn out to be the main donor.

On 9 April, the forward units of the Ninth Army began to arrive in order to take over the sectors of the Second Panzer Army, while at that time its main forces were as before located in the Smolensk area. The Orel bulge because of its challenging terrain was not the most suitable place to conduct a major regrouping. During the muddy season the main burden fell on the railroad network, which was not well-developed here. Therefore, in order both to shift the forces of Model's Ninth Army and to keep it and the divisions of the Second Panzer Army supplied, the double track Briansk – Orel and Orel – Glazunovka railroad lines would be fully engaged. At this moment they became the army's main arteries, even though they had only a modest capacity. Back in 1942 they had been converted to the European gauge, and all the trains had been replaced by German trains. The main unsurfaced road to the staging zone was the road that ran alongside the Orel – Glazunovka railroad; it was 5-6 meters wide and had 2-meter shoulders. In addition, there were lateral roads: Krivye Verkhi – Verkhnee Tagino, Glazunovka – Gremiachevo – Bogorodetskoe, Kunach – Trubitsyno and a number of others, but in the muddy season they were difficult to traverse.

By the end of 10 April, the XX Army Corps and seven infantry divisions that were subordinate to the Ninth Army were already positioned in the first line of its designated sector, which simplified the regrouping and the occupation of the defensive positions by the approaching troops. Nevertheless, judging from the information from captured German documents, the replacement of the units did not go smoothly, and this was connected not only with objective factors. Notes the Ninth Army's journal of combat operation:

> Under the leadership of the army's chief of staff the preliminary work on the preparation of Operation Citadel got started, but it did not go smoothly. The assumption of the Second Panzer Army's sector by the approaching units did not go well. The entire day was taken up with working out detailed agreements with its command and the leadership of the corps. In so doing, the army's chief of staff together with his intelligence chief had to drive out personally several times in an automobile and conduct overflights in order to collect needed material about the disposition of friendly troops and the enemy, which was lacking in the headquarters of the Second Panzer Army.[94]

It is hard to say how much these assertions accurately reflect the real picture. The conducting of such major movements in any army never goes without friction and hitches. In addition, it was just at this time, on 10 April, that an investigation began into the affairs of the commander of the Second Panzer Army Colonel General R. Schmidt, and possibly this might have led

---

94 NARA US, T.312, R.317, F.7886029.

to certain apprehension and confusion in the work of the headquarters. Unquestionably, the muddy season was also considerably complicating the work.

There was one more important problem over which Elverfeldt's headquarters was wracking its brains in early April, and this was increasing the troops' combat capabilities. Its Operations Department noted:

> The main concern of the command remains reconstituting the combat capabilities of the troops, especially those of the assault formations. This concept includes not only bringing up the personnel and materiel to authorized strength, but also first of all – the training and team building within the units. In this connection, the chiefs of staff of the four assaulting corps and the chiefs of operations of the 2nd Panzer, 10th Motorized and 292nd Infantry Divisions should on 6 April begin training the troops. The focus of the training: increasing the maneuverability of the troops.[95]

By 8 April, an analogous order arrived in the headquarters of all the divisions subordinate to W. Model, but because of the weather, the work was virtually idle.

As the American historian Martin Caiden observed, "Operation Citadel, unlike many other moves by the leader of the Third Reich, was no sudden, impulsive stroke ... Citadel emerged slowly."[96] His Order No. 5 from 13 March 1943 is clear evidence of this. However, already by the end of March, the Führer's fervor reawakened, and having tossed aside his prior anxieties, he again began to compile grandiose plans. In the latter half of March, not rejecting the idea of capturing of Kursk with von Kluge's and von Manstein's army groups, he, even before this culminating moment, began to examine options for a number of local operations with the aim of weakening the strength of the Russians opposite Army Group South's front. At his directive, the OKH headquarters sent Army Group South a supplement to Operational Order No. 5 on 22 March that demanded that it quickly start to work up Operation "Goshawk," which was intended to secure the assault grouping that had been created in the Khar'kov area in order to help pinch off the Kursk bulge. The document stated:

> In connection with the fact that the muddy period on the southern flank of the Eastern Front will likely be quite short this year, the Führer has ordered Army Group South first to prepare an attack with the idea of forcing the Donets River, in order to destroy the enemy forces west of Kupiansk. The objective of this attack is seizure of the shortest line in the Lisichansk – Kupiansk – Volchansk sector, in order to secure the rear of the offensive in the direction of Kursk, which will be conducted immediately following the indicated attack. The preparation of these operations must be done with the calculation that they will ensue as soon as the weather and icy conditions on the Donets River allow. For this purpose, it is necessary to free up the main mobile forces for actions on the northern flank of Army Group South. It is necessary to use the time before the attack for the replenishment of these divisions; bringing up the necessary forces, in particular the pontoon bridge park; and so forth. For Army Group Center, the

---

95   NARA US, T.312, R.317, F.7886031.
96   Caiden, M., *Tigry goriat* [*The Tigers are Burning*] (Moscow: Iauza; EKSMO, 2009), p. 77. This is the Russian translation of a book carrying the same title by the author in the English language.

previously issued order about creating an assault grouping in the Second Panzer Army's area of operations remains in effect.[97]

Goshawk was to be a local operation, which was supposed to be conducted with the forces of Army Detachment Kempf and the First Panzer Army. Its intent consisted of pressing part of Lieutenant General P.Ia. Malinovsky's Southwestern Front forces, which were defending southeast of Khar'kov along the Severskii Donets River (along the east of Sovetskoe – Peshchanoe – Chuguev – Andreevka – west of Izium line, and further along the branch as far as where the Krasnaia River enters Severskii Donets) back beyond the river. It was planned that the two assault groups of General of Panzer Troops W. Kempf[98] would force the Severskii Donets River to the north (in the Verkhii and Staryi Saltov area) and south of Chuguev, after which one would pivot and advance to the south, into the rear of the Soviet forces defending along the river, while the other would push on to the east, toward Kupiansk. Simultaneously, the First Panzer Army was supposed to launch an attack along the western bank of the Oskol River to the north, toward Kupiansk, and fix the Southwestern Front's forces in the Izium area. As a result of the operation, the new front line was to run along the south of Sovetskoe – east of Prikolotnoe – east of Velikii Burluk line as far as Kupiansk, and further along the branch of the Oskol River to where it enters the Severskii Donets south of Izium, which meant the Soviet forces would in part be shoved back beyond the Severskii Donets and Oskol Rivers.

From the military point of view, this plan can be considered as fully reasonable. The danger to von Manstein's forces from this area was real. The configuration of the front lines actually might have prompted the Soviet side to initiate active operations in this area. Thus, significant forces would be necessary in order to create just a simple defense here, while even more troops and, most importantly, tanks and self-propelled guns would be required just for the partial reduction of the Izium salient. In the circumstances, though, when not even an assault group had been assembled yet for the offensive toward Kursk, nor had the divisions designated for

---

97 Klink, *Das Gesetz des Handelns. Die Operation "Zitadelle"*, p. 279.
98 Werner Kempf, General der Panzertruppen (1 April 1941). Born 9 March 1886 in Königsberg. He took part in the First World War already as an officer, with the last rank as captain. In the interwar period he served in staff posts, including as an inspector of motorized units. After being promoted to the rank of colonel on 1 April 1935, he was appointed as the commander of Panzer Brigade 4. In early 1939 he received his first general's rank as major general and took command of the Division "Kempf" (which was subsequently converted into the 10th Panzer Division), and took part in the invasion of Poland. On 1 October 1939 he transferred in the same post to the XXXXI Panzer Corps' 6th Panzer Division. In this role he distinguished himself in the campaign in France. When forcing the Meuse River, the 6th Panzer Division destroyed the French 102nd Division. For his successful command of the division, he was awarded the Knight's Cross on 3 June 1940, and on 31 July 1940 he was promoted to lieutenant general. On 6 January 1941 he assumed command of the XXXXVIII Panzer Corps. At the start of Operation Barbarossa, the XXXXVIII Panzer Corps was part of General E. Kliest's Panzergruppe 1 and took part in the encirclement of the Southwestern Front near Kiev. On 10 August 1942 he was bestowed the Oak Leaves to the Knight's Cross, and this became his final high award. On 30 September 1942 he assumed command of Army Detachment Kempf, but on 16 August 1943 Hitler formally removed him from this post for the failure to halt the Voronezh and Steppe Fronts on the Khar'kov direction, and he remained in the reserve command pool until the spring of 1944. Between 6 October and 4 December 1944, Kempf commanded the German forces in the Vosges Mountains in France. He went into retirement after this and passed away in the FRG on 6 January 1964.

it been replenished and refitted, then it was at the very least short-sighted to plan for another operation near Khar'kov. However, Hitler likely had not yet realized this. Just two days later, he issued a new order: To prepare for another, but larger operation in the Izium area under the code name "Panther" (again, prior to the offensive toward Kursk). In the course of its implementation, the First and Fourth Panzer Armies, launching attacks out of the Verkhnii Saltov – Chuguev and Izium – (excl.) Lisichansk areas in the overall direction of Kupiansk, were to drive all of Malinovsky's forces not only back beyond the Severskii Donets, but also beyond the Oskol River, to the Khotomlia River – Dvurechnoe – Nizhniaia Duvanka – Svatovo – Krasnaia River line. According to the preliminary calculations, as a result of the success of Operation Goshawk, all of the territory east of the Donets with an area of more than 8,000 square kilometers would fall under the control of Army Group South, and as a result of the implementation of Panther, an area one and a half times larger (more than 12,000 square kilometers) would come under German control.[99] However, once again I'll emphasize that the essence of the matter consisted not in territorial gain, but in the desire to deprive the Soviet side of a staging area for an attack into the flank of the southern assault grouping, assembled for the thrust toward Kursk.

Thus, by the end of March, three offensive operations in the area of the Kursk bulge, differing in scale, were being worked up simultaneously in Berlin, with the overall aim of bleeding the Red Army white, but with no regard for the inherent capabilities of the German forces. I will remind the reader that they were still engaged in heavy fighting in the Belgorod area and northeast of Kursk. In addition, if it is possible to find a connection between Goshawk and Citadel (under certain circumstances, Goshawk could become a prelude to the summer campaign), there was not one visible between Citadel and Panther. This latter operation was of a completely different scale and required significantly more troops and time. Thus, even to the leadership of the OKH, it was not clear why Panther was even being considered in the run-up to such a major offensive as Citadel, given the existing severe deficit of strength and means.

Erich von Manstein also believed that Hitler's desires far exceeded the possibilities of his army group. At noon (Berlin time) on 22 March, K. Zeitzler phoned von Manstein in order to discuss Order No. 5, and in the course of the talk the Field Marshal unambiguously expressed his attitude toward Goshawk: "I'm against this operation. The basis for my opposition: the frozen Donets, the road conditions and the condition of the troops. If the Führer insists on the operation, we should quickly issue an order."[100] The Chief of Staff of the OKH also expressed unequivocally: "I have exactly the same point of view as the Field Marshal. The order from Obersaltzberg, however, arrived as an ultimatum. I have no choice in the matter."[101] However, in a report from 22 March, the Field Marshal was not so categorical; he did not begin to argue openly, but brought to Hitler's attention first and foremost the main objective problem – the mismatch between the available forces and the assigned tasks, likely not without justification assuming that this would cool Hitler's zeal. The Field Marshal wrote:

---

99 Calculations by the author.
100 Anlagen zum Kriegstagebuch (KTB) Nr. 1 der Heeresgruppe Don/Süd, Ferngespräche (Gespräche des Oberbefehlshabers). Band 2: 4.2.-23.3.1943. Bundesarchiv. Abteilung Militärarchiv. Freiburg im Breisgau [BArch-MA]. RH 19 VI/43. Bl. 45.
101 Ibid.

I consider it my duty to report that the forces of the army group are insufficient for resolving the assigned tasks given to it – a rigid defense of the entire front between Taganrog and Belgorod, which is equivalent to 650 km, while forming a panzer army for use in the northern direction, which is to say, beyond the boundaries of Army Group South's zone of operations.

On the sector of the Sixth Army, there is one division for every 20 km, whereas on the sector of the First Panzer Army and Army Detachment Kempf – 30 km, and all of the infantry divisions are deployed on the defensive front. Such an attenuation of the front does not allow the defense to be considered reliably secure even given the presence of a water obstacle and mobile reserves in the form of two panzer corps: one for the eastern and one for the northern flank. If at least a total of five panzer and panzer grenadier divisions are used for defensive purposes, then there will remain only eight mobile divisions for offensive operations, and notably not a single division will be assigned to the given army.

I'm forced to point out that Army Group South given the length of its 650-km front has only 24 infantry and 13 panzer and panzergrenadier divisions, whereas Army Group Center with a front of 1250 km has 69 infantry and 13 panzer and panzergrenadier divisions.[102]

There was no reaction from Berlin to these conclusions. However, on 28 March a new message arrived that made von Manstein's life even more complicated. Hitler made the decision to hold the Kuban bridgehead (Novorossiisk), and through active operations of a relatively small grouping to fix the entire North Caucasus Front in place, in order to prevent the shifting of forces to the Kursk area. For this purpose, he planned to conduct Operation Neptune on the Taman peninsula between 17 and 24 April 1943 in order to destroy the Soviet bridgehead in the Myskhako area (better known in Russia as the "Malaia Zemlia", or "Little Land"). As a result of this new decision, the Field Marshal was deprived of the approximately 10 infantry divisions promised for him from Army Group A. Now it was proposed that only two infantry divisions be transferred to the group as reinforcements, and at that, neither Goshawk or Panther, nor the offensive toward Kursk was as of yet officially cancelled. Even the question of their sequence was not clear. It was only on 2 April did an order arrive from Hitler that Operation Goshawk would come first. It was to be prepared so that after 13 April, the troops would be ready at any moment within four days of the issuing of the order to conduct the operation. According to forecasts, the breakup of the ice on the Severskii Donets was expected to arrive in the latter half of April, but in reality, the Eastern Front actually reawakened already in the beginning of the month, at a time when Army Group South had only begun to put its troops in order. The reconstitution of the mobile divisions required quite a lot of time. Its shock army – the Fourth Panzer Army – and only recently started forming. Therefore E. von Manstein announced that the panzer divisions could not be ready for combat until the end of the month. As a result, the problem with Operation Goshawk resolved itself. However, Hitler continued to insist on his own highly unrealistic plan of actions that represented a diversion from the planning of Citadel. In response to the Field Marshal's report, he directed that if Operation Goshawk was not ready

---

102 Klink, *Das Gesetz des Handelns. Die Operation "Zitadelle"*, pp. 280-283.

to go by 17 April, then preparations must switch to conducting Operation Panther. Hitler set 1 May as the date by which time the troops should be prepared for it.

The working up of the plans for Operations Goshawk and Panther, as well as the evaluation of their possible results on the future course of combat operations in the East were not circulating in a narrow circle of highly-posted generals and field marshals; the headquarters of all the armies of Army Group South were drawn into their discussions. Toward the end of March and in the first days of April, they presented their ideas. In all the documents it is unanimously noted that their leadership did not share the idea of three successive attacks, considering it to be an intolerable dispersion of strength. The most detailed, substantive analysis of the situation was the report from the commander of the Fourth Panzer Army Colonel General H. Hoth. He pointed out that according to intelligence information, the Russians had a significant quantity of armor forces in this area, and thus in order to achieve the objectives of both operations, it would be necessary to activate the army group's main shock force – all of the panzer and panzergrenadier divisions. Even so, there was no guarantee at all that they could fully meet their objectives. From Army Group South's journal of combat operations:

> Proposals for the conducting of Operation Panther have arrived from the Fourth Panzer Army: On the basis of reconnaissance conducted along the front, Army Detachment Kempf assesses the distribution of enemy tank units in the following manner: two tank corps – at Kupiansk; three tank corps and one mechanized corps – north of Kupiansk; two tank corps – in the area north of Belgorod.
>
> On the basis of this evaluation of the enemy and contrasting it to the fact that only five panzer and four infantry divisions are available for our offensive, the army considers the operational plan of Panther unfulfillable. It is necessary to limit the line of the operation's objectives along the line: Kupiansk – Ivanovka – Alekseevka – Pechenegi – Donets. Here an attack is needed with two panzer corps (each with an additional infantry attached to them for the river crossing) in a strongly concentrated wedge in the direction of Kupiansk in order to destroy the tank units based there. Conduct the covering of the northern and southern flanks from each side with one and later two infantry divisions. Given a further advance, there will probably the need to pivot the northern panzer corps to the north for a defense against Russian tank units conducting a counterattack out of the Valiuki area, while the southern panzer corps together with the two infantry divisions set out to destroy the enemy between the Donets and Oskol Rivers in the Balakleia – Izium direction. The army does not believe that this offensive will yield a decisive success. The objectives set for the offensive – the destruction of the enemy's reserve corps – cannot be achieved, since these forces are positioned outside the operation's operational zone. On the contrary – the occupation of the Kupiansk – Pechenegi line will trigger an enemy counteroffensive. It will be necessary to expend additional forces in order to repulse it.[103]

At the same time, the commander of the Fourth Panzer Army emphasized that it was be impossible to forecast the condition of the troops when coming out of the offensive. Only one

---

103 Kriegestagebuch Ia der Heeresgruppe Don/Süd, März bis Juli 1943. BArch-MA. RH 19 VI/45. Bl. 23.

thing was clear – there would be losses. Pointing to these obvious problems, Hoth also expressed doubt that the OKH afterward would be able to keep its promise to allocate additional forces prior to the offensive toward Kursk. They simply would not be available in the needed amount. The influence that the general's letter had at that moment on Berlin's position is not known; nevertheless, it would play an important role. Soon, Hoth's letter would not only change von Manstein's view toward Citadel's basic tasks, but also force him to alter substantially the already existing operational plan for his army group in this operation. In his message, H. Hoth managed to conceive and distinctly articulate the main, and what was very important at that moment, achievable task for the summer campaign, which prior to that moment had only been forming in the back of the Field Marshal's mind after he had failed to substantiate his plan at the end of March. Hoth's essential idea was not the capture of Kursk and the encirclement of a colossal grouping, but the destruction of a significant portion of the Russian mobile reserves in the process of an offensive in the direction of Kursk.

The headquarters of the OKH also consistently spoke up against the operations in the Chuguev – Izium area. It was thanks to the efforts of K. Zeitzler that this idea finally received a fat X-mark across it. On 11 April he presented a memorandum to Hitler, in which he laid out and justified the plan of an attack toward Kursk, which on 31 March had officially received the code name "Citadel".[104] Hitler agreed with the general's conclusions and already on 15 April signed Operational Order No. 6, which was based on the OKH memorandum. Thereby, under the influence of first of all the military men, Operations Goshawk and Panther finally passed into oblivion, even though preparations for the latter operation continued. This, however, was now only camouflage for the forthcoming attack toward Kursk. This situation plainly shows that in the spring of 1943, Hitler was not yet so obstinate as historians now claim. Sensibility and rational thought could get his attention, and he was making fully deliberated decisions. It was only necessary to convince him with facts and figures.

Order No. 6 laid out the objectives and tasks of the summer campaign in the East, as well as the principle guide for the actions of von Kluge's and von Manstein's army groups. Its essence boiled down to the idea of two concentric, meeting attacks out of the area south of Orel (" … from the line of the Trosna River and the area north of Maloarkhangel'sk") to the south through Ponyri and Ol'khovatka, and out of the area north of Belgorod ("… from the Belgorod – Tomarovka line") to the north through Oboian', in order to split the defenses of two Soviet *fronts* – the Voronezh Front (under General of the Army N.F. Vatutin) and the Central Front (under Colonel General K.K. Rokossovsky[105]), and having linked up in the area east of Kursk, to encircle their forces. The order stated:

> I have decided to conduct Citadel, the first offensive of the year as soon as the weather permits. The attack is of the utmost importance. It must be executed quickly and shatteringly. It must seize the initiative for us in the spring and summer. … Each commander and man must be impressed with the decisive significance of this operation. The victory of Kursk must be a beacon to all the world.[106]

---

104 It is noted in the combat diary of the headquarters of the OKW that the order about the acquisition of the code name "Citadel" arrived on 31 March 1943.
105 Rokossovsky would receive the rank of General of the Army on 28 April 1943.
106 Parot'kin (ed.), *Kurskaia bitva*, p. 520.

The results that Hitler was expecting from the offensive were dazzling. The Wehrmacht was to encircle two Soviet *fronts*, which by their tables of organization should have had more than 1,000,000 soldiers, and to take possession of approximately 23,000 square kilometers of land[107] (if calculated from the nose of the Kursk salient back to the Kursk – Orel railroad), and thereby shorten the Soviet-German front by 240-250 km. However, this was only the pipe dream of a group of men, who already realized that the Ten-Thousand-Year Reich project was crumbling. Unlike the major campaigns of the preceding two years, for the very first time this document contained not a single economic objective. In 1941 the main objective had been Ukraine, with its grain, coal and manganese; in 1942, the Wehrmacht was striving for the Caucasus oil fields and an enormous territory, including the rich Black Earth region; but in 1943, as Hitler had announced back in January, an offensive was being prepared in order to achieve a temporary rest, even though the Germany was continuing persistently to advance down the path toward inevitable catastrophe. The acute deficit of troops (especially infantry) not only for this offensive, but also simply to maintain the stability on the Soviet-German front, as well as the absence of a grand, and more importantly, realistic objective gave the plan of Citadel the nature of an attack into a blind alley. In one word, it was war for the sake of war, and it now could not be anything else. This was openly recognized by one of the participants of the Battle of Kursk as well, the former chief of staff of the Fourth Panzer Army General F. Fangohr, who after the war wrote, "One must therefore conclude that Operation Citadel lacked a truly decisive strategic objective."[108] The recognition of this was also the main source of the anxiety and stress felt in all the key levels of Germany's political and military leadership, which were obvious throughout the spring and early summer of 1943.

Despite the serious problems on the Eastern Front and the threat of an Allied landing in Europe, Berlin still managed to scrape together a sufficiently large force for Citadel. Of the 12 armies and five army groups operating on the Soviet-German front, two armies (Fourth Panzer Army and Ninth Army) and one army detachment (Army Detachment Kempf) were intended to be engaged in the offensive. By the end of 10 April, it was already obvious to everyone that it would be impossible to launch the offensive on 21 April, so in Order No. 6 the start date of the operation was shifted to the first days of May, but even this was not the final postponement:

...
5. The deployment of both Army Groups must exploit all possible means of camouflage, deception and disinformation, so that from 28 April, an offensive can be launched within six days of an order from OKH. The earliest date for the offensive will be 3 May.
...
12. The ultimate objectives of the operation are:
    a) The movement of the boundary line between Army Groups South and Center to line Konotop (Army Group South) – Kursk (Army Group South) – Dolgoe (for Army Group Center);

---

107 Author's calculations.
108 Newton, *Kurskaia bitva: Nemetskii vzgliad*, p. 120.

b) the transfer of Second Army headquarters, with three corps headquarters and nine infantry divisions, as well as other army troops yet to be determined, from Army Group Center to Army Group South;

c) the deployment of three additional infantry divisions from Army Group Center, so that they may be available to OKH northwest of Kursk;

d) the withdrawal of the majority of armored formations from this front for use in different theaters; all of the armored formations of the Second Army will comply with these plans.[109]

If you scrutinize Order No. 6, then just as in the case of the plans for Operations Goshawk and Panther, you can see without difficulty a clear element of adventurism. From the outset, the divisions assigned to the operation were not first-class. At the moment of the document's signing, they did not have the necessary (high) level of combat-readiness and needed significant replenishments of personnel and equipment (especially in the Ninth Army), yet there was not enough of these. Because of this the command of neither army group could count upon reaching the assigned objectives set for such a large offensive, or even accomplish the most pressing task – to create a strong system of defense before the start of the operation. Indeed, no matter how paradoxical it may seem, Hitler and the OKH clearly understood this, and yet steadfastly continued to prepare a powerful blow and to count upon its success.

It should not be thought that the offensive's supporters were completely ignoring this serious problem, but they were treating the resolution of it in a somewhat cursory fashion, without regard for the growing power of the Red Army and the skill of its personnel. In the process of planning for Citadel, no consideration was given to the fact that the Wehrmacht already had a large deficit of manpower in the first quarter of 1943, one which would be very difficult to reconstitute in the prevailing conditions. Thus, in order to ensure (if one can use that term) the achievement of Citadel's objectives, Hitler and the OKH were counting upon the panzers, and first of all the new Pz. V Panthers and Pz. VI Tigers, as well as the support of their attacks by the Luftwaffe. It was this "package" that the German high command would rely upon in order to achieve its goals for the offensive. Back on 18 April Hitler had told von Manstein in Zaporozh'e, "We cannot achieve much with men, because we don't have enough. However, with a massing of our best and heaviest weapons ... a breakthrough can be achieved."[110] This thought was clearly traceable in his Order No. 6 as well: "The offensive forces are to be concentrated on the narrowest possible front, so that with the overwhelming support of tanks, artillery, rocket mortars, etc. they can break through the enemy in one blow ...."[111]

However, already in mid-April it was obvious that the production of armored vehicles was well below the rate that was required. In February-March 1943, Army Group South only had 57 Pz. VI (with the Heavy Panzer Battalion 503 and the II SS Panzer Corps). By 20 April it was planned to supply it with another 10 Pz. VI, and by the end of the month – another batch of 10 Tigers. Meanwhile, the Panther tanks were still not entering service, and according to the most optimistic forecasts, the first of these new panzers were to be handed over to the Wehrmacht only at the end of April or beginning of May. Model had no heavy tanks at all at the moment,

---

109 Parot'kin (ed.), *Kurskaia bitva*, p. 523.
110 Cross, *Operatsiia Citadel*, p. 159.
111 *Velikaia Otechestvennaia voina, 1941-1945*, p. 252.

and his forces were also in acute need of ordinary tank replacements. His operational command reported that on 8 April 1943 it had only 159 Pz. III and Pz. IV, and essentially this was just a bit more than a single full-strength panzer division, yet it had four panzer divisions.[112] The OKH promised it new heavy tanks already within the first ten days of April, but they in fact never showed up. The offloading of Tigers from Germany began only after 23 April, and that was only thanks to a strident protest by Colonel General Model. Thus, there was no basis for the order's demand about massing tanks at the moment the order was signed, and in essence, this was only a pretty turn of phrase.

Serious problems existed in the Luftwaffe as well; it was also in acute need of reinforcements. Here is how General H. von Seidemann, the commander of VIII Flieger Korps, describes the condition of Army Group South's Luftflotte IV by the middle of April: "The winter fighting had greatly weakened all these formations. The vicissitudes of combat in a wide variety of places along the far-flung front, combined with the numerous unit transfers and shifts, necessarily resulted in increasingly lowered technical and personnel serviceability. The physical strength of all our troops had likewise been overtaxed."[113] A military historian, the former Wehrmacht Major General B. Müller-Hildebrandt, second him: "In the struggle against the Soviet air forces, the losses of which were constantly replaced from available reserves, the German air forces could only maintain aerial superiority for several days."[114]

It is extremely difficult to understand the logic of Germany's political leadership at this moment, and I think it is hardly possible to grasp it fully. Unquestionably, Hitler recognized that not simply serious, but virtually all of the available reserves would be necessary for the replenishment of von Manstein's and Model's divisions. Already in January Germany was literally "scraping the bottom of the barrel" in order to patch the enormous gap after Stalingrad, and indeed, the OKW openly referred to this during the discussions. Yet if the offensive failed, it was completely unclear what forces would then be available to withstand the ensuing attacks of the Red Army, which already that spring had numerical superiority over the Wehrmacht. A. Jodl, H. Guderian and those generals that preferred a strategic defense in the East continually pointed to this problem as one of the key ones that had to be resolved before getting an offensive ready to go. In addition, such a large-scale operation required the maximal mobilization of the transportation system, which at that moment was under heavy pressure from partisans, especially in Army Group Center's operational rear. A clear example of their growing strength was the demolition of the Goluboi bridge across the Desna River on 8 March 1943, which had a span of 300 meters, on the single Briansk – Gomel railroad that connected Germany with von Kluge's Army Group Center. After it was dropped, movement on the railroad was only completely restored on 21 March.

The OKH had to take into account the effect of these problems. This was clearly visible even in Order No. 6. That meant there was only one way to plan to launch Citadel even in early May – to go *va banque*. According to historians, adventurism was one of the key characteristics of the Third Reich leader's style of leadership. To them, it is this characteristic that explains the desire of Hitler and the group of generals headed by K. Zeitzler to conduct an extremely dangerous

---

112 NARA US, T.312, R.317, F.7886029.
113 Newton, *Kurskaia bitva: Nemetskii vzgliad*, p. 234.
114 Müller-Hildebrandt, B., *Sukhoputnaia armiia Germanii 1933-1945* (Moscow: Izogrius – EKSMO, 2002), p. 405.

plan within such a compressed time schedule without the necessary forces and means. However, such an approach (to assert that Hitler had no rational basis when making decisions) seems too simplified and detached from the military and political realities in which Germany's leadership operated. However, I will touch upon this matter later.

The command of Army Group South met the announcement of the cancellation of these local operations in the Izium area with relief and actively took up the fulfillment of Order No. 6.[115] Just as before, Manstein continued to support an offensive toward Kursk, considering that the cutting off of this "balcony" in the Soviet lines was the Wehrmacht's main task in the immediate future. Therefore already on 18 April, while still undergoing treatment in Germany, he sent a letter to Hitler via K. Zeitzler, which stated, "It is now necessary to throw all our forces into Operation Citadel for a success; a victory at Kursk will compensate for all of our temporary setbacks on other sectors of the army group's front …. The earlier we start Operation Citadel, the less danger there will be of a major enemy counteroffensive toward the Don basin."[116]

In the sector of Army Group Center, the Führer was still making no attempts to devise similar experiments as Goshawk and Panther; they still lay in the future. The first stage of planning for the Ninth Army's offensive toward Kursk was going rather smoothly, but this does not mean simply. The analysis of documents from its headquarters reveal a note of optimism, albeit measured, regarding the results of the forthcoming operation. The directive from the headquarters of the Ninth Army to the subordinate corps commanders to array the combat formations of the assault wedge in a single echelon can serve as evidence of this, since in its opinion, there was no need there was no need for a greater concentration of attacking forces. Accordingly, there was a certain confidence that the Russian defense would collapse from the initial blow, as had happened back in 1942. Further, it was assuming that the rapid retreat of Soviet forces would begin on the flanks of the Ninth Army's assault groupings, although certain documents note that the expected strength of the Russian defenses (and primarily in artillery) would make intense fighting possible. In this case, the corps were counting on the necessary support of the Luftwaffe.

Intelligence information was first of all the source for this optimism. Throughout the latter half of March and all of April, the Abwehr and the others specialized services were submitting comforting, if not to say soothing reports about the Russians' behavior and their possible plans in the area of the Kursk bulge. Take, for example, the fact that on 23 March the Department for the Study of the Armies of the East reported to K. Zeitzler: "… There is doubt that the enemy is in any condition at all to undertake a decisive summer offensive."[117] On 15 April it was now the OKH that would give at least in general outlines an objective assessment of the Red Army's strength (as we now know), but one that did not permit an understanding of

---

115 In his memoirs, E. von Manstein writes that in April he left for Germany for an operation in connection with a progressing cataract. From the Ninth Army's document it follows that W. Model twice replaced him in command of Army Group South: from the beginning of April to the middle of that month, then from 30 April to 10 May, and in the interval between these two periods of time, it was Field Marshal Baron von Weichs who assumed temporary command of the army group. However, von Manstein maintained continuous contact with both the command of Army Group South and with K. Zeitzler on all major questions. According to the American scholar D. Showalter, the Commander-in-Chief of Army Group South left for treatment in Germany on 30 March 1943.
116 Manstein, *Uteriannye pobedy*, p. 525.
117 Koltunov and Solov'ev, *Kurskaia bitva*, p. 44.

the essence of what was happening in the Kursk area: "The combat capability of the divisions employed at the front should be rated as not very high. Even the newly arrived divisions are not fully equipped and staffed ... The situation as it stands now and the enemy's actions so far do not give clear information to make a judgement about the enemy's future intentions."[118] Five days later the OKH would again report about the lack of clarity regarding the plans of the Red Army's command and the fact that they were only throwing up ordinary defensive works. All of this, naturally, left an impression on the attitudes of both the Ninth Army's command and the higher-standing leadership in Berlin.

The command staffs of the Ninth Army and Army Group Center made the final touches to the initial draft of Citadel's plan (set to begin on 21 April) even prior to the appearance of Order No. 6, in the course of 10 and 11 April. On 10 April Army Group Center's Chief of Staff von Elverfeldt flew off to Zaporozh'e, to the headquarters of the Army Group South, where the Ninth Army commander was temporarily carrying out the duties of von Manstein in his absence for medical treatment in Germany, in order to work out the final resolution of a number of questions. In the course of the meeting, the Model issued a number of instructions, which made a number of notable adjustments to his Ninth Army headquarters' previous plans. One can plainly see the desire to "solve all the problems at one fell swoop" in these instructions, which is to say, under the conditions of an acute deficit of strength, to resolve two major problems simultaneously – to reinforce both the assault wedge and the flanking divisions. In order to do so, he demanded the following changes:

1. In the center of the XXXXVII Panzer Corps' combat formation, to insert the 2nd Panzer Division in between the 20th Panzer Division on the left and the 9th Panzer Division on the right, and to transfer the Jäger Battalions 8 and 13, which were freed up as a result of this, to the XXIII Army Corps on the left in order to reinforce the 383rd Infantry Division.
2. By reducing the sector of the XX Army Corps (as a result of the withdrawal of units of the 102nd Infantry Division), to extend the XXXXVI Panzer Corps' offensive sector substantially to the west.
3. On the first day of the offensive, the forward *kampfgruppen* of the XXXXVI and XXXXVII Panzer Corps after advancing 10-12 kilometers from the line of departure were to close their adjoining flanks. This decision was motivated by the wish, having encircled a portion of the Soviet forces on the boundary between the panzer corps, to destroy them as rapidly as possible in order to take the Trosna – Fatezh – Kursk highway quickly under control in order to organize the bringing up supplies. Simultaneously with this, W. Model was proposing to deprive the Russians of an important transportation artery and to complicate their maneuvering along the front in both directions.
4. To set 15 May as the final date when the troops should be fully ready to step off on the offensive.

118 Ibid.

On the following day, H. von Elverfeldt returned to Smolensk, to the headquarters of Army Group Center to report the final draft of the army's offensive plan, just as Field Marshal von Kluge had directed on 8 April. Judging from revealed documents, despite their strained relationship, both G. von Kluge and W. Model, as well as their respective headquarters, basically had similar, if not identical views on operational matters. This was also observed during H. von Elverfeldt's meeting with H. Krebs on 11 April.[119] Nevertheless, the Army Group Center leadership disagreed with certain proposals made by W. Model. The sticking point was the start date for the operation, but they quickly came to an agreement. It was decided to begin assembling the troops in their jumping-off positions on 24 April, and to move up the date by which the troops were to be ready from 15 May, as Model had requested, to 10 May; and to launch the offensive on 15 May. However, this was only the desire of the operation's direct executors, based on the situation of their troops as it stood in early April. Berlin at this moment had a different point of view. Hitler and the OKH were still preparing to launch the attack on 21 April.

On 12 April 1943 G. von Kluge signed the final order to his troops regarding the offensive and appended to it the initially spelled-out plan for Citadel that had been worked out by the Ninth Army in close cooperation with his headquarters. H. von Elverfeldt received this document on the same day, after which he left Smolensk and flew off to Orel. The scheme that had been presented in the report from Army Group Center on 24 March served as the plan's core. The document's authors based it on the most optimistic intelligence assessments, the essence of which stated that no substantial reinforcement of the Russian grouping directly opposite the sector of the Ninth Army and its nearest neighbors on the Sevsk – Trosna – Maloarkhangel'sk – Novosil' line had yet been noted. According to observation and information from agents, their mobile formations had been withdrawn from the front into the operational rear, and only ordinary defensive works were being thrown up on the forward edge. There was not any evidence at all that the Soviet command was preparing its own offensive. Information arriving from agents about a proposed Soviet attack in the direction of Gomel', which in turn was supposed to secure the Voronezh Front's main offensive toward Khar'kov, had not been confirmed. Therefore, at first glance it seemed that a propitious situation for the implementation of Operation Citadel had come together.

Nevertheless, the document fully sensibly pointed to one obvious circumstance that every level of command should take into account without fail:

> According to available information the enemy intends to hold the area west of the Belgorod, Kursk, Trosna line, won by him during the winter offensive; he is committing all the available forces against the attacking German troops. Therefore, when planning the offensive, the Ninth Army must take into full consideration that the Russians will be occupying a fully prepared defense, primarily along the roads; will conduct diversionary attacks, primarily from the east; and finally, will undertake efforts to break out of the ring of encirclement with major forces from the west. In the course of the further offensive, it is necessary to consider that the enemy, receiving continuous

---

119 NARA US, T.312, R.317, F.7886033.

reinforcements, will do everything to prevent the encirclement of the forces opposite the Second Army.[120]

Thus, a task was placed before the assault grouping of Model's Ninth Army: Without allowing itself to be diverted by threats from the flank, with one decisive thrust by its main forces, having ruptured the Russian defenses between Maloarkhangel'sk and Trosna to the entire depth, to seize Kursk and link up as quickly as possible with Army Group South, the forces of which at the same time would be advancing through Oboian' and Tim to meet it. Its flanking divisions were assigned to create a firm external ring of encirclement (east and southeast) in the Maloarkhangel'sk – Shshigry sector and with active measures fix the encircled forces in the Fatezh – Dmitrievka area (west). The Orel – Kursk railroad was selected as the axis of the Ninth Army's advance. The plan called for the operations of three groups in the Trosna – Maloarkhangel'sk sector:

1. A main group, which would be positioned in the center of the assault formation (the XXXXVII Panzer Corps, with the 20th, 9th and 2nd Panzer Divisions), having broken through the Russian defenses, was to advance strictly to the south as far as the hills north and east of Kursk, and after seizing them take the heights west of the Fatezh – Kursk highway and there make contact with the troops of Army Group South (the Fourth Panzer Army), moving up from Belgorod.
2. An eastern group (the XXIII Army Corps, with the 78th Sturm Division, the 383rd and 216th Infantry Divisions; and the XXXXI Panzer Corps, with the 18th Panzer Division, 86th Infantry Division and 10th Panzergrenadier Division) was to attack to the southeast, screening the left flank of the main group, and thereby create an outer front of encirclement on the east of Shshigry – east of Maloarkhangel'sk line; after the link-up of both army groups, it was to go over to a strict defense.
3. A western group (the XXXXVI Panzer Corps, with the 12 Panzer and 102nd, 258th and 7th Infantry Divisions) received the assignment to screen the main group's right flank and in close cooperation with the XXXXVII Panzer Corps take the sector between Pesochnaia and Usosh' and the area east of Fatezh, before defending against possible attempts to break out by Russian forces assembled in the Dmitrievka area, right up until the moment that the forces of both army groups destroyed them after their encirclement.

W. Model kept two divisions in reserve. The 4th Panzer Division was to assemble immediately behind the main grouping, with the task to operate in the sector of the XXXXVII Panzer Corps, while the 292nd Infantry Division stood ready to develop a success into the depth of the Russian defenses in the direction of wherever the offensive was going more successfully, as well as to bolster the defense of the inner or outer front of encirclement.

The document contained a relatively strict timetable for the operation, but as future events were to show, it was hardly realistic. The Ninth Army's assault wedge was supposed to break

---

120 Klink, *Das Gesetz des Handelns. Die Operation "Zitadelle"*, pp. 287-288.

through the defenses of the Central Front within 48 hours, and to take the hills east of Kursk and the city itself within the next four days. Thus, Model's subordinate corps were given just six days in order to link-up with Hoth's forward units.

Already during the first steps taken to implement Order No. 5 in the latter half of March the muddy season that had started and the partisan attacks on the lines of communication in the Orel bulge showed that more time would be required to prepare the forces and to bring up supplies than previously expected. In the beginning of April, it finally became clear that the prospects of launching the operation even in early May, as G. von Kluge had indicated in his telegram of 24 March, were illusory, so the plan for the offensive from 12 April as prepared by the headquarters of the Ninth Army in agreement with Army Group Center concisely stipulated:

> Considering the level of training and the replenishments of personnel existing at the present time, as well as the time necessary for bringing the divisions of the first echelon up to combat readiness (considering the necessary realignments and the weather conditions), 10 May is proposed as the earliest date for the offensive. This date in fact is based on the following calculations. Any worsening of the weather, even if temporary, will accordingly delay the preparations for the offensive, and first of all the repair of tanks. As far as it is presently possible to judge the future course of events, the delivery of the necessary weapons, in particular the tanks, and also the bringing up of reserves cannot be fully completed by this date. Thus, it is desirable to establish 15 May as the start date for the offensive.[121]

Recognizing the scale of Citadel's tasks and having received information from intelligence sources about the growing strength of the Russian forces and their defenses opposite the Ninth Army, the command of Army Group Center understood the need to reinforce Model's assault grouping, in the extreme case relying on inherent reserves – by means of stripping forces as previously-mentioned from the Fourth Army, even though this notion was still considered rather dangerous. The 12 April plan stated:

> Considering the expected losses in manpower, especially in the infantry divisions, and taking into account the effectiveness of the enemy's artillery fire, it should be considered that the forces committed at the start of the operation will be inadequate for carrying out the numerous assignments (securing the flanks and destroying the encircled foe), and the same applies for the logistical support for the operation. Only by deliberately accepting the risk of significantly weakening the Fourth Army is it possible, beginning in the first days of May, to withdraw its 6th and 98th Infantry Divisions from the front, and under the control of the army group headquarters, send the 98th Infantry Division to the Roslavl' area and the 6th Infantry Division to the area south and southeast of Smolensk. After the completion of the 6th Infantry Division's withdrawal, the 36th Infantry Division will be made fully subordinate to the Fourth Army.[122]

---

121 Parot'kin (ed.), *Kurskaia bitva*, p. 510.
122 Klink, *Das Gesetz des Handelns. Die Operation "Zitadelle"*, p. 288. Regarding the 98th Infantry Division, this calculation would not come to fruition; on 8 June 1943, the 98th Infantry Division would be

One of the first documents under the framework of practical preparation for Citadel, which was sent by the headquarters of the Ninth Army to its subordinate corps in early April, was a directive about the army's acquisition of a code name. Here is the text of this document, dated 8 April 1943:

> For the purpose of deception in the correspondence with the corps, from the present day it is necessary to use the designation "Fortress Staff 11". That's how it is necessary annotate all incoming and outgoing documents. In the header of the documents, it is forbidden to use "1a, 1b, pioneers or artillery", and necessary only to use "For the Fortress Staff". It is now allowed to authenticate the document by personal signature, with no indication of post or rank. It is also permitted to indicate the name of the document's recipient next to the alphabetical designation "1.A.". Extend the designation "Fortress Staff 11" only down to the unit level, and make this known to newly arriving divisions.[123]

However, in the army's war diary the date of the army's acquisition of the code name is given as 31 March. The source of the difference in the text still is not clear.[124] In April, the Ninth Army's subordinate corps and divisions would also receive code names, but this was only the beginning of a series of deceptive measures. Throughout the spring and the first month of summer, Model's army and its subordinate formations would continue to change the code names on several occasions. As a rule, the change coincided with the conclusion or initiation of some important stage in the troops' activity (such as a major regrouping) or an operation. For example, before the start of Citadel the Ninth Army would once again change its code name: From 18 April instead of "Fortress Staff 11", it became "Gruppe Weiss". At this time its main formations were concluding the process of assuming the sector of defense between the left flank of the Second Army and the right flank of the Second Panzer Army. In connection with this, the XXXXVII Panzer Corps would be designated as "Staff Breitenbuch"; from mid-May, when its troops became involved in the anti-partisan sweep "Gypsy Baron", it became "Corps Staff 532", and after its completion, "Rear Area Staff 3"; but on 8 June, its previous designation as "Staff Breitenbuch" would return to it (for more detail see Table 2).

    released from subordination to Army Group Center and begin loading for transport to the Seventeenth Army, to the Kuban bridgehead.
123 NARA US, T.312, R.322, F.7890214.
124 NARA US, T.312, R.317, F.7886029.

Table 2: Code names of the army and certain corps and divisions of Army Group South, used in the period of preparing for the Battle of Kursk[125]

Code Name	Actual Name
Fortress Headquarters 11 (from 31 March 1943)	Ninth Army
Gruppe Weiss (from 18 April 1943)	Ninth Army
Headquarters Breitenbuch	XXXXVII Panzer Corps
Rear Headquarters 3	XXXXVII Panzer Corps
XXXI Corps "East"	XXIII Corps
XXXI Corps "West"	XXXXVI Panzer Corps
407th Infantry Division	7th Infantry Division
418th Infantry Division	18th Panzer Division
404th Infantry Division	4th Panzer Division
492nd Infantry Division	292nd Infantry Division

The problem of concealing the armies designated for the offensive was resolved in an analogous manner in Army Group South. For example, the Fourth Panzer Army until 5 June 1943 would be called in the documents "Reconstituted Staff 'Khar'kov'".

One interesting detail: In the journal of combat operations of Model's Ninth Army, which as is known was preparing for events that were later described in it, in the month of June 1943 its designation as the Ninth Army and "Gruppe Weiss" periodically alternates in the text even on the same page. Why this was done is not clear, but it is impossible not to agree with Steven Newton that today for scholars, especially foreign scholars, who are engaged in the given terms of reference on the basis of German sources, the German practice is certainly befuddling and complicates their work.[126] For the Soviet command, however, this not so clever system of manipulating the names did not present any major problem. Already within two weeks of its arrival in its new sector, the Central Front's intelligence had identified the Ninth Army, and less than one and a half months later, it had even established the precise location of its headquarters. According to frontline standards, in the circumstances of actively conducted disinformation measures and increased camouflage, this was an outstanding result. However, the Soviet side was unable to make use of this information in order to destroy or at least temporarily derail it, whereas the Germans in this respect operated more successfully. As we will see ahead, only by a twist of fate did both N.F. Vatutin and N.F. Rokossovsky avoid certain death within their own command posts.

Incidentally, the leadership of the *fronts* that were defending the Kursk salient and the sectors belonging to it also actively used a system of encoding the troop formations, but not as fanciful

---

125 The table has been compiled on the basis of information contained in reports and the Ninth Army's journal of combat operations
126 Newton, *Kurskaia bitva: Nemetskii vzgliad*, p. 175.

as the German system. Here's an excerpt from the memoirs of I.Kh. Bagramian, who at that time was a lieutenant general in command of the 16th Army:

> In the latter half of April, I was summoned to the headquarters of our Western Front. The Commander-in-Chief General V.D. Sokolovsky read out an order from the Supreme Commander-in-Chief from 16 April 1943: For the valor and combat skill of the troops, our 16th Army had been transformed into the 11th Guards Army. Everyone in attendance warmly congratulated me, but the Commander-in-Chief in addition cautioned: "In the army's correspondence, it will still be called by its former designation, the 16th Army. There is no reason to put the enemy on notice ahead of time ...."[127]

For the sake of justice, I will note that by the start of the battle, the German command also basically knew the composition of the Soviet grouping of the first strategic echelon around Kursk. Only the identity of a portion of the second echelon and the Stavka reserves remained murky to them. However, this knowledge had no substantial effect on the outcome of the summer campaign.

In development of the offensive plan from 12 April, five days later on 17 April the Ninth Army headquarters issued to the corps "General instructions for conducting Operation Citadel" [further in the document, "General instructions ..."] over the signature of H. von Elverfeldt. By its structure this document was similar to G. von Kluge's order from 12 April, but it presented a more detailed blueprint of the operation and the formations were given important suggestions for planning the attack toward Kursk. From the document it follows that both the leadership of Army Group Center and the command of the Ninth Army believed that the Russians in the Kursk bulge intended to remain on the defensive. According to intelligence information, they were already massing forces in the Dmitrov area, had reinforced the artillery grouping between Trosna and Maloarkhangel'sk with four artillery divisions, and were also bringing up the most combat-capable reserves east of the Maloarkhangel'sk – Kursk line. Thus, stubborn resistance along any main roads and counterattacks primarily out of the Maloarkhangel'sk and Shshigry areas should be expected.

In the assessments of von Elverfeldt's staff, the ground on which the Ninth Army was deploying was not very suitable for constructing a defense and massing a large quantity of troops. At the same time, however, it offered the possibility of keeping well concealed the bringing up of troops and their staging for the offensive from aerial reconnaissance and artillery barrages. Yet the area in front of the army's combat formations, where the positions of the Central Front's troops were located, was cut by a large number of deep balkas, ravines and swampy branches of streams, which enabled the Russians in a short period of time to create a strong defense. In connection with this, the "General instructions ..." acknowledged that in the first stage of Citadel, a frontal assault against the defensive belts of Rokossovsky's armies was unavoidable. Thus, the initial task was to determine the most favorable sector for the breakthrough by the army's assault wedge. The "General information ..." noted:

---

127 Bagramian, I.Kh., *Tak shli my k pobede* [*That's how we marched to victory*] (Moscow: Voenizdat, 1988), p. 381.

Given an offensive by a large mass of troops across very hilly terrain in the Fatezh – Kursk – Maloarkhangel'sk quadrant, it is necessary to echelon the troops with the aim of minimizing the difficulties when forcing numerous ravines and streams that cut across the sector of advance. This feature of the sector for the offensive offers little possibility for a bypass maneuver. Thus, the concentration of all types of troops has particular significance for achieving a breakthrough; in other words, an attack against an enemy's exposed flank will <u>unavoidably be preceded by a frontal assault on his positions.</u>

The understanding of the possibility for massing our forces has particular significance for the operation's planning. It is necessary in order to breach the defenses in a favorable sector of terrain, and thereby quickly penetrate to the high ground east of Kursk. Here lies the key to a breakthrough of the enemy's deeply echeloned defenses constructed in front of Kursk and running from east to west. Thereby it will be possible to take the city itself and to cut the lines of supply approaching from the south.[128]

The road with the greatest traffic capacity in the sector of the Ninth Army ran through Trosna, Fatezh and further on to Kursk. It was natural to assume that the Soviet side would undertake every measure in order to create the greatest density of forces and means here. Therefore H. von Elverfeldt demanded of his subordinate staffs: When planning the actions of their troops to take maximum consideration of other routes, right "down to the last field path". Accordingly (and receiving particular emphasis in the document), assuming the movement of major forces along dirt roads, the corps commands strictly had to reconcile the plan of their troops' actions with the weather forecasts.

Relative to the previous documents regarding the planning of the operation, the "General instructions ..." contained a number of changes in the army's assault grouping. For example, the 102nd and 216th Infantry Divisions were dropped from the list given in Army Group Center's document dated 12 April 1943, and their place was taken by significantly weaker formations – Jäger Battalions 8 and 13. This did not happen by coincidence. The Ninth Army command was forced to use these divisions in order to resolve other current tasks, which in W. Model's opinion were extremely important: in the struggle against sabotage and partisan attacks on the lines of communications and the men arriving as replacements for the divisions assigned for Citadel. Noted Army Group Center's Chief of Staff Krebs: "The security of the rear areas and their isolation from areas seized by the bandits has enormous significance for the operation's success. In particular this factor can prove significant for securing the delivery of supplies."[129] The 216th Infantry Division was being directed to secure the rear area of the Ninth Army's assault grouping (additionally, it was reinforced by a regiment of the 251st Infantry Division). At the same time, it, together with the 299th Infantry Division, was regarded as the army's reserve, although it was assumed that the 216th Infantry Division could still become involved in the operation, albeit only in an extreme case. On the other hand, the 102nd Infantry Division was going to be used to set in motion the resolution of a second acute problem with replacements. The Ninth Army was in extreme need for personnel for the infantry divisions, or, as is written in captured German documents, for the "refreshing" of these divisions. However, Army Group

128 NARA US, T.312, R.322, F.7890210.
129 NARA US, T.312, R.322, F.7890212.

Center could offer no help in this; none were arriving from Germany, while the army school in Briansk and other training elements, because of their small number of enlistments, were essentially not in a condition to resolve this problem. Therefore G. von Kluge allowed Model to take an extreme step: to "pluck" soldiers from the combat units of other divisions and to redistribute them among these designated to take part in the offensive. The 102nd and 383rd Infantry Divisions became "donors" for the 7th Infantry Division, while the 72nd Infantry Division was to reassign soldiers to the 78th Sturm Division.

It should be especially noted that H. von Elverfeldt objectively assessed the condition of his own forces in the "General instructions …", and made an honest, though not comforting prognosis: the troops available for the operation, both in number and quality, were insufficient to guarantee its success. As the document stated:

> The latest batch of replacements, the first of which is expected at the end of April, do not permit hope for a radical improvement of the troops' condition in the nearest future. In addition, presently the panzer divisions assigned for the offensive have not more than 150 Pz. III and Pz. IV, including those machines under short-term repair. In this connection, according to plan, they will be reinforced with additional panzer regiments. Thus, the total strength of new and combat-ready panzers, including those returning from factory repairs, can reach 250.[130]

Reading these lines, the question arises: "If this document from the leadership was for subordinates, and not a request to higher command for granting it supplementary forces, then what was the Ninth Army headquarters trying to achieve by laying out the sorry situation of affairs in such detail?" So that subordinates raise questions over every little detail? Unquestionably, this information was honest and expanded the corps commanders' insight into the army's possibilities. However, I think there was little use for a picture drawn in such dark colors, and moreover, the information clearly did not inspire confidence in the success of the forthcoming operation.

However, let us return to the "General instructions …". In order to raise the level of the units' combat capabilities, the corps were advised to use the period of calm to withdraw units from the front systematically in order to conduct training with them in the rear:

> Teamwork presently is not being fostered in the combat elements. At the same time, such training should be conducted for each unit in at least an abbreviated form. Ignoring this demand will not allow us to count on success and will lead to heavy casualties. Therefore, at the first possibility it is necessary to improve the state of affairs regarding this matter.[131]

The headquarters of the Ninth Army detailed the plan of combat operations in significantly more detail than did Army Group Center (almost half of the text was dedicated to this), and not only for the first stage of the operation (the encirclement of Soviet forces in the Kursk salient),

---

130 NARA US, T.312, R.322, F.7890211.
131 NARA US, T.312, R.322, F.7890212.

but also in the future. According to this document, the entire assault grouping was divided into three unequal parts:

> The **Eastern** group (consisting of two corps as before) was supposed to attack to the east of the Orel – Kursk railroad. Its main objective was to prevent the Soviet forces from creating a new defensive front along a line running from east of Shshigry to east of Maloarkhangel'sk. The formations included in it received the following tasks:
> XXIII Corps (78th Sturm Division, 216th and 383rd Infantry Divisions). Secures the deep left flank of the entire army's offensive. The corps assembles its main strength on the right flank, breaks through the defenses, cracks the enemy's expected strong resistance on both sides of Maloarkhangel'sk, and envelops the city. Afterward it takes up a new defensive position along the Mokroe – Sloboda – Panskaia line …
> XXXXI Panzer Corps (18th Panzer Division, 86th Infantry Division and 10th Panzergrenadier Division) in close cooperating with the neighboring corps penetrates the enemy's front on both sides of the Orel – Kursk road with the forces of the 18th Panzer and 86th Infantry Divisions. The corps launches a powerful, unexpected attack to the southeast as far as the line of the Tuskar' River. From there, the corps attacks with the 10th Panzergrenadier Division in the direction of the hills to the south of this sector. Advancing in the eastern direction, the corps expands the breakthrough front right up to the line: hills east of Shshigry – hills located along the Shshigry – Kazinovka – Kasorzha – Alekseevka – Kazakovo, and there takes up a defense. The corps' assault group, attacking to the south, as quickly as possible establishes cooperation with the forces attacking from the south.[132]

The contradiction in the document concerning the 216th Infantry Division calls attention to itself. In the middle of the text, the division is to be withdrawn to the rear in order to guard against possible partisan attacks, yet later in the document, it is included in the XXIII Army Corps' combat group without any qualifying terms. This might testify bear witness to the confidence of the Ninth Army command that it would nevertheless receive, if not a full combat division, at least security units, for addressing the problems in the rear, but by the start of the operation it would still be able insert the division into the front line.

The **Main** grouping (the Ninth Army's assault grouping, one corps) received the task: With a decisive thrust of (only) the panzer divisions, as quickly as possible is to reach the high ground north and east of Kursk, after which it was to take the city with a double envelopment. After the city's capture, its main forces were to advance to the south for the link-up with the Fourth Panzer Army. Meanwhile the right-flanking divisions, in cooperation with the XXXXVI Panzer Corps, were to proceed to repulse attempts by Russian forces, encircled in the Kursk bulge, to break out of the *kessel* [cauldron] and together with the Second Army destroy them. In the "General instructions …" this scheme of combat operations is described as follows:

> XXXXVII Panzer Corps (20th, 9th and 2nd Panzer Divisions). The corps represents the army's assault grouping. It attacks first of all with the forces of the 20th and 9th

---

132 NARA US, T.312, R.322, F.7890214.

Panzer Division and breaks through the enemy front in the Verkhne-Tagino (incl.) – Maloarkhangel'sk (excl.) sector. The corps presses forward into the breach making maximum use of its mobility. The panzer forces seize a line north and east of Kursk. Bring up mobile forces to here in order to screen the penetration's flanks. Use the 4th Panzer Division for this.[133]

I will note that at this moment the 4th Panzer Division was subordinate to Model's army, but judging from the document, from the start of Citadel it was supposed to move out to the Naryshkin area (30 km west of Orel) in order to screen the sector of the XXXXVII Panzer Corps from that direction (insurance in the event of a Russian attack), before becoming subordinate to it in order to cover the flanks.

The third, **Western** group also received an impressive array of tasks, even though it had rather modest capabilities compared to the main group. It was to cut off the Soviet forces in the Fatezh area and to the south (the 60th, 65th and 70th Armies) from the main forces of the Central Front as quickly as possible, and then take up the Dmitriev area and strongly hold it. In addition, it was to form a *kampfgruppe* in order to screen the right flank of XXXXVII Panzer Corps. It was to do all this with just three divisions:

> XXXXVI Panzer Corps, with the forces of the 12th Panzer and 7th and 258th Infantry Divisions breaks through the enemy positions on both sides of the Trosna – Fatezh road. Conduct the massing of forces on the eastern flank [adjacent to XXXXVII Panzer Corps' right flank]. Upon achieving a breakthrough, the corps pivots to the west and rapidly seizes Fatezh and the area south of it. It then moves out to the general Belyi Nemed' – Krasavka line. The XXXXVI Panzer Corps deploys the 258th and 102nd Infantry Divisions on its western flank; they ensure fire pressure on the enemy and probe his defenses with separate assault groups. Upon the detection of the enemy's retreat, it is necessary to organize the pursuit of his with assault groups, with the aim of preventing his organized withdrawal beyond the Svapa River.[134]

The Western group was assigned to collaborate closely with General of Artillery R. von Roman's XX Army Corps. Possessing four infantry divisions (the 251st, 137th, 45th and 72nd Infantry Divisions), it was not only to hold its line securely, preventing the encircled enemy from breaking out to the northwest and the partisans in the army's rear from breaking out of the forests in the west, but also to ensure an artillery cover of the army's right wing, which would become extended in the course of the offensive. At the same time its forward units were supposed to conduct constant and active reconnaissance (including with combat as well), in order to detect a possible withdrawal of Soviet troops in the Kursk bulge in a timely manner.

The Ninth Army headquarters demanded from the corps commands during the offensive to pay particular attention to the flanks of the breakthrough. In any army, they were always one of the main "sore points", and in the circumstances when the Germans plainly did not have enough troops to resolve even the main tasks, the problem of screening the flanks became exceptionally

---

133 NARA US, T.312, R.322, F.7890213.
134 NARA US, T.312, R.322, F.7890212.

important. In the entire period of preparations for Citadel, this problem would give no rest to either Model or his staff, since a possibility of resolving it in a suitable manner never appeared in April, nor in the beginning of June 1943. The Ninth Army's war diary justifiably observed:

> The task of the corps that will be screening the eastern flank (XXXXI Panzer Corps and XXIII Army Corps) does not appear to be simple. The most intense fighting for them can be expected when taking the fortified points and in particular the road hub in Maloarkhangel'sk. Here, the 78th Sturm Division should serve as the shock force. On the whole, the composition of the forces detached for screening the eastern flank does not appear to be fully adequate. In the event of massed Russian counterattacks from the east, the German defensive front can be easily penetrated through and through, to the entire depth of the 15 km occupied by the division. The 292nd Infantry Division will be used in the role of parrying such crises. It should be committed into the fighting so as to prevent the scattering of the panzer units of the assault grouping in order to repulse attacks from the east. The flank screen from the west will be in less dangerous conditions. In order to arrange it, the forces of the 7th Infantry and 12th Panzer Division will be completely sufficient.[135]

In the scheme for the future offensive presented above, the Ninth Army command, not without justification, considered the situation of von Roman's XX Corps to be the most complicated. Since Army Group Center had given it the assignment of holding a passive defense, the thought was to weaken it the most of all in the interests of the assault grouping. At the same time, in the assessments of the Ninth Army staff, a twin danger was threatening his corps: A meeting attack by the Red Army troops from the front (out of the future pocket) and an attack by partisans from the rear (out of the southern portion of the Briansk forests). Model believed that in the event of Citadel's success, one of the most likely directions for the breakout of the Soviet divisions encircled in the Kursk bulge would be precisely to the northwest, toward the area of the Briansk partisan-controlled region. In order to frustrate this, Army Group Center decided to prepare mobile reserves. It was planned to bring at least three reserve divisions up to a condition by the end of April when they would be ready to be shifted quickly over a significant distance. A bit later, when Berlin began to postpone the date of the operation and the danger arose that the Russians would preempt it, the problem of the XX Army Corps' greatly extended front and its weakness would become particularly acute. In connection with this, in May 1943 the suspicions would arise in Model that a plan had ripened on the Soviet side to cut off the Orel salient with two meeting attacks from the north and south – a mirror image of the plan for Citadel. In so doing, he would stubbornly believe that the Russian southern grouping would launch an attack precisely at the boundary between the XX Army Corps and the XXXXVI Panzer Corps. At the end of spring and beginning of summer, this in general was a correct assessment (in mid-July 1943 the Soviet 65th Army would launch an attack in precisely this area) that was stimulated by the high activity in this area of Russian reconnaissance and assault parties.

One by no means unimportant detail calls attention to itself in the "General instructions": they contained little talk about the use of armor. In just two paragraphs (literally several lines

---

135 NARA US, T.312, R.322, F.7886031.

of text) it is remarked that the tanks of the XXXXVI and XXXXVII Panzer Corps were to be given the assignment to attack in the direction of the high ground in the Kursk area. The reason for such neglect of such an extremely important and value tool for resolving the offensive's tasks was their insignificant number in the Ninth Army and the general uncertainty regarding their operational strength that still existed in the middle of April. Model was proposing to crack the main defensive belt of the Central Front with infantry, reinforced with sappers and given ample artillery support. Only after the overcoming of the tactical zone were the panzers to be committed. However, this decision at this moment was not final and fleshed out in detail, since continuous shake ups regarding the army's combat composition were proceeding at the time.

Two serious problems were already clearly noticeable in the initial draft of the Ninth Army's offensive plan: the obvious want of divisions to carry out all the assignments, and the poor combat readiness of the divisions already allotted for the offensive. There also could not be any talk at all about reserves, even the most modest. Thus, von Elverfeldt's staff openly declared: "The army commander does not have a single division in reserve; in connection with this, the maneuvering of the frontline divisions and of the corps reserves has great significance … For the most rapid implementation of the planned measures it is necessary to free up and put into order all the divisions, and particularly the 102nd Infantry Division, the 78th Sturm Division and the 7th Infantry Division."[136]

G. von Kluge also recognized the need for additional reinforcements. In the operational plan from 12 April he wrote: "The divisions employed in the first echelon and the panzer divisions are very poorly equipped with tanks; likely, there aren't enough. Considering the great width of the offensive sector, it will be impossible to detach new forces from the Army Group. Thus, we are asking to assign two more infantry divisions in addition to the Army Group."

It is no secret that there was no prior agreement among all the commanders and military chiefs, who were preparing such large-scale measures, about everything compiled in the initial drafts of the documents. For example, at the beginning of April the OKH firmly promised to send W. Model Tiger tanks for the offensive, but in the 12 April plan, Army Group Center expressed this promise in the form of a request, as a suggestion. Even though the agreement was quite limited, as we will see below, the attempt to violate it on the part of the OKH led to a scandal, which K. Zeitzler himself would have to extinguish. As archival materials show, in mid-April Model was waiting for a more intelligible decision regarding the transfer to him of several infantry divisions (the 6th or 98th Infantry Divisions in particular). Thus, the army's battle formation was being worked out with consideration of their likely arrival. As already noted, he assigned all of the available infantry divisions to the flank groups of the assault wedge and decided to put the bulk of the panzer divisions (four of the six) into the main assault group (the XXXXVII Panzer Corps). Even to someone who has no military background, not to mention an experienced military commander, it is clear that it is impossible to breach prepared enemy positions on the main axis of attack with just tanks and no accompanying infantry, especially with just 150 to 250 available machines. Yet the German plans in addition placed the task on them to seize such a major city as Kursk, which was located in the depth of the enemy defenses at a depth of more than 70 km from the front!

---

136 NARA US, T.312, R.322, F.7890214.

W. Model was an experienced military commander and understood that in the situation that had developed, Berlin's promise might fully remain just empty words, and therefore he hedged, and given the possibility of a negative development of the events, he proposed to strengthen the assault wedge of the XXXXVII Panzer Corps with infantry. This was plainly sketched out in the "General instructions …": "The 292nd Infantry Division is located under the army's direct command in the Orel area. After the offensive's start, it should stand ready to develop the success into the depth or to strengthen the breakthrough's eastern front against enemy counterattacks."[137]

However, it is possible to assume that approximately up to 20 April Model still did not recognize the complete danger of the position into which his army had fallen. Prior to this moment, while at the headquarters of Army Group South, he was not familiar with the real-time intelligence information (or it was not in sufficient volume) about the development of extensive defensive works in the sector of the Central Front. Thus, it is possible that he had a certain confidence that the Russians had not fully recovered from the winter campaign, and therefore an attack with the already available forces in a narrow sector of the front might achieve clear success.

Considering that the preparations for Citadel had entered the active phase, the army headquarters also saw to serious measures to disguise their intentions. They attached great significance to them. For example, immediately after returning from Smolensk, on the afternoon of 12 April Colonel von Elverfeldt, acting as the army's temporary commander in place of Model, personally conducted an inspection overflight of the front lines in order to check the camouflaging of positions.[138] From this time on, such overflights became regular, and were conducted by the commander each day or even more frequently. In addition, the troops were required to devise a number of measures which prior to the start of the offensive were to deceive the Central Front command. In particular it was recommended:

1. To conduct strong artillery barrages over the several consecutive days before the start of the offensive in various sectors, in order to lull the Russians' attention, prevent them from determining the axis of the main attack, and confuse them about the real purpose of the barrages – as the opening of an offensive or as harassing fire. In so doing, by making the enemy accustomed to such heavy barrages, they might take the preparatory artillery fire for the offensive as simply the next ordinary barrage.
2. To execute a number of demonstrative measures, including reconnaissance in force, in sectors that were not to be targeted by the offensive. In the process, they were to include soldiers clad in tanker suits, as well as make a demonstration with individual tanks. The goal was to divert the Russians' attention to a secondary axis.
3. To organize the open movements of trucks and troops in the direction of the front west and northwest of Dmitriev and east of Orel, places where an attack was not planned.

---

137 Ibid.
138 NARA US, T.312, R.322, F.7886033.

Thus, the first stage of planning the offensive toward Kursk by troops of Army Group Center, which lasted from 26 March to 12 April, came to an end. In the course of it, the command had adopted a plan, and the army group's headquarters staff had worked to flesh it out, before submitting it to the subordinate corps for them to make adjustments to it. However, by the middle of April the Ninth Army's assault grouping was still in the process of forming up and neither G. von Kluge nor W. Model had any complete certainty about its composition. It was due to these reasons that once the Field Marshal signed the approximate plan of the operation on 12 April, it almost immediately underwent changes, and by the beginning of July the draft would be completely different; the same fate would befall to the first draft of Army Group South's plan for the offensive. Even so, according to the headquarters of the Ninth Army, this 12 April document played a major role in preparing for Citadel, since "it provided the foundation for further work."[139] This assessment was fully correct, because at 2140 on 14 April, in the course of a telephone discussion between H. von Elverfeldt and H. Krebs, the latter reported that the Führer had in general given his approval to the document. This meant that it contained an approximate balance between Hitler's personal opinion and that of the command of one of the two army groups at Kursk regarding how the offensive should proceed.

A certain clarity about the offensive plan had also appeared among the Army Group South command staff by this time, though doubts about whether it could be successfully and fully implemented were melting away with each passing day. After it became clear that the first option for an offensive toward Kursk – a battering ram attack from Belgorod with the forces of only one army group had lost sense by the beginning of March; a new offensive plan appeared in Order No. 5 – an enveloping attack by von Kluge's and von Manstein's two army groups. However, Hitler had immediately insisted on developing two more operations in the sector of Army Group South within a highly compressed schedule of time. Despite the fact that arguments about the usefulness of Goshawk and Panther were absorbing all of the attention of the army group's command staff, von Manstein throughout this time kept persistently advancing the idea of Citadel. In particular in a letter to the OKH on 29 March about the plans for his troops' actions in the coming month, he wrote:

> Considering the enemy's reinforcement, Operation Panther in particular requires additional units in order to screen the flanks. With the start of an enemy offensive in the area south of Kursk and east of Belgorod, a thrust in the direction of Kursk and to the east together with Army Group Center can be viewed as the initial attack, but in doing so it will be necessary to screen the eastern flank of the attacking forces. Needed forces for covering the eastern direction can be provided by the army group only in very limited strength.[140]

At the close of the letter, he concluded that either Operation Panther or a joint offensive with Army Group Center toward Kursk might be most suitable in the nearest future, but not more than one of them. He understood that such a conclusion, in the first place, would not irritate Hitler, since he, von Manstein, was not out and out rejecting Hitler's option for an offensive

---

139 NARA US, R.312, R.317, F.7886034.
140 Kriegstagebuch Ia der Heeresgruppe Don/Süd, März -bis July 1943. BArch-MA. RH 19 VI/45. Bl. 14.

and agreed with the Führer's proposal. In the second place, von Manstein's proposal in essence buried Operation Panther, since the objectives of the two respective offenses were incompatible. The implementation of Panther was designed to eliminate a threat in the Izium area (which meant it had operational significance), but Citadel's outcome was supposed to achieve a strategic success: it contemplated the capture of Kursk and the destruction of the major enemy grouping west of there. The leadership of the OKH also shared the Field Marshal's point of view. As a result, as already noted, in early April E. von Manstein and K. Zeitzler managed to strike the idea of both Goshawk and Panther from the agenda. So, the headquarters of Army Group South quickly worked out a plan for implementing Citadel's objectives with its own troops. By the middle of April, it appeared as follows:

> Army Detachment Kempf in the course of the offensive, screening its eastern flank with Korps Raus (the 106th and 320th Infantry Divisions), reaches a line running from Nezhegol to Korocha, while the III Panzer Corps (6th, 7th and 19th Panzer Divisions and the 168th Infantry Division) penetrates in the direction of Skorodnoe, in order to adopt a flanking screen in the Korocha – south of Manturovo sector. Later another panzer corps with two divisions thrusts to the east between the rivers Seim and Tim to provide cover from the east.
>
> The Fourth Panzer Army breaks through toward Kursk and links up with the Ninth Army with the SS Panzer Corps (SS Panzergrenadier Divisions *Leibstandarte Adolf Hitler*, *Das Reich* and *Totenkopf*, plus one infantry division for the initial breakthrough) and the XXXXVIII Panzer Corps (*Grossdeutschland*, 3rd and 11th Panzer Divisions) through Prilepy – Oboian' in the general direction of Kursk and to the east, with a subsequent pivoting of XXXXVIII Panzer Corps south of the Seim in order to guard against encirclement. Screen the army's western flank with the forces of the LII Army Corps (255th and 332nd Infantry Divisions).
>
> For this operation the army group needs additional forces in order to free up the XXIV Panzer Corps prior to 27 April, as well as an additional infantry division for the SS Panzer Corps. In the event of the launching of Citadel, the army group on the entire eastern and Donets River front has as a reserve only the 16th Panzergrenadier and 17th Panzer Division. With regard for the greatly extended defensive fronts of the divisions, which will not be able to stave off powerful enemy attacks, the army group considers adding three more divisions to the reserve as unavoidable and absolutely necessary.[141]

The main distinguishing feature of this plan relative to the final plan that would be put into motion on 5 July 1943 concerned the attack of the main forces: the Fourth Panzer Army would attack out of the Tomarovka – Belgorod area strictly to the north, across ground south of Oboian' that presented difficulties for the movement of mobile forces, because it was cut east to west by the Psel River with its wide, swampy basin. While forcing a crossing of it, Hoth's shock grouping almost certainly would come under artillery fire and strong flanking attacks by Soviet tank formations from the east. No one could forecast the consequences of this, but it was obvious that the losses would be heavy, and possible that the entire offensive might stall.

---

141 Ibid, Bl. 40.

Naturally, H. Hoth[142] immediately grasped this and spoke up against the plan. However, in early April, the leadership of Army Group South, which was contending with the proposed Goshawk and Panther operations, was not up to detailing the Fourth Panzer Army's offensive under Citadel. However, the panzer army commander was a highly motived man and very persistent, so as soon as Hitler postponed the start date for Citadel to June, H. Hoth obtained a personal meeting with E. von Manstein, in order privately to persuade him to change the direction of the main and auxiliary attacks. I will dwell in more detail on the results of this very important meeting below.

For now, let us return to the headquarters of the Ninth Army and examine how the preparation of its forces for the operation was going, since it was precisely because of problems with replenishments that became Model's main reason for shifting the operation from May to June. By itself, Hitler's approval of the 12 April 1943 draft plan for Army Group Center's offensive was indeed important, but it was also the only positive news for the Ninth Army command. However, literally within a matter of days, the redrafting of it began and Berlin began demanding the virtually impossible. The OKH announced that it had been decided to alter the the Ninth Army's combat formation – its assault wedge was to be echeloned in depth. Because of this change, the preliminary date for the launching of the operation was postponed from 21 April to 1 May.

This shift in time did not bring W. Model any relief or satisfaction, since it was a half-measure, which complicated the work even more. In the course of a single night, the army's staff was supposed to prepare a new scheme for the regrouping of the troops, who were already

---

142 Herman Hoth (1885-1971), Colonel General. In military service from 1904 and a veteran of the First World War. In November 1938 he was promoted to General of Infantry and formed the XV Army Corps, at the head of which he took part in the conquest of Poland. In 1940 during the war with France, he commanded Panzergruppe Hoth, but in November 1940 assumed command of Army Group Center's Panzergruppe 3. During the invasion of the USSR, his forces together with Colonel General H. Guderian's Panzergruppe 2 were the main force of Army Group Center on the central (Moscow) direction. For his successful performance in the course of the blitzkrieg, in July 1941 Hoth was awarded the Knight's Cross with Oak Leaves. In October 1941, he took command of the Seventeenth Army. Between May 1942 and November 1943, he commanded the Fourth Panzer Army, which was partially destroyed near Stalingrad, later reconstituted, and became the main assault force of Army Group South during the unsuccessful offensive toward Kursk in July 1943. On 10-11 May 1943, during a conference with Field Marshal von Manstein in Bogodukhov (Ukraine), Hoth convinced him to alter the Fourth Panzer Army's operational plan and to establish its main objective in the first stage of Operation Citadel a breakthrough to the Prokhorovka Station area, where it was to encounter anticipated approaching Soviet mobile reserves and destroy them. In the course of 5 to 9 July 1943, his panzer army, having fought its way through two defensive belts of the Voronezh Front, neared Prokhorovka. Hoth's plan had been implemented, and a major battle took place in the fields and woods near Prokhorovka Station. However, this did not yield the anticipated results. Suffering substantial losses and under the threat of encirclement, his forces were forced to begin wrapping up the operation. The main result of Citadel for the Fourth Panzer Army was the wearing down of the divisions, particularly the panzer divisions, and as a consequence, a drop in their combat capabilities. This became perceptible already at the beginning of autumn in 1943. In September 1943, for the combat in Ukraine, he was awarded the Knight's Cross with Oak Leaves and Swords, but in December of the same year he was sent into retirement. On 8 May 1945 he was taken prisoner by the US troops and in October 1948 he was sentenced by the Nuremberg tribunal to 15 years of imprisonment for war crimes. He was released in April 1954.

on the march, and by the following morning present it to Army Group Center. In response H. von Elverfeldt crisply, but very argumentatively retorted to H. Krebs that it was impossible to carry out the given order. Even in the captured German documents that recount this difficult conversation, one can sense the chief of staff's large internal stress. It is also understandable; the situation at river crossing sites and on the roads had significantly deteriorated; everything was sinking into the mud. To alter the previous scheme of regrouping meant to deploy divisions to new areas, which meant they first had to be moved back to Orel (the main forces were moving by railroad), and there given a minimum of supplies, before they once again had to move out on the march to new jumping-off areas. The situation was complicated by the fact that not all the divisions that had been planned to withdraw from the front had done so. For example, this process of disengagement was still underway in the 102nd Infantry Division; two of its regiments had already been withdrawn, but the third was still holding its position in the front lines. Thus, the forces of this division were in several different locations. So, it was physically impossible in the given amount of time for the Ninth Army to carry out such a volume of work.

In the conclusion to his report, H. von Elverfeldt emphasized that the developing situation with the tanks was very alarming. In the Ninth Army's war diary, this correspondence is described in the following manner:

> With respect to the aforementioned problems, it was made explicit to the Army Group chief of staff that it was necessary to allow more time. Since the regrouping of troops on foot requires a significant amount of time, it is necessary to specify a date for an offensive well in advance. The troops are not in a condition to execute the required measures in a matter of ten days, so the army asks in the future not to issue similar impossible directives. "Fortress Staff 11" is hoping that the army commander, who will return from Army Group South on 17 April, will be able to agree upon a precise date for the start of the offensive. The required report about the scheduled regrouping of forces for this reason cannot be prepared in the course of a night and submitted to the Army Group. The date by which the order regarding the regrouping can be carried out must consider that the stockpiling of supplies and bringing the units to order cannot be finished sooner than 10 May. Thus, technically the timing cannot be set any earlier than 5 May.[143]

A chief of staff can give such a declaration to a superior command only when sensing the full support of W. Model, who as is known, on one occasion had the temerity to challenge even Hitler with the question, "My Führer, who commands Ninth Army, you or I?"[144] Model was not exaggerating when he was pointing to the problems of replenishing his worn-out divisions with virtually everything needed (armor, manpower, artillery, and transport) in order to bring them back up to a condition to implement Operation Citadel. The OKH really was dragging its feet in fulfilling its promise to reinforce the Ninth Army with tanks and men prior to the start of Citadel, including with several dozen Tiger tanks as well.

---

143 NARA US, T.312, R.317, F.7886034.
144 Newton, *Kurskaia bitva: Nemetskii vzgliad*, p. 424.

The order about amending the plan arrived at the moment when Model, having returned from Zaporozh'e to the headquarters of the Ninth Army, received intelligence information that the Russians were not only feverishly working to build defensive fortifications at a much faster rate than had been expected, but also over the single night of 12-13 April had assembled twice the amount of artillery than had been previously known to the headquarters. According to its information, at this moment the number of artillery tubes had increased from the 520, which had been identified at the beginning of April, to 960, plus 80-90 Katiusha rocket launchers. It is not clear which artillery – army-level, *front*-level or reinforcements – that the German agents had counted, but 961 guns were in the three artillery and mortar divisions that became part of the 4th Breakthrough Artillery Corps, which began to form on the Central Front in the middle of April. The German Abwehr considered the source of this information as reliable, so H. von Elverfeldt already on the morning of 13 April was directed to issue an order to prepare the troops for a breakthrough of enemy's defensive line in the Kursk area that was already powerful with respect to artillery. Then, at 1745, in the course of conversations with H. Krebs, he requested reinforcements: one Arko [*Artilleriekommandeur*, a corps-level artillery headquarters designed to coordinate the divisional field artillery and separate corps artillery formations], two artillery regiment headquarters, four heavy artillery battalions, one mortar battalion and one super heavy cannon battery; as well as two infantry divisions that should be readied to shift to the army's sector. On the following day, 14 April, at a conference in the headquarters of the XX Corps, he notified General R. Roman that considering the deficit of strength and Berlin's latest demands to echelon the assault force in depth, his left-flank 72nd Infantry Division might be urgently introduced into the sector of the 78th Sturm Division, which would have to be directed into the assault force's second echelon.

Judging from captured German sources, the atmosphere in the headquarters of the Ninth Army at this time was nervous not only because of the orders arriving "from above" that were difficult to carry out, but also because of the lack of understanding about what the Russians were doing, which alarmed H. von Elverfeldt. Intelligence was reporting that almost simultaneously with the reinforcement of the artillery grouping opposite the Ninth Army's front, on 12 April an enemy combat group consisting of one tank brigade, one motorized regiment, four heavy artillery batteries and three heavy anti-aircraft batteries had set out from Kursk in the direction of Staryi Oskol. At this time, there was also an active regrouping of forces underway in the Central Front. Tank brigades and regiments emerging after their forming up process were passing through Kursk (for example, up until 5 April, the 28th Guards Tank Regiment, the 42nd Separate Tank Regiment and the 118th Tank Brigade had been dispatched), and fresh units and formations were arriving (at this time, the 9th Tank Corps was marching through the city, and one of its tank brigades was already located on its southern outskirts).[145] In addition, the Soviet counterintelligence *Smersh* [*Death to spies*] was transmitting several fake radio messages with the aim of misleading the enemy. Thus, even today, it is difficult to figure out how credible the information was from the Abwehr agents, which was laying on H. von Elverfeldt's table. One thing is clear: In the circumstances when its troops were already in movement, the Ninth Army command was extremely sensitive to such reports and was paying fixed attention to any

---

145 *Russkii arkhiv: Velikaia Otechestvennaia. Generalnyi shtab v gody Velikoi Otechestvennoi Voiny: Dokumenty i materialy* [*Russian archive: Great Patriotic War. The General Staff in the years of the Great Patriotic War: Documents and materials*] T-23 (12-3) (Moscow: TERRA, 1999), p. 91.

messages on the activity of the Soviet side, particularly those that were hard to fit into the system of references and coordinates being used by it. Having received no cogent explanation from the intelligence about the group that was moving to the south, the army headquarters decided that the Russians were possibly reinforcing the forces defending the southern face of the Kursk salient. Accordingly, in the event of an offensive toward Kursk from the line north of Belgorod, they might pull their defensive front back to the north, and then launch a flanking attack in the direction of Khar'kov against the group attacking toward Kursk.[146] Even though accurate information was available, considering the presence of the Izium bridgehead, at this moment this supposition seemed fully realistic.

On the morning of 15 April, H. von Elverfeldt once again had a difficult conversation with H. Krebs. Instead of the requested scheme for the new regrouping, he sent up to the army group a document in which he thoroughly analyzed the main objective difficulties that the regrouping that was already underway faced and offered a disquieting conclusion: Considering the new demands given by Berlin (the order from the OKH) to the Ninth Army, there could be no justification to count upon Citadel's success. Army Group Center's headquarters, which was acting as an intermediary between the Ninth Army and the OKH found itself caught between a rock and a hard spot. It knew that it was impossible to ready the Ninth Army to attack within such a limited amount of time (H. Krebs and G. von Kluge understood this no worse than Model and his subordinates), but to support the assessment offered by the Ninth Army headquarters meant to create stress in relations with Berlin. Field Marshal von Kluge decided to act according to the principle of the dutiful soldier: "An order is an order – what happens next is the senior officer's problem". So, H. von Elverfeldt was informed that the Ninth Army's opinion had been passed on to the OKH, but Army Group Center's headquarters once again insistently demanded, without waiting for Model's return, that Ninth Army submit a schedule for the new regrouping before 22.45 of that date (15 April), giving the Ninth Army headquarters the possibility to ascertain the commander's opinion over the telephone. However, Colonel von Elverfeldt firmly stood his ground:

> In the existing conditions, such a decision excludes the possibility of reconstituting the troops, and the departure to the front, in particular of the 292nd Infantry Division, will not allow them to get ready for the offensive. It was also necessary to agree upon the timetable for Citadel with the corps commanders, before reporting it to Army Group Center at 2245. In addition, the plan presently requires the maximum possible trafficability of the roads. Indeed, only given the most favorable conditions can the units be supplied with everything necessary by 29 April.[147]

Both headquarters understood each other well; they were simply striving to avoid being made the scapegoat. Berlin, without looking at the existing realities, was persistently demanding the impossible. The situation was slipping out of its control, and something had to be done. The Russian defense with respect to its fortifications, obstacles and artillery grouping over the past two weeks had substantially been strengthened, and there were simply not enough forces and

---

146 NARA US, T.312, R.317, F.7886034.
147 NARA US, T.312, R.317, F.7886038.

means for an offensive with such deep objectives as the capture of Kursk: there were no panzers, the troops had not been assembled, and no replenishments had arrived for the divisions. Most importantly, neither G. von Kluge nor Berlin had any possibility to reinforce the Ninth Army quickly. However, Hitler still had no intention to cancel Citadel. The OKH decided that there was only one way out: The Ninth Army's assault formation must be urgently echeloned in depth, in order to ensure that the initial attack rupture of the Central Front's defenses (so the new force regrouping had to be conducted in order to create a second echelon), and the offensive had to be launched as soon as possible in order not to give the Russians time to bring up reserves.

At first glance this seemed to be the optimal solution, but in reality, everything was much more complicated than that. The muddy season was still in effect, and because of partisan attacks and Soviet airstrikes on the lines of communication in the Orel salient, the time necessary for trains to reach the Ninth Army had significantly increased. As a consequence, the extremely necessary freights necessary for its divisions were arriving in a trickle, and not in the required surging flood. Furthermore, almost all of Model's forces were already in movement, even though the divisions were worn out, but the necessary minimum of personnel and armor had not even yet been dispatched from Germany. In addition, the regrouping itself and the tight deadlines for the start of the offensive were undermining the plan for the Ninth Army's combat formation that had been agreed upon with Hitler and put down on paper, so there was a need to start the process all over again. Noted the Operations Department of Ninth Army:

> The order regarding the replacement and complete withdrawal of the 102nd Infantry Division from the front, which arrived from the Army Group, disrupted the preparations of the 292nd Infantry Division for an attack in the sector of XXIII Army Corps. The freed-up Jäger battalion should replace the final units of the 102nd Infantry Division released from the front, but instead it was sent into the reserve, into the XXIII Army Corps' second echelon. In addition, the resolution of the task that in the nearest time shall be given to the XXIII Corps prevents the withdrawal of the 78th Sturm Division into the Ninth Army reserve.[148]

In addition, given the build-up of Russian artillery opposite the Ninth Army's front, it followed that the attacking corps must ensure the massing of their own organic artillery, and first of all, the assault guns. This would require both time and equipment (such as prime movers), but both were lacking. Not even a quarter of the number of promised tanks and self-propelled guns had arrived from the Reich.

Besides the sharp and primarily fruitless arguments between the Ninth Army's command and Army Group Center's leadership, on 15 April several important decisions were taken, which might be called compromises. They concerned the XXIII Army Corps and the XXXXVII Panzer Corps. Army Group Center agreed with Model's suggestion to leave five heavy artillery battalions and two battalions of assault guns for the army corps, but categorically rejected to allocate it any armor. As a result, the Ninth Army headquarters emphasized, "… the exceptionally difficult offensive toward Maloarkhangel'sk, which is pursuing a very important objective to screen the left flank and the assault wedge, must be carried out by the corps only with the forces

---

148 NARA US, T.312, R.317, F.7886037, F.7886038.

that are available now."¹⁴⁹ At the same time, the final order that Model had insisted upon arrived (after receiving Hitler's approval), which called for the bulk of the Ninth Army's pioneers and construction units to be concentrated in the XXXXVII Panzer Corps, since during its offensive it would have to overcome a large number of water barriers and deep ravines.

The back and forth between the headquarters of the Ninth Army and Army Group Center continued right up until 16 April, when the Führer's Operational Order No. 6 from 15 April arrived from Berlin. On this day, a new entry appeared in the Ninth Army's war dairy:

> The die is cast! The Führer's instructions have arrived in the form of operational Order No.6/OKH/General Staff of the Army/Operations Department/No.430246/43 for the chiefs of staff from 15 April. The tasks for Army Group Center (Ninth Army): launch an attack from the Trosna – north of Maloarkhangel'sk line, assembling the main forces on the eastern flank with the objective of seizing and firmly holding a line in the east: Tim – east of Shshigry, and further along the Sosna River. On other sectors of the front, launch pinning attacks. Timely make local attacks within the "kessel" to deprive the enemy of the possibility to attack on any other sector of the front.¹⁵⁰

This important document, although it did put an end to the arguments over the offensive's start date and the immediate assignments for the Ninth Army (X-Day was set for 29 April, and the offensive was set to begin on 3 May), at the same time became a catalyst for a new exacerbation of the relationship between Model on one side and the OKH and its supporter G. von Kluge on the other. The analysis of archival sources shows that 18 April 1943 became one of the key moments in the course of preparing for Citadel. On this day there occurred a number of important events, which had a substantial influence on this process.

First, E. von Manstein sent Hitler a document that contained his assessment of the situation regarding Citadel, which proved to be far from optimistic. Even though the Field Marshal sought to keep a sprightly tone, from his opinions it was clear: the operation's prospects were uncertain and this greatly alarmed him. The Soviet command had already implemented substantial organizational and preparatory work within the bulge. The combat diary of his Army Group South lays out the essence of this document in the following manner:

> The large concentration of enemy forces in the Kursk bulge (totaling 124 units) allows the conclusion to be drawn that the enemy will be able to act quickly. In the event of conducting Citadel, the attacks by a large number of mobile units of the Southwestern and Southern Fronts must be expected in the battle for Kursk, and strong diversionary fighting in the area east of Khar'kov, at Izium and on the Mius front. Citadel will put all of the enemy's forces in motion. As a result, the operation will either lead to a rapid, decisive victory, or given specific circumstances, to an insurmountable crisis. In connection with this it is necessary at any cost to deploy a maximum amount of forces on the Mius and Donets fronts, even at great risk. The Army Group has decided to stake everything on the success of Operation Citadel.¹⁵¹

---

149 NARA US, T.312, R.317, F.7886038.
150 NARA US, T.312, R.317, F.7886041.
151 Kriegstagebuch Ia der Heeresgrupped Don/Süd, März-bis Juli 1943. BArch-MA RH 19 VI/45, Bl. 39.

Second, the Ninth Army fully took up its assigned sector of defense opposite the Central Front's line and was readying for the attack, but it still did not have the forces planned for Citadel. Model could not even count upon their arrival in the immediate future.

Third, and this was key, Model, understanding that his army was not in the condition to carry out all the offensive assignments laid upon it, sent a very harsh letter, after which the tension between him and the headquarters of Army Group Center and the OKH rose, even though they promptly promised to send him reinforcements shortly. However, these were just crumbs compared to those that were required for the offensive. The sharpening of this conflict situation would lead to a meeting between Colonel General Model and Hitler, after which the Führer reexamined his view toward the Citadel's prospects and decided to set the offensive aside until the beginning of June. Thus, on 17 April just as soon as Model arrived from Zaporozh'e at his command post in Orel, ugly news began to come in as if out of a horn of plenty. In his later memoirs, von Manstein recalled that Model was capable of pushing his views regarding military questions even in Hitler's presence, and although brave, spared neither himself nor his subordinates in their duties.[152] It was just these particular character traits, doggedness and an abrasiveness that verged on rudeness, which the Colonel General and commander of the Ninth Army in fact demonstrated in full measure at this time. Realizing that the process of regrouping and the reconstitution of his army needed more time because of the changing operational situation at the front, and that the OKH and Army Group Center staff were behaving irresponsibly by issuing orders that were remote from reality, at 1715 Model called H. Krebs. He proceeded in a very harsh, one can even say crude form to demand a clear and precise picture of the Army Group's position on the most important questions, and in the first place, the replenishment of the infantry divisions. Here is how this discussion was presented rather diplomatically in the documentation of the Ninth Army headquarters:

> During the discussions ... Model, mincing no words, pointed out that the situation with the number of personnel in the divisions remains extremely difficult. The Army Group should undertake maximum efforts in order to resolve this problem rapidly. If the situation regarding these points does not change, the army commander believes that he lacks the strength to undertake the operation. From these telephone conversations, the Army Group had to draw the conclusion that it would not be able to carry out the OKH order. During the talks, the Army Group Commander-in-Chief requested that he [Model] put his stated ideas on paper. The report note should indicate the number of necessary march battalions in order to replenish the manpower losses, and in separate indicate the number required for replenishing the pioneer units, since this needed to be reported to the Führer personally. It is also necessary to list everything needed in order to replace the high losses in artillery, heavy infantry guns and anti-tank weapons, first of all for the 4th Panzer Division, which was particularly hard hit in the preceding fighting. During these decisions and the clarifications that followed them by telephone, the army commander formed the impression that given the enormous shortages with respect to all these points, he cannot take responsibility to conduct the operation.[153]

---

152 Manstein, *Uteriannye pobedy*, p. 526.
153 NARA US, T.312, R.317, F.7886043.

By refusing to accept leadership over Citadel on the northern face of the Kursk salient in the conditions that had come together by mid-April, Model was not making some "grandstand play"; he simply had no other way to get Berlin's attention. Consciously or not, the OKH and Army Group Center had placed him in an undoubtedly hopeless situation by demanding that he carry out tasks that the army could not shoulder in the shortest time possible. The fact that a quick, if not to say lightning-like reaction came personally from G. von Kluge, and a bit later from K. Zeitzler, unmistakably shows that the Colonel General was absolutely right in his decision. Already on the following day, 18 April, the Operations Department of Army Group Center reported over the telephone to H. von Elverfeldt that according to Order No.3985/43, signed by the Field Marshal, the bulk of the personnel (and this was three march battalions), which the Army Group was to receive in April, would be sent on to the Ninth Army (including around 900 pioneers). In addition, in the nearest future the Ninth Army would also receive StuG Battalion 177 and 20 Pz. IV tanks with long-barreled guns in order to replenish the panzer divisions.[154] Unquestionably, these forces had a certain significance for W. Model, but considering the strict deadline for the start of the offensive (around 3 May) and the critical situation facing the divisions, they were just "drops in the ocean" and were unable to change the situation fundamentally. In addition, already on the morning of 19 April, after a conversation with the chief of operations of Army Group Center Colonel von Treskow, H. von Elverfeldt once again "had the impression that the Ninth Army would hardly receive the allocated march replenishment (in the size of three march battalions) and tanks in time."[155] The Army Group Center simply did not have armor, and when announcing their allocation the headquarters was only operating on the OKH's promises, which Model in fact had already received, but nothing had in fact been done. At this, considering he had already notified both the Army Group and the OKH regarding the problem of rebuilding his forces with sufficient clarity, the Colonel General hung up the telephone. That afternoon, after making a detailed analysis of intelligence information, Model came to the conclusion that the Ninth Army's present strength in tanks remained absolutely inadequate. Therefore, having gotten in touch with G. von Kluge, in the same abrasive manner as before, he demanded no less than 101 Tiger tanks be immediately given to him.[156] However, the Field Marshal recommended that he address this particular matter to Berlin and Zossen.

The army commander was forced to follow this advice, but in order to make his request more persuasive, he decided to bolster it with the opinion of the leadership of his subordinate corps. For this, he quickly polled all of his corps commanders over the telephone, and the outcome was as expected – the lack of personnel replacements and the deficit in artillery and particularly tanks did not allow Citadel to get underway by the established deadline, around 3 May. He reported about all this to the headquarters of Army Group Center on 19 April in a telephone dispatch addressed to the OKH. In this document, in addition to the aforementioned problems, Model noted that considering the altered situation, the Ninth Army would need an additional day to break directly through the Russians' main belt of defenses (not two, as given in the Army Group's plan, but three), and at least one more full-strength infantry division. In conclusion he added that he had received the personal directive from the OKH Chief of Staff regarding the

154 NARA US, T.312, R.317, F.7886045.
155 NARA US, T.312, R.317, F.7886046.
156 NARA US, T.312, R.317, F.7886045.

start of the regrouping according to the new plan and having the offensive set for the first days of May ready to go, but in light of all that he had laid out above, he asked that Zeitzler repeat it. In a single word, W. Model rather diplomatically (as much as he was able) responded to the demands of the OKH: In such circumstances, his Ninth Army was unable to go on the offensive in early May, and if K. Zeitzler did not agree with him, then the Chief of Staff of the OKH could take on all the responsibility and confirm the demand to launch the offensive on 3 May through a second order.

Inarguably, by bringing the attention of the Army Group and the OKH to the depletion of troops and equipment in his divisions and their impossibility of carrying out orders as stated, W. Model was trying not only to put pressure on Zossen to send him additional forces, but also as an experienced military commander he was thinking about the future. He was striving to divest himself of responsibility and the Führer's possible (if not expected) wrath over the failure of a poorly-prepared operation. However, K. Zeitzler continued to stand his ground. That same evening, Krebs received a response from the OKH: It was impossible to allocate the forces requested by the Ninth Army for the offensive. The OKH could not have failed to grasp the validity of Model's demands, so in the effort to sweeten the deal, on 20 April it informed him of Berlin's decision to postpone the start of the offensive to approximately 15 May. In particular, the telegram stressed that "this was prompted by the impossibility of satisfying the requests for replenishments of manpower, tanks and artillery."[157] By this time, E. von Manstein had received the bulk of that which had initially been promised to him, in addition to the infantry divisions that had been allotted for the projected Operation Neptune. Thus, although on paper the OKH recognized the correctness of the Ninth Army's commander with respect to supplying him (or more accurately, failing to supply him) with everything necessary for the offensive, but this did not make things any easier for W. Model or his army, since the problem had not been resolved.

The Colonel General did not belong to that category of military commanders to whom the orders of staff officers in Zossen were more important than the objective realities of the front. After all, the postponement of the offensive without any additional reinforcement of his army at a time when the Russian defenses were strengthening did not in principle change anything. On the contrary, at this moment time was working to the benefit of the Russians. Therefore at 1830 he called H. Krebs and announced that firstly, the order from the Chief of Staff of the OKH was physically impossible to carry out, given the same forces that he presently possessed, even with the postponement of the start date of the offensive; secondly, going on the offensive with an unprepared army would lead to the operation's failure to attain its objectives and to an eventual withdrawal back to the line of departure. His demand: either shift the offensive start date to after 15 May and send him the requisite reinforcements, or he would take no responsibility for the consequences.[158] With that curt declaration, the Ninth Army commander hung up the phone.

H. Krebs had previously served under W. Model's command for a rather long time and could clearly see the situation in which the Ninth Army's troops found themselves. So, he understood that Model's declaration was not simply an emotional outburst, but a well-considered and final decision under the pressure of objective circumstances. After a certain amount of time had

---

157 NARA US, T.312, R.317, F.7886055.
158 NARA US, T.312, R.317, F.7886050, 7886051.

passed, he called Colonel General Model back and asked to return to the abruptly truncated discussion's subject. Having calmed themselves down somewhat, they quickly reached the one and only proper decision in that situation. The OKH was again sent a telegram, this one No.1a 068/43, but this one designated for Hitler personally. Its essence consisted in the following: only two possibilities to carry out the operation's plan existed: either adapt its objectives with regard to the available forces, or urgently, prior to 15 May, strengthen the Ninth Army with everything necessary.[159] The document repeated the same demands that had been contained in the preceding telegram sent to K. Zeitzler on the prior day. However, it was precisely this document (the second telegram) that in fact entered the history of the Battle of Kursk as W. Model's April letter, which first forced Hitler to ponder the objectivity of Operation Citadel. Field Marshal von Kluge was in agreement with Model that the serious problems to which he was pointing did in fact exist, and understood also that to ignore them was hazardous, while the steps taken so far by the OKH were not only not constructive, but aggravated the situation. Therefore, the command of Army Group Center refused to put any distance between itself and the Ninth Army's position, unlike it had done before, but on the contrary emphasized that it was extremely interested that Hitler take personal part in the resolution of the stipulated problems. This was the optimal approach. In the first place, it protected G. von Kluge from Hitler's wrath in the event of the offensive's failure. Secondly, he was divesting himself of all of Model's demands and accusations that had been addressed to Army Group Center in the ignoring of these problems.

These debates and arguments in the higher headquarters were taking place against the backdrop of the foul weather that was continuing to build and to complicate the force regrouping. A downpour that occurred on the night of 19-20 April over the entire area of the Orel bulge brought the withdrawal of the Ninth Army's divisions from the rear area of the Fourth Army to a complete stop. According to the forecasts of the meteorologists, no improvement in the weather was expected right up to 30 April, so accordingly it was totally impossible to begin anything like an offensive, or even a large shifting of forces, prior to 7 May. This made it unthinkable to resolve the main problems in preparing for Citadel over just a week, by 15 May. Judging from the information gleaned from captured German documents, the Ninth Army command was thinking that this circumstance would bring about a favorable decision from Hitler. Already in the morning of the next day of 21 April, K. Zeitzler personally briefed Hitler on the situation in the Ninth Army and Model's requests. His report made a large impression on the Führer, and he took time to think it over. That same day the Chief of Staff of the OKH informed Krebs about this and expressed the hope that the given questions would be resolved in the nearest future. The Ninth Army command was also informed about Zeitzler's meeting with Hitler and waited for an answer impatiently.

However, it shouldn't be considered that this unquestionably major problem unified the command of Army Group Center and the Ninth Army and that G. von Kluge's jealousy disappeared at a stroke. Far from it. Already on the next day, H. Krebs in a telephone conversation with H. von Elverfeldt demanded a deeper evaluation of the situation in the troops and the forthcoming offensive's prospects, and also recommended not to expect more than the OKH had already agreed upon with Army Group Center, namely not more than 227 tanks and

---

159 NARA US, T.312, R.317, F.7886051.

120 assault guns.[160] This was a clear insult directed at Model, so his chief of staff immediately reacted sharply, stating that the army's leadership would never exaggerate and present a picture of its troops worse than it really was. Thus, it would be useful for the common cause if the Army Group paid more heed to the assessments of the army's leadership. This did not put an end to the dispute; it continued on the following day.

On 22 April the Chief of Staff of Army Group Center took off in an airplane that had been especially sent for him by Model and arrived at the Ninth Army command post in Kishkino with the aim of getting a better picture of the real state of affairs with replenishments directly among the troops. The Ninth Army's documents note: "This was necessary in order to evaluate the justification for Gruppe Weiss' demands."[161] After meeting with Model, he left to inspect the XXXXI Panzer Corps, XXXXVII Panzer Corps and XXIII Army Corps together with H. von Elverfeldt. It is doubtful that H. Krebs really mistrusted both his subordinates and his former commander in a matter that was so significant. The army unquestionably was in a difficult situation, so there was no need to exaggerate the problems it faced. All of this uproar seems theatrical and was plainly organized with the aim of increasing the Army Group's significance as both a controlling organ and as an important participant in the process of preparing for the main offensive in 1943.

As it was in fact possible to assume, the situation in the Ninth Army's divisions proved to be seriously adverse. Therefore H. Krebs even before departing to Smolensk agreed with W. Model and signed Order No.073/43, in which he clarified a number of points of the previous version of the offensive's plan. The general sense of the changes was as follows: through tactical methods, to increase the density of forces on the main axis and to the extent possible to divert a portion of the Russian troops to the army's right flank; more precisely:

a. Subordinate the XXXXVI Panzer Corps to Gruppe Köllner for the purpose of freeing up additional forces;
b. Decrease the sector of the XXXXVII Panzer Corps for the purpose of creating a greater concentration of strength on the main axis of attack;
c. When executing Point b., leave the 86th Infantry Division in its previous place as a main prerequisite for a successful attack in this sector [general direction – east of Ponyri];
d. Shift the boundary between the XXXXI Panzer Corps and XXIII Army Corps 2 km to the west, for the purpose of ensuring a better opportunity for the XXIII Corps to envelop the enemy fortifications in the Maloarkhangel'sk area. This corps is to go on the attack three hours later, in order to give the Luftwaffe the opportunity to support its attack. Also, relocate a portion of the XXXXI Panzer Corps' artillery at the moment of breakthrough;
e. Prepare an attack against the enemy with the XX Army Corps, reinforced by the 251st and 137th Infantry Divisions.[162]

160 NARA US, T.312, R.317, F.7886052.
161 NARA US, T.312, R.317, F.7886029.
162 NARA US, T.312, R.317, F.7886053.

With this order, the General of Infantry Troops J. Freissner's XXIII Army Corps began to take shape in the form that it would take part in Citadel. The 216th and 383rd Infantry Divisions were transferred to it out of the army reserve, as well as the 78th Sturm Division, which the commander of the XX Army Corps was to replace with his 72nd Infantry Division and withdraw it to the rear. I will remind the reader that at this moment, the front was being occupied by the forces of the XX Army Corps, the 20th Panzer Division and the 86th Infantry Division, reinforced with artillery. After the arrival of the listed divisions, the XXIII Army Corps was also supposed to move up into the front line. This was the first official document that authorized such substantial changes in the plan for Citadel already confirmed by Berlin on 12 April 1943. The decisions by H. Krebs and W. Model unquestionably helped smooth out somewhat a few of the individual, acute problems facing the Ninth Army, but they were unable to resolve its main problem. In the condition in which its forces found themselves by the last days of April, they were simply unable to conduct a successful offensive. The higher command in principle understood this, but the situation was not changing. Naturally such a state of affairs on the eve of an offensive that had such ambitious objectives could not help but agitate Colonel General Model, and the aggravations in his relationships with Army Group Center and the OKH continued to grow and reached a peak after 20 April 1943.

Judging from the preserved archival sources, Hitler took the Colonel General's demand very seriously, and reacted favorably to it, but the main thing is he did so quickly. It is possible that a letter from E. von Manstein on the evening before, in which the Field Marshal insistently recommended to exert every effort to ensure Citadel's success, was a positive stimulus to Hitler's reaction to Model.[163] Evidence of this became the completely different attitude of the OKH to the Ninth Army's requests. Here is how the OKH's reaction to Model's maneuver is described in the Ninth Army's war diary for 23 April:

> The tension between the army command and higher command which arose in recent days because of the failure to carry out the orders from higher command today subsided and acquired a fully amicable form. At 1215 the Army Group's Chief of Staff sent the Ninth Army's chief of staff a promise from General Zeitzler to direct a panzer battalion with 50 long-barreled Pz. IV tanks from the west to the Ninth Army. At 1755 General Zeitzler personally called the Army commander and announced that the sending of the 50 Pz. IV with long-barrels was being cancelled, but instead, as had indeed been previously planned, the army would be sent a panzer battalion consisting of 20 Tigers and 25 Pz. III, a battalion of assault guns numbering 40 StuGs, and also radio-controlled tanks. At 1610 the attention of the Army Group's Chief of Staff and the Ninth Army's Chief of Staff was particularly directed to the fact that the 391/5th Labor Battalion numbering 769 men would be placed at the Ninth Army's disposal. Thus, at the final minute, the wish of the Ninth Army commander was able to be satisfied. Thus, all of the obstacles to preparing the offensive according to the plan have been removed. General Zeitzler invited the Army commander to make a second visit to Führer Headquarters on 27 April.[164]

---

163 Manstein, *Uteriannye pobedy*, p. 525.
164 NARA US, T.312, R.317, F.7886055.

The story with the battalion of Tiger tanks would subsequently have its own continuation. On the morning of 11 May, a representative of the OKH Colonel Grunther announced over the telephone to the Ninth Army's Operations Department that as had been promised, the Ninth Army would receive Heavy Panzer Battalion 505, but its composition was changing. Instead of 20 Pz. VI tanks, he would receive 31. The additional 11 Tigers would be sent in place of 11 of its Pz. III.[165] Ultimately, the battalion's strength would be brought up to 45 heavy panzers. In the meantime, it was to consist of four companies, three of which were equipped with Tigers, and one – with Pz. III medium tanks. This decision would strengthen the army's assault wedge, and unquestionably was a result of W. Model's protest against the OKH's inactivity. Even so, despite the efforts that were made, both the Ninth Army and the Army Group Center distinctly understood that this was just a trickle, but the situation required the reinforcement of the Ninth Army with a fully flowing river of men and equipment. Even though at mid-day on 18 April three of the four corps (except the XXIII Army Corps) designated for Citadel reported preparations were going according to schedule, W. Model still did not have an armored fist in order to breach the Central Front's defenses, and he would be unable to form one by month's end.[166]

Thus, the second attempt to launch an offensive toward Kursk, which was already "germinating" after the receipt of Order No. 6, wound up doomed to failure because of objective reasons: Germany's lack of necessary forces and the time to prepare for it. In addition, W. Model's heated arguments with the OKH between 17 and 21 April had plainly demonstrated that the Ninth Army's commander was the only man who demanded a sober approach to matters and activity from the Reich's entire military and political machine. Unlike after the war, the military commanders at the time were not blaming Hitler for all of the miscalculations and blunders, and together with Hitler, they were accepting full and unconditional responsibility for them. This includes those that were committed in the period of Citadel's planning and preparation, since because of their own flaws, ambitions and the factional squabbles within the Wehrmacht's leadership, already in the first stage of preparing for the operation in April, they were unable to organize harmonious, effective work.

In addition to the aforementioned problems, on 18 April the Ninth Army command received one more major headache, which in essence ultimately doomed the decision to begin Citadel not only in the first days of May, but possibly by the middle of the month as well. Until recently, this problem was unknown in the Russian historiography of the Battle of Kursk. First, an ominous message arrived in the headquarters of the Ninth Army from the Second Panzer Army's Operations Department, and then its chief medical officer Colonel Richter personally informed H. von Elverfeldt that a week before, an outbreak of typhus had been discovered in the 4th Panzer Division. At the given moment, already 216 men were sick, and most likely the peak of the epidemic still had not passed, since a quarantine that should have been introduced back on 11 April had not been was not enacted. Because of the failure to take timely measures, the epidemic was spreading, thus any movement of the division for at least the next 8-10 days was undesirable.[167] Thus, in the best case one of Army Group Center's six panzer divisions involved in Citadel became static until 28 April, and even worse, combat training and the influx of men

---

165 NARA US, T.312, R.317, F.7886052.
166 NARA US, T.312, R.317, F.7886045.
167 NARA US, T.312, R.317, F.7886046.

and equipment to refit it ceased. On 19 April, the Ninth Army's Operations Department sent a request to Army Group Center not to move the 4th Panzer Division for at least another week.[168]

"Spotted fever", as this infectious illness was called in everyday speech, broke out in many oblasts of the European portion of the Soviet Union in the first six months of 1943. For example, according to a report from an official of the German military administration, whom the headquarters of the Ninth Army sent on 15 May to analyze the situation in the Lokot' District[169] and the territory adjacent to it, 50percent of the entire population was sick with typhus in the winter of 1942/1943, and over the first 10 days of May up to 700 men tested positive for it, 150 of whom were from the militarized units of collaborationists. In fact, these cases were only those known to the occupational authorities; in reality, there were significantly more people sick with typhus. The main cause was the widespread infestation of fleas among the population.[170]

Major outbreaks of this illness were noted at this time in the troops of the Soviet Central Front as well. The problem became so acute that on 30 April its Military Council appealed to I.V. Stalin with a request to permit in the immediate future only the partial fulfillment of the order from the *Stavka* to remove the civilian population from a 25-km frontal zone, in order not to spread the epidemic.[171] In fact, it received authorization for this.

All of this was happening against the backdrop of the continuing spring thaw, which as before was immobilizing the entire central portion of Russia, Ukraine and Belorussia. On 19 April, the Ninth Army's weather summary indicated that squally winds and strong rains were observed throughout the entire day, so the ground was wet, and the village roads and main roads were passable only for all-terrain vehicles. On the previous day, 18 April, Model, having hastily completed his business in the headquarters, flew off to the XXXXI Panzer Corps. During a discussion of the corps' preparation for the offensive, its commander General Harpe directly declared:

> At the present time, the road conditions remain the factor that is substantially holding up the preparations for the operation. The hope that the weather conditions in the course of several days would permit the roads to dry out have not been justified in the last few days. As a result, the highway and village roads remain impassable. The roads lacking a hard surface will be unsuitable for use for a certain time more, while the hard-surfaced roads can be used only in places. For this reason, the refueling of transport vehicles close to the front has been complicated. At the Zmievka Station, the

---

168 Ibid.
169 A national administrative-territorial body, which functioned under the aegis of the Wehrmacht from 15 November 1941 to 26 August 1943 in the rear of Army Group Center, bounded by the Kursk, Orel and Briansk Oblasts, which included eight of their pre-war districts. In geographical area it was equivalent to Belgium, and in the middle of 1943 more than 580,000 people resided in it. The center of the precinct was the "worker's settlement" of Lokot' (as the Germans called the town) of Briansk Oblast, which housed its administration, various structures of the militarized formation of collaborationists of the "Russian People's Liberation Army" and the headquarters of the Hungarian 102nd Division.
170 *Pod nemtsami: Vospominaniia, svidetel'stva, dokumenty* [*Under the Germans: Recollections, evidence and documents*] (St Petersburg: Skriptorium, 2011), p. 495.
171 TsAMO RF, F.62, Op.321, D.5, ll. 152-153.

fuel trucks cannot reach the 180-tonn fuel terminal, which has been set up between the train station and the highway.[172]

Indeed, no one could argue with this. On 22 April, Krebs ruled out the movement of a battalion of trucks with the total carrying capacity of 900 tonn, which at that moment was located in the Roslavl' area, to the army until the condition of the roads improved.[173] W. Model was forced to issue a directive to make maximum use of horse-drawn transport "since the other types are unsuitable in such conditions."[174] As a result until the end of April, the bulk of the army's troops and artillery were moved to the areas of assembly primarily by horse power, while the tanks and replacements from Germany moved only by rail.

However, the spring of 1943 did not bring only negative surprises. The weather forecasts from Elverfeldt's staff at the end of April seemed absolutely unbelievable. Already on 21 April the rainfall ended, the sun began to warm the earth, a breeze began blowing, and the road conditions began to improve perceptibly, and just three days later the Operations Department stated: "The period of the spring muddy season, which arrived early this year, can finally be considered over, almost three weeks earlier than in the past. Everywhere, corduroying of the roads (where necessary) is being done. Copious dust is already visible everywhere along the roads. Off the roads the soil has also become firm and suitable for the marching of troops. Little green leaves have amicably appeared on all the surrounding trees.[175]

This give the Ninth Army's troops an additional impulse, and their movement from the rear area of the Fourth Army to their assigned lines of departure for the offensive accelerated. An enormous force was moving up to the forward edge of the Central Front, and Model was personally overseeing this process. After arriving from Zaporozh'e, where he had been temporarily fulfilling the duties of von Manstein, who had gone to Germany for medical treatment, he practically spent days located among the troops. He had enough reasons for paying such fixed attention to the march. The main forces were moving at night, with all of the problems that flowed from this: vehicle accidents, traffic jams, collapsed bridges unable to withstand the load, and meetings between officers to clarify the march order, etc. By 25 April, the situation on the main roads along which the army was moving, in spite of the well-known German efficiency and fondness for order, became deadlocked, and the timetable had to be changed once again. The Ninth Army's Operations Department noted: "The marches, which are being conducted on moonless nights, have led to a large number of accidents and heavy losses in transport. In connection with this, today the Army Group demanded that fighter aircraft throughout the day securely cover the routes of movement running through the hills in the Karachev area against low-flying enemy reconnaissance aircraft."[176]

In addition to the objective problems, a multitude of subjective problems arose, connected with the desire of commanders to hasten the movement of their troops along more or less trafficable roads at the expense of their neighbors. As a result, frictions arose even between

---

172 NARA US, T.312, R.317, F.7886045, 7886046.
173 NARA US, T.312, R.317, F.7886054.
174 NARA US, T.312, R.317, F.7886053.
175 NARA US, T.312, R.317, F.7886056.
176 NARA US, T.312, R.317, F.7886078.

division commanders and corps commanders, which only W. Model was able to extinguish on the fly, sometimes through intervening personally on the spot.

Judging from captured German documents, Elverfeldt's headquarters was fearing, and even anticipating, a powerful attack at the moment when the units and formations began taking over their sectors of the front. Various measures were enacted in order to prevent this. For example, on 19 April it sent the 1st *Fliegerdivision* [Air Division] a request to assign the adequate forces and means to take aerial photographs of the ground with the aim of conducting a detailed surveillance of the area of the Central Front's force dispositions and to identify any preparations for an offensive.[177] The document clearly stipulated that the main task was to influence the activity of Soviet forces and not in any event allow "the expected enemy attacks, in particular in sectors of the assembly of our assault groupings, capable of disrupting the regrouping of our troops" as well as "to impede the creation of supply stockpiles and thereby hamper the conducting of an operation."[178] However, these apprehensions turned out to be groundless.

The preparations for the offensive were in full swing, though no decisions had been made yet about how to conduct it. It was relatively quiet at the front and the command at every level sought to use each day so as to prepare better for the forthcoming battle. Tactical exercises were conducted in the divisions that had been withdrawn from the front, and even in those still positioned at the front. This work was reminiscent of a conveyor belt; having run combat-seasoned personnel through the training drills, the divisions commands immediately began breaking in the newly-arrived replacements.

Now let us return to Berlin. As already noted, for the Reich's leadership the entire spring of 1943 passed under the portent of arguments over the future course of the war. Despite the fact that Order No. 6 should have clearly indicated Hitler's resolve to carry out the plan embodied in it, he still had doubts about whether or not his thinking was correct, so discussions about the advisability of Operation Citadel continued even after its adoption. Two groups with diametrically opposed views had formed among the high-ranking military men, who'd been let into the Führer's plans. Those who were opposed to the attempt to liquidate the Kursk salient were now drawing attention to the fact that the time had been missed for such a major offensive; the Russian forces were now firmly dug into their occupied lines and were busily constructing elaborate and deep defensive lines. The Wehrmacht did not have adequate forces to overcome them, and it was senseless to count upon the factor of surprise while preparing such a major operation. Thus, there was no point in throwing forces away on a pre-ordained failure, and better to strengthen their own defenses and create reserves, including for repulsing an attack by the Allies in Europe.

In the latter half of April, information from ground and aerial reconnaissance began to arrive, which captured the colossal scale of the Russians' fortifications at the base of the Kursk bulge. This once again convinced the skeptics that the operation's objectives were too ambitious for the Wehrmacht. Initially only a small group of the Wehrmacht's higher leadership were drawn into

---

177 Later, a specialized unit, Major T. Wienecke's Nahaufklärungsgruppe [Near or tactical reconnaissance] 4 Gruppe was reassigned from Luftflotte VI to the Ninth Army, and distributed among its subordinate corps in the following manner: XX Corps received Geschwader [Squadron] 3 (Bf-110G), the XXXXVI and XXXXVII Panzer Corps received Geschwader 1 (Bf-109G), and the XXXXI Panzer Corps and XXIII Corps – Geschwader 2 (Bf-109G).
178 NARA US, T.312, R.317, F.7886055.

this discussion, but then after receiving the first official documents regarding Citadel from Berlin, the ranks of the skeptics grew with the addition of army commanders, such as the Fourth Panzer Army's Colonel General H. Hoth, the Second Panzer Army's Colonel General R. Schmidt, and the Fourth Army's Colonel General G. Heinrici.[179] Incidentally, the latter left behind an interesting vignette. He recalled that in the course of the plan's discussions, he had the following conversation with his direct superior and an advocate for the offensive, G. von Kluge:

> Heinrici: Herr Fieldmarshal, why do you want a Battle of Borodino?
> Kluge: What do you have in mind?
> Heinrici: That we will run into a powerful adversary at Kursk.
> Kluge: That's now my business.[180]

Such a response from the Field Marshal was understandable. Better informed about the behind-the-scenes machinations in Berlin[181], he understood full well that a rational approach when making decisions that involved the military men played an important role in the case of Citadel, though not a key one. The main reason was Hitler's persistent desire to attack, and the political advantages that he was impatiently expecting from the future victory. The fact that the situation was deteriorating for Germany in Africa unquestionably also had a substantial influence. Nevertheless, as R. Cross accurately observed, the plan of Citadel to a great extent was "calculated in order to refresh Hitler's memory of past victories."[182] According to eyewitness testimony, after the succession of failures on the fronts which shadowed Germany since the end of 1942, its leadership (and I will emphasize not just Hitler alone) were not in the condition to evaluate a situation soberly. With each passing month it was gradually becoming numb to the severity of the losses at the end of 1942 and beginning of 1943; the tendency toward adventurism was growing; and when working out plans, far from realistic assessments of both the potential of the USSR and their own capabilities dominated. Here is just one insignificant example given by A. Speer in his memoirs:

> Such behavior was not the only indication that Hitler had refused to acknowledge the turn of affairs. In the spring of 1943, he had demanded that a three-mile-long road and railroad bridge be built across the Strait of Kerch, although we had long been building a cable railway there; it went into operation on 14 June with a daily capacity of one thousand tons. This amount of supplies just sufficed for the defensive needs of the Seventeenth Army. But Hitler had not forsaken his plan to push through the Caucasus to Persia. He justified his order for the bridge explicitly on the necessity to transport materiel and troops to the Kuban bridgehead for an offensive. His generals, however,

---

179 Newton, *Kurskaia bitva: nemetskii vzgliad*, p. 139.
180 Dashichev (ed.), *Sovershenno sekretno! Tol'ko dlia komandovaniia!*, pp. 495-496.
181 There is one by no means unimportant detail characterizing Gotthard Heinrici and his position in the Reich. He was a strong and resolute man. Having fallen in love with a Jewish woman, he personally asked Hitler to allow him to marry her, and the Führer was forced to grant it. In addition, General Heinrici was very religious and attended church services regularly. Thus, both Hitler and his circle treated Heinrici warily, and in the testimony of some eyewitnesses, even shunned the general.
182 Cross, *Operatsiia Tsitadel'*, p. 103.

had long put any such ideas out of their heads. On a visit to the Kuban bridgehead the frontline generals expressed anxiety over whether the positions could be held at all in the face of the enemy's obvious strength. When I reported these fears to Hitler, he said contemptuously, "Nothing but empty evasions! Jänicke [the commander of the Seventeenth Army] is just like the General Staff; he hasn't faith in a new offensive."[183]

Indeed, in all these debates the question on the viability of an offensive toward Kursk was naturally key.

The diametrically opposed assessments of the generals regarding the Kursk offensive and the fresh intelligence about the scale of the work to fortify the defenses being done by the Soviet troops within the Kursk salient led Hitler into a period of hesitation, and he began to waver. Less than a week after issuing Order No. 6, he decided to make fundamental changes to the plan for the operation, and on 19 April issued a directive to the chief of Army Group Center's transportation service Colonel H. Teske to ponder the possibility of shifting the assault grouping of Model's Ninth Army to the Vorozhba area (in the sector of the Second Army). Having received a reply that Vorozhba was a major rail hub[184], so the movement wouldn't take a lot of time, Hitler called K. Zeitzler and briefly presented his new idea. Its essence consisted in the idea that the divisions of von Manstein's group and Kluge's group should launch an attack not at the base of the Kursk salient, but frontally (in the Second Army's sector), from the west toward Kursk. Understanding that the Führer's anxiety might throw the entire summer campaign into disarray, the Chief of the OKH in the course of the discussion exerted maximum efforts in order to persuade him that the new plan would cause a marked delay to the start of an offensive, and so the risks would substantially grow. However, Hitler was in no mood to take no for an answer. On the following day during a discussion of readying for the offensive, K. Zeitzler reported on the Führer's new idea to the OKH's Chief of Operations Lieutenant General A. Huesinger, Army Group South's chief of staff Major General T. Busse and Army Group Center's chief of staff Lieutenant General Krebs. They all skeptically regarded the prospects of implementing this new idea, pointing to two key complicating factors – the large amount of time it would take to regroup the forces, and the fact that a frontal attack would only drive the Soviet forces out of the Kursk bulge, and not destroy them.[185] Having obtained the opinion of the chiefs of staff of both army groups, K. Zeitzler flew off to Berchtesgaden[186] on 21 April in order to defend Citadel's original plan now in a personal meeting with Hitler. In this, he was successful.

At this time, the situation on all the fronts continued to go extremely unsuccessfully for the Wehrmacht, while problems began to compound rapidly. On 20 April, the Ninth Army's combat diary noted:

---

183 Speer, *Vospominaniia*, p. 354.
184 Vorozhba is a town in Sumy Oblast (Ukraine) and a major rail hub, where the Khar'kov – L'vov, Khar'kov – Minsk, Khar'kov – Orsha, and Kiev – Voronezh railroads intersected. As the crow flies, Vorozhba is 147 km from Kursk.
185 Toppel, *Kursk 1943*, p. 30.
186 A resort town in Bavaria (in the mountainous region of Obersaltzberg, 120 km southeast of Munich); nearby in the mountains was which Hitler's residence of the Berghof, while the town itself had a few buildings holding offices of the Reich Chancellery.

It is important to remark that the situation of the German and Italian troops at the bridgehead in Africa (in Tunisia) has become very critical. At the same time, a danger has arisen of an enemy invasion of southern Europe, as well as on the Atlantic coastline. Simultaneously the enemy is launching powerful air attacks, which have affected the majority of western Germany's areas. Our primary weapon in the West has thus become the submarine fleet, the significance of which has substantially grown. The successes of the submarine fleet over the previous months of this year can be acknowledged as significant. However, Germany's strongest and most dangerous adversary remains the Russians. Against this enemy, the German Wehrmacht stands as the primary defensive wall … Only our complete victory can prevent this danger from the East.[187]

In reality, the events on the Soviet – German front at this time were occupying the central role and presented the main problem for the leadership of Nazi Germany. Operation Neptune, which had been launched by Army Group A, had been a failure. The Red Army had reacted by quickly shifting a significant amount of air power to this area to repulse the German attempt to destroy the bridgehead at Myskhako. The formations of aircraft were able to cover the ground troops that were holding a narrow strip of Novorossiisk's Tsemes Bay. The bitter aerial combats that developed above the Taman Peninsula demonstrated that the Red Army's air force had come a long way since the start of the war, and its commanders were rapidly learning from experience and perfecting their command and control over the fighter formations. It was clear that in the course of Citadel as well, the high activity of the Russian air armies would present a serious complicating factor, and it was reckless not to consider this. Naturally, this flow of negative information from every direction could not help but affect Hitler's decisions that were taken at this time.

However, in the opinion of certain participants of those events and a number of Western scholars, it was nevertheless Model's letter that had the strongest impression on him. It worked just like a catalyst, reinforcing everything that had been said by the offensive's opponents. Having weighed all the pros and cons, on 26 April Hitler issued an order to work out the offensive plan in more detail, and for the first time after the issuing of Order No. 6, postponed its start date to 5 May. He then decided to discuss this matter with all the key figures that had been drawn into preparing for the offensive. Simultaneously, a directive went out to hasten the delivery of armor and other loads in order to refit and replenish the Ninth Army as soon as possible. However, the OKH immediately pointed out the primary causes for the delays in the deliveries – the partisan attacks on the lines of communication and the impossibility of quickly finding a solution to this. The partisan activity had grown so much, especially in the rear of Army Group Center, that it was necessary to issue an order to reduce the speed of the trains in order to avert derailments after an explosion. Thus, in the latter half of April the problems continued to snowball, and there was still no success in working out a unified and well-based opinion as to how to conduct the summer campaign, even though the factor of time at this moment was still playing a key role. Literally with each passing day, the Red Army was building up its forces, and that meant that with each passing day, the possibility of success of either an offense or a defense was decreasing. The German generalship could not help but realize this.

187 NARA US, T.312, R.317, F.7886050.

This is approximately how Russian historians also present the events at the end of April 1943. Next, scholars usually point to a conference that took place on 3 and 4 May in Munich, regarding which two of its key participants, E. von Manstein and H. Guderian have left behind very subjective and muddled recollections. In their memoirs both commanders traced the outline of historical scenes fairly well and offered rather full descriptions of how they struggled against Hitler's mistaken point of view. However, neither one of the military commanders bothered to describe, at least in a few lines, how the document appeared that prompted this conference – Model's report (or letter). From their books it is unclear whether they are talking about Model's letter from 20 April or about something else entirely and say nothing at all about whether or not the commander of the Ninth Army himself was present at the conference. Heinz Guderian writes that the Colonel General was present at the conference[188], but it is impossible to draw the same conclusion from E. von Manstein's narrative. Thus, the memoirs of these two actors, though in fact widely used by Russian historians of the Battle of Kursk, are not reliable as a source, because they are extremely subjective and do not aid in doing a solid analysis of even separate, key clusters of moments during the preparation for Citadel.

In actual fact, as the majority of historians observe, Hitler highly regarded Model's opinion, and as it has become clear after the study of captured German documents I've discovered, the decision to subject the plan for Citadel to a more detailed study, made on 26 April, was a direct consequence of Model's letter from 20 April 1943. In addition, both the further steps taken, such as the postponement of the offensive and the conference held in Munich, were not done without the influence of the Colonel General's opinion. They became a result of an additional meeting Model had with the Führer in the Berghof on 27 April, which is practically unmentioned in the Russian historiography of the Battle of Kursk. It was at this meeting that Model presented documents to Hitler, which painted the completely dismal picture of the Ninth Army's condition just a week before the offensive's proposed start date. Here is how the Operations Department of the Ninth Army described it:

> In the latter half of the day of 26 April, the Army's commander flew off to the Army Group, from whence he headed to the Führer's headquarters in Obersaltzberg as part of a delegation for a conference on the question of conducting Operation Citadel. He took along the plans for substantial corrections of the planned measures, and more precisely the letter from Gruppe Weiss 1a, No.077/43 from 25 April 1943 to Army Group Center. This document once again paid considerable attention to the new information on the enemy's position, which would affect the conducting of the operation. It is necessary to pay maximal attention to the breakthrough of the enemy's first belt of defenses. It is necessary <u>in the shortest amount of time</u> to break through to the Kursk area so as to prevent the enemy's creation of a new defensive front.
>
> Today a new version of the order regarding the conducting of Operation Citadel for the chiefs of staff 1a, No.080/43 was received, which was forwarded to the corps commands. The most substantial change in it is the replacement of the 2nd Panzer Division by the 9th Panzer Division, as well as the rescheduling of the attacks of the XXXXI Panzer and XXIII Army Corps to an earlier time.

---

188 Guderian, *Vospominaniia nemetskogo generala*, p. 337.

At 1545, the Chief of Staff of the Army Group reported to the army's Operations Department regarding a "relief" [the postponement of the offensive for two days, to 5 May]. The army command took this announcement with great satisfaction, since the regrouping of the forces and the stockpiling of supplies was proceeding just as before with large complications and was increasingly falling behind schedule. As a result of the worsening difficulties with the road conditions between Briansk and Roslavl', the assembly of the 10th Panzergrenadier Division and 2nd Panzer Division is being held up for a minimum of 36 hours. The XXXXVII Panzer Corps for this reason issued an order for the powerful forces of the 9th Panzer Division as soon as possible the next morning be moved out to the sector assigned for the 10th Panzergrenadier Division and be held by them until the 10th Panzergrenadier Division's arrival.

Today an order was issued by the Chief of Staff of the Army Group 1a No.4377/43, to which a map had been appended that depicted the tasks of Army Group South during Citadel. In the cover sheet for the map, the main requirements on the part of the OKH are listed. It was indicated that all of the preparations should be completed before X-Day (5 May).[189]

On the afternoon of 27 April W. Model, having arrived at the Hitler Headquarters in Berchtesgaden, personally briefed Hitler about the state of affairs with the preparation of Citadel and offered his assessment of the forthcoming offensive. The Colonel General emphasized that the deficit of time available for shifting the troops and the necessary supply loads was imperatively requiring a postponement of X-Day. The sharp deterioration of the condition of the lines of communication, which made the regrouping of forces and the transportation of supplies impossible, was having a particularly negative affect on the assembly of forces. The divisions that were in movement toward the front had to remain in camps directly along the road sides. He presented a copy of his letter from 25 April (Gruppe Weiss 1a No.077/43) to Army Group Center, which I managed to find in Germany's Federal Military Archives. The document hasn't been used previously by domestic scholars and is interesting by the fact that it not only expands our knowledge about this important stage in the enemy's preparations for the Battle of Kursk, but also because it helps clarify a number of facts, which prior to this had been treated differently in the historiography of the battle. For example, certain Western scholars write that Model at this time supposedly opposed Citadel, since he was recognizing the consequences would be catastrophic for the Wehrmacht whether it was conducted in May or June.[190] It is possible that Model was actually entertaining such thoughts in his mind at this time; however, the document does not confirm this. It contains no expressions of doubt in the need for the operation or criticism of its general plan. Indeed, how could there have been – this was after all the Führer's idea!

By its tone, this letter is laid out in an unadorned manner; its author shared his point of view with the reader concisely and buttresses it with new figures and facts, which details and more thoroughly supports the assessments given by him than those in the documents sent previously to the OKH and the Army Group on matters regarding the preparations for the operation and

---

189 NARA US, T.312, R.317, F.7886059.
190 Newton, *Kurskaia bitva. Nemetskii vzgliad*, p. 471.

the condition of his forces. It was just this information, composed in a crisp, logical chain, that in fact prompted the military and political leadership of Germany to decide to postpone the start of Citadel by more than a month. From the document it follows that the author did not oppose the offensive; he was only striving to point to the major problems, the resolution of which might increase the likelihood of success, and in the first place to the need to reinforce his army.

Walter Model was a professional, so in order to bring up his concerns regarding the state of affairs in the army with the rebuilding of its available divisions and the need for obtaining additional infantry divisions, he relied upon facts and figures, which without any superfluous words would allow even a non-specialist to understand that the Ninth Army still did not have the strength to conduct an operation with such deep objectives as the capture of Kursk. It begins with a description of the enemy's strength and the possible options for his actions at the start of the operation:

> A German offensive in the sector between Belyi Nemed and Maloarkhangel'sk (inclusively) will encounter deep, well-constructed enemy defensive positions, and forces of average defensive strength, which however from previous experience will fight more tenaciously and bitterly when on the defensive. The particular advantage of the defense lies in the large amount of heavy artillery, a powerful anti-tank defense, and strong mobile attacking reserves, in which there are a large number of tanks. The sector on both sides of the Trosna – Fatezh road and the area around Maloarkhangel'sk needs to be mentioned as the centers of the adversary's defense. Here the defensive positions have been maximally strengthened and extended to a large depth; the artillery grouping is also the strongest, and in the given area there is a mass of attacking reserves. In these places, resistance will be the strongest.
>
> Immediately after the start of the offensive and the initial penetrations, one must count upon an attack by reserves of the 13th Army.
>
> The enemy will attempt to destroy any German success in embryo, since at the given moment no further defensive positions have been spotted in the depth of the areas occupied by the enemy, which would allow the enemy to make a planned withdrawal to a new line of defense.
>
> In the further development of the offensive, an attack is expected against the western flank by army reserves of the 70th NKVD Army (two rifle divisions and 1-2 tank units) in the vicinity of Fatezh and to the north, as well as against the eastern flank by reserves of the 48th Army (three rifle divisions and three tank regiments) at Maloarkhangel'sk.
>
> There is doubt in the presence of possible operational reserves, shaken out to the north, in the Kursk – Shshigry area. However, one must expect the appearance of these reserves on the high ground north of Kursk and in the Tuskar sector. Operational reserves have been detected around Dmitriev in the form of two tank corps, as well as enemy reserves west of Livny, which in distinction from the preceding are at the complete disposal of the enemy command for a counterattack against the western and eastern flanks of our offensive. Particularly strong attacks by these units are likely in the area of Fatezh and southeast of there, as well as through Kasorzha and east of Maloarkhangel'sk.
>
> In total, opposite the front of the German offensive there are: Eight rifle divisions, two and a half artillery divisions, two mortar regiments and two regiments of rocket

launchers. As a reserve, the enemy has positioned behind the 13th Army's line of defense: two rifle divisions, one tank corps, one separate tank brigade and one anti-tank brigade.

On the western flank one must anticipate an attack by two rifle divisions and one or two tank units of the 70th Army NKVD and by two tank corps (the 11th and 16th). On the eastern flank, the appearance of reserves of the enemy's 48th Army in the form of three rifle divisions and three tank regiments is assumed.

On the subject of enemy operational reserves in the Kursk – Shshigry area and west of Livny, there is still no information.

2. The assessment of our strength:

A) On the entire sector of front, we have deployed: 11 infantry divisions, one Sturm division, five Jäger battalions, one Panzergrenadier division and six panzer divisions; of these, five infantry divisions, one sturm division, five Jäger battalions, one Panzergrenadier division and six panzer divisions are to take direct part in the offensive …

Excluding the pioneers and labor forces, one can assess the numerical strength in the attacking divisions as sufficient. On the other hand, given the bad weather, the pioneers and laborers are not ready for the amount of work required of them.

The Luftwaffe is ready to employ approximately 400 aircraft (fighters, ground attack aircraft, dive bombers and reconnaissance).[191]

From the information presented in the letter, it follows that the Central Front command already had a superiority in rifle divisions that comprised the bulwark of its defense, which were substantially reinforced with artillery and tank regiments and even corps. Yet as is known, in order to achieve success, the attacking side should have a numerical superiority in forces. In addition, the Ninth Army commander emphasized the presence and strength of the Russians' strategic reserve, and the fact that they should be present. It should be noted that the Abwehr tolerated substantial mistakes when assessing the strength of the Soviet side on this axis; evidence of this is the 11th Tank Corps mentioned in the document, which was supposedly in the second echelon of the Central Front, though early in the month, it left the Central Front for reconstitution. Accordingly, from the letter it flows that it was necessary to consider that the real superiority of the Soviet forces could be even greater, and accordingly, the resistance in the main defensive belt and immediately behind it could be more stubborn and lengthy than previously supposed.

Steven Newton observed:
In order to comprehend what Model was saying … with regard to Operation Citadel, it is critical to understand the situation in the Ninth Army. Following the February withdrawal from the Rzhev salient (Operation Buffalo), the army's constituent divisions had been refitting, absorbing replacements, and hunting down partisans in the Army Group Center rear area. Model's divisions badly needed such a hiatus. Against a ration

---

191 Anlage 3 zum Kreigstagebuch Nr. 8 des Armeeoberkommandos (AOK) 9, Ia, Band 1: Befehle und Meldungen des AOK, Berichtszeit: 30.3 – 2.5.1943. BArch-MA. RH 20-9/136.

strength of 324,924 officers and men in twenty-four divisions, Ninth Army could place just 67,188 combat troops (21 percent) in the trenches. Only two of these divisions were anywhere near their authorized infantry strength, with the remainder hovering at or below 50 percent.

...

Fourteen of these understrength divisions were parceled out to other armies in Army Group Center (most to Fourth Army), and two went to the southern end of the front, leaving Model a nucleus of eight divisions (6th, 72nd, 102nd, 216th, and 251st Infantry Divisions; 2nd and 9th Panzer Divisions), to which would be gradually added another seven infantry divisions, four panzer divisions, and one panzergrenadier division to build the northern assault force for Operation Citadel. None of these divisions could be considered in any sense fresh or at full combat strength when Model received them, all having been pulled out of the line for refitting at about the same time the Rzhev salient had been evacuated.[192]

On 16 May, which is to say after receiving reinforcements, the divisions assigned to the Ninth Army had an average divisional combat strength of 3,307, which amounted to only roughly 60 percent of the authorized strength.[193] Only in two of the divisions did the number of men approach authorized strength, and in the remaining – not more than 50 percent. According to Wehrmacht standards, a division assigned to take part in an offensive should not be less than 75 percent of authorized strength. Indeed, the replenishing of these divisions with manpower was going extremely slowly. The same situation existed with artillery as well; the shortage of cannons and howitzers in the army approached 35 percent.[194]

There was one more important aspect that had Model very troubled – the lack of needed armored vehicles. At the moment he signed his letter (on 24 April), according to the Ninth Army headquarters, in its six panzer divisions (2nd, 4th, 9th, 12th, 18th and 20th) there was a total of 192 tanks (of which 75, or 39 percent were PzKpfw. III and Pz.Kpfw. IV with short-barreled cannons), which meant on average each panzer division had 32 tanks, the equivalent of less than a single panzer battalion.[195] In order to break through the Russians' main defensive belt, he had previously been promised a battalion of new heavy panzers, the Pz.Kpfw. VI, and 200 Pz.Kpfw. V Panthers (see Table 3).

192 Newton, *Kurskaia bitva: Nemetskii vzgliad*, pp. 464-465.
193 Ibid., p. 468.
194 Ibid.
195 NARA US, T.312, R.320, F.7889589, 7889597.

Table 3: Distribution of tanks in the German forces on the Eastern Front as of 4 May 1943 (according to Guderian's report to Hitler)[196]

Divisions	Self-propelled flak guns	Pz.Kpfw. III (short)	Pz.Kpfw. III (long)	Pz.Kpfw IV (short)	Pz.Kpfw. IV (long)	Pz.Kpfw. VI Tiger	Total in repair Number	Total in repair Percent	Total Number	Total Serviceable
18th Army										
Total	-	-	2	1	-	5	3	27.3	11	8
Army Group Center										
2.Panzer	-	2	5	16	23	-	14	23.3	60	46
4.Panzer	-	4	-	12	17	-	7	17.5	40	33
5.Panzer	-	14	7	6	3	-	11	26.8	41	30
8.Panzer	-	21	17	4	11	-	28	34.6	81	53
9.Panzer	-	7	19	2	17	-	21	31.8	66	45
12.Panzer	-	20	8	1	9	-	28	42.4	66	38
18.Panzer	-	10	-	15	1	-	3	10.3	29	26
20.Panzer	-	14	4	6	19	-	16	27.1	59	43
Total for Army Group Center	-	92	60	62	100	-	128	30	442	314
Army Group South										
HvyPzBn 503	-	-	-	13	-	41	4		58	54

196 Arkhiv IVI, F.191, Op.233, D.108 "Reports of Instructor-General of Panzer Forces Guderian to Hitler from 3 May 1941 to 1 June 199", Part 1 (Moscow: Military History Department of the General Staff of the USSR Armed Forces, 1947) (translated from the documents of the TsAMO RF, F.500, Op.12451, D.488, ll. 8–9.

"'Citadel' ... was the final attempt to retain our initiative in the east"   95

Unit										
16.PzGdr	–	2	21	–	6	–	20		49	29
3.Panzer	–	6	22	3	18	–	19		68	49
6.Panzer	11	6	22	–	22	–	38		88 (11)	50 (11)
7.Panzer	–	5	40	34	35	–	21		135	114
11.Panzer	–	3	34	–	15	–	53	50.5	105	52
17.Panzer	–	9	11	1	26	–	23		70	47
19.Panzer	–	5	20	1	18	–	4		48	30
23.Panzer	3	4	14	–	26	–	20		64 (3)	44 (3)
PzGdr. Grossdeutschland	13	2	16	6	55	9	39		127 (13)	88 (13)
PzGdr. LAH	–	–	8	–	36	7	15		66	51
PzGdr. DR	–	2	41	–	9	6	44		102	58
PzGdr. T	–	–	43	4	11	4	45		107	62
Total for Army Group South	**27**	**44**	**292**	**62**	**277**	**67**	**345**	**31.7**	**1087 (27)**	**728**
Army Group A (in the document "Communications from Crimea")										
				14	(+ 8 captured)	16		38	22
13.Panzer	–	–	6	–	–	–	7		13	6

The first 20 Tigers were just now ready to be sent from Germany, but when the factories would produce the first Panthers was not clear; no one had even seen one yet in the combat units of the entire Wehrmacht, including the Ninth Army. Thus, if the offensive was to be postponed for just a few days, the Ninth Army commander could not envision the means he would have to resolve this difficult and very important task, especially regarding the information from aerial reconnaissance about the strengthening of the defenses.

Colonel General Model observed that the superiority of the Soviet side to a certain extent could be offset by the intense training of the combat personnel and concise, well-organized command and control in the course of the fighting, but the training in his units began too late, so it was impossible to achieve the necessary level in the time remaining before the start of the operation. The conclusion suggested itself – his army was unready to launch the operation on 3 May, though Model laid it out rather expansively, but totally clearly:

> The offensive, in addition to breaking through the forward edge in view of the enemy's deeply-echeloned system of defense, presents us with very serious tasks.
>
> Considering the presence of Russian forces in the depth, the offensive should very quickly bypass enemy positions and immediately extend to the south, in order to leave the enemy with no time to set up a new line of defense. In this stage it will be necessary to encircle and destroy hostile units that have been thrown into a counterattack. Both the XXIII Army Corps' and XXXXVII Panzer Corps' diversionary attacks against the enemy and concentrated airstrikes are preliminarily set to begin three hours before the XXXXI and XXIII Army Corps' opening attacks.
>
> The XXIII Corps has very limited strength for a heavy attack at Maloarkhangel'sk. The corps after the start of the offensive must endure a hard, defensive phase. Since the southern wing of the Second Panzer Army[197] has no significant reserves at its disposition, this sector of the front must be bolstered by an additional infantry division.
>
> The offensive of the XXXXVI Panzer Corps must be conducted so as to bypass the large enemy forces on either side of the Trosna – Fatezh road, and after penetrating, quickly pivot around in the opposite direction, thereby creating a ring of encirclement in the western direction. The rapid seizure of the Fatezh area and the creation of a bridgehead south of the Ussosha is important for the effective repulse of the enemy grouping's attack from its position at Dmitriev. This task is too large for the XXXXVI Panzer Corps' available forces. In order to support the southern wing of the XXXXVI Panzer Corps and the timely replacement of the 12th Panzer Division, an additional division is also needed.
>
> The attack of the panzer spearhead (XXXXVII Panzer Corps), after breaking though the defenses, will encounter the expected enemy reserves from out of the Kursk area. This battle will be conducted with the 4th Panzer Division, supported by the right flank of the XXXXI Panzer Corps.
>
> The breakthrough and battle with mobile enemy reserves will be implemented with units that are insufficiently trained for this type of combat, which will quickly

---

197 The Second Panzer Army's right flank joined the left flank of the Ninth Army.

consume strength and mobility, especially in the panzer divisions. In connection with this, the offensive's objective shouldn't be so deep as previously planned.

Given the favorable development of the offensive it will be possible from the area north of Kursk to strike immediately further to the south in order to link up with the Fourth Panzer Army. Above all else, this depends upon how far to the south the forces of the XXXXVI and XXXXI Panzer Corps, which have been directed to encircle the enemy, can advance to the south.

The strength of the panzer wedge should be much larger, which would significantly accelerate the advance toward Kursk and give confidence in the attainment of the objectives; if it would be possible to free up panzer divisions for this with the aim of creating a larger concentration of force, then one or two infantry divisions more are necessary.

The XXXXI Panzer Corps, in connection with the attack to the south and the simultaneous guarding against expected strong flanking attacks from the east, must conduct a corresponding regrouping of strength. After reaching the sector of the Tuskar' River[198], it remains under question whether it will have enough strength for a further attack toward Shshigry. The very same can be said about an offensive as far as Tim for the link-up with the Fourth Panzer Army. Both attacks will be so prepared in order to exploit any opportunity.

The initial plan for the Ninth Army's offensive foresaw that the operation's main phase would last six days: two – necessary for the breakthrough of the Central Front's defensive belt; four – in order to capture Kursk and to link up with the Fourth Panzer Army. No one knew how long it would take to destroy or capture the Soviet forces encircled in the Kursk salient. The line of departure for Model's forces was 75-80 km from Kursk, which meant the average rate of advance after the breakthrough was planned to be 19 - 20 km a day. The German forces had advanced with approximately the same speed back in the summer of 1942. Now, however, the situation had sharply changed. According to R. Töppel, the Ninth Army commander declared that the powerful defenses created by the Soviet troops to a depth of 20 km on the axis of his army's main advance could be breached, but not over two days; it would require six.[199] Accordingly, there should be no expectation of a rapid dash and quick conclusion to the operation. Yet this was only the plan, and how events would develop in reality was naturally unknown to anyone. Such a substantial increase in the time needed to prepare for the offensive and expected to break through the Soviet defenses, as expressed by the Ninth Army commander, could not help but prompt gloomy thoughts in the Reich's leadership, and prod it to rethink the preliminary calculations.

Next Model reworked a joint request of his army and Army Group South for the OKH to issue a new plan for the offensive as soon as possible. This one should take into account all the fresh information about the enemy and postpone the offensive to a later date.

Model's report had a large impact on Hitler. He remained satisfied with the Ninth Army commander. He had asked him to extend his gratitude to the Ninth Army's generals and officers,

---

198 The Tuskar' River is the third largest tributary of the Seim River, and Kursk lies at the mouth of this river.
199 Töppel, *Kursk 1943*, pp. 34-35.

after which he had bestowed Model the Swords to the Knight's Cross, which he received on 3 April 1943. Hitler announced that Model's request about supplies of armaments and tanks would be decided in the near future. As for the postponement of the offensive, the Führer said nothing specific, but promised to examine closely the conclusions set out in the letter. The American military historian Carlos D'Este wrote:

> Hitler, of course, sympathized with Model because he was born into a middle-class family, but the highest professionalism played the decisive significance in his life. When next to the Führer, he never allowed himself agitated outbursts, witnesses to which were his soldiers, but always acted like a confident, sound and balanced man. In all his conduct Model was civil to Hitler, and he easily entrusted the Field Marshal with the highest posts.[200]

As is seen in captured German documents, the Ninth Army commander was extremely alarmed by Hitler's reaction. After all, the situation was not simply complex, but catastrophic, and there was no point in attacking at all. At that time, the troops of his assault grouping were still in motion, yet not nearing their areas of deployment, but still slogging out of their former positions, up to their knees in mud. According to the records of the Ninth Army, between 10 April and the beginning of May, because of the muddy season the rear services were unable to deliver 50 Pz.Kpfw. IV tanks from Orel to the XXXXVII Panzer Corps![201] Recalls the former operations officer of the Second Army Colonel P. von der Groeben:

> The road net in the Orel salient existed in an almost primeval condition as roads go. The Briansk – Orel *Rollbahn* served as the main supply artery for both armies. Several stretches of this *Rollbahn* consisted of gravel road, but most of it was not reinforced in any way except by a one-lane corduroy road that had been completed by German construction troops in 1942. Ninth Army's strategic concentration and its supply phase required at least two north-south traffic arteries of the *Rollbahn* type, which required existing roads to be converted into corduroy roads. Distribution of supplies to dumps and depots, and the maintenance of smooth, uninterrupted flow of supplies once the offensive opened, rendered this an absolute necessity.[202]

In separate areas, the springtime saturation of the soil did not dissipate even at the beginning of summer. Thus, even in June, horse-drawn wagons remained in highest demand in the troops. This was not only because of their ability to keep moving in the mud, but also because of their small loads, since most of the bridges in the area had a load-bearing capacity of not more than 4-5 tonn.

Nevertheless, despite such an unpleasant surprise, Model did not lose heart and quickly went "on the attack". He sent a message to the OKH staff with a report, in which he announced that the movement of the troops could not be hastened in any way. The document also confirmed a report to Army Group Center on 26 April, which indicated that despite extraordinary efforts,

---

200 Barnett, *Voennaia elita reikha*, p. 429.
201 NARA US, T.312, R.317, F.7886064.
202 Newton, *Kurskaia bitva: Nemetskii vzgliad*, p. 138.

more than half of the army's artillery could not be moved into their positions by the indicated deadline. Moreover, a significant portion of the trains carrying supplies had been blocked by partisans on their way to the army's rear zone. Thus, the delivery of even a minimal amount of necessary supply loads remained under question.

The situation was rendered even more acute by the fact that many units had fully expended their ammunition, and the field stockpiles were empty. Immediately after this, Model contacted Elverfeldt and demanded that he in turn also begin to place pressure on the Army Group. During the discussions with H. Krebs that followed immediately, the main request of the Ninth Army's chief of staff was: "Give us time, at least to ready the XXXXVII Panzer Corps for the offensive." The response that followed was curt – the question was closed, and the Army Group would no longer react to requests for postponements. H. Krebs demanded that the Ninth Army hasten the movement of wheeled transportation along all the roads, including the dirt (or better, mud) roads, in order to ensure the concentration of troops within the established deadlines. However, Mother Nature paid no heed to human concerns and passions; on the next day, heavy downpours resumed over the entire area of the Orel salient and all the roads turned into quagmires.

Early on the morning of 29 April, H. von Elverfeldt reported to the headquarters of Army Group Center that the regrouping of the 2nd, 4th and 9th Panzer Divisions and of the 10th Panzergrenadier Division had come to a stop, and the weather forecasts were not promising: the rains would continue for the next two or three days. Thus, the assembly of their units could be ensured at train stations along the Orel – Glazunovka railroad, and they would not be able to arrive in their jumping-off positions any sooner than 9 May. In this connection, he requested that the future planning of Citadel be closely connected with the weather conditions. To this request, H. Krebs again cut off the discussion – a postponement of the offensive was no longer possible. Such a reaction from the military officials shouldn't have been surprising. The Wehrmacht's entire system of command and control was organized around one person who made the all the decisions. Neither G. von Kluge, nor W. Model with all his enormous energy and colossal powers of persuasion, not to mention H. Krebs or H. von Elverfeldt, had the power to change this.

At the same time that the Ninth Army's headquarters was sending out its report, the Colonel General's airplane landed in Smolensk, and Model immediately headed to the headquarters of Army Group Center. From the Ninth Army's journal of combat operations:

> During the meeting with the Field Marshal and the Chief of Staff, a discussion took place on the subject of Operation Citadel's depth. The Ninth Army commander emphasized that the Army Group still had not been able to ensure the arrival of the three divisions assigned for the offensive. On the subject of supplies to the army, the commander held talks with the Chief of the Artillery Headquarters and with General of Artillery R. Martinek on the matter of the most pressing problems. The serious shortage of artillery specialists in the units came up. As a result, the quality of the artillery preparation for Operation Citadel was questioned, as well as the fostering of teamwork with the Luftwaffe and Flak gunners. These talks, including the discussion with the Artillery Headquarters Operations Department and the Operations Department of the 12th

Flak Division wound up by noontime. The result was confirmation that the Flak units could also offer substantial help in resolving the ground force's tasks.[203]

Back on 27 April, while still at the Berghof, Model was present at a reception given by H. Göring. He wanted to discuss the problems of using aircraft during the upcoming offensive and to achieve authorization to use Flak artillery in the struggle against hardened ground targets – tanks and concrete firing positions. In the course of the conversation, the Reichsmarschall gave his approval to use his Flak units as a means of reinforcement for the first echelon. As future events would show, this decision became an important step in strengthening not only the Ninth Army, but also the assault formations of Army Group South, and particularly Army Detachment Kempf.

The stress that enveloped the troops of the Ninth Army after receiving the order regarding the offensive would shake their headquarters for approximately a week, until the moment Hitler decided to postpone the offensive once again to June. Even so, the meeting on 27 April yielded its fruits –the resolution of the problem of replenishing the Ninth Army with manpower, which Model had actively posed at every level over the previous two weeks, was finally no longer at an impasse. Other problems also began to be settled; particularly important was the agreement between the Army Group and the Ninth Army over two issues.

First, on 2 May the decision was made to transfer three additional infantry divisions to Model's assault formation. They were to be distributed as follows: one to the XXXXVI Panzer Corps, one or two to the XXXXVII Panzer Corps, and possibly one to the XXIII Army Corps. However, already on the following day, Kreb's staff reported that the army would receive the 6th and 208th Infantry Divisions in the near future, but the third infantry division was still under question. Such an approach to the preparation of the operation did not inspire trust in the Army Group's command staff and perpetuated the constant tension between Model and von Kluge.

Second, on this same day of 2 May, a directive arrived from von Kluge about sending 15 light infantry guns and six heavy guns from the Fourth Army to the Ninth Army, but without ammunition or the crews for them.[204] On the next day, the first specialized unit arrived in the XXXXI Panzer Corps for breaking through deep defenses – the 311th Company of Goliath Light Charge Carriers.[205] These were small radio-controlled tracked machines that carried 60 or 100 kg of explosives, depending on the model. They were designed for clearing paths through minefields and destroying fortifications. Another company of these Goliaths was en route from Germany by rail and was already located at a testing range between Brest and Minsk. According to the Ninth Army headquarters, it should arrive on 11 or 12 May 1943. It was planned to use the bulk of these Goliaths on the right flank of the assault wedge, in the Panskaia (South) – Hill 250.2 sector. It was intended for the Goliath companies to move out in front of the infantry at the start of the attack, clearing a route for the attackers through the minefields and destroying pill boxes and bunkers of the first, particularly fortified Russian line of defense, and thereby enhance the infantry's ability to breach the defenses.

203 NARA US, T.312, R.317, F.7886065.
204 NARA US, T.312, R.317, F.7886073.
205 NARA US, T.312, R.317, F.7886074.

At the end of April and in the first days of May, loads of supplies began to arrive in the army at an increasing tempo: food, combat supplies, spare parts and ammunition. Naturally, the change in the situation with supplies could not help but make Model happy. In his headquarters' internal documents at this time there is the note: "The latest delay with the start of the offensive should be considered a blessing, since only now has the intensive replenishment of the units begun."[206]

Although not as quickly as Model wanted, nevertheless armored vehicles, including heavy panzers, began to arrive in the armor in larger amounts. According to schedule, the main units of the Heavy Panzer Battalion 505 of Tiger tanks were supposed to arrive on 5 May. Considering that the troops were virtually unfamiliar with the new combat machines, back on 30 April a representative of the Wehrmacht's inspectors of panzer troops Major Kaufmann arrived to get the opinion of the Ninth Army's and Fourth Panzer Army's command staff about the use of Tigers and Ferdinand heavy tank destroyers on their fronts in order to breach the Russian defenses, as well as to determine whether or not the necessary conditions for their receipt and use were present. In the documents of the Ninth Army's Operations Department, there is the note:

> He has been given ultimate authority on location to determine the tasks for the tanks, which will be taking part in the attack. He should particularly strive to ensure that the 90 super-heavy vehicles of the Ferdinand type will be used only on ground suitable for them. He should organize reconnaissance of the terrain in the Ninth Army's sector, as well as in the sector of Army Group South. These "tanks" because of their thick armor have limited mobility. In addition, they still have a lot of mechanical problems. Thus, it is necessary to make sure they don't bog down during the breakthrough of the enemy's main defensive belt and can be used in the subsequent fighting.[207]

The analysis of the terrain and Russian system of defenses in the sector of both armies, the Ninth and Fourth Panzer Armies, as well as an opinion expressed by the latter's command staff about the viability of using the new armor models north of Belgorod led to the conclusion that the Tigers might be used on both the southern and northern faces of the Kursk bulge, but it was better to transfer the Ferdinands to the Ninth Army. In fact, the Fourth Panzer Army's command itself was rejecting the heavy self-propelled guns. On 2 May 1943, Major Kaufmann gave a report on the options with the use of these self-propelled guns in its sector:

> 1. Possibility of use. The area of the offensive is hilly. The entire width of the sector passes over crumbly soil and the mouths of streams, which make the use of the Ferdinands impossible. Only two elevated roads in the direction of the offensive provide the possibility of employing the Ferdinands in a narrow sector just 2-3 km wide.
> a) The ground on both sides of the eastern road [Tomarovka – Bykovka – Iakovlevo] is cut by ravines with crumbly soil and is so narrow that it is possible to use just a single company. However, in connection with the fact that the offensive sector is crossed by

---

206 NARA US, T.312, R.317, F.7886076.
207 NARA US, T.312, R.317, F.7886068.

an anti-tank ditch and the assembly area of the Ferdinands is "conditionally suitable" for this, the Fourth Panzer Army has made the decision to reject their use totally on this axis.
b) The western road [Tomarovka – Butovo – Dubrovo] yields the opportunity of using a battalion of Ferdinands. The assembly area is suitable.
2. The possibilities for unloading:
a) four train stations in the Khar'kov – Belgorod sector;
b) Khar'kov;
c) Bogodukhov and two trains stations east of it;
    A large number of places for unloading them is necessary given the vehicle's low cross-country performance.
3. March routes from the unloading places. The Ferdinands can move to the assembly area without problems. Primarily elevated tracks are at their disposal. In the sector of the Vorskla River at Borisovka, a 60-tonn bridge has been built. All of the other bridges in the direction of the march roads are short and at any moment allow a 65-tonn vehicle to pass over them.
    Conclusions: It has been proposed to use a battalion of Ferdinands in the sector of the Fourth Panzer Army's offensive. The Panzer Army has agreed with this proposal.[208]

In the existing situation H. Hoth's lack of desire to receive a "pig in a poke" before the start of the operation was advantageous to Model, since this type of armor would strengthen his assault wedge. However, the Ninth Army's main problem – the deficit of tanks in the panzer division's panzer regiments still remained unresolved. A significant portion of the promised tanks were still en route, but no one had yet countermanded the start date for the operation. Therefore, the threat of going on the offensive without the necessary minimum of tanks was completely real. However, the arrival of only a few Tigers in the conditions of the muddy season and the large stoppages on the railroads seemed a cumbersome matter for Elverfeldt's staff. The transporting of the 56-tonn machines required heavy railroad platforms and specialized prime movers to transport them to the assembly area, and also placed additional strain on the arterial roads. The unprepared bridges and the washed-out roads also added to the problems of their transportation. Yet the Ferdinand self-propelled guns were even heavier, 68-tonn. By the middle of May, having collided with the impossible of bringing the Tigers up to the forward edge over the available bridges and roads, the Ninth Army's headquarters was forced to issue a directive to the XXXXVII Panzer Corps: "In order to ensure the movement of the Tigers, it is necessary to bring the load-carrying capacity of the crossing sites up to not less than 60-tonn. … It is also necessary to take steps to increase the trafficability of the road net, namely by strengthening the bridges to 16 tonn and by putting up road signs."[209]

However, these were only some of the problems that arose when planning the reception of heavy armored vehicles. The Tigers would be arriving from the German factories exclusively by rail. Yet the intention was to unload them at ordinary train stations, not equipped for such massive loads, for reasons of secrecy and deception. Thus, the question immediately arose regarding the

---

208 NARA US, T.313, R.340, F.8656102, F.8656103.
209 NARA US, T.312, R.317, F.7886091.

substantial reconstruction of the unloading platforms at the stations of arrival and preparing them to receive outsized loads. However, not all the work that ensued was carried out smoothly, nor indeed was the camouflage done carefully so that it wouldn't prompt the particular interest of Soviet reconnaissance; the consequence was airstrikes on the stations. For example, on 5 May during a massed raid of 35 bombers on the Lokiia and Brasovo Stations, 80 tonn of artillery ammunition went up into the air.[210] The Ninth Army headquarters was extremely alarmed by the losses of such an amount of a valuable stockpile and hastily strengthened the cover of these stations with Major General Paul Deichmann's 1st Flieger Division, though the question about the additional assignment of a specialized Flak train here was even considered.

However, even these tanks and assault guns, which in general were arriving in not very large numbers, were continuing to cost the Colonel General a lot of "sweat and tears", even after the conclusion of the hard talks with Berlin and the OKH. Higher command did not always burn with the desire to carry out the given promises. For example, despite the agreement, even at the beginning of May, Army Group Center as good as sabotaged the transfer of the third infantry division to the Ninth Army, and in so doing did not miss the occasion to emphasize that if it in fact did give it up, then it would have no way to ensure replacements for the Ninth Army. Thus, Colonel General Model was supposed to put an end to pestering the Field Marshal and the OKH with demands about sending him even more march battalions. Accordingly, the situation with the OKH's, Army Group Center's and Ninth Army's preparation for Operation Citadel looked approximately as follows: In word, all three echelons of command were pursuing a common cause, but in essence each was primarily thinking about its own interests, but Model was supposed to answer personally for the results.

Now let us return to the position of the adherents to active operations in the East. The purpose of the directive about the start of the attack toward Kursk issued by Hitler after Model's report of 27 April was likely K. Zeitzler's position, who always spoke up against the postponement of the offensive. As documents discovered in Germany's Federal Military Archive show, Hitler understood that for now it made no sense to attack (the assault formation of Model's Ninth Army had not assembled, and there was still an insufficient number of armored vehicles), but this was only part of the problem. All of his steps in the latter half of April (the proposal to shift the offensive into the sector of the Second Army; his postponements; the number of conferences held with key figures of the Wehrmacht) speak to the fact that he was not confident even in the need for just this operation, or in the possibility of reaching all of its objectives. So, without hesitation, he accepted the proposal from the OKH Chief of Staff to discuss the entire complex of problems related to the plan of attack toward Kursk and the summer campaign in full, with the command staff of Army Groups South and Center, and also with key figures who were involved in preparing the operation. The conference was set to take place in Munich on 4 May 1943.

Russian readers and scholars know about this conference from the memoirs of E. von Manstein and H. Guderian. However, the discussion directly regarding Citadel in them receive only cursory treatment. Archival materials uncovered show that before the conference started, at 1200 (Berlin time) Zeitzler gathered the commanders and chiefs of staff of Army Group South and Army Group Center there in Munich in order to lay out the situation which led to

210 NARA US, T.312, R.317, F.7886078.

this conference and his own position, with the aim of soliciting their support. At the start of the meeting, the OKH Chief of Staff announced:

> The Führer after Colonel General Model's report began to doubt whether or not the offensive could penetrate the Russian defenses. The main reason for the hesitations in the Führer's opinion was the arrangement of the enemy's system of defenses in front of the Ninth Army's assault wedge, which has, as they say, a depth of 20 km, with narrow trenches. In order to break through this system of defense, Colonel General Model outlined a six-day offensive plan, on the basis of which the Führer came to the conclusion that:
>
> 1. It is doubtful that the infantry of the Ninth Army's forward units given the planned support of the panzer units would be able to carry out the assignment.
>
> 2. Given such a lengthy process of breaching the defenses, doubt arises in the possibility of creating a kessel. There is the danger that the enemy, relying on the strong defensive system, will be able to withdraw his forces out of the intended encirclement.
>
> Since the Führer in light of the military and political situation is insisting that this operation must become the year's event and yield a tangible result, he believes it is necessary to strengthen the assault forces substantially with tanks and heavy weapons – especially Army Group Center. So, first of all the question arises about the delivery of the Tigers, an anti-tank protection for the Pz.Kpfw. IV tanks, the Hummel [a 150mm self-propelled howitzer], anti-tank guns, and the Ferdinands. Since the necessary number of tanks can be assembled only by 10 June 1943, the Führer wants to postpone the operation. Colonel General Guderian is supporting this decision of his.[211]

Further K. Zeitzler laid out his point of view, which in fact cardinally differed from Hitler's position and, something very important, did not consider the condition of the forces at Kursk. He placed emphasis on the Soviet side's lack of readiness to repulse a powerful attack and the great likelihood that, in his opinion, in a month there would also still be no success in sending the necessary number of armored vehicles to the troops. Yet the Russians over this interval of time might strengthen their defenses to the point that the conducting of Citadel would lose any sense. He persuaded those gathered:

> I'm against any postponements of the start of the offensive, since even without mentioning the fact that the units have already been put into motion and are moving up to the front, the units of the opposing enemy will take advantage of the offensive's postponement. We are giving up our advantage over them in the fact that they aren't now ready to meet us, and the sooner we strike, the more likely it will be that we crush them, and we'll be able to use our operational reserves for other purposes. I also strongly doubt that the delivery of tanks and equipment can be executed within the indicated period of time. Past experience speaks to the opposite. In addition, the Ferdinands "are

---

[211] Kriegstagebuch Ia der Heeresgruppe Don/Süd, März bis Juli 1943. BArch-MA. RH 19 VI/45. Bl. 78-80.

still sick with a large number of childhood illnesses" – the new design is so unfinished that even Guderian is doubtful whether they will be ready for use by June.[212]

At the end of the meeting, the OKH Chief of Staff requested support for his point of view at the meeting with Hitler.

The conference began at 1300 (Berlin time) and continued for approximately four hours. According to the testimony of Army Group South's Chief of Staff, the following men were invited to the conference: K. Zeitzler, E. von Manstein, T. Busse, G. von Kluge, H. von Elverfeldt, H. Guderian, the Luftwaffe's Chief of Staff Colonel General H. Jeschonneck, the Chief of the OKH Personnel Department Major General R. Schmundt and the Chief of the Operations Department Colonel von Scherff.[213] According to the H. Guderian's memoirs, the Minister of Armaments A. Speer was also present at the conference, but this is not confirmed by the archival documents.[214] Already from the first minutes, it became clear to those in attendance that Hitler was doubting that the troops could achieve their objectives by going on the offensive toward Kursk in the nearest future. From the words of T. Busse, here is what was written in Army Group South's journal of combat operations:

> The Führer in a lengthy speech expressed the reasons why he wants to postpone the start of the offensive. The main positions are as follows:
> 1. The schemes of the enemy's fortifications in the sector of the Ninth Army presented by Colonel General Model impressed him greatly.
> 2. The correlation of forces raises doubts.
> 3. The unsuccessful offensive toward Novorossiisk demonstrated that the infantry's attacking energy without the support of panzers is insufficient for breaking through a well-fortified system of defense as well as against a bitterly resisting adversary. He suspects the same thing will happen with the Ninth Army in Operation Citadel, since the Ninth Army intends to attack with infantry, supported by panzer divisions. In addition, Army Group South will be forced in connection with the lack of infantry divisions to make the panzer divisions break through the defenses.
>
> He suspects as well that there is not enough infantry, and the grenadiers and panzers will take a beating during the first attack and will not be in the condition to develop the offensive.
>
> He is concerned that the forming of reinforcements will be completed only by 10 June. That said, when conducting Citadel an economy of force in the course of the struggle with enemy fortified points and knots of resistance has special significance.[215]

---

212 Ibid., Bl. 81-82.
213 Minutes of the conference in Munich, 4 May 1943. Source: Kriegstagebuch Ia der Heeresgruppe Don/Süd, März bis Juli 1943. BArch-MA. RH 19 VI/45. Bl. 80.
214 Guderian, *Vospominaniia nemetskogo generala*, p. 337.
215 Minutes of the conference in Munich, 4 May 1943. Source: Kriegstagebuch Ia der Heeresgruppe Don/Süd, März bis Juli 1943. BArch-MA. RH 19 VI/45. Bl. 80.

As Erich von Manstein recalled, Hitler was planning over the course of a month to reinforce the forces at Kursk, having sent to them all the new models of tanks (the Tigers, the Panthers and the Ferdinand heavy self-propelled guns), and most importantly, increase the number of panzers and self-propelled guns in the divisions. The talk was of doubling the number of tanks and assault guns. Next, he dwelt in detail on two proposals that he had received. The first, from K. Zeitzler, was to begin the operation in mid-May according to the plan based on Order No. 6. The OKH Chief of Staff believed that in the course of it, the Wehrmacht, through better training of the troops and superior command and control over them would suffer fewer losses and substantially deplete the Russian strength in the central sector of the front. This would create favorable conditions for a defense on the entire Eastern Front and positively affect the further course of the war.

The second proposal, submitted as a subject of discussion at this conference, came from Walter Model in absentia. Since 30 April he had again been appointed as the temporarily acting commander-in-chief of Army Group South, therefore in the absence of both von Manstein and von Kluge, he'd been unable to fly to Munich. Hitler detailed the contents of Model's letter from 27 April to those present. H. Guderian wrote, "Model drew the correct deduction … that the enemy was counting on our launching this attack and in order to achieve success we must adopt a fresh tactical approach; the alternative was to abandon the whole idea." [216]

After nearly a 45-minute speech, the Führer asked the commanders-in-chief of both army groups to express their opinion on the question of postponing the operation. It was difficult to raise objections to the arguments of Ninth Army's commander. Therefore, the supporters of the offensive toward Kursk, taking advantage of the fact that the Colonel General was personally unable to respond, sought to avoid specifics in their presentations, instead prioritizing the possible negative consequences of delaying the operation and accusing Model of exaggerating the threats. In the course of the discussion, gradually the attention focused on two problems: the troops lack of readiness for such a far-reaching operation; and a possible Russian offensive in the Donbass region or against the Orel salient. Thus, practically everyone who took part in the discussion dwelt on them, but first and foremost the operation's key figures – the commanders-in-chief of Army Group South and Army Group Center. Manstein's point of view, in the opinion of several generals, was not quite clear. Recalled H. Guderian:

> Manstein, as often when face to face with Hitler, was not at his best. His opinion was that the attack would have had a good chance of succeeding if it had been launched in April; now its success was doubtful and he would need a further two full-strength infantry divisions in order to be in a position to carry it out. Hitler replied that two such divisions were not available and that Manstein must make do with what he already had; he then repeated his question, but unfortunately received no very clear answer.[217]

From T. Busse's entry in Army Group South's combat diary:

---

216 Guderian, *Vospominaniia nemetskogo generala*, pp. 337-338.
217 Ibid., p. 338.

General Field Marshal von Manstein said approximately the following: He could not assess how important and necessary an earlier victory in the East would have been on the basis of an overall picture from the military and political point of view. However, the forces available for his army group in comparison with the enemy's strength was weak, in particularly the infantry. He believes that a success would only happen from a delay in the operation, so that before its expiration, his army group would be given additional infantry divisions. In details:

1. In my opinion a success in the East must be generated before Tunisia falls and the West opens a second front.
2. Waiting means an increase in the risks on the Mius – Donets front. At present the Russians there are probably still not ready for an offensive, but in June they will be ready without fail.
3. Under question is whether or not a rise in our strength will compensate the increase in the Russians' combat capability (the production of tanks over one month on the Russian side, the increase in morale, the recovery from failure, and the fortification of defensive positions). To this, the Führer shot back that it is not worth counting upon infantry divisions in any case and emphasized in a broad sense to replace infantry strength with tanks.[218]

In his own book, the Field Marshal writes that he was advocating for the soonest start of the operation. Indeed, judging from everything, this was not a fruit of postwar thoughts. According to information from the records of the Ninth Army, back on 3 May the OKH informed G. von Kluge that the commander-in-chief of the southern group was insisting on the launching of Citadel on 9 May.[219] In the assessment laid out in von Manstein's memoirs, the postponement of the offensive did not yield anything. In the first place, if you postponed it until the necessary number of tanks and other armaments was received by both army groups, which as was already known would take approximately a month, the Russian forces in the Kursk salient would all the same receive even more armor than the German divisions. According to the information of the Field Marshal, at this time his group possessed 686 tanks and 160 self-propelled guns.[220] In fact, the number of tanks was significantly greater: according to the list, a total of 1,087 (See Table 4), yet the Soviet industry was sending to the front each month no less than 1,500 combat machines.[221] In the second place, the Soviet formations over this period of time would bring themselves back into order and gain significant strength, including with respect to morale. Thirdly, by summer the danger would grow that the Russians would launch their own offensive on the Donets and Mius Rivers to the south.[222]

218 Minutes of the conference in Munich, 4 May 1943. Source: Kriegstagebuch Ia der Heeresgruppe Don/Süd, März bis Juli 1943. BArch-MA. RH 19 VI/45. Bl. 81.
219 NARA US, T.312, R.317, F.7886074.
220 Manstein, *Uteriannye pobedy*, p. 529.
221 Ibid., p. 527.
222 Ibid., p. 528.

Table 4: Plan of the departure of armored fighting vehicles to Army Groups Center and South as of 3 May 1943 (with the calculation that Operation Citadel would start on 12 June 1943)[223]

Period of departure	AFVs of all types	Pz.Kpfw. VI Tigers	Pz.Kpfw V Panthers	Wespe self-propelled howitzers	StuGs
Army Group South					
Before 3 May	616	53		30	
Before 9 May	30	16			
Before 1 June	30			15	
Before 10 June	20	28			40
Total	**696**	**97**		**45**	**40**
Army Group Center					
Before 3 May	286	20		45	
Before 9 May	29				
Before 1 June	121				
Before 10 June	63	31	200		86
Total	**499**	**51**	**200**	**45**	**86**

This possibly might seem strange, but G. von Kluge was also a fervent supporter of an immediate start for Citadel. He unconditionally supported K. Zeitzler and responded critically to the information given by Model. T. Busse wrote:

> General Field Marshal von Kluge unequivocally spoke up against the postponement of the offensive and indicated that Colonel General Model's information about the strength of the enemy's fortification was in his opinion greatly exaggerated. The scheme that prompted the questions depicts a large number of old fortifications, including some of ours from past combat operations. He [Model] was venturing that we should wait until it became necessary to withdraw the units from their assembly areas and that we wouldn't launch attacks at all this year. The Führer objected to Field Marshal von Kluge's utterances, saying that Colonel General Model was very optimistic in his report, and that he himself had brought pessimism to the question.[224]

---

223 Arkhiv IVI, F.191, Op. 233, D.108 "Report of the General Inspector of Panzer Forces Guderian to Hitler from 3 May 1943 to 1 June 1944" Part 1 (Moscow: Military History Department of the General Staff of the USSR Armed Forces, 1947), p. 7 (translated from the documents of TsAMO RF, F.500, Op.12451, D.448, l. 9).
224 Minutes of the conference in Munich, 4 May 1943. Source: Kriegstagebuch Ia der Heeregruppe Don/Süd, März bis Juli 1943. BArch-MA. RH 19 VI/45. Bl. 81.

"'Citadel' ... was the final attempt to retain our initiative in the east"   109

Possibly, it was chiefly a subjective point that was affecting the Field Marshal's stance – jealousy and the strained relations with Walter Model, which were known to everyone. Erich von Manstein recollected:

> Kluge, who plainly felt offended by this report of Model's, declared in the biting form that was characteristic of him, that Model's information that the depth of the enemy's positions reach 20 km is exaggerated. The aerial photographs, in his opinion, only show the now collapsed trenches of previous fighting. Then the Field Marshal pointed out that given a further delay, we would yield the initiative. This might lead to the point where we would be compelled to remove units from the Citadel front. Here, he probably had in mind first and foremost the dangerous situation at the Orel bulge.[225]
>
> Of all those present, only H. Guderian was supporting W. Model's position, and judging from his memoirs, his speech was the most consequential and argumentative. He called Citadel a senseless diversion and emphasized: "If we now begin an offensive according to Zeitzler's plan, then we would suffer heavy losses in tanks, which already in the course of 1943 we wouldn't be able to replace. After all, the shipment of new tanks to the Western Front for mobile reserves is necessary as well, so that we would be able to hurl them against an Allied landing, which will likely take place in 1944.[226]

In addition, the General Inspector of Panzer Troops Guderian declared that the hopes of the OKH Chief of Staff for the Panthers were unreasonably high. Just like any new equipment, they had not been spared of serious teething problems, which industry wouldn't be able to fix before the start of the offensive.

> In the words of T. Busse, the General Inspector of Panzer Troop's position was laid out differently in Army Group South's war diary:

> General Guderian expressed himself so that we must absolutely economize on manpower, having thrown forward reinforced materiel. He is for gathering the maximum number of panzer units in one place – either in Army Group Center or in Army Group South – to strike with a large superiority in force. Colonel General Jeschonnek added to Colonel General Guderian's opinion by saying that he had greater preference for this option, since it would allow the concentration of all of his available aircraft in that place. He announced that the main grouping of enemy aircraft on the Eastern Front had been unmistakably assembled opposite Army Group South, and most likely, a Russian offensive operation would be conducted on this axis. From the point of view of the Luftwaffe, there was no point in waiting for reinforcements through a delay. Two additional groups of dive bombers might be received.[227]

---

225 Manstein, *Uteriannye pobedy*, p. 527.
226 Guderian, *Vospominaniia soldata*, p. 338.
227 Minutes of the conference in Munich, 4 May 1943. Source: Kriegstagebuch Ia der Heeresgruppped Don/Süd, März bis Juli 1943. BArch-MA. RH 19 VI/45. Bl. 82.

The other participants fully shared K. Zeitzler's opinion. Such unanimity and short-sightedness are unsurprising. Not only generals and field marshals participated in this conference, who were planning a concrete combat operation, but also a considerable number of politicians, for whom the military aspect was not key in this matter. Albert Speer wrote, "The world in which we lived forced upon us dissimulation and hypocrisy. An honest word was rarely spoken among rivals … Everyone conspired."[228] No little role was played as well by the desire to avoid jeopardizing one's own position; to maintain the stability of one's own army grouping; etc. Officially, Field Marshal Keitel expressed in plain terms the supporters' main argument for an attack toward Kursk, "We must attack because of political reasons."[229] It was in tune with Hitler's desires, but the Führer's instinct for self-preservation had not atrophied, and likely that was why he took seriously the sober analysis contained in Model's letter.

In this connection it is interesting to understand the motives of G. von Kluge and H. Guderian, who took opposing positions on the process of preparing and implementing Citadel, the latter being the only one of the high-posted military men who consistently opposed the operation. I believe this excerpt from the book by the Western scholar Kenneth Macksey offers the most cogent understanding of their motivations and the reasons for their well-known dispute, which arose back in 1941: "Guderian's strong dislike and burgeoning mistrust of Kluge, which turned to outright hatred along with accusations of incompetence against a soldier who was far from being that, represented a clash between two ways of thinking – between a daring commander who took undiluted, if calculated chances and a prudent general who sought security of his personal well-being besides the safety of his army in battle, preferring to spread rather than concentrate the risks."[230] In these few lines, the British historian accurately noted the essence of each of these two military commanders, which dictated their behavior at the 4 May conference as well. "Clever Hans" as G. von Kluge was called in the Wehrmacht, bore no personal responsibility for Citadel; it had been shifted to Model. It was therefore safer and more convenient for him to serve as a "channel" for the Führer's thoughts and the OKH opinion, and he supported them in everything. Guderian on the other hand had demonstrated back in 1941 that he placed top priority on the task at hand, and therefore in my view, during the deliberations over the attack toward Kursk, he was not thinking about possible damage to his own career, in the event of eliciting Hitler's dissatisfaction with his position, but about an effective resolution of the matters at hand.

Judging from Hitler's further steps, the discussion of the offensive's preparations only hardened the opinion that had formed in him after the meeting with Model – it had to be postponed. Although at the conference, following a short pause for thought, he had not expressed a final point of view. This operation continued to remain for him the most important matter of the summer of 1943, so he decided that it had to be prepared more thoroughly. Even though it is likely that the commander of the Ninth Army prompted Hitler's very serious concerns regarding the possibility of fully realizing the designated plan, he also provided a serious reason to return once again to other options for the summer campaign. Evidence of this are the memoirs of people who surrounded Hitler at this moment. On 7 May 1943 J. Goebbels wrote in his diary about a meeting with Hitler, who had arrived from Munich after the conference: "In the East

---

228 Speer, *Vospominaniia*, p. 351.
229 *Velikaia Otechestvennaia voina, 1941-1945, Kn. 2*, p. 256.
230 Macksey, Kenneth, *Guderian* (Smolensk: Rusich, 2001), pp. 244-245.

the Führer will soon start a limited offensive in the direction of Kursk. He may, however, delay it to see if the Bolsheviks want to beat us to it. That might offer us an even more favorable opportunity than if we took the initiative."[231] On 23 May the Minister of Propaganda again took up this subject in his diary and wrote that the Führer initially wanted the Red Army to start the first offensive, in order then to counterattack it through a mobile defense, which meant in essence Hitler was returning to E. von Manstein's idea from almost four months ago. That Hitler no longer viewed Citadel as that saving straw that would stabilize the situation on the Eastern Front after receiving Model's letter and the conference in Munich is evident as well from his discussion with Guderian on 10 May, which we will discuss below.

To return to the events that immediately followed the 4 May conference, E. von Manstein writes that he learned of Hitler's decision to move the start date of the offensive to 12 June on 11 May.[232] However, the Fourth Panzer Army's chief of staff General of Infantry F. Fangohr asserts that he received the first written order about preparing for a June offensive already on 6 May 1943.[233] In fact, Hitler reached his decision to postpone the offensive again two days after the Munich conference. Possibly, this discrepancy in dates relates to the fact that the Field Marshal was still on a leave of absence at this time and could not follow the situation in detail. He arrived from Berlin back at his army group only on 10 May. Walter Model, however, learned already on 4 May that there was a great probability that there would be a postponement. At 1725 on 4 May, Krebs called him, and even though there was still no official word, confidently advised the Colonel General to prepare to disperse the forces that had already assembled in their jumping-off positions for reasons of deception.[234] The postponement of the offensive for an entire month did not bring any fundamental changes to the essence of the plan, as it had been laid out in Order No. 6. Its overall scheme remained as before – converging attacks at the base of the salient in the direction of Kursk, while just as before, Army Group South would play the leading role. Only the composition of the groupings and the directions of their attacks were subjected to thorough examination.

The decision regarding the delay immediately prompted an objection from not only the OKH, but also from several armies, primarily in von Manstein's Army Group South. For example, on 7 May General of Panzer Troops W. Kempf, the commander of the army detachment of the same name, in a discussion with K. Zeitzler declared that this step would have a negative influence on both operational matters and on the psychological mood of the troops, and that it would bring greater advantage to the Russians than to the Germans. The Chief of Staff of the OKH shared this assessment and promised to bring it up with the Führer.

However, Hitler at this time had no taste for psychology. Unquestionably, he could not completely ignore the opinion of professionals, but the reasons for his vacillations were first of all due to objective matters and were connected with the lack of necessary forces and means. Above all else, the difficult situation with armored vehicles was fostering the doubts in success. In Russian historiography of the Battle of Kursk, this problem has been viewed superficially. However, it was probably just this problem that outweighed all the arguments of the supporters

---

231 Die Tagebücher von Joseph Goebbels. Teil II. Diktate 1941-1945. Bde.8. (München: K.G. Sauer, 1993-1996), p. 314.
232 Manstein, *Uteriannye pobedy*, p. 529.
233 Newton, *Kurskaia bitva: nemetskii vzgliad*, p. 98.
234 NARA US, T.312, R.317, F.7886076.

for going on the offensive as soon as possible. let us turn to Tables 3 and 4. If to rely on Guderian's notes, then G. von Kluge up until 3 May 1943 received a total of 286 tanks from Germany, whereas von Manstein received 616. As of 4 May, there was a total of 442 Pz.Kpfw. III and Pz.Kpfw. IV tanks in all eight panzer divisions of Army Group Center, or which 314 were operational, and 128 (30 percent of the total) were under repair. The average number of combat machines in the panzer regiments of Army Group Center's panzer divisions was only 39, approximately four times fewer than the authorized strength. The 8th Panzer Division was in the best shape, with 53 tanks, while the 18th Panzer Division was the weakest, with only 26 tanks. A report from the Ninth Army's headquarters at 2330 on 3 May shows the condition of its mobile formations; according to it, at this time its six panzer divisions (2nd, 4th, 9th, 12th, 18th and 20th Panzer Divisions) had a total of 231 tanks, including 109 Pz.Kpfw. III and Pz.Kpfw. IV with short-barreled guns, which by this time were considered outdated and no longer able to meet the contemporary demands of combat.[235] Thus, the average strength in panzers in a panzer regiment of one panzer division amounted to 38.5, or four times less than the authorized strength (168).

In Army Group South the situation was better, but not by much. It had a total of 1,087 tanks and self-propelled guns, of which 728 were serviceable. The average strength in panzers of a division was 56, or approximately three times fewer than the authorized strength. The imbalance between the two army groups in panzer strength was a result of the events of February-March 1943 in the southern sector, when the OKH transferred to Army Group South the bulk of the mobile divisions that were operating on this axis, but also all the reserves that were arriving from Europe, in order to conduct von Manstein's "backhand blow". This particular feature of Army Group South (its greater number of panzer divisions and their greater number of tanks and self-propelled guns) was maintained right up to the start of the Battle of Kursk and directly affected its planning. According to the plan's intent, it was precisely von Manstein's assault grouping that had to cover a greater amount of distance (125 km) in order to make the link-up in the Kursk area.

There was also an imbalance between Army Group Center and Army Group South in the supply of Germany's latest tanks, the Tigers and Panthers. According to Table 3, by 4 May 1943, von Manstein had received 67 Pz.Kpfw. VI heavy tanks, but von Kluge and Model had not yet received a single one! This despite the fact that according to the plan as adopted by Berlin, by 3 May Army Group Center was supposed to have received 20 Tigers (see Table 4).

An even more complicated situation had developed with the Pz.Kpfw. V Panthers, which had been promised to the Ninth Army back in early April. These machines had yet to arrive in the Wehrmacht's combat forces, and by the start of the conference in Munich, they were not even ready to be sent to the front. On 10 May a meeting took place in Berlin with Hitler on the subject of their production, since the plan of supplying them to the front had already collapsed, and the prospects were unclear. However, in the course of this discussion the industry representatives promised to make up for the lost time by the end of May and even to overfulfill the previously established target indicators: supposedly instead of the promised 250 Panthers, the Wehrmacht would receive 324. These numbers appeared in writing thanks to Guderian, who first mentioned

---

235 NARA US, T.312, R.320, F.7889556, F.7889563.

them in his memoirs.[236] In reality, however, as archival documents show (in particular his notes to the report at the conference on 4 May, the output plans regarding the supply of these tanks differed. In May it was planned to produce 300 Pz.Kpfw. V, in June – 165, and in July, another 206.[237] It was assumed that the first two Panther battalions would be ready only by 31 May, as well as two heavy tank destroyer battalions consisting of 90 Ferdinands. In order to make these figures more comprehensible, let us recall first the outcome of Citadel, and second the number of these combat machines relative to the other types of armor at the beginning of June 1943 in Model's and von Manstein's assault groupings. In the Ninth Army at that time there were 522 tanks (477 light and medium tanks, plus 45 heavy tanks) and 215 self-propelled guns (125 Marders and 90 Ferdinands), whereas in Army Group South and Army Detachment Kempf there were 1,016 tanks (including 102 Tigers and 200 Panthers) and 247 assault guns.

In these hard conditions, the level of combat readiness of the Ninth Army's infantry divisions was extremely important, but even they were in a sorry state. Notes Steven Newton:

> The twenty divisions assigned to Ninth Army on 16 May had a combined combat strength of 66,137 and an average divisional strength of just 3,306 (roughly 60 percent of the authorized strength, even for six-battalion infantry divisions). According to the standards employed by the German Army, deficiencies in combat strength would have kept all but four of Model's twenty division-equivalents (2nd and 12th Panzer Divisions, 10th Panzergrenadier Division and 78th Assault Division) from being rated as capable of executing even limited offensive missions.[238]

Model in fact laid out approximately the same sorry state of affairs in his report and during his personal meeting with Hitler on 27 April. The numbers spoke for themselves, and came down to just one conclusion: The forces at Kursk still did not have the strength to carry out the offensive's assignments. Therefore, Hitler simply did not have any other choice than to postpone its start for at least a month. At the same time, likely, at this moment he was already beginning to recognize that this decision would in essence bury the very idea of Citadel. In my view, this is shown by his discussion with Guderian immediately after the conference on 10 May on the question of the production of tanks, at which Guderian again attempted to reach out to the rational part of the Führer's brain and to convince him to cancel the operation once and for all. The Inspector General of Panzer Troops asked:

> "Why do you want to attack at all in the East this year? … How many people do you think even know where Kursk is? It's a matter of profound indifference to the world whether we hold Kursk or not."
>
> Hitler's reply was "You're quite right. Whenever I think of this attack, my stomach turns over."

---

236 Guderian, *Vospominaniia nemetskogo generala*, p. 340.
237 Arkhiv Instituta Voennoi istorii (in the future, IVI), F.191, Op.233, D.108. Reports of the General Inspector of Panzer Troops Guderian to Hitler from 3 May 1943 to 1 June 1944 (translated from the German). Part 1 (Moscow: Voenno-istoricheskoe upravleniie Genshtaba VS SSSR, 1947), p. 9.
238 Newton, *Kurskaia bitva: nemetskii vzgliad*, p. 468.

I answered: "In that case your reaction to the problem is the correct one. Leave it alone!" Hitler assured me that he had as yet by no means committed himself and with this the conversation ended.[239]

When introducing the description of this occasion, the main theoretician and practitioner of the German panzer forces noted the important changes that had occurred by this time in Hitler's views (by 10 May): "He could already see the difficulties that confronted us; the great commitment would certainly not bring us equivalent gains; our defensive preparations in the West were sure to suffer considerably."[240] In fact, by the beginning of May the euphoria over the March victories in Ukraine and the soothing intelligence reports about the low combat capability of the Soviet divisions defending Kursk had already begun to dissipate. Against the backdrop of the Red Army's strengthening defenses in the area of the Kursk bulge and the substantial lagging of the Reich's industry in producing the new tanks, the problems at which the opponents of Citadel kept pointing became obvious to Hitler as well. However, as time would show, this was a period of only partial sobriety. The idea of ending all of Germany's major problems with one stroke and again taking the initiative in the East into his hands were firmly embedded in his mind.

Albert Speer, who was a long-time close acquaintance of the Führer, somewhat differently assesses the motivations behind Hitler's decisions in his memoirs. The Minister of Armaments believed that at this moment, Hitler was evaluating Germany's situation and chances completely rationally; it was simply that the hopelessness and apprehensions before an imminent collapse had enveloped him. In his memoirs, he writes:

> It was as if he was were running along an unalterable track and could no longer find the power to break out of it.
>
> Underlying all this was the impasse into which he had been driven by the superior power of his enemies. In January 1943 they had jointly issued a demand for Germany's unconditional surrender. Hitler was probably the only German leader who entertained no illusions about the seriousness of this statement. Goebbels, Goering and the others would talk about exploiting the political antagonisms among the Allies ... But now, during the situational conferences, he more and more often declared, "Don't fool yourself. There is no turning back. We can only move forward. We have burned our bridges."[241]

Both of the evaluations offered above in principle do not contradict each other and, I believe, give an accurate assessment of Hitler's motivations and mood.

The first half of May 1943 proved to be for the Reich's leadership extremely stressful and unsuccessful. Almost immediately after the decision to postpone the start date of Operation Citadel, a catastrophe erupted in North Africa. On 15 May a message arrived at Führer Headquarters in East Prussia that two days previously, von Arnim's grouping in Tunisia had capitulated to the Allies: the entire grouping, including the Italians. The Allies captured

---

239 Guderian, *Vospominaniia nemetskogo generala*, p. 340.
240 Ibid.
241 Speer, *Vospominaniia*, p. 383.

270,000 Axis servicemen, including approximately 94,000 German soldiers and officers.[242] The command of the German Kriegsmarine, including Gross Admiral K. Dönitz himself, viewed this country "as a strategic position of the first order."[243] Therefore, such a colossal defeat and the loss of this important region substantially worsened Germany's position in the Mediterranean region. This event had been expected, but Hitler was hoping that it would take place later, at least in June or July, and after Citadel, so he would have the opportunity to shift freed-up forces to the West to shore up the situation there. However, the hopes were unjustified.

On the following day, Gross Admiral K. Dönitz reported to Hitler that "Germany was in a great crisis in the Battle of the Atlantic, since the enemy, employing new equipment to detect the submarines, has made the submarine war impossible and is inflicting heavy losses on us."[244] This was in fact the start of a turning point in the struggle for the Atlantic. Having activated all of their entire scientific and industrial potential, the Allies had begun to swing the situation regarding their sea lines of communication to their advantage. Over the month of May 1943 alone, the German Kriegsmarine had lost 40 submarines.[245]

Thus, the threat had grown of an Allied landing on the European continent not only from the United Kingdom, but also from the south. It now seemed that Jodl's conjecture about a Second Front was slowly, but surely beginning to take shape. In this connection, the OKW once again proposed to abandon the offensive toward Kursk. In the OKW war diary, its position was concisely articulated:

> If we were able to repulse an invasion quickly and energetically, even at the cost of yielding territory in Russia, then it might be possible to avoid the need to apprehend further actions by the Anglo-Saxons this summer. This would then reflect on the Russian theater of combat operations. Therefore, the General Staff of the OKW would prefer now to send mobile formations from the Eastern Front to northern Italy, in order to have the opportunity to move them from there into Italy, France or the Balkans depending on the situation of the invasion front. No other significant reserves for these purposes are available.[246]

A number of historians maintain that in the situation when the questions of defending Italy and the Balkans was changing from a theoretical question to a practical matter, Hitler's doubts on the advisability of Citadel was increasing. A number of utterances from Germany's military and political actors supposedly show this. For example, on 14 May G. von Kluge in a conversation with H. Heinrici acknowledged that now it was no longer possible to speak with any confidence about the date for the start of an offensive toward Kursk. Joachim Goebbels announced on 24 May that Hitler intended to allow the Russians the opportunity to attack first. However, all of this, including the conversation with Guderian mentioned above, should be viewed as Hitler's "smoke screen" and the speculations of his inner circle, which were based upon personal,

---

242 Müller-Gillebrandt, *Sukhoputnaia armiia Germaniia 1933-1945*, p. 362.
243 Töppel, *Kursk 1943*, pp. 16-17.
244 Ibid., p. 16.
245 Ibid.
246 Kriegstagebuch des Oberkommandos der Wehrmacht (in the future, KTB/OKW). Bd. III. Hb.II (Frankfurt am Main, 1963), p. 1622.

deeply subjective impressions from contact with him. They were recording only the external manifestations of the Führer's vacillations, which not infrequently were only a "play to the public" and did not give evidence of his real desires and intentions. There was simply no other way out to the resolution of the tasks (how realistic they were is a separate question) that he had placed before himself. So, he was only choosing a suitable moment in accordance with the Wehrmacht's possibilities and his own view of the military and political situation, which at that time was turning not in Germany's favor. Perhaps a period of vacillations was necessary for Hitler, which would seemingly be an obligatory step or personal ritual as he weighed a final decision on a very important matter – and his circle could not always, in his opinion, immediately grasp the correctness of his decision.

It is difficult to say on what basis von Kluge and Goebbels made their statements cited above, but neither at this time nor in the future did Hitler make a single more or less substantial step toward cancelling Operation Citadel, nor would he. The planning and preparation of the attack toward Kursk between April and the beginning of July would be subordinate to one, single goal – to mobilize as much strength as possible and to perfect the operation's plan. The repeated postponement of the operations should also be seen from this vantage point; after all, the aim of all these decisions were not to cancel the operation, but only to create the most favorable conditions for it. Nothing was going to sway Hitler from this path, not even the major setback in Tunisia or the serious arguments made after it by the OKW regarding the threat of an Allied landing on the continent. He did not regard them as significant and as before was basing his strategic plan on the calculations that the USSR's allies wouldn't open a Second Front in 1943.

He unambiguously made this known already at a conference on 19 May: "Nothing will happen in the West; I've fully convinced in this."[247] To be on the safe side, he only directed in the event of an Allied landing to work out a plan for shifting forces from the Eastern Front to France and Italy, and the strengthening of the Balkans, which entered history under the code names *Alarich* and *Constantine*.

Hitler actually believed in his star and believed that the plan of Citadel would bring Germany, as had happened more than once before, the expected success. He nurtured his illusions on a number of objective factors as well. After all the main instrument of war – the armed forces – were still not only combat capable, but still very strong. K. von Tippelkirch justifiably remarked:

> The past year to a varying degree distinctly demonstrated both the increased agility of the Russian command in resolving operational tasks and the previous significant tactical superiority of German troops on the battlefield ... The German Army had acquired such combat experience and was feeling that in spite of all the losses suffered to this point, as well-prepared, and recognizing its superior over the enemy to such an extent that it stood fully equal to the tasks flowing from the strategy of struggle to exhaust the enemy by means of operational maneuvering. The period of the muddy season, the shortening of the front lines and the period of lull that followed were very fortunate for the German divisions.[248]

---

247 *Hitlers Lagebesprechungen. Die Protokollfragmente seiner militarischen Konferenzen 1942-1945* (Stuttgart, 1962), p. 219.
248 Tippelskirch, *Istoriia Vtoroi mirovoi voiny*, p. 23.

In May 1943, thanks to the efforts undertaken within the framework of "total mobilization", the Wehrmacht reached the pinnacle of its strength in manpower over the entire years of the war; at this time, it numbered 10.3 million men. Germany had 196 divisions or 71percent of their total number operating on the Eastern Front, plus 39 allied divisions.[249]

New Pz.Kpfw. V and Pz.Kpfw. VI tanks had begun to roll off the factory lines, and although they unquestionably had high combat qualities, they were also suffering from a number of teething problems. Their guns could reliably inflict damage on any of the Red Army's tanks from a range of 1500 meters or more. At the same time, the most widespread Soviet tank, the T-34, had to close within a range 500 or 600 meters in order to knock out an enemy tank. In the spring, a German prototype of the Soviet "Katiusha" rocket launchers, but one more powerful and with ten 150mm barrels, mounted on an armored self-propelled transport (the PzWrf 42), began to enter the Wehrmacht's mobile formations and in particular the SS panzer corps. In addition, the first models of the 105mm self-propelled howitzer (the Sd.Kfz.124 Wespe) began to arrive. The German divisions were replenished with new equipment and other types of troops. For example, from April 1943 the production began of the Focke-Wulf 190F-1 ground attack aircraft, and a bit before that Henschel 129-B equipped with two 30mm cannons, as well as the tank-hunting Junkers 87 G-1. All of this taken together enabled the formation of rather powerful groupings for the attack toward Kursk.

I will point out one important detail. The forces assigned for Citadel seemed impressive as well because German intelligence had managed to reveal only the first strategic echelon of the Soviet defenses around Kursk. The Abwehr had been unable to establish the genuine strength of the *Stavka*'s strategic reserves, which had been assembled and deployed behind the Central and Voronezh Fronts, nor had it yet recognized the scale of the steps taken by the Soviet leadership in the spring and early summer of 1943 to strengthen its armed forces. Even according to the standards of today, they were colossal – on the border of the Kursk Oblast and in the Voronezh Oblast, a new, fully-equipped and manned *front* appeared. Its troops began to receive not only regular weapons and gear, but also updated versions, as well as new types of ammunition. After the war, Erich von Manstein wrote about the impressions of his army group's command staff regarding the Soviet preparations for the summer 1943 campaign: "We, of course, did not anticipate such large organizational capabilities from the Soviet side, which it demonstrated in this matter, as well as in the development of its military industry."[250] Manstein likened it to fighting the Hydra – in place of one severed head, two new ones would grow.

Serious influence on the length of Hitler's phase of "hesitations and wavering" was the unhealthy atmosphere that had enveloped around him – the long-standing conflict with the highest army leadership, augmented by the stresses that were accumulating with each passing month in the relationships with the generals because of the growing problems at the front and the planning of the summer campaign. Major General D. von Holtitz wrote:

> The constant admonitions coming out of the General Staff before the war regarding the thoughtless embracing of political decisions only strengthened the hostile attitude toward it on the part of Hitler and his circle … However, it seemed that

---

249 Bleier, et al., Germaniia vo vtoroi mirovoi voine (1943-1945), p. 258.
250 Manstein, *Uteriannye pobedy*, p. 504.

Hitler was proved right each time both in peacetime and during the war. Neither the remilitarization of the Rhein District, nor the *Anschloss* with Austria, and not even the absorption of a part of Czech territory prompted armed resistance, as the General Staff feared. The victories won by Hitler in the first years of the war, and their unexpectedness and striking speed gave even greater weight to his conceptions. There are no doubts that this string of luck shook somewhat the normal confidence of the General Staff. If previously it worked out plans coolly and logically, on the basis of the analysis of forces, space and time, now in the light of the initial successes, all of this seemed unnecessary ... Hitler, meanwhile, because of his inarguable successes, became convinced in his own infallibility. He not only came to believe in his capability to handle the Reich's military and political situation all by himself, but also in his pre-destination to direct combat operations personally. He increasingly concentrated the decision-making regarding major operations in his own hands. This reached the point where he interfered in the actions of mid-level and even major formations and units, thereby disrupting the traditional principle in the German Army, which required that each commander be the complete master of making decisions within the framework of his own competences. Constantly and thoughtlessly mingling political and manufactured factors, hitting upon ignorance regarding the situation in various sectors of the front, and taking no account of the situation of the troops, the Führer was issuing foolish orders to hold positions that there was no possibility of holding. The was leading to the loss to the dearest of what we possessed – men ... Hitler refused to acknowledge the obvious, that the correlation of forces was changing not in our favor. He did not wish to see that after Tobruk and Stalingrad, military fortune had turned its back on us. In his eyes the following consequences were not the result of his own mistaken calculations. On the contrary, he was assigning blame for them on his "incompetent" generals and officers of the Generals Staff who were losing faith in victory.[251]

The defeat in front of Moscow substantially changed his attitude toward the army's military leadership for the worse, and after Field Marshal von Paulus walked into captivity, Hitler's exasperation grew even larger. For example, once he remarked about Erich von Manstein, whom many considered in the Wehrmacht as the leading military commander, that "the field marshal's horizons ... [are] the size of a toilet seat."[252] Here is one more striking assessment: On 9 May 1943, J. Goebbels wrote in his diary, "He is absolutely sick of the generals. He cannot imagine anything better than having nothing to do with them. His opinion of all the generals is devastating ... All generals lie, he says ... he simply cannot stand them."[253]

An impressive part of the Wehrmacht's higher command staff was experiencing similar feelings for the Führer, particularly after the disaster on the Volga. After all, it is no accident that three assassination attempts, organized by the high command staff, were undertaken against

---

251 Holtitz, *Soldatskii dolg*, pp. 145-146.
252 Showalter, *Bronia i Krov': Bitva na Kurskoi duge* [*Armor and Blood: Battle at the Kursk bulge*] (Moscow: AST, 2013), p. 57. This is the Russian translation of the author's book *Armor and Blood: The Battle of Kursk* (Random House, 2013).
253 As cited by Cross, *Operatsiia "Tsitadel'"*, p. 40.

him between March and the end of April 1943. After a number of highly-posted generals had been sent into retirement back in December 1941, Hitler himself stood at the helm of the German Army, and the complicated, but already well-tested system of planning combat operations and command over the troops began gradually to fall apart. Albert Speer recalls:

> In the summer of 1943, General Guderian, Inspector General of the Tank Forces, asked me to set up a meeting with the Army Chief of Staff Zeitzler … But it turned out that Guderian had more in mind than the settlement of minor disputes. He wanted to discuss common tactics in regard to the matter of a new Commander in Chief of the army …
>
> The differences between Zeitzler and Guderian rapidly dwindled to nothing. The conversation centered on the situation that had arisen from Hitler's assuming command of the army but not his exercising it. Zeitzler thought the interests of the army as against the two other branches of service and the SS must be represented more vigorously. Hitler, as Commander-in-Chief of the Armed Forces, ought to remain non-partisan. A Commander-in-Chief of the Army, Guderian added, had to maintain close personal contact with the army commanders. He should be looking out for the needs of his troops and deciding fundamental questions of supply. But Hitler, both men agreed, had neither the time nor the inclination to act on this practical level, nor to uphold the special interests of one branch of service. He appointed and deposed generals whom he hardly knew. Only a Commander-in-Chief who associated with higher-ranking officers on a personal basis could decide such questions of personnel. The army knew, Guderian said, that Hitler scarcely interfered in the personnel policies of his Commanders-in-Chief of the Luftwaffe and Kriegsmarine. Only the Heer was exposed to this sort of treatment.[254]

Further the Minister of Armaments writes that Field Marshals von Kluge and von Manstein were supporting this position.

Incidentally, the Commander-in-Chief of Army Group South was the first to attempt to correct this unhealthy situation back on 6 February 1943, when he asked Hitler to receive him for discussions. However, the problem of Hitler's distrust of the generals arose as well in this meeting. Hitler's adjutant, Colonel von Below, later recalled:

> He [von Manstein] was expecting much for himself from this meeting with the Führer. The problem of the structure of the Wehrmacht's high leadership had been occupying him ever since the Führer had become the Commander-in-Chief of the OKH and had taken personal command of Army Group A in October 1942. Manstein wanted to ask Hitler to appoint a Commander-in-Chief of the OKH or at a minimum put a general in charge of all of the forces on the Eastern Front. If the Führer did not agree to this, then at least he should give thought to curtailing the duplication in the work of the General Staff of the OKH and the leadership of the Wehrmacht's operations staff by creating a joint general staff. The Führer handled the conversation in a calm and

---

254 Speer, *Vospominaniia*, p. 353.

businesslike form, discussed all of the points put forward by Manstein, but could not make any concessions. He simply did not know of a single German Army general in whom he felt enough trust in order to share such powers of authority with him. Thus, the structure of the high command staff remained just as it had been.[255]

In reality, the situation at times bordered on the absurd; more or less major operations even on the divisional level were implemented only after obtaining Hitler's approval. The Führer maintained that "anyone could direct such a trifle as a military operation." In connection with this, the highly-posted officials of the Nazi Party and of the governmental structures had a steadfast desire to "instruct" the military men how it was necessary to fight, but also to give them a little operational guidance themselves. At the front this was sensed right away, when the troops began to receive harebrained missions and orders that failed to reflect the real situation at the front, particularly in units that were holding territory or using a mobile or so-called "elastic" defense. Recalled the former commander of the Fourth Army General G. Heinrici recalled:

> Hitler always tried to make us fight for every yard, threatening to court martial anyone who did not . No withdrawal was officially permitted without his approval – even a small-scale withdrawal. This principle was so hammered into the army that it was a common saying that battalion commanders were afraid "to move a sentry from the window to the door". These rigid methods cramped us at every turn.[256]

In their turn, the military commanders initially as a response simply removed any absurdities in the orders to the troops and replaced them with more or less manageable tasks in line with the initial directives arriving from above. Such subterfuges took place on the tactical level. As concerns strategic operations similar to Citadel, the military commanders could not act that way. They therefore attempted to find other approaches. The process of working out the operational plan of Army Group South at Kursk can serve as an illustrative example of this. Colonel General H. Hoth, the commander of the Fourth Panzer Army, who'd been given von Manstein's grouping as the assault formation, did not believe in the possibility of encircling two Soviet *fronts* simultaneously with his available forces. So, having no influence on the process of strategic decision-making, he persistently sought to advocate a more realistic, in his opinion, task for his panzer army – the destruction of the Red Army's mobile reserves. General Hoth decided to tilt the command of the Army Group South in his direction. Naturally, he sought to plant this idea in Erich von Manstein and to get him to recognize it as the main objective, at least during the first stage of Operation Citadel, in order to include it in the process of operational planning. He looked for any convenient opportunity to discuss his proposal in detail with the Field Marshal, and such an encounter took place on 10-11 May 1943 in Bogodukhov (Ukraine), where the headquarters of the Fourth Panzer Army was located.

Erich von Manstein had been disappointed by the results of the conference in Munich. As a professional he understood Model's situation and his position when discussing the offensive.[257]

---

255 von Below, H., *Ia byl ad'jutantom Gitlera* [*I was Hitler's adjutant*], translated into Russian from the German by G. Rudnyi (Smolensk: Rusich, 2003), p. 406.
256 Liddell Hart, *Po druguiu storonu kholma*, p. 330.
257 Manstein, *Uteriannye pobedy*, p. 526.

The postponement was objectively favorable for his troops as well. However, the main thing he took from the discussion at the conference was that the Ninth Army should not expect any substantial help during the operation. However, it still did not have any clear picture of how to carry out such a complicated task in the new conditions. The Field Marshal recalled H. Hoth's letter, written back at the beginning of April, in which Hoth had picked to pieces the plans for Goshawk and Panther. In addition to the doubts in the success of these operations, Manstein caught the letter's main idea – the author's persistent desire to find an optimal way to destroy the Red Army's mobile reserves in the southwestern sector of the Eastern Front, which were growing with each passing day. This task was indeed important, but at the same time significantly more realistic than the encirclement of two *fronts*. If this was not addressed in the nearest future, the impressive Russian forces accumulated in the course of the springtime might by summer become a major threat not only for his troops. According to H. Hoth's estimates, already in early April opposite Army Group South, there were eight Soviet tank and mechanized corps to the north of the Kupiansk – Belgorod sector alone.[258] Without a doubt, the Soviet command would be using them in order to frustrate Operation Citadel, as well as an assault wedge in the event of their own offensive in Ukraine. Hoth's idea was in accordance with Manstein's own thoughts. Therefore, when Hoth proposed to discuss his new version of the plan for the future operation at his headquarters, as well as his opinions and suggestions regarding a number of operational and tactical questions, von Manstein immediately agreed.

The Colonel General's idea could not help but catch the Field Marshal's interest. In the first place, it better corresponded to the essence of the entire policy of Germany and its armed forces with respect to the Soviet Union at that moment, which H. Himmler had unambiguously laid out in his presentation to the SS Panzer Corps' command staff on 25 April 1943 in Khar'kov, than anything else:

> We should conduct the war and our approach with the thought of how best to deprive the Russians of human resources – alive or dead? We do this when we kill them or capture and leave them with genuine work; when we seek to take an occupied area and when we leave the adversary a de-populated territory. Either they should be driven to Germany and become its labor force or be killed in combat. But to leave the foe with people, so that it again has a working and military force, is generally speaking absolutely incorrect. Such cannot be tolerated. If this line to destroy people will be deliberately pursued in the war, I'm convinced there will come a time when the Russians already in the course of this year or the following winter will run out of strength and bleed out.[259]

In the second place, the possibility of a powerful attack by Red Army with the reserves, gathered into a fist, was fully realistic. The data upon which Hoth relied proved even to be an underestimate. On 1 April 1943, the three *fronts* opposing Army Group South had a combined 10 mobile corps formations, including three tank and one mechanized corps in the

---

258 Kriegstagebuch Ia der Heeresgruppe Don/Süd, März bis Juli 1943. BArch-MA. RH 19 VI/45, Bl. 23.
259 *Voina Germanii protiv Sovetskogo Soiuza 1941-1945. Katalog dokumental'noi vystavki. K 50-letiiu so dnia napadeniia Germanii na Sovetskii Soiuz.* [*Germany's war against the Soviet Union, 1941-1945. A catalogue of documentary displays on the 50th anniversary since the day of Germany's invasion of the Soviet Union*] (Berlin, 1994), pp. 103-104.

Voronezh Front;²⁶⁰ two tank and one mechanized corps in the Southwestern Front; and three mechanized corps in the Southern Front. ²⁶¹ In addition, the 5th Guards Tank Army's 5th Guards Mechanized Corps and 29th Tank Corps were assembled behind the Voronezh Front as part of the Reserve Front (which was renamed as the Steppe Military District on 13 April 1943). If you consider that the authorized strength of a tank corps amounted to 187 tanks and self-propelled guns, and that of a mechanized corps – 214 tanks and self-propelled guns, then the Soviet mobile reserves might amount to 2,406 tanks and self-propelled guns on this axis. In fact, this does not even include the separate tank and self-propelled artillery regiments that were located in the troops of these *fronts*. In addition to the indicated formations, at this moment the Stavka possessed 10 more tank and mechanized corps, three of which (1st Mechanized Corps, 10th Tank Corps and 18th Tank Corps) would be activated in order to repulse Army Group South's future offensive.

After Erich von Manstein arrived in Bogodukhov to see H. Hoth, for the next two days they not only discussed a circle of major problems connected with the Fourth Panzer Army's and Army Group South's participation in Citadel, but also reached important decisions which lay at the basis of the second version of the plan for their offensive toward Kursk, and it was namely Colonel General Hoth who was the initiator of the key ideas which then took shape in the decisions. Hoth's scheme, which he expressed over these two days, first became widely known from the notes of General of Infantry F. Fangohr, made after the war for the US Army's military history program. Hoth thought that given terrain features, an attack out of Belgorod toward Kursk along a direct line through Oboian' shouldn't be conducted, as was called for by the initial (April) plan of the offensive. The passable sectors for tanks south of Obioan' are narrow, restricted by the basins of three rivers and a number of deep balkas, so the German mobile formations, in the event of advancing directly to the north, might suffer heavy losses. F. Fangohr observes:

> General Hoth also had to assume that Soviet strategic reserves – including several tank corps – would enter the battle by pushing quickly through the narrow corridor between the Donets and Psel Rivers at Prokhorovka ... Accordingly, following our penetration of the enemy's defensive belt, II SS Panzer Corps would advance not due north across the Psel, but veer sharply to the northwest toward Prokhorovka in order to destroy the Russian tank forces we expected to find there. Such a maneuver had the advantage that it would place us much nearer to the intended thrust of *Armeeabteilung* Kempf's III Panzer Corps, raising the possibility of the coordination of the two interior army wings on the battlefield.²⁶²

---

260 Including the 1st Tank Army's 3rd Mechanized Corps and 6th Tank Corps, which were located in the *Stavka* reserve, but already in the process of moving up to join the Voronezh Front.
261 *Voenno-nauchnoe upvravlenie Genshtaba Sovietskoi Armii. Boevoi sostav Sovietskoi Armii v gody Velikoi Otechestvennoi voiny. Chast' 3 (ianvar'-dekabr' 1943)* [*Military-Academic Department of the Soviet Army's General Staff. Combat composition of the Soviet Army in the years of the Great Patriotic War. Part 3 (January-Decemeber 1943)*] (Moscow, 1972), pp. 87-89, 96-97.
262 Newton, *Kurskaia bitva: nemetskii vzgliad*, p. 100.

He also proposed to change the XXXXVIII Panzer Corps' mission. Once the offensive kicked off, it wouldn't advance strictly to the north across the Pena River, as had been previously planned, but instead in close coordination with the left wing of the SS Panzer Corps, thereby screening it, including after the SS Panzergrenadier divisions' veered to the northeast, toward Prokhorovka. This would enable the commander of the II SS Panzer Corps SS-Obergruppenführer Paul Hausser to exert maximum force in the assault wedge and at the decisive moment of the clash at Prokhorovka to count upon the assistance of his neighbor. At the same time, H. Hoth believed that the process of breaking through the Russians' powerful system of defenses would be costly. Therefore, it would be impossible to count upon his panzer divisions reaching operational space until the Fourth Panzer Army overcame the Noven'koe – Teterevino line (27-30 km south of Oboian'), where in fact it expected to meet the approaching Soviet reserves. However, if the battle of Prokhorovka was won, the forces of Army Group South would break through the interfluvial area of the Oskol, Donets, Psel and Seim Rivers, from where they would be able to attack in any direction.

On 14 May Hoth followed up with a letter to von Manstein, in which he clarified details of his plan and in connection with this, briefly laid out the new scheme of the offensive on its first day and the arrangement of using the forces of the two primary corps. In the first portion of the document the Colonel General proposed amending two important points of the first (April) version of the plan for Army Group South's offensive: the boundary line between its forces and Army Detachment Kempf, and the composition of his panzer army's assault wedge immediately before the start of the operation, and then proceeded to make a case for them:

> In addition to my verbal comments on 10 and 11 May, I propose the following related to the conducting of Operation Citadel:
>
> 1. The shifting of the boundary line between Army Detachment Kempf and the Fourth Panzer Army: as far as the road fork 6 km southwest of Shopino just as it was before, further Shopino (Fourth Panzer Army) – Visloe – Smorodino (AD Kempf) – Luchi – Prokhorovka – Ol'khovatka – Saraevka – Subbotino (Fourth Panzer Army) – Tim (AD Kempf). Justification: Such a boundary line permits the panzer army, with an attack across the land bridge leading to the north through Prokhorovka, to bypass to the east of the Psel sector with the SS Panzer Corps, while the bulk of the XXXXVIII Panzer Corps strikes to the northeast of Oboian'. Thus, the entire operation will target enemy units standing in the Miropol'e – Sudzha area and east of there, and in connection with this the more rapid breakthrough in the direction of Kursk is possible. The command of Army Detachment Kempf agrees with this decision.
> 2. The employment of the 3rd Panzer Division from the start of the offensive on the forward edge of XXXXVIII Panzer Corps' western flank, and not in the second wave. Justification. It is necessary to prevent a situation where the *Grossdeutschland* Panzergrenadier Division would be forced to detach units in order to screen the western flank. Since the available infantry for these purposes is insufficient, the 3rd Panzer Division should be activated in the first line. In addition, experience

shows that a panzer division placed in the second wave, as a rule, advances with great difficulties (traffic jams and so on), and is always badly delayed.[263]

This is the first document in which Hoth proposes to commit his last operational reserve, which was the 3rd Panzer Division, into combat from the first minutes of Citadel, and thereby, in fact deprives himself of a lever of influence on the situation in the breakthrough sector. This decision has long been known and certain scholars, not without justification, consider it mistaken, but I've managed to find only now the arguments of the army commander in its favor. In fact, it must be said that they don't seem convincing. When analyzing each argument separately, the second point causes surprise. Is it possible at all to compare the presence of an operational reserve in the hands of a commander at the start of the battle with the rather dubious assertion about the difficulty of introducing the division into battle from the second echelon? After all, that is the way reserves have always been brought forward. However, this approach does not undermine Hoth's motive. It is more effective to view both factors taken together – the desire not to sap the Panzergrenadier Division *Grossdeutschland*'s strength and the difficulty of quickly introducing a division into combat. Even more one panzer division was necessary for him in the first hours of the offensive in order to create first of all the utmost concentration of forces and means in order to guarantee the steamrolling of the Russians' line within a short period of time. Moreover, Hoth was concerned about the possibility of strong tank counterattacks in the flank already in the first belt of defenses. Accordingly, his main motivation becomes understandable, even though it was not openly stated in the letter: Already in mid-May, the Colonel General lacked confidence in the possibility of quickly breaching the Voronezh Front's main defensive belt.

In addition, it was in this document that Hoth first proposed to von Manstein to conduct a limited operation on the day before the offensive started in order to seize the ground south of Cherkasskoe, a large village and powerful knot of resistance on the 6th Guards Army's right flank, where the village of Butovo and the adjacent high ground served as positions for the combat outposts of the Soviet Guardsmen. In essence, this would become the first step in realizing Citadel's plan.

Thus, Hoth's "plan" was in fact proposing to execute Operation Citadel in two stages. In the first stage, Fourth Panzer Army was first supposed to break through two of the three defensive belts of the Voronezh Front, before destroying the Soviet operational and strategic mobile reserves together with Army Detachment Kempf in the vicinity of Prokhorovka Station. Only after this would the opportunity appear to push on to the Shshigry area to link up with Model's troops. Hoth believed that if these first two tasks could be resolved quickly and successfully, without high losses, then nothing could stop his panzer army. Even so, he was not confident that the Russians would roll over and allow six of their armies in the Kursk salient to be isolated and destroyed. Therefore, although the main objective of the second stage was clear – meeting up with the Ninth Army, he believed that the panzer corps should be given concrete assignments only after the battle at Prokhorovka.[264]

263 NARA US, T.313, R.370, F.8656081, F.8656082.
264 Newton, *Kurskaia bitva: nemetskii vzgliad*, p. 101.

Accordingly, the destruction of the Soviet mobile reserves near Prokhorovka was a decisive step for Citadel's further elaboration. Manstein agreed with Hoth's conclusions. His plan was sufficiently fleshed out and adapted to the terrain, and took full consideration of the strength of the Soviet defensive system as it stood in early May, the possibilities of the army group and its strength (the quality of the panzer divisions) and weaknesses (the lack of infantry), and was also spared of any hint of adventurism. In addition, it contained a sober and logical prognosis of the responses of the Soviet command, depending on the operational situation that should take shape in the course of the Fourth Panzer Army's and Army Detachment Kempf's operations. In K. von Tippelskirch's opinion, Hitler also arrived at the idea expressed by Hoth in May, but later, just before the start of the Battle of Kursk:

> The events of the preceding year nevertheless apparently had made an impact on Hitler's operational views. In one of his speeches given by him not long before the start of the offensive in front of members of the higher command staff, who'd been given responsibility for conducting the operation, he announced his firm decision to go over to a strategic defense [probably, he's talking about a conference on 1 July 1943]. Germany, he said, should henceforth grind down the adversaries' strength in defensive battles, in order to stick it out longer than they could; the pending operation had as its objective not the seizure of a significant amount of territory, but only to straighten out the bulge, which was needed in the interests of economizing strength. The Russian armies positioned in the Kursk bulge should be, in his words, destroyed, and it was necessary to force the Russians to expend all of their reserves in fighting until they were depleted, and thereby weaken their offensive strength for the oncoming winter. The main idea of these considerations fully coincided with the point of view of the military leadership, and moreover, the idea of wearing down the enemy's forces was virtually implemented.[265]

Five days later, on 18 May, von Manstein sent a letter to the troops, in which the Field Marshal gave recommendations to the command of the armies and corps involved in Citadel, primarily, but not only, regarding questions of command and control of the troops. The letter's contents plainly reflect the conference in Bogodukhov and the thoughts that Hoth expressed at it. For example, it describes the need directly before the attack kicks off to conduct a limited operation to seize the no man's land at a point where it was very wide, in order to gain time and strength for the breakthrough on the first day of the operation. However, the most interesting point, in my view, is the Field Marshal's affirmation of the obvious fact that the offensive would not be a surprise for the Soviet side, although efforts must be made to achieve it in certain sectors. I particularly want to emphasize this point, since in the historiography of the Soviet period, and even in academic works, a number of scholars made the completely contrary assertion.[266] Here is an excerpt from this document:

---

265 Tippelskirsch, *Istoriia Vtoroi mirovoi voiny*, p. 24.
266 See, for example, *Istoriia Velikoi Otechestvennoi voiny 1941-1945*, p. 257.

A) The conducting of combat operations
1. Operation Citadel foresees the breakthrough of strong and deeply developed defensive fortifications. This requires the most accurate training, which regards not only the initial attack, but also takes into consideration all the possibilities relating to the enemy positions in the rear, in order not to allow the mobility of the combat operations to slacken.
   The offensive in general is divided into three phases:
   a) The breaching of the forward positions (including the approaches). A planned attack with the application of a large amount of ordnance is conducted. For this it is necessary to train for the closest collaboration of the infantry, panzers, sappers and artillery. The objective of this phase must be the destruction of the Russian divisions positioned on the forward edge of defense to such a point that there is no question about a struggle for the second line.
   b) A rapid penetration to the second line. In this stage, typical combat operations with panzer divisions comes into effect. Concentrate strength and advance with rapid drives. It is necessary to ensure the close contact of the artillery and the mobility of the infantry after the breaching of the first line. On the other hand, in the event that the second line of defense is occupied by large enemy reserves, the command must be ready to halt the advancing panzer divisions at the front, and if necessary, to strike the second line with a planned attack in order to break through the defenses. Give prior thought to the sectors in which this will be necessary, as well as the places of the assembly of forces for these attacks.
   c) The fighting in unobstructed territory with the enemy's operational reserves
      The less that the panzer divisions up to this point have had the need to participate in planned attacks in positional fighting, the more thorough must be the training of the leaders and the more imperative the training in the field.

…

3. Tactical surprise, at least regarding the selection of the point of breakthrough and the start time of the offensive, must be ensured by all types of camouflage and diversionary actions.
   When bringing up the panzer units and assembling them prior to the offensive, all movements must be concealed from enemy reconnaissance by any means. Groups necessary for instructing the attacking units must be sent forward stealthily in separate machines, while the bulk should be brought up as late as possible. There, where it is possible, create areas of assembly on X-1 day or X-2 day in the direction of the offensive's primary objectives. Any movements should be completed before sunrise. Limit the number of machines for transporting the sappers to the minimum. The machines of the panzergrenadier regiments should be left far behind, and send only machines equipped with heavy weapons to the assembly areas, while the panzer grenadiers come up on foot. Heavily restrict all other movement. Separately, groups of troops are ordered to conduct diversionary measures.

   …

5. A surprise attack promises success during the offensive against the first line of defense only at separate objectives (forward observation points, strong points,

etc.). When breaking through the deep fortifications, surprise correspondingly dissipates, but it should be replaced by intensified fire. In this way, speed does not fall, for which purpose it is necessary to give prior thought to firepower. After the penetration of the forward positions, surprise can be gained only by means of an unexpectedly rapid attack against the second line.
6. Positions in front of the forward edge. Wherever there is the perception that the enemy has pulled back his main line of defense into the depth, leaving in front only forward outposts or advanced fortified points, take these places even before the start of the attack or early in the morning on the day of the offensive, using the effect of surprise. The purpose of these advances, in addition to the capture of the observation posts, is to give access to enemy minefields in order to clear them before the start of the offensive, and also to distract enemy artillery and anti-tank defenses. In those places where the main line of defense hugs our line, the attack must begin directly from it. [By hand, the letters "SS" had been jotted down.][267]

The Ninth Army command on the contrary took the postponement of the offensive with relief. The situation was improving, including for Model personally. The period of preparations for Citadel had been extended by a month, and this meant the army would receive a respite, fresh forces, and be able to conduct intensified training of the troops. Certain participants of the Battle of Kursk, for example, the former operations officer of the Second Army Colonel von der Groeben claims that Model was inclined to cancel the attack towards Kursk altogether.[268] So the 6 May decision gave him hope that in the end, the operation would be closed down. These thoughts were not without substance.

On 15 May, the problem of the struggle against the saboteurs and partisans on the rear lines of communication began to be resolved: This time not by the next, local punitive operation, but on a large scale, with the use of major combat formations, although the effectiveness of such a measure even before its application raised doubts. The Ninth Army was also supposed to take part in this operation. In order to destroy the partisan detachments in the woods south of Briansk, it detached its shock formation – the XXXXVII Panzer Corps – and the headquarters of the Second Army was to take charge of the operation. Model understood that it was an extremely tall order to conduct an operation with regular divisions equipped with tanks and heavy weaponry in swampy terrain that was even difficult for an individual to cross on foot, and then quickly and efficiently return them to their jumping-off positions by 12 June (in less than a month). It would be even more difficult to regroup them afterward in the conditions of Orel's lack of good roads, and to get the troops ready for a strategic operation over a maximum of three to five days was sheer fantasy. This circumstance once again confirmed the Ninth Army commander in the thought that the start date of the offensive, set by Hitler as 12 June, wouldn't be the last. Even if after the anti-partisan actions Citadel was not cancelled altogether, then with a great deal of probability, its start date would be postponed once again.

---

267 NARA US, T.313, R.340, F.8656364-8656367.
268 Newton, *Kurskaia bitva: nemetskii vzgliad*, p. 139, 142.

No fundamental changes had been made in Order No. 6, and accordingly the basis of Army Group Center's plan for the operation remained in effect, so its headquarters was able somewhat to set planning aside and focus attention on the control over the arrival of equipment and replacements, their allocation to the combat units, and combat training. In a word, from mid-May, by frontline standards a rather unhurried and routine schedule of work settled over the headquarters of the Ninth Army. So, Model in fact decided to get some rest. Considering that his leave of absence in April had been interrupted by his appointment as acting commander-in-chief of Army Group South, on 19 May he received permission to turn over his duties and on the next day he departed to Germany for a leave of absence until 10 June.

The question about who was carrying out his duties in his absence has been neglected by the majority of historians, and in general the events in the area of the Kursk bulge in the latter half of May and early June 1943 have been poorly illuminated in the military history literature. Some scholars, for example Stephen Newton, make a mistake and assume that General of Infantry W. Weiss was serving in Model's place.[269] In reality, the acting commander from the evening of 19 May was the commander of the XXXXI Panzer Corps, General of Panzer Troops Josef Harpe. This is unambiguously shown in the Ninth Army's journal of combat operations.[270]

However, let us return to the events in the Orel salient. Over recent times, in connection with the publication of documentary sources and research based on new historical material, a point of view has arisen and strengthened among historians and in society that the effectiveness of the partisan movement has been exaggerated in Russian historical literature. The real results of their activity supposedly had no substantial influence on the Red Army's combat operations, while the image of the "Red partisan" has been excessively embellished by Soviet propaganda. Unquestionably, this is true to a considerable extent. However, the given subject of study shouldn't be approached one-dimensionally, only in comparison with the army's standards. In the first place, the partisan detachments were not combat formations in the full sense of the term. For the most part they consisted of civilians (with the exception of special detachments and NKVD operational groups), who had no regular military service; frequently by their composition and physical abilities, they were not ready for service in regular units (they had women, old men and adolescents in them). Accordingly, it is not serious to expect indicators of performance equal to combat units from civilians who've taken up rifles and pitchforks. In this connection it is hard not to agree with Doctor of Historical Science A. Mertsalov, who emphasizes:

> Bowing before their heroism, we'll recall that those who resorted to joining the irregular forces did not always come from good lives. Their combat capabilities and effectiveness were much lower. They suffered more casualties than did professionals. For the Stalinist methods of warfare, the use of primitive means of struggle was totally characteristic – Molotov cocktails, grenade bundles, the actions of suicidal attackers (the ramming of tanks and aircraft, blocking of enemy firing points with their own bodies, calling fire down upon oneself, etc.).[271]

---

269 Newton, *Pozharnik Gitlera – fel'dmarshall Model'* [*Hitler's fireman – Field Marshal Model*] (Moscow: AST, 2007), p. 264.
270 NARA US, T.312, R.317, F.7886121.
271 See Mertsalov's article "Gor'kii dym" ["Bitter smoke"] in *Rodina*, No. 6 (2004), p. 12.

In the second place, as of today not all of the Red Army's major operations, which employed partisan formations, have yet been fully analyzed on the basis of the documentary records of the opposing sides, and their influence on the results of the operations hasn't yet been determined. The poor study of the subject "The participation of partisans in the Battle of Kursk", especially in the period of Army Group Center's preparations for it between April and June 1943 can serve as an example of this. Yet it would seem that the Briansk partisans at this time had a substantial effect on the timetable of the preparations for Citadel. They engaged and harassed major forces of not only security divisions, but also those of the Wehrmacht, and forced the enemy to expend valuable material resources that were extremely necessary for Operation Citadel with meager results. Thus, I consider it still premature today to draw a generalized conclusion on the contribution of the partisans both in specific battles of the Great Patriotic War, and in our overall victory over the Nazis.

By the spring of 1943, the partisan movement in the rear of Army Group Center had grown to a substantial size. Especially painful for the occupiers were their attacks on transportation lines (railroads and bridges), and on targets of their logistical support system (water supply stations, water pumphouses, sawmills, prepared railroad ties, and so forth). According to German records, already by the middle of 1942 their sabotage attacks had become a headache for the command of Army Group Center. From an appendix to a report from its main railroad department from 28 July 1942:

> Partisan attacks during the course of July have taken on a menacing scale that has not only reduced the railroad traffic to a point significantly lower than established norms, but in general the situation in the nearest future will prompt the most serious concerns. The number of partisan attacks: January – 5, February – 6, March – 27, April – 65, May – 145, June – 262, July – 304 … At the same time, it should be particularly considered that over recent times, the strength of the attacks has grown significantly and accordingly their consequences have risen. The losses in men and especially in valuable materiel are very high.
>
> … For example, the number of trains daily crossing the border and moving in the direction of the front amounted in the course of the week between 12 July and 18 July to an average of 116 per day, and in the course of the week between 19 July and 25 July 1942 to only 111, at the same time that the norms according to the running times foresees 128 trains for each 24 hours. It has been necessary to hold trains carrying coal, separate trains carrying combat loads … and even the transportation of troops for a time.
>
> At present, 200 locomotives alone have detonated mines, of which 110 are undergoing repairs … in Germany. These locomotives have been knocked out of service for no less than six months. Thus, only in the zone of Army Group Center's Main Railroad Department, a number of locomotives have been damaged or destroyed by mines equal to the monthly production by Germany's locomotive plants. In addition, 38 locomotives have been derailed. These train engines have been knocked out of service for no less than a year.
>
> Thus, locomotives are being rendered non-operational for months and are not only unable to carry out their main function, but also require the involvement of a significant amount of labor to repair them at steam engine repair factories and depots. At the government locomotive repair plants for the months of May, June and July,

approximately 4,000 labor hours have been expended to repair locomotives that have triggered mines. The number of man-hours spent to repair them in locomotive repair depots is much greater.

   … The number of badly damaged and completely knocked out railcars: January – 0, February – 0, March – 57, April – 45, May – 166, June – 218, and 1-25 July – 287.

   … The number of lightly damaged railcars, which are revealed only after thorough inspection by foremen, is much greater … The delay of trains varies between 10 and 120 hours. If you consider that on average each train is late by 36 hours, then for 100 trains, daily moving in the same direction, this amounts to: 100 x 40 x 36/24 = 6,000 railcars, and a total of 12,000 railcars that could be used daily for the army's needs or for military industry and the economy.

   … The influence of the partisans on the local workers is constantly increasing. To an ever-increasing degree, indifference and idling are manifesting themselves among workers and office employees. Over the previous weeks 242 people on traffic duty have left work, and 437 on other duties, for a total of 679 individuals. During the partisan attacks it is often discovered that local railroad workers were implicated or took part in them. Often, the top workers turn out to be partisans or even the leaders of partisan organizations and detachments. Thus, the number of arrests among local railroad workers is constantly increasing. In conclusion, one can say that given the further increase in partisan attacks, the railroad traffic, which has already fallen below the necessary level, will continue to decrease even more. In such a case, the requirement of armed combat personnel on railroad trains cannot be satisfactory. Moreover, there is reason to be concerned that the partisans by systematically increasing their operations, will paralyze entire railroad junctions.[272]

Logemann, who'd been authorized to oversee military transportation, and who signed this document, proved to be absolutely correct. With the passage of time, the effectiveness of the partisan attacks only grew. Berlin reacted to such reports with cruel repressive measures. For example, on 31 August 1942, the Chief of Operations of the OKH General Adolf Heusinger signed an order regarding the creation of special storm groups in the military formations positioned in the rear in order to struggle against the "bandits". Other measures were also undertaken, including the development of an extensive network of agents by the Abwehr and other special services for the struggle against the partisans with the aim of if not completely destroying them, at least of reducing their activity. However, there was no success in achieving the desired effect; on the contrary, the scale of the sabotage attacks only grew, including as a reaction to the cruel terror of the occupiers. In the course of the intensifying punitive raids, the occupiers were killing more civilians than partisans. The Germans clearly understood this and deliberately embarked on war crimes. For example, on 29 March 1943, the command of one of the army corps sent a proposal to the Third Panzer Army to carry off all the civilians that they came across during round ups and operations, and to kill them later in remote places, so that an impression might form among the local population: Their fellow villagers were being detained as prisoners of war and would soon be released.

---

272 Dashichev (ed.), *Sovershenno sekretno! Tol'ko dlia komandovaniia!*, pp. 402-405.

According to Army Group Center's Operations Department, as of January 1943 a total of more than 100,000 people had been killed as "partisans". The absolute majority of those counted were civilians, who had no direct connection to paramilitary groups. The German scholar N. Müller writes: "Such a cruel competition played out sometimes between the troop commanders responsible for conducting punitive operations and the representatives of Himmler's agency, as is clear from a telegram sent by Jeckeln[273] on 24 March 1943 regarding Operation "Winter Sorceries" as conducted by Wehrmacht units. He was complaining that the troops who had taken part in it had utterly burned all the villages down to the ground, although this, properly, should have been done by SS units."[274] A similar approach by the occupiers to their victims and to the meticulous tracking of the numbers would be preserved even in the future, for example, in the course of the punitive operation "Gypsy Baron", which was conducted before the launching of Citadel.

According to the estimates of German academics, already by the summer of 1943 the partisans were controlling more than 200 square kilometers, which represented approximately 1/6 of the entire occupied Soviet territory.[275] Considering that the concept of "controlling" is rather nebulous, I believe that this figure should be treated with a certain amount of caution. Nevertheless, it is obvious that the number of partisan organizations began to increase significantly from the latter half of 1942, especially after the encirclement at Stalingrad, through an influx of civilians (who before this time had primarily been following a "wait and see" approach), and the effectiveness of partisan attacks grew.

In March and April 1943, when the preparations for Citadel began, the partisan attacks on Army Group Center's lines of communication became a major headache, since the situation with respect to the regrouping of the Ninth Army and the transportation of supply loads was very stressful. The rear area personnel were under a time crunch. According to the calculations of Krebs' staff, at this moment, only the minimal and most essential supplies needed by Model's forces in order to resolve the operation's tasks amounted to: fuel – 11,000 cubic meters (12 trainloads, ½ a refill during the breakthrough, 4 refills during the exploitation of a success, and 5.5 refills in army stockpiles); shells – 12,300 tons (28 trainloads); and food – 8,220 tons (21 trainloads).[276] All of the supplies had to be delivered to the designated point before 25 April. To this figure, several dozen trainloads of equipment, weapons, replacements and ammunition should be added. This was in fact only for the Ninth Army, and yet other armies were also located in the Orel salient. At the end of April and beginning of May 1943, the Germans in the Orel salient managed to get less than four trains through per day by rail. On 3 May 1943 the headquarters of the Ninth Army set a task before its chief quartermaster: To bring the rail traffic up to 8.5 trains, though 16-20 were required![277] These figures from captured German

---

273 Friedrich Jeckeln served as the Higher SS and Police Leader of northern Russia and the Baltic republics, including the rear area of Army Group Center. He was the commander of one of the largest collection of Einsatzgruppen death squads and was later sentenced to death by a Soviet military tribunal for war crimes and executed in 1946.
274 Müller, N., *Vermakht i okkupatsiia* [*Wehrmacht and occupation*] (Moscow: Veche, 2010), p. 168.
275 Ibid., p. 158.
276 NARA US, T.312, R.317, F.7886032.
277 NARA US, T.312, R.317, F.7886074.

documents plainly demonstrate what high results the Briansk partisans and NKVD special groups managed to achieve in their combat work in the course of the preparations for Citadel.

Moreover, according to the calculations of the Ninth Army's headquarters staff, in the course of the offensive the troops were supposed to make a total advance of up to 200 km. Therefore, first the rear services would have to expand the available storage space in pace with the arrival of supply loads by constructing new warehouses and preparing stockpile locations; and second, plan the work and prepare to move supplies, ammunition, fuel and food directly in the wake of the advancing troops.

For sake of comparison, I will cite the data for the planned shipment of ammunition for the Fourth Panzer Army's artillery. Already after the postponement to June, its headquarters received a directive to assemble the following for Citadel prior to 24 May:

A. For the artillery preparation: 1,625 tonn of artillery shells, and 530 tonn of ammunition for the heavy infantry guns, for a total of 2,155 tonn.
B. Before penetrating the enemy's second positions: 4,300 tonn of artillery shells, 210 tonn and 800 tonn for the anti-tank guns and the main guns of the panzers, for a total of 5,310 tonn.
C. For the following days of the offensive: 310 tonn of artillery shells, 60 tonn for the heavy infantry guns, and 100 tonn for the panzer and anti-tank guns.[278]

As we have seen, in comparison with Model's army, the anticipated expenditure of ammunition by Hoth's troops was significantly lower, only 4,365 tonn of artillery shells following the artillery preparation. The volume of work for supporting the Ninth Army was assumed to be large, and with the available modest transportation means, it would be extremely difficult to carry out by the established deadline. In those conditions, the bulk of the motorized transports with a large carrying capacity had been assembled with the artillerymen, and there was nothing to substitute for it. The army had to make a difficult decision: Given the need, to use combat transports for the delivery of rear loads of supply, and to move personnel and equipment on foot or on horseback. Naturally, this order negatively affected the mobility of the combat divisions, yet even so it could not resolve the problem with bringing up supplies, because the Ninth Army was catastrophically short of trucks and prime movers. Even a month later, on 16 May, the headquarters of each of its 13 divisions were reporting that they were around 2,000 vehicles short of the authorized strength in total.[279] This is precisely why the Germans tried to find a way out of the problem by resorting to horse-drawn wagons. For example, in the month of April, the 18th Panzer Division alone received 2,500 horses in order to try to meet its needs.[280] A panzer battalion of 18th Panzer Division still employed a significant number of horse-drawn wagons, and needless to say the situation was even worse in the infantry and panzergrenadier divisions.[281] Altogether, by the start of the Battle of Kursk, Model's Ninth Army possessed 50,000 draught horses.[282] However, even though this was a substantial, but auxiliary resource,

---

278 NARA US, T.312, R.317, F.8650561.
279 Newton, *Kurskaia bitva: nemetskii vzgliad*, p. 469.
280 Ibid., p. 466.
281 Ibid.
282 Haupt, *Srazheniia gruppy armii "Tsentr"*, p. 238.

it could only provide assistance in the frontal zone. Shipments from Germany and the main volume of loads (the movement of troops and equipment) moved along railroads of all types in the Orel salient, including regular tracks and narrow-gauge tracks.

In connection with this I will provide one interesting detail. In April the Soviet army-level intelligence noted this characteristic of the enemy's use of rail and horse to deliver supplies opposite the Central Front. However, the conclusions drawn from this were not quite correct: It believed the Germans were only cutting back on road work. From an intelligence bulletin of the 48th Army's Intelligence Department on 5 May 1943:

> The enemy, in the period of the spring thaw, has sharply restricted the use of roads suitable for motorized transport. In this period, the supply of the forces with everything necessary for combat is being implemented for the most part by railroad transport. The Orel – Zmeevka – Glazunovka line in the period of the spring thaw has seen increased traffic, up to 10 trains a day in comparison with the winter season. Simultaneously the enemy has curtailed motorized traffic along the improved unpaved road between Orel and Glazunovka and along other roads leading from the railroad to the front lines. As a result of this, the enemy has kept a section of the roads in good condition, without calling upon the expenses for their improvement.[283]

Therefore, in the springtime, the railroad arteries in fact became the main target of attack by both the Soviet air forces and partisans. From the recollections of Army Group Center's Chief of Transportation Oberst Teske:

> April, like March, was marked by heavy troops transport requirements within the army group. Accordingly, Soviet air assets attempted to interfere primarily at points of approach and intervehicle communications near the front-line area, as well as at unloading stations. The increasingly frequent partisan raids, by contrast, aimed at our communications lines in the rear, upon which we depended for supply and individual troop transports. Nevertheless, Field Railroad Headquarters 2 achieved maximum efficiency along the Smolensk – Briansk – Orel line, which was critical for the strategic buildup.
>
> During May the number of troop and supply transports decreased, as the strategic concentration for Operation Citadel had in general been completed. On the other hand, the number of troop transports moving through our area to Army Group South, which were intended for the southern attack wing out of the Kharkov – Belgorod area, increased. Accordingly, the Soviets aimed their air and partisan attacks at the points of main effort, which in this case meant the important railroad stations at Gomel, Orsha and Minsk, as well as the critical short stretch of track between Zhlobin – Gomel. In May alone that section of railroad came under attack sixty-nine times, resulting in 156 hours of blockage on the single-track line and 222 hours along the double-track line. We also lost thirty-five locomotives and 106 cars.[284]

---

283 TsAMO RF, F.62, Op.323, D.19, l. 139.
284 Newton, *Kurskaia bitva: nemetskii vzgliad*, p. 267.

In April, the Soviet air forces launched 626 attacks on the sector of the Minsk – Gomel railroad track; it required the Germans 12 days to repair the damage.[285] In the following months, despite the German efforts to stop them, the activity of the Red Army Air Force and the partisans against the lines of communication of Army Groups Center and South continued to grow, with the exception of a slight pause. An increase in Moscow's organizational activity contributed to this. On 26 April 1943 the Politburo approved an operational plan for Ukrainian partisans for the spring and summer period, which gave them the mission to paralyze the work of 26 major railroad junctions, including the Shepetovka, Kovel', Saransk, Zdolbunov and a number of other rail hubs that fed Army Group South. In May 1943 major aerial operations were conducted that would yield clear results, which were particularly noticeable in the first days. For example, on 4 May alone, in the course of an air raid on Orsha, the adversary lost 300 trucks together with their loads. Thus, in April and early May 1943, the main factors that were complicating the preparations for Citadel were the weather conditions and large deficit of vehicles, as well as the rising activity of the partisans and Soviet air attacks.

The raids on the lines of communication and the sabotage attacks of the partisans were causing an increase in not only the direct loss of men and equipment and disrupting the timetables for keeping the troops supplied with food and combat supplies, but also something very important, were causing the Germans to divert significant forces of manpower to guard the supply routes and to conduct anti-partisan operations. For example, in the summer and autumn of 1942, according to incomplete data, a total of around 350,000 German soldiers were assigned to protect the lines of communication in the occupied territory of the USSR and to anti-partisan duties, and in May alone 1943 Himmler's SS was employing more than 327,000 men for these purposes.[286] On 9 May 1943, the Chief of Army Group Center's Rear Area Max von Schenckendorff felt compelled to report to von Kluge that the 59 security and police battalions under his command could not handle the protection of 3,300 km of railroads and paved roads, as well as the large number of industrial and military targets, so he requested reinforcements.

The Reich's leadership at this time came to the conclusion that only large-scale punitive operations employing Wehrmacht combat formations could reduce the growing pressure of the partisans on the rear infrastructure and wipe out the accomplices, who occupied a significant share of the occupation administration. It decided to conduct the first operation in the rear of Army Group Center in May, while preparing for Operation Citadel, because it was here, in the large wooded areas around Briansk that major partisan regions had sprung up which covered a significant portion of the supply arteries on the central axis of the Soviet-German front.

On 27 April 1943, literally just a day after the Politburo's decision regarding the partisans' combat work in Ukraine, Hitler signed Operational Directive No. 14 about the anti-partisan struggle, which demanded:

> The Russians are ever more intensively rolling out banditry in the struggle. They are appointing generals as commanders of the bands, organizing systematic communications and supply with the help of couriers, radios and aircraft; bandits are even being brought out by aircraft for leaves of absence. According to available information, approximately

---

285 Liubchenko, D., "Kolesa dolzhny krutitsia na pobedu" ["Wheels should turn toward victory"] *Nauka i tekhnika*, No. 12 (2013), p. 61.
286 Müller, *Vermakht i okkupatsiia*, p. 159.

80,000 people make up the partisan bands that are functioning in the areas of combat operations, and this number excludes the numerous detachments in western Ukraine, Belorussia and the Baltics.

In recent time the partisan bands have inflicted serious damage to railroad transport and agriculture, have disrupted the floating of lumber along rivers, etc. Based upon this, we should conduct the struggle against banditry even more intensively and thoughtfully ...

I am ordering:
1. To consider the struggle with banditry equivalent to combat operations at the front. The operations departments of armies and army groups should direct it. This struggle must be conducted systematically.
2. All forces suitable for the given purpose must be used. In those places where such forces are insufficient, it is necessary, considering the circumstances, to create composite units and in the course of a specific period of time engage them in the struggle against banditry. This will serve as well the purposes of combat training and increase the combat capabilities of the units made part of them.

...

8. Banditry – is such a foe that uses every possible means in the struggle, and only by such means of equal cruelty can it be stamped out.
9. It is necessary to use every means of deception and camouflage. The organization of auxiliary detachments made up by local citizens in German service and operating under its leadership has justified itself. With the help of such detachments, important information can be collected and corresponding experience can be accumulated.[287]

The Commander-in-Chief of Army Group Center received the coded message from Zossen, which laid out the essence of this directive and simultaneously demanded the quick planning and conducting of a major anti-partisan operation in its rear on 11 May, although its headquarters had already been informed about Hitler's order.[288] The letter from the OKH particularly emphasized that the date designated on 6 May 1943 for the start of Citadel was set in stone, so the pacification operation simply run until 12 June, but should be completed as soon as possible, in order to have time to ready the troops for the offensive. In addition, the army group was directed to pay maximal attention to the concealment of the withdrawal of forces from the front, so that the Russians wouldn't attack its weakened front at this time. The Ninth Army was interested in this operation, because it was counting upon resolving a number of its pressing problems through its implementation. Judging from archival documents, its command in the first place was hoping to weaken the pressure on the sector of the railroad between Briansk and Kamarichi, a significant portion of which ran along the edge of the forested area south of Briansk, and to eliminate the partisan formations in the triangular area where the Seva and Nerussa Rivers came together in the rear of the XX Army Corps on the right.

---

287 Klink, *Gesetz des Handelns. Die Operation "Zitadelle"*, pp. 302-303.
288 NARA US, T.312, R. 317, F.7886087.

Although it had been planned that the XXXXVII Panzer Corps would take full part in the punitive operation, which was to cover a large portion of the Ninth Army's rear area, nevertheless, considering that it was fully overshadowed by the preparation of the attack toward Kursk, responsibility for carrying out the directive was placed on its neighbor, the Second Army. It had considerable experience and had already more than once conducted large-scale anti-partisan operations, including with the use of regular units, such as "Bird Call", "Triangle", "Quadrangle", "White Bear" and others in the latter half of 1942, although not one of them had been able to achieve its goals in full measure. From mid-May 1943, the struggle against the partisans began to take on a major scope. For the first time, troops of four armies were simultaneously detached for it – the Fourth and Ninth Armies, and the Second and Third Panzer Armies. With their participation, a number of operations would be conducted prior to the Battle of Kursk in order to neutralize the partisan pressure on the roads in the Orel salient, such as "Hired Gun" (an attack against the forested area northwest of Briansk and the Smolensk – Briansk road), "East" (the woods northeast of Briansk and the Briansk – Orel railroad), etc.

However, the Operation "Gypsy Baron" became the largest anti-partisan sweep. The grouping for it was formed completely on the basis of General of Panzer Troops Joachim Lemelsen's XXXXVII Panzer Corps, which was supposed to coordinate its actions with the 442nd Special Purpose Headquarters (also known as "Headquarters Borneman").[289] This organ was carrying out the functions of a coordinator of all the forces (police, punitive and army) with the aim of using them effectively in circumstances that were unusual for them. Five combat divisions were committed against the partisans – the 10th Panzergrenadier Division, the 4th and 18th Panzer Divisions, and the 7th and 292nd Infantry Divisions. On 8 May Elverfeldt's headquarters sent an order to these divisions about their temporary subordination to the Second Panzer Army for the operation's planned period of 14 days. In addition, the 98th and 221st Infantry Divisions were shifted from the Fourth Army in order to cordon off the forested areas west of Briansk (to the south of Roslavl'). As a result, according to Soviet information on the operation, more than 50,000 men were pulled together for Operation Gypsy Baron (including so-called Ost Battalions of non-German foreign troops and Wehrmacht combat units).[290] Opposing them

---

289 Major General Karl Bornemann (1885-1979), an Austrian. He began his military service in the Austro-Hungarian Army. In 1937 he received the rank of major general. A year after Austria's *Anschloss*, he was discharged from the army, but on 1 February 1940 he was called up into the Wehrmacht. With the start of the war with the Soviet Union, he was sent to the front and placed in charge of the 442nd Special Purpose Divisional Headquarters (Headquarters Bornemann), and engaged in the anti-partisan struggle in the rear areas of Army Group Center. For this, in February 1943 he was awarded the German Cross in Gold. After Operation Gypsy Baron, Headquarters Bornemann was made responsible by Army Group Center for the transportation of supplies in the rear zone, and from 9 June 1943 it was made subordinate to the Ninth Army. In 1944, he took command of the 410th Infantry Division. On 1 September 1943, Karl Bornemann found his way into detective history. In the woods south of Briansk, the partisan brigade "For the Motherland" attacked his column. He survived, but lost his briefcase and general's coat, which became proof of his supposed death. The episode with the "killing" of a Wehrmacht general is encountered in a number of publications from the Soviet era, for example, M.F. Kovalev's *Lesnoi front. Dokumental'naia povest'* [*Forest front. Documentary tale*] (Moscow, 1983), p. 201, and V.E. Bystrov's "Sovetskie partizany v period Kurskoi bitvy" ["Soviet partisans in the period of the Battle of Kursk" in *Kurskaia bitva* [*Battle of Kursk*] (Moscow: Nauka, 1970), p. 400.
290 AP RF, F.3, Op.50, D.475, l. 49.

were the 12 combat forces of the Joint Partisan Headquarters covering the southern portion of Orel and Sumy Oblasts under the leadership of Hero of the Soviet Union D.V. Emliutin.

The decision to employ such significant forces from the acting army for the struggle against the partisans was more emotional (the desire to put an end to a long-standing problem) than rational. In the first place, the army group command approached the task rather formally; not only were the possible results of the undertaken steps ignored, but also their effect on Citadel. Secondly, having become familiar with captured German documents, it is hard not to separate from the feeling that they contain an element of the failure to understand the essence of the partisan problem and apprehension over the growing partisan movement and its large inherent potential. The army command approached the analysis of this problem and the elaboration of its optional decisions in a purely standard form, which is to say in a routine manner, relying only on its own interpretation of the events and life values, without troubling itself to consider the mindset of a Soviet citizen and especially the details of his or her character. As a result, the combat tactics employed to destroy the partisan area proved ineffective and did great harm to the occupiers.

The operation began on 16 May 1943. Taking advantage of its numerical superiority, combat equipment and the relatively high mobility of the troops, as well as the confusion in Emliutin's headquarters in the first days, which led to poor direction of the partisan detachments, within a matter of five days the enemy's assault groups made a deep penetration into the partisans' base area and isolated a number of its detachments. The Shchors Brigade (731 men), the Kravtsov Brigade (more than 600 men) the 1st K.E. Voroshilov Brigade (up to 550 men) and the Death to German Occupiers Brigade (around 1,000 men) fell into encirclement together with D.V. Emliutin's headquarters, and in the process contact with a majority of the partisan detachments was lost. From the Ninth Army's journal of combat operations for 20 May:

> The anti-partisan operation Gypsy Baron is proceeding according to plan. The operation's objectives for the day have been easily achieved with no significant enemy resistance. However, they have been substantially complicated by the incessant rains and poor road conditions. Enemy losses in this operation with the inclusion of previous successes amount to 145 killed, 30 wounded, 36 captured, and 242 – dispersed. Captured gear: three light machine guns, eight rifles, as well as a certain amount of munitions and explosives. Fifteen bandit camps have been destroyed.[291]

Already, on 21 May, German forces seized the sector of railroad between Mikhalovsky and Unecha, and movement along it toward the front was resumed. The situation in the encircled areas rapidly deteriorated for the defenders; the partisans were running low on food, medications and ammunition. The Central Front command became involved in the struggle. Bomber divisions of the 16th Air Army struck aggregations of enemy troops in the areas of Altukhovo, Glinnoe, Suzemka, Krasnaia Sloboda, Kokorevka and Ostrye Luki. In addition, once the sun set, aircraft were delivering vital supplies to the Briansk forests, but their amount was not large, and the situation worsened with each passing day.

291 NARA US, T.312, R.317, F.7886095.

The documents of the Ninth Army regarding the operation in the first five days of it were filled with victorious rhetoric. However, already on 21 May its Operations Department recognized: "In the rear area of the Second Panzer Army, the anti-partisan Operation Gypsy Baron is running behind schedule. The enemy is putting up fierce resistance to the 18th Panzer Division attacking in the center."[292] Just a day before this, Harpe, realizing that the operation was beginning to bog down, decided to commit a grouping from the Second Panzer Army to the anti-partisan operations: the 709th Special Purpose Ost Truppen; Ost Battalions 328, 582, 628, 629 and 640; and the Ost Companies 102 and 178. A week later, the headquarters of the Ninth Army, anticipating that the partisans might slip away into Ukraine, began urgently bringing up fresh forces to the Briansk forests, including a battalion of the German special service Regiment Brandenburg-800. Both decisions were aimed not at reinforcing the already available forces, but in order to enhance their effectiveness and to keep the losses of the regular combat units low. That their casualties and loss of equipment were substantial could no longer be concealed. The Ninth Army's journal of combat operation notes, "The enemy resistance has weakened, and they have frequently begun to withdraw without combat. However, on our side there have been numerous casualties from minefields. The future attack must focus on the objective of freeing the supply routes."[293] So already on the seventh day of the operation, the destruction of partisans in this area was no longer front and central, but at a minimum to reestablish control over the lines of communication.

The partisans fought fiercely, using every available means of struggle, as well as such things as tanks, which were unusual for "forest warriors". For example, on 27 May the 7th Infantry Division captured a T-34 tank, which the partisans had used during a counterattack against its units.[294] Altogether, according to the account of Army Group Center's headquarters, over the three weeks of operations, three T-34 tanks were captured. These tanks had previously belonged to the armies of the Briansk Front, which for various reasons back in 1941 had been forced to leave them behind when breaking out of encirclement, and they had been found and put back into service by partisan tinkerers.

Other than tanks, in photographs taken by Soviet frontline reporters who visited partisan formations in the Orel area in the spring and summer of 1943, one can also see BA-10 armored cars, which were also restored to service and took part in the struggle with occupiers even in the summer of 1943.[295] Likely, the use of these heavy types of weapons by the "bandits" was unexpected for the men of the Wehrmacht's army units and made an especially chilling impression on the enlisted men. However, there were only few of these tanks and armored cars, so their employment did not yield a big result. Significantly more effective were the methods of struggle typical for partisans. Here's how the commander of the 98th Infantry Division General of Infantry Martin Gareis describes its participation in Gypsy Baron:

> On 20 May the four kampfgruppen stepped off to create the first of the concentric rings around the vast green labyrinth of boggy mounds, reeds and shrubs in the dense thickets,

---

292 NARA US, T.312, R.317, F.7886097.
293 NARA US, T.312, R.317, F.7886098.
294 Töppel, *Kursk 1943*, p. 38.
295 Today these photographs are preserved in the Russian State Archive of Film and Photo Documents in Krasnogorsk.

where even in Tsarist times shadowy folk sought and found shelter. In the damp, sultry air, judging from the radio messages, the first objective has been achieved. There is no apparent enemy between the edge of the forest and the troops. Then scouts headed into the labyrinth, a blocking force was established, communications equipment was moved up, and most importantly, secure communications were established between the units. The conditions were other worldly. The command stayed in place and directed the operation over the radio.

The sappers had work up to their necks: to clear the mined trails and to lay bridges in place of those that had been destroyed or were too short. The efforts expended on this in order to force or cut our way through these thickets were not in any comparison with the expected success. On 21 and 22 May, the assembled troops engaged in bitter combat – only not with a living enemy! Each inch of the wilderness or swamps had to be won from the forest step by step. In addition, on 22 May the rain persisted from sunrise to sunset. And what was the result? Earthen fortifications abandoned by the partisans. The nest was empty! The bird had flown away!

… On 24 May at 0700 after the next rainy night, the ring of encirclement closed in to the final cordon. However, the net had been cast in vain. It contained neither the colonel [according to the German version, a colonel was commanding the partisans], nor a unit of 2-3,000 partisans. The encampment had been abandoned, the fish had swum off, though to all it was obvious that it just been there! But the net closed around nothing. The losses in our ranks were not many, but the partisan band also did not suffer … Having scattered into small groups, using ingenuity, the forest residents had dissolved into the thickets.[296]

Even so, by the end of the month, grievous damage had been done to the partisans, their resources had virtually dried up, and starvation had begun in certain detachments. On 31 May the Germans seized the partisan airfield at the village of Smelizh and had pushed back three of the partisan brigades to the Desna River. The total area now being defended by them had dwindled to approximately 6 square kilometers.

From a special report of the 1st Department of the USSR National Committee of State Security's 4th Directorate in the name of B.Z. Kobulov, a 2nd Rank Commissar of State Security:

All of the partisan brigades have been badly battered; two brigade commanders and the commanders of many detachments have been killed, and many partisans have been captured by the enemy. Some of the partisans of one of the brigades slipped away to the police. The situation is extremely grave; armed men in the brigades and detachments have become fewer, and hunger is occurring. The enemy is isolating the partisans. For the struggle against the partisans, the Chief Kaminsky's police brigade of the Lokots' District has been moved out into the forests.[297]

---

296 Gareis, M., *98-ia pekhotnaia diviziia* [*98th Infantry Division*] (Moscow: Tsentrpoligraf, 2013), p. 223.
297 *Ognennaia duga: Kurskaia bitva glazami Lubianki* [*Bulge of Fire: Battle of Kursk in the eyes of the Lubianka*] (Moscow, 2003), p. 273.

At this critical moment, Moscow at last took a number of decisive steps to save the partisans. It started with a change in command. The Central Headquarters of the partisan movement reported to Stalin on 1 June:

> The commander of the Joint Headquarters of the Briansk detachments Emliutin in the first days showed complete confusion, lost command and communications with the units, and completely removed himself from the organization of resistance ... As a result, he did not consider it necessary and did not insist on helpful steps on our part. Disorganization and desertions became evident in the detachments and brigades. In this situation with the sanction of the Secretary of the Orel Oblast Committee of the All-Union Communist Party of Bolsheviks Comrade Matveev decision was made on the spot to appoint Lieutenant Colonel of Border Troops A.P. Gorshkov and Commissar Hero of the Soviet Union Comrade Bondarenko in command of the partisan groups and detachments.[298]

D.V. Emliutin was a man who not only had managed to survive the hardest period of creating a resistance movement at the end of 1941 and beginning of 1942, he also stepped forward as one of its prominent organizers. It was to his credit that a number of major successful operations and large diversions was prepared and conducted (including the blowing up of the Goluboi Bridge), for which he was deemed worthy of the Gold Star. Nevertheless, it was difficult to demand from a former chief of a district department of the NKVD, which he was before the start of the war, the accurate, calibrated actions on the level of a commander of a large combat formation (virtually a division) – especially moreover in the conditions where the enemy had a five-times superiority in forces and means. Yet at the same time a question arises: "If in the course of two successive weeks he could not grasp the situation, then what was the Chief of the Central Headquarters of the Partisan Movement Lieutenant General P.K. Ponomarenko, who was located at that time in the headquarters of the Central Front as a member of its Military Council together with two of his headquarters, that of the Central Headquarters of the Partisan Movement and the Briansk Headquarters of the Partisan Movement, doing at that time? For the sake of justice, I will note that collaborationists serving in the German Ost battalions that were taking part in the punitive operations were also deserting to the partisans. For example, more than 800 servicemen of the Ost battalions at this time joined the partisan detachments.

In the second place, Moscow began to increase the delivery by air of the most necessary loads at the end of May. This, however, came too late.

Finally, and most importantly, the decision was made to assemble quickly the remnants of the partisan detachments and brigades and to pull them out of the pocket. The Germans from the first days of the operation were in fact concerned about this possibility, especially if a dual attack was launched from the front and rear of the XX Army Corps, which was extremely weak, and did everything to prevent this from happening. Back on 18 May, the Operations Department of the Ninth Army's headquarters observed: "The successes achieved yesterday with the conducting of Gypsy Baron allow the consideration that it will be finished on schedule.

---

298 AP RF, F.3, Op.50, D.475, l. 51.

However, it is not rendering any large influence on the situation at the front, and here, as before, one must consider the possibility of coordinated attacks from the front and rear."[299]

On the night of 1-2 June 1943, remnants of the partisan formations that had managed to assemble quickly around the new leadership, entered the breakthrough at the hamlet of Pionersky. In the course of bitter fighting and suffering heavy casualties, they nevertheless managed to break out to friendly lines. The isolated pockets of partisans remaining in the forests continued to fight on, but from this moment on, the intensity of the combat operations began quickly to subside.

On 6 June, Operation Gypsy Baron officially came to an end, or more accurately, it was wrapped up, because in essence it had not achieved any of its goals – the destruction of the partisan formations in the Briansk forests. The main reason for this was the time pressure that Model's Ninth Army was already under, as well as the substantial lagging of the anti-partisan operation behind the schedule: the two weeks that had been set aside for it had turned into almost an entire month. Therefore, the question of the need to withdraw the forces from Briansk forests quickly became acute. After all, Hitler's order about starting Citadel on 12 June still had not been cancelled and there were no signs yet that he would do so. Field Marshal von Kluge by this time had returned from Germany and was brought up to date by his staff about what had been happening in his absence. On 31 May, after the next meeting with "Corps Breitenbuch", during a conversation with Harpe, he openly acknowledged that the elimination of the bandits was taking place in extremely difficult conditions and that the combat operations had become excessively prolonged. The Field Marshal understood that he wouldn't be able to share equally the responsibility with Model for the failure to assemble the assault grouping of the Ninth Army in its jumping-off positions on time. So, on 1 June 1943, he reported to the OKH (as did von Manstein at the same time) that in the current situation, the troops wouldn't be ready to implement Citadel any sooner than 25 June. The OKH took heed of this circumstance and on 5 June issued a preliminary directive to postpone the offensive until 20 June, but the precise date for it would be determined later.

Two days later, H. von Elverfeldt issued a report about a victory in the Briansk forests:

> Operation Gypsy Baron, which pursued the objective of sweeping clear the triangular area where the Seva and Nerussa Rivers merge, has been successfully concluded. The Second Panzer Army in today's report announced its results: 1,568 prisoners, 869 turncoats, and 1,584 killed. A large quantity of weapons has also been captured. Gratitude has been expressed to all the units and headquarters that took part in the operation. After the conclusion of Operation Gypsy Baron, the Corps Headquarters 532 that was responsible for its coordination became renamed as Reserve Headquarters 3. From 8 June it will be made subordinate to Gruppe Weiss, after which it will acquire its old designation, "Headquarters Breitenbuch".[300]

---

299 NARA US, T.312, R.317, F.7886094.
300 NARA US, T.312, R.317, F.7886115.

According to the information of the German historian R. Töppel, all of the partisans that were captured alive were subsequently shot, pursuant to an order about how to handle "bandit" prisoners.[301]

On 9 June the Ninth Army headquarters again returned to this subject and emphasized: "The insurance of security in the rear area is no longer a matter of top priority."[302] However, these "incantations" shouldn't be taken seriously. In essence, this was a grain of wheat in a mountain of chaff. In fact, at this moment the number of sabotage attacks against the rear lines of communication in the zone of the Ninth Army had noticeably declined. However, this lull did not last for long, and later that same month in the rear of von Kluge's Army Group Center, explosions began to thunder and trains began to fly off the rails. Colonel Teske honestly recognized:

> In June, the last month of strategic concentration, we saw another increase in troop movements for the attack units. Simultaneously, the number of interruptions in traffic and partisan raids increased to an average of twenty-four per day, culminating in the loss of 298 locomotives, 1,222 cars, and forty-four bridges throughout Army Group Center's area. Soviet air raids were limited to the immediate area of the strategic buildup and struck the railroad stations at Briansk, Orel and Karachev. A counteraction against the partisans in the badly infested woods south of Briansk – Gypsy Baron – involved eleven front-line divisions and brought only temporary relief.[303]

Now for the sake of comparison, here are a few figures, now from the documents of Army Group Center about the partisan activities on its line of rail communications. If in April 1943 626 sabotage attacks, 210 attempts to cause train crashes, and the demolition of 1,760 linear meters of rails were noted, then in June these indicators grew and amounted to 841, 272 and 1,780 respectively.[304]

At the same time, the official German figures regarding the harm done to the partisans by the punitive forces pale next to the forces involved in the operation. For three weeks, 50,000 men together with tanks, artillery and air support were beating through the forested areas in order to eliminate less than 4,000 lightly armed people who were unprepared to take on a regular army! In addition, the divisions that took part in Gypsy Baron also suffered losses in killed and wounded, and their personnel became exhausted. Here is just one case: the 7th Panzer Division lost a total of 859 men, including 37 killed or missing in action (four officers and 33 enlisted men and junior officers; and 828 wounded (183 officers and 639 enlisted men and junior officers).[305] On 5 June, the XXXXVI Panzer Corps received an order from the headquarters of the Ninth Army: "Pay attention to the fact that in recent days, the 7th Panzer Division has valiantly engaged in heavy combat in almost impassable wooded terrain. Therefore, it needs rest and the

---

301 Töppel, *Kursk 1943*, p. 38.
302 NARA US, T.312, R.317, F.7886119.
303 Newton, *Kurskaia bitva: nemetskii vzgliad*, p. 268.
304 *Pod nemtsami: Vospominaniia, svidetel'stva, dokumenty*, p. 485.
305 Töppel, *Kursk 1943*, pp. 38-39.

opportunity to bring itself back into order as soon as possible. It is necessary to anticipate all these steps as far as is possible."[306]

I will add that in addition to the aforementioned forces of Army Group Center, there were other divisions drawn into participating in Operation Gypsy Baron and used in the struggle against the partisans at this time, which also suffered casualties before being sent to take part in "Citadel". In particular the 6th Infantry Division had been activated for Operation Free Defense, which was conducted in parallel with Operation Gypsy Baron between 21 and 30 May 1943 in the rear area of the Second Panzer Army. Yet in the beginning of July 1943, this division would be deployed on the axis of main attack of Model's Ninth Army.

According to certain documents, the command of Army Group Center was assuming that this operation would not only alter the situation in its rear, but also in the course of it the divisions of the XXXXVII Panzer Corps would receive a unique form of combat training and seasoning prior to the offensive toward Kursk. Field Marshal von Kluge and his chief of staff Krebs during Operation Gypsy Baron more than once visited the corps headquarters in order to look into the details, obtain briefings on the combat operations, and try to grasp how far the expectations for it were being justified. However, in practice everything proved much more difficult. Already after the war, the Second Army's operations chief Colonel Peter von der Groeben rightfully acknowledged: "Unfortunately, the anti-partisan operation consumed time and resulted in considerable losses, especially in motor vehicles. Although it can be argued that the spearhead divisions participating in this operation did receive valuable training while engaging in "bush warfare," this experience could by no means be considered sufficient to prepare them for the kind of fighting they would have to do in open terrain, assaulting prepared Soviet positions."[307]

Moreover, the men of the infantry and panzer divisions of Lemelsen's panzer corps that took part in the operation became physically worn down and psychologically stressed. The spring thaw and the swampy forested areas did not allow the wide use of motorized transport for the troops. The Wehrmacht officers and soldiers that were involved in the operation had trouble getting accustomed to the partisan tactics, when they could virtually look the enemy in the eye, and when they could expect a bullet or the detonation of a booby trap from each hillock or patch of shrubs. In this respect, the collaborationist units had an advantage, since they had been built up from local residents as well (for example, Kaminsky's brigade). This factor had a serious effect on their psyche of the German soldiers. One of the consequences of this became concentrated artillery strikes throughout the forested areas (just like before an attack against field positions), where it was possible (!) that partisans might be lurking. However, the preliminary reconnaissance was not always thorough, and sometimes they had to rely on the information from turncoats, which was not always so reliable, so the barrage effects proved modest: often, there were simply no partisans in the attacked areas, while shells and mortar rounds often hit empty space. The expenditure of ammunition was accordingly excessive. Even before the "victorious announcements" subsided, this problem became extremely acute. On 10 June the Ninth Army headquarters noted:

---

306 NARA US, T.312, R.317, F.7886113.
307 Newton, *Kurskaia bitva: nemetskii vzgliad*, p. 138.

> The Oberquartermeister is reporting on the large expenditure of shells at the front over recent days and the large expenditure of ammunition during Gypsy Baron by the units that were operating in the army's rear. As a result, an unfavorable situation has emerged with the supply of shells for Citadel. It might take a long time to make up for the shortage. Therefore, aid has been requested in resolving this problem.[308]

It is interesting that the German military machine, as praised by its memoirists for its smooth teamwork and precision, was working in this manner. From whom was the army command seeking help? After all, back on 5 June, Army Group Center's Operations Department had informed H. von Elverfeldt through Telegram No.3398/43:

> The situation with shells for light field howitzers designated for Operation Citadel has worsened and the build-up of needed stockpiles of shells remains under question. In addition, complications with the supply of machine-gun bullets, the expenditure of which has exceeded the planned indicators in view of the enemy's high activity, is observable. Army Group Center has requested the full supply of the necessary reserves of ammunition.[309]

The circle had closed!

Skipping somewhat ahead in the events, I will note that there was no success in resolving this problem prior to the Battle of Kursk. This would hamper the troops already in the offensive's first days. In conclusion, I will offer one more citation. On 8 July, the OKH Headquarters in a report on the partisan activity over April to June 1943 observed: "Partisan activity on the entire eastern expanse over the preceding quarter of the year is continuing to strengthen. ... Our measures regarding the struggle with the partisans, despite the commitment of major forces (for example, for the first time in the southern region of Army Group Center we introduced significant forces by postponing Operation Citadel in order to pacify the main area of partisan activity in the Briansk region) have not brought the desired success."[310] This, of course, is a rather candid evaluation.

The partisan pressure on the lines of communication in Army Group South's rear was also building at this time. In a report from the General Staff Headquarters of the OKW, there is the note: "The partisan movement in Ukraine has become especially widespread, and this is adversely affecting the supply of our army with food."[311] However, because of the absence of expansive forested tracts and the better developed road network, the partisan problem did not become as acute as it did in the Orel salient. General P. Sudoplatov, one of the leaders of the subversive work in the Wehrmacht's rear, observed:

---

308 NARA US, T.312, R.317, F.7886120.
309 NARA US, T.312, R.317, F.7886113.
310 *Sovetskie partizany: Iz istorii partizanskogo dvizheniia v gody Velikoi Otechestvennoi voiny* [*Soviet partisans: From the history of the partisan movement in the years of the Great Patriotic War*] (Moscow, 1963), pp. 261-262.
311 KTV/OKW. Bd. III, p. 775.

> In the steppe oblasts and districts of Ukraine, it was exceptionally difficult to organize partisan formations and sabotage acts on the railroads. In the western forested territories, our operational groups achieved great successes. However, their operations were complicated by the constant combat contacts with bandits of the OUN Ukrainian nationalists, who actively cooperated with the Nazi occupiers.[312]

It was precisely this reason why Erich von Manstein did not have to pull any of his panzer corps back into the rear in order to combat partisans prior to the attack toward Kursk, unlike Walter Model.

After the postponement of the start of Citadel, the work to put the finishing touches on the plan became a secondary matter in the headquarters of the Ninth Army, even though the problems of the future offensive remained a priority just as before. From mid-May the main attention of its subordinates General Harpe and H. von Elverfeldt, who had returned from a short leave on 19 May, was focused on resolving problems along three directions: monitoring the decisions of the Russian command and preparing measures to reveal its immediate intentions; training and increasing the combat readiness of the troops; and improving the logistics infrastructure and replenishing the forces with the necessary supplies of fuel, ammunition and food. All of these problems were closely interrelated, so it was difficult to assign priority to any one of them.

However, if to analyze the documents of its headquarters thoroughly between the end of April and the beginning of June, it is plainly discernible that nevertheless more attention was given to revealing the intentions of the Soviet side. Indeed, this was not simply because Hitler back in Order No. 5 had set one of the main tasks for the troops to preempt the Russians' offensive as much as possible. The Ninth Army's headquarters was staffed with professionals who were highly qualified for those times, and there was no need to explain to them that the army was not ready at this time to implement Citadel. Its subordinate forces still had not been brought back up to strength, and the defense of the Orel salient was openly weak. Meanwhile, the Red Army was rapidly building up its forces. Messages about this were going out throughout all the channels of command. The Chief of Staff of Luftflotte Six, General of Fliers Friedrich Kless, recalled:

> Strong ground forces had been moved into the Kursk salient, deployed in defensive lines that were unusually strong and uncommonly far echeloned in depth. Beginning in April, these forces received a steadily swelling stream of equipment and personnel reinforcements that gradually exceeded the size of anything required by a purely defensive deployment. The only rail line feeding the Kursk area (which ran Voronezh – Kastornoe – Kursk) was carrying trains in uninterrupted succession while reconnaissance flights frequently discerned major nighttime movements approaching and/or starting for Kursk on the highways. The same was partially true of daytime movements on the highways. Aerial photographs also revealed an extraordinary increase in the number of still-unoccupied but completely constructed artillery emplacements. We likewise identified a strong Soviet buildup in the Sukhinichi – Kozelsk – Belev area,

---

312 Sudoplatov, P., *Pobeda v tainoi voine 1941-1945 godov* [*Victory in the secret war of 1941-1945*] (Moscow: OLMA-PRESS, 2005), p. 339.

which was closely watched for strategic reasons. Between these two concentrations, reconnaissance identified tactical points of potential enemy main effort near Novosil and southwest of Bolkhov.[313]

In a communique dated 23 May 1943, this is how Elverfeldt's staff assessed the Soviet movements and their plans for the nearest future:

> The enemy has ceased the intensive steps to strengthen the defenses and has shifted to the second phase of implementing their supposed plan. The enemy's significant artillery forces and the presence of their major reserves has created good possibilities for parrying the German attack in any direction. This also does not exclude the presence of enemy plans of launching an attack himself with the aim of breaching the front of the Orel bulge.[314]

The powerful airstrikes launched by Soviet aircraft and conducted between 6 and 8 May on the major airfields in the area of the Kursk bulge and lines of communication, as well as the increased reconnaissance activity of the Central Front also heightened the concern of the Ninth Army's command, because they were taken as a clear sign of preparations for an offensive.[315]

In connection with this, Ninth Army command was paying particularly focused attention to the flanks of the Orel salient. Model's troops were holding its southern face, while the majority of the bulge (its northern and eastern faces) was being defended by the Second Panzer Army. In Russian historiography of the Battle of Kursk, undeservedly little attention has been paid to this German panzer army, and if any attention is given to it at all, it is described as weak and playing no significant role. In reality, like all the armies of von Kluge's Army Group Center, throughout the entire preparatory period for the summer campaign, the Second Panzer Army served as a "donor" to the Ninth Army. Thus, the situation in its forces became extremely difficult. According to Steven Newton, by the beginning of July, its total strength amounted to 160,000 men, which was 54,000 less than the establishment strength. The most dangerous aspect of this was that the majority of the personnel shortage was found in the combat formations. Of its 15 divisions, only eight carried a rating of "attack capable" (which is to say fully combat-ready), while four were rated as "capable for limited attacks only" (worn), one was rated as "defensive-capable only" (meaning it had suffered substantial losses), and two were rated as "limited-defensive", the lowest category for a line division. It should be added that it was at this time that the table strength of artillery, the most important means for conducting defensive fighting, was reduced. In the batteries of the divisional artillery, the number of guns fell from four to three, and the army was short of its authorized number of artillery pieces by 119 light and 32 field howitzers. Yet the sectors being held by the Second Panzer Army's divisions were significantly extended (up to 30 km per division), while virtually the army's entire motorized transport had been removed from it in order to bolster the Ninth Army.[316] Only the ground where its troops were deployed aided the defense; it made it difficult to employ large armored

---

313 Newton, *Kurskaia bitva: nemetskii vzgliad*, pp. 192-193.
314 NARA US, T.312, R.317, F.7886099.
315 NARA US, T.312, R.317, F.7886090.
316 Newton, *Kurskaia bitva: nemetskii vzgliad*, p. 537.

formations and contained a system of lines, saturated with artificial obstacles, that had begun to be constructed back in 1942.

The Orel salient, which was advantageous for the launching of converging attacks by the Russians at its base, plus the weakness of the Second Panzer Army, was prompting the German command to the thought that the Soviet side might execute a plan similar to Citadel here – and was probably even preparing for one. The Ninth Army's war diary from 24 May states:

> With respect to the assembly of major enemy strength on the Second Panzer Army's front to the north of the Orel salient, the question has arisen about the possibility of an enemy attack in this area. Therefore, the need to earmark strong mobile reserves from Gruppe Weiss has appeared, which in the event of danger can be shifted to the north. It was decided that the commanders or the chiefs of staff of the 2nd, 9th and 12th Panzer Divisions will establish direct communications with the LIII Army Corps for this purpose, so in case of necessity the forces of these divisions can be quickly transferred to the north, into the sector of the LIII Corps. New ideas have arisen as well on the matter of commanding the forces located at the tip of the Orel salient, if the enemy launches an attack from north to south. In the event of this it is sensible to change the allocation of responsibilities between the army headquarters, in order to guarantee the uninterrupted command and control over the forces. This conclusion was immediately reported up to the army group.[317]

Because of the threat of a Soviet offensive, the constant concern of the command staff of Model's Ninth Army right up to early July was the elaboration of measures to strengthen the front of the Orel bulge (especially on its right flank, in the sector of the XX Army Corps, which was holding the southern base of the salient), and to form a strong mobile reserve and keep it combat-ready. On 15 May the Ninth Army's Operations Department sent an order to the corps, which directed the consideration of the possibility of the urgent movement of the 9th and 12th Panzer Divisions, which were located at that time in the army's reserve, and to reconnoiter additional routes of movement for them quickly. On 8 June, with consideration of fresh alarming intelligence, the army issued an order regarding a schedule of movement for the mobile divisions that were located in the reserve at that time: the 4th and 18th Panzer Divisions, as well as the 10th Panzergrenadier Division, which was already in the sector of defense of the Second Panzer Army's XXXV and LV Army Corps (holding the northern base of the salient and its tip, respectively).[318]

The concern of Model and his staff over the situation in the XX Army Corps, which was unquestionably justified and stemmed from the significant problems which had accumulated in this army that were difficult to resolve at this time, and the high activity of the 65th Army that was holding the Soviet line opposite it. One of the most complicated questions concerned transport communications. Even in early June 1943, the roads in its sector were hardly passable for ordinary motorized transport. Naturally, this affected the possibility of maneuvering the forces in case of an enemy attack. There was only one way out – corduroying the roads with

---

317 NARA US, T.312, R.317, F.7886100.
318 NARA US, T.314, R.1126, F.000134.

logs, but in the meantime there was neither the manpower nor the trees for this, while the fortification of the main belt of defense and the struggle with partisans were ongoing.

Nevertheless, the main problem was the low strength of its divisions, especially if you consider that it was positioned not only at the base of the Orel bulge, but also at the boundary between the Ninth Army and Second Army. Any more or less noticeable movement in the sector of the Soviet 65th Army that was opposing it immediately caused alarm bells to ring in Elverfeldt's headquarters. It was continuously stimulated by the poor knowledge of the situation beyond the Soviet forces' tactical zone (even 10-15 km in the depth) and the recognition that the forces and means in the army were still inadequate even for a defense.

Thus, for example, on 15 May the Ninth Army's Operations Department noted: "Ground and aerial observation over the Russian 65th Army's rear area haven't permitted the detection of significant changes. Thus, the supposition of the enemy's preparation for an attack in this area hasn't been confirmed."[319] A bit later, in the course of Operation Gypsy Baron, information again arrived that supposedly a Soviet breakthrough attack was in planning here, but it also proved to be inaccurate: "According to the testimony of deserters, the partisan bands remaining in the woods have been forced to search for a way to break out through the front lines. For this the Russians are planning a frontal attack with army units. In anticipation of this, on 1, 2 and 3 June the divisions of XX Corps will be brought up to full combat readiness in a defensive arrayal. Gruppe Weiss has appealed to Army Group Center today for authorization to send understaffed battalions of the 45th Infantry Division in order to create free march battalions."[320] In the early days of June, a serious incident would actually occur in Roman's corps, but the German command, despite its focused attention on this area, wouldn't be ready for it.

Operation Samara, which had been devised back in April, also shows the significance which the command of Army Group Center attached to the XX Corps' sector. In the historiography of the Battle of Kursk (neither in Russian nor in foreign) has it ever been mentioned, yet in captured German sources this plan comes up often. When preparing this book, I contacted a number of Western scholars, but they were also unable to make clear what this operation was about. This was not in fact because the operation was so secret. It is simply because scholars did not understand how seriously the Germans regarded specifically the possibility of a Russian attack from out of this area and in general the encirclement of their forces in the Orel salient when preparing for Citadel. In addition, the question of a possible preemption of the Wehrmacht offensive toward Kursk by the Soviet side was closely intermingled here with Model's lack of desire to conduct it at all.

The main objective which the command of the Ninth Army set for Operation Samara was to determine the Russians' genuine intentions, and the main assignment for the troops involved in its implementation was to reduce (straighten out) the 45th Infantry Division's sector of the line, and thereby free up part of its strength in order to form a corps reserve. Thus, the success of this local operation was supposed to expand the capabilities of Roman's corps on the defensive, even if not very significantly. As is observed in documents of the Ninth Army's headquarters from 15 May: "As a result of the shortening of the front, a more advantageous line will be achieved, as well as the ability to free up two battalions. <u>In addition, this operation should be viewed as</u>

---

319 NARA US, T.312, R.317, F.7886092.
320 NARA US, T.312, R.317, F.7886112.

a "general rehearsal" prior to Citadel. (!) The main task of such a rehearsal is the study of the enemy's behavior at the start of a German offensive."[321]

The word "rehearsal" shouldn't be understood literally. The operation's idea stemmed from Walter Model, and its plan was approved by G. von Kluge on 16 May. At this time the offensive toward Kursk was a future matter, so the main thing that the command of the Ninth Army was seeking was to provoke the 65th Army, in order to reveal the disposition of its troops (whether defensive or offensive), and to assess their level of training and degree of cooperation. If defensive, then belief in victory would have increased, but if it became clear that the Russians themselves were ready to attack and only waiting for the right moment, then that would be one more reason to cancel Citadel altogether. In addition, in the course of the fighting, definite knowledge would be gleaned about the system of fortifications and drawn from the experience of overcoming them. The fact that this operation was countermanded immediately after Hitler reached his final decision about conducting Citadel shows that it was these factors, and not the two battalions made available for a reserve, were primary. As the Ninth Army's journal of combat operations notes on 22 June: "At 1900, the Operations Department over the telephone issued a directive to the operations officer of the XX Army Corps that in the interests of ensuring a strong defense, the conducting of Operation Samara has been cancelled at an order from the army group. The corps is to report the quantity of needed mines and building materials promptly."[322]

The command of the Ninth Army was devoting significant efforts at this time to the combat training of the troops, as was the southern assault grouping, Army Group South. They were not simply conducting tactical exercises regularly; there was also a concise order to the subordinate corps: Make sure that all of the battalions, including the march battalions [of new replacements] and those who have already joined the army, have undergone rehearsals in the field. In the process, ensure both the standard array of training is tested (the ability to take up a defense quickly, to camouflage positions, to operate as part of a unit, etc.), and teach the soldiers to overcome Soviet positions, taking into account the arriving aerial reconnaissance information from the areas of the Kursk bulge. For example, the Fourth Panzer Army's headquarters, relying on aerial photographs of the Voronezh Front's positions, replicated sectors of them in the Khar'kov area, where assault teams of the infantry divisions went through training. In Army Detachment Kempf, artificial bodies of water (ponds) were built, which imitated conditions similar to those on the Severskii Donets River and taught the grenadiers to cross them in boats while under fire.

In the Ninth Army as well, work was in full swing each day until the late evening hours, but it had its own particular details. In the first days of May, Tiger tanks began to arrive, an innovation of the German tank building industry, which were still unknown to its troops, so they were immediately forwarded to testing areas. The commander of the 2nd Panzer Division Lieutenant General Vollrath Lübbe recalled:

> The division in early May was transferred from the area west of Smolensk to the area south of Orel ... While the division was located in the rear south of Orel it underwent intense combat training. Tactical exercises went on around the clock, both at the squad

---

321 Ibid.
322 NARA US, T.312, R.317, F.7886133.

and platoon levels, and as part of companies and battalions, all the way up to the reinforced panzer division. During these exercises, march drills and the actions of panzer and panzer grenadier units when closing with the enemy (reconnoitering of the terrain, reconnaissance) and in combat stood front and center. Particularly important significance was given to the thorough training of the radio operators and maintaining direct contact over the radio. The panzer battalion of Tigers, which had been assigned a special task as part of the 2nd Panzer Division, conducted separate tactical exercises.[323]

The first joint training between units of the 2nd Panzer Division and the crews of the new Tigers of Heavy Panzer Battalion 505, which Model personally attended, took place on 15 May. In the Ninth Army headquarter's document file, there is the note:

> The training brought great satisfaction. However, significant shortcomings were also revealed, which require elimination. Among them, the most substantial was the fact that the 2nd Panzer Division's evacuation and repair battalion since the moment of the end of the latest fighting hasn't increased its level of training. The commander ordered this unit, and also the reconnaissance battalions of the 2nd and 9th Panzer Division, to conduct intensified training urgently.[324]

Not everything went smoothly with the Tigers either. In early summer, on 2 June, tests of their off-road capabilities were held. The task was not very difficult: two Pz.Kpfw. VI were to make a forced crossing of a boggy creek ranging from 4.5 to 7.5-meters wide, but both attempts ended in failure; both heavy tanks became stuck, and they had to use prime movers to extract them. It became clear that the offspring of Erwin Anders and the Henschel firm was not up to such obstacles. This conclusion forced the battalion command to seek a solution to the problem, because the forthcoming operation was going to cross broken ground cut by streams and deep ravines. Within a certain amount of time, the following decision was proposed: to remove the turrets from outdated Pz.Kpfw. III tanks and convert them into bridge layers. The commander of the XXXXVII Panzer Corps General of Panzer Troops J. Lemelsen supported the idea but could not get Model to agree with it. As a result, a sorry scandal kicked up a din before the start of Citadel. These were the first, but far from last training exercises of Heavy Panzer Battalion 505. Indeed, they all, for understandable reasons, drew the focused interest of the Ninth Army's higher command staff. The final exercises would take place just before the Battle of Kursk, on 25 June, and the commander of the XXXXVII Panzer Corps himself would be present to monitor them.

One interesting detail: The delivery of the Tigers to this area became known to the Soviet command almost as soon as the train carrying them arrived in Orel. This information became available by random chance. The intelligence summary from the Central Front's headquarters for 7 May 1943: "A captured pilot of a Focke-Wulf 190 fighter, who had to make a forced landing on 5 May in the area 20 km northeast of Maloarkhangel'sk, testified that during a mission on 3 May, while above the Orel railroad station he saw the unloading of 30 Tigers."[325]

323 TsAMO RF, F.15, Op.11600, D.1063, l. 88-89.
324 NARA US, T.312, R.317, F.7886091.
325 TsAMO RF, F.62, Op.323, D.11, l. 33.

There were fewer of the heavy machines than that – just 20, but 25 Pz.Kpfw. IV tanks had arrived together with them. They, probably, had been unloaded first, so the pilot was counting both the heavy tanks and the medium tanks still remaining on the platform cars. However, the fact is that Tiger tanks really were at the train station in Orel, and the Soviet command found out about this already on 5 May – that is the case. The train carrying the heavy machines was not the last arrival of armored vehicles for the Ninth Army in this month. On 25 May it received another 10 Pz.Kpfw. III tanks with the long-barreled 75mm gun, five of which went to the 4th Panzer Division and the other five to the 20th Panzer Division.

The artillery was undergoing more substantial reinforcement at this time. Not only through the arrival of materiel, but also new formations. For example, on 5 June the Ninth Army headquarters received a message that the following formations had been allocated to it from the OKH Reserve: the Heavy Mortar Regiment 53, the headquarters of the Special Designation Artillery Regiment 41, Light Artillery Battalions 425, 851 and 855, II Battery of Heavy Artillery Battalion 64, and StuG Battalions 242 and 245. All of these units and elements, other than the assault guns, were supposed to arrive from Germany in the Mogilev area, while the self-propelled guns were already located near Gomel'. The arrival of the trains in Orel was planned on the night of 14-15 June. On 7 June, Mortar Regiment 51 arrived (two battalions of 150mm mortars and two battalions of 210mm mortars), and was promptly handed over to the XXIII Army Corps. The headquarters of the Heavy Mortar Battalions 18 and 19 had already been allocated to the XXXXVI and XXXXVII Panzer Corps, but these units had just formed up and had no combat experience. Therefore, the army headquarters ordered to move them up immediately after their arrival and be placed at the disposal of the corps commands for training and the development of their cooperation with the corps command. In addition, the arrival of the 2nd Battery of Artillery Battalion 59 (also for the XXIII Corps) and StuG Battalion 244 (for the XXXXI Panzer Corps) was anticipated from day to day.

The German command was also paying a large amount of attention to the psychological conditioning of the troops, especially of the arriving replacements. For example, back in early May, von Kluge had personally recommended to Model: "In order to bolster the combat spirit, it makes sense to inform the men about the mass murder in Katyn."[326] In addition, according to the recollections of veterans of the Battle of Kursk with whom I've been able to talk, during such "political discussions", a documentary film about the shooting of German prisoners by Soviet troops in Rostov back in 1941 was often shown. It is hard to say whether or not what was shown in the film actually happened, but as my conversation partners stated, after viewing it animosity toward the Red Army increased.

In parallel the OKH devised and on 7 May began to conduct a major propaganda operation, which received the code name "Silver Braid". The operation was directed at affecting the morale of the Red Army troops along the entire Eastern Front and undermining their resolve, and became one of the elements of the preparations for Citadel. At its basis was OKH Order No. 13 from 20 April 1943 "On the military personnel of the Red Army, who've voluntarily gone over to the side of the German Army." As the well-known specialist in the realm of the psychological warfare V.G. Krys'ko writes:

---

326 NARA US, T.312, R.317, F.7886072.

Its main task consisted in compelling as many Soviet soldiers as possible to cease resistance and surrender from the outset of the German offensive. In this, particular hopes were placed on General A.A. Vlasov's Russian Liberation Army, which had just started the process of forming. Therefore, the main slogan of the operation was: "Russians crossing over to Russians." A portion of the leaflets were signed by representatives of Vlasov's headquarters. The Vlasovites also were participating in the implementation of sound broadcasts. The operation's second task ... consisted in frightening Soviet soldiers with the threat of the use of the latest tanks (such as the Tiger and Panther tanks, as well as the Ferdinand self-propelled tank destroyers) and other weapons that were still unknown to them, and thereby prompt them to surrender or desert.

Finally, all the Soviet military personnel who declared themselves to be foes of Soviet power were promised a number of benefits during the period of their captivity. These benefits were confirmed by OKW Order No. 13 ..., which was issued with Hitler's approval. In the order it was emphasized that each serviceman of the Red Army who abandoned a unit at his own initiative and made his way on his own over to the German side would "be considered not prisoners of war, but a man who had voluntarily gone over to the German Army." Soviet officers who "voluntarily came over" were promised, in addition to a plentiful food ration and good treatment, one orderly for every three officers up to the rank of captain, one orderly for each two majors and above, and an individual orderly for each general.[327]

In the sector of Model's army, this operation was put into practice in the latter half of May. It is not clear why its command believed that it would be successful among the troops of the Central Front. On 11 May, Elverfeldt's headquarters noted: "Soon the start is anticipated of a planned operation, at the Führer's order, to stimulate deserters. The essence of 'Silver Braid' consists in scattering leaflets from aircraft. It is being assumed that it will be successful in the sector of Gruppe Weiss, so it is necessary to assign adequate effort to it."[328]

This large-scale propaganda campaign was conducted for almost the next three months. Over May and June 1943, 1,000,000,000 copies of leaflets were dropped over the entire Soviet-German front, and more than 32,000,000 leaflets alone were dropped in the area of the Kursk bulge in May 1943. In the sector of Army Group North, 49,000,000 leaflets were dropped, plus other propaganda material. However, the operation was a failure; the adversary did not see an enormous flow of turncoats. For example, in the sector of Army Group North, over the month of June 1943 only 655 servicemen of the Red Army went over to the enemy's side.

Unquestionably, the arriving replacements and heavy weapons, the daily training, and even the cunning operations described above on the whole increased the combat capability of the Ninth Army and nurtured hope for Citadel's successful outcome. However, even so, this was insufficient to meet the operation's objectives. First of all, an increase in the delivery of weapons and manpower had to be multiplied many times over, and Germany was not ready for such a surge, even in early June. Everyone concerned in the preparations for Citadel recognized this

---

327 Krys'ko, V.G., *Sekrety psikhologicheskoi voiny* [*Secrets of the psychological war*] (Minsk, 1999), p. 122.
328 NARA US, T.312, R.317, F.7886088.

serious problem, and the search for a solution to it was primarily the arguments that particularly flared up at the end of May.

Step by step with the approach of summer, stress began to grow on both sides of the front line. At the end of May, the Abwehr was continuing to report about the Russians' intensive work to fortify their positions and to assemble significant forces in the operational rear. Here is how the XXIII Corps wrote about this process:

> At the end of April, the construction of field fortifications was in an early stage. At the same time, the enemy's combat strength was around one rifle divisions. First the arrival of units of the 5th and 12th Divisions was identified; they took position in the second echelon primarily in the area of Maloarkhangel'sk. Striving to anticipate the execution of our plans, the enemy command from this moment on began swiftly to feed their northern Kursk front with a large quantity of fresh forces. This reinforcement particularly concerned the western flank of the 13th Russian Army, where fresh divisions from the Kursk area arrived. As a result of these measures, in the course of May the line of contact that extended from west to east developed into a powerful defensive line, centered around Maloarkhangel'sk. The 13th Army command possesses the exceptionally strong 8th Rifle Division, as well as powerful tank units: one tank brigade and two separate tank regiments, located in reserve. The approach of new units in order to reinforce the 13th Army's and 48th Army's reserve is expected.
>
> The combat strength of the enemy rifle companies, which at the end of April did not exceed 45 men, as a result of the arrival of march replacements, now varies between 60 and 80 men, which is approximately 33percent greater. The enemy field fortifications have become particularly stronger in comparison with where they stood on 1 April. More precisely, it has been fleshed out with a trench network, firing positions, artificial obstacles and minefields. The information from aerial reconnaissance, prisoner testimony and in part ground observation shows that the enemy command has exerted every effort in order to create a continuous, deeply-echeloned field defense. High ranking officers were constantly sent to organize and keep watch over these works. If the enemy command also has a plan for an offensive operation, then according to the available information it is impossible to draw any conclusions regarding it, at the very least regarding the sector of our corps.[329]

Similar information was coming in from several sources, and therefore not without justification it seemed to be fully correct, and it was hard to argue with these conclusions. However, in the first days of June 1943, the activity of Russian reconnaissance and assault parties rose significantly along the entire front of the Ninth Army. This quickly prompted an outburst of fresh concern. They were operating particularly aggressively in the sector of the XX Corps and on the right flank of the XXXXVI Panzer Corps, and in the opinion of Elverfeldt's staff, an alarming situation had unfolded here. For example, at 2030 on 1 June, after a brief artillery barrage, four penal companies of the 65th Army's 69th Rifle Division went on the attack against

---

329 NARA US, T.314, R.688, F.000754.

positions of the 45th Infantry Division's Infantry Regiment 133 and captured the villages of Samara, Usazha and Iamnoe. Prisoners and German equipment were seized.[330]

On the night of 1-2 June, a reconnaissance party of the 60th Army's 112th Rifle Division sallied forth against the combat positions of the 137th Infantry Division of the very same German corps, and wiped out up to a platoon of infantry and captured a situational map and other important documents.[331] At 0500 on 3 June, a penal company of the 65th Army's 354th Rifle Division attacked the positions of the 251st Infantry Division in the area of Trostenchik, which was located on the left flank of Roman's infantry corps, and took it. According to a report from the headquarters of the Central Front, thanks to the effect of surprise, up to 250 soldiers and officers were wiped out in this combat, and six prisoners of Infantry Regiment 471 were captured as well as impressive trophies: two anti-tank guns, four machine guns, six submachine guns and 12 rifles. At 1600, only in the course of the fifth counterattack was the Russian assault group driven back and the village retaken, though bitter fighting on its outskirts continued.[332]

On 4 June the 70th Army's 280th Rifle Division with four rifle companies attacked positions of the 258th Infantry Division's Infantry Regiment 479 in the vicinity of Hill 253.0 (3 km northwest of Tureika) after a 30-minute artillery preparation. The Soviet infantry took the first line of trenches and dug in there. In the following several days, all of the counterattacks in strength of up to a battalion with the support of tanks were fought off by them; 19 prisoners and German gear were taken, and four tanks were knocked out. In the bunker of one of the 258th Infantry Division's battalions, Soviet scouts discovered codes for the exchange of open and encoded telegrams that had been abandoned in panic by the fleeing radio operators. This attracted a serious investigation in the 258th Infantry Division and the guilty men were sent in front of a military tribunal.

Even though in a number of cases the German side plainly understood what was going on, they reacted slowly. For example, during the attack against Hill 253.0 on 6 June, the headquarters of the Ninth Army indicated:

> The enemy has brought up the 84th Guards Mortar Battalion and additional infantry forces to the left flank of the 258th Infantry Division. In the vicinity of Hill 253.0 it is possible to expect the enemy to go over to the defense. The expected enemy attack against the projecting hill is likely pursuing the aim of combat reconnaissance, <u>as well as the occupation of more favorable positions for a subsequent large offensive.</u> [Author's emphasis]

On the following day it was already regretfully reporting: "As a result of the lack of vigilance and poor defensive preparations, in the early morning hours in the sector of the 258th Infantry Division an enemy attack took place that had been readied since the prior evening. As a result, the enemy took Hill 253.0 practically without combat."[333]

Taking repossession of this hill cost the division dearly. In the documents of the army's headquarters, there is the note:

---

330 TsAMO RF, F.62, Op.321, D.104, l. 56.
331 TsAMO RF, F.62, Op.321, D.104, l. 60.
332 TsAMO RF, F.62, Op.321, D.104, l. 63-64.
333 NARA US, T.312, R.317, F.7886116.

In order to eliminate this penetration in the sector of the 258th Infantry Division, at 1800 two groups of dive bombers from the 1st Flieger Division and 64 pieces of artillery were assigned as reinforcements. At 2000 hand-to-hand combat with the enemy began on the hill. As a result, the situation was restored. However, our units suffered heavy losses in the process: 329 wounded, 85 killed and 105 missing in action.[334]

From 7 June, anticipation of a Russian offensive rose even higher. The Operations Department of the Ninth Army emphasized, "All of this taken together compels us to expect a Russian attack in the nearest future. This conclusion is confirmed as well by statements of Russian deserters."[335] Just as before, Model was particularly concerned about his right flank. Having no possibility to strengthen it substantially with a full-strength combat formation, he hastily sent there at first mobile units – the 2nd Panzer Division's reconnaissance battalion and elements of the 10th Panzergrenadier Division, but then Roman's corps was reinforced with artillery. In the process, Model had to remove artillery units that had been intended to reinforce the Ponyri direction, which in the Ninth Army's opinion was critical. On 8 July, at the order of Colonel H. von Elverfeldt, Light Artillery Battalion 860 that was arriving from the Briansk forests was directed to Roman's XX Corps, even though it had been previously designated for the XXXXI Panzer Corps. Then the 2nd Battery of StuG Battalion 909 was shifted to the 45th Infantry Division, and on 9 June, the 258th Infantry Division, which had suffered substantial casualties, was sent a full-strength march battalion as reinforcement. Simultaneously, fearing an attack into the rear of the XX Corps by groups of partisans left in the Briansk forests, the army headquarters directed by 10 June to shift the 308th Ost Battalion to Komarichi to serve as the corps' operational reserve.

Certain other details gathered in bits and pieces in the course of combat reconnaissance patrols also spoke to the fact in the opinion of the Ninth Army's headquarters, the Russian activity was connected with offensive plans. For example, at sunrise on 6 June, 5/Grenadier Regiment 531 of the 383rd Infantry Division with the support of combat engineers conducted a probing attack against the positions of the 48th Army's 143rd Rifle Division, where alongside the firing positions and bunkers, the Germans discovered several trenches that were leading across no-man's land toward the first line of trenches of 5/Infantry Regiment 531. Then other patrols found such trenches in other places as well. They could have been used to conceal the movement of rifle units directly toward the forward edge of the German defenses, but initially the Soviet troops had dug these trenches for artillery spotters and intelligence purposes (in order to listen in on the enemy). Thus, on the eve of Citadel, the series of attacks against their front line and the stratagem with the approach trenches were taken together by the German command staff as unequivocable proof of the Red Army's preparations for a major offensive in this area. In the light of these events, the Ninth Army's regrouping that had started in order to form an assault wedge raised the suspicions of von Elverfeldt and his staff that the Russians wanted to attack precisely at that moment when the Ninth Army's forces were no longer dug in and ready to receive an attack. Therefore, between 9 and 17 June the army's command made active preparations to repulse a possible attack by taking steps that adequately met their supposition.

---

334 NARA US, T.312, R.317, F.7886115, F.7886117.
335 NARA US, T.312, R.317, F.7886115.

On 8 June the Second Panzer Army issued an order regarding the return of the XXXXVII Panzer Corps' divisions to their previous areas after Operation Gypsy Baron. It was assumed that their forward units would begin to arrive in place within approximately 3-4 days, and the final assembly would be completed between 16 and 20 June. However, because of the threat of an attack by the Red Army, already on the next day, 9 June, "Headquarters Breitenbuch" underwent a reorganization. Prior to this moment it was in essence an auxiliary command post of the Ninth Army, created for the anti-partisan operation out of staff officers of the XXXXVII Panzer Corps, and constituted an integrated entity with the corps' main headquarters. Now however it increased in membership in order to create a nearly independent temporary command structure, which was to carry out an important task within a short period of time – to assemble the army's assault grouping as a whole for Citadel as quickly as possible. All of the forces of the XXXXVII Panzer Corps, which were coming out of the area of the Briansk forests were made subordinate to it, as well as command over all of the transports in the army's rear area and the reserve divisions of the Ninth Army and the units and formations of other armies that were located in its rear (the reserve of Army Group Center). Thus, Headquarters Breitenbuch, which as before contained the XXXXVII Panzer Corps, was simultaneously supposed to take command of the rear area, the panzer corps itself, and even a part of the Ninth Army. Meanwhile, the XXXXVII Panzer Corps' main headquarters received the order to monitor the situation at the front, and in the event of the start of a Russian offensive, to conduct the combat operations in its sector with the forces of two divisions of the front line – the 20th Panzer Division and 86th Infantry Division, supported by the forces of Arko 130.

On 9 June Headquarters Breitenbuch received subordinate to it the 2nd, 4th and 9th Panzer Divisions; and the 6th and 31st Infantry Divisions. On 15 June it took command of the Heavy Panzer Battalion 505 (minus one company), and on 16 June – the 12th Panzer Division, 10th Panzergrenadier Division, the headquarters of the Pioneer Regiment 678, and subsequently it was vested with the function as the primary responsible authority in command of all of the army's engineer troops. On 10 June J. Lemelsen began to form the semblance of an operations department in Headquarters Breitenbuch. For this purpose, he directed a number of experienced staff officers from the corps headquarters to it. Their task was in the event of the start of combat operations, to prepare and commit the army's assault grouping into combat from the second echelon.

In fact, as the former commander of the 65th Army Lieutenant General P.I. Batov testified, the Central Front's Military Council was striving with this series of local operations to create an impression in the enemy's mind that not only was a major offensive ready, but it would take place precisely in his army's sector, which was on the northern face of the Kursk bulge. The purpose of this scheme was to divert a portion of the German strength from the Ponyri axis (which the Soviet command believed was the main one) to the Central Front's left flank, which is to say to compel the Germans to create a larger grouping at the boundary between the Ninth and Second Armies than the one opposite the 13th Army.[336] Simultaneously, it was assumed that these limited combat actions would obtain fresh information about the enemy's degree of readiness (the speed of reacting to the attacks, the presence of reserves, etc.). This aim was

---

336 Batov, P.I., *V poxodakh i boiakh* [*In campaigns and battles*] (Moscow: Voenizdat, 1974), p. 294.

not fully achieved, but the attacks did cause the enemy to get nervous and to shift some of its strength to this area as the Central Front command hoped.

These measures had one more, albeit hidden, but positive effect for the Soviet side: they prodded Walter Model to hasten the preparations for Citadel. After the series of these local attacks, he decided to accelerate the assembly of the XXXXVI Panzer Corps at the boundary with the XX Corps. Its commander General Horne was issued an order: using all of the available transport, to shift at least the 7th Infantry Division, which had just emerged from the Briansk woods for rest, as quickly as possible to this area, and then endeavor to bring up the remaining divisions. As a result of this haste, strain increased in the troops, traffic jams and confusion arose on the roads, and the amount of work in the headquarters sharply increased.

Even so, the headquarters of the Ninth Army should be given its due credit; it rather quickly (in the course of six to eight days) fully handled the operational situation in the southern area of the Orel salient and parried the attempts by Rokossovsky's troops to consolidate their gains in the captured sectors. In addition, having quickly analyzed the results of the combat engagements, H. von Elverfeldt issued a number of important orders in order to strengthen the troops' readiness for surprise attacks. In the first place, he directed to start improving the lines quickly, in order to be able to reliably defend against possible new attacks. Secondly, he increased the readiness of the units of the first echelon to repulse not only sorties by small reconnaissance and assault parties, but also a major offensive. Thirdly, Elverfeldt assigned forces especially for organizing short, sharp counterattacks from out of the depth. For this purpose, each division was to withdraw one regimental group to form a shock reserve and bring it up to a heightened state of combat readiness, having supplied it with motorized transport and mobile means of communication.

I believe it will not be without interest for the reader to learn the sector being held by Model's army at this time. This is how the command of the Soviet 5th Air Division described Ninth Army's system of defenses opposite the 13th Army as it stood at the end of June 1943, which is to say, after the first steps were taken to strengthen it:

> The first line of defense: Saburovo, Krivtsovo, Glazunova, railroad hut 1 km south of Maslovo, Arkhangel'skoe, Verkhnee Tagino. Second line: Hills 245.0, 253.1, 254.0, 253.7, 265.2, 264.1 and 264.0, Sen'kovo, Sadovod State Farm. Third line: Hill 251.6, Kunach', Krivye Verkhi, Malye Bobriki, Bogomolovka. Fourth line: Novopolevo, Staropolevo, Shuterevo, Gremiachevo, Bogoroditskoe.
>
> The enemy's defenses relies on a sufficiently saturated system of fire, with careful use of the terrain. The adversary is camouflaging his means of fire well. The primary defensive positions are infantry entrenchments and dedicated machine-gun positions, connected between the hills by full-profile trenches. In addition, there are a significant number of well-camouflaged earth and timber bunkers with one or two firing embrasures (16-17 each per each center of resistance), which are positioned in tactically advantageous places with good fields of vision and fire.
>
> The combat positions of the infantry are echeloned in depth and represent a network of company strong points, connected into battalion centers of resistance and calculated for all-round defense. The density of firing positions along the forward edge amounts on average from 8 to 12 machine guns for each kilometer of the front. According to prisoner testimony, each machine gun has three or four alternate weapon pits. They are placed so that the entire ground in front of the forward edge is swept by multi-layered

frontal and flanking fire. The firepower of the enemy's defense is augmented by the concentration of tanks in small groups in direct proximity to the forward edge of the defense.

The enemy infantry is located in bunkers positioned on the reverse slopes of hills and dug into the banks of gullies and ravines. The men of the second echelon are quartered in populated places and woods, in bunkers, homes and tents. The bunkers are calculated to hold five or six men and covered by three or four layers of logs and railway ties.[337]

Reading through this document, it is hard to imagine that the German side was intending to attack, and not to defend, given how impressive their defensive works looked like at this time. In fact, as veterans of the Battle of Kursk recalled, when the German arrogance diminished a little, they openly feared us and always dug a bit deeper into the ground. In addition, at this time the Ninth Army command began working in detail on the matter of moving out a reinforced line of combat outposts, which in case of a strong Russian attack were supposed to delay it for a short time before falling back to the main line of defense. However, a final decision on this matter was set aside.

In addition, the open nervousness and concern which was being observed in Elverfeldt's headquarters, especially between 8 and 12 June, was connected with the fact that despite the plain signs of the preparation for an offensive, the Russians were still holding back, and in the meantime, there were no intelligible signals coming from Berlin regarding Operation Citadel. The uncertainty was bedeviling everyone, and the troops were waiting with impatience: Which direction was the pendulum swinging? From the documents it is apparent that both the army's leadership and a significant share of the senior command staff were waiting for the offensive with excitement, considering it the only way out of the extended period of uncertainty and the main way to swing the situation in Germany's favor. However, there remained not a few of those who continued to consider Citadel a reckless undertaking, which might lead to tragic outcomes. Judging from the documents of the Ninth Army, after 1 June there was no confidence in them or the others that the operation would begin immediately after 12 June.

When you familiarize yourself with the materials of the Wehrmacht headquarters at key moments of battles or operations, it is impossible not to notice the surprising ability of their officers and generals (at the tactical and operational level) to focus quickly on the main problem, while setting aside intrigues and everything personal. In this connection the relations between Army Group Center and the Ninth Army in the final phase of preparing Citadel can be cited as a plain example of such "professional mimicry". As soon as the threat arose of a Soviet offensive, their headquarters began to work on this question in detail, professionally and with no emotions; the views of the key figures regarding most of the problems became unified. For example, on the morning of 11 June a number of telephone conversations took place between the army and the army group, in the course of which the overall operational situation and the likely options of the German forces' actions in the Orel salient (primarily the Ninth Army) in the nearest future (before 25 June) were discussed. From the documents it is distinctly clear that notes of the discussants' alarm are traceable in connection with a possible Russian attack, but they were

337 TsAMO RF, F.5 ad, Op.1, D.18, l. 176 obr., 177.

not predominant. The main point in the discussion regarded finding out what would happen in the next 10-15 days. The leadership of both command organs believed that it was this problem that was the key one, and at the same time difficult to resolve, primarily because of the lack of clarity in Berlin's position. Nevertheless, they formed a common position, the essence of which was as follows: The situation was extremely unstable, and in the next two weeks, events might develop according to one of four likely directions:

1. Before 25 June, an order would arrive to start Citadel with the available forces;
2. The Russians would go on the offensive against the Ninth Army and its troops would conduct combat actions in their own defensive positions;
3. The Red Army would launch a general offensive along the entire front of the Orel salient, and accordingly force Army Group Center to defend with all its forces;
4. Berlin would be forced to issue an order to abandon the Orel bulge in order to use the freed-up forces on other fronts.

As is known, the first alternative proved to be the most accurate, although in those circumstances the leadership of both the army and the army group could not exclude the other three. Naturally, such divergent trains of thought did not add any clarity to the situation, though they arose due to objective causes.

The first ten days of June proved to be very hard for the Ninth Army command, especially in the psychological sense. Skepticism with respect to Citadel's prospects against the backdrop of the Ninth Army's difficult situation was increasing with each passing day, and Berlin's nearest plans were absolutely totally murky. In fact, up to this moment all of the key decisions regarding the East Front (and at times even insubstantial ones) were being made by Hitler alone. However, the preparation of this operation became a model of super centralization of all and everything, so at this moment the Führer's closest circle could only conjecture about what he might decide. Three months after the signing of Operational Order No. 5, Model's forces had been replenished to some extent, but even so, they were far short of being able to meet the tasks that had been given to them. The Ninth Army was located in a dispersed condition; there was no armor for deep breakthrough of the Russian defenses, nor was there the necessary amount of artillery shells; the divisions of the XXXXVII Panzer Corps, which were to comprise the shock wedge of the offensive, had not even yet arrived from the Briansk forests after taking part in Operation Gypsy Baron. The moment when the main factor of success was viewed as the weakness of the Russian forces and their defenses and been missed long ago. Now therefore many believed that the chances of realizing the plan of a rapid dash to Kursk were illusory. At the same time, a Russian offensive in the middle of June was being viewed, even by Krebs' headquarters, as almost a certainty: "The army group has come to the conclusion that the enemy opposite its front has been substantially reinforced and in order to prevent his inevitable offensive in the nearest future, the sole response remains the conducting of Citadel as soon as possible; the army group considers the presence of the enemy's offensive plans in the nearest future obvious."[338]

Thus, the problem of maintaining possession of the Orel salient was being worked on at this time in parallel with the plan for Citadel, and just as deeply and thoroughly. It is sufficient to

---

338 NARA US, T.312, R.317, F.7886121.

say that already in early June (!), documents of the Ninth Army mention a preliminary decision that in the event the Russians went on the attack first, Walter Model would be made responsible for the defense of the entire Orel salient. Krebs, on behalf of the commander-in-chief of Army Group Center, even sent a number of instructions to Model, which he should follow at this time.

First, in the meantime Model was to conduct an active defense, thereby securing the troops' occupation of their jumping-off positions for Citadel. Second, he was to conduct systematic work to improve the trafficability of the roads in the army's sector, especially in the XX Corps. It was recommended to corduroy the main dirt roads quickly with logs in the rear of Roman's corps. Third, Model was to intensify the process of setting up a rear belt of defenses along the Desna River (the so-called Hagen Line) for the Ninth Army. For this purpose, von Kluge directed to use even cadets of the army's school in Briansk on the fortification works, in order not to divert troops from the front, and to make the work a systematic and uninterrupted. As Colonel P. von Groeben wrote, Model's decision, reached back in May, about constructing the Hagen Line as insurance in the event of the abandonment of the Orel salient, went opposite to Hitler's instructions and the plan of preparing for Citadel, but von Kluge was fully supporting him.[339] However, the amount of construction work was still too large, so the existing decision about using men of the army group's 4th Panzer and 10th Panzergrenadier Divisions for this construction work had also not yet been countermanded, and with this, the matter came to a pause. Then the Field Marshal ordered on 16 June to transfer the 4th Panzer Division all the same to XX Corps for use in setting up positions along the line of the Sevsk and Nerussa Rivers (40 km southwest of Karachev) and northeast of there. A group of officers was immediately sent there to reconnoiter the ground, headed by the commander of Panzergrenadier Regiment 2 Colonel Buk. However, Hitler's decision to launch the offensive effectively repudiated this order, and the 4th Panzer Division began to take up its jumping-off positions.

Finally. von Kluge recommended that all of the panzer divisions, particularly the 20th Panzer Division, be withdrawn into the second echelon in order simultaneously to form both the assault wedge for Citadel and the army's mobile reserve. In addition, two infantry divisions – the 6th and 31st – were transferred from the army group to reinforce the Ninth Army. Model, with von Kluge's approval, intended to replace the tankers at the front quickly with them. However, the OKH had other plans for them. In the documents of the army group, it is especially emphasized that these measures (the replacement of the divisions) provided the basis for the final version of Citadel's plan as worked out by Army Group Center in order to create a quasi-third echelon for the Ninth Army, which would have a dual role: both for the breakthrough of the Russians' first belt of defenses in the course of an offensive, and as a counter measure in the event that the Russians attacked first. Both von Kluge and Model believed that if the offensive toward Kursk went successfully, then the army's panzer divisions and the army group's reserve might become an effective means to develop it. On the other hand, if the Russians attacked, they would become the main means to break it up, if they were located in the second echelon. Thus, both military commanders considered it senseless to throw them against mines in the first wave of the attack; there was not nearly enough armor, and each tank was highly prized.

Operation Gypsy Baron and the tense situation at the front somewhat distracted the Ninth Army's command from the planning of Citadel. The perfecting of the plans for the formations

---

339 Newton, *Kurskaia bitva: nemetskii vzgliad*, p. 141.

and units when conducting it (the breakthrough process, the exploitation of a success) with regard to the changing situation was unquestionable still continuing, but sluggishly so. For example, on 6 June J. Harpe met at the army's command post with top staff officers and the commander of the 6th Infantry Division Lieutenant General H. Grossman, at which possible alternatives for using this division when breaking through the main belt of defenses were discussed. The matter was not settled. Model was in Germany, and it made no sense to come to a decision without him. Even more, the army group itself, in expectation of a final decision from Berlin, still had not conclusively determined whether it made sense in its view to replace the panzer divisions with the infantry divisions, or to leave everything as it was in the meantime. If to recall, just one week remained before X-day, 12 June, which had been set by Hitler as the date for the start of the offensive, and at first glance such passivity of the generals might seem strange. However, this is only from the vantage point of an onlooker; those who gathered at the command post of the Ninth Army were already assuming with a great deal of likelihood that Berlin was planning to postpone Citadel once again.

Just a day before this, on 5 June, Krebs was requested to submit a valid schedule as to when precisely all of the preparations for executing the operation might be finished. The request had a clear provision: to ensure the process ended no later than 20 June. Therefore, it was not hard to guess that Berlin's anticipated decision wouldn't come on 12 June. Even prior to this, it was clear to Elverfeldt's staff that without the XXXXVII Panzer Corps, which was chasing after partisans through the Briansk forests, the offensive would not begin. Thus, the majority of the generals of those who had been involved in the planning of an attack toward Kursk back in May, after the start of Operation Gypsy Baron, were aware that if Citadel did in fact get underway, then considering the modest transport means and the difficult ground they had to cover when moving, it wouldn't start any earlier than the middle or latter half of June.

On 10 June, Model returned to Army Group Center. Along the way to the front, he had made a stop at the OKH, where he met with the Chief of Operations Lieutenant General A. Heusinger, but the latter could not say anything definite about Citadel; they were waiting for Hitler's decision. Under the surface it was clear to everyone that the offensive was not ready, though they understood that this was not an argument for Hitler. On the morning of 11 June, Model met with Günther von Kluge in Smolensk. The Colonel General reported on his return from leave and laid out the latest information that he had received the evening before from his Operations Department. The Field Marshal in turn brought Model up to date on the situation, and after this "it became clear to the army commander that the decision regarding a German general offensive in the East wouldn't be reached in the nearest future."[340] Günther von Kluge remarked that a large amount of work would have to take place in the next few days. With consideration of the latest events (the strengthening of the Russian defenses, primarily), substantial changes were made in the planning of Citadel both with respect to the composition of the assault grouping and its combat formation. The Ninth Army would have to exert every effort so that all of the planned measures (including with the shuffling of sectors for the divisions) would be implemented within the indicated period of time. Walter Model's hunch was not wrong: on the following day an official announcement came from the OKH: The offensive was

---

340 NARA US, T.312, R.317, F.7886120.

once again postponed for another 11 days. From this moment, the final phase of the planning and preparations for the Battle of Kursk began for the Ninth Army.

Considering that one of the key problems that influenced Hitler's postponement of Citadel from the first days of May to 12 June was the lack of the necessary number of armored vehicles in the Ninth Army, it is important to understand how the strength of its tank park changed over this period of time. According to a report from its headquarters at 2235 on 10 June, in addition to the six mobile divisions (the 2nd, 4th, 9th, 12th, 18th and 20th Panzer Divisions) under its command, only one more unit had appeared – Heavy Panzer Battalion 505. In total they had 402 tanks, which means that over the month of May and early June, the Ninth Army received an additional 171 tanks (a 74percent increase). The tanks that came in were new, updated Pz.Kpfw. IV (141) and Pz.Kpfw. III (22) with long-barreled guns, which unquestionably enhanced the quality of the tank park. This circumstance and the total number of arriving tanks at first glance offers justification to speak about considerable results. However, if to turn to other indicators, then the situation looks somewhat differently. Especially if you consider that we're talking about an army that was getting ready to play a key role in the year's main offensive operation. For example, at this time each panzer division had an average strength of 63.8 tanks, and of the 231 promised Pz.Kpfw. V and Pz.Kpfw. VI, which Berlin viewed as breakthrough tanks, Model had received only 19 Tigers. If you add the obvious fact that Model's army had yet to assemble into an assault fist, and some of its divisions were still thrashing around in the Briansk forests, then the decision to postpone Citadel was completely rational, and the man who made the decision does not look like a dilettante who had absolutely no understanding of the principles of conducting major military operations, like the community of his generals made Hitler out to be after the war.

Now let us return to the area south of Orel. Back on the evening of 10 June, immediately after arriving by aircraft, Model drove out to the headquarters of Luftflotte VI. He was placing great hopes on its support in the course of Operation Citadel. Especially now, when he lacked either the armor or the manpower for the offensive, and yet an additional problem had emerged – the divisions arriving back from Operation Gypsy Baron were not in the best shape. Therefore, he was proposing to maintain close contact with the command of Luftflotte VI. As noted in the documents of the Ninth Army's Operations Department:

> There the army commander quickly set about exchanging information regarding the situation with Luftflotte VI's chief of staff. As a result, real assignments were formulated for the aircraft in the event of actions on the defensive. In particular, with respect to the enemy artillery and operational reserves, as well as the Russian points of command. In the event of Citadel, the massed use of air support was agreed upon. On the basis of the results of discussions that had taken place recently, the air fleet's chief of staff expressed the opinion that the achievement of complete superiority in the air over the enemy shouldn't be anticipated. This could happen only under particularly favorable circumstances.[341]

341 NARA US, T.312, R.317, F.7886119, F.7886120.

This announcement by the Luftwaffe command did not sound comforting to Model. The tense situation at the front also did not bring any optimism. Colonel General Model was sharing his concerns about a possible Russian offensive with his staff. Therefore, his first decision after taking up the matter with J. Harpe on the afternoon of 11 June became the orders "About increasing the level of readiness by bringing the men up to a state of alert in the units all along the front", which contained provisions about preparing for a gas attack. The command of the troops positioned in the second echelon and operational rear must ensure the readiness of their units for a march in no less than two hours from the receipt of an order. Just two days later, on 13 June, a new "major" order was issued regarding the army's defense, which extended throughout the army the previous orders to separate divisions, and specified concrete defensive assignments for each corps in the nearest future.

The alarm about the matter of the Russians' possible use of chemical weapons arose from a number of pieces of evidence. In the first place, radio operators of the XX Corps had intercepted a rather ambiguous discussion between Soviet officers on this topic. The Abwehr interpreted it as preparations for a gas attack already at the tactical level. Secondly, the Germans had long before been using gas in isolated sectors of the Soviet-German front, though in a very limited fashion. For example, back in February 1942 the Military Council member of the Southwestern Direction N.S. Khrushchev reported to Moscow that troops of the 21st and 40th Armies east of Prokhorovka Station in Kursk Oblast had been hit by mortar shells with chemical warheads, and several soldiers had been poisoned. In the same year of 1942, the Nazis had been using gas in the city of Kerch against partisans in the Adzhimushkai quarries and other places. Throughout the entire war, the idea of initiating the massed use of chemical weapons periodically bobbed up in the political leadership of Germany. The thought therefore that the Russians might be thinking in the same way was not so unexpected for the Ninth Army command, especially since information had come from agents in May 1943 that work was underway to equip Il-2 ground attack aircraft with chemical weapons in units of the 2nd Air Army. The OKH was extremely alarmed about this, and the Abwehr received an order to re-check this information, but on 16 May 1943 Major General O. von dem Gabo had arrived from Berlin to the Ninth Army in order to discuss the problem of chemical defense with its command staff and the corps leadership.[342]

In reality, judging from documents found in the TsAMO RF [Central Archives of the Russian Federation's Ministry of Defense], the Soviet side, having unverified evidence of the enemy's repeated use of gas, was concerned that if the Germans wound up in a losing situation this summer, they might resort to chemical warfare. Thus, the Soviets took steps to act preventively, though they were not planning to start it first. For example, special equipment for dispersing chemical agents were in fact mounted on the Il-2 aircraft of the 2nd Air Army. For the successful completion of this work, a number of its commanders received honors; in particular, the Chief of Chemical Services of the 1st Ground Attack Aviation Corps' 290th Ground Attack Aviation Division Major I.A. Asfand'iarov was put up for the Order of the Red Star on 26 June 1943. In the recommendation for the award, it states, "… Under his personal leadership and the direct participation of the division's flight staff, the Il-2 was made fully ready to use chemical weapons, in particular the ZV [incendiary agents]."[343]

---

342 NARA US, T.312, R.317, F.7886092.
343 TsAMO RF, F.33, Op.682526, Ed. xr. 767.

On 14 June, the headquarters of the Ninth Army sent Order No.0123 from the commander to the subordinate corps, which accounted for the latest changes in the situation, and in connection with this, defined more precisely the assignments for the main formations designated for Citadel. This document became evidence of the Abwehr's successful work and the intense discussions of its command with the headquarters of the OKH throughout the day of 13 June and the morning of 14 June. In early May it had been decided that the penetration of the Central Front's tactical zone to a depth of 10 km would be conducted in two places with two assault groups: with the forces of the 2nd and 9th Panzer Divisions supported by the 6th Infantry Division, and the 12th Panzer Division in cooperation with the 31st Infantry Division. The remaining panzer divisions were to advance in the second and third echelons together with the infantry, in order to complete the breakthrough and to ensure a rapid advance in the direction of Kursk.

It was planned to use the 31st Infantry Division in order to screen the right (western) flank of the attack grouping and in order to create an inner front of encirclement, while the 6th Infantry Division (after overcoming the Russians' main defensive belt) was to strengthen the left (eastern) flank of the assault wedge. The XXIII Corps had the assignment to operate in the direction of Maloarkhangel'sk, in order to form the outer front of encirclement and to parry possible Soviet counterattacks from the east. It was being assumed that two more infantry divisions, which Model was requesting in addition from G. von Kluge, would be sent to the same place. However, when information began to come in about the reinforcement of Soviet troops in the Dmitriev and Fatezh area, doubts arose regarding the capabilities of the 31st Infantry Division. Ninth Army headquarters observed:

> The attack of the 31st Infantry Division together with the 12th Panzer Division must ensure both the necessary infantry screen for the attacking panzer wedge, and also the defense of the XXXXVI Panzer Corps' western flank. However, it is not clear that the 31st Infantry Division is in the condition to cover such an extended front all the way to Fatezh, without losing the capability to support the 12th Panzer Division's attack. Here it will probably be appropriate to use one of the infantry divisions transferred from the army group. This will enable deeper penetration by the 12th Panzer Division into the enemy's defenses and relieve it of the need to defend its flanks, which would unavoidably weaken the force of the attack on the main axis of advance.[344]

The matter that remained was a small one – to find two more infantry divisions and to persuade Günther von Kluge to transfer them to Model together with the 6th and 31st Infantry Divisions. However, in the meantime, until the Colonel General's return from leave, a coded telegram of a new proposal was going around; intelligence had presented irrefutable evidence that in the depth of the Russian defenses, another powerful mobile reserve had been formed out of several tank corps. This circumstance sharply strengthened Model's opinion regarding the demands about sending him not two infantry divisions (the 6th and 31st Infantry Divisions), but four infantry divisions. This information proved to be so substantial that it forced both the Ninth Army and Army Group Center to reexamine the combat formation of the assault wedge and

344 NARA US, T.312, R.317, F.7886125.

the tasks of the corps included in it. The appearance of Order No.0123 mentioned above was connected with this shake up.

The aim and tasks of the Ninth Army remained unchanged in the document. Its main thought was that the effect of surprise had been lost; the Russians were not only expecting an offensive, they had substantially strengthened their lines, including in the rear, so it was impossible to count upon breaking their resistance with the initial attack. As Model noted:

> In the Trosna – Maloarkhangel'sk sector, where the enemy is anticipating the main attack, defensive measures have been completed. Here he possesses a particularly strong, fortified system of positions; a carefully arranged tank defense; and unprecedentedly strong artillery and a large number of Katiusha rocket launchers. In the depth of the enemy's area, especially near Kursk and Maloarkhangel'sk, a multitude of ground units have assembled, the shock power of which consists primarily of tank formations. The number of enemy aircraft corresponds to the number of its ground troops … In the event of our attack, the enemy is preparing for bitter resistance at the front, supported by a multitude of strong tank formations from the east and southeast, directed to conduct counterattacks and offensive actions with the aim of diverting forces.[345]

From this, essentially correct conclusion, it followed that the offensive plan had to change so as to take account of not only the buildup of Russian artillery opposite the assault wedge, but also the possibility of numerous mobile reserves brought up by the Soviet side to the breakthrough sector. Thus, the flanking corps received new individual assignments:

a. XXXXVI Panzer Corps (102nd, 258th, 7th and 31st Infantry Divisions) were to repulse the attack by the Russian grouping deployed east of Dmitriev against the western flank of the XXXXVII Panzer Corps' assault wedge and as soon as possible, having broken through the defenses with its main forces, to take control of the Trosna – Fatezh road and to link up with the XXXXVII Panzer Corps' left flank divisions, while Manteuffel's group was also to capture Fatezh;

b. XXXXVII Panzer Corps (2nd, 9th and 20th Panzer Divisions and the 6th Infantry Division) in the first hours of the offensive was to support the XXXXI Panzer Corps' offensive with all its means of fire. Then the 20th Panzer Division and 6th Infantry Division were to break through in the sector: west of Verkhnee Tagino – Novyi Khutor, and with the support of aircraft, exploit the offensive in the direction of an area north of Kursk. In addition, depending on the operational situation, it should be ready to operate together with the XXXXI Panzer Corps' mobile groups in a southern direction in order to link up with forces of Army Group South. It was assumed that in order to exploit the success of the XXXXI Panzer Corps, possibly Model's mobile reserve formed from the 4th and 12th Panzer Divisions and the 10th Panzergrenadier Division, would be transferred to it.

---

345 BA-MA. AOK 9 (Ia). KTB Nr.S.IV. Bd.3 (35939/14).

c. The XXXXI Panzer Corps and XXIII Corps were to repulse possible counterattacks against the eastern flank of the XXXXVII Panzer Corps and to take up a defensive front along the Shshigry – Sozha line.

XXXXI Panzer Corps (the 86th and 292nd Infantry Divisions and the 18th Panzer Division), reinforced by Heavy Panzerjäger Regiment 656, in the early hours of the offensive in cooperation with XXIII Corps was supposed to achieve the primary objective – a breaching of the line on the left flank of the army's assault wedge, west of the Orel – Kursk railroad. Afterward it was to give support to the left-flank divisions of the XXXXVII Panzer Corps (with the aim of exploiting their success into the depth) and the offensive of the XXIII Corps south of Maloarkhangel'sk; given the need, the forces of Panzerjäger Regiment 656 were to repulse Russian tank attacks from the south and southeast.

The XXIII Corps (78th Sturm Division and a kampfgruppe of the 383rd Infantry Division [II/Regiment 1 of the 383rd Division, II/Regiment 1 of the 36th Infantry Division and reinforcing guns of the 383rd Infantry Division], in cooperation with the XXXXI Panzer Corps, with the support of aircraft, was to break through the positions of the 13th Army on both sides of Maloarkhangel'sk, occupy the Mokroe – Panskaia line, and create a firm defensive front.

The new plan did not cancel the Ninth Army's request about sending it two additional infantry divisions, and on the contrary demanded reinforcement with panzer formations as well. These demands were fully justified. Thus, the commander of the XXIII Corps General of Infantry Johannes Friessner pointed out:

> Our troops would be weaker by the end of the offensive's second and beginning of the third day. It was at this moment that the approach of powerful enemy reserves was anticipated, and our losses would reach a maximum. Accordingly, the offensive's success at this moment would depend on the availability of fresh forces from which kampfgruppen should be formed ... Since the offensive requires the assembly of all the corps' strength and a proportional weakening of its defensive front, the threat arises of a breakthrough of it by the enemy. In order to prevent this, as well as to augment the strength of the attack in the depth of the enemy's defenses, an additional division should be positioned behind the corps' right flank, which is to say behind the boundary between the 86th Infantry Division (XXXXI Panzer Corps) and the 78th Sturm Division (XXIII Corps).[346]

On 17 June, Friessner called Model in order to discuss his proposal. The Colonel General considered his opinions to be fully legitimate. Back in early June, the Abwehr had identified the arrival of not only powerful Russian artillery reserves in the area of Livny, but also several tank regiments for the 48th Army. Indeed, this was actually the case. However, the army commander had no way to help him, especially because at this time large problems had arisen as well on

---

346 NARA US, T.314, R.688, F.000756.

the main axis of advance; he was extremely disturbed by the condition of the XXXXVI and XXXXVII Panzer Corps' divisions.

At 1120 on 14 June, a lengthy telephone discussion took place between H. Krebs and H. von der Elverfeldt, in the course of which they came to the same opinion regarding two important questions. In the first place, unquestionably the 6th and 31st Infantry Divisions had to be transferred quickly to the Ninth Army. In the second place, the 31st Infantry Division was not in the condition to get ready for the offensive in time. There was one solution: to bring up the 4th Panzer Division and 10th Panzergrenadier Division that were still being held in reserve, and to move them into the second defensive line (second echelon). However, such a regrouping required the agreement of both of their commanders, so the decision was set aside until the next morning. Even so, an order was immediately issued for the 6th and 31st Infantry Divisions to get ready for a march, in order to ensure their rapid transfer to direct subordination to Model.

Günther von Kluge did not like his chief of staff's proposal at all. Regarding the infantry divisions, he gave his agreement for their transfer, but preferred not to move up the 4th Panzer Division and 10th Panzergrenadier Division, because this would leave him effectively without any reserves. Moreover, there was one more important aspect to this question. Together with these divisions, he would gradually lose a degree of influence on Model's actions and become more distant from any role in Citadel. Therefore, that evening (at 2015) both chiefs of staff held another lengthy and extremely tense conversation, which went nowhere. Good sense demanded that the 4th Panzer Division and 10th Panzergrenadier Division be transferred all the same to the Ninth Army, but the Field Marshal was just as before categorically opposed to this. On the following day Günther von Kluge visited Model's command post, and having handed the Colonel General a copy of his order from 14 June about changes in the plan of Citadel, he announced that the army would receive the 6th and 31st Infantry Divisions, although principal agreement on this matter had already been reached long before. However, the Field Marshal turned this mechanical procedure of handing over a document into a grand ceremony, which would testify to his magnanimity, his understanding of the army's difficult situation, and his active participation in resolving its problems. With this, the pleasantries ended. The Field Marshal did not give any clear answer to Model's question about whether or not he would in the nearest future two more infantry divisions subordinate to him, as well as the 4th Panzer Division and 10th Panzergrenadier Division. Kluge only promised to give an answer within the next three days.

The re-subordination of the 6th and 31st Infantry Division was unquestionably substantial help for the Colonel General, even though in essence these were not means of reinforcement for the assault grouping; they were only patching holes discovered in the course of making the finishing touches to the plan of the operation. True, their combat readiness at the time still was not high. As has already been noted, throughout the course of the entire three-month period of preparing for the offensive, including in the final stretch (from the middle of June 1943), the forces of the Ninth Army were constantly located in a jumbled condition, and its command under extreme time pressure. The plans of both the operation itself and the regroupings were regularly overturned, sectors were shifted and re-allocated, and divisions were continually being re-subordinated to various corps, armies and the army group. At this time, it is hard to find even a full two weeks when the divisions designated for the main offensive of 1943 (!) were not being shifted to some point or being engaged in matters that were essentially secondary for them. For example, even by 13 June, the main forces of the 7th and 292nd Infantry Divisions were still positioned in the Briansk forests.[347] It was only three days later that their units started to move out to their jumping-off positions according to Citadel's plan. Indeed, the first units of the 31st Infantry Division did not begin to arrive in the army's sector until 18 June!

At this time, the army's most pressing problems (personnel replacements, replenishment with equipment, logistics and combat training) were agitating Model and his headquarters. The rebuilding of the infantry divisions was proceeding slowly and by 15 June (just eight days before the next start date set for the offensive), it had not been completed even at a minimum. Having become familiar with the captured German documents, it is impossible not to note how Elverfeldt's staff rejoiced at the arrival of each march battalion, just as if it was a precious gift! A similar situation was unfolding in the panzer divisions. As of 16 June, the four panzer divisions of the shock XXXXVII Panzer Corps had a combined 244 tanks, including 18 Pz.Kpfw. III with short-barreled cannons (2nd Panzer – 59, 4th Panzer – 91, 9th Panzer – 33, and 12th Panzer – 61) [For more detail see Table 5].

---

347 NARA US, T.312, R.317, F.7886124.

Table 5: Dynamics of the replenishment of tanks and their introduction into service in certain panzer divisions of the Ninth Army between 9 and 30 June 1943 (according to divisional reports) [348]

	a) 2nd Panzer Division				
	Tanks				
Date	Pz II	Pz III 50mm short-barreled	Pz III 75mm short-barreled	Pz IV 75mm long-barreled	Pz IV command
6 June		4	16	29	
10 June[349]	1/-	7/4[350]	20/18	33/29	3/3 1/0
11 June		-/4	-/18	-/29	-/3
12 June		5	17	30	3/-
13 June		11	19	32	3/-
14 June					
15 June					
16 June[351]		11	18	30	3/-
17 June		11	18	30	3/-
18 June		10	18	30	3/-
19 June		10	19	29	3/-
20 June		10	19	29	3/-
21 June					
22 June					
23 June					
24 June		11	19	30	3/-
25 June		11	18	29	3/-
26 June		11	18	29	3/-
27 June		11	19	31	3/-
28 June		11	20	31	3/-
29 June		11	19	30	3/-
30 June		10	19	58	3/-

348 Based upon reports from the division to the headquarters of the XXXXVII Panzer Corps, and on reports from the XXXXVII Panzer Corps' headquarters to the headquarters of the Ninth Army.
349 On 10 June the 2nd Panzer Division reported on the presence of one Pz.Kpfw. II and nine artillery observation panzers, two of which were in repair for 14 days, as well as 13 Sd.Kfz. 251/5 assault engineer halftracks. In subsequent reports, there was no further mention of these tanks and halftracks.
350 In this and the following entries for 10 June, the number to the left of the slash gives the known establishment number of tanks, which should be kept in mind for the rest of the entries in each column. The number to the right of the slash shows the number of serviceable tanks of that type on that date.
351 The report from the 2nd Panzer Division indicated the presence of six Sd.Kfz.251/5 flame-throwing halftracks.

Date	b) 4th Panzer Division					
	Tanks					
	Pz II	Pz III command	Pz III 50mm L/42 or L/60	Pz III 75mm L/24	Pz IV long-barreled	Pz IV command
6 June						
10 June		2	38	15		16/2
11 June	5	4		15	69	15/3
12 June						
13 June		4		15		17
14 June						
15 June						
16 June	5	4		15	72	8/3
17 June						
18 June				15	72	5/3
19 June						
20 June				15	72	5/3
21 June				9	72	6/3
22 June				9	71	6/3
23 June						
24 June				9	74	6/3
25 June						
26 June				9	74	-/3
27 June						
28 June						
29 June						
30 June				9	73	6/1

Date	c) 9th Panzer Division					
	Tanks					
	Pz III 50mm L/42 or L/60	Pz III 75mm L/24	Pz IV command	Pz IV long-barreled	Command	Artillery observation
6 June	24		4	26	4	
10 June	30/23	8	7/3	30/26	6/5	2[352]
11 June	-/25		-/3	-/27	-/4	
12 June	-/25		-/3	-/26	-/5	
13 June	-/25		-/4	-/26	-/5	
14 June						
15 June	-/25		-/5	-/27	-/5	
16 June	-/28		-/6	-/27	-/5	
17 June	-/28		-/6	-/25	-/5	
18 June						
19 June						
20 June	-/28		-/6	-/29	-/6	
21 June	-/28		-/5	-/29	-/5	
22 June	-/28		-/4	-/29	-/5	
23 June						
24 June	-/27		-/2	-/28	-/4	
25 June	-/27		-/1	-/29	-/2	
26 June	-/27		-/1	-/29	-/3	
27 June	-/27		-/2	-/30	-/5	
28 June	-/25		-/4	-/30	-/5	
29 June	-/26		-/4	-/30	-/5	
30 June	-/25		-/4	-/30	-/5	

352 On 10 June the 9th Panzer Division reported that it had two authorized artillery observation panzers (both in a 14-day repair period), 12 Sd.Kfz.251/5 halftracks (11 operational, one under repair) and three Sd.Kfz.253 observation light halftracks. Subsequently, these tanks and halftracks weren't noted in reports.

Date	d) 12th Panzer Division					
	Tanks					
	Pz III 50mm short-barreled	Pz III 50 mm long-barreled	Pz III 75mm L/24	Pz IV short-barreled	Pz IV long-barreled	Artillery observation
6 June						
10 June						
11 June						
12 June						
13 June						
14 June						
15 June						
16 June[353]	12	8	6	1[354]	35	3[355]
17 June						
18 June	13	8	6	1	34	3
19 June	13	8	5	1	34	3
20 June	13	8	5		34	2
21 June	13	8	5	1	34	4[356]
22 June	13	8	6	1	34	4
23 June	12	14	6	1	34	2
24 June						
25 June	1	14	6		34	4[357]
26 June	3	14	6		31	2
27 June	1	13	6		33	2
28 June	1	12	6	1	33	4
29 June	1	8	6		32	2
30 June	1	12	5		24	2

353 On 16 June, the 12th Panzer Division reported also having three authorized experimental V.K. 1601 light Panzer II Ausf. J reconnaissance tanks.
354 Prior to the start of the Battle of Kursk and throughout its course, this tank was located at the army school in Briansk.
355 Two command tanks and one short-barreled Panzer III command tank.
356 On 21 and 22 June, the 12th Panzer Division reported on the presence of two command tanks and two short-barrelled Panzer III command tanks, as well as two serviceable V.K. 1601 light Panzer II Ausf. J reconnaissance tanks.
357 On 25 June, the 12th Panzer Division again reported on the presence of three serviceable V.K. 1601, but on 27 June they were completely absent in the report.

I will remind the reader that the establishment strength of a single panzer division from January 1943 was supposed to amount to 167 combat machines. According, the level of equipment varied between 35 and 55percent of authorized strength. The "super weapons" that had been promised by the Führer a month before – the Ferdinand self-propelled gun and the Panther tanks – remained only an empty promise. The army stockpiles of artillery ammunition were half-empty. Nevertheless, both the OKH and Hitler in complete seriousness were planning to be in Kursk by the end of June!

Berlin showed similar behavior (on one hand the indifference to the needs of those who would be implementing Citadel, and on the other the chest-pumping on the subject of its expected results) not only with respect to Model's army, but also von Manstein's army group. This can be plainly seen in the example of the Panzer Brigade 10 of Panthers, which at the end of June would be transferred to the Fourth Panzer Army. From the beginning, Hitler announced that he was placing very great hopes on this formation. In essence, it was his offspring, but it was completely unready for combat. It would be incorrect to blame only the workforce for this. The German military-bureaucratic machine in the spring and summer of 1943 was still working efficiently for the most part; it would begin to show serious breakdowns only in 1944, under the relentless Allied bombing. Therefore, I will repeat that the root of all of Model's and von Manstein's problems should be searched in the very idea of seizing the initiative from the USSR in the summer of 1943, which from the outset was beyond Germany's capabilities. Even so, later certain participants in those events, for example, General Hans Speidel, would attempt to persuade the public that Citadel might have succeeded, but only in March 1943, immediately after the recapture of Belgorod.[358] Or as von Manstein wrote, it might have been successful if launched in May or early June 1943. However, these assertions aren't realistic. The facts unambiguously show that the Wehrmacht never had the necessary forces and means for the successful execution of Citadel. After Stalingrad, the idea that lay at its basis was already verging on fantasy. Just one detail plainly shows that this was not understood in Berlin or in Lötzen – the scale of the combat operations in the course of the Wehrmacht's summer campaigns in the East in the first three years of the war. If in 1941 Germany's armed forces attacked (and accordingly had the forces for this) on a front of more than 2,000 kilometers, then in 1942 the sector of active combat operations had decreased by more than three times, to 600 kilometers; Citadel was to take place in sectors that had a total length of just 150 kilometers, which was four times less than in 1942. Even so, back then, in 1943, Berlin had announced not without justification that its start date had more than once been postponed for objective reasons – because of the shortage of troops and equipment.

A recently disclosed transcript of the telephone conversations between Field Marshal von Kluge and the commander of the Third Panzer Army Colonel General Georg-Hans Reinhardt on 17 June 1943, found in the TsAMO RF, shows the difficult state of affairs in the troops before Citadel, in particular in Army Group Center. The Third Panzer Army at that time was part of Army Group Center and was occupying a defense on the important Moscow axis. The document is rather lengthy, so I will cite its most important moments that touch the problems under discussion:

---

358 Speidel, H., *Vtorzhenie 1944* [*Invasion 1944*] (Chicago, 1950), p. 57.

Colonel General: I am disappointed on the subject of pulling the SS Motorized Infantry Brigade 1 out of the line in connection with the need to use it for the struggle against bandits in the Borisov area.

Field Marshal: The use of SS Infantry Brigade 1 against bandits is unknown to the army group; this needs checking.

Colonel General: The removal of SS Infantry Brigade 1 from the front means the extending of the front, and hence, its weakening. Over recent time, we have lost the following weapons at the front: around 350 light and heavy machine guns; 12 light infantry guns; 13 light and 20 75mm anti-tank guns; 24 20mm Flak guns; two 88mm Flak guns; 20 76.2mm guns (Russian); and two batteries of 155mm heavy field howitzers. The delivery of more than 9 tonn of ammunition per day is possible only with the assistance of the army group. In the future this means as well the cancellation of bringing up one supplementary reserve battalion each to the XXXXIII and LIX Corps. This has been prompted by the lack of prepared reserve battalions. Thus, the replacement of the SS Brigade can be conducted only by means of expending all of the rear's possibilities. It is important that all the field works [the building of the system of defense] be conducted according to plan, so each time I have to monitor that the works aren't shown only on paper. I consider it necessary to emphasize this once again, so that in the future no one is surprised about this matter [if the defenses aren't ready for a Russian attack].

Field Marshal: Your situation is somewhat better than in the Second Panzer Army, where one of the divisions is holding a front of defense that stretches for 56 km, and two others each are holding a 40 km front. Thus, the troops are very badly overextended. The density of the front of the Second Panzer Army with weapons and manpower is very inadequate, especially when you consider the enemy's massing of forces in this sector. I don't see a substantial threat on our front, and don't expect one in the foreseeable future. The Russians have assembled all their forces in the Khar'kov area, somewhat to the north, in the Kursk area and at Leningrad. The Eighteenth Army in the nearest future anticipates an attack with the objective of liberating Leningrad.

Colonel General: When the Russians launch an attack anywhere, it would be desirable to fall back, thereby forming a salient that protrudes to the west, with the aim of weakening the enemy with a counterattack from the direction of Riga, since our forces are insufficient to hold a front by other means.

Field Marshal: In this case, we'll have to give you additional help. However, at this time I consider your sector to be completely quiet.

Colonel General: However, we have very few men at the front and the front is poorly fortified.

Field Marshal: I've rarely encountered a good state of affairs on this point at the front. However, the front in any case must be held in its entirety.

Colonel General: The setting up of the positions in the zone of responsibility of the II Luftwaffe Field Corps is completely unsatisfactory. The men in it are always acting like children.

Field Marshal: I am struck by this news. I am ordering the army's chief of staff [who was present during the telephone discussion and at one point appears to pick up the phone] to contact the commander of II Luftwaffe Field Corps promptly.

Colonel General: I'm in full agreement with you. The Luftwaffe Field Corps has been simply ignoring a multitude of orders. Partially this is due to stubbornness, and partially due to the lack of proper discipline. It is an incontestable fact that the Luftwaffe Field Corps becomes weaker with each passing day, though no replacement is foreseen for it. Will this lack of discipline and ignorance of orders ever come to an end?

Field Marshal: Alas, I cannot help you in any way with this. We must now urgently accumulate reserves in Europe, using for this everyone non-essential. The plan of Citadel has been confirmed; beginning tomorrow and for the next eight days, it can be put into operation at any time. It is clear to all of this that this will be the decisive battle of this year. The condition of the Second Panzer Army is dispiriting. Russian attacks against it will lead to the immediate wrapping up of Citadel. <u>Everyone agrees that it would be better if the Russians would start their offensive first.</u> [Author's emphasis]

Colonel General: I am reporting on the condition of the division's sectors: 206th Infantry Division – will soon be in full readiness for a defense; 330th Infantry Division – is in good condition, but lacking depth; 87th Infantry Division – moderately ready: the right flank prompts concerns, and on the left flank the situation is bad; the Luftwaffe Field Corps – from satisfactory to bad; 263rd Infantry Division – in part the communication trenches haven't been finished, but the division is making efforts to complete them; 291st Infantry Division – excellent, on its left flank the rear area hasn't been fully set up, especially the hilltop; 181st Infantry Division – is working diligently, but suffering continuous casualties; SS Infantry Brigade 1 (mot.) – in places good, in places satisfactory; 20th Panzergrenadier Division – good; 205th Infantry Division – there are both leading and lagging units, which has been discussed in detail in our report.

Field Marshal: Regarding the matter raised by the army commander regarding the terrain in the Rossono area[359], I've emphasized that it is impossible to conduct an operation here in mid-July, because at this time Operation Citadel will be underway.

Colonel General: In that case the bandits will cut the Daugavpils – Smolensk road which is important for the army group, and will bring it to such a condition that it cannot be restored.

Field Marshal: I can offer no help, because all available means have been gobbled up by Citadel. Recently the Führer had a conversation with Rosenberg and Sauckel. Rosenberg to a great degree represents our position, which the Führer opposes, protesting that our proposal might be implemented. He knows that the [Vlasov] Russians promise us nothing, and he has no formula on how to hold them back. The main problem now is the situation with the labor force in Germany, no one can forget

---

359 In 1942-43, on the territory of Kalinin Oblast's Idritskii District, there existed the Republic of Rossono. Its leaders – the socialist revolutionaries Librikh and Griaznov and the anarchist Martynovsky – proclaimed a simple ideology: For Russian socialism without Nazis and Stalinists. At the end of 1943, Rossono was destroyed together with almost its entire population by Latvian and Ukrainian death squads.

this. The Führer sees great danger in the creation of the Committee;[360] he does not want to give anyone firm promises on this question, and he is not interested in the dissatisfaction because of this. He needs a labor force in Germany and insists that everyone was subordinate to this objective … It is more than likely that Vlasov's act will fade with the passage of time. The Führer explained that he would be content if the formation of any sort of Eastern forces was avoided, and instead if the flow of labor force to the Reich intensified.

Colonel General: This means that the dispatch of workers to Germany will soon become a major pain for us.

Field Marshal: I'm in complete agreement!

Colonel General: I believe that for propaganda purposes, in our notices about labor obligations, the restoration of property rights should be immediately announced. However, no documents on this matter should be issued by the panzer army.

Field Marshal: I don't have any idea what to make of all this … This means for us that we must now bury all of our hopes. Our main concern becomes the question: How to send as many workers as possible to Germany?

Colonel General: When will at last our situation with ordnance improve? The French guns have long been standing without shells. Deliveries occur only as an exception. The [captured] Russian guns are also practically without shells. Shells arrive to us literally one by one. Recently even situation with ammunition for the German machine guns has become intolerable.

Field Marshal: I have had to hear this from practically everyone. As for the bullets for the machine guns, this problem has become very acute everywhere. The army group's chief of staff thinks that that we'll be able to deal with this problem no sooner than in six weeks. Possibly you've been informed that the main stockpiles of ammunition will be in the process of relocation in the nearest future.

Colonel General: An extreme shortage is being felt as well in anti-tank guns. The army group's chief of staff anticipates that in the nearest future, there will not be a single division left that has more than eight heavy anti-tank guns. The panzer army needs urgent reinforcement with heavy anti-tank battalions. The means for towing the anti-tank guns at present are completely unsuitable for the current conditions.

Field Marshal: The production of tanks and assault guns has sharply improved. The lagging in heavy weapons on the whole has been overcome; it is possible to hope that by the beginning of winter, our supply with materiel will become as good as we've ever had.

Colonel General: It is precisely because we cannot control whether or not the Russians will be able to launch an attack against us at the moment when we will be withdrawing to the west, and whether or not this attack will be launched in the direction of Daugavpils.

---

360 By this Hitler means the attempt by A.A. Vlasov to form a Committee of the Liberation of the Peoples of Russia on the basis of the "Smolensk Declaration" from 27 December 1942 and the deployment of a formation of the Russian Liberation Army, made up not only of prisoners of war, but also residents of the occupied territories of the USSR.

Field Marshal: The Russians can hardly be so strong after they've suffered serious losses in the course of Citadel. Recently it is not only we that have been experiencing certain difficulties caused by the enormous mass of Russians. At present, like never before, we can see the hard situation with supplying the Russian population, the poor condition of the transport, and the shortage of men.

The Colonel General heeded the Field Marshal's reply, pointing to the absence of pessimism in his evaluations. He then declared: The state of affairs in the panzer army is such that we are not able to offset the shortage of men and weapons. The discussion resumed:

Field Marshal: According to the plan of Citadel, the 8th Panzer Division should be withdrawn to Smolensk. The panzer army must agree with this. Obviously, the apparitions of Sukhinichi linger before the panzer army's command. However, this is not simply a personal opinion, although he [the Field Marshal] of course understands that the Russians can launch an attack here even in the event of the conducting of Citadel.
Colonel General: There exists the hard and fast requirement that each gun suitable for anti-tank defense must be distributed across the front at an interval of 500 meters, but according to the reports of the corps commanders, because of the intolerable ground condition, it is impossible to meet this responsibility in certain sectors.
Field Marshal: In the future it is hardly possible to count upon the allocation of a large number of guns suitable for anti-tank defense, which can be used in any sort of manner. He also considers it established that the requirements indicated by the Colonel General don't relate to all of his army's positions.[361]

Unquestionably, the most interesting point in this document is von Kluge's statement about the elusive dream of the Reich's generals that the Red Army be first to go on the offensive in the summer of 1943. Despite of the bold, and judging from everything, sincere declarations about the success of the future offensive, both the Field Marshal and other generals perfectly recognized how unfavorable Citadel was at this moment for the Wehrmacht, and the hazards stemming from it.

The subject of the conversation, which is connected with the discussion of what to do about "Vlasov's act", requires broader explanation. In early 1943, because of the growth of the partisan movement in the rear areas, including that of Army Group Center, and the shortage of manpower in the combat units and rear security forces, the Wehrmacht command jointly with Himmler's agency decided not only to expand the use of prisoners and the local population in service, in the so-called Ost battalions, but also to form a Russian Liberation Army (RLA) under the leadership of the Red Army's former Lieutenant General A.A. Vlasov. According to their scheme, the RLA was supposed to shatter the wave of popular resistance in the rear and attract Russians to the German side for the struggle against the Red Army and partisans. In addition, hopes were also that the RLA would take over the responsibility for rounding up civilians for slave labor in Germany. For this purpose, the OKW had organized two trips by

---

361 TsAMO RF, F.500, Op.12451, D.79, ll. 1-6.

A.A. Vlasov to the territory occupied by Army Group North, and there were even plans to organize two divisions out of prisoners and capture Oranienbaum and Kronstadt with them – the "Ray of Light Act" – in order to unleash from there "a genuine struggle for the liberation of Russia from Bolshevism". The headquarters of Army Group Center was actively involved in all this, hoping to derive advantages from it; after all, it was being contemplated to conduct the "Ray of Light Act" in order to support Citadel, as well as to make broader use of the local population on building defensive works. Also, it was thought to form several more Ost battalions in order to guard the rear, so that combat units wouldn't have to be withdrawn from the front for this purpose, as had happened back in mid-May. However, Hitler had no taste for A.A. Vlasov's excessively bold plans and pronouncements made during his trips and ordered W. Keitel to stop fooling around with "this Russian". It was regarding these unrealized hopes that Günther von Kluge was lamenting when he mentioned Hitler's conversation with Rosenberg and Sauckel.

Now, however, to return to the area of the Orel bulge. The unclear situation with the Russians' intentions was also deeply troubling Model's neighbor – the Second Panzer Army. At this time its front was in a greatly weakened condition, since the bulk of the replenishments and reserves had gone to the Ninth Army. As a result, the resources of its command on the eastern and northeastern sectors of the Orel salient had substantially diminished. In connection with this, on the morning of 19 June its chief of staff held talks with Elverfeldt, during which they discussed the possibility of a Russian tank attack in the Novosil' area. On this occasion the Second Panzer Army requested to work out a route of movement for StuG Battalion 245, which had been promised to it by the army group, but was still located with the Ninth Army, to an area 19 km southeast of Orel. Relying on intelligence information, which identified numerous positions for Katiusha rocket launchers at Novosil' and the active movement of Soviet forces on the roads north of Kursk to this area, Model shared his neighbor's concern and made no protest against the immediate transfer of StuG Battalion 245 to the Second Panzer Army's XXXV Corps, which was done immediately following the conversation. In addition, almost simultaneously with this, von Kluge issued an order to move a regimental kampfgruppe of the 9th Panzer Division, reinforced with self-propelled guns, to an area east of Orel (in the rear of Second Panzer Army), to serve as his personal mobile reserve.

A tense atmosphere, connected with the delayed start of the summer campaign and a possible Russian offensive toward Orel was reigning in the offices in Berlin and Lötzen. By this time, the disagreements regarding Citadel still had not been smoothed over in the Wehrmacht's leadership. Now, however, the two sides, in addition to the conclusions they had drawn back in springtime, were pointing at the lost time as a key problem. The operation's opponents, which as before were united around the OKW's operational leadership, were insisting that the period when it might have been possible to take advantage of the temporary weakness of the Russians (in the spring) had slipped away into the past. By now, they had not simply brought the frontline forces back up to strength, but had also substantially built up their reserves. The hope to encircle a million-strong Russian grouping with a whirlwind attack was now illusory.

On their part, the proponents of Citadel, headed by the OKH, were asserting that a collision with the Red Army's main forces in the nearest future was unavoidable, so the Wehrmacht should be first to take the initiative, since it no longer had the troops for a passive defense of a front that extended more than 2,000 km. K. Zeitzler's main motivation was obvious and had no direct relationship with the matter. The cancellation of the operation threatened serious consequences for the OKH's position in the hierarchy of Nazi Germany. After all, if Hitler rejected the offensive, he would be accepting the OKW's proposal about forming strategic reserves, a significant portion of which would be allocated to the Western theater of operations in order to guard the continent against a possible Allied landing, and thus be automatically subordinated to the OKW.

After the war, certain foreign authors maintained that by this time, supposedly even von Kluge and von Manstein opposed an offensive toward Kursk. In this connection, an excerpt from a publication by the former OKH staff officer Eike Middeldorf, as cited by G.A. Koltunov and B.G. Solov'ev in their book, is interesting: "With regard for the replenishment of the offensive's panzer divisions with materiel, at first this was set for the end of May. When this deadline was ignored, the offensive was designated to take place in mid-June. The OKH and the commanders-in-chief of the army groups unanimously believed that this deadline must be absolutely the final one for the offensive to be successful."[362]

In fact, throughout the entire period of preparations for Citadel, both of the field marshals were consistent supporters of Citadel, and the cited passage is nothing other than a clear example of the notion that appeared in Germany right after the war ended – "The Führer was stupid, the generals smart". This was called upon to free the Reich's generals from guilt and place all of the blame for the major failures in the Second World War in the eyes of the public on Hitler. Erich von Manstein recollected in his memoirs:

> If to view now the situation back then, then one can say that the commanders of the army groups in connection with the repeated postponements of the start of Operation Citadel should have informed the OKH that this offensive had lost its sense and mustn't be implemented ... As for me, then I assumed (which was apparently a mistake) that the operation had to be conducted for the following reasons. In the first place, the rejection of Operation Citadel would have brought about a further period of waiting in the East ... At the time it seemed that the Soviets actually had no wish to hurry with their own offensive .... Secondly, the command of Army Group South was convinced that the offensive would be hard, but successful. We were less confident that we would be able to repulse an enemy offensive in the Donbass. However, we were convinced that after a victory at Kursk, we would be able to put an end to the crisis in the Donbass, and perhaps achieve great victories here.[363]

Günther von Kluge based his assurance that the offensive had to be conducted even after such a long pause on approximately the same arguments. On 18 June, in a telegram addressed to K. Zeitzler (with a request to report its contents to the Führer), he maintained that a further delay or the complete cancellation of Citadel would allow the Russians to launch an offensive against Army Group South with the aim of breaking through to the Dnepr River. Moreover, in his opinion, it would inevitably be coordinated with a landing by the Allies in Europe, so accordingly Germany faced a dual threat. He stressed:

> Purely defensive operations, the aim of which would be the holding of our presently occupied positions, would lead to the rapid dispersion of our strength. Even having held

---

362 Koltunov and Solov'ev, *Kurskaia bitva*, p. 46.
363 Manstein, *Uteriannye pobedy*, pp. 532-533.

out in this defensive battle, we would all the same be apparently compelled to abandon the Orel salient with the aim of economizing forces, which is extremely undesirable, because the Orel Oblast is especially fruitful and valuable. From this, the conclusion may be drawn that since a collision with the main Russian forces is unavoidable, the best decision would be to implement our offensive in accordance with Citadel's plan. An obligatory condition of conducting it will be the use of the maximum number of tanks and the strong support of the Luftwaffe, as well as the replenishment of the forces with troops and equipment, in order to conclude successfully this exceptionally hard battle.[364]

This is a well-known document, but in the course of my work over this manuscript, I discovered a letter written by von Kluge on 25 June 1943 addressed to the OKH about the situation in his sector in the files of the US National Archives. The document's contents are inconsistent. Its author plainly wants to prove the need to attack toward Kursk, but does this rather erratically, since his arguments don't present a consistent chain of facts. The Field Marshal dedicates the first part of the document to the question of a possible Red Army offensive targeting the Orel salient. He openly acknowledges that unlike his tactical reconnaissance, his operational intelligence was working poorly. Therefore, in Berlin it should be understood that it was fully possible that the Russians were preparing a lot of surprises, which were unknown to Army Group Center. However, he is convinced that they would not start first:

Recently intense movement is observed in the Kursk area, which once in a while subsides for several days. The intensive transport of troops is happening out of the Novosil' area. At the same time, however, it is possible to draw a conclusion about the lack of readiness of these troops for a major offensive. However, presently it is rather problematic to check the accuracy of this conclusion, which contradicts that which we've been expecting for a long time. Such assessments [the identification of readiness for an offensive] can be made only with respect to a restricted amount of time and in narrow sectors of the front. So, all of the assertions expressed at the present time about the reliability of the forecasts of an enemy offensive cannot be accepted, and the intentions of the Russian command regarding the start of its offensive must be acknowledged as unknown to us. Each time our reconnaissance has unexpectedly, at the last moment, stumbled upon major enemy forces that have regrouped unnoticed from the rear area around Belev. These forces are showing up opposite weakened sectors of our front, thereby creating such a correlation of force that our thin defensive lines, in the event of an attack, would not be able to be held without the commitment of major reserves. In the Sukhinichi area, on the contrary, no major changes in the enemy grouping or the high intensity of transport movements has been noticed.

In this connection our available grouping does not permit the effective repulse of a strong Russian attack against the center and left flank of Gruppe Weiss or against the center and right flank of the Second Panzer Army. An attack in the western direction on the Zhizdra – Kirov front seems unlikely. Countermeasures against the

---

364 See the *Voenno-istoricheskii zhurnal*, No. 6 (1959), p. 91.

long-expected Russian attack with the aim of enveloping the grouping in the Orel salient seem excessive, since we've been unable to identify major shifts of hostile forces to the west. All of the above allows me to draw a conclusion that we shouldn't expect an offensive on an operational scale in the near future. In particular, one directed at achieving a double envelopment.[365]

Further on, the Field Marshal turns to an assessment of the Red Army's possible actions in the event that the Ninth Army goes on the offensive and the condition of its defenses. The purpose of these several paragraphs is as follows. First, to convince Berlin that he, Günther von Kluge, is in firm control of the situation both in the sector of his army group and with respect to the preparation for Citadel (even though formally Model was in charge of the operation), taking an active part in the preparations, and helping the Ninth Army as far as he was able. Second, to show the great difficulties that both the army group and the Ninth Army were encountering, and also, despite Hitler's sharp rebuke at the 4 May conference to Erich von Manstein's request for reinforcements, to convince the OKH all the same to send to Model the two additional infantry divisions that he was requesting.

In addition, from the document it follows that the von Kluge believed Citadel was unquestionably the only way out of the existing situation, basing his position on the fact that the Russian defenses were supposedly still far from ready. However, the main reason that the Wehrmacht absolutely had to attack was the thinned front of his entire army group, especially that of the Second Panzer Army, since it was here that Soviet forces were showing high activity with the movement of significant reserves. Günther von Kluge also gently hints that for the success of the operation, Berlin must not only render assistance, but also hasten with it. He wrote:

> At the same time, because the Russian strength is fully adequate, in particular with the inclusion of a large number of mobile formations, they are capable of cutting off the attacking wedge of our forces in the event of a breakthrough of their front. The threat of this is especially large given our offensive on the right flank and in the center of the Second Panzer Army. In this case the army group will possess plainly insufficient reserves, which consists of the main bulk of the 36th Infantry Division, 112th Infantry Division and 5th Panzer Division; in the event of a serious danger, the 8th Panzer Division and 183rd Infantry Division can also be used. The need exists to remove the 83rd Infantry Division, which is located now in reserve behind the front of the Fourth Army and Third Panzer Army, to the reserve on this direction.
>
> In the event of any development of the situation, the army group must ensure the maximal reinforcement of Gruppe Weiss in the amount of not less than two infantry divisions. <u>For a more rapid penetration of the enemy's defenses, it makes sense to move the 31st and 6th Infantry Divisions up into the first echelon. Thus, Gruppe Weiss, just like the army group, needs to be allocated additional infantry divisions.</u> Nevertheless, the danger remains that this request cannot be satisfied, in particular if there is no success in stabilizing the front of the Fourth Army. In this connection each corps must,

---

365 NARA US, T.312, R.320, F.78885222.

to a maximum extent, prepare to repulse Russian attacks in its sector and to hold intact the front's outline, without permitting any serious withdrawal.

For Gruppe Wiess, just like for the army group as well, great hopes are connected with being allocated the latest panzers (the Panther), since the 3rd Company of Tigers is experience great delays en route. Meanwhile the movement capabilities of the small units of Hornisse [Nashorn] tank destroyers remain a question. The total number of tanks thus far is substantially below the planned level. This also concerns the anti-tank means. Thus, the task stands in front of the reserve group [the administrative echelon] to assemble both battalions of assault guns allocated to reinforce Gruppe Weiss and the Second Panzer Army as quickly as possible in the Gomel' area. The weakest eastern and northern sectors of the Second Panzer Army should be substantially strengthened in an anti-tank respect. All the reinforcements must be directed to the Second Panzer Army's front, thereby indirectly easing the resolution of Gruppe Weiss's tasks. Thus, a panzergrenadier battalion of the 25th Panzergrenadier Division remains their only source of field artillery, and they are deprived of their own anti-tank means. The sectors of the divisions in the Novosil' – Belev sector are now excessively stretched, and the means in them are inadequate. The army group does not have the possibility of properly reinforcing them with heavy anti-tank guns. Instead of this, the sectors subjected to attack must be covered by one of the two available StuG battalions, which are at present only now arriving in the army [Second Panzer Army]. I want to point out particularly all those responsible for the extraordinary importance of this task.

Since a straightforward decision exists: the main attack will be launched by Gruppe Weiss, and this attack must have the maximum possible strength, I offer the following assessments. It is not known to anyone when the Russians will launch an attack or whether one will take place at all. They can under certain circumstances hold off on this attack until winter or even longer, while in the meantime strengthening their forces with tanks and other contemporary weapons. Such a development would be extremely undesirable for us.

In order to prevent it, the best solution is the timely launching of our attack! The longer we wait, the harder it will be to launch it. Thus, it is necessary to prepare for an offensive as quickly as possible. Thereby all of the enemy's efforts to set up their positions, upon which they are placing great hopes, will be reduced to null. <u>In order to set up the positions, the enemy must conduct such lengthy measures as evacuating the civilian population, the delivery of a large quantity of timber, the construction of new transportation routes and the rehabilitation of existing ones. For all this work, he has not more than one or two months left before the onset of the autumn muddy season.</u> However, we also have in our possession only this small amount of precious time. Indeed, as soon as at least a short attack will be launched, in my opinion, the enemy will have to commit a large quantity of reserves in order to repulse it, in the circumstances when only a portion of his reserves will be ready for commitment into combat.

I am reminding you – the Second Panzer Army's front is so thin, that any Russian attack can be repelled only with the immediate introduction of reserves into the battle from the depth. With regard for this, whether we want to or not, we must position our forces in such a way that it will be possible to ensure their immediate use for short attacks or counterattacks. <u>We must take all possible measures for the soonest start of</u>

our own offensive. In this case we will have the possibility of choosing the time of an attack or remaining on the defensive, and also <u>given the need, to abandon the occupied area until the end of summer</u>, while in the process preserving offensive possibilities. [All author's emphasis][366]

I have intentionally cited this document virtually in full, so that in it, the point of view of the command of Army Group Center with respect to Citadel just two weeks before its start has been presented in the Commander-in-Chief's own words. I emphasized a few of the most pressing problems that stood before him and his proposals of ways to resolve them. Of particular interest is the final line in the letter. Prior to this, we see Günther von Kluge as he was in May 1943 – a politician-general and a convinced adherent of active operations, who in support of the Führer's position was ready even to distort the facts in order to emphasize the correctness of the earlier chosen course. In the last line, however, in spite of all of the above listed arguments in favor of an offensive, a professional takes the center stage (though not distinctly so), who in the document of a strategic nature permits the thought of abandoning the Orel salient in the nearest future, since he considers the failure of the entire summer campaign to be possible, even though according to Hitler, it must surely end successfully. It is hard to say whether or not the Field Marshal sincerely believed in Citadel's success, while remaining a consistent advocate for it. However, the impression forms that in June 1943 he was already preparing a basis to be able to say in the event of failure: "I also had doubts in the achievement of the objectives embodied in the operation's plan, but I believed in the Führer and the implementation of it until the end."

At the army level at this time there was also more than a few advocates of the attack toward Kursk; such key figures as Walter Model and Hermann Hoth can be assigned to this group, albeit with some stretch. Today it is impossible to establish how the commander of the Ninth Army personally assessed the need for Citadel. If to rely on the captured documents of the Ninth Army, then at this moment he also saw the only way out of the prolonged operational pause as an immediate attack toward Kursk, although he was not holding his breath regarding a victory. Therefore, parallel with the preparation for the operation, its troops were actively throwing up defensive works along a rear line in the Orel salient. In the preamble to the final version of the Citadel plan, he wrote:

> The enemy opposite Gruppe Weiss stands with large forces in expectation of a German offensive. In the Trosna – Maloarkhangel'sk sector (inclusively), where the enemy in all likelihood has determined for himself where the main attack of the forthcoming offensive will land, all of the measures for preparations of the defense have long ago been completed. The enemy possesses a particularly strong, well laid-out system of trenches and works that is sufficiently manned with infantry; a strong, well-considered echeloned anti-tank defense; and particularly strong artillery and a large quantity of Katiushas. They've also assembled a local attacking reserve, having tanks.
>
> In the depth of the enemy's territory, especially at Kursk and Maloarkhangel'sk, army and front reserves have been assembled, the strength of which is their mobility, since basically these are armored units. In addition, a command reserve is positioned

---

366 Ibid., F.78885223-78885225.

on the Kastornoe – Livny – Verkhov'e [a village in Orel Oblast] line. At the present moment the arrival of supplementary forces at the indicated areas is continuing. The replenishment of the hostile units standing opposite the Gruppe's right flank in the Dmitriev area has basically been completed. Reinforcements were also brought up here a certain time ago. The strength of the enemy air force rivals the strength of our ground forces.

In the event that the German offensive does not take place, it is necessary to count upon the enemy's offensive operations. If the German offensive does in fact occur in the direction of Kursk, it will encounter bitter resistance of an enemy that has prepared for a defense along the entire front, and later strong, numerous armored formations, which will be conducting diversionary attacks and counterattacks, likely from the east and southeast. Enemy attempts to break out from the west must also be expected.[367]

By the middle of June, Hermann Hoth, who was the main "architect" of the offensive plan for an attack toward Kursk from the south, was showing greater concern about the correlation of forces on his panzer army's front, even though he rarely spoke out against the attack. He believed that the effect of surprise had vanished long before, and in order to repulse the counterattack of the 1st Tank Army and engage in the expected battle with the Soviet's approaching strategic mobile reserves at Prokhorovka, only two panzer corps (the II SS Panzer Corps and the XXXXVIII Panzer Corps) under his direction were now insufficient. On 14 June 1943 he sent to the headquarters of Army Group South a document containing his assessment of the situation in the sector of the Voronezh Front and the likely intentions of its command. In it, the general demonstrated a clear understanding of the logic of the actions on the Soviet side, although his level of information did not extend beyond the second army-level belt of defenses. In the middle of June, he could not even say with confidence whether or not the Soviet defenses included a third line of defense on the axis of his panzer army's main attack (although work had already started on one long before) and spoke about it only in a speculative tone. Wrote the Colonel General:

> The Russians are anticipating a German offensive in order to straighten out the front in the Kursk area. They only don't understand where this offensive will begin. At first, the steps taken to strengthen the positions were indicating that the enemy is expecting attacks along the main roads between Belgorod and Tomarovka. Now it appears that he is expecting an attack southwest of Rakitnoe.
>
> Significant strengthening of the Russian defense is evident on the entire front. The bringing up of a rifle division to a point south of Krasnaia Iaruga, the further increased construction of positions, including the digging in of tanks and the deployment of minefields are obvious to the naked eye. The enemy's artillery positions have multiplied. At the forward edge, in addition to all else, the enemy has strengthened the anti-tank defenses.
>
> Anti-tank ditches south of Cherkasskoe have been extended as far as the ravine 2 km west of Berezovyi, so that on the entire offensive front, the gaps between

---

367 Klink, *Das Gesetz des Handelns. Die Operation "Zitadelle"*, p. 321.

natural obstacles have been blocked to tanks. One more anti-tank ditch is under construction southwest of Dubrovo on both sides of the road. Here, like at Iakovlevo, lies a significantly reinforced second line of defense. In the rest, the main location of identified works is located west of the Soldatskoe – Rakitnoe line.

According to prisoner testimony, it must be expected that a third line of defense is being built along the Psel River.

The main direction of enemy reconnaissance activity and reconnaissance-in-force operations in the proposed areas of the offensive lie in the vicinity of Erik and Butovo. On the rest of the panzer army's front, there has been activity only at Trefilovka opposite the center and fight flank of the 57th Infantry Division. The Russians thus far are not shelling our batteries. Their harassing fire is irregular and has recently become lighter.

By means of the increased dispatching of agents and particularly nighttime aerial reconnaissance without bombings, the Russians are attempting at any price to clarify the situation.

The attack conducted by the Russians on 13 June with the forces of a regiment against the fortified point of Trefilovka was exclusively a local operation. Future attacking intentions have so far not been revealed.

In step with the increase of the striking power of our units, the Russians' operational reserves are growing as well. It is especially necessary to count upon a significantly greater number of tanks and their better equipage than counted upon previously.

The fortification of our defenses is moving forward in very small steps, because the divisional sectors are too broad and the units are occupied with continuous defense. The construction of the artillery positions and second line of defense has begun. Since for these purposes there are only local residents without the proper number of supervisors, the construction is going very slowly. The army's sapper battalions are engaged in improving the roads and bridges. The divisional sapper battalions are undergoing training for special assignments.

Improved training of the units is badly needed. Nevertheless, the spirit of attack and the willingness to advance are above all praise. The provisioning of supplies nevertheless hasn't improved in general. The insufficient fitting out of the tanks in the 3rd and 11th Panzer Divisions prompts reflection. So far not all of the tanks have been fitted with armored skirts. There are no other admonitions that need to be met urgently.

The shipment of materiel to the divisional combat schools and the panzer army's district school is below the provisioning of the units with supplies, since replacement equipment is not arriving.

Conclusion: I believe that each day of delay with the start of the Citadel offensive is working only in favor of the enemy.[368]

The fact that all of Hoth's assessments primarily relate to the area of the first and second defensive belts and the problems of the insufficient equipping of the panzer divisions, which are

---

368 NARA US, T.313, R.340, F.8656227, 8656228.

the key instrument for a breakthrough, testified to Hoth's great disturbance with the degree of fortification of Vatutin's defenses and a lack of confidence that his panzer army would be able to penetrate it quickly. On 19 June, the 11th Panzer Division numbered 84 tanks and 21 assault guns, including five outdated Pz.Kpfw. II tanks, four command tanks and three flamethrower tanks, while the 3rd Panzer Division was even in worse shape – 63 tanks and 21 assault guns.[369] This was approximately 30-40 machines less than the smallest establishment strength, but the situation was similar in the divisions of the adjacent Army Detachment Kempf. Manstein had no other tanks, and Hoth already knew that he would be given the brigade of Panthers, so he could not expect additional forces from Berlin. Therefore, by the start of the offensive (4 July 1943), the 3rd Panzer Division would only receive five more tanks, but at the same time be deprived of 11 assault guns, while the 11th Panzer Division would receive nothing at all.[370]

Even so, Hoth was hoping that the men's high level of training and the superiority of the German armor over their Soviet counterparts would play the decisive role in achieving victory, at the very least, in the offensive's first stage. On 20 June 1943 his headquarters produced an interesting document entitled "The assessment of the situation for conducting Operation Citadel and its continuation", which stated: "The enemy ... has moved up the 1st Tank Army. Despite this, a successful implementation of Operation Citadel is still possible ... For the continuation of the operation, it is not territorial gain that is important, but the destruction of the enemy's new major formations."[371]

Despite the unfavorable conditions, the commander of the Fourth Panzer Army's hope was still smoldering according to his chief of staff, F. Fangohr:

> Finally, General Hoth remained convinced that the German Army had lost the element of surprise through the repeated postponement of the offensive. Accumulating and reorganizing six panzer divisions south of the Kharkov – Akhtyrka area over a period of several months simply could not have escaped the Soviet attention despite all the deception measures.
>
> Even so, General Hoth appeared confident of achieving at least a limited victory. With regard to the breakthrough attack against the Russian defensive system, he anticipated complete success.[372]

Judging by the revelatory documents, most of the pessimists were among the commanders at the operational and tactical levels, which is to say, among those who directly faced the problems of carrying out the operation. Moreover, they spoke out more openly and categorically. For example, the commander of Army Group South's 7th Panzer Division Major General von Funck did not keep concealed his sharply negative attitude toward the plan of Citadel and in the presence of senior officers of his division asserted that the war was lost, and that the Germans had bitten off more than they could chew.[373] Certain commanders of Army Group Center also provided a

---

369 NARA US, T.313, R.340, F.8656227, 86562202.
370 Zetterling, N. and Frankson, A., *Kursk 1943: a statistical analysis* (London: Frank Cass, 2000), p. 186.
371 Parot'kin (ed.), *Kurskaia bitva*, p. 514.
372 Newton, *Kurskaia bitva: nemetskii vgliad*, p. 74.
373 Cross, *Operatsiia Tsidadel'*, p. 133.

similar assessment regarding the forthcoming offensive. Lieutenant General Lubbe recalled a situation in the XXXXVII Panzer Corps prior to the Battle of Kursk:

> Through rumors from the corps headquarters I found out that opposite the front of the Second Panzer Army (80-90 km east of Orel), very large enemy forces had been detected, which were continuing to strengthen all the time. In addition, I learned that our Second Army (on the right of the Ninth Army) ... was not ready for an offensive and even worse, had almost no mobility. This information ... naturally gave rise to serious doubts in the success of Citadel among many, including myself. However, no one talked openly about this.[374]

In the final phase of Citadel's preparations (in June 1943), both in Army Group Center and in Army Group South an interesting situation emerged with the arrangement of combat forces of the main armies. Model and Hoth separately were changing their approaches to the task of breaking through the main belt of the Soviet defenses. The Ninth Army commander began to echelon his assault wedge in depth, while the Fourth Panzer Army in contrast issued an order on 27 June to move its last reserve – the 3rd Panzer Division – into the front line. Although the decision to do this had been made back in May 1943, Hermann Hoth had refused to cancel it for the next one and half months. This might show that they had become firmer in their opinion that the possibility of rapidly breaking through the Russian defenses would push their forces to the limit (and perhaps was now already beyond their capabilities). Hoth was an adherent of the theory that tanks were the decisive factor, so he emphasized the massing of armor from the first minutes of the offensive along the entire front, so the army could exert all of its power in the initial attack. Model's assigned breakthrough sector was narrower, so his headquarters decided to "grind through" the lines of the Central Front in a different way: to maintain a high density of forces and means at the tip of the attacking spearhead by continually bringing up units from the second and third echelons right up to the full breakthrough of the tactical zone. In particular, he planned to give the artillery of the divisions of the third echelon to the divisions of the first wave for the first day of the offensive. For example, on 18 June General of Infantry Horn, the commander of the XXXXVI Panzer Corps, reported that the reserve 12th Panzer Division was moving up its only Flak battalion and all of its artillery to the frontline divisions, as well as transferring two batteries of assault guns to reinforce the 7th and 31st Infantry Divisions.[375] It was also under consideration to handle infantry units in the same way, in the event that the forward divisions suffered very high casualties.

On 18 June, Hitler held a conference in the Berchtesgaden, in order once again to review the situation and to make a final decision about the offensive. The OKW was uniformly recommending the cancellation of Citadel. It was characterizing the operational situation in early summer 1943 as a period of growing instability in every theater of combat operation. It was, therefore, recommended to form two powerful reserve groupings. One, consisting of the strategic reserve, would be deployed in Germany, and the second would combine the two armies on the Eastern Front that were to be employed in the attack toward Kursk, and instead assemble

---

374 TsAMO RF, F.15, Op.11600, D.1063, l. 90.
375 NARA US, T.312, R.322, F.7891358.

them behind the operating forces in areas offering a good rail network, so if the need arose, they could be quickly shifted to crisis points, for example, to Italy or the Balkans.

Guderian, who was attending the conference, also spoke up categorically against an attack toward Kursk. Back during a meeting with Hitler two weeks before, he reported the hopelessness of the undertaking with Citadel, pointing to the concrete example that the Panthers still were not ready for combat. Even now, he once again emphasized to those gathered the same fully objective arguments: the panzer divisions were not in any condition to meet their objectives set by the operation, and the hopes being placed on the Panther brigade were unwarranted. The Inspector General of Panzer Troops stressed, "In addition to the technical imperfections of the new tanks, the crews and officers aren't sufficiently familiar with each other, and some of them have no combat experience."[376] However, these arguments did not budge Hitler from his position. He parried Guderian's arguments with the rather dubious assertion that "never before have the German troops in Russia been better trained, and never have they been so well-equipped with heavy weapons."[377] To the OKW's proposal, he replied that he highly valued the opinion of his officers, but he had already made the decision to go on the offensive toward Kursk, and he promised to give his start date a bit later.

For the command of the Ninth Army, the situation with the offensive finally became clear on the evening of 20 June. At 1800, in the office of the Operations Department, "a deep sigh of joy and relief filled the room" – that's how the narrow circle of officers and generals involved in Citadel's planning greeted the news from the army group that the Führer had made his final decision to conduct the operation. The armies received the order: Within eight days, the troops must be ready for active operations. Even so, it would be a full five chaotic days later before Berlin would announce the final start date – 5 July 1943. The final correction was connected with the continuing struggle between proponents and opponents of the offensive. The OKW's Deputy Chief of Operations General Walter Warlimont recalled:

> On 18 June therefore the OKW Operations Staff submitted an evaluation to Hitler leading up to the proposal that, until the situation had been clarified, Citadel should be cancelled and that a strong operational reserve at the disposal of the Supreme Command be constituted both in the East and in Germany, the latter by the formation of new units. The same day Hitler decided that 'although he appreciated the point of view of the OKW', Operation Citadel should definitely be carried out, and he laid down the date of the attack as initially 3 and subsequent 5 July. … Jodl had returned from leave at the end of June and he also raised emphatic objections to the premature commitment of the central reserves in the East; he pointed out both verbally and in writing that a local success was all that could he hoped for from Operation Citadel and that it could have no strategic significant for the overall situation. Hitler was clearly shaken but was eventually influenced by others and stuck to his decision.[378]

---

376 Guderian, *Vospominaniia nemetskogo generala*, p. 342.
377 *Wehrwissenschaftlihe Rundschau*, No. 9 (1965), p. 537.
378 Warlimont, W., *V stavke Gitlera: Vospominaniia nemetskogo generala* [*Inside Hitler's Headquarters: Memoirs of a German general*] (Moscow), pp. 361-362. This is the Russian translation of Warlimont's *Inside Hitler's Headquarters 1939-1945* as published in English by Presidio Press as a reprint of the 1964 copyright held by Weidenfeld & Nicholson, Ltd.

A minute, but important detail: This quote, just like the entire process of preparing Operation Citadel as presented in captured German documents refutes the assertion of some highly-placed members of the Russian special services that Soviet agents already "at the end of April, two and half months before the start of the Battle of Kursk, transmitted complete information to Moscow that the German offensive would begin in early July."[379] Just how was it possible to learn the precise date of Citadel in April, if Hitler himself did not know it prior to 18 June?!

The sole outcome of Jodl's demands became the next scandal. Zeitzler did not miss the occasion to submit a complaint that the OKW, just as before, had exceeded its authority and was interfering in the matters of the OKH, which Hitler reviewed for several days. The Supreme Command of the Wehrmacht was in this state right up to the start of the summer campaign. It needs to be said that stress and tension were also apparent at this time in the command of the Red Army. It's no wonder, because the realization of the colossal responsibility for reaching decisions that were fated to have such large consequences was weighing down on the Soviet generals and marshals to no less a degree. Surprising is the synchronicity of the events that unfolded in Moscow and Berlin that were essentially similar. It was just at this same time, after 20 June, as arguments were going on in the Fuhrer Headquarters, that N.F. Vatutin appealed to Stalin with a request: To launch the Red Army's offensive right away, and the Supreme Commander also hesitated.

Let's return to the headquarters of the Ninth Army. The evening of 20 June passed in an elevated mood. Its officers quickly prepared and distributed to the troops two important directives from H. von Elverfeldt. In the first under No.0142/43, he provided an assessment of the situation, information on the enemy, described its available and reserve forces, and once again pointed to the need to strengthen the army with two additional infantry divisions. In the second, No.0136/43, considering the possibility that the offensive would get underway soon and lacking confidence that the two requested infantry divisions would arrive, he "demanded to work out a plan to shift the 10th Panzergrenadier Division (altogether or in batches) to the left flank of the 78th Sturm Division and to scout out previously planned routes of movement for its commitment into the battle in the sector of the 383rd Infantry Division."[380]

However, despite the prospect of Citadel's execution that had appeared, the tension connected with a possible preemptive Russian offensive lingered in the headquarters. Even so, on this day Elverfeldt in his daily communique to Army Group Center reported that despite the fact that the Russian activity at the front had increased somewhat, he had seen no radical change in the composition of their forces. Nevertheless, the command of the Ninth Army was still anticipating a Russian offensive and had decided for itself that it would begin on 22 June. In connection with this, Headquarters Breitenbuch, the commanders of the XXXXI and XXXXVI Panzer Corps, on this same day received a telegram about detaching mobile reserves from each division and scouting routes for their rapid lateral movement to the supposed areas of the Russian attacks.

The following day, 21 June, began and ended differently, very wretchedly for Model and his headquarters. The first unpleasantness arrived from Smolensk early in the morning: the expected arrival of Battalion 655 of Ferdinands, the Panther Battalions 51 and 52, and the self-propelled

---

379 *Tainye stranitsy Velikoi Otechestvennoi* [*Secret pages of the Great Patriotic War*] (Moscow: Kuchkovo pole, 2009), p. 128.
380 NARA US, T.312, R.317, F.7886130.

guns for resurrecting the assault gun battalions expected at 0915 had been cancelled.[381] The army had been deprived of this reinforcement and replenishment. The Colonel General was enraged; this news became the last drop to his next open conflict with Army Group Center's leadership. Certain foreign scholars, in particular Steven Newton, maintain that following the May conference, Model had so infuriated other key players that "neither Zeitzler nor von Kluge had any particular interest in acting as his audience ...."[382] As archival sources show, this was far from being the case. I cannot say this about the Chief of the General Staff of the OKH without any particular confidence, but von Kluge in the course of May and June met personally with the Ninth Army commander on more than one occasion, and spent a long time discussing the problems of the forthcoming offensive with him. I suspect that given the need, Zeitzler acted in the same way.

This does not mean that they were delighted with each other. Model was never a beloved figure among a significant portion of the Wehrmacht's generals. In the first place, he was not a "true Prussian" – a hereditary military man. Second, Model was distinguished by his sincere faith in the ideas of National Socialism, while the majority of the generals and field marshals adhered to the principle that a soldier must remain outside of politics. Third, he really was a capable general, but in the opinion of some of his colleagues, he had advanced in rank too quickly – in just three years, he had risen from colonel to colonel general. This was annoying, and those envious of him were inclined to believe such a rapid career climb was due to his adherence to Nazism. The former commander of the 86th Infantry Division General of Artillery Helmut Weidling while in prison after the war wrote the following about Model:

> Model was a big specialist in the military sphere. He enjoyed authority among his troops and the latter felt confidence under his command. He was a resourceful man, who was able to find a way out of any disadvantageous situation. Therefore, Hitler sent him to those sectors where the situation was particularly difficult. He was an enthusiastic supporter of Hitler.[383]

In fact, the Colonel General did not hide his desire to have close contacts among the Reich's governing elite. For example, while still acting as the commander of a panzer corps, he had asked SS Reichsführer Himmler to assign him a SS officer as an adjutant, which prompted a storm of indignation among the army officers who were jealous of these leaps in rank.[384]

Fourth, and finally, many considered Model to be a martinet because of his tendency toward extremely harsh discipline and order, even according to the standards of the German Army. Even so, there was no one who could behave like an aggrieved school boy in his high rank, not Model, not von Kluge, nor Zeitzler. An obvious example was Field Marshal G. von Kluge's challenge to Guderian to a duel in May 1943. At the time, Hitler through his adjutant had sharply put him in his place: A war was going on, and such juvenile behavior was impermissible!

---

381 NARA US, T.312, R.317, F.7886131.
382 Newton, *Pozharnik Gitlera – fel'dmarshal Model*, p. 266.
383 *Generala i ofitsery vermakhta rasskazyvaiut: Dokumenty iz sledstvennykh del nemetskikh voennoplennykh* [*Generals and officers of the Wehrmacht talk: Documents from the investigative cases of German prisoners of war*] (Moscow: MFD, 2009), p. 215.
384 Manstein, *Uteriannye pobedy*, p. 526.

In fact, throughout the entire period of preparation for the Battle of Kursk, constant tension between the leadership of the Ninth Army, the OKH and Army Group Center is traceable. Their key figures carried on intrigues in back rooms and whenever possible threw their comrades-in-arms under the bus, although they did not seek to aggravate a personal situation openly, since they were "all in the same boat", so to speak. Even more so, they were aware of the Model's prickly nature. Emotional outbursts took place rarely, only with respect to isolated and major questions, and only when he had clearly run into a brick wall of opposition. One such moment was the Ninth Army's deprivation of the Ferdinands and Panthers. Here it was impossible for Model to restrain himself; they had stripped him of even the elusive chance for success. It must be said that the conflict over the armor had been ripening under the surface for the entire last month, and it was von Kluge's decisions that were aggravating him. In early June, 30 Pz.Kpfw. IV tanks had arrived, but the Field Marshal, instead of passing them on to the Ninth Army, had transferred them to his reserve 8th Panzer Division. Between 12 and 27 June, 11 Tigers and 112 Pz.Kpfw. IV tanks were to arrive, of which at his order 60 of the Pz.Kpfw. IV tanks had already been set aside once again for his reserve, this time the 5th Panzer Division. Neither of these panzer divisions were planned to be committed into the fighting, either as part of the first or the second echelons, while at this time Model's divisions were experiencing an acute deficit of armor. Even so, the army commander over all this time did not put forward any demands, and only on occasion did he mention that the army was in bad need for armored vehicles.

Having received the shocking news about depriving him of the Panthers and heavy self-propelled guns, he called the army group and spat out all the anger that had been accumulating inside him over this time. It should be noted that although this conversation was extremely tense, the Colonel General was from the outset in a constructive mood. He immediately agreed with Hitler's decision to give the Panthers instead to von Manstein, but he categorically demanded to have the Ferdinands returned to him and in addition to send him one more StuG battalion, since "both these battalions are vitally necessary for the offensive."[385] However, he could not change the situation right away with either well-founded argumentation or with resolute insistence. After this, he switched to a discussion with Elverfeldt of the offensive plan based upon the new realities.

Literally just minutes later, Krebs called him and added fuel to the fire. The army group had called off Operation Samara. At the same time, the army group's chief of staff emphasized that he personally considered it a significant point for Citadel's success and the understanding of the Russians' attitude. Secondly, at von Kluge's decision, the third echelon of troops (10th Panzergrenadier Division, 12th Panzer Division and Gruppe Esebeck), which had been assigned for Citadel, would remain in his reserve right up to the start of the offensive. At the same time, the artillery of the divisions of the third echelon, as had been previously planned, would operate in the interests of the divisions of the first wave only on the first day. Finally, the army group did not agree with the transfer of units of the 10th Panzergrenadier Division to reinforce the 383rd Infantry Division as the Model had proposed. In order to soothe somewhat the bitter pill to swallow, Krebs added that it was under consideration to reinforce the army with the 36th Infantry Division and, perhaps, some other division.

385 NARA US, T.312, R.317, F.7886131.

Model, who still had not cooled down from the first conversation, replied in a sharp tone that the third echelon was an essential need for the army; otherwise, it would be impossible to lend support to the forward divisions in the first, most difficult stage of the offensive. He stressed at the end of the discussion, "I've studied the ground well, and I request to give me personal responsibility for the positioning of the forces, since I am answering for the operation's results."[386]

It is possible to understand the emotional intensity of the army commander. In one hour, he had been stripped of the Ferdinands and Panthers, and had thus been deprived not only of his sole hope for success in the first days of the offensive, but also of any possibility of reinforcing the combat wedge when breaking through the main belt of defenses. Yet responsibility for the operation still lay on his shoulders. On the following days, he therefore continued his sharp polemics and put constant pressure on the army group with the aim of reinforcing his army.

Kluge's arguments in return were that the heavy self-propelled guns were extremely important for reinforcing the Second Panzer Army's front, and the third echelon was his only means for repulsing a Russian offensive, should it immediately follow in response to the start of the Ninth Army's offensive. It is hard to call them convincing. Unquestionably, he had the right to take precautions in the event of a Red Army offensive, but not to such an extent! After all his decisions took no consideration of the Ninth Army's condition or Hitler's assertion that Citadel would be the year's main offensive. It also did not tally with the Field Marshal's own declaration, which he made during a telephone conversation with Model back on 2 May: "The operation has particular significance for the struggle on the entire Eastern Front, since its success is capable of freeing up substantial reserves. Each soldier must be imbued with the importance of his task in this battle."[387] He was personally aware that at this moment, even the army's shock unit – the Heavy Panzer Battalion 505 – had still not been brought up to strength in tanks; on 25 June it numbered only 27 Pz.Kpfw. VI and 12 Pz.Kpfw. III armed with the 50mm cannon, instead of the established 45 Pz.Kpfw. VI.[388] For his part, the Colonel General as much as he was able tried to exert influence on the strengthening of this important breakthrough instrument. For example, on 27 June he directed that "the above-establishment Pz.Kpfw. III with the L60 cannon (long-barreled cannon) be returned again to Heavy Panzer Battalion 505."[389] Even so, it is difficult to call this even a half-measure; there had been 12 Pz.Kpfw. III in the battalion, and naturally they could not replace the heavy tanks, which the first echelon acutely needed. It is difficult to separate from the thought that the Field Marshal's order about transferring the Ferdinands was dictated not by concern for the common cause, but more likely by von Kluge's own deeply personal motivations.

On the following day, Krebs confirmed everything that had been reported over the telephone on the prior evening with his Directive Ia No.6623/43, with one correction: the army group agreed to move the 10th Panzergrenadier Division's Panzergrenadier Regiment 10 to the spearhead of the 383rd Infantry Division's attack.[390] In addition, one infantry regiment from the 36th Infantry Division was directed to the 383rd Infantry Division. This was impressive

---

386 NARA US, T.312, R.317, F.7886031.
387 NARA US, T.312, R.317, F.7886072.
388 NARA US, T.315, R.386, F.000499.
389 NARA US, T.312, R.317, F.7886136.
390 NARA US, T.312, R.317, F.7886032.

reinforcement for the XXIII Corps, which was prompted by Model's large doubt that it (just like the XX Corps) would be capable of meeting its objectives, especially after intelligence in June had detected tanks in the depth of the Soviet defenses. Initially it had not been planned to switch any armor to Friessner's corps, with the exception of two StuG battalions, so after the Abwehr's report, Model was extremely worried over the murky prospects of developing combat operations in this sector in the first days of the offensive. In fact his concern was so serious that with the aim of strengthening the preparation to repulse possible Russian tank attacks from the east during the offensive, he issued an order to initiate work to expand the trench network here on 26 June, and on 27 June, to reinforce the sector of the 383rd Infantry Division in the next three days with another regimental group from the 292nd Infantry Division.

The Field Marshal's only decision with which Model fully agreed was the cancellation of Operation Samara. Like von Kluge, he also believed that on the eve of the offensive, it was not worth provoking the Russians, but better to strengthen the sector of the XX Corps with obstacles and fortifications. On the evening of 22 June, Roman's headquarters received a telegram, which stated, "In the interests of ensuring a strong defense, by an order of the army group, the execution of Operation Samara is being cancelled. The corps must quickly make known its need for mines and construction materials that are in short supply for the defense."[391] On 28 June, while the troops were already moving into their jumping-off positions, Model hastily removed even combat units from the front – the reconnaissance battalions of the 2nd and 9th Panzer Divisions – and sent them in order to assist the XX Corps' 251st Infantry Division get its positions ready more quickly. This decision plainly demonstrates not only the Ninth Army commander's deficit of strength, but also how seriously he was alarmed by the situation in this sector. So naturally, in such a murky situation, he considered it thoughtless and more importantly even fruitless to provoke the Russians in this sector once the decision to launch Citadel had been taken.

At the end of the month, despite the army group's firm stance with respect to self-propelled guns, Model was nevertheless able get what he wanted. First, on 30 June the StuG Battalion 245, which he had only recently been directed to send to the XXXV Corps, arrived from the Second Panzer Army and placed at his disposal. Second, yielding to his pressure, von Kluge agreed to return the Ferdinand heavy tank destroyers as well to the Ninth Army, as long as all the conditions were created to ship them quickly back to the Second Panzer Army if the need arose because of the renewal of the threat of a Russian attack in its sector. In execution of this agreement, on 3 July H. von Elverfeldt personally informed the army group:

> In the event of the need to move the Ferdinands up to meet an attack in sectors of the front north and northeast of Orel, their shipment by rail has been planned. In order to organize this, the following steps have been taken by the present time:
> a) Special railcars and heavy Russian platforms have been prepared at several stations west of Orel. Their use is only with the authorization of the Gruppe Weiss's Department of Armor or of the corps.

---

391 NARA US, T.312, R.317, F.7886133.

b) Stations in the Glazunovka – Orel sector have been equipped with loading and offloading means (strong access ramps at the Glazunovka, Zmievka and Orel railroad stations).

In order to move the heavy Ferdinand machines across to the sector of the XXXV Corps, sectors of roads have been improved, bridges have been reinforced, and a signal communications and traffic control have been agreed upon with the command of the Second Panzer Army.[392]

When analyzing in detail the situation in the Ninth Army before the Battle of Kursk, it is impossible not to note the persistent and constant effort of Army Group Center's command to encroach upon Model's turf, to have a role in the preparation of Citadel and to direct the troops, even at a tactical level, where such a high headquarters shouldn't handle such matters. This despite the fact that at this time Walter Model and his subordinates were demonstrating operational efficiency and the necessary quality of work. The motivations for this are understandable. The army group once again wanted to show who was boss and to emphasize its status as a superior headquarters, especially in a situation when nothing was threatening it, because it was Model who was bearing personal responsibility for Citadel. In addition, it was thought that the offensive would be difficult, and the prospects for success unclear, but present, and Hitler was counting on them. Both von Kluge and Krebs, therefore, did not consider it excessive to take steps in advance, so that in the event that clear results were achieved, it would be possible to speak about the joint success of the Ninth Army and Army Group Center, and not only that of Model alone. Here is one of the examples of how Krebs' staff was "disturbed" by army headquarters' ability to organize properly the commitment of two full companies (!) of armor into battle. As noted in a document of Ninth Army headquarters for 28 June:

> The Army Group has ordered the Operations Department by 1045 to report on the status of the combat readiness of the company of self-propelled guns and the 1st Panzer Company of the 12th Panzer Division. These units, which don't possess armored assault guns, have been designated for the first echelon of the offensive, despite the fact that the army was directed to use their men as a reserve to replace men put out of action. The demand to withdraw these units into the reserve was issued by the Army Group's Chief of Staff to the Ninth Army's Chief of Staff during a telephone conversation at 1800.[393]

To find flaws and to order corrections is the responsibility of each officer, whatever the post he is holding. However, it is hard to believe that the Ninth Army command was planning to commit tank and assault gun crews without their machines to break through the Soviet first line of defense. At the very least, I've never come across such precedents. Unfortunately, I've been unable to find out how this matter was settled right before the start of the operation. However, judging from available captured German documents, a portion of the 12th Panzer Division, including its panzer battalion as well, took active part in Operation Citadel.

---

392 NARA US, T.312, R.321, F.78861048.
393 NARA US, T.312, R.321, F.7886137.

From the mid-May, using the relative lull in operations, Model's staff put an emphasis on the combat training of the troops of the divisions assigned to the assault wedge. However, they were unable to do this systematically, because of their participation in Operation Gypsy Baron, and then the lengthy process of regrouping, in the course of which their assembly areas were changing repeatedly.

In addition, some of the divisions had been transferred to the army back in early June only "on paper", and they arrived at its disposal only in the latter half of the month. So, these divisions received no replenishments, and there was not sufficient time left to work out questions of their cooperation during the operation or to prepare the troops according to the overall scheme of training.

Finally, as documents reveal, the bulk of the march battalions arrived in the beginning of June, and there was no time to train the men properly. A similar situation developed with respect to the Ferdinand battalions. They were being viewed as a most important asset for breaking through the Central Front's defenses, but they had not seen any fighting yet. Therefore, it was important to understand their capabilities and to work out their cooperation with the divisions with which they were to operate in the first echelon. However, the heavy self-propelled guns also arrived just several days before the operation kicked off, when they were in no condition yet for training, and the army faced a different, important task – not to disclose their areas of assembly.

Even so, Elberveldt's staff persistently strove to carry out the preparation plan completely, and in this effort they had Model's full support. Particularly intensive work was done in the last ten days of June. On 15 June an order had been issued about conducting large training exercises in the area of Staff Breitenbuch's location (south of Orel), in the course of which new anti-tank munitions were tested. On the following day, the 31st Infantry Division, which had only just finished setting up its lines, received an order to switch to reinforced training of the units at the training areas. In addition, all of the divisions at this time were ordered to conduct firing exercises with the use of the new machine-gun rounds.

On the morning of 18 June, map exercises began at the command post of the XXXXVII Panzer Corps in the presence of the army commander, with the aim of working out the first stage of the offensive plan – the breakthrough of the Soviet defenses by the 6th and 20th Panzer Divisions. Five days later, Model took part in large maneuvers done by Staff Breitenbuch with the simultaneous participation of all three divisions, the 6th Infantry, the 2nd and the 9th Panzer, which had been prepared by the Colonel General personally, and on 25 June he again held map studies, this time in the XXXXVI Panzer Corps. Indeed, such high activity on the part of the army commander in matters of preparing the troops can be seen in captured German documents right up to the start of the Battle of Kursk. I suppose by this time he had clearly come to terms with the fact that Citadel was not going to be postponed again, while at the same time he recognized that the army was not ready for it. Colonel P. von Groeben wrote:

> Seasoned veterans who had been tried and proven in many a critical battle since the very start of the Russian campaign composed the divisions earmarked to spearhead the offensive. These divisions reorganized in rear areas in early spring, filling their ranks with new soldiers and – to some extent – receiving new weapons and equipment. Thus, despite a cadre of experienced troops, in their new organization and composition these divisions completely lacked combat experience and – to be more specific, experience in staging attacks through heavily fortified defenses. It was absolutely necessary that these

divisions receive this kind of training prior to the large-scale offensive envisioned by OKH. Carefully planned, well-disciplined and -controlled training was indispensable and would require at least four weeks.[394]

It was with just such energy that Model, striving to make up for lost time in May and June 1943, worked on elaborating the elements of the operation with divisional staff officers, and demanded that the division commanders conduct daily training exercises and to inspect the troops in person.

Unfortunately, the hopes for reinforcement with even that minimal amount of armor and "wonder weapons" that Hitler had promised in May were not realized. Model and his staff officers had to rely on infantry, and by mid-1943 it was not in the best shape. Here is how the commander of the 7th Infantry Division Lieutenant General Fritz-Georg von Rappard described the situation in it to his superior in March 1943:

> Dear General,
> You won't have any pretenses toward me if I touch upon several questions regarding the infantry:
> 1. In the conditions of the present positional war, all of the fighting costs the infantry an incommensurate amount of blood; even during well-prepared operations with good support, the casualties rarely amount to less than 25 percent. Casualties of 50 percent or more aren't a rarity. The causes of this are as follows:
>   a. The stubborn resistance of the Russians, who so artfully arrange their defensive fortifications, so in spite of thorough reconnaissance, they remain in part undisclosed and the infantry has to take them by storm;
>   b. The inadequate training of the infantry commanders, who don't know how to combine fire and maneuver correctly. In the best case, this only is seen in the initial breakthrough. They fail with improvisation, which is necessary in the course of an offensive. Commanders don't know how to lead their units. The infantry goes on the attack in large, undispersed masses of riflemen. The will to attack is present, but tactical skill is wanting;
>   c. The training of the soldier, who does not fully know his weapon, does not know how to use the terrain when moving, does not know how to camouflage, and is not adroit in handling a shovel is insufficient.
>   d. The weakness in manpower of the units does not allow the men the opportunity to rest.
> 2. The heavy casualties have a substantial influence on the question regarding the command staff. The inadequate education and training of the soldiers force the commanders to go in front. The more experienced officers we lose, the larger the casualties among the soldiers as well. We're using up those men, which with additional training and accumulated combat experience might become junior officer cadres, in such a way that the losses among commanders and soldiers alternately keep rising above one other, thus closing the accursed circle.

---

394 Newton, *Kurskaia bitva: nemetskii vzgliad*, pp. 137-138.

3. The command echelons apparently take no consideration of this catastrophic breakdown in the infantry. When issuing orders, they take no account of whether an infantry regiment consists of two battalions or three, or whether there are 600, 400 or only 200 men in the battalion. A battalion is considered a battalion and receives a corresponding order. I know of cases when battalions, which had been whittled down to 150 men in the shortest amount of time, still remained at the front for a long time as "irreplaceable".

    Given such a state of affairs, the spirit of the infantry, which has firmly endured all the casualties, cannot remain unshakeable for very long. Up to the present, we have made the artillery obligated so that while the infantry is on the defense it does not suffer even greater losses. ... I'm speaking here not on the subject of my own division, which is in better shape than many other divisions, but in general. Our people don't have the staying power of the Russians.[395]

This rather self-critical and fully objective document requires no additional commentary, especially when you consider that its author was not a novice in his profession and was not in his first year at the front. The following data alone emphasize the general's accurate assessment. In the course of the offensive toward Kursk, the 7th Infantry Division, which was operating on an auxiliary axis as part of the XXXXVI Panzer Corps, over the first five days of the fighting would suffer the highest casualties in the corps (both in absolute numbers and as a percentage of fighting strength [60 percent]). Among all of the divisions of the Ninth Army, it would occupy second place in the loss of men over this period. The main reason has been laid out in the cited excerpt.

The difficult situation with the most basic type of troops was no secret for Berlin. Take, for example, Hitler's directive from 22 June 1943. In the document, there is no desire to correct the situation fundamentally or at least attempt to resolve some of the accumulated problems. His purpose was to soothe and show that the Führer knew all and took everything in account, so the situation would soon improve. Nevertheless, together with the typical propagandistic blathering, aimed at improving the morale of the combat troops, something obvious has also been noted in it: "In the war's fourth year, by itself it stands to reason that it is the infantry which suffers the heaviest casualties and loses its best men, so the well-known shortcomings in the training, in the reserves and in the professional aptitude of the junior officers becomes apparent, and complicates the replenishment of their ranks with young men."[396]

However, in order to overcome these difficulties, the steps laid out in the directive are plainly inadequate and show boundless faith. In the first place, there is the notion that "the German soldier, just as before, was superior to his Russian counterpart in everything, and will always be so". In the second place, there is the belief that "these shortcomings were inherent in the adversary's infantry to a much greater extent ...; the foe cannot eliminate the majority of such shortcomings or fill its current gaps, while we can do so." If, however, blind faith did not help, then the Führer demanded of his commanders "to be ruthless at the sign of any withdrawal

---

395 "Voina 1941-1945. Vestnika Arkhiva presidenta Rossiiskoi Federatsii [The War, 1941-1945. Annals of the Archive of the Russian Federation's president] (Moscow, 2010), p. 125.
396 Klink, *Das Gesetz des Handelns. Die Operation "Zitadelle"*, pp. 292-293.

of subordinate units and elements and make every effort and use every available means at his disposal to intervene and restore the position."[397]

All of the other remaining measures, proscribed in this directive, had been implemented in the Wehrmacht even before this, but had no effect in improving the situation, and were no longer even able to change it. Both of the cited documents by von Rappard and Hitler have a symbiotic relationship and testify to one and the same thing: The hardened combat core of the regular Wehrmacht (from the level of the private to the battalion commander), which had been trained and gone through its breaking-in period with combat in the first phase of the Second World War, had been lost forever. Germany had fallen into the same never-ending circle that plagued the Red Army in 1941 and 1942: The reason for the high casualties was the poor individual training of soldiers and commanders of the tactical level, but there was no time to train them better, because the high loss of manpower in the acting army required its rapid replenishment with men. In this situation there was no choice; the requirements for candidates for a post kept dropping and the time to train this most important category of servicemen of the active formations decreased. Naturally, this immediately told on the results of their combat performance in more casualties.

It should be noted that such major problems with the organization of training is not traceable in the documents of Model's neighbor to the south. From the moment that the forming up of von Manstein's assault grouping concluded in April 1943, its composition never changed fundamentally. Prior to the start of the Battle of Kursk, the Fourth Panzer Army only received one major formation as a reinforcement – the First Panzer Army's 3rd Panzer Division, but its units basically had time to carry out its training plan before 5 July. Moreover, Hoth's and Kempf's subordinate divisions did not take part in any anti-partisan operations, and were only busy with preparations for Citadel. Yet even so, according to the testimony of P. von der Groeben, Erich von Manstein complained that he had not been able to complete the four-week plan of training the troops assigned to Citadel before the end of June. Then what could be said about Model's Ninth Army, which had undertaken this work only in the latter half of June, when so much time had already been lost? The description of the results of this can be found in the recollections of the commander of the Ninth Army's 18th Panzer Division, Major General K. von Schlieben, who wrote the following about the men of his division in the course of Citadel: "It happened that entire companies, having caught the sound of the rumble of enemy tanks, jumped into their machines and fled to the rear in wild panic."[398]

To return again to the headquarters of the Wehrmacht's assault groupings at Kursk. On 27 June at 1505, Erich von Manstein received a telegram from the OKH, which introduced the final adjustment to the date of Citadel's start: the troops must be ready to initiate it at dawn on 5 July.[399] In parallel, the same information arrived at the headquarters of the Ninth Army as well. Approximately two hours later, its operations command made known to the subordinate corps commands that Model's preliminary order from 25 June 1943 about movement up into the jumping-off positions should be put into motion. All of the army's divisions assigned for the attack toward Kursk should be assembled in the areas designated for them by the end of 3 July, so that after a day's rest they could launch a decisive attack.

---

397 Ibid.
398 Newton, *Kurskaia bitva: nemetskii vzgliad*, p. 538.
399 NARA US, T.312, R.365, F.8650566.

What were the Ninth Army's numerical and combat strength on the eve of Operation Citadel? Despite the fact that quite a bit has been written about this in the historical literature, there is nevertheless no clarity regarding this matter. It is very important, however, both for understanding the overall intent of Germany's summer campaign and more specifically for Operation Citadel, to determine the potential of the forces included in conducting it and in order to assess the contribution made by the armies of each of the six Soviet *fronts* that took part in defeating the Wehrmacht's final strategic offensive on the Soviet-German front. The reasons for this lack of clarity are several, but two stand out: Firstly, from the outset, access to the documents in the Western archives was blocked for Soviet scholars, since in the USSR the information contained in them was considered a priori false. In the years 1946-1956, domestic military scholars who were aggregating the combat experience in the war for the benefit of strengthening the country's defensive capabilities were forced to use two groups of sources: captured German documents and the materials of Soviet intelligence organs (interrogations of prisoners, deserters and so forth). However, the original documents of the Wehrmacht were as a rule disorganized and did not provide an overall picture of the events, while the testimony of prisoners of war proved to be uninformative for the most part and often unreliable. Other materials, for example, the documents of the army-level and *front* intelligence organs, were of a superficial nature, and the enemy's potential in them was as a rule exaggerated. An especially significant amount of unreliable information came from the intelligence services of the acting Red Army in the first stage of the war, which compelled the Supreme Command twice (in the autumn of 1942 and spring of 1943) to conduct their reorganization.[400] Therefore, prior to 1991 all of the research on the Battle of Kursk was based primarily on sources from domestic archives, and their reliability on matters that touched upon the Wehrmacht was not very high. Sometimes our historians used information from the publications of ideological allies (like the GDR), or in the extreme case, those of "neutral" Western authors, but they played only a secondary rule in their works. Secondly, when the opportunity appeared in the 1990s for Russian scholars to work in foreign archives, it became clear that in order to select, systematize and analyze the large quantity of documents even on such a simple question as the condition of the German forces at Kursk in the summer of 1943 would require a significant amount of time. Moreover, it proved hard for historians to obtain the necessary number of sources in order to conduct a comprehensive study first of all due to financial reasons.

Nevertheless, the first publications on this problem began to appear in Russia in the early XXI Century. However, they were only concerned with the shock armies of Army Group South – the Fourth Panzer Army and Army Detachment Kempf.[401] In the summer of 1944, the Ninth Army fell into encirclement near Minsk. The command managed to evacuate the bulk of the documents of its headquarters and formations to Germany, from where in 1945 they wound up in the US National Archives. However, a significant number of documents were captured by

---

400 See the People's Commissar of Defense's Order No. 0072 from 19 April 1943 (*Russkii arkhiv: Velikaia Otechestvennaia voiny: Prikazy Narodnogo komissara oborony SSSR (1943-1945)* [*Russian archive: Great Patriotic War: Orders of the USSR People's Commissar of Defense (1943-1945)*], Vol. 13 (2-3) (Moscow, 1997). pp. 127-129.
401 Lopukhovsky, L.N., *Prokhorovka: Bez grifa sektretnosti* [*Prokhorovka: Without the seal of secrecy*] (Moscow: Iauza, 2005); Zamulin, V.N., *Kurskii izlom: Reshaiushchaia bitva Otechestvennoi voiny* [*Kursk turning point: The decisive battle of the Patriotic War*] (Moscow: Iauza, 2009).

Soviet troops and then went to the Central Archives of the Russian Ministry of Defense, to its captured archive. Primarily it consists of documents of an operational nature, which touch directly on combat operations; there are practically no statistical materials or accounts. Likely, this also played no small role in the fact that despite the large volume of sources on the Ninth Army for 1943, today we know least of all about the combat potential of this Wehrmacht army both before and during the Battle of Kursk. I've happened to spend 15 years working with materials of the US National Archives regarding the Second World War. The analysis offered below lays primarily on new materials that I've uncovered in the course of this research and which haven't been previously introduced in academic circulation.

So, what was the combat and numerical strength of Model's forces on the eve of Operation Citadel? In foreign and domestic literature, this question has been raised more than once, but a significant portion of the data cited in publications and monographs vary even on basic indicators. Soviet historians, as a rule, used aggregate figures either for the entire German grouping in the area of the Kursk bulge (Fourth Panzer Army, Ninth Army and Army Detachment Kempf), or for the entire Army Group Center, including the forces that were defending the Orel salient, but not assigned to Operation Citadel. However, even here there is no common opinion. For example, the authors of the first open Soviet work on the Battle of Kursk by G.A. Koltunov and B.G. Solov'ev set the overall strength of the soldiers and officers of Army Groups South and Center, which were involved in Operation Citadel, as "around 900,000".[402] However, their colleagues from the Institute of Military History write instead "more than 900,000", because in their opinion Model possessed 22 infantry and panzer divisions.[403]

In the early 21st Century, domestic scholars continued to discuss this question heatedly. L.N. Lopukhovsky maintained: "The northern [grouping] included the Ninth Army and part of the Second Army ... a total of 26 divisions and 460,000 men."[404] In the work of the aforementioned Institute of Military History entitled *Ognennaia duga* [*Bulge of fire*], a new figure received mention that diverged significantly even from what its colleagues had cited previously – 24 infantry, 6 panzer and one motorized division with a total strength of 460,000 men.[405]

It should be noted that G.A. Koltunov, a veteran of the Battle of Kursk, was the only Soviet historian who throughout the lengthy postwar period persistently sought to grapple with the problem of the strength of Model's assault grouping, and not without success. According to his information, in the 10 divisions of the Ninth Army's first echelon, which went on the offensive on 5 July 1943, there were 160,000 active men.[406] If you set aside the erroneous number of divisions indicated by him, and only add the number of men of all the army's divisions that were actually located in the first echelon on that day, the figure virtually coincides with the real one, with a difference of only several hundred men. Moreover, it needs to be considered that this theoretical calculation was made back in the early 1970s only on the basis of captured German documents in the TsAMO RF and his own experience.

---

402 Koltunov, G.A. and Solov'ev, B.G., *Kurskaia bitva* (Moscow: Voenizdat, 1970), p. 47.
403 *Velikaia Otechestvennaia voina 1941-1945, Voenno-istoricheskie ocherki* [*Great Patriotic War 1941-1945): Military History Essays*], Book 2 (Moscow, 1998), pp. 253, 254, 259.
404 Lopukhovsky, *Prokhorovka: Bez grifa sekretnosti*, p. 27.
405 *Ognennaia duga* [*Bulge of fire*] (Moscow, 2003), p. 596.
406 *Voenno-istoricheskii zhurnal*, No. 6 (1968), p. 67.

A number of foreign scholars have also wrestled with this problem, but they also have failed to resolve it fully. For example, D. Glantz and J. House cite practically the correct figure for the overall strength of the Ninth Army by the start of the Battle of Kursk – 335,000 men.[407] However, it is hard to work with it. It does not give a picture of either the strength of some or another division, or about the combat strength of its assault divisions, so it is impossible to grasp the degree that the entire army and its separate divisions were understrength. Thus, it does not address such questions as: What strength was directly activated by Model, both as a whole in the attack toward Kursk, as well as in separate directions in the course of attempting to breach the Central Front's tactical zone?

The main reason for the appearance of different figures is one and the same – the incomplete base of archival sources. let us turn to the reports from the headquarters of the Ninth Army to the command of Army Group Center and the OKH, uncovered in the US National Archive. So, on 1 July 1943 Model's army had five corps – two army corps (XX and XXIII) and three panzer corps (XXXXI, XXXXVI and XXXXVII). Together, they had a total of 18 divisions: 14 infantry and one sturm division [6th, 7th, 31st, 45th, 72nd, 86th, 102nd, 137th, 216th, 251st, 258th, 292nd and 383rd Infantry Divisions and the 78th Sturm Division) and four panzer divisions (2nd, 9th, 18th and 20th Panzer Divisions).[408] In addition, the XXXXVI Panzer Corps received Gruppe Manteuffel as a general reserve (Jäger Battalions 9, 10 and 11), while XXIII Corps received Infantry Regiment 86 of the 36th Infantry Division and Jäger Battalions 8 and 13. As a result, the total strength of the Ninth Army amounted to 331,131 men, including 9,316 officers, 59,296 junior officers and 259,881 enlisted men.[409] This figure does not include the 3,421 officers, service personnel and enlisted men located in the medical-sanitation units on 1 July 1943, or the men of Heavy Mortar Regiment 18 and the 312th Company of Radio-Controlled Demolition Carriers, the headquarters of which failed to submit reports in time. Therefore, it is still not possible to determine their manpower strength on the basis of archival documents.

Moreover, in the event that offensive developed successfully, in order to reinforce Model's assault grouping G. von Kluge formed a reserve consisting of the 10th Panzergrenadier Division (less one regiment) and Gruppe Esebeck[410] (the 4th and 12th Panzer Divisions), although at the start of the Battle of Kursk this group was directly subordinate to the Field Marshal and was considered his personal reserve. On 4 July 1943, in all the divisions designated for Citadel (other than the 12th Panzer Division[411]) and in the two reserves (of XXIII Corps and Gruppe Manteuffel[412]), there was a total of 191,755 men (189,786 in the divisions and 8,312 in the reserves).

Thus, according to the staffing establishment, on 1 July 1943 the Ninth Army had an overall shortage of 48,233 men, including 42,658 in the divisions and 5,575 in the units directly

---

407 Glantz, D. and House, J. *Kurskaia bitva: Reshaiushchaia povorotnyi punkt Vtoroi mirovoi voiny* [*The Battle of Kursk*] (Moscow, 2006), p. 356.
408 In addition, the Ninth Army had two security divisions, the 203rd under the command of Generalleutnant Rudolf Pilz, and the 221st, under Generalleutnant Hubert Lendle.
409 NARA US, T.312, R.322, F.7890947.
410 This group was named after the surname of its commander, Generalleutnant Hans-Karl von Esebeck.
411 Information is sparse for this panzer division in the US National Archive; on the basis of archival sources, I've only been able to establish its strength in combat effectives for 4 July 1943 – 4,456 men.
412 Named after the surname of its commander, Oberst Hasso von Manteuffel.

subordinate to the corps and army.[413] These figures include the following categories of service personnel: enlisted men for the regular formations and units – 23,606 (21,583 for the divisions and 2,023 for the units subordinate to the army and corps); enlisted men for the divisions' reserve field battalions – 3,007; Hiwi[414] – 15,198 (12,564 and 2,634 respectively); and German soldiers holding positions in the Hiwi – 6,422 (5,504 and 2,634 respectively).

For an army preparing for a general offensive, such a large shortage of men was a substantial problem. Judging from captured sources, Model, von Kluge and the OKH leadership all understood this. However, because of the general deficit of manpower in Germany, they were unable to resolve it before the start of the operation. However, it must be acknowledged that quite a bit was done to address the problem. Immediately prior to Citadel, it was under consideration to reduce the shortage of enlisted men by approximately one-third. On 30 June the OKH informed Colonel H. von Elverfeldt that nine march battalions (5.5 for the infantry divisions and 3.5 for the panzer divisions) with a total of 5,000 to 7,000 men had embarked upon trains for the Ninth Army. They were scheduled to arrive in Orel prior to X-Day (5 July 1943). Therefore, already on the night of 30 June and 1 July, a directive went out to the troops about distributing these replacements. According to this document, less than half of the new recruits should be sent directly to the front:

> In the nearest time, the arrival of replacements is anticipated. They should be used in order to replenish the shortage of personnel at the front as follows: 137th Infantry Division – 450 men, 251st Infantry Division – 450 men, 6th Infantry Division – 600 men, 10th Panzergrenadier Division – 300 men, 258th Infantry Division – 300 men, and 292nd Infantry Division – 300 men, as well as for sending to the junior officer's school as a form of divisional reserve. In particular, 1.5 march battalions should go through training in the technical school. A portion is to comprise the basis of a training battalion in Lokta and a reserve for Gruppe Weiss with direct subordination to XX Corps. One march battalion is to be sent to the technical school in Briansk for training in the panzergrenadier training battalion. For the training of the two remaining march battalions (as panzergrenadiers), place responsibility on Staff Breitenbuch. Position both battalions in the Kromy area.[415]

However, just two days later a new message arrived that the replacements would arrive between 5 and 9 July, begin to enter the troops only by the end of 9 July, which is to say, after the main combat operations in the Ninth Army's sector (within the framework of Citadel) were to be wrapping up. In particular, the XXIII Corps' 216th Infantry Division, which suffered

---

413 NARA US, T.312, R.322, F.7890947.
414 The Hiwi, the German abbreviation for *Hilfswilliger* (or voluntary assistants for the Wehrmacht), were gathered (or compulsory mobilized) from the local population of the Soviet occupied territories and prisoners of war. From October 1942, in the establishment table of a German infantry division, a correlation of 10,708 servicemen to 2,005 Hiwi was set; a year later, the Hiwi were included in the establishment strength of an infantry division.
415 NARA US, T.312, R.322, F.7890980, 7890981.

particularly heavy casualties in the course of the offensive, would receive March Battalion 124 on 9 July with a total number of 963 men.[416]

Serious problems existed with the quality of the called-up contingent as well. The heavy losses of personnel forced the Wehrmacht command to lower the level of standards for new recruits. At this time, even the SS field troops were taking no longer taking in only pure-blooded Aryans or volunteers ethnically close to them (according to race theory), but any males from occupied countries that were in suitable good health, including those not belonging to the "Nordic race": Poles, Czechs, Slovenians and even Soviet prisoners of war, which from January 1943 began to transfer from labor teams of the infantry divisions to their manning table as "volunteers".[417] At the same time, the major setbacks at the front were seriously shaking confidence in the Reich's ultimate victory; in the occupied countries, anti-war sentiments were growing, and their population was striving by any means to avoid participating in the global war. Therefore, within the Wehrmacht, the number of deserters, turncoats and objectors (including incidents of self-inflicted wounds) was rising relative to previous years, and this was the first indicator of the decline in the troops' combat spirit and the loss of their inner reservoir of courage. An order from the commander of the Second Panzer Army's XXXV Corps General L. Rendulic that was passed down to each serviceman testifies to the fact that serious problems with discipline arose in the divisions of Army Group Center before the Battle of Kursk, which the commander was proposing to correct in no other way than by a firing squad. In part, the order stated:

1. In one division that does not belong to the corps, the infantry units a while back only under the effect of enemy preparatory artillery fire abandoned the trenches, which they'd been entrusted to defend. The circumstances were revealed in every detail and had the result of several death sentences, which were carried out.

    …

7. Each soldier who has been found absent from his unit during a battle, each, who has been declared by a doctor as not being wounded or sick, will be tracked down at a dressing station and subject to arrest. He must be immediately subject to a drumhead court martial. If a soldier is found in any of the above situations, only sentences that foresee capital punishment can be handed down.
8. Divisions and regiments, as well as each local commandant of the rear area, must with the assistance of a dense network of patrols take steps to take complete control in its area. In addition to this, the corps is to introduce patrol service in the field gendarme right up to the area of combat operations.
9. The given order does not apply to the overwhelming majority of our soldiers. They've been shown to be dutiful, dedicated and courageous sons of the German people in many battles and in numerous undertakings. However, the order is directed against those few, who are present in any organization and who always think first about themselves, and who have no wish to recognize their responsibilities with respect to the organization. If nevertheless I have directed that the given order be made known to all the soldiers, then the reason for this lies in the fact that

---

416 NARA US, T.312, R.689, F.000405.
417 Rass, K., *Chelovecheskii material: Nemetskii soldat na Vostochnom fronte*, p. 375.

a conscientious solder will keep watch over those, who will weaken at a critical moment, so that he might raise his spirits and still be saved for the organization.[418]

The final paragraph should not receive special attention. It is a banal propagandistic stamp, called upon to sweeten a bitter pill and to emphasize once again that the Wehrmacht still was a menacing weapon in the hands of the Führer, who would lead the German people to a happy future. However, the facts noted in it are only a portion of those that arose on this path, and through common efforts they had to be eradicated as quickly as possible, so as not to ruin the heroic image of the Wehrmacht's struggle against the "subhuman race". However, in any army, corps orders devoted to discipline speak only on the basis of isolated incidents, and only when it becomes clear that a negative tendency has become evident and needs to be combatted. Since it is necessary to use with caution such a serious instrument in the hands of a commander as a written order. It is not only called upon to give offices at the tactical level the right to execute undisciplined soldiers, and to remind the latter of their duty to be steadfast, but also causes servicemen to think about what is happening. After all, it plainly testifies to the fact "everything is not going so smoothly in our hierarchy" if there is a statement about this even at the corps level. Indeed, the command of a Wehrmacht formation knew this perfectly well.

In the documents of the German Army, desertion is recorded throughout the entire war, but at different periods its scale varied: up to the beginning of 1943, the size of this problem can be assessed as insignificant. This can be explained first of all by the powerful influence of propaganda; and second by the understanding of the military men themselves of that degree of atrocities that they were perpetrating in the USSR and that they faced a reckoning for this according to any legal system. Finally, the number of recruits from the occupied countries in the acting army on the Soviet-German front was not very significant. After Stalingrad the situation began to change. The lack of confidence in the soldiers and even junior officers about the possibility of victory in the war soared, and as a result, the desire to save one's own skin was growing. At the same time, so-called replenishments of Volksdeutsch [ethnic Germans who lived outside the German borders], Slavs and even Russians began to enter the ranks of the Wehrmacht in large numbers, as well as recruits from such traditionally unsteady lands, in the opinions of German officers, as Alsace and Lorraine. The contingent called up from the conquered countries as a rule replenished the infantry divisions. Before the start of the Battle of Kursk, in some of them (for example, in Army Group South's 168th Infantry Division) foreigners comprised up to 40percent of the manpower.

In certain foreign publications, it is possible to encounter the assertion that by the start of the Battle of Kursk, defeatist attitudes in both German army groups at Kursk had been wiped out. K. von Tippelskirch writes: "The period of the muddy season, the reduction of the front lines and the period of calm that followed were very fortunate for the German divisions. The "Stalingrad shock", in only the troops of the southern sector of the front that had previously experienced bad defeats, was in the end overcome even there."[419] The former Wehrmacht general probably wanted very much to present the desirable rather than the actual situation, so that is why this passage that is so far from reality about the supposedly local manifestations of a dejected mood

---

418 Khristoforov, V.S. (ed.), *Velikaia otechestvennaia voina,1943 god: Issledovaniia, dokumentov, kommentarii* [*Great Patriotic War, 1943: Research, documents and commentary*] (Moscow, 2013), pp. 670-672.
419 Tippelskirch, *Istoriia Vtoroi mirovoi voiny*, p. 23.

in the winter and early spring of 1943 appeared in his book. Documentary sources of both sides paint a different picture in all the divisions of the German Army on the Eastern Front. In this connection indicative is the order from Army Group South on 13 April 1943, which demanded from the army commands: "In the divisions that have arrived from the West, it is necessary to track casualties attentively. In the event that as a result of their first combat encounters, the number of men in a company falls to 80 men, the threat arises of their loss of combat capability, since their level of morale makes them sensitive to casualties."[420] It is interesting that the headquarters of the Fourth Panzer Army recalled this order just several days before the Battle of Kursk and demanded that the command staff of the divisions strictly implement it. It is hard to imagine that this order concerned, for example, the II SS Panzer Corps, which had also just arrived from the West, since the winning mindset of its men was incomparably higher than in the Wehrmacht formations. However, one thing is clear: even just before Citadel, the combat morale of the German soldiers was beginning to decline everywhere, and the German command was seeking any means to stop this process.

If to trace the evolution of the morale and political attitude of the German troops, for example, that were located opposite the Central Front from March to the end of June 1943, then according to Soviet intelligence information, a tendency to strengthen the discipline and combat spirit of the troops was actually evident. However, to maintain that a defeatist mentality had been wiped out by the start of the Battle of Kursk is a clear exaggeration. From a briefing sheet from the 13th Army's Intelligence Department on the condition of the enemy troops opposite its front on 28 June 1943:

> The mood of the majority of the German soldiers is rather depressed; fatigue from the prolonged war is perceptible. The defeat of the German forces, suffered in the winter of 1942-1943, has undermined the soldiers' faith in the possibility of Germany's victory. Such attitudes are particularly prevalent among the soldiers called up from the reserve (of older ages), and soldiers not of a German nationality. That portion of the soldiers who still continue to believe in victory are staking all their hopes on the 1943 summer offensive. However, these soldiers don't have complete confidence in a favorable outcome of the war for the Germans. For example, according to the testimony of Deringer, a soldier of the 20th Panzer Division's Panzergrenadier Regiment 59, talks are going around the soldiers to the effect that "If the summer offensive of 1943 fails, then in the winter the Germans will have to retreat to Poland, and the war will be lost."
>
> The extended lull at the fronts in the USSR is acting oppressively on the soldiers. They say, "Better to move to the west than to stand on spot." (From the testimonies of a soldier of the 78th Sturm Division Franz Jurkowitsch). Among the latest replacements for the enemy's Ninth Army are a large number of soldiers of non-German nationality or Germans from territories not previously part of Germany (Slovenians, Luxembourgers, Alsatians), who in their majority have a defeatist attitude and have no desire to fight for the Germans. A soldier who has come over from Sturm Regiment 215 of the 78th Sturm Division Franz Kugel has declared, "I'm not a soldier, I'm a Luxembourger." So, he says he has no wish to fight for Germany. These defeatist attitudes often come from the rear,

---

420 NARA US, T.312, R.365, F.8650576.

in letters from family members. The British bombing of Germany's western areas is continuing to have a large effect on the declining morale of the German soldiers.[421]

Captured German sources also testify to the decline in combat morale and a drop in the level of discipline. In them, there is note of the dangerous tendency in the Wehrmacht of the voluntary going over to the Red Army side by German servicemen. For example, on 17 June 1943 the Operations Department of the Ninth Army reported to the army group that an extraordinary incident had taken place in the 78th Sturm Division: six Germans had crossed the lines to the Russian side, among which were four Volksdeutsch. Such incidents had happened even previously, and they were taken very seriously. The army's intelligence leadership was instructed to look into the reasons for it very closely, and the rear staff was told to delay the planned departure to the front of around 150 Volksdeutsch recruits. In addition, Elverfeldts' staff demanded a closer examination of the arriving replacements in the training units.[422] Evidence of the fact that this tendency was growing is the fact that during the offensive toward Kursk, a number of servicemen of the Ninth Army went over to the Soviet side, among which was the acting commander of the 9th Panzer Division's II/Panzergrenadier Regiment 11 Senior Lieutenant H. Frankenfeldt, a German by nationality.[423] It is hard to imagine such an event taking place in the course of a German offensive, say, back in 1942. Even so, our opponent should be given due credit: The German war machine at this time continued to operate efficiently, even with the growing strain on it. The Soviet army-level intelligence therefore justly indicated that "On the whole, the morale of the enemy units operating opposite the 13th Army remains satisfactory."[424]

Now let us take a look at the strength of Model's assault grouping, which is to say, those forces that were directly assigned to execute Citadel. It was planned to use all of the Ninth Army's divisions in the operation, except for XX Corps and the XXXXVI Panzer Corps' 102nd Infantry Division, which even so, were supposed to support their attacking neighbors with fire from place. Accordingly, 18 divisions formed the assault wedge: 13 of the army's divisions (four panzer – the 2nd, 9th, 18th and 20th; and nine infantry and sturm divisions – the 6th, 7th, 31st, 86th, 216th, 258th, 292nd, 383rd and 78th Sturm), and three – from out of Army Group Center's reserve (the 10th Panzergrenadier Division (minus the panzer regiment) and the two divisions of Gruppe Esebeck (the 4th and 12th Panzer Division). For the roster and combat strength of these divisions on 4 July 1943, see Table 6.

421 TsAMO RF, F.361, Op.6081, D.53, l. 343.
422 NARA US, T.312, R.321, F.7886129.
423 TsAMO RF, F.361, Op.6081, D.54, l. 19-21.
424 TsAMO RF, F.361, Op.6081, D.53, l. 343obr.

Table 6: Roster strength, combat strength and deficit of infantry in the Ninth Army's divisions as of 4 July 1943[425]

Division	Roster strength	Combat Strength	
		Unit	Reporting for duty
XX Army Corps			
241 Infantry	10,385	I/451 GR	351
		III/451 GR	345
		I/439 GR	373
		II/439 GR	364
		I/471 GR	362
		II/471 GR	359
		Security Bn.	350
		Sapper Bn. 251	232
		Total:	2,736
137 Infantry	10,396	I/447 GR	320
		II/447 GR	313
		I/448 GR	324
		III/448 GR	325
		I/449 GR	344
		II/449 GR	352
		Reserve Bn. 137	345
		Panzerjäger Bn. 137	217
		Sapper Bn. 137	286
		Total:	2,826

425 Source: NARA US, T.312, R.322, F.7890958

45 Infantry	10,770	I/130 GR	430
		II/130 GR	439
		I/133 GR	523
		I/135 GR	479
		II/135 GR	533
		III/135 GR	474
		Recon Bn. 45	248
		Panzerjäger Bn. 45	221
		Sapper Bn. 81	200
		Total:	**3,747**
72 Infantry	11,846	I/105 GR	405
		II/105 GR	392
		I/124 GR	387
		II/124 GR	388
		I/266 GR	415
		II/266 GR	423
		Divisional battalion	345
		Panzerjäger Bn. 72	246
		Sapper Bn. 72	308
		Total:	**3,309**
		XXXXVI Panzer Corps	
102 Infantry	11,436	I/84 GR	372
		II/84 GR	384
		II/232 GR	356
		III/232 GR	367
		I/233 GR	363
		II/233 GR	360
		Security Bn.	293
		Sapper Bn. 102	254
		Total:	**2,930**

258 Infantry	11,249	I/478 GR	429
		II/478 GR	441
		III/478 GR	424
		I/479 GR	429
		II/479 GR	382
		III/479 GR	370
		Divisional battalion	354
		Panzerjäger Bn. 258	258
		Sapper Bn. 258	305
		Total:	**3,392**
7 Infantry	11,871	I/19 GR	425
		III/19 GR	439
		I/61 GR	377
		III/61 GR	353
		I/62 GR	413
		II/62 GR	497
		Recon Bn. 7	419
		Panzerjäger battalion	325
		Sapper Bn. 7	384
		Total:	**3,532**
31 Infantry	11,692	I/12 GR	422
		III/12 GR	427
		I/17 GR	472
		III/17 GR	474
		I/82 GR	457
		II/82 GR	459
		Sapper Bn. 31	357
		Total:	**3,068**
Gruppe von Manteuffel	3,765	Jäger Bn. 9	649
		Jäger Bn. 10	715
		Jäger Bn. 11	661
		Total:	**2,025**

		XXXXVII Panzer Corps	
20 Panzer	12,154	I/59 PzGR	477
		II/59 PzGR	484
		I/112 PzGR	473
		II/112 PzGR	530
		Panzer Recon Bn. 20	542
		Sapper Bn. 92	325
		Total:	**2,831**
4 Panzer	12,932	I/12 PzGR	606
		II/12 PzGR	508
		I/33 PzGR	483
		II/33 PzGR	643
		Panzer Recon Bn. 4	744
		Sapper Bn. 79	565
		Total:	**3,549**
2 Panzer	13,522	I/2 PzGR	710
		II/2 PzGR	626
		I/304 PzGR	744
		II/304 PzGR	703
		Panzer Recon Bn. 2	812
		Sapper Bn. 38	467
		Total:	**4,062**
6 Infantry	11,352	I/18 GR	422
		II/18 GR	435
		I/37 GR	405
		III/37 GR	399
		I/58 GR	379
		III/58 GR	386
		Recon Bn. 6	331
		Sapper Bn. 6	364
		Total:	**3,121**

9 Panzer	14,234	I/10 PzGR	625
		II/10 PzGR	657
		I/11 PzGR	598
		II/11 PzGR	587
		Recon Bn. 9	711
		Sapper Bn. 86	393
		Total:	**3,571**
	XXXXI Panzer Corps		
18 Panzer	12,028	I/52 PzGR	554
		II/52 PzGR	543
		I/101 PzGR	470
		II/101 PzGR	453
		Recon Bn. 18	580
		Sapper Bn. 93	304[426]
		Field Works Bn.	575
		Total:	**3,479**
10 Motorized	12,734	I/20 GR	464
		II/20 GR	466
		III/20 GR	470
		I/41 GR	598
		II/41 GR	616
		III/41 GR	593
		Recon Bn. 110	739
		Sapper Bn.	376
		Total:	**4,322**

---

426 Minus one company

Division	Strength	Unit	Count
86 Infantry	11,576	I/167 GR	432
		II/167 GR	447
		I/184 GR	422
		II/184 GR	427
		I/216 GR	411
		III/216 GR	410
		Storm Bn. 186	455
		Panzerjäger Bn. 186	281
		Sapper Bn. 186	365
		Total:	**3,650**
292 Infantry	10,880	I/507 GR	394
		II/507 GR	410
		III/507 GR	390
		I/508 GR	393
		II/508 GR	392
		III/508 GR	388
		Divisional battalion	503
		Panzerjäger Bn.	212
		Sapper Bn. 292	402
		Reserve battalion	230
		Total:	**3,714**
		XXIII Army Corps	
78 Storm	15,971	I/14 SR	625
		II/14 SR	562
		I/195 SR	603
		II/195 SR	636
		I/215 SR	601
		II/215 SR	585
		10./14 SR	129
		8./195 SR	123
		8./215 SR	95
		Recon Bn.	123
		Sapper Bn. 178	463
		Total:	**4545**

8 Jäger Battalion	1,325		722
13 Jäger Battalion	1,243		685
216 Infantry	10,059	I/348 GR	363
		II/348 GR	352
		III/348 GR	380
		I/396 GR	356
		II/396 GR	353
		III/396 GR	319
		Recon Bn. 216	379
		Sapper Bn. 216	300
		Total:	2,802
383 Infantry	11,209	I/531 GR	379
		II/531 GR	365
		III/531 GR	No data
		II/532 GR	435
		III/532 GR	No data
		I/533 GR	307
		II/533 GR	251
		III/533 GR	303
		Security Bn.	344
		Sapper Bn. 383	269
		Total:	2633
		I/87 GR	482
		III/87 GR	519
		Grand total:	3634
12 Panzer (Ninth Army reserve)		I/5 PzGR	751
		II/5 PzGR	746
		I/25 PzGR	724
		II/25 PzGR	771
		Recon Bn. 12	900
		Sapper Bn. 32	564

Incidentally, in his memoirs Erich von Manstein notes that Army Group Center supposedly received not one, but two motorized divisions for the offensive.[427] A.V. Lobanov even identifies

---

427 Manstein, *Uteriannye pobedy*, p. 522.

it – the 20th Panzergrenadier Division and added that it was in von Kluge's reserve together with the 8th Panzer Division.[428] Possibly, the Field Marshal had in mind the 36th Infantry Division. At one time it actually had been motorized, but long before the Battle of Kursk. Already in mid-1942 this division was equipped as an ordinary infantry division, and in the captured documents of the Ninth Army for July 1943, it was already recorded, just like its regiments, as infantry. As for the 20th Panzergrenadier Division, in the archival sources for the Citadel period, this division is not even mentioned in the Orel salient.

As is clear in the presented information, Model was forming the backbone of his assault wedge according to a principle different from his neighbor, Field Marshal Erich von Manstein. He was basing his assault grouping around infantry divisions, not panzer divisions as in the case of Army Group South, which numbered 118,583 men (with the inclusion of the five jäger battalions, their combat strength numbered 39,212 men), which is to say 35.8percent of the Ninth Army's total manpower or 61.8percent of the men involved in Operation Citadel (not including the 12th Panzer Division).[429] The average numerical strength of one infantry division remained low and amounted to 11,853 men, with an average combat strength of 3,578 men and an average strength of one infantry battalion amounting to 392 men. Of all the divisions, only the 78th Sturm Division noticeably stood out with respect to manpower strength; it had the most men of any of the Ninth Army's divisions, with 15,961 on 4 July 1943 and a combat strength of 4,545 men, yielding an average strength of 660 men for each of its six battalions. The 216th Infantry Division was the weakest, with just 10,059 soldiers and officers, a combat strength of 2,802 and just an average of 354 men for each of its six battalions.

Nevertheless, Model's average infantry division, even given that it was not fully manned according to establishment strength, exceeded the numerical strength of its counterpart in the Central Front (the rifle division) by approximately 4,000 men. However, if you consider that it was the infantry divisions that were supposed to resolve the main task of the first, most important stage of Citadel – to penetrate the deeply-echeloned Soviet defenses, then these figures don't seem so significant, and it becomes clear why Walter Model throughout the entire course of the preparations for Citadel was persistently presenting both before von Kluge and the OKH two main needs: strengthening the army with heavy armor and manpower for the infantry divisions. Moreover, his infantry divisions possessed a rather modest amount of artillery. By 27 June all five corps of the Ninth Army had a total of 1,189 guns, including 620 light, 477 heavy and 92 Flak (see Table 7). The bulk of this artillery was concentrated in four shock formations. The XX Corps had only 161 cannons and howitzers (120/41), or an average of 40 tubes per division.[430] This was the lowest indicator for the Ninth Army. For sake of comparison, for example, not even the strongest division in first echelon of Central Front's 13th Army, the 8th Rifle Division, had not only its establishment strength of 294 artillery pieces (140 guns, 125 mortars and 22 M-8 rocket launchers) but also attached assets with 407 additional artillery pieces (respectively 202, 169 and 22).[431]

---

428 *Voenno-istoricheskii zhurnal*, No. 8 (2003), pp. 10, 12.
429 Considering that the 10th Panzergrenadier Division and 78th Sturm Division did not have a panzer regiment, when calculating this they were treated as infantry divisions.
430 NARA US, T.312, R.322, F.7891349.
431 TsAMO RF, F.62, Op.321, D.139, l. 39.

Table 7: Amount of German artillery deployed in the sector of the Ninth Army on 27 June 1943 and the estimate of the number of Soviet guns deployed opposite its corps (according to the Ninth Army's intelligence information) [432]

Corps	German artillery[433]			Soviet artillery		
	Light	Heavy	Total	Light	Heavy	Total
XX Army	120	41	161	220	12	232
XXXXVI Panzer	147	66	213	280	105	385
XXXXVII Panzer	115	123	238	64	30	94
XXXXI Panzer	127	109	236	108	48	156
XXIII Army	111	138	249	232	66	298
Total:	620	477	1097 + 92 Flak guns	904	261	1,165
Calculated number of artillery pieces per one division of the Ninth Army [434]						
Corps	Number of divisions		Total number of guns in the corps		Number of guns per division	
XX Army	4		161		**40**	
XXXXVI Panzer	4		213		**53**	
XXXXVII Panzer	3		238		**60**	
XXXXI Panzer	3		236		**79**	
XXIII Army	3		249		**83**	

The panzer divisions (12th Panzer Division exclusive) had a total of 64,870 men, which is to say 19.6percent of the Ninth Army's available manpower or more than 33.8percent of the personnel of its assault grouping and von Kluge's reserve for the Ninth Army. The mobile divisions had more men (except for the 12th Panzer) than the infantry divisions (with the exception of the 78th Sturm Division); they numbered on average 12,974 soldiers and officers with an average combat strength of 3,506 men. The strongest was the 2nd Panzer Division, which had 14,234 men on its roster (and a combat strength of 3,571), and the weakest was the 18th Panzer Division, having 12,028 men in formation with a combat strength of 3,479. For the implementation of a major offensive, these were acceptable numbers, though in comparison, the panzer divisions of Army Group South had more manpower.

---

432 Source: NARA US, T.312, R.322, F.7891349.
433 The total number of guns includes the artillery of all the divisions deployed in the first and second lines, the 4th and 12th Panzer Divisions, and the 10th Motorized Division, which was located in reserve, except for 10 pieces of artillery left in the 10th Motorized Division.
434 Source: Newton, S., *Kurskaia bitva: Nemetskii vzgliad* (Moscow: Iauza, 2006), p. 184.

The situation with the analysis of the number of tanks and self-propelled guns in the formations and units of the Ninth Army prior to the Battle of Kursk is very similar to the problem of determining their staffing with manpower. In the Soviet historiography, only an overall figure for the number of armored vehicles in both army groups for the operation has been given, without details for the armies or much less the divisions – 2,700 armored vehicles.[435] It is not clear where the authors obtained this figure, or how they derived it, since they provided no footnotes in their book. The figure for the number of tanks and self-propelled guns in Model's army before the offensive was first published by Russian scholars in 1998. In the aforementioned multi-volume work, the members of the Institute of Military History indicate that the Ninth Army had 746 tanks, of which 45 were Tigers and 280 were assault guns.[436] However, this data as well lacks a reference to sources, which unquestionably lowers the degree of trust in them. In the following years, there was no new data on this subject in the publications of Russian authors. Abroad, scholars also showed interest in this matter; in the past 20 years alone, Thomas Jentz, Niklas Etterling and Anders Frankson, and David Glantz and Jonathon House all addressed it. However, even now, there is no common opinion, and the majority of authors also cite figures without providing the sources. For example, it is not clear why the American scholars D. Glantz and J. House maintain that each of Ninth Army's StuG battalions, except for the 909th, (which the authors, by the way, did not consider as part of the Ninth Army) had 36 assault guns.[437] According to their table of organization and equipment at that time, they should have had only 31. That this establishment strength in the troops was primarily met is shown by captured German records from the US National Archive.[438] The only exception was StuG Battalion 185, which on 1 July 1943 numbered 32 assault guns. Such a disagreement is observed with the numbers of panzers as well. Relying primarily on the archival materials of the Ninth Army, which previously haven't entered academic circulation, and also the work of Zetterling and Frankson [*Kursk 1943: A statistical analysis*], which in my view is the most reliable at the present time, I've managed to determine the number of armored fighting vehicles in all of the formations and units of Army Group Center that were designated for Operation Citadel. The aggregate data are shown in Table 8.

---

435 Koltunov and Solov'ev, *Kurskaia bitva*, p. 47.
436 *Velikaia Otechestvennaia voina, 1941-1945*, Book 2, p. 254.
437 Glantz and House, *The Battle of Kursk*, p. 349.
438 NARA US, T.314, R.317, F.000383.

Table 8: Number of tanks and assault guns in the units and formations of Army Group Center assigned for Operation Citadel, and in the Second Panzer Army on 1 July 1943

Designation of units and formations	Pz.If/Pz.II	Pz.III short-barreled	Pz.III long-barreled	Pz.IV short-barreled	Pz.IV long-barreled	Pz.VI Tiger	Command tanks	Total tanks	Self-propelled guns	Total tanks and self-propelled guns
Ninth Army										
XXIII Army Corps	-	-	-	-	-	-	-	-	-	**63**
StuG Bn. 185	-	-	-	-	-	-	-	-	32 (27/5)	32
StuG Bn. 189	-	-	-	-	-	-	-	-	31	31
XXXXI Panzer Corps	/3	20	16	40	12	-	3	94	207	**301**
656 Heavy Panzerjäger Regiment — Bn. 653 Ferdinands	-	-	-	-	-	-	-	-	45	45
Bn. 654 Ferdinands	-	-	-	-	-	-	-	-	45	45
Bn. 216 SP Infantry Support Gun Brummbär	-	-	-	-	-	-	-	-	45	45
313 and 314 Cos Tracked Mines	-	-	-	-	-	-	-	-	10	10
Separate tank company	/3	15	7	-	-	-	-	-	-	
StuG Bn. 177	-	-	-	-	-	-	-	-	31(22/9)	31
StuG Bn. 244	-	-	-	-	-	-	-	-	31(22/9)	

Unit										
XXXXVII Panzer Corps	/21	18	80	14	144	31	18	326	62	388
20 Panzer Division	/9	2	15	9	40	-	7	82	-	82
9 Panzer Division	-	-	26	4	45	-	5	80	-	80
2 Panzer Division	/12	8	32	1	59	-	6	118	-	118
XXXXVII Panzer Corps (cntd)										
21 Sep. Panzer Brigade ("Brigade Burmeister") / 32 Co. Radio-controlled tracked mines	-	-	-	-	-	-	-	-	-	-
505 Heavy Panzer Bn.	-	8	7	-	-	31	-	46	-	46
StuG Bn. 245	-	-	-	-	-	-	-	-	31 (22/9)	31
StuG Bn. 904	-	-	-	-	-	-	-	-	31	31
XXXVI Panzer Corps	-	-	-	-	-	-	-	-	31	31
StuG Bn. 909	-	-	-	-	-	-	-	-	31	31
Total for the Ninth Army:	/24	38	96	54	156	31	21	420	363	783
Reserve of Army Group Center, planned for the Ninth Army (Gruppe Esebeck)										
4 Panzer Division (on 30 June 1943)	-	-	9	1	73	-	6	89	-	89
12 Panzer Division	5/6	8	15	1	36	-	4	75	-	75
Total for Gruppe Esebeck	5/6	8	24	2	109	-	10	164	-	164
Total for Operation Citadel	5/30	46	120	56	245	31	31	584	363	947
Second Panzer Army										
5 Panzer Division	-	-	17	-	76	-	9	102	-	102
8 Panzer Division (OKH Reserve; at the front from 12 July 1943)	/14	24	34	8	14	-	6	101	-	101
Total for Second Panzer Army	/14	25	51	8	90	-	15	203	-	203

As of 1 July 1943, the four corps in Model's Ninth Army had a total number of 783 armored vehicles, of which 420 were tanks (including 31 Tigers) and 363 were self-propelled guns (together with the Ferdinand heavy self-propelled tank destroyers). In addition, another 164 tanks were located in Gruppe Esebeck. Thus, in order to conduct Operation Citadel, Army Group Center on 1 July 1943 had 947 combat machines (584 tanks, and 363 self-propelled guns and Ferdinands).

The Ninth Army's armor was primarily concentrated in four panzer divisions that had a combined 513 combat machines; Heavy Panzer Battalion 505 had 46; and Heavy Panzerjäger Battalion 656 had 25. Each panzer division had an average of 87 combat machines, or approximately 81percent of establishment strength.[439] The most powerful was the 2nd Panzer Division, which had 118 combat machines, including six command tanks and 12 light, outdated Pz.Kpfw. II tanks, which could not be used for combat purposes in an offensive against Red Army defenses. The 18th Panzer Division was the weakest, with only 69 tanks, five of which were command tanks.

Nevertheless, I consider it necessary to warn that even these figures might receive some adjustments in the future. In the course of work with archival materials, two considerations became clear, which will make a correction almost certain. First, because of the acute deficit of armor, panzers and assault guns were being shuffled between both formations and units in Model's assault grouping, and between his army and Gruppe Esebeck, which was subordinate to von Kluge. To further complicate things, each transfer of armored vehicles was not always mentioned in all the combat reports. For example, after the headquarters of Army Group Center informed Colonel H. von Elverfeldt that the army was not going to receive the promised Panthers, Model made an attempt to address the acute situation with armor in the Ninth Army's first echelon, at least with half-measures. On 27 June he directed that the Pz.Kpfw. III with the long-barreled L/60 cannon be again returned to Heavy Panzer Battalion 505.[440] However, this particular piece of information was only discovered in the journal of combat operations; there is no mention of this directive in the army's reports and messages. Virtually half of the combat machines of Gruppe Esebeck's 12th Panzer Division were transferred to formations and units of the Ninth Army. Of the 88 tanks it possessed on 1 July, 12 short-barreled Pz.Kpfw. III were now with Heavy Panzerjäger Battalion 656; eight long-barreled Pz.Kpfw. IV and one short-barreled Pz.Kpfw. III were with the 258th Infantry Division; one short-barreled Pz.Kpfw. III was with the 102nd Infantry Division; seven long-barreled Pz.Kpfw. III and one short-barreled Pz.Kpfw. III were in Heavy Panzer Battalion 505; one short-barreled Pz.Kpfw. IV was in Briansk with the training unit; and four long-barreled Pz.Kpfw. IV and three Pz.Kpfw. I were undergoing light repairs (a repair requiring not more than 14 hours to complete). However, up to the Battle of Kursk, only a single message from the 12th Panzer Division at 1915 on 1 July 1943 mentioned these transfers. Therefore, it cannot be excluded that in the future, other such transfers might appear in other divisions that are unknown today. Secondly, a portion of the armored vehicles arrived in the army literally just several days before the start of the fighting and were recorded by assorted departments. Considering the significant amount of documentation for both Ninth Army and Army Group Center, it is impossible to assert with any confidence

---

439 The calculation includes 13 tanks of the 12th Panzer Division that were transferred to Heavy Panzerjäger Battalion 656 and Heavy Panzer Battalion 505's Tigers, which is to say, 88 machines.
440 NARA US, T.312, R.317, F.788136.

that no division or other received new combat machines just a day or two before the offensive, which hasn't been discovered by us today. In addition, in the final four days before the operation, a certain number of tanks might have returned to their units, which was not mentioned in the reports. As a result, the total number of tanks and self-propelled guns might rise, though I think not by a substantial number.

Incidentally, this supposition to a great degree also relates to Model's neighbor, von Manstein's Army Group South. Here, a significant number of armored vehicles were arriving right up to the start of Citadel. For example, if to judge from the schedule of arrival of armored vehicles in the Fourth Panzer Army, which its headquarters sent to Army Group South on 1 July 1943, at that moment, of the two battalions of Panthers, only one, the Panzer Battalion 51 (104 Panthers) had arrived; Panzer Battalion 52 with 100 Panthers was still en route and was supposed to arrive approximately on 3 July.[441] So far, the time of its arrival hasn't been found in documents; it is only known that in a message of the XXXXVIII Panzer Corps at 1915 on 2 July, it still was not recorded on its list of units.[442] Considering that the arrival of a company of Panzer Battalion 51 (to Bogodukhov, Novaia Bovariia and Odnorobovka) fell behind schedule by 7 to 15 hours, then with a great amount of confidence it is possible to state that this Panther battalion might have arrived on the eve of the Battle of Kursk.

Regarding the armored vehicles that might have been transferred to the Ninth Army once the offensive was underway between 5 and 11 July 1943, either in separate groups or as part of divisions, then judging from revealed documents, this proved to be extremely few. The sole substantial replenishment was the already mentioned 14 Tigers of 3./Heavy Panzer Battalion 505, which began to arrive on 8 July. There was one more relatively large group of tanks and self-propelled guns, about which the Ninth Army received a report on 8 July. It consisted of 24 150mm Bison self-propelled howitzers (sIG-33) for the 2nd and 4th Panzer Divisions; 10 Sturmpanzer infantry support guns (known as the Brummbär ["Grouch"] by the Allies) for StuG Battalion 216; two command tanks for the 2nd Panzer Division; 12 Hummel self-propelled guns armed with a 150mm howitzer for the 12th and 18th Panzer Divisions; and six light halftracks armed with guns for the 18th Panzer Division.[443] However, this batch of armored vehicles was not expected to arrive until 9-10 July, and in the troops, a day or two later, thus none these tanks and self-propelled guns were able to take part in Model's offensive, so they shouldn't be considered when assessing the condition of the Ninth Army during Citadel.

In addition to tanks, a significant role was given to assault guns in the execution of the Ninth Army's offensive. As the information in Table 9 shows, they comprised a bit more than 38 percent of the assault grouping's total number of armored fighting vehicles.

441 NARA US, T.313, R.368, F.8654240.
442 NARA US, T.313, R.368, F.8654350.
443 NARA US, T.312, R.322, F.7890982.

Table 9: The number of tanks and self-propelled guns in the separate panzer brigades, regiment and battalions attached to Army Groups South and Center on 4 July 1943 for Operation Citadel[444]

Designation	Attachment	Pz-II	Pz-III (L24)[445]	Pz-III (L42)	Pz-III (L60)	Pz-V	Pz-VI	Ferdinands	Brummbär	StuG G and StuG H	Sd.Kfz 301
					Ninth Army						
Pz Brigade 21	XXXXI PzK		8		7		31				
Hvy Pz Jäger Reg 656	XXXXI PzK[446]	2	3	10 (+2[447])	7			83 (+4,+2[448])	42 (+1, +2[449])	10/-	72
StuG Bn 177	XXXXI PzK									22/9	
StuG Bn 185	XXIII AK									27/5	
StuG Bn 189	XXIII AK									31/-	
StuG Bn 224	XXXXI PzK									22/9	
StuG Bn 245	XXXXVII PzK									22/9	
StuG Bn 904	XXXXVII PzK									31/-	
StuG Bn 909	XXXXVI PzK									31/-	
Total:		2	11	10 (+2)	14			83 (+6)	42 (+3)	228 (196/32)	72

444 Zetterling and Frankson, Kursk 1943: a statistical analysis, p. 65
445 The designation within parentheses indicates the length of the gun barrel.
446 Zetterling and Frankson, Kursk 1943: a statistical analysis, p. 65, 27.
447 Two under repair for up to 14 days.
448 Four under repair for up to 14 days, two under repair for more than 14 days.
449 One under repair for up to 14 days, two under repair for more than 14 days.

Designation	Attachment	Pz-II	Pz-III (L24)[445]	Pz-III (L42)	Pz-III (L60)	Pz-V	Pz-VI	Ferdinands	Brummbär	StuG G and StuG H	Sd.Kfz 301
Army Group South (Fourth Panzer Army and Army Detachment Kempf)											
Pz Brigade 10						200					
Hvy Sep Pz Bn 503	III PzK (AD Kempf)						45				
StuG Bn 228	III PzK (AD Kempf)									22/9	
StuG Co. 393	Korps Raus (AD Kempf)									12/-	
StuG Bn 905	Korps Raus (AD Kempf)									23/9	
StuG Bn 911	XXXXVIII PzK (Fourth PzA)									22/9	
Total:						200	45			106 (79/27)	
Total for Ninth Army and AG South		2	11	10(+2)	14	200	76	83 (+6)	42 (+3)	334	72

When planning the combat formation adopted by the army's assault wedge, Model concentrated a large portion of the armor, 689 combat machines (420 tanks and 269 self-propelled guns) in the XXXXVII Panzer Corps and XXXXI Panzer Corps, which were to operate on the main Ol'khovatka axis and the auxiliary Ponyri axis. Of the tanks, 326 were allocated to the XXXXVII Panzer Corps, while 207 of the assault guns and Ferdinands went to the XXXXI Panzer Corps. The flanking corps, the XXXXVI Panzer Corps and the XXIII Corps, received only crumbs – three battalions of assault guns with a total number of 91 self-propelled guns. In order to break through the main belt of defenses of Rokossovsky's troops and to repel possible armored counterattacks, Model planned to use two powerful armored formations as an armored battering ram in the XXXXVII and XXXXI Panzer Corps, which were equipped with the latest models of armor: Panzerjäger Regiment 656 under the command of Lieutenant Colonel E. von Jugenfeld (XXXXI Panzer Corps) and Colonel A. Burmeister's Separate Panzer Brigade 21, which the German documents refer to as Panzer Brigade Burmeister (or simply, Brigade Burmeister). The panzerjäger regiment consisted of Major B. Kall's StuG Battalion 216, Major H. Steinbach's Panzerjäger Battalion 653, Haupt K-H Noak's Panzerjäger Battalion 654 and a separate panzer company under the regiment's command. The StuG battalion was armed with 45 150mm StuG IV Sturmpanzer assault guns, and the two panzerjäger battalions were each equipped with 45 Ferdinand heavy tank destroyers. The separate panzer company consisted of Pz.Kpfw. III tanks armed with 50mm or 75mm guns. In addition, as an asset (for screening the company of radio-controlled Goliaths), the regiment received 10 StuGs.

The sole armored unit of the Separate Panzer Brigade 21 was Major B. Sauvant's Heavy Panzer Battalion 505, which according to its establishment was supposed to have 45 Pz.Kpfw. VI Tigers. Before the start of the fighting, the Tigers were arriving in batches and replacing the Pz.Kpfw. III tanks that were temporarily assigned to the battalion on a tank by tank basis. However, by the start of Citadel, the number of Tigers in the battalion did not manage to reach their authorized number. In Russian historiography on the Battle of Kursk, despite the significant number of publications on the subject, there is still no clarity on the matter of the Heavy Panzer Battalion 505's composition and use. The main reason for this is the authors' failure to make use of archival materials and the use by the majority of them of only open foreign sources, often with mistakes. In certain works, one encounters open contradictions, because of which it is hard to figure out what the author is trying to say. In M.B. Bariatinsky's book, we read: "Initially the battalion was equipped according to the old table and by 20 April 1943 numbered 20 Tigers and 25 Pz.Kpfw. III. By 6 May, Heavy Panzer Battalion 505 was in the process of moving to the Eastern Front, to Army Group Center, aboard several trains. On 10 July 1943 the Pz.Kpfw. III tanks were removed from the battalion, and another 14 Tigers arrived in place of them, and the battalion reached its authorized strength of 45 heavy panzers [sic]." Just three pages later, something quite different is given by the author: "By 5 July 1943 the Heavy Panzer Battalion 505 had only 31 Tiger tanks. The point is that its 3rd Company arrived in the area of combat operations only on 8 July."[450] It is not clear why if another 14 Tigers arrived to join with the 20 Tigers in the battalion, they did not number 34 Tigers, but the authorized strength of 45 Tigers. At the same time, according to the author's assertion, until 5 July the battalion numbered only 31 Pz. VI! According to M. Kolomiets, prior to the Battle of Kursk the

---

450 Bariatinsky, M., *Tigry v boiu* [*Tigers in battle*] (Moscow, 2008), pp. 143, 146.

Heavy Panzer Battalion 505 "had its authorized number of Tigers – 45 machines, and all were operational by the morning of 5 July."[451]

What was the actual number of Tigers in Sauvant's battalion at the moment of entering combat? In captured German documents it is noted that prior to the start of Citadel, all of the planned Pz.Kpfw. VI had not arrived in the Ninth Army. Between 10 and 15 June, it received the last batch of these combat machines prior to the operation, but not 14 of them, only 11. All of the Pz.Kpfw. III tanks present in the battalion at that moment were replaced by them, but as already mentioned, at Model's personal order, all of the Pz.Kpfw. III tanks were returned again to Sauvant, since the arrival of the remaining Tigers was being significantly delayed. So, on the morning of 5 July, Heavy Panzer Battalion 505 went on the offensive as part of the XXXXVII Panzer Corps with 44 tanks of two types: 31 Pz.Kpfw. VI and 13 Pz.Kpfw. III armed with the 50mm gun. The remaining Tigers of the 3rd Company did not arrive until the fourth day of the operation.

The German command took into account the significant depth and high density of the minefields in the Central Front's defenses, which were covered by a powerful artillery grouping, particularly in the main defensive belt. Therefore, in order to reduce the loss of heavy armor in the first stage of the offensive, Jugenfeld's regiment and Burmeister's brigade were given three companies of radio-controlled Sdkfz. 301 Goliaths; in particular, Heavy Panzer Battalion 505[452] received the 312th Company, and the Heavy Panzerjäger Regiment 656 received the 313th and 314th Companies.

As already mentioned above, in addition to the four panzer divisions, Heavy Panzer Battalion 505, Separate Panzer Brigade 21 and Heavy Panzerjäger Regiment 656, the Ninth Army's assault wedge also consisted of StuG and StuH assault guns. By 5 July, Model had seven separate battalions of these, which had a total of 218 StuG/StuH assault guns. All of the battalions were intended for use as part of the divisions of the first echelon. This was a significantly larger number of assault guns than in Army Group South. Hermann Hoth and Walther Kempf had only three assault gun battalions and one separate company, which had a total number of 106 StuG/StuH, or 10.4percent of the armor it had designated for Citadel (refer to Table 9). Because of their weak armor protection and small numbers, the assault guns could play only a limited role in Army Group South's offensive. Therefore, the plan anticipated using them primarily as an asset for the infantry divisions in order to breach narrow sectors of the front, or as a mobile anti-tank reserve of the division commanders. Even so, it did not preclude the use of these battalions in support of the armored units in the course of massed armored attacks, especially in the early days of the operation.

When comparing the main indicators between the condition of Model's and von Manstein's subordinate divisions that were directed toward Kursk, the Ninth Army was significantly inferior to its neighbor (see Tables 10 and 11). For example, let us take as an example the important consideration of manpower strength. The Fourth Panzer Army and Army Detachment Kempf, which constituted Army Group South's attacking forces (on the main and auxiliary directions

---

451 Kolomiets, M., "Tigry na vostochnom fronte (ot Rostova do Kurskoi dugi)" ["Tigers on the Eastern Front (from Rostov to the Kursk bulge"] *Frontovaia illiustratsiia*, No. 6 (2005), p. 48.
452 On 24 June 1943, this battalion had a total of 835 servicemen, including 24 officers, 7 servants, 184 junior officers and 620 enlisted men. Its combat strength consisted of 374 men, including 19 officers, 100 junior officers and 255 enlisted men.

respectively), had between them five corps, three panzer (the III, XXXXVIII and II SS Panzer Corps) and two army corps (LII Corps and Army Corps "Raus"), which consisted of 17 divisions: eight infantry (57th, 106th, 167th, 168th, 198th, 255th, 282nd and 320th Infantry Divisions) and nine panzer and panzergrenadier (3rd, 6th, 7th, 11th and 19th Panzer Divisions, and the *Grossdeutschland*, SS *Leibstandarte Adolf Hitler,* SS *Das Reich* and SS *Totenkopf* Panzergrenadier Divisions), which had a total number of 297,831 men, which was 106,076 more than Model had. Naturally, this substantially increased the manning levels in von Manstein's divisions. On average, Hoth's and Kempf's infantry and panzer (and panzergrenadier) divisions had respectively a ration strength of 16,537 and 18,552 men, which exceeded their counterparts in the Ninth Army by 4,999 and 2,145 men respectively. Meanwhile, the average combat strength of an infantry division of von Manstein's Army Group South almost doubled that in Model's Ninth Army and amounted to approximately 6,344 men.[453]

---

453 Newton, *Kurskaia bitva: nemetskii vgliad*, p. 472.

Table 10: Number of tanks and self-propelled guns in the panzer divisions of Army Group South and Army Group Center, assigned for participation in Operation Citadel, as of 1 July 1943[454]

Panzer Division	Pz I	Pz II	Pz III	Flame/command	Pz IV	Pz VI	T-34	Total tanks	StuG	Marder	Wespe	Hummel
Army Group Center												
Ninth Army												
2nd	-	12	40	/6	60	-	-	118	-	30	12	6
9th	-	-	26	/5	49	-	-	80	-	16	-	6
18th	-	-	14	/3	52	-	-	69	-	8	-	-
20th	-	9	17	/7	49	-	-	82	-	30	-	-
Total:	-	21	97	/21	210	-	-	349	-	84	12	12
Gruppe Esebeck												
4th	-	-	9	/6	74	-	-	89	-	25	12	6
12th[455]	5	6	36	/4	37	-	-	88	-	16	-	-
Total:	5	6	45	/10	111	-	-	177	-	41	12	6
Total for AG Center	5	27	142	/31	321	-	-	526	-	125	24	18
Army Group South												
3rd	-	7	59	-	23	-	-	89	2	14	-	-
6th	-	13	52	13/-	28	-	-	106	-	14	-	-

454 Zetterling and Frankson, Kursk 1943: a statistical analysis, p. 46.
455 This includes all of the 12th Panzer Division's tanks, including those transferred to the operational subordination of other divisions. In actuality, the 12th Panzer Division had 75 tanks in its assembly area.

Panzer Division	Pz I	Pz II	Pz III	Flame/command	Pz IV	Pz VI	T-34	Total tanks	StuG	Marder	Wespe	Hummel
7th	–	12	62		38	–	–	112	–	6	6	6
11th	–	8	62	13/–	26	–	–	109	–	11	–	6
19th	–	4	38		38	–	–	81	–	12	–	–
PzG GD	–	4	28	14/–	68	15	–	129	35	20	12	6
PzG LAH	–	7	13		83	13	–	116	35	21	12	6
PzG DR	–	1	70		33	14	26	144	34	12	12	6
PzG TK	–	–	63		52	15	–	130	35	11	12	6
Total for AG South	–	57	447	40/–	389	57	26	1,016	141	121	54	36
Grand Total	5	84	589	40/31	710	57	26	1,542	141	246	78	54

Table 11: Manpower strength of the divisions of Army Group Center and South, assigned for Operation Citadel, as of 4 July 1943

Army Group Center[456]		Army Group South	
Division	Total Manpower	Division	Total Manpower
6th Infantry	11,352	57th Infantry	16,048
7th Infantry	11,871	106th Infantry	19,848
10 Motorized	12,734	167th Infantry	14,347
31st Infantry	11,692	168th Infantry	15,880
78th Sturm	15,961	198th Infantry	14,641 (on 8 July)[457]
86th Infantry	11,576	255th Infantry	14,107
216th Infantry	10,059	320th Infantry	20,030
258th Infantry	11,249	322nd Infantry	15,959
292nd Infantry	10,880	SS PzG *Adolf Hitler*	23,160
383rd Infantry	11,209	SS PzG *Totenkopf*	19,795
2nd Panzer	13,522	SS PzG *Das Reich*	20,303
4th Panzer	12,932	3rd Panzer	13,968
9th Panzer	14,234	6th Panzer	20,229
18th Panzer	12,028	7th Panzer	15,705
12th Panzer	?	11th Panzer	15,894
20th Panzer	12,154	19th Panzer	14,906
Gruppe Manteuffel	3,765	PzG *Grossdeutschland*	23,011 (on 5 July)
XXIII Army Corps reserve: 8th and 13th Jäger Btns. and 36th Infantry Division's Infantry Regiment 87	4,547		

There were two primary reasons for such a substantial difference in the manning of the divisions: the overall deficit of manpower and equipment in Germany, and the different magnitude of the assignments standing before the two army groups. The Germans planned to execute the offensive in relatively narrow sectors, which in their total amounted to less than 14 percent of the entire Soviet-German front. Army Group South's offensive was primary, since it faced more ambitious tasks. To reach the designated link-up in the Kursk area, Model's forces had to make an advance of approximately 75 kilometers, while von Manstein's troops would have to

---

456 NARA US, T.312, R.322, F.7890958
457 The 198th Infantry Division arrived in Army Detachment Kempf's sector of the offensive on 8 July 1943.

cover almost twice that distance, 125 kilometers.[458] In addition, every time the screw of tension tightened, connected with the receipt of fresh information about the substantial growth in the Soviet defenses inside the Kursk salient, both Hitler and the OKH primarily reinforced the southern grouping, not the northern grouping. The decision in the latter half of June might serve as an obvious example of this: the 200 Panthers, which had previously been promised to the Ninth Army, went instead to Hoth's Fourth Panzer Army. In addition, because Army Group South had already been assigned significant forces in order to conduct von Manstein's backhand blow toward Khar'kov, already at the end of March 1943 it had considerably more combat potential than the Ninth Army. Having received additional forces in the period leading up to Citadel, by 5 July Army Group South's strength had almost doubled. Model had no such possibility to augment his forces.

In addition, the analysis of captured sources show that subjective factors also had a noticeable effect on the manning and equipping levels of the Ninth Army. In April 1943, the headquarters of the OKH ignored the army's needs for plainly unjustified reasons for virtually the entire month; only Model's letter addressed to Hitler finally and immediately got the ball rolling.[459] The prolonged transfer of the last batch of replacements – the nine march battalions, which was sent to Model back on 28 June, but did not arrive in place because of procrastination and delays until the end of Citadel, can serve as another clear example. After all, the problem with replacements was a key one, and all the major figures of the Wehrmacht were aware of it back in the springtime, yet no one except for Elverfeldt's staff even lifted a finger in order to hasten its arrival by at least the start of the fighting. There were also other factors: the lack of a good working relationship between von Kluge and Model; the poor condition of the roads in the Orel salient; the partisan attacks on the railroads; the numerous combat encounters with Central Front's reconnaissance patrols and assault teams in the course of May and June, which resulted in substantial losses in the divisions that forced the army to replace the casualties with entire march battalions (for example, in the 258th and 7th Infantry Divisions);[460] and the sluggishness of the rear services.

In the documents of the headquarters of the Ninth Army one also encounters simply blatant instances of the indifference of all the responsible structures of supply to the needs of its troops, who were readying to take part in a general offensive. For example, already in the first days of June, its divisions were living on a shoestring budget: there was a clear lack of shells for the field and anti-tank guns. Model and his staff began reporting about this from the beginning of June to all levels of higher command, including to Berlin as well. In the course of a final meeting before Citadel, Model even personally requested Hitler's assistance at least with the anti-tank shells, but the Führer paid no heed. Already once the fighting was underway, he reminded K. Zeitzler of this request, but he wouldn't receive them even before the end of the operation.

At first glance, it is impossible not to touch upon such "non-military" reasons for the lower strength of Model's divisions, as illness with subsequent hospitalization. In the Russian historiography of the past war, the given problem hasn't received due attention unfortunately. However, it had a direct influence, including on the course of combat operations. In the historical literature, one often comes across the assertion based on the memoirs of former frontline

---

458 *Velikaia Otechestvennaia voina 1941-1945*, Book 2, p. 254.
459 NARA US, T.312, R.317, F.7886050.
460 NARA US, T.312, R.317, F.7886119.

veterans that soldiers did not get sick in the trenches, because their bodies had become adapted to extreme conditions.[461] This is true, but not the full truth. Archival documents testify to a different state of affairs; here is just one small example: Between 1 and 30 June 1943, the total loss of officers and men reporting for duty in the Ninth Army's 6th Infantry Division amounted to 288 (or 2.5percent of its total number of personnel), including 216 who were absent due to illness. Almost all of the hospitalized men, 215 soldiers and junior officers, were from combat units, which amounted to 6.8percent of the division's combat strength given an average strength of 407 men for each infantry battalion. At first glance this figure seems small, but if we recall that at this time the division was not engaged in combat, then its significance unquestionably grows, since it shows that in a rear area (virtually at rest), just one division was deprived of the equivalent of 53percent of an infantry battalion. There were 21 such divisions in the Ninth Army. If we then conduct a simple arithmetic operation, 21 x 215, the result is 4,536, which is a figure equivalent to the combat strength of the 78th Sturm Division, which was the strongest infantry division in Model's army. Naturally, the rate of illness was not as high at this time in all of the divisions, but in several it was even higher. For example, in the 4th Panzer Division because of the outbreak of typhus in April 1943, the number of men hospitalized increased noticeably.

The very same problems existed in the Soviet troops as well. In the spring of 1943, because of the lack of fats in the rations, the soldiers in a number of the first-echelon divisions of the Voronezh Front were struck with night blindness. After sunset, the soldiers had trouble seeing even nearby objects. As a result, a stressful situation arose in the divisions that had a lot of men from Central Asia.[462] Their commands were forced to send only Russians, Ukrainians and Belorussians, who were not so affected by this illness, out on reconnaissance patrols, picket duty and nighttime vigil at machine guns. The daily around-the-clock duties were exhausting the men. In the frontline conditions, the problem was extremely acute, so two of the Front's headquarters – the Sanitary and Rear Service command staffs – were involved in resolving it.

One more example – cases of suicide in the units of the 5th Guards Army at Prokhorovka. On 10 and 11 July 1943, while preparing for the frontal counterattack, there was a wave of suicides among the junior officers who had just arrived from the reserve and had not yet seen any fighting: company commanders, platoon commanders and commanders of mortar batteries. Nervous disorders were a constant in all of the active armies, and grew in correlation with the intensity of the fighting. For example, at the start of the British combat operations in Tunisia (during the Second World War), neuropathies comprised 2percent of all casualties. However, the number of cases of "shellshock" grew to up to 15percent of all casualties in pace with the demands of a combat situation. In the armies of the United States, over the entire period of the Second World War, approximately one million cases of nervous and psychological disorders were diagnosed, and for this reason approximately 525,000 men were discharged from the army.[463]

---

461 See for example the recollections of a doctor of the 52nd Guards Rifle Division, Senior Lieutenant V.A. Mikhinaia, "Mediki v boiakh na Kurskoi duge" ["Medics in the fighting at the Kursk bulge"], which is preserved in the Kursk Oblast Museum of Local History.
462 Zamulin, V.N., *Zabytoe srazhenie Ognennoi dugi* [*Forgotten battle of the Bulge of Fire*] (Moscow: Iauza, 2008), p. 98.
463 *Army Information Digest*, January 1957, p. 30.

Incidents of nervous breakdowns and disorders of varying degrees of severity were not few in the Red Army over the years of the war, even among experienced, hardened military commanders. Even so, this important factor of combat life in the troops has practically not been elucidated in Russian historiography. Marshal of the Soviet Union A.M. Vasilevsky related one such story in his memoirs:

> Stress and distress – this happened with people in the war and occurred not only at the time when we had only just begun to win, but also much later – nerves simply were not holding up. I recall, for example, one such case on the Mius River[464], when an offensive had already been prepared in Gerasimenko's army.[465] Gerasimenko was not playing a major role in the forthcoming offensive … but his army also had offensive assignments. So, on the morning before the offensive, we arrived at the command post together with Tolbukhin. We spoke with Gerasimenko. Everything was normal. Even before this, I had spent time with him. He was ready for the offensive, and neither I nor Tolbukhin had any particular criticisms for him. During the discussion, I asked:
>
> "Well, how are your troops, how are they feeling?"
>
> Then suddenly, raising his voice to a shout, he said:
>
> "The troops … the troops …", and giving a wave of his hand, he added: "We'll certainly fail!"
>
> "What do you mean, fail?"
>
> "We're going to fail."
>
> I summoned the army's chief of staff and asked his opinion of the units' readiness for the operation. He said that everything was in order, everything was ready, and he had confidence in success. Then I was compelled to say in Tolbukhin's presence that since the army commander did not believe in the operation's success and had announced this before the offensive even got underway, we'd have to submit the question of his dismissal to the Stavka, because it was impossible to go on the offensive with such an attitude.
>
> Then suddenly, Gerasimenko somehow slumped over and spoke up, one can say, almost with tears in his voice, and his appearance was completely tormented:
>
> "Forgive me, I don't know what came over me, or how all this erupted out of me. I'm exhausted. I haven't slept a wink all night, thinking about how we'd move out, and what might happen … I'm overstrung and have become overwrought … I'm tired. I need to sleep."
>
> We did not report to the Stavka that he should be dismissed from the army. He had a good night's sleep, pulled himself back together, and in the future, carried out the assignment that he'd been given.[466]

---

464 The Donbass offensive operation, conducted between 17 July and 2 August 1943 with the aim of pinning down Wehrmacht forces and preventing them from shifting reserves from the Donbass to the area of the Kursk bulge.

465 Vasilii Filippovich Gerasimenko (1900-1961), a lieutenant general. Between December 1942 and December 1943, he commanded the Southern Front's 28th Army.

466 Simonov, K.M., *Glazami cheloveka moego pokoloeniia* [*Through the eyes of my generation*] (Moscow, 1988), pp. 456-457.

All of the aforementioned problems in isolation played no substantial role, but taken together, their influence on the lower combat capabilities of the Ninth Army's forces on the eve of the Battle of Kursk were perceptible. Did the above listed problems exist in Army Group South when preparing for the Battle of Kursk? Unquestionably, but first of all, not all of them and not to the same extent. For example, it did not have to conduct a major anti-partisan operation like Gypsy Baron, for which the entire XXXXVII Panzer Corps was activated, though the struggle with them was actively proceeding in the northern portion of Zhitomir Oblast as well, which was the location of one of the major partisan bases, and in other places. However, these operations were substantially smaller in size, and most importantly, did not involve forces of the assault grouping that had been formed for Citadel. Second, Erich von Manstein did not have such a strained relationship with Hermann Hoth or Walther Kempf, as Günther von Kluge did with Walter Model. The Field Marshal was personally responsible for the success of Citadel, and thus did everything possible for them, even at the expense of the defense on other sectors of his army group. The transfer of the 3rd Panzer Division and 198th Infantry Division from the First Panzer Army to the Fourth Panzer Army can serve as an example of this. Erich von Manstein believed that once the decision had been reached about the offensive, "everything had to be done to ensure Operation Citadel's complete and rapid success."[467] Indeed, it should be acknowledged that throughout the entire period of preparations for the summer fighting, he tried to stick to this principle, and even though this did not always happen, I want to emphasize once again that a strong foundation for this had already been created in his army group earlier that spring.

Then finally, the transportation network and flow of supplies to Army Group South was better developed and not as intensively subjected to partisan attacks as was the case in the Orel salient. Moreover, in the south there had been no need for such large-scale force regroupings, as Model had to do.

Now let us look at the final version of the Ninth Army's plan for an offensive toward Kursk, which had been first put to paper on 14 June 1943, but continued to be "polished" almost right up to the start of the operation. Its main parameters – objectives, assignments, and timetables – had already been settled by this time. Disputes went on between the command of the army group and the army regarding the composition of the assault grouping and the reserves (divisions for exploiting a success), as well as on a number of tactical matters, which sometimes snowballed into major problems, such as the redrawing of sectors for the offensive.

Thus, Ninth Army was to launch the main attack along the Orel – Fatezh – Kursk road, and a subsidiary attack along the Orel – Ponyri – Kursk railroad. Both thoroughfares ran from north to south through the line of contact between the opposing sides. The distance between the two points where these routes cut through the frontline was approximately 40 km, and 75 km further to the south, they came together at the same point – the city of Kursk. This city was to become one of Model's two main objectives; the other, linking up with the Fourth Panzer Army in the Shshigry area. Thus, between themselves these two thoroughfares delineated the territory in the form of a narrow wedge, which cleaved the ground in this area (where the defenses of the Central Front stood like an enormous breakwater). Both of the roads were laid down along the most passable terrain and the German command took this circumstance into account. It

---

467 Manstein, *Uteriannye pobedy*, p. 524.

was thus here where Model planned to deploy the army's assault wedge, which consisted of two mobile formations – General of Panzer Troops J. Lemelsen's XXXXVII Panzer Corps (the 2nd, 9th, and 20th Panzer Divisions and the 6th Infantry Division) and General of Panzer Troops J. Harpe's XXXXI Panzer Corps. They received the following missions according to the order for Operation Citadel on 14 June 1943:

> XXXXVII Panzer Corps (20th, 2nd and 9th Panzer Divisions and the 6th Infantry Divisions) supports the echeloned attack of the XXXXI Panzer Corps for three hours prior to Y-hour and up to the moment start of the attack, after which at Y-hour it attacks in turn with the support of the Luftwaffe and the XXXXI Panzer Corps' strong artillery group as the army's main group with the 20th Panzer Division and 6th Infantry Division spearheading the breakthrough of the enemy fortifications in the sector: west of Verkhnee Tagino – Novyi Khutor.
>
> Decisive will be the fact that the corps after a successful breakthrough in deep cooperation with aircraft and with the use of all its mobility and striking power penetrates to the area of heights north of Kursk. Here it is necessary to ensure the rapid moving up of the second echelon (2nd and 9th Panzer Divisions) through the breaches made by the 6th Infantry Division.
>
> The 6th Infantry Division after completing its assignment – upon reaching the Stanovoe – Vozy road, must be ready, while holding the road for the movement of the panzers, to switch to the army's direct command and to take part in combat operations in the sector of the XXXXI Panzer Corps or XXIII Corps, either from behind the left flank of the XXXXVII Panzer Corps or according to the situation.
>
> After achieving the area of heights north of Kursk, XXXXVII Panzer Corps must be ready to operate according to the situation: either in cooperation with the XXXXI Panzer Corps' mobile units; or to advance further to the south; or to link up with the Fourth Panzer Army at Kursk and east of it. Be prepared for a further breakthrough toward Shshigry with the pivoting of XXXXI Panzer Corps' southern wing.
>
> The task of the XXXXI Panzer Corps and XXIII Corps is the prevention of enemy influence against the panzer wedge's eastern flank and the creation of a new front of defense on the Shshigry – Soshny sector line. XXXXI Panzer Corps (292nd and 86th Infantry Divisions and the 18th Panzer Division) for the three hours up to Y-hour in close contact with the XXIII Corps and the powerful support of the heavy armored vehicles (Panzerjäger Regiment 656 on the corps' left flank west of the Orel – Kursk railroad and the strong work of the XXXXVII Panzer Corps' artillery breaks through along both sides of the given railroad with the 292nd Infantry Division. From Y-hour, the corps with all of its forces and all of its artillery supports the offensive of the XXXXVII Panzer Corps' eastern group. Later, according to the development of the situation it is necessary to prepare the employment of Panzerjäger Regiment 656 in the role of supporting the XXIII Corps' offensive south of Maloarkhangel'sk or in the offensive's depth as an anti-tank defense against enemy tank attacks from the south or southeast. Subsequently, developing the offensive, XXXXI Panzer Corps seizes the Bugorskii – Mokroe line with the forces of the 86th Infantry Division, organizes a defense there, and breaks through with mobile units up to the Tuskar River sector. Here, the 10th Panzergrenadier Division, which is located in the reserve of the army group commander, might be necessary. The corps must be ready after the 292nd

Infantry Division's advance to strike toward either Shshigry or toward Kursk with mobile units, in close contact with the XXXXVII Panzer Corps. The rapid regrouping of forces (artillery and anti-tank units), the assignment of reserves, and the rapid construction of defensive positions by all possible means will have decisive significance for the XXXXI Panzer Corps' and XXIII Corps' newly created defensive front. Forces and materiel for constructing fortifications (strands of wire, mines and machines) will assigned by a separate order.[468]

Accordingly, the main result of the operation's first stage for Lemelsen's and Harpe's divisions was to consist of the breaching of the 13th Army's and 70th Army's three belts of defenses in the course of 72 hours, and the emergence of their divisions in operational space. The entire offensive's goal was a breakthrough to the depth of 75-80 km in seven days, the capture of Kursk, and the encirclement of the Central Front's and Voronezh Front's forces in the Kursk salient together with von Manstein's assault grouping.

General of Infantry J. Friessner's XXIII Corps was supposed to guard the left flank of the XXXXVII and XXXXI Panzer Corps' combat wedge. As follows from this document, after overcoming the main defensive belt (in close cooperation with the XXXXI Panzer Corps) and the capture of the primary center of resistance in this area, Maloarkhangel'sk, its three divisions (78th Sturm Division, 216th and 383rd Infantry Divisions) were to repulse anticipated counterattacks by Soviet mobile formations and to create an outer front of encirclement along the line: east of Shshigry – east of Maloarkhangel'sk. According to intelligence information and the calculations of the XXIII Corps' command staff, on the third day of the operation, which is to say by 8 July, the Soviet command would be ready to bring up three brigades and three regiments with a total number of up to 215 tanks to the sector of the 78th Sturm Division's and 216th Infantry Division's offensive.[469] This information was muddled and in essence, not accurate. For example, German intelligence had assigned the 129th Tank Brigade to this group, but it was located significantly to the west of this sector, in Ponyri, which is to say, in the center of the XXXXI Panzer Corps' offensive, and had according to Friessner's Intelligence Department somewhere around 25 tanks in total, not the 53 that it had in reality.[470] Supposedly, the 3rd Tank Corps would also be brought up to this sector, but only with two brigades, in which there might be not the authorized number of 106 machines, but for some reason only 76. The impression forms that this was not confirmed intelligence information, but only speculations, based on the elementary principles of conducting a defense and mingled with the apprehension of a powerful counterattack, which would be hard to repel because of the lack of necessary forces here. Nevertheless, in the opinion of Elverfeldt's staff, this danger was completely real; the Abwehr had identified a supposedly hidden concentration of a major armored grouping in the Livny area, so an order was issued: After the commitment of the XXXXVII Panzer Corps' panzer divisions into the breakthrough, its 6th Infantry Division should be quickly directed to the east, to the assistance of the XXIII Corps.

At this moment, the XXIII Corps was actually weak, and it did not have the necessary strength even for reaching its primary objectives – the capture of Maloarkhangel'sk and the

---

468 Klink, *Das Gesetz des Handelns*, pp. 322-323.
469 NARA US, T.314, R.680, F.001049.
470 Ibid.

creation of an outer front of encirclement. Therefore, Friessner was forced to resort to steps, which both he and his subordinates considered incorrect. For example, having failed to persuade Model to assign him not only an additional division, but also units to create a minimal corps reserve, he did not find anything better to do than to remove Jager Battalion 8 and Pioneer Battalion 746 from the assault group's 78th Sturm Division, which was supposed to be the corps' main instrument in achieving its objectives. In response, the commander of the 78th Sturm Division Lieutenant General H. Traut sent him a written objection, in which he noted that this was "not a propitious decision", and having carried it out, his division would be not only unable to bring up its forces and means to the forward edge to support the offensive, but also unable to help break through the first two lines of positions at the village of Soglasnyi or to seize the tactically important Hill 254.6 (the task for 5 July). Traut emphasized, "[The division] does not have the reserves to exploit a success, and accordingly, it won't be able to take advantage of a favorable opportunity that comes up as a result of the surprise attack."[471] Putting it plainly, Traut was saying that with this decision to strip it of the two battalions, his division's offensive was as good as over, and that meant the corps' offensive was as well. Likely, in order not to leave the corps' command in an awkward situation, H. Traut proposed to alter this decision only in part: to leave Jäger Battalion 8 in the division up until moment that that it took Hill 254.6, and only afterward send Jäger Battalion 8 into the corps reserve, but he did not make any mention at all about the Pioneer Battalion 746. On 25 June, without objections, this proposal was confirmed by Friessner.[472]

The command of the Ninth Army and of the subordinate corps in these final days before the offensive frequently encountered problems of a similar type. Therefore, I will emphasize once again that it is hard to imagine that if the sober-minded generals of the Wehrmacht (which they considered themselves to be), who took part in planning the attack toward Kursk, were unable to grasp that if the commander of a shock division was haggling with his superior over one single battalion right before the year's general offensive, it was simply laughable to expect to achieve those grandiose objectives that were embodied in the plan of Citadel. However, let us return to the offensive's scheme.

General of Infantry H. Zorn's XXXXVI Panzer Corps was supposed to screen the right flank of the XXXXI and XXXXVII Panzer Corps' attack. It was supposed to operate on both sides of Trosna and to the west of there with the forces of three infantry divisions (the 258th, 31st and 7th Infantry Divisions). It had the mission to split the defenses on the 70th Army's left flank, take Fatezh and the ground south of it, before actively opposing the Russians' major grouping in the Dmitriev area, so that it wouldn't be able to delay or disrupt the XXXXVII Panzer Corps' offensive. The Ninth Army's plan laid out its tasks as follows:

> XXXXVI Panzer Corps (102nd, 258th, 7th and 31st Infantry Divisions) has received the mission to prevent the pressure of enemy units positioned east of Dmitriev against the western flank of the panzer wedge. It must in close cooperation with XXXXVII Panzer Corps break through as quickly as possible and with a rapid advance retake the Trosna – Fatezh road. Take Fatezh and organize a defensive front on the Belyi

---

471 NARA US, T.314, R.680, F.000058.
472 Ibid.

Nemed' – Krasovsk – Putchino – Usozha River line as far as the mouth of the Ruda River [a tributary of the Usozha], and a staging area south of Fatezh on the Khomel' to Melokovka – Vasilevskoe line and east of there. According to the development of the situation, a replenishment with additional sapper means is under consideration.

If the enemy's situation permits, plan the use of forces here to reach and hold the Pesochnia – Usozha River – Ruda River line and south of there. Later, bring up Gruppe von Manteuffel to Fatezh. The reserve 12th Panzer Division will be released in the wake the 31st Infantry Division for a rapid breakthrough to Fatezh and the area south of Fatezh only if necessary and at that only temporarily.[473]

The main forces of infantry (85,746 men, or 44.7percent of the infantry involved in the Ninth Army's offensive), artillery (474 tubes, or 39.8 percent), all of the army's tanks, and a significant portion of the assault guns and self-propelled tank destroyers (689, or 88 percent) were concentrated in the XXXXVII and XXXXVI Panzer Corps. In its four divisions, the XXXXVII Panzer Corps had a ration strength of 51,262 men and possessed 395 armored vehicles and 238 guns, while the XXXXI Panzer Corps had respectively 34,484, 311 and 236. In addition, after the emergence of the forward units on the heights south of Ponyri Station, the 4th Panzer Division was to be committed into the sector of the XXXXVII Panzer Corps from out of von Kluge's reserve in order to exploit the success; it had 12,932 men, 89 tanks and 25 Marder self-propelled tank destroyers.

The three infantry divisions and the combined-arms reserve of the XXIII Corps (8 and 13 Jäger Battalions and Infantry Regiment 87) numbered 41,776 men and 249 guns (or 83 barrels per division, which was more than in any other of the corps; the XXXXVII Panzer Corps had 238 guns, the XXXXI Panzer Corps had 236, and the XXXXVI Panzer Corps had 213). They also had two StuG Battalions. In addition, as already noted, on the first day of the operation the plan was to shift the 6th Infantry Division and a battalion of Ferdinands into its sector. The western wing of Model's grouping was the weakest in the combat formation. XXXXVI Panzer Corps had on its list just four divisions, but it was planned to use only three of them for the offensive – the 7th, 31st and 258th Infantry Divisions, as well as the reserve Gruppe Manteuffel (with a combined total of 38,577 men of the corps' total of 50,013 men and 213 guns). This was connected with the fact that major Russian forces had been discovered in the Dmitrov – L'gov area, though their posture plainly testified to the Russians' defensive intentions. German intelligence mistakenly believed that there were no Russian tanks here, and only infantry and artillery made up this enemy grouping. Thus, Model was counting upon the fact that given the fire support of XX Corps (161 guns), Zorn's corps would have enough strength to tie down and hold the Russians until the army's main forces had created a solid outer ring of encirclement. Even so, no one could guarantee that in the first stage of the operation, the XXXXVI Panzer Corps wouldn't get bogged down in the enemy's defenses, or that Russian armor wouldn't make an appearance here. In this case, Model with von Kluge's agreement put the 12th Panzer Division into reserve (with 75 tanks in its inventory) and issued it a preliminary order to scout out routes for movement to this direction and to work out matters of collaboration with the XXXXVI Panzer Corps.

---

473 Klink, *Das Gesetz des Handelns*, pp. 322-323.

The Ninth Army commander believed that such a combat arrayal of the assault grouping was optimal given the circumstances, although it was hard for him to believe that with the available forces it could achieve Citadel's objectives. Two problems particularly troubled him: the weakness of the divisions on the main axis, and the possibility that the Russians would go on the offensive against the Second Panzer Army in his rear. According to his calculations, Lemelsen's and Harpe's panzer corps would be able to batter their way through the Russian defenses, albeit with great difficulty. However, he did not have the forces available to exploit a success, even given the reinforcement of the 4th Panzer Division, which in the future would be pinned down at this moment in combat with Russian mobile formations. It was assumed that this would be the most precarious moment for his Ninth Army and the most advantageous time for the Soviet forces. Therefore, he asked G. von Kluge to bring up additional forces to the Orel salient. In particular, he insisted on the 5th Panzer Division, which was in the army group's reserve in the Ul'ianovo area (north of Orel) and the 36th Infantry Division, which at his request the Field Marshal moved out to the east of Orel on 30 June, "to be in constant readiness and even if offensive's first stage is successful, they should remain in the area of Gruppe Weiss."[474]

Given the deficit of strength, when preparing the offensive Model paid a large amount of attention to devising an effective plan for the artillery's use. He pointed out: "Since our artillery is insufficiently strong, it is necessary to achieve its massing on the breakthrough sectors within the boundaries of each corps ... When breaking through the enemy defenses, it is absolutely necessary to use the tactics of assault groups, which should advance to a depth of 10-12 kilometers in such a way that they quickly capture ground defiles (the bottlenecks) between watercourses and ravines that have a key significance for the advance."[475]

As has been already mentioned, with the aim of increasing the density of artillery means, back at the end of April 1943 Model had received H. Goering's permission to use Flak guns to combat ground targets. He considered their use especially important in the first stage of the offensive. On 2 May, with regard for this decision, the army headquarters released a directive regarding its use. The document accented three main points:

a. The Flak guns crews should be used in order to suppress accessible firing points (bunkers and dug-in tanks);
b. It was necessary to make timely use of the bulk of the 88mm guns involved in the artillery offensive to combat aerial targets;
c. Light flak guns in the initial stage of the offensive should be used exclusively to counter low-flying aircraft.[476]

The Commander-in-Chief of Army Group South signed the final order about the offensive to its main forces significantly later, only on 28 June. In order to achieve the objectives of the first stage of Citadel – the destruction of the 1st Tank Army and the Soviet mobile reserves in the Prokhorovka area, according to H. Hoth's calculations, it was necessary on the first day of the offensive to penetrate the defenses of the 6th Guards Army quickly as far as the Teterevino – Noven'koe line and to engage the 1st Tank Army and defeat it. It was assumed that

---

474 NARA US, T.312, R.317, F.7886138.
475 NARA US, T.312, R.317, F.7886069.
476 NARA US, T.312, R.317, F.7886072.

in step with the army's advance into the depth of the Voronezh Front's lines (on approximately the third or fourth day of the operation), the Russians would bring up the reserve tank and mechanized formations that had been formed and brought up to strength that spring to the Prokhorovka area. By this time, two of the Fourth Panzer Army's shock formations – General of Panzer Troops O. von Knobelsdorff's XXXXVIII Panzer Corps and *Obergruppenführer* P. Hausser's II SS Panzer Corps – should be joining combat with these Soviet reserves, having first repulsed the counterattack of the 1st Tank Army's main forces. During the breakthrough to Prokhorovka, the right flank of Hausser's SS panzer corps was to be covered by the 6th Panzer Division of Army Detachment Kempf's III Panzer Corps, and the left flank, by XXXXVIII Panzer Corps' 11th Panzer Division.

Hermann Hoth thought that the decisive battle at Prokhorovka Station would begin in the period between 7 and 9 July. It was expected by this moment the XXXXVIII Panzer Corps would have had time to batter the 1st Tank Army's forces, force a crossing of the Psel River south of Oboian', and having deployed a blocking force to the north, pivot part of its armored forces (it was assumed that this would be the Panthers of Panzer Brigade 10) to the assistance of II SS Panzer Corps at Prokhorovka Station. Colonel General Hoth was anticipating the arrival of significant number of Soviet armored forces, so in his opinion the main forces of Army Detachment Kempf should take part together with the divisions of the II SS Panzer Corps and the XXXXVIII Panzer Corps in the expected battle at Prokhorovka Station. Hermann Hoth wrote:

> It can be assumed that after breaking through both of the enemy's defensive belts, the task of the Fourth Panzer Army will be the smashing of the Russians' 1st Tank Army, since without its destruction the operation's further conducting will be senseless. Meanwhile, the Russian motorized and tank forces located east of the Kursk salient will collide with Kempf's group. According to the information available today, the number and strength of these formations are such that Kempf's group alone will not be able to destroy them. Probably, this will require a pivoting to the east of the Fourth Panzer Army with both of its panzer corps in order to take part in the clash of armor, having first secured its rear with infantry divisions. It would be incorrect to assign for this only one of the Fourth Panzer Army's panzer corps and leave the other to attack toward the north [toward Oboian']. It is necessary to deprive the enemy of attacking means as much as possible. This is possible only if all of the armored forces of Kempf's group and the Fourth Panzer Army will be turned for an attack in close cooperation against the enemy's eastern flank [toward Prokhorovka]. Only after completing this local operation will it be possible to link up with the Ninth Army.[477]

Hoth summed up the final tasks for von Knobbelsdorff's and Hausser's divisions in Order No. 194/43, which he signed on 28 June 1943:

1. Opposite the front of the panzer army's offensive are presumably four enemy rifle divisions in the first belt of defenses and two more rifle divisions – in the second.

---

477 Parot'kin (ed.), *Kurskaia bitva*, p. 514.

It can further be assumed that one tank corps is positioned in the second defensive belt or immediately behind it, and another tank corps is south of Oboian'. The enemy's behavior indicates that he, relying on his deep and well-organized system of defenses, intends to hold the Kursk salient and is using for this the tank forces positioned close to the front in the struggle for the first belt of defenses.

After breaking through the second defensive belt [Teterevino – Noven'koe], the attacks of armor in strength of several tank corps should be expected against the eastern flank of the entire attacking grouping [out of the area of Prokhorovka] as well as the attacks of 3-4 rifle divisions that have been brought up by the enemy against the western flank.

2. Fourth Panzer Army goes on the Citadel offensive in order to encircle and destroy the enemy in the Kursk bulge. For this, on X-day [5 July] the panzer army, in accordance with the plan, breaks through the enemy's first position in the sector of high ground northwest of Belgorod and Korovino, having preliminarily on the afternoon of X-1 day [4 July] taken the hills on both sides of Butovo and south of Gertsovka with the forces of XXXXVIII Panzer Corps.

The army quickly crushes any resistance in the enemy's second line of defenses, destroys the enemy's armored forces [1st Tank Army] hurled against it, and then launches an attack in the direction of Kursk and east of there, bypassing Oboian' to the east. The operation is secured from the east by Army Detachment Kempf's offensive. In order to implement this, the army detachment attacks with its left flank (6th Panzer Division) out of Belgorod through Sabynino in the direction of Prokhorovka.

3. II SS Panzer Corps, supported by panzers, after a strong artillery preparation, executing the planned offensive, breaks through the enemy's forward edge of defense in the Berezov, Zadel'noe sector. Occupy the hills necessary for artillery observation the night before this. One division, echeloned to the right, attacks out of the area of Zhuravlino and takes the Belgorod – Iakovlevo road.

After concluding the combat for the enemy's first position, the corps immediately goes on the offensive against the second position between Luchki and Iakovlevo. Screen the left flank along the Vorskla River with one-third of the 167th Infantry Division's strength.

After breaking through the second position, the corps regroups, so that having adopted a formation that is echeloned to the right, it can attack with its main forces to the northeast south of the Psel River, and with its right flank – through Prokhorovka.[478]

The plan was to deploy Army Detachment Kempf's assault grouping on the right of the Fourth Panzer Army, in the Belgorod area and to the south of there. It was formed of two corps (III Panzer Corps and Corps Raus, which was named after the surname of its commander General of Panzer Troops Erhard Raus), for operations on a secondary direction with the aim of creating an exterior front of encirclement. It faced two very difficult tasks – to cover the Fourth Panzer

478 Ibid., p. 516.

Army's right flank, the II SS Panzer Corps, reliably, and in pace with the latter's advance, create the outer front of encirclement around the Russians in the Kursk salient. At the same time Army Detachment Kempf would have to conduct an active defense on its own right flank (XXXXII Corps), in order to pin down the Russian forces in this area. In the first stage, the army detachment's axis of advance was set as the Belgorod – Korocha – Skorodnoe line, which extended for approximately 65 km. In an updated order for Operation Citadel from 1 June 1943, Kempf wrote:

2. … Fourth Panzer Army breaks through the enemy's defenses in the direction of Kursk, advancing across the Mar'ino (27 km north of Prokhorovka) – Oboian' line, and establishes contact with the Ninth Army attacking from the north as quickly as possible.
3. Army Detachment Kempf has the task of securing the entire operation, by conducting an offensive to the east. For this it holds a line on the Donets River from the right flank as far as the mouth of the Nezhegol' River, and seizes Nezhegol' River – Korocha River line up to the city of Korocha.
4. Together with panzer forces, it launches an attack in the overall direction of Skorodnoe, in order to take for itself a screen of the right flank in the Korocha, bend of the Seim River, south of Manturovo sector.[479]

Accordingly, the task to break through to Prokhorovka and to achieve the primary objective of the first stage of the operation – the destruction of the Soviet reserves – was not given to Hoth's and Kempf's troops "on the fly", which is to say, already in the course of the operation on the basis of the current operational situation, as has been generally accepted in Soviet and Western historical literature, but had been set before them back in May 1943, during Citadel's planning, and was ultimately adopted just a week before the operation's start.

In order to screen the flanks of Army Group South's combat wedges, the plan proposed using three army corps, consisting of two or three infantry divisions each, reinforced with artillery and assault gun units, but without tanks. They faced an array of extremely difficult tasks, considering their low strength: to fortify seized territory, to cover the flanks of the breakthrough, and in extreme cases to serve as donors for the panzer divisions, in order to plug gaps and cover boundaries. The LII Corps (57th, 255th and 322nd Infantry Divisions) was located on the Fourth Panzer Army's left flank, while General of Infantry F. Mattenklott's XXXXII Corps (39th, 161st and 282nd Infantry Divisions) was located on Army Detachment Kempf's right flank.

The plan to breach the defenses of Lieutenant General I.M. Chistiakov's 6th Guards Army was relatively simple and thus predictable. Hermann Hoth was placing his main hopes on the panzers, for the attacks of which in the first stage assault guns would be indispensable. They that faced the task of breaking the Soviet lines with the powerful support of the Luftwaffe and artillery. It was not easy to find a suitable sector of ground for the simultaneous deployment of several major panzer formations opposite the 6th Guards Army's front. The terrain in which the Guardsmen had dug in was difficult – a plain cut by a large number of deep ravines, with

---

479 Ibid., p. 518.

a significant number of villages and hamlets. In addition, on the left flank, opposite the II SS Panzer Corps front and the right flank of the XXXXVIII Panzer Corps, was the valley of the Vorskla River and its tributary, the Vorsklitsa with its swampy basin. In the center, opposite the XXXXVIII Panzer Corps' front, 12 km from the forward edge, was a significant section of the 6th Guards Army's second army-level line that had been set up in the bend of the Pena River (the "Pena bulge"). Thus, the lowland of these rivers themselves presented a serious natural obstacle to an offensive toward Kursk from the south.

According to the assessment of the 6th Guards Army's headquarters, 42percent or approximately 28 km of its sector presented difficult ground for the movement of armor. There were 13 routes that offered good ground for tanks, of which four were primary, because they featured main roads leading to the north and northeast (toward Iakovlevo, Oboian', etc.). Each of the 13 directions ("corridors") had a width of 0.5 km to 20 km. Natural obstacles – balkas, river basins and swampy branches significantly strengthened the defenses, and given proper, and often not even very large-scale work by engineers, they could become a serious anti-tank obstacle. There were quite a few such obstacles on the tank-vulnerable directions in the 6th Guards Army's sector. Hoth's headquarters had attentively studied the information from observation posts and aerial reconnaissance photographs, and thus knew that the Soviet side was doing large-scale defensive work on its lines, and was very skillfully tying together the system of fire with the lay of the ground.

Hoth therefore probably decided not to take a risk, and chose a proven method for creating breaches in the 6th Guards Army's main and secondary defensive belts, as was in fact being anticipated by the Soviet command – a breakthrough by panzer wedges along major roads. However, he was planning to launch the main attack not out of one area alone, as had been the previous practice, but out of two areas simultaneously – with the forces of the II SS Panzer Corps along both sides of the Tomarovka – Bykovka – Iakovlevo road, and the XXXXVIII Panzer Corps from out of the Butovo – Cherkasskoe area along the road toward Iakovlevo. Both of the panzer corps were supposed to link up as quickly as possible in the area of Iakovlevo. A rapid advance along these two graded roads would bypass the relatively impassable and well-fortified basins of the Vorskla and Vorsklitsa Rivers, and if the offensive went successfully, without getting bogged down in heavy fighting, encircle the defenders in the bottom land.

The XXXXVIII Panzer Corps was positioned in the center of the Fourth Panzer Army's combat formation, but on the first day of the operation the leading role was allocated to the II SS Panzer Corps; it faced clearing a path for itself to Prokhorovka while creating the conditions for the deployment of the XXXXVIII Panzer Corps' main forces in the Iakovlevo area (on the Belgorod – Kursk highway, which would subsequently drive toward Oboian', screening its left flank, to engage the 1st Tank Army in battle. The three divisions of the II SS Panzer Corps faced overcoming the 6th Guards Army's main and second line of defenses west of the Belgorod – Kursk road, and having cleared a corridor up to Iakovlevo inclusively, they were to pivot to the east (to the right) toward Prokhorovka, yielding its place to its more powerful neighbor, von Knobelsdorff's panzer corps.

Both of the Fourth Panzer Army's panzer corps were among the Wehrmacht's best mobile formations. Their strength was the fact that both were almost up to their authorized levels of men and equipment; had a significant number of updated medium panzers, new heavy panzers, self-propelled guns and anti-tank guns; and their men and especially the command staff had a large amount of combat experience.

A German panzer corps was a large and very powerful combat formation. It is hard to compare with any Soviet formation or army of the time. In strength it was approximately equivalent to a Soviet combined-arms army consisting of two corps, which was reinforced with three tank corps. let us turn to the main indicators of von Knobelsdorff's panzer corps (the 3rd and 11th Panzer Divisions and Panzergrenadier Division *Grossdeutschland*). On 1 July 1943 it numbered a total of 61,692 men, of which 50,729 were servicemen and 1,963 were civilian employees. The full strength 167th Infantry Division had a total of 17,837 men. In addition, 3rd Panzer Division had another 1,106 Hiwi. A certain number of them already in the first days of the fighting were taken prisoner by units of the 1st Tank Army. Among them were even some who had captured by the Germans back in the Kiev area in September 1941.

In its armor strength, the XXXXVIII Panzer Corps was an uncommonly strong formation; at that moment its pool of armored vehicles was greater than in any other Wehrmacht formation. On 4 July 1943, it had 647 armored fighting vehicles, including 464 panzers and 147 assault guns and self-propelled guns. The Panzergrenadier Division *Grossdeutschland*, commanded by General W. Hörnlein, particularly stood out in this respect. It was the strongest German panzer division of all those involved in the attack toward Kursk. In addition to its own panzer regiment, it was reinforced with Panzer Brigade 10's Panthers, consisting of Panzer Regiment 39 with a two-battalion composition (200 Pz. V). As already noted, the brigade had been especially attached to the corps for the struggle with the 1st Tank Army, which as Hermann Hoth anticipated, would go into battle in the sector of von Knobelsdorff's panzer corps. On 1 July 1943 the Panzergrenadier Division *Grossdeutschland* numbered 329 panzers (in the panzer regiment and Panzer Brigade 10) and 55 assault guns and self-propelled Marder tank destroyers, which amounted to 63percent of all of the XXXXVIII Panzer Corps' armor (384 out of 609). As the course of combat operations would show, particularly on 5 July, the decision to concentrate such a large number of tanks and self-propelled guns in the hands of the command of just one division did not justify itself. Thus, by the start of Citadel von Knobelsdorff's XXXXVIII Panzer Corps was comparable in strength to a Soviet Guards army of two-corps composition, like, for example, the 5th Guards Army. At the same time, it had more armored fighting vehicles than the entire 1st Tank Army.

The II SS Panzer Corps had significantly more personnel than the XXXXVIII Panzer Corps, but fewer tanks and self-propelled guns. By the start of the summer fighting it had 73,380 men on its roster, and a combat strength of 39,106 men. Of its subordinate divisions, the SS *Leibstandarte Adolf Hitler* had a ration strength of 20,933 men and a combat strength of 12,893; SS *Das Reich* had 19,812 and 10,441 respectively; and SS *Totenkopf* – 19,176 and 10,214, while the corps' organic assets had respectively 8,800 and 5,558.[480] By 1 July 1943, it had received 390 tanks and 148 assault guns and Marder self-propelled tank destroyers. At the beginning of the operation, II SS Panzer Corps had Grenadier (Infantry) Regiment 315 and II Battalion of the Artillery Regiment 238 attached to it from the 167th Infantry Division. In addition, the corps received Colonel Gröwen's 3rd Mortar Division. This was a powerful formation, consisting of Mortar Training Regiment 1, Mortar Regiment 55 (159-210mm mortars) and one heavy mortar regiment (280-320mm). Each of them had approximately 1500 men, 54 mortars and 10 76mm capture Soviet guns.

---

480 NARA US, T.354, R.605, F.0000162, 0000167, 0000169 and 0000171.

Genera of Infantry E. Ott's LII Army Corps had three infantry divisions: the 57th, 255th and 322nd Infantry divisions. The latter, throughout the course of Operation Citadel would be several times resubordinated to XXXXVIII Panzer Corps depending on the operational situation. On 1 July Ott's formation had a ration strength of 51,638 men, including 45,666 servicemen and 3,411 Hiwi.

Thus, by the start of Operation Citadel, there were 223,907 men in the Fourth Panzer Army. This included 63,290 SS personnel, 143,290 army officers and men, 9,853 Hiwi and 6,492 civilians.[481]

One important thing should be noted. Among the historians that study the events of the summer of 1943, there is no single opinion on the number of tanks and self-propelled guns in Hoth's panzer army. In their works, they provide figures that vary considerably. For example, Glantz and House maintain that the numbers cited above for the II SS Panzer Corps, which I took from the book by the Swedish scholars N. Zetterling and A. Frankson are for 1 July, but on 4 July their number had dropped to 356 tanks and 96 assault guns.[482] There is also no agreement about the number of armored fighting vehicles in XXXXVIII Panzer Corps either. According to Glantz and House, on 1 July 1943 it had 535 tanks and 66 StuG, but on 4 July the number of them had fallen substantially and amounted to 464 tanks and 89 StuG. The documents of the Fourth Panzer Army and Army Group South that I managed to uncover show that despite the number of mistakes made by the Swedish scholars in their book, their data are more accurate, so in this work I've primarily resorted to them. For the number of tanks and self-propelled guns in the panzer divisions of the Fourth Panzer Army and Army Group South for 4 July 1943, see Table 12.

481 NARA US, T.313, R.390, F.00057.
482 Glantz and House, *The Battle of Kursk*, pp. 350, 351.

Table 12a: Equipping of Army Group South's formations and units with tanks and self-propelled guns, 4 July 1943

Formation	Pz I	Pz II	Pz III	Pz IV	Pz V	Pz VI	Command	T-34	Flamethrowing	Total tanks	Marder	StuG	Hummel	Wespe	Total self-propelled guns
II SS Panzer Corps[483]															
LAH	-	4	11	79	-	12	9	3	-	118	21	34	6	12	73
Das Reich	-	-	48	30	-	12	8	18	-	116	8	33	6	12	59
Totenkopf	-	-	59	47	-	11	8	-	-	125	11	28	6	12	57
Total for corps	**-**	**4**	**118**	**156**	**-**	**35**	**25**	**21**	**-**	**359**	**40**	**105**	**18**	**36**	**189**
III Panzer Corps															
6 Panzer	-	13	52	28	-	-	-	-	13	106	14	-	-	-	14
7 Panzer	-	12	62	38	-	-	-	-	-	112	6	-	6	6	18
19 Panzer	3	2	38	38	-	-	-	-	-	81	12	-	-	-	12
Sep Hvy Panzer Bn 503	-	-	-	-	-	45	-	-	-	45	-	-	-	-	-
StuG Bn 228	-	-	-	-	-	-	-	-	-	-	-	31[484]	-	-	-
Total for corps	**3**	**27**	**152**	**104**	**-**	**45**	**-**	**-**	**13**	**344**	**32**	**31**	**6**	**6**	**75**
XXXXVIII Panzer Corps															
3 Panzer[485]	-	-	30	38	-	-	-	-	-	68	15	2	-	-	16

483 Information for the II SS Panzer Corps is according to a report at 1945 on 4 July 1943 (NARA US, T.354, R.605, F.000470).
484 31 StuG III assault guns
485 Information for the 3rd and 11th Panzer Divisions is according to a report from the XXXXVIII Panzer Corps (NARA US, T.313, R.368, F.8654268, 8654269).

"'Citadel' … was the final attempt to retain our initiative in the east"   245

11 Panzer	-	-	50	22	-	-	4	-	8	84	9	22	6	-	17
Grossdeutschland	-	-	22	62	-	14	-	-	14	112	20	34	6	12	72
Panzer Brig. 10	-	-	-	-	200	-	-	-	-	200	-	-	-	-	-
StuG Bn 911	-	-	-	-	-	-	-	-	-	-	-	31[486]	-	-	-
Total for corps	-	4	102	122	200[487]	14	4	-	22	467	44	89	12	12	105

Table 12b: Number of operational tanks, self-propelled guns and anti-tank weapons in the divisions and corps of the Fourth Panzer Army on 4 July 1943[488]

Type	Panzer Brig. 10	3rd Panzer Division	11th Panzer Division	*Grossdeutschland*	XXXXVIII Panzer Corps	*Leibstandarte Adolf Hitler*	*Das Reich*	*Totenkopf*	II SS Panzer Corps[489]	Fourth Panzer Army
Pz II	-	-	-	-	-	4	-	-	4	4
Pz III short-barreled	-	3	8	2	13	-	1	-	1	1
Pz III long-barreled	-	27	42	20	89	11	47	59	117	170
Pz IV short-barreled	-	17	-	7	24	-	-	5	5	29
Pz IV long-barreled	-	21	22	55	98	79	30	42	151	196

486 22 StuG III and nine StuH
487 192 Panthers present in the subordinate battalions plus eight command tanks.
488 Information for Table 12b has been gathered from the reports of the divisions and corps (NARA US, T.313, R.368).
489 The totals for the II SS Panzer Corps have been counted up by the author; information for the tables were taken from a report submitted by its headquarters at 1845 (Berlin time) on 4 July 1943 (NARA US, T.354, R.605, F.00470) and from the book by R. Toppel, Kursk 1943: Die groste Schlacht des Zweiten Weltkriegs (Paderborn: 2017), p. 96.

Type	Panzer Brig. 10	3rd Panzer Division	11th Panzer Division	Grossdeutschland	XXXXVIII Panzer Corps	Leibstandarte Adolf Hitler	Das Reich	Totenkopf	II SS Panzer Corps[489]	Fourth Panzer Army
Pz V	200	-	-	-	200	-	-	-	-	200
Pz VI	-	-	-	14	14	12	12	11	35	49
T-34	-	-	-	-	-	3	18	-	21	21
Flame-throwing	-	-	8	14	22	-	-	-	-	22
Command	-	-	4	-	4	9	8	8	25	29
Total tanks	200	68	84	112	464	118	116	125	359	823
Assault guns (StuG)	-	2	22	34	58	34	33	28	95	153
Self-propelled anti-tank guns	-	15	9	19	43	21	10[490]	11	42	85
75mm PAK (Sfl)	-	10	5	22	37	18	16	19	53	90

Note: The Wespe and Hummel were respectively 105mm and 150mm self-propelled howitzers; the Marder was a self-propelled tank destroyer; and the StuG (SturmGeschutze) was an assault gun for direct infantry support, but in the Battle of Kursk operated as a self-propelled anti-tank gun.

Source: Zetterling and Frankson, *Kursk 1943: a statistical analysis*, Table 3.22; for Panzer Brigade 10, M. Kolomiets, "Pantery na Kurskoi duge" ('Panthers' in the Battle of Kursk) [TankoMaster No. 5] (1999), p. 25.

490 Two self-propelled 75mm anti-tank guns, and eight self-propelled 76.2mm anti-tank guns.

So, by the start of Operation Citadel (4 June 1943), in the three panzer corps of Army Group South that had been directed to break through the Voronezh Front's defenses, there were 1,167 tanks and 341 StuG and Marder tank destroyers, including 823 and 278 respectively in the Fourth Panzer Army. Noteworthy is the fact that in the shock corps of Hoth's panzer army the overwhelming majority were updated Pz.Kpfw. III and IV tanks with long-barreled guns, Pz.Kpfw. V Panthers and Pz.Kpfw. VI Tigers: these amounted to 86.4percent of the XXXXVIII Panzer Corps' tank park, and 84.4percent of the II SS Panzer Corps' armor. Moreover, in von Knobbelsdorf's formation, almost 46percent of the tanks were Panthers or Tigers. After the Battle of Kursk, the Wehrmacht never again had the possibility of assembling such a significant quantity of tanks for conducting an offensive within the framework of an army group.

Army Detachment Kempf was significantly weaker. Based on his given missions, Werner Kempf arranged his forces in the following manner. He assigned two corps to the assault grouping: III Panzer Corps (to serve as a battering ram) to breakthrough in the direction of Skorodnoe, and Korps Raus – for screening III Panzer Corps' right flank with the aim of reaching the line of the Nezhegol' and Korocha Rivers and to set up a defensive front along the right bank of the Korocha River. His XXXXII Corps was to hold in place in order anchor the right flank along the course of the Severskii Donets River.

Before the start of Operation Citadel, General of Panzer Troops H. Breith's III Panzer Corps was supposed to take position on the army group's right flank and during the offensive screen the right flank of the II SS Panzer Corps. From the spring, its 168th Infantry Division had been holding a bridgehead on the left bank of the Severskii Donets River at Mikhailovka, which had two small bridges. The army detachment command staff viewed this small clump of land as a very important line. In a directive from its chief of staff Major General Hans Speidel, issued to the corps for putting together of the plan of actions in the course of Citadel, he noted that Breith's formation should launch the main attack simultaneously with all three divisions out of the Mikhailovka bridgehead and across two other bridges at Dorogobuzheno and Solomino. In Kempf's opinion, in the conditions he faced, this was the optimal version. In the first place, the positioning of its strongest corps on the left flank would ease the army detachment's task to screen the right flank of the Fourth Panzer Army. Secondly, an attack from here presented the shortest path to the main objective – the village of Skorodnoe.

At the same time, however, when planning III Panzer Corps' offensive, especially in the first stage, this situation would place its leadership in a problematic situation. Considering that three panzer divisions were to be located in the first echelon simultaneously, it was extremely important to resolve the problem with crossing sites and to reinforce them with infantry, which were to create on the eastern bank the conditions for a normal movement of the armor across the river and the deployment of its significant forces for the attack. Intelligence information was showing that the Russians were throwing up extremely powerful fortifications around the Mikhailovka bridgehead, while at the same time this patch of earth was not large in size. Therefore, Breith decided to give both bridges there to the 6th Panzer Division alone, while the 7th and 19th Panzer Divisions and the two infantry divisions of Korps Raus – the 320th and 106th Infantry Divisions – were to force a crossing of the Severskii Donets River from the march, using their organic and handy bridging means and fords.

Breith's plan to reinforce the kampfgruppen of the panzer divisions proved rather debatable. Under the circumstances of an acute deficit of infantry, he proposed to split up the 168th Infantry Division and assign one of its grenadier regiments, a battalion of artillery and a sapper company to each of the panzer divisions. The intention was to form assault groups out of these units and elements, as well as the panzer divisions' own panzergrenadier regiments, which would be first to cross the river in order to expand the bridgehead (in the 6th Panzer Division's sector) or create bridgeheads (in the sector of the 7th and 19th Panzer Divisions). Only after these groups drove the Guardsmen back into the depth of the first belt of defenses would the opportunity appear to cross the armor and heavy weapons to the eastern bank, and allow the kampfgruppen of the 6th, 7th and 19th Panzer Divisions to enter directly into action. In order to support the assault groups on the eastern bank of the Severskii Donets River in the first hours of the offensive, Breith decided for a StuG battalion to move up to the vicinity of the bridges, and to allocate a company of Tiger tanks to the 19th Panzer Division. These assets were to be used initially from the western bank of the river in order to destroy enemy firing positions in the forward edge of the 7th Guards Army's first belt of defenses, and then after the penetration of its defenses, cross the river and follow in the wake of the grenadiers as they advanced, suppressing enemy resistance now in the depth of the first defensive belt.

Breith laid out these proposals in the course of a command staff map exercise conducted on 3 June 1943 with the participation of the leadership of the army detachment and Army Group South. Writes the American scholar S. Newton:

> Kempf wondered if the regiments of the 168th Infantry Division, even supported by the assault guns, Tigers and corps artillery assets, would have enough strength to penetrate the first Soviet defensive line quickly enough to expand the existing bridgeheads for the commitment of the main bodies of the 6th and 19th Panzer Divisions. He questioned Breith's decision not to attach a Tiger company to 6th Panzer Division and mandated an increase in size of the infantry attachment to 7th Panzer (Breith had originally allocated von Funck only a single battalion). Field Marshal von Manstein expressed his own doubts about a tactical plan that required the 168th Infantry Division to be dismantled and then reassembled in the middle of the battle; he pointed to the absolute necessity of having that division available to relieve the pressure on II SS Panzer Corps' eastern flank.[491]

Furthermore, the Field Marshal questioned Breith's proposal not to conduct a lengthy artillery preparation directly before the attack, but only a brief artillery barrage. He pointed out that the complicated terrain and the Russians' superb camouflaging of their positions wouldn't allow targets to be identified accurately, and so the effectiveness of the fire in the course of a relatively short artillery barrage might prove to be minimal. However, Breith responded to this that in the event of increasing the time allotted to the preparatory fire, this would mean the wastage of artillery shells to no purpose.

All of these concerns had real justifications, and it is possible that the commander of III Panzer Corps recognized this. However, at the same time all of those gathered at the map exercise realized that the plan was being worked out under the strict limitations of a deficit of forces and means. Opposite the front of Army Detachment Kempf, the Soviet side had erected a deeply-echeloned, powerful defense, the strength of which the river would substantially bolster in the first hours of the offensive, while in its depth, reconnaissance had already detected numerous

---

491 Newton, *Kurskaia bitva: nemetskii vzgliad*, p. 503.

tactical reserves. Neither Erich von Manstein nor Werner Kempf had any way to reinforce the III Panzer Corps, so Breith's proposals were accepted without substantial changes. Thereby, the chief executives of both the army detachment and the army group were demonstrating their attitude toward the problems under consideration: in the existing situation, the corps commander had the best view on how to arrange his forces; after all, in the end he would be the one to lead the troops into battle and also be responsible for its outcome.

The greatest weakness in the plan of Army Detachment Kempf's offensive, and incidentally in that of the Fourth Panzer Army as well, was the absence of reserves available for both the corps commanders and their superiors. This was prompted first of all by the meagerness of the forces that were assigned to Citadel and the clear lack of confidence on the German side that without committing all of their available forces into the opening attack they would be unable to penetrate the Russians' powerful field fortifications within the designated time. Thus, despite established military doctrine, which stipulated keeping a reserve available to exploit any success, the German commanders were throwing all of their available forces into the initial attack.

In a number of sectors, there was the intention to arrange the forces so densely, that they would be more likely to get in each other's way than to assist each other; not only the command staff of Army Detachment Kempf and its corps ran into these problems, but also that of its neighbor. In particular, a very similar situation developed in the XXXXVIII Panzer Corps' initial advance.

Hermann Breith had the reputation of being an experienced and successful panzer commander, and he could not help but understand that the absence of reserves would substantially limit his influence on the operational situation. Therefore, even in the event that one of his divisions managed to break through the defenses, he would be unable to exploit this tactical success. He nevertheless made no protest against the insistence of Speidel's staff to commit all three panzer divisions into the fighting simultaneously, even though on less significant matters he clearly expressed his position and in general they were resolved just as he had proposed.

Yet the general could not help but realize that an excessively high concentration of troops would be created (four divisions in a span of 16 kilometers) within the designated breakthrough sector of his divisions, so that difficulties in the command, control and even maneuvering would be inevitable, even given smaller forces. It was obvious as well that both the crossing and the combat operations of the 6th Panzer Division in the Mikhailovka bridgehead would be very difficult. As a professional, he had to understand that the Soviet side was viewing this area as the most likely place for an attack by the Germans, so they had fortified it better than on any other sector of the front. Altogether, this prompts the thought that moving up the 6th Panzer Division into the frontline on the first day of the operation was not the best idea; it would have been better to keep it in the second echelon and use it as the corps commander's operational reserve or for exploiting a success on the offensive's second or third day.

In addition, when analyzing the combat dispositions of Kempf's forces before the start of the battle, it is impossible not to call attention to the following, rather important, aspect. The concept of the "axis of the main attack" was distinctly determined only at the level of the army group, but was completely lacking in the III Panzer Corps. Its divisions were arranged in a single line and received an order to operate practically along parallel directions. In the German terminology, there was no *Schwerpunkt*, or main point of attack. Such an equal distribution of effort allowed the Soviet side, using details of the terrain and its system of defenses, to shift successfully both the fire of heavy artillery and tactical reserves from one sector to another, wherever the threat of a breakthrough arose. For their part, the commanders of the III Panzer Corps' panzer divisions could not count on the commitment of corps reserves (there simply were not any), nor on the help from its stronger neighbor, and so they were forced to rely only on their own strength and means. This tactical miscalculation in combination with the objective problem of the army detachment's and corps commanders' lack of reserves would substantially hamper the actions of Kempf's forces, especially during the first and hardest two days of the operation.

A decision by Army Group South's command compounded the aforementioned problems for Army Detachment Kempf: To commit all of the missions flown by Fliegerkorps VIII to the sector of Fourth Panzer Army's main attack on the first day of the operation. The bombers were directed to II SS Panzer Corps' sector, and the fighters – to sweep clear the airspace above the Fourth Panzer Army. As a result, the auxiliary axis was in effect left exposed, and Army Detachment Kempf's divisions, which had to cross the Severskii Donets under concentrated fire, would be forced to cover themselves only with their own modest forces of Flak artillery, which were also supposed to be used against firing positions in the first belt of the 7th Guards Army's defenses. Even the planned diversion of a squadron of tank-hunting aircraft to support Kempf's forces on the second day of the operation (or on the first, in the event of a powerful tank attack by the Russians already on 5 July) went fitfully because of bureaucratic procrastination, among other reasons.

As in the case of the Ninth Army, Army Detachment Kempf was experiencing an acute deficit of armored vehicles for a breakthrough. In order to gird the assault wedge with armor, the command of Army Group South sent Werner Kempf new tanks, but their number was few: Fourth Panzer Army received 257 Tigers and Panthers, but Army Detachment Kempf received only 45 Tigers. At the same time, despite the justified requests of Kempf and his staff, by the start of the Battle of Kursk the III Panzer Corps had not been brought up to establishment strength in either armored fighting vehicles or artillery. By 5 July 1943, its best equipped division, the 7th Panzer Division had only 112 tanks, while the 6th Panzer Division had 106 and the 19th Panzer – just 81. Moreover, in the 6th and 19th Panzer Divisions, just 60 of the total number of tanks (or 57 percent) were Pz.Kpfw. III or IV, while the rest were flame-throwing tanks or even outdated Pz.Kpfw. II tanks. Thus, these divisions could use for the breakthrough of the Soviet defenses only a little more than half of their available tank park. These panzer divisions also failed to receive their battalions of self-propelled artillery (six 150mm howitzer Hummel and 12 105mm howitzer Wespe) that they were supposed to have, while only 12 of the self-propelled artillery howitzers arrived in the 7th Panzer Division instead of the 18 promised it.

Striving to enhance the shock power of the III Panzer Corps, Werner Kempf assigned it the 45 Tigers of Heavy Panzer Battalion 503 and Assault Gun Battalion 228 (22 StuG and nine StuH). This was a substantial reinforcement, especially for the troops of the first wave, and the total number of armored vehicles in the corps increased noticeably after this, by 67 machines. Moreover, it was very important that the guns of these tanks and self-propelled guns had long barrels and a caliber of between 75mm and 88mm. However, skipping ahead of the events, I will note that the capabilities of both the Panthers and the Tigers had been plainly overestimated. These machines were brand new or relatively new for the army, so the units that had been specially-created for them – the separate battalions – had not even adequately worked out the proper tactics for using these tanks. Therefore, already on the first day of the offensive, Heavy Panzer Battalion 503 would be deprived of virtually all of its Tigers because of mishandling, without obtaining any noticeable results. For more detail on the equipping of the divisions of Army Detachment Kempf with armored vehicles on 4 July 1943, see Table 12.

When directing the troops of Army Detachment Kempf toward a struggle against Soviet mobile formations in the course of the breakthrough of the 7th Guards Army's first and second belts of defenses, and later in the vicinity of Prokhorovka, the command of Army Group South understood that three understrength panzer divisions assigned for this were inadequate. So, from the outset, it had been decided to compensate for the shortage of armored vehicles with the latest models of self-propelled guns, the Hornisse, which arrived to arm Heavy Panzerjäger Battalion 560 in the spring of 1943. At the end of May, this unit was placed at Erich von Manstein's disposal, who subsequently transferred it to Kempf. However, later it was decided not to commit it into the fighting because of the lack of readiness of these heavy tank destroyers.

In the conditions of an acute lack of forces and means, the command of Army Detachment Kempf was staking great hopes on the artillery, including the Flak artillery, even though it had very few of them. By the start of the battle of Kursk, Arko 3, which was subordinate to Breith's panzer corps, had on its unit roster: II/Artillery Regiment 62 (105mm light howitzers), II/Artillery Regiment 71 (150mm howitzers), Separate Heavy Artillery Battalion 875 (210mm howitzers), and Flak Artillery Regiments 99 and 153; at the beginning of the operation, Artillery Regiment 612 was also attached to it. Korps Raus received more substantial artillery forces; its Arko 153 possessed: I/Artillery Regiment 21 (105mm light howitzers), I/Artillery Regiment 77 (105mm light howitzers) and II/Artillery Regiment 54 (105mm light howitzers); Flak Artillery Regiments 4, 7 and 48 (88mm Flak guns); StuG Battalion 905 (31 StuG) and the 393rd StuG Battery (12 StuG). As Erhard Raus recalled, the bulk of the artillery assets planned for his corps began to arrive already at the end of April 1943. He later wrote:

> The *Armee-Abteilung* placed reorganizing units in the vicinity or west of Kharkov. Units committed at the front rotated one-third of their strength (one reinforced regimental *Kampfgruppe*) at a time, for purposes of reorganizing near the front. Since the original attack date had been set for 4 May, maximum efforts were made to move up required personnel and materiel …
>
> The three flak regiments, fielding a total of seventy-two 88mm and approximately 900 smaller flak guns, had been attached to XI Corps to serve as a substitute for missing medium artillery. According to Luftwaffe policy, the subordination of flak officers to army unit commanders was forbidden; the corps artillery commander therefore depended on the voluntary cooperation of the senior flak commander. This led to repeated minor frictions but worked out quite well in general.[492]

However, Hitler had postponed the attack toward Kursk that had been planned for early May, and Army Group South had the possibility of continuing the replenishment with troops. By early June, Army Detachment Kempf had a total of not less than 100,000 military servicemen for Citadel, of which 32,000 to 34,000 were directly part of combat formations.[493] Breith's panzer corps and Korps Raus had a total of 36 infantry battalions, 344 tanks, 75 assault guns, 32 Marder tank destroyers, 317 field artillery pieces, 216 Flak guns (including 72 88mm guns), and 126 six-barreled rocket launchers. See Table 13 for more detail on the numerical strength and types of weapons arming the divisions of Army Detachment Kempf at the start of Operation Citadel.

---

492 Raus, *Tankovye srazheniia na Vostochnom fronte*, pp. 294, 295.
493 Newton, *Kurskaia bitva: nemetskii vzgliad*, p. 500.

Table 13: Manpower and primary types of weaponry in the formations of Army Group South on 1 July 1943 (per the list), which were called upon to implement and support the offensive toward Kursk

Formation		Number					
		Ration strength, men	Combat strength, men	Infantry battalions	Tanks, StuGs, Marders	Field artillery pieces	Rocket launchers
Fourth Panzer Army[494]							
LII Army Corps		51,638		12		91	
XXXXVIII Panzer Corps		61,692		29	640 (527, 68, 45)	244	39
II SS Panzer Corps		73,380		21	538 (390, 104, 44)	179	138
Total for the Fourth Panzer Army		223,907		62	1,178	514	177
Army Detachment Kempf[495]							
III Panzer Corps	6 Pz D	16,702		21	407 (344, 31, 32)	200	54
	7 Pz D	15,394[496]					
	19 Pz D	13,780					
	168 ID	?	5,515[497]				
	198 ID	?	5,572				
Korps Raus	106 ID	15,099[498]	6,577	18	44 StuG	117	72
	320 ID	14,494	5,995				
XXXXII Corps	39 ID			6		33 (105, 150mm)	
	161 ID			8	45 Hornisse	48 (105,150mm)	
	282 ID			9		36 (105, 150mm)	
Total for AD Kempf:				62	496		126
Grand total:				124	1,674	831 (?)	303

494 NARA US, T.313, R.390, F.00057.
495 NARA US, T.354, R.605, F.000162, 000167, 000169; T.354, R.607, F.000566.
496 As of 27 June 1943
497 The combat strength in manpower for the 106th, 198th and 320th Infantry Divisions as of 4 July 1943.
498 Including 503 Hiwi; this number doesn't include the division's reserve infantry battalion, which at the time of the Battle of Kursk was located in Germany.

All of the above taken together (the miscalculations in Breith's plan; the deficit of strength and the lack of needed air support; and the 7th Guards Army's elaborate system of defenses) would become the main reasons for the high losses experienced by Army Detachment Kempf's troops already from the first minutes of the operation, and as a result of this, the failure to carry out its assignments according to schedule. Thus, to consider only the main problems left unresolved by the first days of July 1943 by the command of Army Group South, which was the strongest of the two Wehrmacht force groupings in the area of the Kursk bulge, these were the plain lack of strength and means in the Fourth Panzer Army and Army Detachment Kempf for achieving such far-reaching objectives of the forthcoming offensive; and the deficit of authorized equipment and weaponry available in their divisions, especially the panzer divisions. Taken together with the main dangers that faced them (the significant number of operational and strategic reserves that had been accumulated by the Soviet side in the spring and the high degree of fortification of the 6th Guards Army's and 7th Guards Army's defenses, which were even stronger for the latter because of the Severskii Donets River), then one can state with confidence that the objectives that had been officially set in Citadel's plan were beyond the capabilities of its forces to reach, and this, together with the all of the problems facing the Ninth Army discussed above, once again plainly demonstrates the adventuristic nature of the entire idea behind the plan of an offensive toward Kursk.

Thus, the cited data show that on 5 July 1943, the assault grouping of Model's Ninth Army was the weaker of the two involved in implementing Operation Citadel. This includes not only the number of formations assigned to seize Kursk, but also their numerical strength. Despite the significant efforts made to rebuild the divisions of the Ninth Army and the repeated postponement of the offensive's start date, Germany's military and political leadership proved unable to meet even the minimal needs of Model's troops, which is to say bringing them back up at least to authorized strength. In order to carry out such large and extremely complex tasks, it should have at least received additional means of reinforcement, and primarily artillery and heavy armor. However, due to objective reasons this was not done, which is one of the main reasons for the failure of the Wehrmacht's general offensive on the Soviet-German front in the summer of 1943.

In conclusion of the discussion of this complicated, but very important period of the Wehrmacht's preparations for the largest battle of the Second World War, I will try to highlight its most important aspects. I will also express my point of view regarding a number of debated questions, which are today being discussed by historians.

Thus, the initial scheme of an operation to break through to Kursk (slicing off the southern sector of the bulge) arose in the headquarters of Army Group South spontaneously, as a reaction to its successful operations in February and March 1943 in Ukraine. Originally its main goal was exploit the successful counterblow at Khar'kov to the maximum, and to resolve important, but nevertheless local problems of von Manstein's army group on the eve of the summer period of the fighting, which would be hard in every respect. At this moment the Field Marshal's proposal was not the only one, and in the assessment of the OKH and OKW, was not optimal, since Erich von Manstein was first of all thinking about the particular interests of his own army group. Even so, he attempted to persuade Berlin that his ideas coincided with its strategic goals as well.

Germany's political and military leadership, which was in a grievous state of morale and psychological condition after the shock of Stalingrad and recognizing that after the defeat at the Volga victory was illusory, were feverishly searching for an acceptable option for the further conducting of the war. Therefore, Hitler and the OKH, inspired by the results of von Manstein's counterattack, began to take a look at a plan proposed by Colonel General Schmidt, which in essence developed the Field Marshal's idea to form the basis for the entire summer campaign.

Three main objective factors lay at the root of the Wehrmacht's springtime success in Ukraine. First was the exhaustion and tattered state of the Soviet troops, which had not had any respite from combat for three months and had become distantly separated from their rear services. Second was the concentration in Army Group South of the bulk of the German mobile divisions on the Eastern Front, as well as the substantial amount of reserves that had been transferred from Europe. Third was the lack of reserves for the Soviet side on this axis. Thus, in the initial plan of an offensive toward Kursk, neither von Manstein nor Schmidt took into account the meteorological conditions (and the spring of 1943 came early), the sorry condition of Army Group Center's troops, or the potential capabilities of the Red Army. The operation, which had been originally conceived as a logical continuation of Army Group South's counterblow, although it did require additional forces. The plan primarily counted only on the temporary weakness of the Soviet forces on this direction for success, but could not be executed prior to the start of the spring thaw for objective reasons. Because of the mud-locked roads, active combat operations came to a halt, while the Soviet command using the rail system quickly reinforced its grouping in this area. Meanwhile Model's Ninth Army had only started the process of assembling its divisions on the southern sector of the Orel bulge, but after the winter fighting, they were in no condition to take part in a major offensive. Therefore, when von Manstein says in his memoirs that he was counting upon the success of the springtime offensive, this is only an attempt to "save face". Neither in March 1943 nor in early April 1943 was the German Army in any condition to conduct an offensive, and at that moment no soberly thinking military commander could count upon a success of one even theoretically.

By mid-April, Hitler, objectively viewing the Eastern Front as the key theater of military operations for Germany and finding no better option for further conducting the war, settled on Citadel as the general offensive in 1943. By this time a certain sobering of thought had come over him regarding the Wehrmacht's possibilities and the Soviet side's potential. First, having properly considered the arguments of the military men, he rejected the idea of eliminating the Izium salient, albeit with difficulty, and decided to concentrate every effort on preparing an attack toward Kursk. Secondly, thanks to Walter Model's letter, Hitler began to recognize that although the success at Khar'kov was a major victory, on the scale of the entire war it was still only a local one. Germany was unable to regain the initiative after it, as had been expected. At the same time, the Red Army was accumulating forces and rebuilding formations after the winter at a pace that noticeably exceeded von Manstein's and von Kluge's assault groups, and Berlin could do nothing to alter this. In this situation, it was dangerous to rely only upon the Wehrmacht's superiority in command and control and the level of training of its troops, as the supporters of Citadel were doing. By early May the Soviet Union had already possessed significant power, and its army was experienced and strong, so the early plan and the available troops were unable to achieve the expected result. Model's conclusions, cited by him in the letter from 21 April 1943, were not simply those of a general, but close to the views and spirit of an ordinary man – he argued that it was impossible and even dangerous to attack before the middle of May. His opinions resonated with Hitler's internal unease and became the main argument in favor of postponing the operation from May to the first ten days of June.

The postwar assertions of the German generals and the historians close to them, that Hitler was only a politician who had no understanding of the laws and principles of conducting large-scale operations, and his decision to postpone Citadel was unjustified and only deprived the Wehrmacht of the effect of surprise, which became the main factor behind the failure of the glitteringly planned offensive of the OKH, are far from the truth. It was simply impossible to conceal the assembly of two strategic groupings with a total number of more than 600,000 men in areas that were most suitable for an offensive. Many Wehrmacht commanders acknowledged this. For example, a veteran of the Battle of Kursk, Major General F. von Mellenthin noted, "It is an accepted fact that plans and preparations for an operation of such magnitude cannot be kept secret for any length of time."[499] Thus, none of those participating in Citadel assigned paramount importance to the effects of surprise. Captured German documents also show this. Both Hitler and the OKH (albeit in varying degrees) considered the available forces and means necessary for implementing the tasks assigned in the operation as the main factor of success, but Germany would never have enough even according to minimal German calculations. So Model, who was soberly assessing the potential of his army, continually argued with both Günther von Kluge and the OKH, pointing to the uncertainties regarding the offensive. It was precisely this problem that became the main one for Hitler between April and June 1943, including as his primary motive when making his decisions to postpone Citadel repeatedly. Everything else was only secondary.

Although by the Battle of Kursk the German command would be able to build up significantly the number of all types of armaments in the troops in the East (the number of tanks doubled up to 2,845 between April and 20 June[500]), given the growing power of the Red Army, the Wehrmacht was unable at that moment to hold such an extended front. In comparison, on 1 June 1943 the Soviet Union's acting Red Army possessed 12,311 tanks.[501] Germany's own industry could not even approach such indicators. The German troops were also experiencing serious shortages of other types of weapons.

The empty rhetoric of the memoirists, which was adapted by researchers and journalists, pursued the aim first of all to rehabilitate the Wehrmacht's generals in the eyes of society, to conceal their blunders and omissions, as well as their incapability to separate from their smarting vanity and ambitions when preparing for such a complex operation in such adverse conditions for Germany. This primarily relates as well to the bickering and squabbling between the OKH and the OKW, and between Model and von Kluge. Occupied with the cliquish problems and the struggle for influence, even those of the generals who considered Citadel to be the only correct decision, for not always comprehensible reasons, hampered the preparation of the troops to conduct it, and turned a blind eye to the dissipation of combat power. Clear examples of this can be the "dust-up" between Walter Model, Günther von Kluge and Kurt Zeitzler between 17 and 20 April 1943, and also the diversion of XXXXVII Panzer Corps for actions as part of Operation Gypsy Baron.

Unquestionably, the rising partisan attacks on the lines of communication of both Army Group Center and the Ninth Army required the taking of decisive measures. However, the OKH's idea to use regular army divisions, including panzer divisions, in punitive operations on the eve of the year's general offensive was not well-considered and led only to unjustified losses, the expenditure of valuable resources, and the excessive fatigue of the men. In addition, the prolonged anti-partisan operation, together with the breakdown in the delivery of heavy armor,

---

499 Mellenthin, *Bronirovannyi kulak vermakhta*, p. 321.
500 Müller-Gildebrandt, *Sukhoputnaia armiia Germanii, 1933-1945*, p. 401.
501 TsAMO RF, F.38, Op.11353, D.1173, l. 44-45.

was one of the main reasons for postponing the start of Citadel from 12 June to 5 July 1943. The divisions of the Ninth Army that had been engaged in the struggle against partisans received an order to move out of the Briansk forests to their staging areas only on 8 June 1943. In fact, the main divisions did not assemble in full for the offensive until 20-22 June, while the heavy armor arrived even later. Thus, all this taken together was not only a consequence of Germany's objective incapability to execute such an ambitious plan, but also of the mistakes by the supreme command of its armed forces.

When comparing the combat potential of Model's and von Manstein's assault groupings, it should be noted that while the German side sought to allocate its available strength in a sufficiently balanced manner with respect to the missions, the Fourth Panzer Army, after receiving the entire brigade of Panthers, had an excessive number of armored vehicles, while at the same the Ninth Army was experiencing an acute deficit of them. As the events of 5 July would show, Hoth was unable to handle properly the capabilities he'd been given. Already in the stage of planning, he made a major mistake. By moving up all his panzer divisions into the first echelon and having concentrated an excessively large number of armored vehicles on his left flank, the commander first of all deprived himself of the possibility of influencing the operational situation, and second created chaotic traffic among the panzers and assault guns in the sector of the XXXXVIII Panzer Corps, which would lead in the final account to the breakdown in the timetable for the offensive and heavy, unjustified losses.

Model's emphasis placed on breaking through the defenses of the Central Front with infantry divisions also did not bring success; for this purpose, he needed significantly more artillery, but he did not have any. Nevertheless, after the war a number of key Wehrmacht figures maintained they not only believed in victory, but also that the Germans had a real chance for success. On what is this obvious delusion based, if you don't consider the natural desire of the side that has suffered defeat to "save face"?

First, it was based on the firm belief that the system of organization and command of the troops was substantially superior in the Wehrmacht than in the Red Army. Second was the confidence of the superiority of the German soldier over his Red Army counterpart in both combat training and weaponry. Hitler asserted in one of his directives on the eve of the Battle of Kursk, "The German soldier, just as before, is superior to the Russian in everything, and will always be so. He is more steadfast than the Slavs."[502] This was not simply a propagandistic boilerplate. Many generals of the German Army continued to believe in it sincerely. Third, the German command believed that the main reason for the past defeats, first of all at Stalingrad, was of a political nature. They simply did not want to see their own miscalculations in them. Assessing the Wehrmacht before the Battle of Kursk, Kurt von Tippelskirch wrote: "The German Army had acquired such combat experience, and felt that despite all the defeats suffered prior to this it was sufficiently well-prepared and aware of its superiority over the enemy to the extent that it was equal to the tasks flowing out of the strategy of the struggle to wear out the enemy by means of operational maneuvering."[503]

Finally, there was the excessively optimistic intelligence information. I've already cited the example of the substantial mistake made by the Abwehr when assessing the number of armored

---

502 Klink, *Das Gesetz des Handelns*, p. 292.
503 Tippelskirch, *Istoriia Vtoroi mirovoi voiny*, p. 24.

vehicles in the Central Front. I will present one more fact, found in the documents of the US National Archive and the Russian Ministry of Defense's Central Archives. If you analyze captured German maps showing information regarding the Central and Voronezh Fronts, then you must recognize that the German intelligence operated in a fully professional manner. On 1 July 1943, the composition of the armies and corps of both *fronts* were revealed almost precisely. The enemy had already established the presence of armored formations – the separate tank corps (5th Guards, 2nd Guards, 9th and 19th Tank Corps), the 1st and 2nd Tank Armies, and their composition and places of assembly. However, it is not clear why the Abwehr officers included the 3rd Tank Corps in the 13th Army, and the remaining 16th, 9th and 19th Tank Corps in the 2nd Tank Army, when both the 3rd Tank Corps and 16th Tank Corps formed the basis of the 2nd Tank Army, while the other two tank corps were located in the *front* reserve. In addition, the enemy had revealed a significant portion of our artillery grouping. Tippelskirch wrote:

> The sparse network of Russian railroads and highways could be easily monitored by aircraft, thanks to which the German command could opportunely find out about the redeployment of Russian troops. The painstaking work of radio intelligence, which monitored the enemy's radio communications, always yielded an accurate picture of its command's network of communications. In addition, the intensive activity of troop reconnaissance ensured the obtainment of information of a tactical nature. Artillery flash and sound intelligence normally determined the strength and position of Russian artillery accurately during the unavoidable registration of fire, despite all of the Russians' crafty maneuvers.[504]

However, everything did not go as smoothly as the general lays out, precisely regarding the strength of the artillery, and the most substantial blunders occurred, primarily with respect to the Central Front and the 13th Army. The Ninth Army's intelligence officers did not accurately determine the numerical strength of the artillery and mortars in all three of the armies opposing it (the 48th, 13th and 70th Armies). For example, according to the table giving an estimate of the number of Soviet artillery pieces opposite its front on 27 June 1943, according to the German calculations all three of the armies should have had 1,165 heavy and light field guns, but in reality, they had 2,046 tubes (not including 45mm anti-tank guns).

The reason for the mistake is that the Abwehr staff members plainly did not understand the structure of a breakthrough artillery corps, which first appeared in the Red Army after 12 April 1943, and did not have any information regarding the number of its subordinate formations. Therefore, they failed to establish the actual composition of the 5th and 12th Artillery Divisions that were part of the 13th Army. In particular, they did not know about the presence of the 9th and 86th Heavy Artillery Brigades, the 5th Guards Mortar Division of rocket launchers, or about an entire number of howitzer regiments. The Germans also mistakenly believed that the 13th Army had only six regiments of Katiusha rocket launchers, although in reality it had received an additional very powerful grouping of rocket launchers – 12 battalions of M-30 rocket launchers. The enemy also was not aware of the numerical strength and assembly area of the Central Front's artillery reserves. As a result, the leadership of the Ninth Army, while plainly

504 Ibid., p. 27.

recognizing the superiority of the Russians in the number of armored vehicles, unjustifiably believed it had an approximate equality with them in artillery.

There is an additional detail of some importance connected with how the Wehrmacht command perceived the intelligence information, as noted by Tippelkirch: "Hitler was unable to free himself from the old desire to underestimate the strength of the Russians constantly. So he unceremoniously rejected the results of the processing of intelligence in the General Staff of the OKH, believing without any justification that they were exaggerating the enemy's strength and overstating the case."[505] If to add to all the above the fact that German panzer formations actually could operate successfully against Russian tank corps at a correlation of 1 to 6 against them, as certain German generals maintained, then it becomes clear on what the Germans based their optimism prior to Citadel.

Even so, those who worked out the plan of Citadel were experienced professionals. For them, all of these factors could not obscure the two major problems that lay on the surface, which clearly demonstrated its large degree of hazard, and which in general should have cooled the ardor of the fiercest supporters of the offensive. In the first place, the Wehrmacht, by throwing virtually all of its reserves into Citadel, was left with nothing. For any commander in war, this is the first sign of an approaching defeat. Secondly, both in Berlin and Zossen, they knew that the offensive plan for the most powerful grouping at Kursk, Army Group South, had only been worked out in detail for the first 8 to 10 days of operation, which is to say, up to the conclusion of the fighting for Prokhorovka. No one knew what would come next, or what Hoth would have available after this battle.

A similar situation was observed with the Ninth Army's plan for the offensive as well. It was more or less understood how the forces should operate up to the point of the breakthrough to the hills south of Ponyri, but beyond that things were murky.

Therefore, many historians, even today, don't fully understand the key motivation for the Wehrmacht's leadership that caused it to support a decision so persistently, which deprived it of any possibility to affect the operational situation on the entire Eastern Front, especially under circumstances when even the success of such a large operation was far from certain. Before the start of the Battle of Kursk, with the aim of masking Germany's inability to organize a large offensive from the German people, the German Army and the broader global public, and most importantly when realizing that it might end in defeat, the Chief of the Operations Staff of the OKW Alfred Jodl issued a directive to the Wehrmacht's Propaganda Department to call Citadel not an offensive, but a counteroffensive. This "would down play the enemy's offensive strength and emphasize the strength of our defenses and reserves in the East."[506] It would also prepare a footing for the German propaganda in the event that the operation failed. Thus, it is hard to call the attack toward Kursk as anything other than a risky gamble, and as facts show, its progenitors and active participants understood this perfectly well.

---

505 Ibid., p. 24.
506 *Russkii arkhiv: Velikaia Otechestvennaia voina: Kurskaia bitva. Dokumenty i materialy 27 marta – 23 Avgusta 1943*, Vol. 15 (4-4) (Moscow: TERRA, 1997), p. 436.

Photo 01: A Kamfgruppe of an SS Panzergrenadier Division attacks with the support of Tiger tanks on the Khar'kov direction in March 1943. (RGAKFD)

Photo 02: Units of the SS Panzergrenadier Division Leibstandarte Adolf Hitler enter a village. The division's tactical emblem is visible on the assault gun, Khar'kov direction, March 1943. (RGAKFD)

Photo 03: The Commander-in-Chief of Army Group South Field Marshal E. von Manstein (in the center) greets Adolf Hitler on the airfield in Zaporozh'e on 10 Marcy 1943. (RGAKFD)

Photo 04: Participants in the conference at the headquarters of Army Group South in Zaporozh'e studying a map. From left to right, the Commander-in-Chief of Army Group South E. von Manstein, the commander of Army Group "A" Field Marshal E. Kleist, Hitler, the OKH chief of staff Colonel General K. Zeitzler and the commander of the First Panzer Army General of Cavalry E. von Mackensen, 10 March 1943. (RGAKFD)

Photo 05: The Commander-in-Chief of Army Group Center, Field Marshal G. von Kluge, 1943. (RGAKFD)

Photo 06: The commander of the Second Panzer Army Colonel General R. Schmidt, 1943. (RGAKFD)

Photo 07: The OKW's Chief of Operations, General of Artillery A. Jodl. (RGAKFD)

Photo 08: The temporarily acting Commander-in-Chief of Army Group South in April 1943, Field Marshal M. von Weichs. (RGAKFD)

Photo 09: Street fighting in Khar'kov. Note the command halftrack situated on the left, March 1943. (RGAKFD)

Photo 10: A grenadier of one of the SS Panzergrenadier divisions scans the battlefield from behind a knocked-out Soviet T-34 tank in the Belgorod area. (RGAKFD)

Photo 11: Spring 1943 came early. The crew of a German HK 101 Kleines Kettenkraftrad on a road south of Orel, April 1943. (RGAKFD)

Photo 12: A German panzer crew in the process of removing a track from their combat machine, Belgorod area, April 1943. (RGAKFD)

Photo 13: The first page of a copy of Hitler's Order No. 6 from 15 April 1943, which arrived at the headquarters of the Ninth Army at 1900 on 16 April 1943. (NARA US)

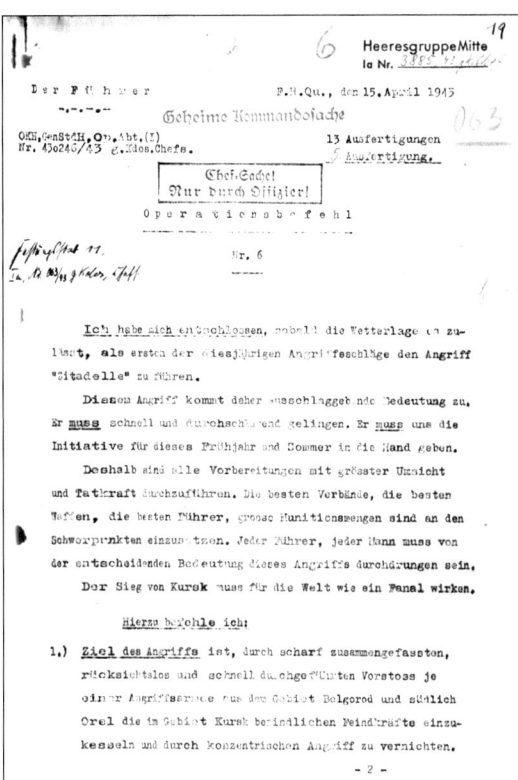

Photo 14: The crew of a Marder tank destroyer of a panzerjäger battalion of Army Group Center's 10th Motorized Division, photographed in front of the self-propelled gun in a village south of Orel, April 1943. (Author archive)

Photo 15: The commander of the Ninth Army Colonel General W. Model talks in a trench with a subordinate division commander, April 1943. (RGAKFD)

Photo 16: The chief of staff of Army Group Center Lieutenant General H. Krebs, 1944. (RGAKFD)

Photo 17: The commander of the Ninth Army's XXXXI Panzer Corps, General of Panzer Troops J. Harpe, 1943. (RGAKFD)

Photo 18: The commander of the Ninth Army's XXXXVII Panzer Corps, General of Panzer Troops J. Lemelsen, 1943. (RGAKFD)

Photo 19: The commander of the Ninth Army's XXIII Army Corps, General of Infantry H. Zorn, 1943. (RGAKFD)

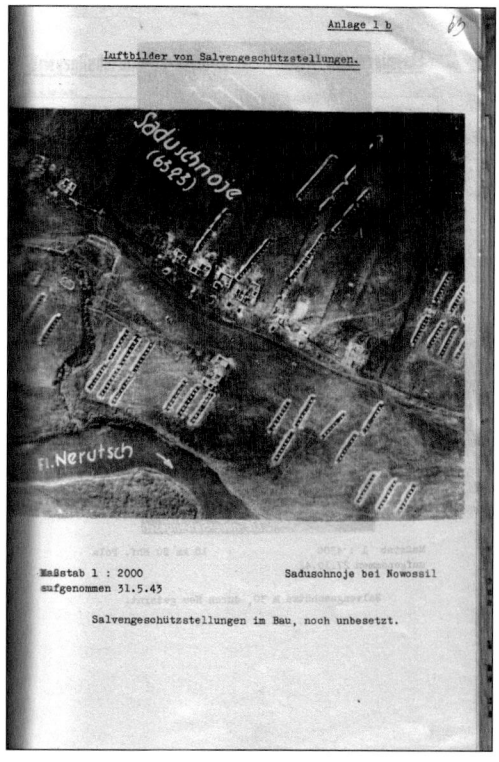

Photo 20: An intelligence summary of the headquarters of Army Group Center with photographs of Katiusha rocket launcher positions on the Central Front in the vicinity of the Neruch River at the village of Zadushnoe, in Orel Oblast's Novosil'skii District, 31 May 1943. (TsAMO RF)

Photo 21: Colonel General H. Hoth, commander of the Fourth Panzer Army, in his headquarters, the photograph was presumably taken in the period between May-July 1943. (RGAKFD)

Photo 22: General-Inspector of Panzer Troops Colonel General H. Guderian (second from the right) inspecting a new Tiger tank of SS Panzergrenadier Division Leibstandarte Adolf Hitler's heavy panzer company. (Open source)

Photo 23: H. Guderian (standing second from the left in the foreground) during a visit to the SS Panzergrenadier Division Leibstandarte Adolf Hitler of the II SS Panzer Corps, which was subordinate to the Fourth Panzer Army. (Bundesarchiv)

Photo 24: General-Field Marshal E. von Manstein (in the foreground) studies the operational situation in the sector of Army Detachment Kempf with the commander of III Panzer Corps, General of Panzer Troops H. Breith, June 1943. (RGAKFD)

Photo 25: Commander of Army Detachment Kempf, General of Panzer Troops W. Kempf, 1943. (RGAKFD)

Photo 26: Major General H. Speidel, chief of staff of Army Detachment Kempf, 1943-44. (RGAKFD)

Photo 27: The commander Army Detachment Kempf's Korps Raus, General of Panzer Troops E. Raus, summer 1943. (Bundesarchiv)

Photo 28: Commander of II SS Panzer Corps Obergruppenführer P. Hausser, 1943. (RGAKFD)

Photo 29: The commander of the Fourth Panzer Army's XXXXVIII Panzer Corps, General of Panzer troops O. von Knobbelsdorf, 1943. (RGAKFD)

Photo 30: The commander of the Fourth Panzer Army's LII Army Corps, General of Infantry E. Ott, 1943. (RGAKFD)

Photo 31: The commander of the Luftflotte Four's VIII Fliegerkorps, General H. Seidemann, 1943. (RGAKFD)

Photo 32: A tank-busting Ju-87D-5. Ordinarily, these aircraft were equipped with 20mm guns to destroy ground targets like Soviet armor and vehicles. However, Stuka pilots desired a more powerful weapon, so prior to the Battle of Kursk, some of the Ju-87D, such as this one, were retrofitted with 37mm cannons as an intermediary step prior to the widespread introduction of the Ju-87G. (Open source)

Photo 33: A Pz.Kpfw. V Panther tank, fresh off the MAN factory line. This tank model, a novelty of the German tank industry, was rushed into service especially for the Battle of Kursk. (TsAMO RF)

Photo 34: A German Hummel self-propelled 150mm howitzer, which was first widely employed by the Wehrmacht in the course of the offensive toward Kursk in July 1943. (Author archive)

Photo 35: A German Borgward IV remote-controlled heavy demolitions carrier standing next to its diminutive kin, a Goliath remotely-operated demolition tankette, on a proving ground. These demolition carriers would receive widescale use for the first time on a relatively narrow sector of the front in the summer of 1943 north of Kursk. (TsAMO RF)

Photo 36: Field Marshal von Manstein pores over a map of the operational sector of the forthcoming offensive together with General Hoth and a group of Fourth Panzer Army's staff officers, 21 June 1943. (Bundesarchiv)

List of Maps

1. OKH Operational Order No. 6 from 15 April 1943. — II
2. Tomarovka – Iakovlevo – Syrtsevo sector. — III
3. Prokhorovka – Psel River sector. — IV
4. Kursk Bulge Soviet defence plan and German offensive scheme within the framework of Operation Citadel. — V
5. "Vatutin's Plan": 7th Guards Army Voronezh Front defences and anticipated direction of German offensive. — VI
6. Lipovyi Donets – Northern Donets sector. — VII
7. 7th Guards Army main and second line defences, 1 July 1943 (15th Guards Rifle Division and 36th Guards Rifle Division exclusive). — VIII

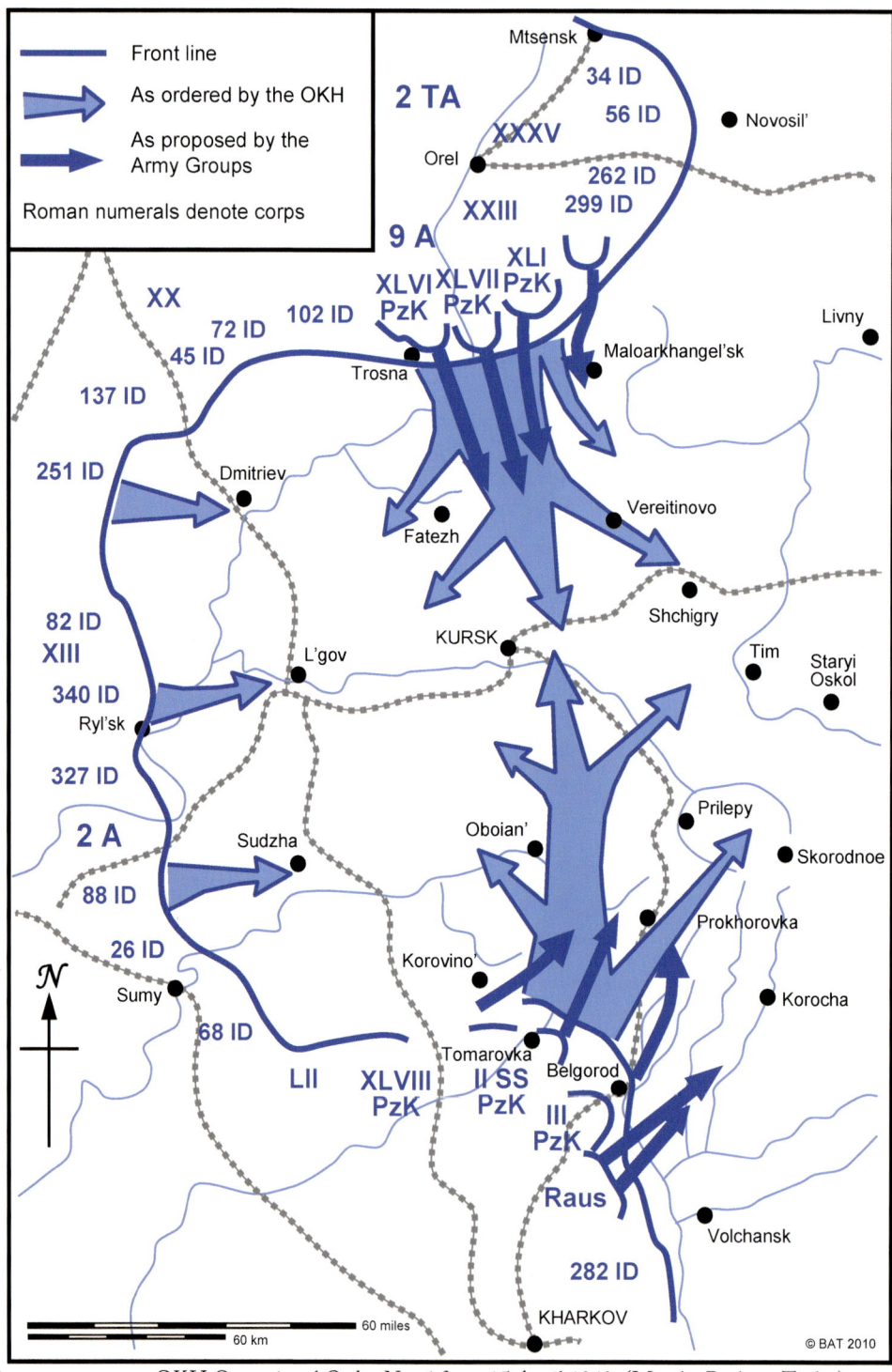

1. OKH Operational Order No. 6 from 15 April 1943. (Map by Barbara Taylor)

III

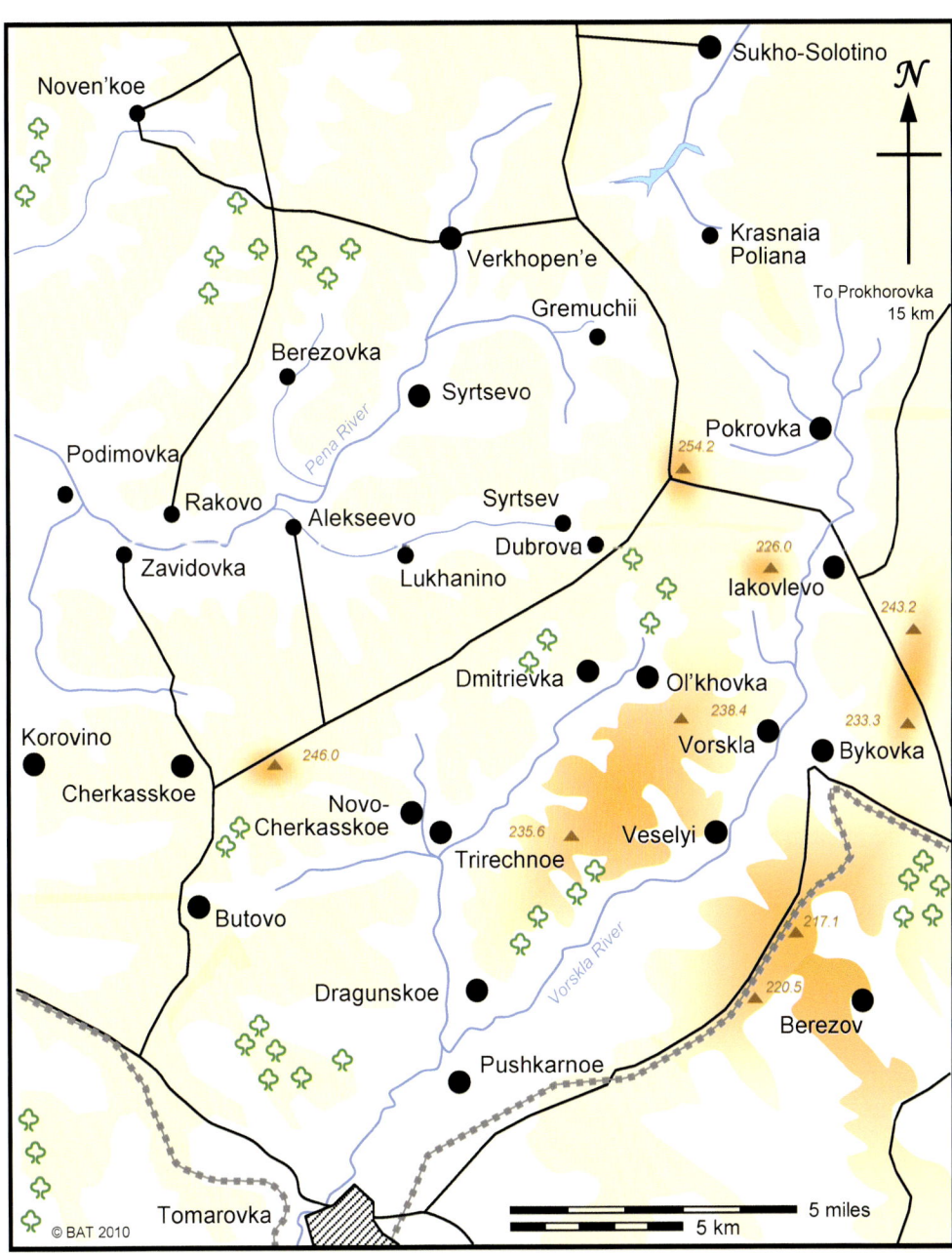

2. Tomarovka – Iakovlevo – Syrtsevo sector. (Map by Barbara Taylor)

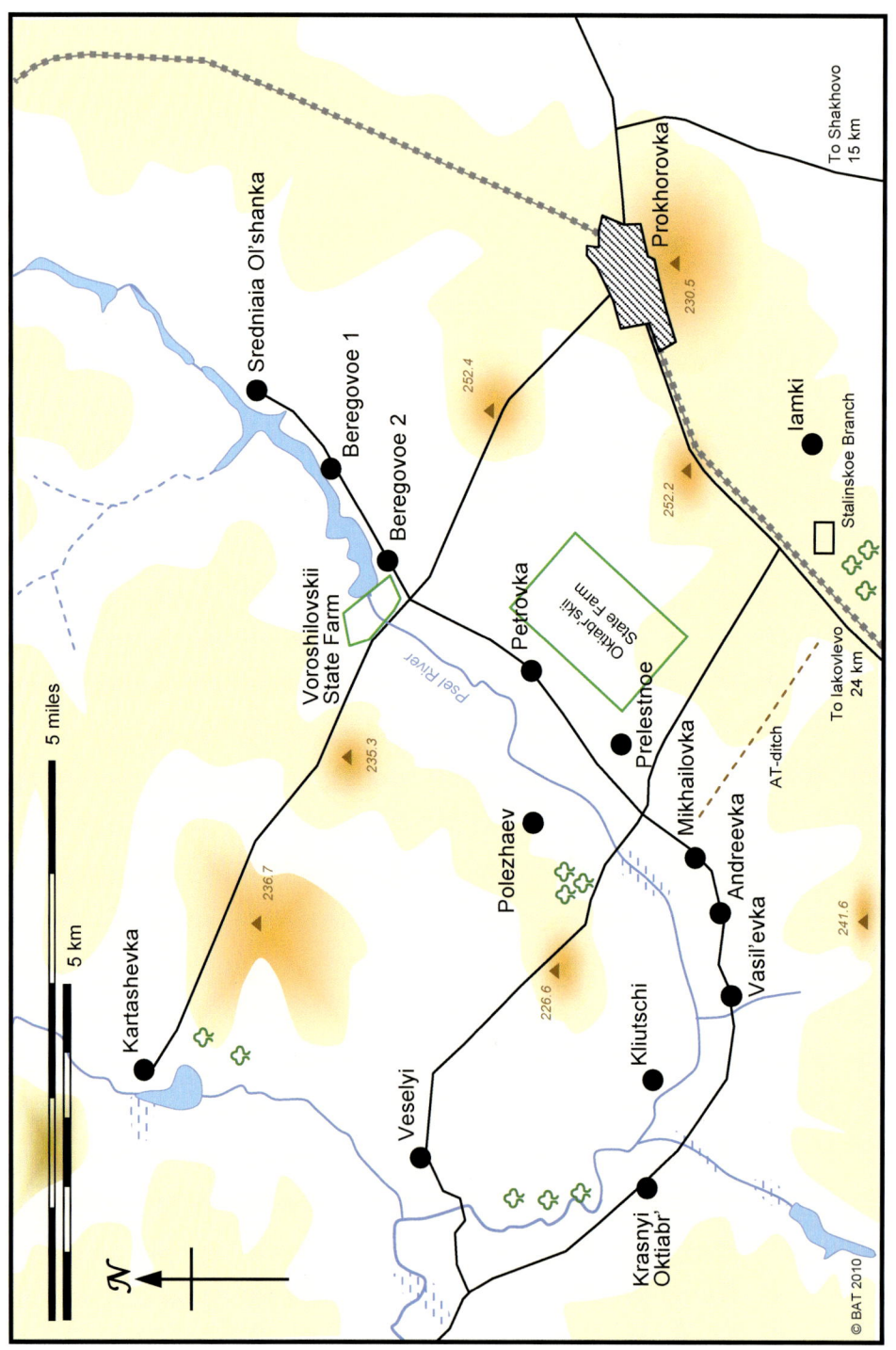

3. Prokhorovka – Psel River sector. (Map by Barbara Taylor)

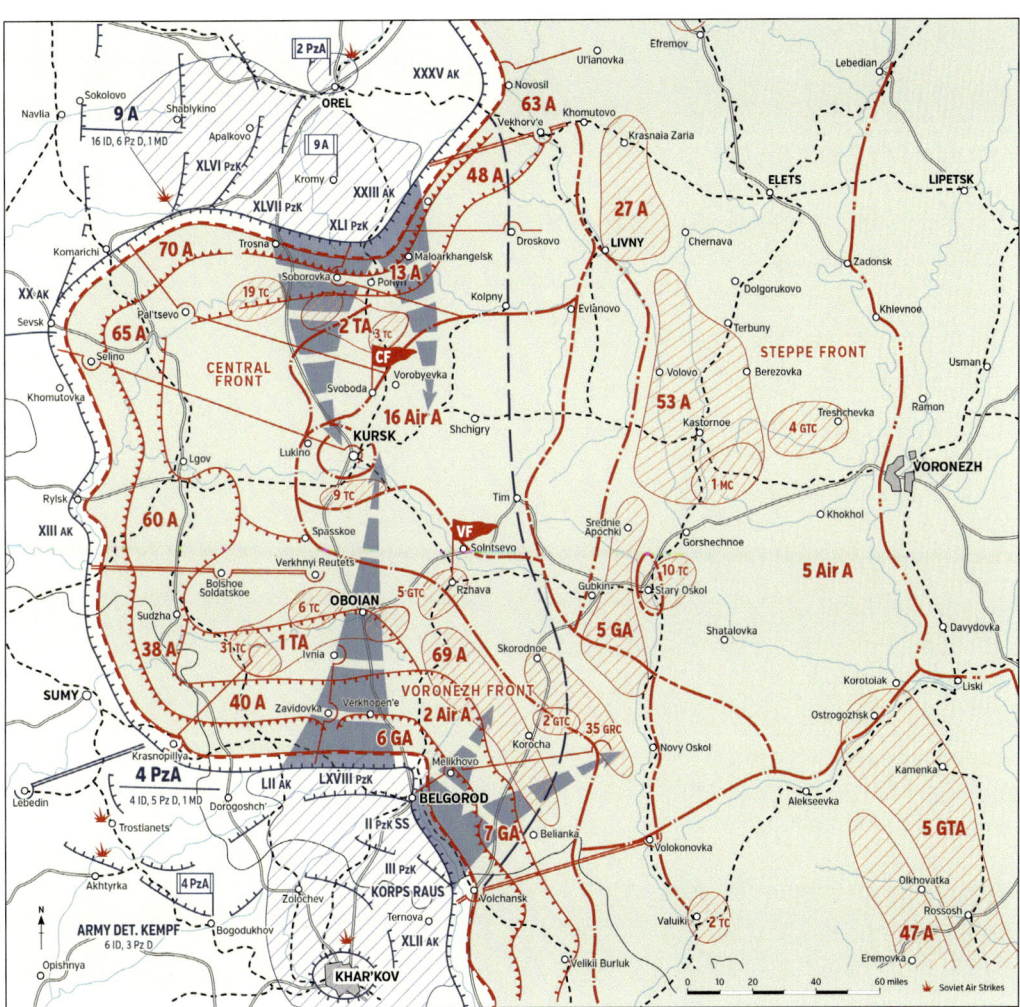

4. Kursk Bulge Soviet defence plan and German offensive scheme within the framework of Operation Citadel. (Map by George Anderson)

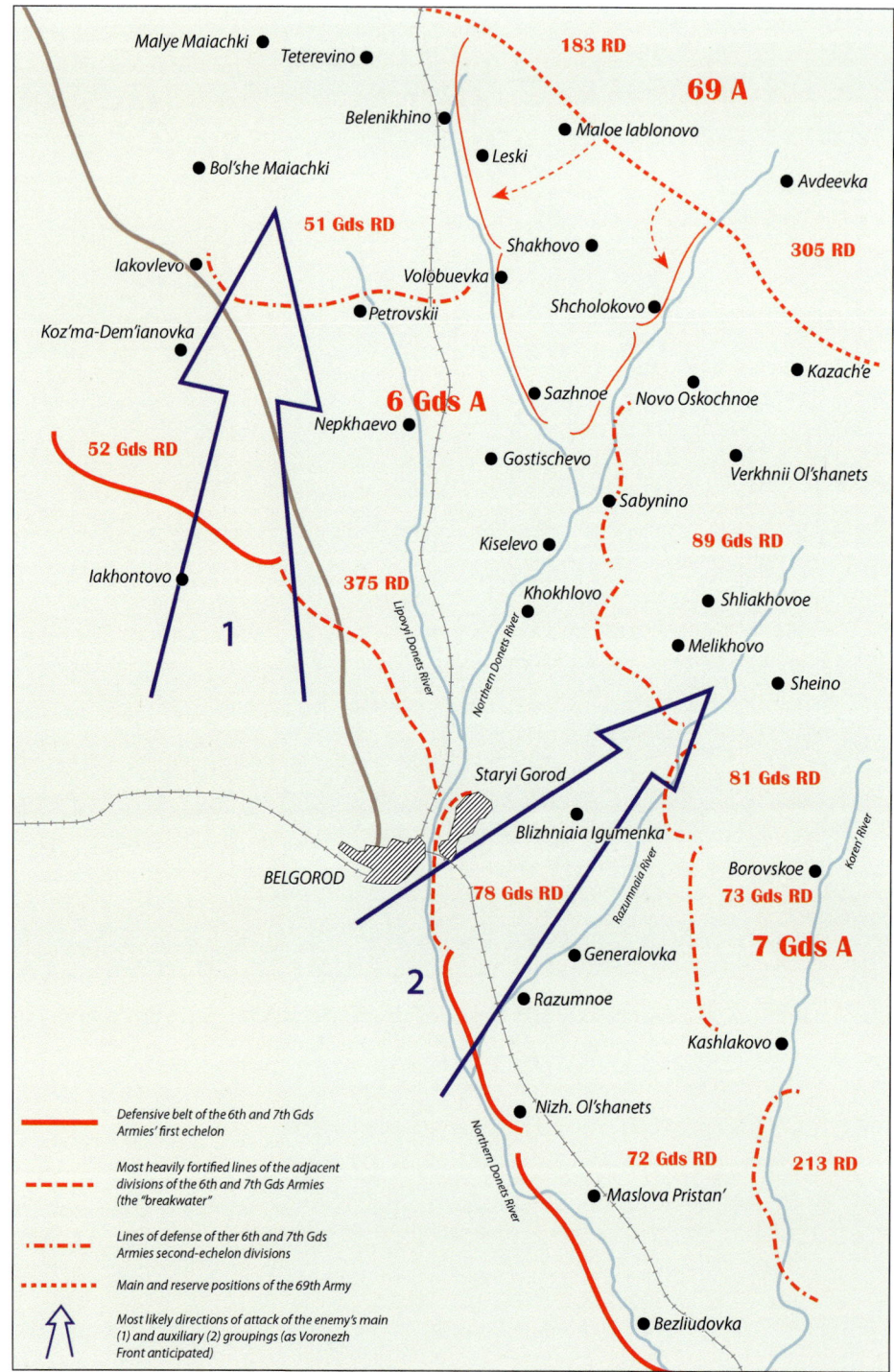

5. "Vatutin's Plan": 7th Guards Army Voronezh Front defences and anticipated direction of German offensive. (Map by George Anderson)

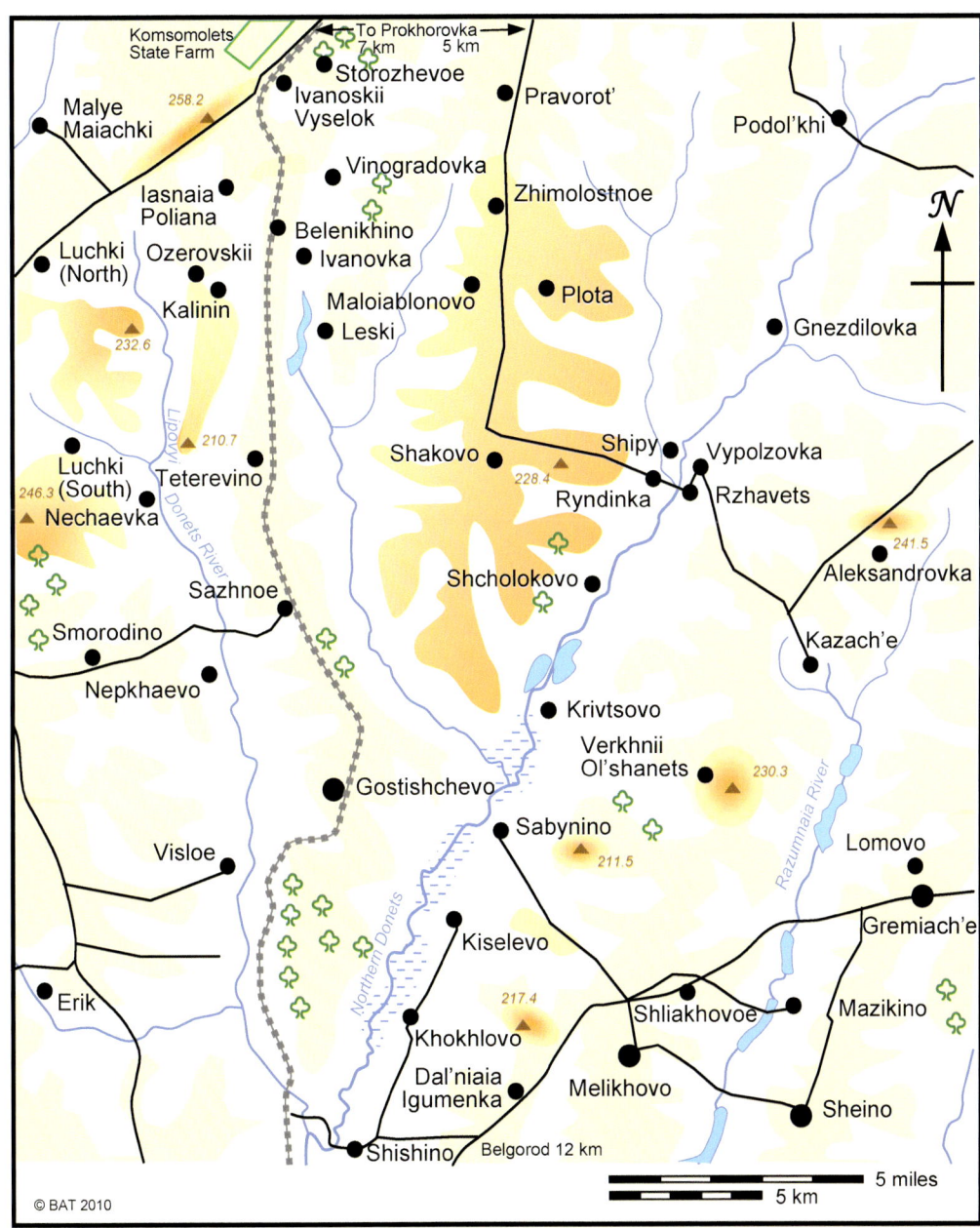

6. Lipovyi Donets – Northern Donets sector. (Map by Barbara Taylor)

VIII The Planning and Preparations for Kursk Volume 1

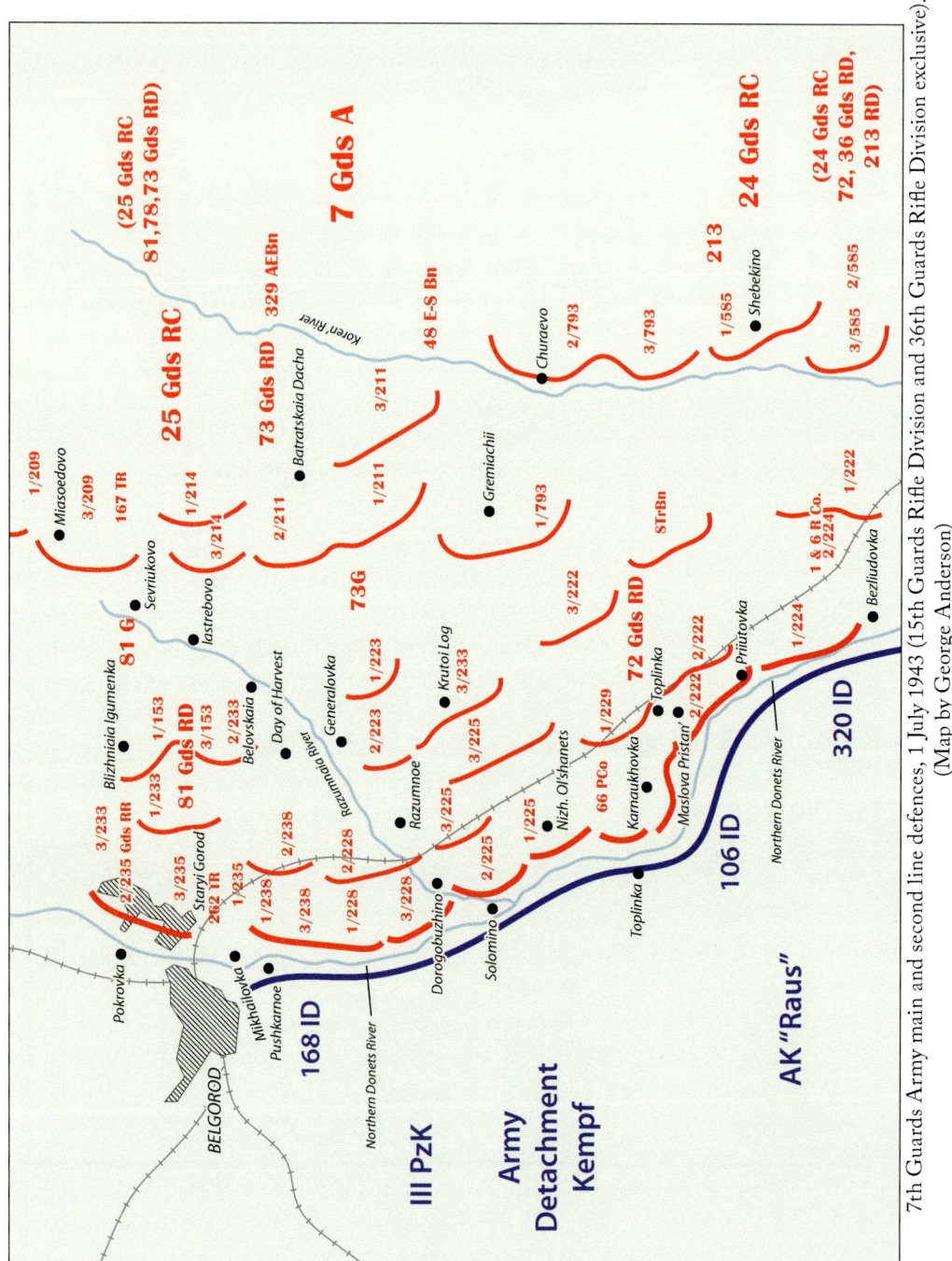

7. 7th Guards Army main and second line defences, 1 July 1943 (15th Guards Rifle Division and 36th Guards Rifle Division exclusive). (Map by George Anderson)

Part II

"It would be better if we grind down the enemy on our defenses …"

2.1 How the decision was made to adopt a premeditated defense

The line contained in the title of this chapter comes from a report to I.V. Stalin written by his deputy, Marshal of the Soviet Union G.K. Zhukov from 8 April 1943.[1] It was precisely this report that became the basis of the plan for the Kursk strategic defense operation, which became the key element of the entire summer campaign, although its planning had begun approximately two months before this time. It is possible to divide all of the *Stavka*'s and General Staff's work on the given matter into three separate phases.

The first lasted from January to 12 April 1943 inclusively. Its main features were the concentration of the Red Army's forces and the mustering of the country's resources to reinforce

---

1   Zhukov, Georgii Konstantinovich (1896-1974), Marshal of the Soviet Union (1943), four-time recipient of Hero of the Soviet Union (1939, 1943, 1944 and 1956). Zhukov was a participant in the Russian Civil War and the military conflict at Khalkin Gol (1939). From 1940, he commanded the forces of the Kiev Special Military District. In January – July 1941, he served as Chief of Staff of the Red Army, and from 26 August 1942 until the end of the war, as the Deputy Supreme Commander. From 26 August 1942, Zhukov also served as the USSR Deputy People's Commissar of Defense. Between 17 and 27 March 1943, he was located at the Voronezh Front as the *Stavka* representative, with the aim of limiting the breakthrough made by Army Group South in the Belgorod area. He was one of the key organizers of the defense at Kursk and the preparation of the Red Army for the summer 1943 campaign. Zhukov was also the *Stavka* representative between 4 and 9 July 1943 on the Central Front, between 10 and 12 July 1943 on the Western Front, from 13 July and until the end of the Battle of Kursk – on the Voronezh and Steppe Fronts. In February 1944 Zhukov took command of the 1st Ukrainian Front, and from November 1944 until the end of the war, the 1st Belorussian Front. On 8 May 1945, in the name of the Supreme Commander-in-Chief of the Red Army, he accepted Germany's capitulation. For his contribution to the defeat of the adversary in the years of the Great Patriotic War, Zhukov was deemed worthy of two of the highest commander's Orders, the Order of Victory (No. 1 and 4). On 24 June 1945, Zhukov led the Victory Parade in Moscow. In the years 1945 and 1946, Zhukov was the Commander-in-Chief of the Group of Soviet Forces and the head of the Soviet Military Administration in Germany, before becoming Commander-in-Chief of the Army and of a number of military districts. In the years 1955 to 1957, Zhukov served as the USSR Minister of Defense. He retired in 1958. Zhukov described the preparation of the Red Army for the Battle of Kursk and his own participation in it in his memoirs, *Vospominaniia i razmyshleniia* [*Reminiscences and reflections*], which was published in 1970.

them; the development of a general plan for the defensive stage of the summer campaign and the acceptance of a preliminary decision to adopt an intentional defense. At the end of this period, the document cited above was also prepared by Zhukov.

The second stage did not last as long; it continued between 13 April and the middle of May. In this phase, the *Stavka*'s 12 April 1943 decision was generally implemented, the results of which became: the complete readiness of the troops of the Voronezh Front and Central Front for a defense; the completion of the work to fortify the first line of defenses in the Kursk area and the initiation of work on the second; and the conclusion of the initial stage of planning for the summer campaign.

The third phase lasted from mid-May to 4 July 1943. In the course of it, the *Stavka* finally confirmed the preliminary decision to adopt an intentional defensive posture, and with it to conduct the first (defensive) stage of the summer campaign, which entered history as the Battle of Kursk, or the repulse of the German attack within the framework of Operation Citadel. The deeply-echeloned defenses within the Kursk bulge also took on their final form, and in the process Rokossovsky's and Vatutin's troops underwent intense combat training and prepared to use the defenses. In addition, staff officers fully completed and elaborated the plan for the summer campaign, while the General Staff and command staffs of the Western, Briansk, Central, Voronezh and Southwestern Fronts did all the necessary paperwork for the forthcoming operations, including and especially the offensive operation that would follow the defeat of Citadel.[2] Subordinate headquarters as well conducted command post exercises. Finally, the forces of the *Stavka* strategic reserve, in the form of the Steppe Military District, were fully equipped and trained. Together with the Voronezh and Southwestern Fronts, it was supposed to become the main instrument for the offensive stage of the summer campaign in the southwestern sector of the Soviet-German front, the main objective of which was the destruction of Army Group South and the liberation of Ukraine.

When beginning to analyze the first stage, it is important to recall the situation in which the Soviet Union was located at this time, and the capabilities that its armed forces had. In the period between 22 June and the beginning of November 1941 alone, it had been deprived of territory, upon which 42 percent of the population lived; where 33 percent of the aggregate production of the entire Soviet industry was produced; where 71 percent of the raw iron and approximately 60 percent of the steel were smelted; contained 47 percent of its cultivated area for crops; and was the source of 38 percent of its total output of grain and almost 60 percent of the pig stock and 38 percent of the cattle.[3] All of this was lost over the first four months of the war alone! There followed the tragic events at Khar'kov in 1942, the enemy's breakthrough to the Volga River and the northern Caucasus, and the enormous human sacrifices and material damage. Nevertheless, the "colossus on clay feet", as the creator of the Third Reich called the USSR, had not simply remained standing. Having evacuated a significant portion of the industrial enterprises, it restored the industry in the country's eastern areas, which already in

---

2   The usual documented plan for the offensive operation "Polkovodets Rumiantsev" was not ready; the *Stavka* directive regarding its adoption was signed on 6 August 1943, already in the course of the operation.

3   Kurotkin, S.K. (ed.), *Tyl Sovetskikh vooruzhennykh sil v Velikoi Otechestvennoi voine 1941-1945* [*Rear of the Soviet armed forces in the Great Patriotic War 1941-1945*] (Moscow: Voenizdat, 1977), pp. 101, 500, 501.

the first half of 1942 began gradually to increase the output of military production. Already just a year later, by the end of January 1943, the volume of its output grew to such an extent that the leadership of the Red Army's General Staff, understanding the impossibility of achieving a final turning point in the war without powerful reserves, considered it possible to appeal to Stalin to dispatch new armaments and equipment to cover the army's not only current needs, but also to form strategic reserves.

At the same time, it should be emphasized that Germany, despite the enormous potential that it had activated in this war, including the industrially developed countries of occupied Europe, simply could not compete with the USSR in military production. According to the data of G.A. Koltunov and B.G. Solov'ev, in 1943 the military production in our country had grown 4.3 times with respect to its pre-war output, while in the Third Reich, the comparable indicator was just 2.3 times.[4] Thus, despite the shocks and losses, the Soviet economic model proved itself to be not only viable in wartime conditions, but also more effective than that of any other countries of Europe, including Germany, which had swallowed virtually all of Europe. Naturally, back then these figures were unknown to the opposing sides, but the fact that the power of the Soviet Union had consolidated and grown at a rapid pace was evident by the serious successes of its armed forces in early 1943 following the heavy defeats of 1942.

Thus, relying on the impressive industrial potential that had been created in the Volga region, the Urals and in Siberia and the major victories at the front, Moscow, reached an important political decision at the end of the winter of 1942/1943: the moment had come at last to drive the aggressors beyond the borders of the USSR and to move all of the combat operations onto their territory. The Red Army faced the task of completely clearing the adversary from the occupied areas of the country by the end of 1943. However, the twenty months of bloody fighting had not been wasted. In the documents of the *Stavka*, one can begin to see, especially after the Germans' recapture of Khar'kov, the desire to abandon "gung-ho" approaches when resolving strategic problems, as had been the case in early 1942, and to evaluate the country's potential and Germany's own capabilities in a more sober manner. Although the Kremlin also understood that profound changes had already taken place in the course of the war, even so, the euphoria that was observed in the Soviet command after the complete destruction of Paulus's Stalingrad grouping, began to fade in the *Stavka*'s major decisions. The Soviet political leadership realized that the country and its armed forces still faced a hard struggle against a strong and still far from vanquished foe. Stalin's Order No. 95 from 23 February 1943 plainly demonstrates this:

> The enemy has suffered a defeat but has still not been vanquished. The German-fascist army is experiencing a crisis in view of the blows it has received from the Red Army, but this still does not mean that it cannot recover. The struggle with the German aggressor has not yet ended – it is only expanding and becoming more intense. It would be stupid to assume that the Germans will abandon even a kilometer of our land without combat. The Red Army faces a severe struggle against a cunning, cruel and still powerful adversary.[5]

---

4   Koltunov and Solov'ev, *Kurskaia bitva* [*Battle of Kursk*] (Moscow: Voenizdat, 1970), p. 16.
5   Stalin, I.V., *O Velikoi Otechestvennoi voine Sovetskogo Soiuza* [*On the Great Patriotic War of the Soviet Union*] (Moscow: Gosudarstvennoe izdatel'stvo politicheskoi literatury, 1947), p. 91.

Indeed, literally within a matter of days after the publication of this document, the situation on the southern and southwestern directions of the Soviet-German front would take a turn for the worse, which only confirmed the accuracy of the assessment of the enemy given by it.

The *Stavka* took its first major steps to prepare for the achievement of its given goal for 1943 – the liberation of the entire country – already on 29 January, by issuing a directive about beginning the concentration of military resources and the creation of field reserves at both the *front* and strategic level, which meant to initiation of creating instruments for resolving the designated ambitious tasks. The command staffs of the Southwestern, Southern and North Caucasus Fronts were given a directive to form a permanent reserve, while the command staff of the Don Front was ordered to withdraw the headquarters of the 57th Army and the army's units and services into the *Stavka* Reserve.[6]

Moscow was planning to lean upon the assistance of its Allies as well in this important and at the same time complex matter. At this time, not only foodstuffs and deficit raw materials were arriving from the USA and England, but also weapons, transport vehicles, tanks and aircraft. In a private conversation, G.K. Zhukov openly recognized:

> It mustn't be denied that the Americans were sending us a lot of materiel, without which we could not have formed our reserves and wouldn't have been able to continue the war … We did not have explosive charges or gunpowder. There was nothing with which to fill our rifle cartridges. The Americans really did bail us out with gunpowder and explosive charges. And how much sheet metal did they send us?! Really, would we have been able to get the production of tanks up and running so quickly, if the Americans had not helped us with steel?[7]

However, already at the beginning of spring 1943, this flow of supplies would be substantially reduced, and fully restored only in August 1943, after the conclusion of the Battle of Kursk. This situation once again confirmed I.V. Stalin's pernicious conviction that the Allies at any moment could let him down, so in the fierce struggle against the Nazis, the Soviet Union must count upon primarily only its own efforts, despite the fact that the people had already laid colossal sacrifices on the altar of Victory that would be difficult to replace.

The country's leadership took the next step to create a foundation for the future victories on 1 March 1943. The Deputy Commander of the Red Army's Armored and Mechanized Forces Lieutenant General N.I. Biriukov received a directive from Stalin to strengthen the combined-arms armies that had been withdrawn into the Stavka Reserve. For this purpose, their tables of organization and equipment should include two separate tank regiments for direct infantry support, as a rule of a composite nature (39 T-70 and T-34 tanks). At the time, this was no small force; these tanks arrived in the reserve of the army commanders and substantially expanded their capabilities, especially when attacking. Just 10 days later, a new order arrived: to withdraw seven tank and mechanized corps from the front to the Ostrogozhsk, Staryi and Novyi Oskol,

---

6   *Velikaia Otechestvennaia voina: Stavka VGK, dokumenty i materialy 1943* [*Great Patriotic War: The Headquarters of the Supreme High Command, documents and materials 1943*] Vol. 16 (5-3) (Moscow: TERRA, 1999), p. 42, 43.
7   Zin'kovich, N., *Marshaly i genseki* [*Marshals and General Secretaries*] (Moscow, 1997), pp. 161-162.

Alekseevka, Kastornoe area and to reassemble them promptly.[8] The Supreme Commander-in-Chief's signing of a directive on 11 March regarding the formation of the Reserve Front consisting of three combined-arms armies (2nd Reserve, 24th and 66th Armies) and three tank corps (4th Guards, 3rd and 10th Tank Corps) became the logical conclusion of the first stage of this process to build a strategic reserve. Initially, its headquarters was to form on the basis of the Briansk Front's headquarters, which had been abolished, while its forces were being transferred to the newly-created Central Front in the Kursk area as reinforcements. However, because of the deteriorating situation near Khar'kov at that time, the implementation of this decision had to be halted temporarily, and then revised. However, the mechanism of the withdrawal from the front of major formation and armies that were to comprise the Reserve Front had been put into motion, and their re-establishment in rear areas never ceased entirely.

Already on 30 March 1943, when it became clear that von Manstein's counteroffensive had been stopped, Moscow again returned to the question of resurrecting a most important instrument for future large-scale operations – the mobile formations. At this time the *Stavka* requested that five more tank and mechanized corps (the 1st Guards Mechanized Corps and the 2nd, 23rd, 2nd Guards and 5th Guards Tank Corps) be brought up to combat readiness between 5 and 20 April.[9] However, it had managed to return to the organizational work regarding the creation of the Reserve Front even earlier. Judging from the decisions he made, Stalin was assigning great significance to this matter. For its creation, he brought together the most experienced cadres, who had proven their abilities, including from the civilian sphere. Recalled Politburo member A.I. Mikoyan:

> On 27 March 1943 after 1:00 in the morning, I arrived at Stalin's nearby dacha in Volynsk in response to his summons. He told me that according to intelligence information, the Nazis were concentrating major forces for an offensive in the area of the Kursk bulge. "Apparently," said Stalin, "they are attempting to take the strategic initiative, having a further bead on Moscow. In order to prevent this, we must urgently organize a strong Reserve Front, which we might then commit to battle at the most acute and decisive moment of the fighting and with a subsequent switch to a counteroffensive."
>
> This question, judging from everything, had already been thoroughly considered by him and discussed in the *Stavka*, because he promptly expressed concrete ideas not only about the designation and character of this *front*, but also about the area where it should form up, as well as about the schedule of staffing it with personnel. In his opinion, the Reserve Front should be formed, first of all, by means of those military units that have been withdrawn to the rear after battle for rest and replenishment with personnel and combat equipment.
>
> "The point is that this is very important and necessary for the war's future prospects," Stalin continued; "It is necessary so that when you take on the responsibility of organizing this Reserve Front as a member of the State Defense Committee it will be good that our material resources are concentrated in your hands. The selection of

---

8 Biriukov, N.I., *Tanki – frontu* [*Tanks – to the front*] (Smolensk: Rusich, 2005), pp. 314, 318.
9 Ibid., pp. 321-322.

the Front's command staff, as usual, will be the General Staff's business, and all the rest – yours."

Such an instruction was not only unexpected by me, but also unusual, since I had never before been engaged in the matters of troop formations, having directed since the outbreak of the war the supply of the Red Army broadly with gear, food, fuel and artillery shells.[10]

It is important to understand how the Supreme Commander-in-Chief determined the tasks of this new *front* at the end of March 1943. Despite the fact that the main objective (the liberation of the country) for the troops had already been formulated, and the strategic reserves had been primarily prepared just for this purpose, as is apparent from the cited excerpt, at this moment Stalin was viewing them first of all as a powerful lever of influence on the current situation at the front. He would adhere to this position, even when planning the summer campaign in the course of April and May, although the former chief of the General Staff's Operations Department General S.M. Shtemenko[11] recalled that at this time the General Staff had not at all intended to commit them into the fighting prior to that moment when the Red Army went over to a general counteroffensive. I.V. Stalin disagreed with this approach. In early April, when working out a directive regarding the Reserve Front, he demanded that the bulk of these forces be deployed behind the troops that were holding the most threatened direction (the area of the Kursk bulge at that moment had already come to the fore), and their commanders received the assignment to work out alternative ways of rendering assistance to the formations of the Central and Voronezh Fronts positioned in front of them.[12] This clearly shows that Stalin had a certain lack of confidence in the Red Army, and his desire to prevent a repeat of the tragic mistakes of the first half of 1942. The "syndrome of last year's failures", albeit in dots and dashes, would nevertheless be traceable in all of the *Stavka*'s important decisions taken in the period of

---

10   Mikoyan, A.I., *Tak bylo* [*As it was*] (Moscow: Vagrius, 1999), p. 320.
11   Shtemenko, Sergei Matveevich, General of the Army (1968), was born on 20 February 1907 into a peasant family in Don Oblast's Cossack village of Uriupinskaia. He joined the Red Army in 1926. He completed the Sevastopol School of Anti-aircraft Artillery in 1930, the Military Academy of the Red Army's Motorized and Mechanized Forces in 1937, and Military Academy of the General Staff in 1940. From August 1941, Shtemenko served as the deputy chief of a department in the General Staff's Operations Directorate. In June 1942 he was appointed chief of a department of the Operations Directorate. From April 1943 he was the First Deputy, and then from May 1943 the chief of the General Staff's Operations Directorate. Between November 1948 and June 1952, Shtemenko was the Chief of the General Staff and Deputy Minister of the USSR Armed Forces. In June 1953 after Lavrentii Beria's arrest, Shtemenko was reduced in rank from General of the Army to Lieutenant General and was appointed chief of staff of the Western Siberian Military District. In August 1956, he became chief of the Military Intelligence Agency and acquired the rank of colonel general. In October 1957, he warned Minister of Defense G.K. Zhukov, who was on an official trip to Yugoslavia, that he was going to be replaced, for which he was reduced in rank from colonel general to lieutenant general and appointed first deputy commander of the Baltic Military District. In February 1968, Shtemenko once again gained the rank of General of the Army, and in August 1968 became the First Deputy Chief of the General Staff and the Chief of Staff of the Warsaw Pact's Allied Armed Forces. Shtemenko passed away in Moscow on 23 April 1976.
12   Shtemenko, S.M., *Generalnyi shtab v gody voiny* [*General Staff in the war years*] (Moscow: Voenizdat, 1968), p. 156.

preparing for the Battle of Kursk, and only after it would Stalin manage to rid himself of it, at least outwardly.

Now let us turn to the second phase in the preparations for the summer campaign, the process of planning the combat operations, which I will remind you continued for approximately a month, from 13 April to mid-May. Recalled S.M. Shtemenko:

> At the end of March and throughout April, an exchange of opinions regarding where and how best to resolve the main tasks of the war in the summer of 1943 took place in the *Stavka* and the General Staff. On this account, they consulted the authoritative military commanders who had represented the *Stavka* in the acting army, as well as certain *front* commanders-in-chief. The question "Where?" did not appear very difficult back then. There was only one response to it – the Kursk salient. After all, it was precisely in this area that the enemy's main shock forces were located, which concealed two menacing possibilities: a deep envelopment of Moscow, or a pivoting to the south. On the other hand, it was precisely here, opposite the enemy's main grouping, that we could use our forces and means, primarily the large armored armies, most effectively. On all the other directions, even if our operations were successful, they wouldn't promise the Soviet armed forces such prospects as the Kursk bulge. The *Stavka*, the General Staff and the *front* commanders-in-chief all eventually came to this conclusion.
>
> The second question – How best resolve the war's main tasks? – was more difficult. Responses to it did not follow right away and were far from the same.[13]

Formally, G.K. Zhukov should be considered the author of the idea to neutralize the German offensive by means of adopting a defensive posture. On the basis of the analysis of the operational situation and the enemy behavior, it was he who first officially proposed (in a document of a strategic nature, the report to I.V. Stalin mentioned above) that the Germans would soon attempt to cut off the Kursk salient and it would be more sensible for the Red Army to bleed their assault formations white in well-prepared defensive lines. Even so, a number of key figures in the Red Army's leadership had already come to this conclusion, especially A.M. Vasilevsky.[14] From the

---

13 Ibid., p. 150.
14 Vasilevsky, Aleksandr Mikhailovich (1895-1977), Marshal of the Soviet Union (1943), twice Hero of the Soviet Union (1944, 1945). He entered the Great Patriotic War in the role of Deputy Chief (1941), and from June 1942 – Chief of Staff of the Red Army. One of the authors of the plan for the 1943 summer campaign, the kernel of which were the events around Kursk. Together with Marshal of the Soviet Union G.K. Zhukov and Colonel General A.I. Antonov, he took part in a conference held in the Kremlin on 12 April 1943, where the decision was made about the Red Army's adoption of a strategic defense at Kursk. In the course of March to June 1943, Vasilevsky did a large amount of work to organize the defenses of the Central and Voronezh Fronts in order to repulse the enemy's attacks in the area of the Kursk bulge. Between 6 and 14 July 1943, he was the *Stavka* representative with the Voronezh Front, and at I.V. Stalin's directive, he was personally responsible for the commitment of the strategic reserves (the 5th Guards Tank Army and 5th Guards Army) in the battle at Prokhorovka on 12 July 1943. From 14 July 1943 Vasilevsky served as the *Stavka* representative with the Southwestern Front. In 1945, he took command of the 3rd Belorussian Front. In August and September 1945, he was the commander-in-chief of the Soviet forces in the Far East during the destruction of the Japanese Kwantung Army. For his large contribution to the victory over Germany, he was deemed worthy of two

moment that the development of the summer campaign began and throughout the operational pause at the front, both marshals consistently shared the same point of view about how to conduct it. Both men believed that in the first stage, it was necessary to grant the initiative to the enemy. Only later, after having sapped the strength of the German main assault groupings, would the strategic reserves, that had been formed up in the spring, go on the offensive. This point of view rather quickly (in comparison with the process of preparing for Citadel) reigned in the *Stavka* and became the working plan of the country's entire political and military leadership, because it was in accordance with I.V. Stalin's own internal leaning (to demonstrate caution in active offensive operations), which he had already clearly shown already in March 1943 when he was deciding how best to use the reserves.

Between 18 March and 11 April 1943, first A.M. Vasilesky and then G.K. Zhukov visited the Central and Voronezh Fronts at the Supreme Commander's special assignment in order to check the implementation of the *Stavka* directives regarding the stabilization of the situation, and simultaneously with the aim of obtaining preliminary suggestions regarding how to conduct the summer campaign. In the course of their visits, both marshals together with N.F. Vatutin and K.K. Rokossovsky inspected the line of the armies of the *front*'s first echelon and discussed in detail the enemy's behavior, his possible plan, and the entire complex of problems connected with the summer campaign with their command staffs. Even so, G.K. Zhukov was the first to suggest to the *Stavka* the idea of adopting an intentional defense, since he independently, in his own name, prepared the first report that contained this idea, and the General Staff, after studying it, supported his proposal. Marshal Zhukov's aide, Major General L.F. Miniuk, left behind interesting recollections of this work in his diary:

> **17 March** (1943): We left by train to Kursk at 11:00 A.M.
> **18 March**: We arrived in Kursk in the afternoon and met with A.I. Antonov, who briefed the Marshal on the situation as it stood in the Kursk salient, then immediately headed to the village of Streletskaia, where the headquarters of the Voronezh Front was located.
> **19 March**: In the morning, we traveled to the Belgorod area to General I.M. Chistiakov's 21st Army, to its 52nd Guards Rifle Division, which had made contact with the enemy's *Totenkopf* Panzer Division.
> **20 March**: Back again to the 52nd Guards Rifle Division to inspect its positions. Recommendations were given about where to position combat outposts and where to set up the forward edge of defense.
> **20-21 March**: We stayed in the village of Streletskaia and traveled to see Chistiakov in Kochetovka and to Moskalenko's army [the 40th Army]. We were primarily not at the headquarters, but in the field, where the defense was being established. We made decisions about setting up close cooperation with fire at the boundaries and the preparation of counterblows and counterattacks in the event of an enemy breakthrough toward Oboian'.

---

of the highest commander's Orders, the Order of Victory (No. 2 and No. 7). From 1946, Vasilevsky was Chief of the General Staff. In the years 1949 to 1953, he was the USSR's Minister of Armed Forces, and in the years 1953 to 1957, the USSR Deputy Minister of Defense. Vasilevsky retired in 1968.

21 March: General Vatutin arrived and replaced the Commander-in-Chief of the Voronezh Front Golikov. Zhukov met with Vatutin, discussed the situation and the necessary measures to take first.
22 March: Once again to the 52nd Guards Rifle Division together with Vatutin. A conference convened with the command staff.
23 March: Now to Moskalenko's 40th Army – the same matters.
24 March: We traveled to the Central Front to visit Rokossovsky in the village of Svoboda.
From **25 March to 8 April**, we spent time not only at the Front headquarters, but also worked primarily in Pukhov's 13th Army together with Rokossovsky. We visited the front, after which there was a meeting with the army's command staff, then traveled to Lieutenant General I.V. Galinin's 70th Army, and also spent time in P.I. Batov's 65th Army, before heading north to P.L. Romanenko's 48th Army. Later we returned to Kursk, and Zhukov, having drawn on a map the most likely directions of the enemy's attacks, gave me his opinion about the fascist command's most likely plan of actions, and ordered me to put together a report to Stalin. I remember, when I read it to Zhukov, he asked:

"To whom are you writing this? Remember, you're writing to none other than Stalin – the Chief of the General Staff!"

He told me about how Poskrebyshev reads reports to Stalin, and about the Supreme Commander's work style. He also talked about his manner of speech, his superb memory, and that in reports only the surnames of the commander's should be given, since Stalin clearly remembered which armies they were commanding, and about a lot of other things I did not know.[15]

However, it should be emphasized that at first the Supreme Commander took the proposal from his deputy with caution. It was too important that he should be the one to make all the decisions. Therefore, he ordered a thorough analysis of the proposal while drawing into the discussion a wider circle of generals who had a direct relationship with it. From this point of view, for the time being he remained silent. A.M. Vasilevsky recalled:

Once I was with I.V. Stalin when he received a report. It was known to the Supreme Commander that the General Staff was supporting Zhukov's point of view. Having read Zhukov's report, Stalin said: "I need to consult with the *front* commanders" – and directed to get their opinions. He ordered the General Staff to get a special conference ready in order to discuss the plan for the 1943 summer campaign. He himself called N.F. Vatutin and K.K. Rokossovsky and asked them to present their observations and assessments regarding their *fronts*' situations and the plan for their forthcoming operations.[16]

---

15 Mirkin, A.D. and Iarovikov, V.S. (ed.), *Marshal Zhukov: polkovodets i chelovek* [*Marshal Zhukov: Commander and man*], Vol. 1 (Moscow: APN, 1988), p. 262.
16 Vasilevsky, *Delo vsei zhizni* [*Cause of an entire life*], Book 2 (Moscow: Politizdat, 1988), p. 17.

Having arrived at the General Staff, A.M. Vasilevsky took a number of steps to obtain the information for the looming conference. He instructed the Main Intelligence Department and the Department of Fronts' Intelligence to analyze the information about the enemy's intentions, his concrete steps in this direction, and to present their conclusions by 12 April. After this he flew off to Bobyshovo, to where the headquarters of the Voronezh Front had moved and where Zhukov was located, and together over the next two days they worked out the main principles for the plan of the summer campaign, and also prepared a *Stavka* directive about the areas of assembly for the main strategic reserves, a draft of which had already been sent to Stalin on 10 April. S.M. Shtemenko recollected:

> On the whole, the course of the anticipated events drew the following picture for us. On the offensive, the enemy would chiefly rely on tanks and aircraft. The infantry would be given a secondary role, since it was weaker than in preceding years. The disposition of his assault groupings gave a clue to operations along converging directions: the Orlov – Kromy grouping – toward Kursk from the north, and the Belgorod – Khar'kov grouping – toward Kursk from the south. An auxiliary attack, splitting our front, was deemed possible from the west out of the Vorozhba area between the Seim and Psel Rivers toward Kursk. ... Thereby, the German-fascist command could count upon the encirclement and destruction of all of our armies that were occupying a defense along the Kursk bulge within a short period of time. It was assumed that the enemy was planning to reach the Korocha, Tim, Droskovo line in the first stage of the offensive, and in the second stage – to launch an attack into the flank and rear of the Southwestern Front through Valuiki and Urazovo. It was being assumed that to meet this attack, an offensive would be conducted out of the Lisichansk area to the north in the direction of Svatovo and Urazovo. Attempts by the Germans to seize the Livny, Kastornoe, Staryi and Novyi Oskol line and the railroad running to the Donbas, which was important for us, also weren't excluded.[17]

A substantial dilemma confronted the intelligence services and was the source for such a wide array of enemy alternatives. Of course, the situation did demand that the command staff consider every possible enemy action without exception and to seek the most effective ways of frustrating his intentions. N.F. Vatutin's[18] "error in judgement" (in fact an abundance of caution)

---

17 Shtemenko, *General'nyi shtab v gody voiny*, p. 158.
18 Vatutin, Nikolai Fedorovich, General of the Army (1943). Born on 16 December 1901 in Kursk (today Belgorod) Oblast's village of Chepukhino in the Valuiki District, one of the many children (nine) born to a middle-class peasant couple. Due to its socio-economic position, he received a good education. In 1913 he completed the fifth grade of a rural school, then two years of a county secondary school in Valuiki and three years of a business school in Urazovo. Until 1917 he lived in his father's family and worked in agriculture. Vatutin was called into the Red Army in April 1920 as part of a mobilization drive. In 1920 and 1921, he participated in the fighting against Makhno's band and Ataman Belen'ky on the territory of the Lugansk, Poltava and Khar'kov oblasts. Vatutin graduated from the Poltava Infantry School in 1922, the Kiev Higher Army Military School in 1924, and the Frunze Military Academy in 1929. He commanded first a squad, then a platoon and a company. From June 1929, he served as a staff officer as the assistant chief of the 7th Rifle Division's Intelligence Department in the city of Chernigov, before being assigned the assistant chief of the North Caucasus Military District's

that certain scholars would note after the war arose precisely from this circumstance. In the sector of the Voronezh Front, there were many directions that offered good ground for tank operations, so he had to consider not only powerful German attacks in the most likely directions from Belgorod, toward Oboian' and Staryi Oskol (which were obvious), but also toward Sudzha (on the Front's left flank), where the command of Army Group South had no intention to launch an offensive and had not even considered one.

The initial period of preparations for the Battle of Kursk has received little attention in domestic historiography, because documentary sources on the routine work of the *Stavka* in this period are almost completely lacking, with the exception of its directives, which were published in 1999. A number of other problems have also existed. Back in the 1970s, A.M. Vasilevsky observed:

> Until recently, the question about the planning and preparation for the Battle of Kursk in both academic and especially memoir literature hasn't been covered accurately at all; the large creative and organizational activity of the *Stavka* and its working organ, the General Staff has either been deliberately or involuntarily understated, while the role of the frontline chains of command, and first of all the Voronezh Front's Military

---

Operations Department in Rostov. Vatutin continued his staff work as the chief of staff of the 28th Mountain Rifle Division in Ordzhonikidze; the chief of operations in the headquarters of the Siberian Military District in Novosibirsk. After completing the Military Academy of the General Staff in July 1937, Vatutin became the deputy chief of staff of the Kiev Special Military District, before becoming the chief of staff in November 1938. Between 26 July 1940 and 13 March 1941, Vatutin was the Deputy Chief of the General Staff and simultaneously the Chief of Operations. Between 13 February 1941 and 30 June 1941, Vatutin served as the First Deputy Chief of the General Staff for operational matters and logistics. On 30 June 1941, Vatutin became the Chief of Staff of the Northwestern Front. In mid-July 1942 at his personal request and with the support of A.M. Vasilevsky, Vatutin assumed command of the Voronezh Front, before being transferred to the same position with the Southwestern Front. Under his leadership, this Front performed successfully in the Battle of Stalingrad, but which on 7 December 1942 Zhukov was promoted to the rank of colonel general. On 12 February 1943, he became General of the Army and was awarded the Order of Suvorov 1st Class, and on 28 March 1943 he took command of the Voronezh Front again. N.F. Vatutin was one of the best prepared and promising generals of the cohort of *front* commanders. His characteristic style of leadership was his deep elaboration of an operation, activity, and the ability to organize powerful armored blows into the depth of the enemy's defenses with a singleness of purpose. General Vatutin had a calm, poised nature. As N.S. Khrushchev and K.S. Moskalenko recalled, he was distinguished by his considerate attitude toward subordinates, and in his work, he sought to allow them to show their initiative. However, he had a difficult relationship with I.V. Stalin. The Supreme Commander more than once justly criticized Vatutin's mistakes in command of the Voronezh Front and expressed dissatisfaction with his leadership methods. In particular, there is evidence that he harshly criticized Vatutin's actions in the course of repulsing the German attack toward Kursk in July 1943, during Operation Polkovodets Rumiantsev, and also in the Korsun – Shevchenkovskii operation. Even so, for his performance in the Battle of Kursk, he, like the other *front* commanders-in-chief, was awarded the Order of Kutuzov 1st Class. However, despite the fact that from the middle of 1942, Vatutin was directing a number of *fronts* on the most critical directions and taking part in some of the largest battles of the war, right up until his tragic death he was never deemed worthy of the highest command rank, Marshal of the Soviet Union, or the Gold Star of the Hero of the Soviet Union. He passed away on 15 April 1944 in a Kiev hospital after being wounded in an ambush set by Ukrainian nationalist partisans in the sector of the 60th Army on 29 February 1944.

Council, has been exaggerated ... Moreover, a number of important details haven't been mentioned at all in documents, because they were discussed at the highest levels of command among a narrow circle of men, who were directing the preparation for the Battle of Kursk. In addition to I.V. Stalin, G.K. Zhukov, A.I. Antonov and the author of these lines, this relates to other comrades who were working in the State Defense Committee, the *Stavka* and the General Staff during the war years.[19]

In fact, I.V. Stalin, concerned about the possible disclosure of strategic information, banned the production of any transcripts of meetings and conferences held in the Kremlin. He also demanded that the participants remember any decisions or assignments, and then to write them down in secret notebooks upon their return to their offices; after a certain passage of time, these notebooks were destroyed. So, the details of the process of working out the most important strategic decisions and plans of the USSR's military and political leadership, as well as the opinions and proposals of its key figures, have been to a great extent irretrievably lost. In recent decades, sources which at first glance seem to cast light on this problem have entered academic circulation. However, after an attentive analysis of them regarding certain matters, the situation has become even murkier.

For example, one can cite the logbook of visitors to I.V. Stalin's office – Party and government figures during the war years (henceforth, the Logbook). This document was not kept systematically, and one might even say it was done carelessly. It does not observe a strict chronology; the visit to the Supreme Commander by a number of military commanders was not registered, even though other sources mention them; and given family names in the Logbook are garbled. Unfortunately, a number of researchers use the information from the Logbook without any critical analysis or consideration of the details of the Soviet system of government administration that existed at that time. For example, the Logbook shows that late in the evening on 11 April 1943, I.V. Stalin convened a meeting in his Kremlin office with V.M. Molotov, G.K. Zhukov, Deputy Chief of the General Staff Colonel General A.I. Antonov[20], K.K. Rokossovsky and the Chief of the Red Army's Engineers Lieutenant General M.P. Vorob'ev. The details of

---

19 Vasilevsky, *Delo vsei zhizni*, Vol. 2, p. 18.
20 Antonov, Aleksei Innokent'evich, General of the Army (7 August 1943), was born on 15 or 26 September 1896 in Grodno (Belorussia) to the family of a Russian officer and the daughter of a Polish man who'd been sent to Siberia. In 1916 he completed the Pavlovsk Infantry School, and took part in the First World War as a warrant officer. He joined the Red Army in 1919 and fought in the Russian Civil War. In 1931 and 1933 Antonov graduated from two departments of the Frunze Military Academy (each time passing through the full course of study), and one course of study of the Military Academy of the General Staff. In March 1941 Antonov became the deputy chief of staff, and from 24 June 1941, the chief of staff of the Kiev Special Military District. On 27 August 1941, Antonov became the chief of staff of the Southern Front, before switching to take the same post in the North Caucasus Front on 28 July 1942. In the words of the deputy commander-in-chief of this *front*, R.Ia. Malinovsky: "He doubtlessly possessed remarkable organizational capabilities, a genius understanding of the enemy's plans, and the ability to confound them cunningly." From November 1942 Antonov served as the chief of staff of the Trans-Caucasus Front, and from 11 December 1942, as the chief of the Operations Department and a deputy chief of the General Staff. From May 1943 Antonov was the First Deputy Chief of the General Staff, before becoming the Chief of the General Staff on 4 February 1945. On 4 June 1945, Antonov was awarded the Order of Victory, the sole General of the Army to do so among all of the 14 Marshals and Generalissimos deemed worthy of this honor. In March 1946, he

this meeting are unknown, but judging from those invited, the plan of the summer campaign of 1943 was under discussion. Yet if you consider that there is no mention in the Logbook of the arrival in the Kremlin of G.K. Zhukov, A.M. Vasilevsky and A.I. Antonov late in the evening on 12 April, when the preliminary decision about going over to a strategic defense was reached, then plainly several mistakes appear simultaneously. In the document, either the identity of those who gathered on 11 April has been mixed up, since neither G.K. Zhukov nor K.K. Rokossovsky never made any mention of it, or the date of this meeting is wrong, and it did not happen on 11 April, but 12 April, while instead of A.M. Vasilevsky the name of K.K. Rokossovsky has been given. However, the latter man never made any mention about participating in such a major historical decision, while G.K. Zhukov writes in considerable detail about everything that was connected with this meeting. However, in so doing he also mentions that late on the evening of 11 April, having arrived from the front, he met with A.M. Vasilevsky, who passed along I.V. Stalin's instructions to prepare an operational map and documents of the situation in the area of the Kursk salient for both of them, and to appear together in the Kremlin on the evening of 12 April. A.M. Vasilevsky confirms this. Thus, the information presented in the Logbook about those who were with Stalin on these two days is inaccurate, and this can be understood by comparing the Logbook with the memoirs of each of these two marshals.

Nevertheless, for example, Boris Sokolov ignores the inconsistencies noted above in the Logbook. Relying on this unsubstantiated basis, he interprets the absence of N.F. Vatutin from the 11 April meeting (who had no possibility of attending) as a manifestation of I.V. Stalin's greater trust in K.K. Rokossovsky's opinion than in that of the Commander-in-Chief of the Voronezh Front.[21] In fact, a number of eyewitnesses have taken note of the Supreme Commander's more focused attention to Konstantin Konstantinovich, especially after Stalingrad.[22] An incident with the German's recapture of Zhitomir in December 1943 also confirms this version, when Stalin sent Rokossovsky to Vatutin with ambiguous authority – whether to check on him and relieve him, or to assist him as a comrade and commander of a an adjacent *front*.[23]

However, before making such assumptions as the ones used by Sokolov, it is necessary to look into the chronology of the events in detail, or else they will seem unconvincing, and second, one should not attach too much significance to the influence of I.V. Stalin's emotions on strategic questions in general, or in this question in particular. I will risk venturing that if in fact Rokossovsky was present at the 11 April meeting in the Kremlin, then likely this was due to a specifically "personal" matter. At this time Stalin was extremely preoccupied with the Moscow axis. We find confirmation of this in the memoirs of the veterans of those events, including G.K. Zhukov.[24] Therefore, he might have wanted to find out specifically how sound it would be to connect the defense of the capital with the questions regarding the future operation at Kursk. Indeed, K.K. Rokossovsky's Central Front would have to play one of the key roles in either case. Yet neither *front* commanders-in-chief could take part in preparing and making preliminary decisions of a strategic nature. This was a prerogative of *Stavka* members and State

---

again became the First Deputy Chief of the General Staff. In 1955, Antonov became the Chief of Staff of the Warsaw Pact of forces. He passed away in Moscow on 18 June 1962.
21 Solov'ev, B.G., *Rokossovsky* (Moscow: Molodaia gvardiia, 2010), pp. 255-256.
22 Chuev, F., *Soldaty imperii* [*Soldiers of the empire*] (Moscow: KOVCHEG, 1998), p. 340.
23 Rokossovsky, *Soldatskii dolg* [*A Soldier's duty*] (Moscow, 19997), pp. 304-305.
24 Zhukov, *Vospominaniia i razmyshleniia*, Vol. 3 (Moscow: Novosti, 1990), p. 22.

Defense Committee members, which N.F. Vatutin and K.K. Rokossovsky[25] never were, unlike G.K. Zhukov and A.M. Vasilevsky. If to adhere to B.V. Sokolov's logic, then it is clear from the Logbook that in the three months prior to the Battle of Kursk, both *front* commanders-in-chief each visited the Supreme Commander twice. In so doing, each of them was summoned to these meetings for a very important matter, but only one which was strictly within their competence – with accounts on the status of their *front*'s troops and proposals for their use; Vatutin – on 25 April and 28 June, and Rokossovsky – on 11 April (?) and 28 April.

As concerns the question "Was K.K. Rokossovsky's opinion more authoritative to I.V. Stalin than N.F. Vatutin's?", it provides little to the understanding of both the history of the entire war and the concrete events of the spring of 1943. The Supreme Commander-in-Chief made strategic decisions on the basis of a complex analysis of all incoming information on the basis of military and political realities, not the subjective assessments of separate commanders, even those stellar commanders that he personally liked. G.K. Zhukov wrote, "In general, I.V. Stalin never discussed the conception of an entire campaign with the *front* commanders. He limited the discussion to just one specific operation of a *front* or group of *fronts*."[26] Both the transfer of K.K. Rokossovsky from the 1st Belorussian Front in the autumn of 1944 and the decision to adopt a strategic defense at Kursk are evidence of this. After all, initially, in the first days of April, the Central Front leadership was proposing active operations, but the *Stavka* nevertheless opted to defend. Later, in May and June, after the Voronezh Front had received additional forces, N.F. Vatutin also proposed not to wait for the enemy's attack, but to go on the offensive instead. However, the first to express such a thought was his neighbor, the headquarters of Rokossovsky's Central Front, although at this moment hardly any attention has been given to this in domestic historiography, because it is hardly compatible with the persisting belief in our society that Rokossovsky fought better at Kursk than did Vatutin. In an internal memo sent by the Central Front to the General Staff on 10 April 1943, there was the following proposal: "In

---

25   Rokossovsky, Konstantin Konstantinovich (1896-1968), Marshal of the Soviet Union (1944), Marshal of Poland (1949). A veteran of the Russian Civil War. Being the commander of the 5th Cavalry Corps, he was arrested in August 1937, but rehabilitated in March 1940. He met the Great Patriotic War in the post of commander of the 9th Mechanized Corps, then headed the Western Front's 4th Army for a short time. In the Battle of Moscow, Rokossovsky commanded the 16th Army. Between July and September 1942, Rokossovsky was Commander-in-Chief of the Briansk Front, and between September 1942 and February 1943, he commanded the Don Front, which conducted the liquidation of Paulus' encircled grouping at Stalingrad. On 4 February 1943, the Don Front became transformed into the Central Front and was deployed west and north of Kursk. At the end of March 1943, after an unsuccessful offensive toward Briansk, Rokossovsky's troops took up a defense on the northern face of the Kursk bulge. In the period of the springtime operational pause, he personally did a lot of organizational work for the planning and preparation of the Battle of Kursk. Between 5 and 12 July 1943, the Central Front under his command successfully repulsed the Ninth Army's offensive under the plan of Citadel, before launching a counteroffensive on 15 July 1943 with the objective of eliminating the Orel salient. For his skill demonstrated in the course of the Kursk defensive operation, Rokossovsky was deemed worthy of the Order of Kutuzov 1st Class. In the autumn of 1944, Rokossovsky switch to the post of commander-in-chief of the 2nd Belorussian Front. On 24 June 1945, he commanded the Victory Parade on Red Square in Moscow. For his enormous contribution in the defeat of the German aggressors, he was awarded the highest commander's Order of Victory (No. 5). From 1949 to 1956, he served as Poland's Minister of Defense. Between 1956 and 1962, he was the USSR Deputy Minister of Defense. Rokossovsky discussed his role in the Battle of Kursk in his memoirs, *Soldatskii dolg*.
26   Zhukov, *Vospominaniia i razmyshleniia*, p. 180.

the circumstances of the existing situation, the following measures should be considered viable: to destroy the enemy's Orel grouping through the joint efforts of the Western, Briansk and Central Fronts, thereby depriving him of the possibility of launching an attack out of the Orel area through Livny toward Kastornoe; to take the Mtsensk – Orel – Kursk railroad, which is vitally important for us; and to deprive the enemy of the possibility to use the Briansk network of railroads and graded roads."[27]

Thus, in essence the Central Front command was proposing to implement in a truncated form the February – March 1943 operation on the Briansk axis that had failed. This document was not signed by K.K. Rokossovsky, but by his chief of staff Lieutenant General M.S. Malinin[28]. However, Rokossovsky, judging from everything, was in agreement with his chief of staff's position, because never once anywhere did he speak out against it, nor did M.S. Malinin have the right to send such a document to the *Stavka* without the knowledge of the Central Front Commander-in-Chief. After all, Moscow was requesting not the point of view of the chief of staff alone, but the collective opinion of the Front's Military Council. Therefore, in my view, the Supreme Commander's relative trust in K.K. Rokossovsky and N.F. Vatutin when preparing for the Battle of Kursk is a contrived notion, and only someone distant from a deep understanding of the events of those time could deliver it to a wide audience and aim it at the lack of erudition of a reader.

The work on the plan for the defensive operation in the Kursk area proceeded in parallel with the German planning of Operation Citadel, and several of their moments coincided within a day of each other. In addition, just like in Germany's leadership, the Soviet command initially

---

27   TsAMO RF, F.233, Op.2307, D.3, l. 33.
28   Malinin, Mikhail Sergeevich (1899-1960), General of the Army (1953), Hero of the Soviet Union (1945), In the Red Army from 1919 and a veteran of the Russian Civil War and the Winter War with Finland. In April 1940 Malinin became the chief of staff of the 7th Mechanized Corps (Moscow Military District). In the first days of the war, the corps was shifted to the Western Front, where it took part in the heavy fighting in Belorussia, and was eventually encircled. Colonel M.S. Malinin together with the corps headquarters and a significant number of the men came out of the pocket in the Smolensk area, whereupon he was appointed chief of staff of the Western Front's Iartsevo grouping commanded by Major General K.K. Rokossovsky. From this time on, Malinin became Rokossovsky's right-hand man and close friend. On 19 August 1941, Malinin became the chief of staff of Western Front's 16th Army, which performed well in the Battle of Moscow. After K.K. Rokossovsky assumed command of the Briansk Front, Major General M.S. Malinin became his chief of staff. On 30 August 1942 with K.K. Rokossovsky's appointment as commander-in-chief of the Don Front, Malinin assumed an analogous post in his headquarters. After the Don Front was transformed into the Central Front in February 1943, he remained Rokossovsky's chief of staff. Malinin took part in the planning and conducting of the offensive toward Briansk in February-March 1943 in this post. In April to July 1943, he was one of the key organizers of the successful defense of the Central Front's troops in the course of the Battle of Kursk on the northern face of the Kursk bulge, even though he personally believed that at Kursk the Red Army should be the first to go on the offensive. He laid out this point of view in the documents submitted to the *Stavka* in April 1943. Malinin was considered a fine organizer and hard-bitten leader, although he never held an independent command post (as the commander of an army or *front*). For the successful conducting of the Kursk defensive operation, he was deemed worthy of the Order of the Red Star. In the autumn of 1944, K.K. Rokossovsky assumed command of the 2nd Belorussian Front and for the first time in the war he parted from his headquarters. Working now under the command of Marshal of the Soviet Union G.K. Zhukov, who took over the *front*, M.S. Malinin distinguished himself in the Vistula to Oder operation and the Berlin offensive.

did not have a single viewpoint regarding whether to take the offensive first or whether it would be better to adopt a defensive posture. In connection with this, I.V. Stalin's organizational capabilities should be given due credit, and his ability to listen to specialists and heed them, though he did not accept all of the important and well-based proposals of the military chiefs. Even so, thanks to this flexibility of thought, at the very least by the spring of 1943, he managed to arrange more clear-cut and effective work with his generals and People's Commissars (who took direct part in supporting the acting army), unlike Hitler, and to a greater degree based it on the realities of the operational situation as opposed to the Führer's tendency to rely upon assumptions, sycophants and beliefs when conducting it. Many of those who were alongside Stalin, including those who later became his fierce opponents, note the positive changes that took place in him as the Supreme Commander-in-Chief while preparing for the Battle of Kursk. Wrote A.I. Mikoyan:

> Without touching upon here those aspects of Stalin's activity that were subsequently properly condemned by our Party, it must be said that Stalin during the course of the war, and especially at its outset, on the whole held to a correct political line, as I thought back then and as I think now. He was much less capricious and arbitrary, which began to appear when our military affairs turned for the better and before he simply became too full of himself. To be sure, there were also shameful episodes at the start of the war connected with stubbornness and the unwillingness to consider genuine facts. For example, there was the categorical ban against withdrawing the entire army in Ukraine from the developing pocket, even though Khrushchev and Bagramian kept insisting on this. I recall that he did not even go to the telephone when Khrushchev called about this question, and asked Malenkov to respond. This seemed to me to be impossible highhandedness. As a result, an entire army fell into a cauldron, and the Germans soon took Khar'kov, and then broke through toward the Volga. However, such never had its place over the history of the Steppe Front.[29]

N.S. Khrushchev repeated him: "He was already feeling differently and now showing self-assurance. I would even say that at this time it was even pleasant to report to him, unlike it had been a year previously. He was also showing a more correct understanding of the situation and a more proper attitude toward the questions brought up by the *fronts*."[30] G.K. Zhukov recalled:

> After I.V. Stalin's death, the story appeared that he exclusively made all the military-strategic decisions. This is not at all the case. If questions were reported to the Supreme Commander based on knowledge of the matter, he took them into his attention. Indeed, I know cases when he rejected his own opinion and previous decisions. Such was the case in particular at the start of many operations.[31]

---

29 Mikoyan, *Tak bylo*, p. 350.
30 Khrushchev, N.S., *Vospominaniia: Izbrannye fragment* [*Recollections: Selected fragments*] (Moscow: Vagrius, 1997), p. 148.
31 Zhukov, *Vospominaniia i razmyshleniia*, Vol. 3, p. 14.

Erich von Manstein also indicated in his memoirs that by this time, the Soviet command when resolving operational matters was not so rigidly tied to political or military-economic frameworks of thought.³² It is hard to figure out on what the Field Marshal was basing this opinion, but as we will see ahead, the results of the work of the Soviet military and political leadership in the spring and summer of 1943 would prove to be substantially more productive than the German work, and the personal contribution of the top public officials more weighty. Therefore, scholars who reject or keep silent about this fact are deliberately distorting the historical truth. Unfortunately, today there are more than a few such authors.

Let us now return to the events of 12 April 1943. At mid-day, the Military Council of the Voronezh Front gave a briefing to the *Stavka*. N.F. Vatutin, while presenting a thorough analysis of the operational situation and the potential threats, nevertheless declined to offer any concrete proposals regarding the ways and methods to foil the enemy's anticipated offensive. He provided a clear point of view only regarding the Germans' general plans in the nearest future: "The enemy's intention consists in launching concentric attacks out of the Belgorod area to the northeast and out of the Orel area to the southeast with the objective of encircling our forces positioned to the west of the Belgorod – Kursk line. Subsequently, an enemy attack is expected in the southeastern direction into the flank and rear of the Southwestern Front."³³

So, by the start of the conference, the majority of the key figures in the *Stavka* leadership, the General Staff and of the *fronts* were fully sharing G.K. Zhukov's valid assessment, when he wrote:

> In the first stage the enemy … launches an attack … outflanking Kursk from the northeast and … southeast … The enemy will strive … to encircle our 13th, 70th, 65th, 38th, 40th and 21st Armies. The final objective of this stage might be the enemy's emergence on the Korocha River – Korocha – Staryi and Novyi Oskol line … He will rely mainly on his tank divisions and aviation.³⁴

Thus, the Soviet command already in the first phase of planning had accurately determined Citadel's objective (the destruction of the armies defending the Kursk salient), and the main tools for achieving this (armor and aircraft).

The meeting in the Kremlin began late in the evening; in addition to Stalin, it included G.K. Zhukov, A.M. Vasilevsky and his deputy, and General of the Army A.I. Antonov, who headed the Operations Department. All three were key figures in the military leadership, and the Supreme Commander entrusted only this narrow circle of military chiefs to prepare the entire array of materials for the final decision about the summer campaign. This shows I.V. Stalin's highest faith in these men, and his desire to prevent any leaks of information regarding a strategic topic.

G.K. Zhukov writes that the Supreme Commander listened to all of the Marshals' presentations very attentively. After a thorough and careful analysis, those present came to the opinion that the conclusion offered by Zhukhov in his report from 8 April was the correct one: "I believe it is

---

32   Manstein, *Uteriannye pobedy*, p. 545.
33   Glantz, D. and House, J., *Kurskaia bitva: Reshaiushchii povorotnyi punkt vtoroi mirovoi voiny* [*Battle of Kursk: Decisive turning point of the Second World War*] (Moscow: Astrel', 2006), p. 388.
34   Zhukov, *Vospominaniia i razmyshleniia*, Vol. 3, p. 14.

inadvisable for our forces to go on the offensive in the coming days with the aim of preempting the enemy."[35] In their opinion, it should become the basis for the development of the operational plan. During the further discussion, I.V. Stalin showed particular apprehension over only two problems: Whether or not the Soviet forces would be able to withstand the enemy's concentrated attack, and whether or not they would succeed in reliably protecting the Moscow direction. The thought of the previous failures was plainly giving him no peace, and he insistently strove to prevent any possibility of a repeat of the tragedies of 1941 and 1942. Both Marshal Zhukov and Marshal Vasilevsky replied with conviction. Wrote Vasilevsky, "This was not 1941 ... The Red Army had been tempered in battles and had acquired enormous combat experience ... Now the fascists were already fearing us. Indecision and doubt had been cast aside."[36]

It is impossible to agree with the assertion that the Soviet political and military leadership already in April 1943 had acquired full confidence that the Red Army would be able to answer successfully the questions that troubled I.V. Stalin. Doubts and vacillations were seen both in May and June 1943. Indeed, they were being fueled as well by the recent tragic experience of 1941 and 1943, as well by certain intelligence information, which although was not considered substantiated, together with Moscow's fully understandable alarm on the matter of the unclear prospects of the start of the summer campaign, created considerable stress in the *Stavka* of the Supreme High Command.

However, let us return to the conference in the Kremlin. As a result of the lengthy, detailed consideration of the problem, the participants came to three fundamental decisions, which to a large extent predetermined our victory in the Battle of Kursk.

First, they settled on the Kursk bulge as the most likely sector of the Soviet-German front for the Germans' possible summer offensive. Therefore, it was precisely here that they expected the main events in the nearest future to unfold and decided to focus all their efforts. The plan was to foil the enemy's scheme, inflict heavy losses on the attacking German troops, and in the future go over to a decisive offensive in this same area.

Second, the participants took the preliminary decision to adopt a deliberate defense. In connection with this, the *Stavka* instructed the command staffs of the Voronezh and Central Fronts to rebuild the forces' combat capabilities within the shortest period of time; to set about planning the general Kursk strategic defensive operation between the two *fronts*; to initiate the construction of a powerful field defense with an elaborate, saturated system of anti-tank artificial obstacles and emplacements, with consideration for the fact that the Germans would choose most likely armored vehicles and aircraft as their main means for a breakthrough. In order to reduce the capabilities of the Luftwaffe's formations, it was recognized as useful to prepare and launch powerful strikes by the *fronts'* air forces against enemy airfields and base complexes, stockpiles of supplies in the Kursk area, and also railroad lines that were feeding the German army groups with supplies of fuel and ammunition.

Third, they decided to initiate planning for the summer campaign as a whole, and to include as a key addition to the defensive operation the launching of a general strategic offensive by the Red Army in Ukraine and Belorussia. In addition to the Voronezh and Central Fronts, the headquarters of the Western, Briansk and Southwestern Fronts should be included in this

---

35   Ibid., p. 15.
36   Vasilevsky, *Delo vsei zhizni*, Vol. 2, p. 17.

process. As a result, in the course of the combat operations in the summer period, the follow-on offensive would liberate the eastern regions of Belorussia, the entire area of Ukraine east of the Dnepr River and the Taman peninsula, thereby creating the conditions for completely clearing the aggressors out of the country by the end of the year. In addition, even before the conference on 12 April 1943, the *Stavka* had considered it expedient within the framework of the preparations for the summer campaign to issue orders to get work going quickly to increase the trafficability of the railroads; to complete the formation of the Reserve Front by the end of April; to overhaul the entire system of military intelligence with the aim of improving its effectiveness (I.V. Stalin's order from 19 April 1943 became the result of this); and to preserve the secrecy veiling the entire array of preparatory measures for the forthcoming operations.

Wrote A.M. Vasilevsky, "When talking about the plan for the Battle of Kursk, I want to emphasize two aspects. First, that this plan was at the heart of the general strategic plan adopted by the *Stavka* for the summer and autumn campaign of 1943; second, that the highest organs of the strategic leadership – the *Stavka* of the Supreme High Command and the General Staff – played the decisive role in working out this plan."[37]

In conversations with me, certain foreign historians have offered a novel argument that essentially echoes von Manstein's point of view, that after the failures of the Soviet forces in Ukraine in March 1943, the Wehrmacht had temporarily seized the initiative, so Moscow, by adopting a premeditated defense, was supposedly acknowledging this fact. I consider this position to be unjustified. The decision taken on 12 April 1943 did not signify the Soviet side's loss of the initiative. At this moment the USSR was in possession of far greater potential than Germany, and it is extremely important to see that the Soviet command had already learned to use this in comparison with the initial stage of the war. The Red Army had a numerical advantage in almost every indicator of combat strength. The decision was not an obligatory step, but a calculation toward a future objective. By going over to the defensive, the *Stavka* was only striving to conserve strength and to create the most favorable conditions for the soonest and complete liberation of the country's occupied territory.

In addition, it was acknowledged at the meeting that if the Germans would substantially dawdle with the start of their offensive, then the Red Army should be first to initiate active operations, bypassing the planned defensive phase connected with waiting for the enemy's attack toward Kursk. The participants instructed the General Staff to familiarize the command staffs of the five *fronts* mentioned above with the *Stavka*'s overall plan, and to issue orders to each of them to devise offensive operations with regard for the overall objectives and tasks of the summer campaign. For its part, Moscow also undertook a number of important steps in order to facilitate and to increase the effectiveness of the troops' combat work. For example, on this same day the "tools" of the *front* commands when implementing offensive tasks were significantly expanded; I.V. Stalin signed the State Defense Committee's Resolution No.3164ss regarding the creation of four breakthrough artillery corps and eight heavy cannon brigades. Only one of the artillery corps, the 4th Breakthrough Artillery Corps, was assigned to the *fronts* that were holding the Kursk salient –Rokossovsky's Central Front. The decision about subordinating the new artillery corps to the Central and Briansk Fronts was based in the first place upon their proximity to the capital and the strength of the enemy's defenses. The artillery was being viewed

---

37 Ibid., p. 18.

as an important element in the system of defenses covering the Moscow direction, in the event that the enemy attacked out of the Orel area to the north, and simultaneously as a reinforcement of the forces planned for eliminating the Orel salient. Thereby the *Stavka* was attempting to take into account the woeful experience of a number of previous, unsuccessful offensives around Viaz'ma and to provide the *fronts* with a powerful means for breaking through the casemated and well-developed defenses that the Germans had been creating here for more than a year. The elimination of the German Orel grouping was strictly tied to the Kursk defensive operation of the Central and Voronezh Fronts. So Rokossovsky's neighbor, the Commander-in-Chief of the Briansk Front, also received two of the breakthrough artillery corps, the 2nd and 7th. It was being contemplated that they would remain under the Briansk Front's control right up to the start of the Orel operation, at which point the 7th Breakthrough Artillery Corps would be sent to the southern side of the Kursk bulge in order to pulverize the enemy's lines immediately prior to the start of the offensive toward Khar'kov and on into Ukraine. However, these plans weren't fully realized; by the end of July, the Voronezh Front had not received both of the breakthrough artillery corps, but only a portion of their divisions. On the other hand, by 5 July 1943 the 4th Breakthrough Artillery Corps was already subordinate to K.K. Rokossovsky and ready for combat. It would play a very important role in the defeat of Citadel and then render substantial assistance to his forces when launching the counteroffensive, even though by this time its brigades, especially the howitzer brigades, had suffered conspicuous losses.

Finally, at the meeting in the Kremlin on 12 April 1943, the participants finally determined the assembly areas for the strategic reserves. A week before this, on 6 April, the decision about the introduction of a totally new organizational form of forces on a single axis – the Reserve Front – was adopted and formalized.[38] The plan was to include 50 percent of all forces directly subordinate to the *Stavka* of the Supreme High Command. Somewhat later, the Reserve Front became the Steppe Military District, and then the Steppe Front. It was planned to form the headquarters of the Steppe Front on the basis of the field command of the 41st Army, including in its composition six combined-arms armies (the 2nd Reserve, 24th, 53rd, 66th, 47th and 46th), one air army (the 5th Air Army), and one tank army (the 5th Guards Tank Army), as well as six tank corps (the 1st Guards, 3rd Guards, 4th Guards, 3rd, 10th and 18th) and two mechanized corps (the 1st and 5th). In addition, five cavalry corps (the 2nd, 3rd, 5th, 6th and 7th) would be simultaneously transferred to it on 27 April, after which it would become the largest and most powerful amalgamation of armies and corps in the Red Army. Of the seven *fronts* that would take part in the Battle of Kursk and the following Operation "Polkovodets Rumiantsev", only two – the Steppe and Briansk Fronts – would possess cavalry corps, while only the cavalry divisions of the latter *front* would take direct part in the fighting. The territory of the Steppe Military District amounted to 102,000 square kilometers, centered around Voronezh.

The District's forces would be fully deployed in May along the Livny – Staryi Oskol – Korocha line. S.M. Shtemenko recalled: "I.V. Stalin believed that in any case, the Steppe Military District need to be positioned in advance on the central axis in the rear of the acting *fronts*, having in mind the possibility of using it as well in the defensive phase of the operation, if by that time the situation called for this."[39] At the end of June 1943, the Supreme Commander would delineate

---

38 Russkii arkhiv, *Stavka Verkhovnogo Glavnokomandovaniia: Dokumenty i materialy 1943*, (Moscow: TERRA, 1999), pp. 114, 115.
39 Shtemenko, *Generalnyi shtab v gody voiny*, p. 156.

more specific possible tasks for the District in the defensive phase of the Battle of Kursk in a conversation with its new commander-in-chief, Colonel General I.S. Konev:

> Plainly, a very large battle is looming, and it is in the cards for the Steppe Front to play a major role in this battle. This means that if the enemy breaks through our defenses, the Front will have to create a shock grouping, launch a powerful counterblow, destroy the attacking enemy, and then go on the counteroffensive. When readying the troops for these active operations, it is necessary now to bring the entire sector of the Steppe Front into a defensive stance ... Stalin brought my attention to the fact that both directions, the Orel and the Belgorod, would be equally important.[40]

However, this would be later; in the second stage of preparations, two weeks after the meeting in the Kremlin, on 23 April, the *Stavka* sent the Steppe Military District's command Directive No.30107, which determined the tasks for the nearest future:

> 1. In the period of bringing the Steppe Military District's forces up to strength, simultaneously with the tasks of combat training, place the following tasks on the District's troops:
>   a) In case the enemy goes on the offensive before the District's forces are set to be ready, keep in view to screen the following directions strongly:
>   1. Livny, Elets, Ranenburg;
>   2. Shshigry, Kastornoe, Voronezh;
>   3. Valuiki, Alekseevka, Liski;
>   4. Roven'ki, Rossosh', Pavlovsk;
>   5. Starobel'sk, Kantemirovka, Boguchar and the Chertkovo – Millerovo area.
>   The District commander is accordingly to organize within the force grouping the thorough study of these directions and the lines possible for deployment by the commanders of the formations and units and their headquarters staffs;
>   b) Take up, study and prepare a line along the Don River's left banks for defense: Voeikovo, Lebedian', Zadonsk, Voronezh, Liski, Pavlovsk, Boguchar. The line is to be ready by 15 June 1943;
>   c) Reconnoiter a defensive belt along the Efremov, Izmalkovo, Chernova, Borki, Izbishche, Rep'evka, Alekseevka, Roven'ki, Belovodsk, Diatkino Station, Kamensk line as far as the Severskii Donets with the aim of determining the condition of the defensive works present along it, and the correctness of choosing this line in accordance with the terrain conditions. Pay particular attention to the utilization of commanding heights with the aim of creating the most advantageous conditions for observation and the system of fire.[41]

Nevertheless, Stalin placed particular emphasis in the document on what he considered to be the Steppe Military District's primary objective, for which it had been originally created – the

---

40 *Znamia*, No. 12 (1987), p. 93.
41 Russkii arkhiv, *Stavka Verkhovnogo Glavnokomandovaniia: Dokumenty i materialy 1943*, Vol. 16 (5-3) (Moscow, 1997), p. 127.

liberation of Ukraine. Therefore, in the second part the *Stavka* demanded that the Steppe Military District immediately to initiate the training the troops for this offensive:

> The troops, headquarters staffs and commanders of the formations are to prepare primarily for offensive fighting and an operation to break through the enemy's defensive belt, as well as to deliver powerful counterblows by our forces; for the rapid fortification of seized lines; to repulse enemy counterattacks; to counter massed attacks by tanks and aircraft; and for nighttime operations. Work out the questions regarding the command of the troops and the concerted action of types of troops in each phase of a battle and an operation particularly meticulously.
>
> Pay special attention to instruction in force-on-force training against the adversarial intelligence, having as the objective the uncovering of the system of defense and his grouping. Demand the compulsory and direct involvement of important representatives of headquarters at every level, up to the army and *front* inclusively, in probing the enemy, particularly on the most important directions.
>
> Conduct the training of staff, as a rule, incessantly and over many days, with means of signals and intelligence.
>
> Conduct the training with the troops from the battalion and above in the course of several days, working out a number of questions between themselves while making the training conditions and the off-duty life of the troops as close as possible to combat activity.[42]

Considering Stalin's demand to cover the Moscow direction securely, the decision was made to position the rest of the reserves behind the right flank of the Briansk Front in the Kaluga – Tula – Efremov area. However, according to the recollections of highly-posted generals who were veterans of those events, already in the beginning of April there were no doubts in Moscow or in the *fronts* that the main events in the forthcoming campaign would unfold in the sectors of the Central and Voronezh Fronts. This confidence only rose with each passing day. Nevertheless, in the early stage of the elaboration of the Kursk defensive operation, especially during the visits to Rokossovsky's and Vatutin's troops, G.K. Zhukov became convinced that the Germans might also launch a powerful attack at the boundary between the Voronezh and Southwestern Fronts, approximately in the same place where their offensive had started in the summer of 1942. Colonel General R.Ia. Malinovsky, who at the time was commanding the Southwestern Front and who on 28 April 1943 became a General of the Army, shared Marshal Zhukov's opinion. Both men persistently maintained this point of view right up to the start of the Battle of Kursk. Thus, as a measure of insurance, the *Stavka* assembled the 5th Guards Tank Army and a number of other reserve formations in the Liski area, behind the boundary between these two *fronts*, and on the extreme left flank of the Voronezh Front's 7th Guards Army, and at G.K. Zhukov's behest, the defenses would be constructed in two echelons, so that in the second army-level defensive belt, two full-strength rifle division would be positioned in line behind another full-strength rifle division that would be deployed in the main defensive belt.

42 Ibid.

This is one of the facts that plainly show that in the course of planning for the summer campaign, not only the Supreme Commander recalled the mistakes of the previous year, but also his deputy, who in addition also strove to take into account the tragic experience of the summer of 1942. In addition, likely because of his high level of professional intuition, G.K. Zhukov had a more accurate perception of the enemy's intentions than did I.V. Stalin. In his opinion, the Izium salient, because of the forces of the Southwestern Front that were positioned in it, although standing in no comparison with Kursk salient, presented a serious threat to Army Group South, which could not help but shackle the initiative of its command staff. Accordingly, it was highly likely that it would attempt to liquidate this bridgehead across the Donets River, and in general this might happen during the preparations for Citadel. I will remind the reader that given a successful development of the offensive toward Kursk, Hitler noted in his Operational Order No. 6 to be ready to launch an attack to the southeast (a version of the Panther plan), just as G.K. Zhukov was in fact assuming. G.K. Zhukov wrote:

> Thus, already in the middle of April, a preliminary decision about a pre-meditated defense had been made by the *Stavka*. To be sure, we returned to this question more than once, and a final decision about an intentional defense was taken by the *Stavka* in early June 1943. At this time, for all intents and purposes it had already become known that the enemy intended to launch a powerful attack against the Voronezh and Central Fronts with the participation of a large armored grouping and the use of the latest Tiger and Panther tanks and the Ferdinand self-propelled gun.[43]

As unclassified documents reveal today, the Red Army was completely ready to go on the offensive first already in May 1943, which by the way was something that the Germans greatly apprehended. However, Moscow choose a different path. It must be acknowledged that when making this decision, the *Stavka* members showed a certain amount of courage, since over the preceding 20 months of the war in the course of strategic operations, the Soviet command had repeatedly failed to prevent a breakthrough of its field defenses by Wehrmacht panzer wedges. In the best case the enemy had been stopped in the operational depth by hastily formed new armies and even *fronts*. In the process, our troops would suffer appalling losses, while the adversary would take control of a large amount of territory. The *Stavka* could no longer allow such a thing to happen again. The Kursk bulge was being held by two *fronts*, which numbered a total of more than 1,000,000 men, and the destruction of such a powerful grouping would have catastrophic consequences.

In 1999, in a group discussion that I attended, the Doctor of History Colonel F.D. Sverdlov, who back in early 1960 had happened to hear a presentation by K.K. Rokossovsky in the Frunze Military Academy, recalled:

> The Marshal particularly emphasized that already on 28 April, during a discussion in the Kremlin of the Front's plan of defense, I.V. Stalin set a task before its leadership: By all means, to prevent a deep penetration by the German armored groupings into the defenses, to contain them within the tactical zone, and to bleed their assault formations

---

43 Zhukov, *Vospominaniia i razmyshleniia*, Vol. 3, p. 23.

– the panzer and motorized divisions – white. The Voronezh Front's Military Council received the same task in the Kremlin from the Supreme Commander a bit earlier [on 25 April 1943].[44]

Already after the events at Kursk, in the autumn of 1943 Stalin laid out the main reasons that compelled him to take the decision to adopt a pre-meditated defense in a conversation with the commander of the 5th Guards Tank Army Colonel General P.A. Rotmistrov. This despite being aware beforehand that the acting Red Army was exponentially stronger numerically than the enemy in manpower and main types of armaments:

> Our infantry and artillery are very strong when on the defense and inflict heavy damage to the Nazi's attacking forces. In a maneuvering combat, however ... the infantry is not as strong. Our armored forces ... are fully able to conduct a battle of maneuver. However, in the conditions when the fascists had almost the same number of tanks as the Red Army, but possessed a numerical advantage in heavy tanks, a risk was unjustified.[45]

I will note that the Wehrmacht's panzer and panzergrenadier divisions were the most important means not only for an offensive, but also when on the defensive (for launching counterattacks). Accordingly, the main task that the *Stavka* set for its troops in the Kursk area in the first stage of the battle (just like that of the Army Group South command when planning Citadel) was the annihilation of the German mobile formations in the previously prepared army-level defensive belts, or at least inflicting the heaviest possible losses to them, in order to deprive the enemy command of a critical instrument for foiling the Red Army's upcoming offensive in Ukraine and Belorussia.

One of the important and extremely murky questions in the history of the Battle of Kursk is the activity of the Soviet intelligence organs to reveal Berlin's idea in the stage of discussing the Citadel plan, as well as their contribution to illuminating the preparations by the Germany Army for an attack toward Kursk in the spring of 1943 and its start date. As is known, not a single scout or intelligence officer can win a battle or war, but depending on their degree of effectiveness, as a rule they can render a large amount of assistance to this. Even so, recently one often encounters publications, in which certain members of the domestic intelligence services assert that a key role in the victory at Kursk belonged precisely to the Soviet intelligence, because supposedly all of the colossal work of the USSR's political and military leadership and the Red Army when devising and preparing for the Kursk defensive operation began only after the information from the intelligence service in the spring of 1943 had been conclusively checked and verified. For example, Lieutenant General V.A. Kirpichenko wrote:

> John Cairncross at the end of April, two and a half months before the start of the Battle of Kursk, transmitted to Moscow the complete information that the German offensive would begin in July. This was a decoded telegram to Berlin sent by the German General

---

44 Author's personal notes.
45 Rotmistrov, P.A., *Vremia i tanki* [*Time and tanks*] (Moscow: Voenizdat, 1972), p. 162.

von Weichs, who was preparing the German offensive in the south of the Kursk bulge ... the information was checked and re-checked dozens and dozens of times! ... When it had been repeatedly confirmed, the rapid development of the plan for a premeditated defense was initiated.[46]

One comes across even more debatable assertions in the literature. For example, the former Chief of the NKGB [People's Commissariat of State Security]'s Fourth Department P.A. Sudoplatov wrote that our intelligence even had an effect on the repeated decision to postpone Operation Citadel.[47] A member of the foreign intelligence service Colonel Iu. Modin emphasized that "the Soviet victory in the great tank battle in the Kursk bulge at Prokhorovka in July 1943, when 2,000 tanks became locked in a bloody fight that continued for two days and nights, could be partially attributed to John Cairncross's credit."[48] However, the "facts" given by the aforementioned authors are unfortunately not confirmed by either documents or the events in the first half of 1943.

In Soviet historiography, this question has yet to be fully explored, primarily for objective reasons: by this time, the 50-year classification of archival documents, established by law, had not expired. Accordingly, there was nothing meaningful to discuss. In the works of domestic historians, therefore, the intelligence activity in March to June 1943 was treated superficially. This had somewhat of a reflection on the book by the leading Soviet specialists on the Battle of Kursk G.A. Koltunov and B.G. Solov'ev:

> At the assignment of the General Staff, the intelligence services did thorough work in the sectors of the Central, Voronezh and Southwestern Fronts. A task was given to the Intelligence Department and the Central Headquarters of the Partisan Movement – to reveal the presence and dispositions of reserves in the enemy's operational depth and the areas of assembly of the forces that had been transferred from the west. Already in the beginning of April, they managed to establish that the enemy was bringing up major forces for a large summer offensive to the area of the Kursk bulge. This could not but affect the decisions of the Soviet command and its plans.[49]

Indeed, with this statement the discussion of the matter ended. Next the authors turned to describing the process of reaching the decision regarding a pre-meditated defense.

Thus, approximately up until the first half of the 1980s, when examining this topic, the main attention was given to the description of the General Staff and the astute foresight of the Soviet commanders, and to a lesser extent – the combat work of the military intelligence organs and partisans; the work of strategic intelligence and its concrete results received virtually no

---

46 Bondarenko, A.Iu. and Efimov, N.N., *Tainye stranitsy Velikoi Otechestvennoi* [*Secret pages of the Great Patriotic War*] (Moscow, 2009), pp. 128-129. [Ed. note: John Cairncross was an intelligence officer and spy during the Second World War. As a Soviet double agent, he passed raw Tunny decrypts to the Soviet Union, which purportedly influenced the Battle of Kursk.]
47 Sudoplatov, P., *Pobeda v tainoi voine 1941-1945* [*Victory in the secret war 1941-1945*] (Moscow: OLMA-PRESS, 2005), p. 321.
48 Modin, Iu., *Sud'by razvedchikov: Moi kembridzhskie druz'ia* [*Fate of the intelligence agents: My Cambridge friends*] (Moscow: OLMA-PRESS, 1997), p. 167.
49 Koltunov and Solov'ev, *Kurskaia bitva*, p. 28.

analysis. For example, separate authors noted the important role played by NKVD member N.I. Kuznetsov in assembling valuable information regarding Citadel; he was operating under the assumed identity of Senior Lieutenant P. Siebert in occupied Soviet territory.[50] However, it is still difficult today to assess his activity as an intelligence agent. In the books *Eto bylo pod Rovno* [*It was at Rovno*] and *Sil'nye dukhom* [*Strong in spirit*], N.I. Kuznetsov's former commander Colonel D.N. Medvedev, who led the "Victors" partisan detachment, talked about Kuznetsov's conversation with Ukraine's Reichscommissar E. Koch, which took place on 31 May 1943, in the course of which Koch supposedly announced the big "surprise" that Hitler was preparing for the Bolsheviks at Kursk, and advised "Seibert" to return to his unit all the sooner.[51] These publications that describe these events were fiction, but in an introductory article the author emphasized that everything he wrote was based on fact.[52] Therefore, the information became widely used, including in academic literature.[53] P.A. Sudoplatov also confirmed that such a conversation had occurred and that N.I. Kuznetsov actually did pass the information regarding Kursk on to the Center.[54] However, in 1988 the well-known author and researcher of the history of Soviet intelligence T.K. Gladkov published an excerpt from Kuznetsov's report about that memorable meeting, but there was no mention of Kursk in it. In the conversation with E. Koch, the subject was totally based on the opinion of German servicemen "regarding the preparation for an offensive in the East."[55] No indication of the place or date is given. However, even if there had been mention of Kursk, at the moment this information would have yielded little to Moscow. It might only confirm what was already known: the Germans were preparing for a major offensive against the Central and Voronezh Fronts that were defending the Kursk salient.

Gradually, at the end of the Soviet era, articles began to appear in the open press about the active participation of strategic intelligence in readying the defensive operation. Finally, after the collapse of the Soviet Union, documents from the special services began to appear in academic circulation, memoirs of the former members began to be published, and books of research on the subject that contain important information began to come out in print. However, the fact that the archives with the necessary sources often belong to different agencies (for example, the TsAMO – to the Ministry of Defense; the special files of the NKVD and SMERSH military counter-intelligence agency – to the Federal Security Bureau; the documents regarding international matters – to the archive of the Ministry of Foreign Affairs; and the documents regarding internal affairs – to the Ministry of the Interior), each with its own rules, boundary lines and departmental regulations, which often slow and complicate the work of scholars, and greatly hampers the process of gathering the needed information. Nevertheless, relying on known materials that have been uncovered by the author, like the documents from the Central Archive of the Russian Federation's Ministry of Defense and the US National Archive, which have recently become accessible to Russian scholars, I will attempt to reproduce the process by

---

50 Lukin, A.A., and Gladkov, T.K., *Nikolai Kuznetsov* (Moscow: Molodaia gvardiia, 1971), p. 82.
51 Medvedev, D., *Eto bylo pod Rovno* [*It was at Rovno*] (Moscow: Pravda, 1987), p. 156; and Medvedev, D., *Sil'nye dukhom* [*Strong in spirit*] (Moscow: DOSAAF, 1984), p. 200.
52 Medvedev, *Sil'nye dukhom*, p. 5.
53 *Istoriia Vtoroi mirovoi voiny, 1939-1945* [*History of the Second World War, 1939-1945*] Vol. 7 (Moscow: Voenizdat, 1976), p. 115.
54 Sudoplatov, *Pobeda v tainoi voine*, p. 344.
55 Gladkov, T.K., *S mesta pokusheniia skrylsia* [*I absconded from the place of the assassination attempt*] (Moscow: Geia, 1998), p. 242.

which the main intelligence reports on the given subject arrived at the *Stavka* in chronological sequence, and based on the events that took place try to grasp whether or not it affected the decision-making of the Soviet command and to what extent Moscow might have used it when making key decisions during the preparation of the Battle of Kursk.

So, in March and early April 1943, the intelligence services had been given a task: to reveal the enemy's intentions once the ground hardened from the spring thaws; to determine the objectives and assignments; the forms of their implementation; and the assembly areas of the enemy's main assault groupings. A.M. Vasilevsky recalled: "The analysis of the information was indicating that it was precisely here [the Kursk bulge] that the fascist leadership was attempting to give a decisive battle. However, there was more to it than that; the assumptions needed confirmation by intelligence, since in the history of warfare, more than a few cases are known when the enemy attacks not where it was expected."[56] The first information about Berlin's plans in the Kursk area arrived in the *Stavka* from foreign agent sources in Switzerland controlled by the Intelligence Department of the General Staff on 16 March 1943, which was virtually right after the Germans recaptured Khar'kov and Hitler signed his Operational Order No. 5. A radio message from a resident in Bern, Sádor Rádo (code name "Dora"), observed, "The German High Command intends to use the strong, combat capable units that have been freed up after the shortening of the [Army Group] Center's lines for the recapture of Kursk."[57]

A message from this same source about a conference involving H. Goering with representatives of Germany's industries and the OKW, which arrived two days later on 18 March, indicated that Hitler's deputy was speaking about a plan to capture Kursk like it was an established fact:

> A conference just took place in the Hubertusstock Castle under the chairmanship of Goering with the participation of leading representatives of the OKW and the most important representatives of the German economy, led by Rechling and Pfleuger.
>
> Goering gave a report about the strategic, political and organizational plans of the German High Command. According to this report, the German High Command after the capture of Khar'kov and Kursk is expecting a new offensive by the Red Army, but only after a certain passage of time, in the course of which the German command hopes to be able to ensure the defense between the front and the Ostwall line in the necessary manner.
>
> Goering expressed confidence that the German command will succeed, thanks to the lack of agreement between the Anglo-Saxons and the USSR and will successfully overcome the critical period experienced by the German army up until the middle of April. After 15 April the shortening of the Eastern Front [the elimination of the Kursk salient, which had initially been planned for 27 March] and the results of "total mobilization" will allow once again the strengthening of the western and south European fronts with the army's strong formations and a Luftflotte, and the gradual return of the situation to normal there.[58]

---

56 Peskov, V., "Komandnaia tochka" ["Command post"], *Izvestiia*, 8 May 2008.
57 Lota, V., *Bez prava na oshibku* [*Without the right to make a mistake*] (Moscow: Molodaia gvardiia, 2005), p. 85.
58 Ibid., p. 86.

The information obtained from Switzerland on 22 March became the most detailed of all those that Moscow obtained prior to the conference in the Kremlin on 12 April (and that are known to us today). Dora's radio message continued:

> German aerial reconnaissance has established that Soviet forces in the Kursk area have been reinforced to a much greater degree than the Germans expected, and also that the construction of fortifications for creating the best conditions for putting the Soviet artillery into action has been going on around Kursk at an increased tempo, much more than was possible at Khar'kov.
> The German military command is accelerating in every possible way the massing of forces for launching an attack in the direction of Kursk. Troops and panzer units are being withdrawn from the Khar'kov area and are being readied for an offensive toward Kursk through Sumy to the north.
> Motorized divisions are located in a combat-ready condition as part of Group "Weichs" [sic] for the attack against Kursk.[59] The majority of the mobile reserves are still tied up in the Khar'kov area, and in connection with their heavy losses still cannot be transferred to a new area. Among these attacking reserves are the Panzergrenadier Divisions *Adolf Hitler*, *Das Reich*, and *Totenkopf*. Of these three divisions, only the *Totenkopf* Division is located at present in a combat-ready condition and can be transferred.[60]

On 3 April 1943, when Zhukov and Vasilevsky had already started work in the troops that were defending the Kursk bulge, another message arrived from Bern regarding the enemy's intentions, which confirmed the previously submitted information and expanded it: "The intention of the General Staff to cancel the offensive toward Kursk has been called off by Hitler and Goering, in connection with the fact that for diplomatic reasons, the government is obligated to regain all of the jumping-off positions for the summer offensive of last year."[61]

So far, there has been no success in finding all of the material from military intelligence on the given subject that was accumulating at this time in the *Stavka*. Only the report, "On the possible plans of the German command for the spring and summer of 1943", signed on 29 March 1943 by the chiefs of the General Staff's Department of Military Intelligence Department under Major General L.V. Ovianov, has emerged. This document is very interesting and important, since it enables us to see the prognosis of the Soviet Union's military intelligence regarding Berlin's ideas at the start of the planning of the summer campaign not through the interpretation of contemporary scholars, which are today a dime a dozen, but from the direct source.

In the opinion of the authors of this report, the German forces in the northern sector of the Soviet-German front would go over to the defense over this period of time. This was confirmed by the withdrawal of the forces of the Fourth and Ninth Armies on the Moscow axis by 100-200

---

59 This is a mistake. Army Group "B", which was being commanded by Feldmarschall M. von Weichs, had been smashed in February 1943, and at this time Felmarschall Erich von Manstein's Army Group South was operating in the south and southwest of the Eastern Front. M. von Weich's was von Manstein's deputy.
60 Lota, *Bez prava na oshibku*, pp. 86-87.
61 Ibid., p. 19.

kilometers. Instead, they would undertake active offensive operations "in the southern sector of the Eastern Front, along the Voronezh and Rostov operational directions."[62] Their main objective would be to shatter the defenses of the Red Army at its key link, and to seize the main roads to the west of the Don River that connect the central area of the USSR with the Caucasus. For this purpose, they might conduct an operation with "a limited objective, which is to say to achieve the maximal reduction of the Red Army's ability to resist by means of gradually knocking out manpower, weapons and equipment."[63] According to the information of intelligence specialists, two shock groups were already in the process of forming for this offensive: one around Orel (Second Panzer Army) and one around Khar'kov (the First and Fourth Panzer Army), and the latter grouping was intended to be the main one. Most likely, the main task of the operation was to be the encirclement of the Kursk (Central and Voronezh fronts) grouping or the Kupiansk (Southwestern Front) grouping of Soviet forces. In addition, the formation of a third grouping in the Donbas was not excluded, in the Slaviansk – Debal'tsevo area (First Panzer Army and the Sixth and Seventeenth Armies). According to the first offensive option, the Orel and Khar'kov groupings would launch an attack in the direction of Voronezh (with a distance of 200 km between the two groupings). The depth of the operation would be 200 km. According to the second alternative, the encirclement would take place in the Kupiansk salient, Khar'kov and Slaviansk area (with a distance of 200 km between the two groupings), in an overall direction of Boguchar. The depth of this operation would be 200-250 km.[64] In addition, the Second Panzer Army would be operating in a pinning direction (toward L'vov) along the Sevsk, Sumy, Tomarovka line (at the boundary between the Central and Voronezh Fronts). The depth of its offensive would be 300 km.

The report also paid attention to the date of the offensive and to how it might be possible to counter the enemy as well. In the opinion of the military intelligence officers, if the Wehrmacht did not attack in the next five to 10 days, which is to say between 3 and 8 April, then the offensive should be expected in the first half of May. The report stated that it might be possible to disrupt the German plans only by launching an attack against the Khar'kov grouping; otherwise to undertake active operations against the Orel grouping might allow the Wehrmacht command to be in a condition to execute its offensive plan. The report summary observed:

1. With the liquidation of the southern front [Army Groups A and B], the enemy is renouncing offensive attempts toward the Caucasus and in the direction of the bend in the Don River;
2. The operational assembly of the enemy armies indicates the enemy's strengthening opposite the Central Front's [Army Group Center] and Southern Front's right flank [Army Group South];
3. All of the enemy's panzer divisions on the Eastern Front, with the exception of just two or three, are concentrated in the southern sector, to the south of the Orel – Briansk line, which confirms the supposition that the enemy's main actively operating fronts will be opposite the Central Front's right flank and the enemy's entire Southern front.

---

62 TsAMO RF, F.15, Op.11600, D.1475, l. 4.
63 Ibid.
64 Ibid., l. 5obr.

Likely operational directions of an offensive by the forces of the enemy's [Army Group] South.
Two possible alternatives flow from the operational assembly of the German armies:
1. An offensive with the aim of reaching the Don River between Voronezh and Boguchar, the Kalitva River and the bend in the lower course of the Northern Donets River with the capture of Rostov.
2. An offensive toward Voronezh with a subsequent offensive in the direction to the northeast bypassing Moscow to the east …

   Both offensive options would pursue a common task: an attempt to encircle subsequently and destroy our Kursk and Kurgan groupings …

   An offensive by the Khar'kov grouping in cooperation with the Orel grouping in the direction of Voronezh …

   The 1943 offensive operation does not preclude the possibility of repeating the 1942 offensive operation with regard to the selection of the main axis of attack, with a sharp change of the direction in order to reach the operational rear areas of the defending side …[65]

It is impossible not to acknowledge the high degree of professionalism of the members of the Military Intelligence Department and their perspicacity. Even so, I will note that the document is uneven in quality and not all of the conclusions laid out in it were proven correct. Unquestionably, the assessments were accurate on the whole about where the main events would take place, and regarding separate important matters, such as the offensive's objective, the approximate sectors, and the distribution of the Wehrmacht's mobile formations across areas of the Soviet-German front. However, concerning Berlin's general concept for the 1943 campaign, then here the report was mistaken. The Soviet estimates makes the enemy's possible plan seem too ambitious. The reasons for this are likely the fact that at this moment the Soviet intelligence lacked information about Germany's real capabilities or how seriously the Wehrmacht's possibilities had declined after Stalingrad. In addition, I believe that the Wehrmacht's victories in 1941 and 1942 still continued to weigh upon the Department's leadership, so it plainly exaggerated the German capability to plan for a decisive lunge into the depths of the Soviet Union, toward the Don and even east of Moscow. The report's first point, which consists entirely of a quote from the Supreme Commander, shows this: "But they [the Germans – Leonid Olianov] are still sufficiently strong enough to organize a serious offensive on any one direction – Stalin." Even so, at the moment this information was sufficient for the *Stavka* to form a general impression about the adversary's possible plans and to focus its main attention and efforts on the Kursk bulge, as the key area where mostly likely the main events of this year would unfold.

Information on this subject was also flowing up other channels to the Soviet strategic intelligence service, and not only of a military nature, but also of a military-economic character; it was also testifying to the fact that Germany was preparing a major offensive, and it would likely take place in the Kursk area. If to rely on special report from the 1st Department of the NKGB's information office addressed to the People's Commissar of State Security, Commissar of State Security of the 1st Rank V.N. Merkulov on 27 May 1943, then the General Staff's

---

65 TsAMO RF, F.15, Op.11600, D.1475, l. 6 obr, 7.

intelligence network at this moment stood foremost in the delivery of valuable information regarding Citadel. The leadership of the NKGB believed a report from its spy network in London from 30 April and an intercepted telegram from Army Group South to Berlin from 25 April to be its first, critical information regarding Kursk.[66] However, for the sake of justice, it should be stressed that the NKGB already on 10 April had also received interesting information, in particular from the Chief of the Czech Military Intelligence Colonel F. Morawicz, who was cooperating with us. According to his evidence, the line that the Wehrmacht's formations intended to reach by the conclusion of the operation was being set as Voronezh. He maintained, "With this offensive, the Germans are pursuing the objective of disabling the Soviet army at the very least for the next six months."[67]

Nevertheless, even if to analyze just the information from military intelligence together with at least the reports from the Voronezh Front's Intelligence Department, in the first place they were much in accordance with each other, and secondly, they clearly showed the Germans' offensive intentions in the area of the Kursk salient with the aim of eliminating the bulge. Just one example: In March at first Voronezh Front's 313th Radio Battalion got a fix on all of the radio stations of the SS divisions that were mentioned in Dora's report, and on 20 March, after a combat action near Belgorod, units of the 52nd Guards Rifle Division acquired papers from dead SS soldiers of the SS Panzergrenadier Division *Totenkopf*. Thereby the information from two completely different sources regarding the transfer of this elite division to the southern face of the Kursk bulge was confirmed.

However, far from everything went so smoothly. For the command staff at any level and in every army, a decisive factor to answer the question as to whether or not to use the intelligence is the trust in the source of the information. In this respect, by April 1943 Moscow had serious problems with the Bern station. As was maintained after the war by the former chief of the 4th (Intelligence & Sabotage) Department of the NKVD-NKGB Lieutenant General P.A. Sudoplatov, the information from the *Red Orchestra*, one of the leaders of which was S. Rádo, "was of a secondary nature for us".[68] There were several reasons for this. One of the main suppliers of information on Germany was the Lucy spy ring run by a German emigrant Rudolf Roessler, who supposedly had a broad network of informants in the Reich itself; however, he persistently refused to provide their names and posts, explaining this by the desire to ensure the people's safety. Lucy's information, which passed to Dora for more than a year, was very interesting and kept arriving on the fly, which in wartime conditions is a large plus, but which also could not help but raise concerns. In radio messages the Center praised this source for his good work and kept funding Dora, but in reality, Moscow was not trusting his reports. A comparative analysis of the information from various sources, and primarily from members of the "Cambridge Five", led the Center to the conclusion that the British had inserted its own agent into Dora's network and through him was "pumping" filtered information to Moscow. P.A. Sudoplatov in his book recalls this double agent; he was the group's main radio operator under the code name "Jim":

---

66 "*Ognennaia duga*": *Kurskaia bitva cherez glazami Lubianka* [*Bulge of Fire: Battle of Kursk through the eyes of the Lubianka*] (Moscow: Moskovskie uchebniki i Kartolitografiia, 2003), p. 266.
67 Ibid.
68 Sudoplatov, *Pobeda v tainoi voine 1941-1945*, p. 305.

> In the spring of 1943, several weeks before the start of the Battle of Kursk, our station in London received from the Cambridge group information regarding the specific objectives of the planned German offensive under the code name "Citadel". The report from London contained more exhaustive and accurate information about the German offensive plans than had been received from Lucy in Geneva along the lines of military intelligence. It became clear to the leaders of the military intelligence and the NKVD that the British were sending us controlled batches of information through Dora, but at the same time they wanted us to defeat the German offensive.[69]

Whilst the evidence from Lucy was useful for the Soviet side as ancillary information, at any moment, however, the Allies might palm off "bogus stories" through it as well. This danger always existed, but in particular it began to rise in the early spring of 1943, when serious tensions arose in the relations between the Soviet Union and its allies. In March 1943, Great Britain and the United States of America halted the shipment of armaments and equipment via the northern convoys, which seriously complicated the work to rebuild the Red Army after the hard winter campaign. Moreover, petty intrigues began regarding the postponement of the opening of a Second Front, which had been promised by the leadership of the USA and England in August-September 1943, to a year later.

The analysis of archival sources and the memoirs of S. Rádo allowed certain Russian scholars to go even farther and to assert that the majority of the information regarding Germany had been prepared for Dora by the Reich's special services, and was skillfully fobbed off to Roessler's sources, in particular to "Werther", and it was possible that even he was himself an agent of the Reich's special services.[70] This judgement is not without justification. let us turn to one of S. Rádo's reports published in his book *Pod psevdonimom "Dora"* [*Under the pseudonym of "Dora"*], which Lucy had transmitted to him on 18 April 1943:

> The composition of the Fourth Panzer Army under the command of General Hoth: the 3rd, 25th and 27th Panzer Divisions and SS Division *Wiking*; the 12th, 26th and 103rd Motorized and Light Divisions; the 9th and 11th Panzer Divisions have been temporarily removed for replenishment; the 6th and 7th Panzer Divisions have been removed for reforming. The forming up of the Fourth Panzer Army for summer operations should be completed only in May.[71]

This information widely diverged from the information available to the intelligence departments of our *fronts*, opposite which the indicated adversarial army was operating. The radio message from Bern failed to include the three panzergrenadier divisions of the SS Panzer Corps, which the Fourth Panzer Army command had received back in February 1943, and which from this moment up until the end of the Battle of Kursk remained subordinate to it. Meanwhile, the 7th, 9th, 25th and 27th Panzer Divisions, the 12th, 25th and 103rd Panzergrenadier Divisions

---

69 Sudoplatov, P.A., *Razvedka i Kreml': Zapiski nezhelatel'nogo svidetelia* [*Intelligence and the Kremlin: Notes of an objectionable eyewitness*] (Moscow, 1966), pp. 168-170.
70 B.V. Sokolov in his book *Razvedka* [*Intelligence*] substantiated this speculation in the most nuanced manner.
71 Rádo, S., *Pod psevdonimom "Dora"* [*Under the pseudonym "Dora"*] (Moscow: Voenizdat, 1973), p. 200.

and the SS Division *Wiking* neither before the battle of Khar'kov nor after it were subordinate to the Fourth Panzer Army. The 3rd Panzer Division at this time was under the command of the First Panzer Army and was transferred to Hoth only in June; the 25th Panzer Division was based in Norway; the 27th Panzer Division was located in Germany; the 9th Panzer Division was part of Army Group Center, while the 12th, 26th and 103rd Panzergrenadier Divisions never in fact existed as part of the Wehrmacht.[72] In addition, other large inconsistencies were discovered in other reports from Lucy. A few coded messages from Dora look like complete fantasies: "Beginning in mid-April 1943, the first new panzer divisions will start to arrive, which Guderian is forming in Germany itself and in the General-Governorate [a German zone of occupation established after the invasion of Poland]. Guderian has the intention to send one panzer division every 15 days to the German High Command."[73]

I will remind the reader that at this moment, Berlin was not even giving any thought to forming new panzer divisions; it was scraping the bottom of the barrel in order to rebuild the existing ones, if not to establishment strength, then at least to something close to it, and the production of new tanks was not going smoothly. As is known, this became one of the official reasons for the postponement, at the very least, of the first date set for Citadel in May. This report from Dora is reminiscent of N.S. Khrushchev's declaration made in the early 1960s that the USSR was making rockets out of sausages. However, the words of the head of the Soviet government were just propagandistic flimflam. The report from the Swiss station on the other hand were *a priori* of a different status. Likely, because of this and other excessively unrealistic information, suspicion arose in Moscow (or more accurately, the lack of trust strengthened) with respect to the Bern station and its sources. Therefore, its messages wound up in a category, in the best case, "for rechecking", and then the time arrived as well for a thorough investigation of its work, the results of which weren't stunning for those who came into close contact with it. Notes O.V. Karimov:

> The verification of the messages from the Dora station conducted by the GRU [General Intelligence Department] of the General Staff revealed that quite often disinformation arrived in Moscow from the source concealed under the pseudonym of "Werther". Werther was providing extensive information on the enemy's armed forces and the plans of Germany's High Command. Between 7 November 1942 and 25 July 1943, Werther submitted 84 messages, the contents of which touched upon these major questions. With double-checking it was established that only 15 of these were fully reliable and arrived on time; 29 were reliable but arrived only after a delay; and 23 contained disinformation. Of the latter, 17 contained disinformation that had the aim of disguising the intention of the German command. Thus, the verification demonstrated that almost half of Werther's reports were of a disinformation nature.[74]

---

72 Müller-Gillebrandt, B., *Sukhoputnaia armiia Germanii 1933-1945* [*The German Army, 1933-1945*] (Moscow: Izogrius; EKSMO, 2002) pp. 764-768.
73 Kondrashov, V.V., *Voennaia razvedka vo vtoroi mirovoi voine* [*Military intelligence in the Second World War*] (Moscow: Kuchkovo pole, 2014), p. 343.
74 Khristoforov, V.S. (ed.), *Velikaia Otechestvennaia voina; 1943: Issledovaniia, dokumenty, kommentarii* [*Great Patriotic War; 1943: Research, documents, commentary* (Moscow: Izdatel'stvo Glavnogo arkhivnogo upravleniia Moskvy, 2013), p. 192.

I will note that this process of verification took place already after the Battle of Kursk, but the reason for it was the serious doubts about the messages from Bern that arose precisely in the period of preparation for the summer campaign. In order to show the sort of communications the Center assigned to the category "Reliable, but arrived with a delay", and why it did so, I will cite an excerpt from a report received by Dora on 5 June and sent to Moscow on 11 June 1943:

> a) Pending a change of the situation, at the end of May the German High Command was planning to launch an offensive on the Soviet-German front (a breakthrough of the front) with the following forces: The First and Fourth Panzer Armies, the Sixth Army and the newly reformed XI Corps, which consists of five divisions and comprises the assault wing of the Second Army. The simultaneous offensive of all these forces is not anticipated.
>
> The German High Command intends to strike first with the forces of the First Panzer Army and a portion of the Sixth Army toward Voroshilovgrad in the direction of the lower Don.
>
> After mid-May, under consideration is a plan for an offensive at first with the forces of the Fourth Panzer Army and the XI Corps toward Kursk. Despite certain vacillations, the divisions of Manstein's group that have been prepared for an offensive continue to remain in their jumping-off positions ...[75]

Information from the first two paragraphs don't raise serious doubts; this is a brief summary of various proposals and alternative plans for combat operations in the southern sector of the Kursk bulge and to the south of there, which were under discussion in Berlin throughout the entire spring (Operation Panther and so forth). However, by the beginning of June, even this partially reliable information lost its relevance. Possibly, that is why they were stealthily planted by Dora's sources in order to enhance their authority in the eyes of Moscow. Disinformation has been sprinkled throughout the entire text. First, XI Corps at this time was not part of the Second Army, but was positioned south of Belgorod in Army Detachment Kempf. Accordingly, it could not become part of Second Army's "assault wing". Second, an attack by the Fourth Panzer Army toward Kursk was being viewed as a priority not from the middle of May, but from the beginning, from March and April 1943. Third, neither at the end of May nor at the beginning of June were the assault divisions of von Manstein's army group that were designated for Citadel, moved up into jumping-off positions for an offensive toward Kursk; as before, they were continuing to remain in the rear for rest and replenishment. At this time, it had already become clear that the established start date for Citadel was not 12 June, since the necessary number of armored vehicles had not been delivered, while significant forces of the Ninth Army (an entire corps) was bogged down in the Briansk forests, taking part in Operation Gypsy Baron, so they were not ready for an offensive. Yet here is a message, the contents of which were called upon to disguise the enemy's real intentions:

> 27 June 1943. To the director. Flash. From Werther. Berlin, 21 June. The OKH is conducting a regrouping of the armies of Manstein's army group. The aim of the

---

75 Ibid., p. 234.

regrouping is the creation of a threat to the flanks of the Red Army in the event that it undertakes an offensive out of the Kursk area to the west – in the direction of Konotop. Dora.

I recall that on 21 June, Hitler had finally decided to begin Citadel in the first days of July and confirmed a tentative start date for it – 3 July – but after several days he changed it to 5 July. The Ninth Army and Army Group South began moving up their assault groupings into their jumping-off positions on 27 June, and it was precisely on 21 June that the agent Werther received information from Berlin that in the nearest days, a regrouping would begin at the Kursk "balcony", which the Russians with a great deal of probability would try to detect. Therefore, the message clarified that the movement of the enormous mass of troops was purportedly insurance against a possible attack by the Red Army, and not preparation for an attack against Kursk. Such reports were one of the elements of the German disinformation plan to disguise Citadel. Today it is understood that the information contained in this report from the Swiss station, and in others like it, were a fabrication, but back then this was far from clear. Therefore, Moscow just a week later could see "great value" in Werther's information. Yet here is a report from this same source on 6 July 1943, forwarded from Bern on 10 July, which did not require any time to grasp its essence, and it immediately went to the category of disinformation:

> To the director. Flash. From Werther. Berlin, 6 July.
> 1. The order regarding a preventative offensive by the Germany Army, which took place on 4 July with the forces of one to two divisions, to which the Red Army responded on 5 July with a concentrated counterattack against a local German offensive in the Tomarovka area, had the objective of conducting a deep reconnaissance in connection with the fact that the Germans were apprehensive about the course of the events between Velikie Luki and Dorogobuzh.
> 2. Having established the size of the Red Army's offensive blow between Khar'kov and Kursk, the [German] command ordered to begin an offensive with two armies in the Kursk sector. On 6 July the German command was nevertheless viewing the fighting as defensive and was gradually committing new reserves into it, primarily through Khar'kov, Lebedin and Konotop.[76]

On 4 July 1943, the German forces on the southern face of the Kursk salient did not conduct any "deep reconnaissance probes" whatsoever. Within the framework of the preparations to execute Operation Citadel, all four divisions of the XXXXVIII Panzer Corps instead conducted a local operation north and northeast of Tomarovka with the objective of seizing elevated ground and the fortified villages of Gertsovka and Butovo, which were located out in front of the 6th Guards Army's right flank. On 5 July, the Soviet side did not undertake any counterattack or any active offensive operations whatsoever in the sector of the Voronezh Front. On the contrary, on this day the main forces of Army Group South went on the offensive toward Kursk. Already by the morning of 6 July, the Front command activated all of its reserves in order to try to repulse the Germans, but that afternoon the Fourth Panzer Army's II SS Panzer Corps, having

---

76 Rádo, *Pod psevdonimom "Dora"*, p. 252.

broken through two of the 6th Guards Army's defensive belts, shattered two of its reinforced rifle divisions that were defending the Oboian' – Prokhorovka direction and encircled the reserve 5th Guards "Stalingrad" Tank Corps, which N.F. Vatutin had moved up in order to bolster the defenses in this area. In connection with this, on this very day the Front command was compelled to appeal to the *Stavka* for additional forces. It was against this backdrop that soothing dispatches were arriving from Bern that stated Berlin was viewing all of these events as nothing other than defensive actions against the Soviet forces. It is hard to imagine that they might have believed this fiction in Moscow and actually did value Dora's sources. Incidentally, it may seem surprising, but even in the early 1970s, S. Rádo himself continued to consider all of his messages, including those mentioned above, as completely honest.[77]

It is therefore impossible to agree with certain Russian authors that by the beginning of April 1943, Soviet intelligence had supplied the country's leadership with all of the necessary information about Citadel. Information really was coming in to the *Stavka*, but not in a wide stream, and the *Stavka* rightfully chose not to rely on the intelligence it had received by early April. So, it was forced to undertake major efforts in order to other information through alternative channels.

It also must be acknowledged that at this time, the intelligence information arriving from the acting army was also often distant from the truth. For example, according to the information of the General Staff's Main Intelligence Department, as cited by S.M. Shtemenko in his book, by 8 April 1943 the Germans had supposedly assembled 15-16 panzer divisions numbering a total of 2,500 tanks and self-propelled guns opposite the forces of Rokossovsky and Vatutin.[78] In fact, at this time, the Wehrmacht did not have this many armored vehicles on the entire Eastern Front. On 1 April 1943 Army Groups Center and South possessed 1,283 tanks and self-propelled guns (396 and 887 respectively), of which only 570 (181/389) were operational. On the entire Eastern Front, the enemy had 1,336 combat machines, of which only 45.8 percent (or 612) were serviceable.[79] The erroneous information that the enemy had such a significant armor grouping around Kursk unquestionably was making the Soviet side extremely nervous. After all, on 29 March the Central Front had just 539 serviceable tanks, including 232 T-34 and KV tanks; the rest were light tanks or foreign models.[80] The Voronezh had even fewer; on 9 April it had 276 combat machines operational and 44 more on the way.[81] In addition, Moscow had to take into consideration the Wehrmacht reserves, and also its ability to reinforce the divisions in this area with armor shifted from quiet sectors of the front. Thus, hypothetically, all of this taken together could yield a very significant force for an offensive – but only hypothetically.

Paradoxically, it was just this disquieting, but ultimately false information that helped the *Stavka* to work out and take the most correct decision to this at this moment to adopt an intentional defensive posture, since the General Staff based its analysis of the operational situation and the correlation of forces at Kursk. which were presented to I.V. Stalin on 12 April 1943, on this information. For this reason, within a relatively short period of time after the

---

77 Ibid., pp. 250-259.
78 Shtemenko, *General'nyi shtab v gody voiny*, p. 159.
79 NARA US, T.78, R.587, F.00078723.
80 TsAMO RF, F.62, Op.321, D.16, l. 37.
81 Zamulin, V.N., *Kurskii izlom: Reshaiushchaia bitva Velikoi Otechestvennoi* [*Kursk turning point: Decisive battle of the Great Patriotic War*] (Moscow: IAUZA/EKSMO, 2008), p. 98.

conference in the Kremlin, the commanders of the Central and Voronezh Fronts received a directive to consider the primary task of the troops when preparing for the defensive operation to be the destruction of enemy armor, and to prepare the entire system of the Front's defenses primarily as an anti-tank defense. G.K. Zhukov recalled, "We wanted to meet the expected German offensive with a powerful defensive means, causing them losses and primarily to smash the enemy's armored groupings."[82]

Incidentally, here it is impossible not to recall a similar mistake by Soviet intelligence when estimating the strength of Paulus' grouping before the counteroffensive in November 1942 at Stalingrad. Here, the estimate was not off just by two times, like at Kursk, but off by more than three times – they were expecting to encircle 85,000 to 90,000 Germans, but in the pocket, there were 300,000![83]

At the same time, the mistaken intelligence information mentioned above about the German strength in armored vehicles also had an extremely negative affect on the planning of the Kursk defensive operation. At the end of April, the *Stavka*, relying upon it, made one more decision, a mistaken one, that the Wehrmacht's main attack would be launched against the Central Front, since the intelligence services believed that it was within the Orel salient that the Germans had assembled their main forces, including armored forces, that comprised Model's assault wedge, in order to take Kursk and possibly follow it with an attack toward Moscow. This information was being confirmed by our special services both in May and June 1943. For example, an intelligence summary from the Red Army's Armored and Mechanized Forces for 15 June 1943 indicated:

> The majority of the enemy's armored forces on 15 June 1943 are located opposite the Red Army's Western, Briansk, Central, Southwestern and Southern Fronts in the following assault groupings:
> a) in the Briansk – Orel – Kromy area, six panzer divisions (5th, 9th, 2nd, 12th, 18th and 20th Panzer Divisions) totaling up to 1,600 tanks and self-propelled guns;
> b) in the Belgorod – Khar'kov – Bogodukhov area, seven or eight panzer divisions (the 6th, 7th, 11th, *Adolf Hitler*, *Das Reich*, *Totenkopf*, *Grossdeutschland* [Panzer or Panzergrenadier Divisions] and presumably the 4th Panzer Division) with a total number of 1100 to 1200 tanks and self-propelled guns.[84] [See Table 3]

Within this document, the strength of the enemy groupings has in fact been reversed by the headquarters of the Red Army's Armored and Mechanized Forces. According to captured German documents, on 1 June 1943 Model had only 783 armored vehicles, of which 420 were tanks (including 31 Tigers) and 363 were self-propelled guns (including the Ferdinand heavy self-propelled tank destroyers). Altogether, Army Group South marked 947 combat machines for Citadel. Yet according to the information of the Western scholars, for example, David Glantz and Thomas Jentz, at this time Model's assault grouping directed toward Kursk had 1,514 armored vehicles (1,259 tanks and 245 self-propelled guns).[85]

---

82 Zhukov, *Vospominaniia i razmyshlennia*, Vol. 3, p. 23.
83 Vasilevsky, *Delo vsei zhizni*, Vol. 1, p. 283.
84 TsAMO RF, F.38, Op.11353, D.199, l. 248.
85 Jentz, T.L., *Panzertruppen: The Complete Guide to the Creation & Combat Employment of Germany's Tank Force, 1943-1945* (1996), p, 82.

This mistake first became known from the memoirs of G.K. Zhukov, which was published several decades after the victory over Germany. Even though the Marshal rather highly assessed the activity of the intelligence services during the run-up to the Battle of Kursk, nevertheless he acknowledged:

> The *Stavka* and the General Staff believed that the enemy was creating the strongest grouping in the Orel area for operations against the Central Front. In fact, the grouping opposite the Voronezh Front proved to be stronger, where eight panzer divisions (1,500 armored vehicles) were operating. Opposite the Central Front, six panzer divisions (1,200 armored vehicles) were operating. To a significant extent, this also explains why it was easier for the Central Front to handle the repulse of the enemy's offensive, than it was for the Voronezh Front.[86]

This error cost us dearly. It had to be remedied not only by the troops of the Voronezh Front, but also by significant forces of the Steppe Military District and reserves of the Southwestern Front. I will remind the reader that in addition to all of Vatutin's forces and reserves, Moscow during the Kursk defensive operation would also be forced to commit here two additional Guards armies and a tank corps (between 8 and 11 July), which would commit all of their inherent forces into the fighting. In addition, in the concluding stage of the operation, the entire Steppe Military District would be brought up to the battle area.

Unfortunately, the information (already culled and filtered), which became available to the NKGB's leadership from its 4th Department (from partisans and operational teams operating in the enemy rear) was often contradictory and hard to analyze. In order to understand the quality of the information that arrived after its "screening" in the 4th Department, I will offer excerpts from two reports supplied by the 4th Department on the same day of 10 May 1943 that were addressed to the Deputy People's Commissar of the NKGB B.Z. Kabulov. First:

> From the Briansk area. Through the testimony of deserters from a Russian-German battalion activated against the partisans, it has been established that one of the enemy's main tasks on the southern outskirts of the Briansk forests is the capture and restoration of the Khutor Mikhailovsky – Unechi railroad. For this purpose, German sappers have arrived and set to work. During the interrogation it also became clear that the Germans have removed combat units and equipment from guarding the Briansk woods and are concentrating forces for a decisive attack toward Moscow, Kursk, and in the direction of Orel. The general offensive is expected sometime after 20 May.[87]

Second report:

> From the Ovruch area, Zhitomir Oblast. Information has been received about the increased movement of enemy troops from Gomel' in the direction of Kalinkovichi and Mozyr' … According to local residents, the troops from the Kursk and Briansk

---

86 Zhukov, *Vospominaniia i razmyshleniia*, p. 475.
87 TsA FSB RF [Central Archive of the Russian Federation's Federal Security Bureau], F.4, Op.1, D.473, l. 137.

directions are traveling for rest. There are Finns, Russians, Ukrainians and Germans among the soldiers.[88]

If the adversary was concentrating forces for an attack toward Kursk and even removing combat units from guarding woods (although Operation Gypsy Baron would already get underway in mid-May), then why were his troops traveling for rest from the Kursk and Briansk directions? At a minimum, this meant that an offensive would not take place in the near future, but the other document indicates its start date – at some point after the next ten days. It is hard to believe that trainloads of personnel were traveling on leave from the front just two weeks before a general offensive. From the documents it is also difficult to determine the direction of the enemy's main attack. The information that the Germans were planning to attack both toward Moscow and Kursk was of such importance for the Soviet command on 10 May, then the NKGB would have announced that Germany was looking to conquer the USSR. Yet in the report, as they say, this was only half of the trouble, but what did "in the direction of Orel" mean? After all, this city was already in the enemy's possession, and if to attack in the direction of Orel, this meant the German forces had to among the positions of the Soviet forces. Indeed, such documentary head scratchers that were coming in from all of the specialized services had to be puzzled out each and every day in the Lubianka, the General Staff and the *Stavka*.

Unquestionably, Moscow knew about the dissatisfactory condition of the intelligence services, particularly regarding the talent pool of the analytical offices and their low effectiveness. Therefore, an NKO [People's Commissariat of Defense] order from 19 April 1943 appeared about reorganizing and improving their work. However, even before this, due to the absence of complete and reliable information about the enemy's plan, the *Stavka* took steps to increase the quality and diversity of intelligence information on the given matter. On 3 April I.V. Stalin signed a directive to the leadership of the military intelligence organs, first of all those of the *fronts*, in which he issued tasks "to monitor continuously the changes in the enemy's grouping and timely establish the directions on which he is conducting an assembly of troops and, especially, armored units."[89]

Unfortunately, prior to the start of the Battle of Kursk, the intelligence organs of the acting army were unable to develop into an effective means for obtaining information of high quality about the enemy for the command. A tendency to exaggerate his strength in their reports remained, and just as before they were continuing to identify hundreds of tanks in places where there were none and pinpointing non-existent armies and corps on their maps while at the same time failing to notice the most powerful grouping opposite their own lines. By the end of 1943 the situation began to change for the better, but not dramatically so, and right up to the final surrender of Nazi Germany, the intelligence service remained one of the most vexing problems in the Red Army. After the war, these and many other problems of the Red Army were hushed up, and movie films that were remote from reality and done in the style of a detective show were viewed by a wide audience, in which our "combatants on the invisible front" always successfully outplayed the dim-witted Nazis and purloined their most important secrets. Over the last 70 years, fictional works and military history books of the same genre were written and published

---

88 Ibid., l. 141.
89 Pavlov, A.G., "Sovetskaia razvedka v 1941-1945 g.g." ["Soviet intelligence in the years 1941-1945"] *Novaia i noveishaia istoriia,* No. 2 (1995), p. 35.

in millions of copies. All of this taken together formed in the public mind a distorted image of both the nature itself of the hard, dangerous work of an intelligence agent and the contribution of the special services in the victory over the foe in the war, including the victory at Kursk. It should be acknowledged that even today, despite certain positive changes that have occurred in academic history, an honest and detailed assessment of the results of the activity of Soviet intelligence members in the years of the Great Patriotic War still hasn't been given in book or film.

However, the reports of the special services were only a portion of the informational base, which the *Stavka* used when devising the plan for the summer campaign. The second important block of information about the enemy and his plans was accumulated and simultaneously generated by the minds of key figures of the country's military and political leadership, and first of all G.K. Zhukov, A.M. Vasilevsky, A.I. Antonov and the *front* commands. Nurturing their own impressions formed directly in the course of combat operations while commanding the troops, and during the interrogation of prisoners, relying on their own personal experience and intuition, they came to the same assessments and conclusions, which intelligence was also mostly reporting: The Germans were intensively preparing for an offensive, and it would get underway in the area of the Kursk bulge right after the end of the muddy season.

Thus, the information of the special services on this subject, which arrived after the meeting on 12 April 1943, although both quite checkered and interesting, had no independent, decisive significance for the *Stavka*, because the intelligence was unable to report anything that was previously unknown about the enemy's intentions. The reports from Bern weren't prompting trust for fully objective reasons, while the NKGB's network of agents, upon which the Kremlin was placing great hopes, at that time still could not acquire the necessary information. However, this should not cast a shadow over the results of unquestionably the heroic work of hundreds of people, who each day risked their lives for victory over the common foe. The primary result of the intelligence activity was the information that confirmed the point of view of the *Stavka*'s and General Staff's key figures, which had already been formed before this on the basis of the analysis of the situation they had conducted by the end of March and the beginning of April, and their personal observations, impressions and intuition. For the men who were making such important decisions, which such major events as the defense of the Kursk bulge would later follow, the possibility to refer to other sources and to contrast their assessments with other, independent information, was extremely important. Therefore, the intelligence information, even when it was not always accurate, was highly valued.

As the results of the conference in the Kremlin show, its participants were considering the enemy to be experienced and cunning, so accordingly, mistakes had to be avoided. Therefore, the decision to go over to a temporary defense, I will stress, was a tentative one, and given changes in the situation, it might be reversed. In addition, the intelligence information, even that which seemed reliable, had to be revalidated by means of issuing to all the intelligence organs a repeated order to collect information on the plans of the Germans in the Kursk area as a matter of top priority.

Recently, an article appeared on the internet which claimed that at the 12 April 1943 conference, an unsigned copy of Hitler's Operational Order No. 6 lay on table in front of I.V. Stalin; it had purportedly been acquired by Dora's agents. I will allow that Soviet intelligence might have received this extremely important document, but up to the present day it hasn't been published in Russia, and I've not come across such information in Western sources; moreover, the information on the Internet was given without any references to sources.⁹⁰ Therefore, I don't consider it proper to use it for our analysis.

After the conference in the Kremlin, reports about the Germans preparation for an offensive continued to come in systematically from the military intelligence's network of foreign agents. Moreover, they were now more detailed and specific, and their source was also our military attaché in London Major General I. Skliarov ("Brion") and an analyst of the British Government Code and Cypher School at Bletchley Park John Cairncross (Soviet agent "Liszt" or "Moliere", one of the notorious "Cambridge Five"), who was operating under the direction of the NKGB. Here are just two of the "Brion's" radio messages received by the chief of the General Staff of the Red Army's Intelligence Department on the day of 16 April:

> Taking into account all of the received reports, it is possible to assume that the OKW has reached a decision that given the present strategic situation, there is the possibility of launching a new large offensive in the East. The basis for such a decision by the OKW, on one hand, is the calculation that an Allied invasion in the West is likely this year, but Allied operations against Sicily and southern Italy, or Crete and Greece, will not be able to divert major German forces. On the other hand, the OKW has the opinion that at the present time, the Red Army is operating with the forces it had during the winter period, and that the OKW has its final chances to achieve a success in the East this year ….
>
> The concentration of German forces in the Belgorod and Orel areas demonstrates that the Germans want to use this sector for an operation, the overall direction of which should lead approximately to the Voronezh area. This supposed axis of advance would lead the German armies to the Moscow area against the nucleus of the Soviet Army. The Caucasus front should recede into the background …⁹¹

The second radio message was not only confirming the already known intentions of Berlin, but also reported the code name given to the offensive operation – Citadel, and provided accurate information on the specific formations that the Germans were planning to draw upon to execute it:

> On 14 April an order from the Luftwaffe Command in the East (of the air forces operating in a sector stretching approximately from Smolensk to Kursk, where possibly the formations of VIII Fliegerkorps were based) was intercepted, which indicated that the forward elements for Operation Citadel would quickly begin moving. VIII Fliegerkorps has been included in this operation and the indicated forward units are in the process of moving out of Germany. According to available information, the British intelligence believes that this operation might be the nucleus of a future German offensive in the area of the Kursk salient.⁹²

---

90 Available at ru.wikipedia/org>wiki/Kurskaia bitva
91 Lota, *Bez prava na oshibku*, p. 89.
92 Ibid., p. 90.

However, a radio telegram addressed to the OKH from the headquarters of the Army Group South sent on 25 April 1943, which was intercepted and decoded by the British with the help of a prototype of the German Enigma encoding machine, became the most important item for confirming the decisions that had been made and prompted the trust of the Soviet side. This document was acquired by John Cairncross and quickly translated by a resident of the NKGB in Moscow who specialized in special communications. In it, the acting commander-in-chief of Army Group South Field Marshal M. von Weichs[93] in fact was only giving an estimate of the forces of the Voronezh Front in the sector of the designated offensive under Citadel; even so, the operation's master plan became much became clear from the document. On 7 May 1943 the People's Commissar of State Security V.N. Merkulov sent it to the State Defense Committee. The radio telegram read:

> The main concentration of enemy forces, which obviously a certain time ago was on the northern flank of Army Group South, might clearly be discerned in the area of the future operation: Kursk – Sudzha – Volchansk – Ostrogozhsk.
>
> ... In order to oppose the implementation of Citadel's plan, the enemy has approximately 90 divisions, which are located to the south of the Belgorod – Kursk – Maloarkhangel'sk line. The offensive by Army Group South's units will meet stubborn resistance in a deeply echeloned and well-prepared zone with a multitude of dug-in tanks, artillery and local reserves. The primary defensive efforts will be concentrated in the main Belgorod – Tomarovka sector ...
>
> At the present time it is difficult to predict whether or not the enemy will try to avoid the threat of encirclement by means of withdrawing to the east, which will follow after the breakthrough of the main sectors on the frontline: Kursk – Belgorod – Maloarkhangel'sk.
>
> In conclusion, it is necessary to note that the events are indicating that the enemy's intentions are more defensive than offensive. This is infallibly correct with respect to the sector of the front held by the Sixth Army and First Panzer Army. It is possible to speculate that in the event of the shifting of reinforcements to the area north of Army Group South's front and with the initiation of the advance of the strategic reserves toward the front lines or their amalgamation into larger formations, enemy offensive

---

93 Maximilian von Weichs, whose full name was Maximilian Maria Joseph Karl Gabriel Lamoral Reichsfrieherr von und zu Weichs an der Glon, was a German military commander and Feldmarschall-General (1943). He was born on 12 November 1881 in Dessau. From July 1942, he commanded Army Group B, which was attacking in the direction of Voronezh. Weichs made wide use of Flak artillery in the ground fighting, for which he received the nickname of "the Flak general". In the spring of 1943, in turn with Walther Model, he temporarily replaced Erich von Manstein, who had departed for treatment in Germany, in command of Army Group South, and in July 1943 he was assigned to the High Command reserve, before becoming the commander-in-chief of Army Group F in the Balkans. In February 1945, he was awarded the Oak Leaves to the Knight's Cross. On 25 March 1945, he was again sent into the command reserve. On 2 May 1945, von Weichs was captured in Bavaria by US troops. He was subjected to interrogation in the course of the Nuremburg trials, but was not at the time condemned or sentenced due to medical reasons. He spent the years 1945 to 1948 in an American prison for war crimes. Weichs passed away on 27 September 1954 in Bornheim (Rhineland) near the city of Bonn.

actions become more likely, but in that condition, he won't succeed in even preempting the implementation of our Citadel plan.[94]

It is not worthwhile to pay attention to the final lines of this message; they are either the desire to convince oneself in something that you don't even believe yourself, or simply the boasting of a self-confident military commander. The Soviet side was not interested in one thing or the other. For Moscow, the following was important in this document. First, it confirmed the German intention to launch an offensive in the Kursk area. At the same time, it was clear that the preparation for it had already passed the initial stage of reaching agreement and the operation's plan was now ready. Second, the document indicated the likely area of Army Group South's main attack, and something that was very important, it coincided with the area that N.F. Vatutin had already predicted. Third, in the first stage of the offensive, the Germans weren't intending to implement a deep penetration right off the bat, like, for example, as they had in the summer of 1942; the discussion so far was about the link-up of concentric attacks by the forces of two army groups from Belgorod and Maloarkhangel'sk toward Kursk (as incidentally did happen). Fourth, the enemy was aware that the Red Army was fundamentally preparing for an offensive in the very same sector designated for Citadel, but he did not know its real strength. Finally, the command of Army Group South did not feel inherently confident in the success of the designated offensive; it was warning Berlin ahead of time about the expected Russian bitter resistance. It understands that if the defense did not collapse from the initial blow and the Soviet command was able to bring up serious reserves, then it was impossible to predict the outcome of the operation. It was just this prospect that compelled von Weichs to write the encouraging chatter at the end of the telegram.

It should be mentioned that this document, like all of the intelligence information that concerned Citadel, played an important role in determining only the enemy's immediate plans, and did not touch upon, and in fact could not touch upon the full complex of problems regarding the entire summer campaign of 1943, which were of great importance, because it would mark a fundamental turning point in the war for better or for worse. Citadel's failure was only one of its elements, albeit a very important one, although it still did not mean the achievement of the full campaign's objectives. Thus, the assertion met in the literature that Soviet intelligence, having revealed Citadel's master plan and the place where the Germans would conduct it, had thereby resolved the problem of achieving this fundamental turning point for the better is not essentially true.

However, let us return to the cited document. Trust in the intercepted radio telegram rose after new information was received from the USA (via the GRU) and England (via the NKGB), which confirmed Berlin's readying of a major offensive. The first document arrived from London on 29 April – "The assessment of the possible German intentions and plans for the Russian summer campaign of 1943", which had been prepared especially for Prime Minister Winston Churchill. According to V. Lota, who judging from his book was personally familiar with it, this was a very large volume that was expansive in its sweep of the analyzed questions. Regarding the Kursk area, the British analysts noted that at the end of March 1943, British

---

94 *Organy gosudarstvennoi bezopasnosti v Velikoi Otechestvennoi voine: Sbornik dokumentov* [*Organs of state security in the Great Patriotic War: Collection of documents*]; Vol. 4, Book 1 (Moscow) pp. 444-445.

military intelligence had identified a large concentration of "German armored divisions to the northeast of Kursk (the Orel salient), possibly for offensive operations, and it was probable that the Germans would assemble forces to eliminate the Kursk bulge. This should shorten their frontlines and regain the defenses that they had been holding in this area the previous spring …"[95] That Germany was only capable this year of conducting an offensive with limited objectives had been reported to Major General Skliarov back in mid-April. According to his information, at the end of March an expanded conference of the committee that oversaw the production of armaments took place under the chairmanship of Hermann Goering. The following decisions were reached at it:

a. To preserve the output of aircraft at the level of the 1942 average annual production;
b. To increase the production of artillery guns by 16 percent ;
c. To retain the number of panzer divisions and to bring them fully back up to the establishment strength in tanks;
d. To increase the production of transports, especially locomotives, flatcars and boxcars.[96]

All this plainly showed that the Reich's industry was working at its limits and the Germans were trying at a minimum to replace the enormous losses they had suffered at Stalingrad and on the southwestern axis immediately following the elimination of Paulus' Sixth Army. Accordingly, there could no longer be talk of any grand offensive, like in 1942.

The second announcement that the USA had acquired important information regarding Citadel arrived in Moscow on 30 April, but the information itself arrived later, in the first ten days of May. Its essence was contained in several lines: "… the Germans had set as their task for the current year not the conquest of new territory, but the destruction of the Red Army. The German main attack in the summer campaign will be out of the Kursk – Orel area in the direction of Voronezh …."[97]

It is obvious that this information was similar to M. von Weich's coded message and the information from the chief of the Czech intelligence service F. Morawicz, which he had passed along to the NKGB agent back on 10 April. So, by early May Soviet strategic intelligence had efficiently and in full volume confirmed the correctness of the decisions reached by the *Stavka* on 12 April, and the accuracy of the Voronezh Front command's prediction about the area where E. von Manstein's forces would launch the main attack.

In the future, in May and June 1943, both the GRU and the NKGB continued to work rather successfully on the given matter. For example, despite the fact that nothing had happened after three intelligence warnings that the Germans were likely going on the offensive in May, an assessment of the incoming information and an accurate prognosis of the enemy's next steps was given in a special report from the NKGB's 1st Department's intelligence office on 27 May:

---

95   Lota, *Bez prava na oshibku*, p. 29.
96   Ibid., p. 26.
97   Ibid., p. 43.

1. The announcement that the German command will undertake no offensive this year does not correspond to the reality, which indicates reinforced preparations for an offensive.
2. The information about the limited nature of the offensive is plausible, because according to all of the information, Germany lacks the necessary strategic, human and material resources for a large offensive this year.
3. The information ... about the preparation of a major operation in the Kursk – Belgorod area is most serious.[98]

Even so, the intelligence information remained albeit a necessary, but nevertheless secondary instrument for Moscow's taking of key decisions. Relying on the files of the Voronezh and Central Front's in the TsAMO RF, it is possible to assert that although the information received by the Soviet High Command was fully sufficient for understanding the general tasks of Manstein's and Kluge's assault groupings, Moscow did not know important details regarding the future operation. The miscalculation made in determining where the main blow would land in the Kursk area became a consequence of this. At the same time, it should be observed that the intelligence information arriving in May and June 1943 could not help quickly resolve one more important question: What were the reasons for the several postponements of the start of Citadel? This was the source of the anxiety that arose at this time in the *Stavka* and the headquarters of the Voronezh Front. Therefore, both in April, just as in the following two months, a human factor played the main role in maintaining restraint and sticking to the chosen course – the talent and intuition of the key figures in the highest Soviet military leadership.

2.2 Preparation for the battle of Kursk: The planning and construction of field defenses, and the rebuilding and replenishment of forces

The conference on 12 April 1943 marked the end of the initial, very important stage of the Soviet High Command's preparation for both the Battle of Kursk and the entire summer campaign. The second stage began from 12 April and was no less important and stressful. It featured not only the "war of nerves" between Moscow and Berlin, but first of all the colossal work done to create a most powerful system of field defenses around Kursk and the assembly of the strongest possible combat groupings to hold them. If in January to April 1943 the complicating factor was the rapidly changing operational situation at the front, then in the at this time the main problems were presented by the onset of the muddy season and the uncertainty surrounding the enemy's intentions, which from early May grew into a war of nerves.

Immediately after the conference in the Kremlin, the meticulous work of the General Staff and the *Stavka* representatives with the *front* commands that were holding the central and southwestern directions of the Soviet-German front got underway. In the process, Moscow paid particularly focused attention to the situation on the southern face of the Kursk salient. The enemy's advance in the sector of the Voronezh Front was finally brought to a halt in the last ten days of March 1943. The front lines became stabilized along the line: Snagost', Bliakhova, Alekseevka, Molotov State Farm, Volkhov, Bititsa, Ol'shanka, Dibrova, Glybnia along the

---

98 *"Ognennaia duga": Kurskaia bitva glazami Lubianka*, p. 268.

right bank of the Syrovatka River to (excl.) Krasnopol'e, (excl.) Novo-Dmitrievka, Vysokii, Zavertiachii, Nadezhda, Novaia zhizn', Trefilovka, Berezovka, Trirechnoe, Dragunskoe, Zadel'noe, (excl.) Blizhniaia Igumenka, Staryi gorod and further along the left bank of the Severskii Donets River to Sovetsoe-1.

The *Stavka*'s concern was prompted primarily by the condition of N.F. Vatutin's forces, and the intelligence information that concerned this operational direction. First, in comparison with the Central Front, its corps and divisions had become exhausted and heavily attenuated after the Khar'kov operation. The divisions that had been transferred from Stalingrad, particularly those of the 21st Army that had been deployed on the primary tank-vulnerable (Oboian') direction were not in the best shape. In the course of discussions with N.F. Vatutin on 29 March, I.M. Chistiakov had reported:

> I need primarily replenishment with troops. My reserve regiment is still back in Stalingrad, and it, according to a report, is being broken up in order to replenish Zhadov's household (the code name for Lieutenant General A.S. Zhadov's 66th Army). Five of my blocking detachments there have already been taken away from me.
>
> Supplies, especially of fuel and ammunition, are in an exceptionally unsatisfactory state. Comrade Dontsov [K.K. Rokossovsky, to whom the 21st Army had been subordinate prior to the transfer to N.F. Vatutin's command], pursuant to a *Stavka* order regarding my transfer to you, was supposed to provide 15 days' worth of rations and two standard loads of ammunition. but failed to do so. Fuel is now running low; today we just have 0.4 refills, and only 0.7 of a combat load of ammunition. A number of the army's rear units are still near Stalingrad and require 19 trains [in order to bring them up]; they were promised yesterday, but none arrived. I request assistance.[99]

I will note right away that this was not a rebuke with respect to K.K. Rokossovsky; the army commander was merely explaining why his troops were short on rations. At this moment the Central Front was in acute need for assistance, including with both provisions and the transportation of them. An ignoble example was the multiple cases of death from starvation in its 70th Army that were noted at this time.

On 2 April 1943 the commander of the 21st Army again raised the question regarding replenishments:

> I have begun forming five anti-tank rifle battalions. I'm submitting to you a requisition document for their weapons, and that they be fully staffed with men. My own resources – 4,200 newly-mobilized men; the local residents are completely untrained and are being held in a temporary reserve regiment. I still haven't received uniforms for them; they are being allocated in bits and pieces. I can send one march battalion [in essence, of untrained men] to the units on 5 April 1943. I have no weapons for them, nor for the divisions that I must replenish in the first place. My available weapons are still in stockpiles back in Stalingrad.[100]

99 TsAMO RF, F.203, Op.2843, D.469, l. 30.
100 Ibid., l. 33, 37.

The Soviet command was expecting in the nearest future a strong attack with tanks from Khar'kov toward Kursk. This was directly mentioned in N.F. Vatutin's Order No. 0093 from 31 March 1943.[101] Therefore, I.M. Chistiakov, in addition to his own divisions, had to rebuild the 160th Rifle Division that had been transferred to him for reinforcement, form two destroyer anti-tank brigades, and bring four destroyer anti-tank artillery regiments, two destroyer anti-tank artillery brigades, and three engineer battalions up to a state of combat-readiness in a short interval of time. The rifle division had been badly handled by the Germans; in essence, it was now nothing more than an understrength rifle regiment. On 25 March 1943, the 160th Rifle Division had just 1,768 men, 1,021 rifles, 13 heavy and 11 light machine guns, 160 PPSh submachine guns, 24 mortars of all types, seven field guns, six anti-tank rifles, 728 horses and 17 vehicles.

However, the Front was experiencing its own acute deficit of resources. It could satisfy to a certain extent the army's need with respect to light infantry weapons and uniforms, but it did not have the ability to address its other needs. For an illustrative purpose, I will cite an example of how N.F. Vatutin handled the replenishment of the 21st Army with personnel and fuel. He directed to shift the assignment of 6,000 men, which were heading to I.M. Chistiakov's neighbor, the 64th Army, to the 21st Army, with the calculation that M.S. Shumilov was "wealthier" in manpower resources and not defending such a dangerous direction, and therefore he could wait a bit, until the 21st Army's remaining forces and means arrived from Stalingrad. When doing so, the General of the Army without equivocation declared to the commander of the 21st Army that he knew that "it [the batch of replacements] wouldn't cover all of your needs", but he should not count on anything more. However, he also on the spot noted that he would petition the General Staff "regarding the quickest movement of your main reserve regiment and weapons from Stalingrad."[102] Yet when I.M. Chistiakov reported to him that the 1440th Self-propelled Artillery Regiment, which had been transferred to the army, was standing in a field several dozens of kilometers from its designated place "with empty fuel tanks", N.F. Vatutin personally directed to issue it diesel fuel from the Voronezh Front's miniscule reserves. In early April, the larger portion of the Soviet forces that were defending the Kursk salient, including the Central Front as well, were in just such a state.

Second, the intelligence organs were continuing to report about the assembly of significant forces opposite Rokossovsky's and Vatutin's *fronts*, up to 16 panzer divisions that were already fully equipped with tanks and self-propelled guns. Moreover, in the opinion of battlefield intelligence, the strongest grouping was positioned precisely in the area of Belgorod and Khar'kov opposite the Voronezh Front. At this time, the estimate was that it had eight infantry divisions in the first line and eight panzer divisions, with the possibility of increasing the infantry divisions to 20 and the panzer divisions to 11 through transfers from the southern flank of von Manstein's grouping. Today we know this information was far from accurate, but back then this still was not understood. In addition, the reports of strategic intelligence about the preparations for Operation Citadel in the Kursk area were increasing the alarm. I.V. Stalin demanded that A.M. Vasilevsky give a directive to the Voronezh Front's Military Council: to

---

101 TsAMO RF, F.203, Op.2843, D. 323, l. 1.
102 TsAMO RF, F.203, Op.2843, D.469, l. 38.

prepare rapidly a briefing on the status of the forces and their needs, after which N.F. Vatutin would be called up to the *Stavka* to present it.[103]

On 21 April the Military Council submitted the document to Moscow, and after the General Staff analyzed the contents, it became the subject of a three-day conference held in the Kremlin. In the papers, Zhukov not only briefly and concisely spelled out the replenishment of the troops, the preparations of the defense, and provided an assessment of the enemy and his intention, he also offered a developed plan for a preemptive offensive operation, the objective of which was to be the complete routing of the Germans in eastern Ukraine and the establishment of a bridgehead on the Dnepr River. Later, in the latter half of July, this scheme was offered to the *Stavka* as the basis for devising an operation to defeat the German Belgorod-Khar'kov grouping, which entered history under the code name "Polkovodets Rumiantsev", but in April Stalin did not support him, in my view due to political reasons, although it was most optimal relative to the version that was eventually adopted. The Military Council reported:

> In connection with the certain delay in the arrival of weapons and uniforms, the process of re-arming and re-forming the armies of the first echelon will be completed by 25 April 1943, and in the 69th Army – by 5 May 1943. By that time the divisions will have been brought up to the strength of 7,000 to 8,000 men each. The tanks for the 2nd and 5th Guards Tank Corps have already partially arrived, and the equipping of them will be completed approximately by 25 April[104]. It was assumed that all of the Front's remaining tank units would be fully equipped with tanks by 1 May 1943, chiefly through the return of repaired tanks. In addition, the 7th Separate Rifle Corps, which has been made part of the Front, will arrive in its new designated area.
>
> On the whole, there are a total of 540 tanks, 101 fighter aircraft, 173 ground attack aircraft, 170 daylight bombers, 43 nighttime bombers, for a total of 487 airplanes on 17 April 1943.
>
> During the period of rearming and reforming the forces, the Front has the task to hold the occupied positions strongly and to prevent any encroachment by the enemy. In the event of an enemy offensive, it is to smash him in defensive fighting, and then having selected the right moment, to go on the offensive and destroy him.
>
> Suggested foundations for the defense:
> 1. The creation of a deep defense, which will not only have a number of prepared defensive belts, but which will also be occupied by troops. This will not allow the enemy to achieve an operational breakthrough.
> 2. The organization of a dense anti-tank defenses to a great depth, especially on tank-vulnerable directions;

---

103 Vasilevsky, *Delo vsei zhizni*, Vol. 2, p. 19.
104 It was anticipated that according to *Stavka* Directive No. 346091 from 30 March 1943, these corps would receive: 2nd Guards Tank Corps – 98 T-34 and 70 T-70 by 5 April 1943; 5th Guards Tank Corps – 98 T-34 and 68 T-70 by 10 April 1943, after which by 7 April and 12 April 1943 respectively their respective build ups should be completed. However, because of the untimely arrival of tanks from the *Stavka* reserve, the deadline was shifted to the end of April.

3. The organization of a sturdy anti-tank defense by means of building shelters for the combat units, camouflage, and the wide use of anti-aircraft weapons on the important directions.
4. The preparation and execution of maneuvers as the basis of a successful defense.[105]

Late in the evening of 25 April, this document, as presented by N.F. Vatutin and the first member of the Voronezh Front's Military Council Lieutenant General N.S. Khrushchev, was discussed in the Kremlin by *Stavka* members for more than four hours. The conclusion was the recognition that the first half of the report, the operational plan of defense, answered the demands of the *Stavka* directives and took full account of the situation in the Front's sector, and the rebuilding of the forces was basically proceeding according to the timetable. Therefore, it was approved without any substantive changes. The day of 10 May 1943 was set as the final date for the Front to be completely ready for a defense.[106]

The proposal about going over to the offensive also received detailed analysis. However, considering the already approved tentative decision regarding a premeditated defense, as well as the need to discuss this matter with the command staff of the Southwestern Front as one of the proposed sectors for the offensive operation, the *Stavka* decided it would be sensible to set aside the second half of the presentation, in order to work on it in greater detail. Even so, the Front command received an order to ready the troops for active operations before 1 June. On 28 April, the Voronezh Front received Lieutenant General M.E. Katukov's 1st Tank Army as a reinforcement, which for the time being was to be reserved for the subsequent offensive, and only later, at the end of May, was it considered beneficial to use it in the course of the defensive fighting, both for launching counterattacks and as an armored shield behind the 6th Guards Army. For this purpose (preparations for the future offensive), the *Stavka* demanded that N.F. Vatutin withdraw the 7th Guards Army into the *front* reserve, and in the event of an offensive into Ukraine, it was proposed to use it together with the 1st Tank Army on the axis of the main attack. Thus, Moscow highly valued the work of the Voronezh Front's Military Council regarding the preparation of a defense, while at the same time making it clearly understood, as M.S. Shumilov remarked, "the idea of a preemptive attack was still not being discarded, but kept in the background."[107]

Beginning in the 1960s, the "mistake" made when planning the defense of the Voronezh Front before the Battle of Kursk became a point of active discussion in Russian historiography, and one that continued to be discussed. In private conversations and even at official public meetings with former generals of the war, this question was being raised more than once already in the late 1950s, though it did not appear in open press for the first time until 1965, in the book *Velikaia Otechestvennaia voina 1941-1945: Kratkaia istoriia* [*Great Patriotic War 1941-1945: Brief history*]:

> How is it possible to explain the idea that the Voronezh Front with its available forces could not grind down and attrite the enemy's assault grouping, or stop its offensive without calling upon fresh forces, despite having a superiority in manpower and

---

105 Glantz and House, *Kurskaia bitva*, pp. 390-392.
106 TsAMO RF, F.16-A, Op.1720, D.14, l. 23.
107 Shtemenko, *General'nyi shtab v gody voiny*, p. 154.

equipment over the foe at the start of the defensive battle? In contrast to the Central Front, the Voronezh Front's command was not able to determine precisely the axis where the enemy would be launching the main attack. It overextended its subordinate forces in a sector that was 164-km wide, without massing forces and means on the direction of the enemy's main assault.[108]

G.K. Zhukhov, a direct participant in the discussions, did not agree with this argument. In his article published in the *Voenno-istoricheskii zhurnal*, No. 9 (1967), he assessed the combat work of the Voronezh Front in the first stage of the Battle of Kursk rather judiciously and completely objectively and rejected the notion that N.F. Vatutin erred when planning the system of defense and the distribution of his forces. He wrote:

> The critics … of the Voronezh Front's command rests on an inaccurate calculation of the density of forces and means in the specific conditions of an operational-strategic situation … It mustn't be forgotten that the enemy on the first day launched an assault with almost five corps (II SS Panzer Corps, III Panzer Corps, XXXXVIII Panzer Corps, LII Corps and a portion of Korps Raus) against the 6th and 7th Guards Armies, at a time when Central Front's defenses [were attacked] by three corps. It is easy to grasp the difference in strength of the German forces between the Orel direction and those out of the Belgorod area.[109]

However, already at the end of September 1967, there followed an unexpectedly sharp reaction to this article from Marshal of the Soviet Union K.K. Rokossovsky. However, not in the open press, but in a letter to the journal's chief editor V.A. Matsulenko, which later became public in 1992. You often don't come across a document of such strong inner emotional heat and at the same time so distant from the historical truth. The arguments presented by K.K. Rokossovsky are contradictory to the real events, which even at the time were generally known by many in our country. Rokossovsky wrote:

> The enemy's shock grouping that was operating against the Voronezh Front consisted of 14 divisions, five of which were infantry, eight were panzer, and one was motorized [panzergrenadier], while the enemy shock grouping that operated against the Central Front consisted of 15 divisions, eight of which were infantry, six were panzer, and one was motorized. Thus, if the enemy grouping that was operating against the Voronezh Front was somewhat superior in the number of tanks, then his grouping that was operating against the Central Front was significantly superior in the number of infantry and artillery.
>
> Central Front's more successful actions are explained not by the quantity of enemy troops, but by the more properly arranged defenses.[110]

---

108 *Velikaia Otechestvennaia voina 1941-1945: Kratkaia istoriia* [*Great Patriotic War 1941-1945: Brief history*] (Moscow: Voenizdat, 1965), p. 244.
109 Zhukov, *Vospominaniia i razmyshleniia*, pp. 490-491.
110 *Voenno-istoricheskii zhurnal*, No. 3 (1992), p. 31.

This is a very debatable assertion. K.K. Rokossovsky probably forgot that on 5 July 1943, his *front*, even according to the estimates of Soviet historians, had 2,740 more pieces of artillery than did the Voronezh Front.[111] In addition, he must have overlooked the fact that Army Group South, which was operating against Vatutin's troops, had 1.5 time more armored fighting vehicles than did the Ninth Army's assault grouping, which was attacking south of Orel. Altogether, it was not 14 German divisions that were involved in the attacks against the Voronezh Front, but 17. Meanwhile, the enemy hurled only 15 full-strength divisions against his *front*.[112] In addition, the level of equipping and staffing of the German divisions differed: it was lower in the north of the Kursk bulge it was lower, and much greater in the south. I will cite only two facts as proof of this. The 10th Panzergrenadier Division that was operating in the north did not have its constituent panzer regiment[113], while the *Grossdeutschland* Panzergrenadier Division that was under Army Group South did; by the start of the battle, it had 112 tanks and self-propelled guns.[114] Moreover, the German assault grouping attacking north of Belgorod in addition to its panzer and panzergrenadier divisions had Panzer Brigade 10, which in numerical strength was equivalent to two panzer divisions and had more than 200 of the new Pz.Kpfw. V Panther tanks.[115]

The arguments of the two sides, their points of view and their cited facts became a most valuable source of information for historians, although unfortunately in the 1960s they did not reach specialists and the broader public in full. The "competent organs" weren't interested in allowing this dispute between two of the most famous military commanders in the country to become widely known, and without looking into the matter, sought to keep it hushed, and in the best case the stamp "For service use" was placed on all the documents, including Rokossovsky's letter.[116] However, no matter how odd it might seem, it was not scrubbed from the memoirs of either Marshal of the Soviet Union. As a result, the reader was given the possibility to learn K.K. Rokossovsky's position, which he subsequently described in detail in his memoirs, while there was no possibility to look into G.K. Zhukov's arguments regarding those events. Therefore, the opinion of Vatutin's supposed mistake when preparing for the Battle of Kursk became consolidated in the public conscience. Recently declassified operational and account documents of both *fronts* for 1943, stored in the Russian Federation Ministry of Defense's Central Archives, permit a detailed analysis of this problem with the use of documents that were previously known only to a narrow circle of the Red Army's highest command staff.

Thus, when elaborating the scheme for the Kursk defensive operation, the work on which began in the middle of April, N.F. Vatutin had to resolve several important and at the same time extremely complicated tasks: to determine the most likely directions of the enemy's main and auxiliary attacks; to prepare an action plan for the Front's troops with the aim of the unconditional fulfillment of the *Stavka*'s demand to stop the enemy within the tactical zone

---

111 *Istoriia Vtoroi mirovoi voiny 1939-1945* [*History of the Second World War 1939-1945*], Vol. 7 (Moscow: Voenizdat, 1976), p. 155.
112 NARA US, T.314, R.988, F.000148-000155.
113 NARA US, T.315, R.556, F.000138.
114 NARA US, T.313, R.368, F.8654350.
115 Ibid.
116 Rokossovsky's letter, which sparked the argument, was first published only in March 1992.

of operations; and to devise a primary scheme for the assembly of its troops and for erecting defensive lines in order to contain the enemy offensive.

K.K. Rokossovsky faced these same problems, but N.F. Vatutin from the outset was in a more difficult position. In order to contain Army Group South's forces within the tactical zone, it was necessary to create a high density of forces and means in it.[117] Yet it was precisely these that he was lacking. In the sector of the Central Front, there were only three likely directions of German attack in a sector that extended for 95 km (or 31 percent of its defensive sector), where the adversary, when going on the offensive, might create a serious threat, and 40 km where he most likely would deliver the main attack. In the south of the Kursk bulge, in contrast, the adversary would be able to use no less than four directions within a sector of up to 170 km (or 69 percent of the Voronezh Front's defensive line), and moreover the main attack might be delivered anywhere within a sector that was three times wider, 111 km. Meanwhile both commanders were receiving approximately the same number of troops and heavy weapons: On 5 July 1943 the total number of combatants in the Voronezh Front amounted to 467,179[118] servicemen for a defensive sector that stretched for 306 km, which amounts to 1,526 men per km, while Central Front had 417,451[119] to hold 245 km of front, or 1,703 per km of front. Therefore, the cost of a mistake in Vatutin's expectations was significantly higher than for Rokossovsky. This forced him to approach the planning more carefully and creatively, and to use fully all the possibilities to strengthen the lines of his troops.

Failing to possess the forces and means to create a high tactical density on all of the enemy's likely directions of attack, without stripping his reserves, N.F. Vatutin decided to strengthen the resilience of his defenses by increasing the operational density, which is to say by increasing its depth in the center and on the Front's left flank.[120] The plan of defense devised by him was complex and multi-leveled. It had not one, but at a minimum two primary tasks:

a. To halt and bleed white the enemy within powerful defensive belts in the tactical zone (from the outset it demanded that the troops contain the Germans within the first two army-level belts);
b. To prepare favorable conditions (first of all to create a suitable staging area) for the deployment of attacking forces with the aim of launching a counterstroke toward Khar'kov and subsequently on to the Dnepr.

The General of the Army took two obvious circumstances as reference points. First, the main objective of the first stage of the German offensive should be viewed as a breakthrough to Kursk, the largest city and administrative center within the salient. In a report to Stalin on 21 April 1943, he wrote:

---

117 Tactical density, according to the *Kratkii slovar' operativno-takticheskikh i obshchevoiskovykkh terminov* [*Abridged dictionary of operational-tactical terms common to all arms*] (Moscow: Voenizdat, 1958), is the saturation of a specific sector of the front with troops and combat equipment, expressed in the number of battalions, tanks, guns and other types of combat equipment per 1 km of the front.
118 TsAMO RF, F.203, Op.2843, D.426, l. not given.
119 TsAMO RF, F.62, Op.321, D.138, l. not given.
120 Operational density is the average density of force groupings on a specific operational axis (or within the boundaries of an operational force). *Kratkii slovar' operativno-takticheskikh i obshchevoiskovykh terminov.*

> The enemy ... will launch concentric attacks to the northeast out of the Borisovka – Belgorod area and to the southeast out of the Orel area, in order to encircle our forces that are positioned west of the Belgorod – Kursk line ... A major attack will be undertaken against the Voronezh Front out of the Borisovka – Belgorod area in the direction toward Staryi Oskol and with part of the strength toward Oboian' and Kursk. Auxiliary attacks can be expected ... toward Volchansk, Novyi Oskol and Sudzha, Oboian', Kursk.[121]

This calculation proved to be surprisingly accurate. I will remind the reader that Order No. 6 from 15 April 1943 indicated: "Army Group South with concentrated forces launches an attack from the Belgorod – Tomorovka line, breaks through the Prilipy – Oboian' front and links up at Kursk and east of it with Army Group Center's attacking army. In order to screen the offensive from the east, reach the Nezhigal' River – Korocha River – Skorodnoe – Tim line as quickly as possible."[122] As is known, Tomarovka is located next to Borisovka, while the Nezhigal' and Korocha Rivers and the village of Skorodnoe lay right along the Staryi Oskol' direction. Accordingly, based on the combat dispositions of the Voronezh Front, attacks by the main grouping (which is to say, the forces for creating the inner and outer fronts of encirclement) could be expected against its center and left flanks, or more specifically, against the defenses of the 40th Army (an auxiliary attack designed to divert the defenders' strength from the main targeted sector), at the boundary between the 40th Army and 6th Guards Army; against the 6th Guards Army and its boundary with the 7th Guards Army (the main attack); and possibly at the boundary between the Voronezh and Southwestern Fronts (another auxiliary attack). By the way, G.K. Zhukov insisted on the latter option right up to the start of the battle.

Second, the German idea was to implement this plan with only a powerful panzer grouping. K.S. Moskalenko recalled:

> Vatutin ... more than once reminded us that Manstein, an experienced and cunning foe, was commanding the forces of Army Group South. Nikolai Fedorovich told us that in the course of the war, he had twice encountered him: the first time, on the Northwestern Front in 1941, and the second time, on the Southwestern Front in January – March 1943. Both time Manstein used one and the same approach – a panzer breakthrough. It seemed unlikely that he would use it again this time, but Vatutin demanded that the troops be ready to repulse tanks.[123]
>
> Only three sectors were deemed most suitable for the massed use of armor:
> -- along the Belgorod – Oboian' road (the Oboian' highway);
> -- along the line: Belgorod – Iakovlevo – Prokhorovka – Mar'ino;
> -- the interfluvial area between the Northern Donets River and Razumnaia River from Belgorod in the general direction of Korocha and further on toward Skorodnoe.

---

121 Glantz and House, *Kurskaia bitva*, p. 389.
122 Parot'kin (ed.), *Kurskaia bitva*, p. 521.
123 Ibid., p. 106.

Two of these directions were located in the sector of the 6th Guards Army, the headquarters of which characterized the area where its troops were deployed as follows: "By the nature of its natural obstacles which are present in front of the army's forward edge, there are 28 km rated as difficult ground for the passage of tanks, and 13 directions vulnerable to armor exploitation with a width of 0.5 to 5 km and a total frontage of 38 km. Of the 13 tank-vulnerable directions, four are considered primary, with a total frontage of up to 20 km ... This was giving the enemy the possibility of moving out up to 2,000 tanks simultaneously, with no need for echeloning them."[124]

For the sake of comparison, as already noted, Army Group South's offensive plan for Kursk changed twice. Prior to Hoth's May meeting with Manstein in Bogodukhov, the Fourth Panzer Army was supposed to attack out of the Tomarovka – Belgorod area directly toward Oboian', while Army Detachment Kemp was simultaneously supposed to advance from Belgorod through Prokhorovka and Korocha toward Skorodnoe. After altering the plan, Hoth's panzer army was supposed to operate along the Tomarovka – Iakovlevo – Prokhorovka – Oboian' direction, and Kempf's forces: Belgorod – Korocha – Skorodnoe. Thus, in both cases, the enemy command was going to use all three main tank-vulnerable "corridors", which Vatutin considered to be the most dangerous and likely for a breakthrough by the enemy's main grouping.[125] It needs to be noted as well that the General of the Army immediately (in mid-April) with a high degree of accuracy gave the expected strength of the German panzer grouping, which would attempt to penetrate his front. Nikolai Fedorovich observed, "It should be expected that the enemy will create a shock grouping in strength of up to 10 panzer divisions and no less than six infantry divisions, with a total of up to 1,500 tanks and self-propelled guns, the assembly of which should be expected in the Borisovka – Belgorod – Murom – Kazach'ia Lopan' area."[126] On the basis of intelligence information, these forces should be assembled by early May, once the muddy season came to an end, and the foe would then be ready for the offensive. We will recall that in order to implement Citadel, in Operational Order No. 6 from 15 April 1943, Army Group South was assigned seven infantry and nine panzer or panzergrenadier divisions. In fact, during the July offensive, a total of nine panzer divisions and 1,508 armored fighting vehicles would be committed into the fighting here, the bulk of which arrived already in May.[127]

Starting from these two assumptions, N.F. Vatutin proposed that it was most likely that Army Group South would try to overrun the line of Lieutenant General I.M. Chistiakov's 6th Guards Army with panzer wedges supported by large numbers of aircraft. The opening attack would strike the (excl.) Trefilovka – Voskhod – southern fringe of the woods southwest of Cherkasskoe – southern outskirts of Trirechnoe – Zadel'nyi ravine – Lapin ravine – southern outskirts of Berezov – Gremuchii – Erik – Shopino – Hill 211.6 – woods east of the Home of Invalids – Chernaia Poliana line[128] (65 km, the main attack), and Lieutenant General M.S. Shumilov's 7th Guards Army on the Shishino – Staryi Gorod – forced labor colony – Bezliudovka – Volchansk (excl.) line[129] (53 km, auxiliary). Accordingly, the width of the sector where it was possible to

---

124 TsAMO RF, F.355, Op.5113, D.235, l. 12.
125 Glantz and House, *Kurskaia bitva*, p. 389.
126 Zhukov, *Vospominaniia i razmyshlenia*, Vol. 3, p. 20.
127 Zetterling and Frankson, *Kursk 1943: a statistical analysis* (London, 2003), Table 3.8 on page 32.
128 TsAMO RF, F.335, Op.5113, D.235, l. 6.
129 TsAMO RF, F.203, Op.2843, D.386, l. 2.

expect the main attack amounted approximately to 118 km, or 48.2 percent of the defensive sector according to the layout of the forward edge of defense.

Stemming from this, Vatutin worked out the following scheme for distributing his Voronezh Front's forces. He devoted his main efforts to strengthening the left flank and center (an extent of 170 km), in order to block the most dangerous directions of attack by Army Group South's main forces. Already on the sixth day after assuming command of the Voronezh Front, with his Order No.0093 from 31 March he precisely marked this sector as the most dangerous in his view and the steps he was taking to strengthen it: "For the purposes of successfully carrying out the Front's assignments and for a stouter occupation of the defenses, I have decided: by means of a regrouping to strengthen the Front's left flank and to occupy the directions Belgorod – Oboian', Belgorod – Korocha; Volchansk – Novyi Oskol particularly strongly. Create a defense of great depth, for which occupy not only the main defensive belt with troops, but also intermediary and rear lines, and keep strong assault groups ready in order to conduct counterattacks and to go over to a counteroffensive."[130]

Vatutin proposed moving up three combined-arms armies (the 40th, 6th and 7th Guards Armies) into the first echelon here. They were to set up the first two army-level defensive belts, which the commander-in-chief considered to be the most important factor for preventing an operational breakthrough and occupy them with troops. The plan was to deploy the 69th Army in the third army-level belt, in the rear of the 6th and 7th Guards Armies, and the 35th Guards Rifle Corps behind it in the first *front*-level belt of defenses (along the Krivosheevka – Stolbishche line). This was the first, April 1943 version; in the latter half of May, having received the 1st Tank Army, and also having determined the enemy's plans more precisely, he planned to move up forces of the 1st Tank Army in order to occupy separate sectors of defense on the Oboian' direction, and the 5th Guards Tank Corps to the Prokhorovka direction, as well as to position the 2nd Guards "Tatsinskaia" Tank Corps in the sector of the 7th Guards Army.

In addition, from the beginning it was proposed to direct all of the mobile reserves that the Front possessed (the 2nd Guards Tank Corps, the 5th Guards Tank Corps and the 1st Tank Army) and the majority of the anti-tank artillery reserves (the destroyer anti-tank artillery regiments and brigades) to the center and left flank of the Voronezh Front (Chistiakov's, Shumilov's and Kriuchenkin's armies).

As a result, 22 of the 35 rifle divisions that were subordinate to N.F. Vatutin were directed to assemble on the Oboian' – Prokhorovka and Korocha directions. Consequently, along the entire front each rifle division on average would be responsible for 10 km of frontage, and on the axis of the anticipated main German attack – 5.2 km of frontage. In addition, the Front was to transfer 44 of the artillery regiments of reinforcement, including destroyer anti-tank artillery regiments, of the 70 available (or 68 percent); 50 percent of the six infantry support tank brigades and 10 infantry support tank regiments; and eight Guards mortar regiments (of Katiusha rocket launchers) or 73 percent of the 11 available to Chistiakov's 6th Guards Army and Shumilov's 7th Guards Army.[131]

Thus, in order to hold the most important directions, Vatutin planned to move up 63 percent of his rifle divisions, between 50 percent and 73 percent of armored divisions and artillery, and

---

130 TsAMO RF, F.203, Op.2843, D.323, l. 1.
131 *Bitva pod Kurskom: Ot oborony k nastupleniiu* [*Battle of Kursk: From the defense to the offensive*] (Moscow: AST Khranitel', 2006), p. 48.

to occupy four defensive lines with a depth of up to 60 km (from the first trenches of the main defensive belt back to the final trenches of the first army-level belt of defenses) with the troops of the armies of the first strategic echelon and the Front's reserves. Such a significant distance was determined by the uneven lay of the land. The space between the first and second army-level defensive belts substantially varied on different directions (as a rule, to the greater). Because of this, intermediary lines were planned (and then constructed) in the Front's center and on the right flank. They became one of the distinguishing features of the system of defense in the south of the Kursk bulge, since there was no need for them in the north.

The Central Front would follow the same path, but the tactical density here was even higher. K.K. Rokossovsky would subordinate colossal forces and means to Lieutenant General N.P. Pukhov's 13th Army, which was holding the most likely axis of the main German attack, and his main reserves would also be directed to Pukhov's sector. Pukhov's troops would also occupy four defensive belts (three army-level and the first front-level). However, due to the terrain, the distance between them would be approximately half that of the Voronezh Front. Therefore, the depth of the defenses on the direction of the most probable attack here was not 60 km, but 30 km. However, because of the 13th Army's narrow defensive front (32 km) and the enormous forces that were concentrated in the hands of its leader (12 divisions), it would have much higher tactical density, on average just 2.7 km for each of its rifle divisions, which was half the average width of a sector for each of the Voronezh Front's divisions on the main directions. Most importantly, forces of the 4th Breakthrough Artillery Corps of the Soviet High Command's reserve (more than 2,000 guns and mortars) would be deployed in the first two defensive belts, and it was thanks to this that an unprecedented density of artillery would be achieved here, to an extent that the Voronezh Front could not even approach. Accordingly, it was the artillery that would become the foundation of the defenses of the 13th Army's infantry and permit the Soviet side to stop the adversary's offensive rather quickly here relative to the Voronezh Front in the south. K.K. Rokossovsky wrote: "In the most threatened sector, where knowing the German tactics we expected the enemy's main attack would come on a front of 95 km, we assembled 58 percent of the infantry, 70 percent of the artillery, and 87 percent of the tanks and self-propelled guns … The second echelon and the Front's reserves were also positioned on the direction of the main enemy grouping's likely offensive."[132]

G.A. Koltunov and B.G. Solov'ev back in 1970 were the first to note Rokossovsky's larger capabilities in artillery units than Vatutin's. They wrote, "The operational artillery density on both *fronts* was equivalent, but the possibility of resisting the enemy's initial concentrated attack was greater on the Central Front than on the Voronezh Front. This is explained by the fact that the Central Front had 2,140 more guns and mortars than the Voronezh Front."[133] However, this most important factor did not become widely known, so it is not often used by Russian scholars when analyzing the results of the Battle of Kursk.

Thus, both Vatutin and Rokossovsky used one and the same principle of constructing a defense on the likely direction of the enemy's main attack but had different means at their disposal. K.K. Rokossovsky, having a narrower corridor for the possible enemy attack than Vatutin had in the south, created his defensive depth within the 13th Army alone, having girded

---

132 *Voenno-istoricheskii zhurnal*, No. 3 (1992), p. 31.
133 Koltunov and Solov'ev, *Kurskaia bitva*, p. 66.

its first echelon with the 4th Breakthrough Artillery Corps, while N.F. Vatutin was forced to flesh out the troops of the 6th and 7th Guards Armies with subordinate corps of the 1st Tank Army and Front reserves. Moscow probably agreed with him that it was too risky to mass rifle divisions in the sector of the 6th Guards Army (for example, at the expense of the 40th Army) without the availability such an artillery "fist" like the 4th Breakthrough Artillery Corps, given the danger of an enemy attack along several separate directions. Indeed, it could not have been otherwise, because all of the planning went under the supervision of single center, the General Staff, and all of the principle questions were resolved there. In fact, only after receiving its stamp of approval could the leadership of the two Fronts submit their plan of defense to the *Stavka*.

Nevertheless, after the war, in the arguments over "Who fought better at Kursk?", K.K. Rokossovsky used just this difference in means with the aim of proving that he and his staff, having created Pukhov's "super-army", the forces of which virtually covered all three likely directions of the Ninth Army's main attack, acted properly, while N.F. Vatutin, by drawing upon his reserves in order to create an operational density, supposedly acted recklessly when he scattered his strength along the entire 170-kilometer sector and failed to create the necessary tactical density there, where the enemy actually struck. However, in doing so he kept silent that it was impossible for the Voronezh Front to do what he did due to objective factors. Insisted K.K. Rokossovsky: "The correct determination of the most dangerous direction of an enemy offensive for a *front*'s forces, and matching this with a grouping and the maneuver of forces and means in the process of the battle are the main reasons for the more successful actions of the troops of the Central Front than of the Voronezh Front, where the primary main forces of this Front were distributed almost equally across its entire sector."[134] This was to say that in Rokossovsky's opinion, N.F. Vatutin should have moved up part of the 69th Army and 35th Guards Rifle Corps from the *front*-level belt of defenses into the army-level defensive belts, behind the armies of the first echelon, in order to create a high tactical density. In his opinion, this would have stopped the adversary already within a distance of 10-15 km, as happened in the course of the fighting on the northern side of the Kursk bulge.

However, such an approach was not viable for the situation that the Voronezh Front faced, since the enemy grouping that was operating here really was stronger than the one opposite the Central Front, and K.K. Rokossovsky had substantially more artillery than did N.F. Vatutin. It is not clear why when calculating the density of the defensive forces in the sector of the 13th Army, K.K. Rokossovsky believed that he should include the divisions that were covering all three directions and were positioned in all four belts of defenses (the three army-level and the one *front*-level), but when making this same calculation in the sector of the Voronezh Front, the troops of the 69th Army and 35th Guards Rifle Corps were excluded. After all, just like Pukhov's divisions, they were occupying the rear army-level defensive belt and the first *front*-level defensive belt that were blocking the main axis of the enemy attack – the Oboian' and Korocha directions.

Unquestionably, formally the commander of the Voronezh Front was not using his reserves for their intended purpose. Regulations stated that if these were "purely" reserves, then they should not be strictly tied to specific sectors of the defense, since at any time they might be needed to localize a breakthrough or to reinforce a direction that was under heavy enemy

---

134 *Voenno-istoricheskii zhurnal*, No. 3 (1992), p. 31.

pressure somewhere else. However, the war was requiring a creative approach to the operational art, and moreover there were solid reasons for Vatutin's decision. First, the *Stavka* had assigned enormous reserves to the Voronezh Front according to the standards of those times, and this was no accident, because of the larger number of tank-vulnerable direction in its sector than on the Central Front. Second, it is right to assume that it was up to the *front* commander-in-chief to choose how to use them, and he prudently decided that there was no justification to create a high tactical density with the forces of the 69th Army and 35th Guards Rifle Corps on the most important directions, since it would be impossible to shift them quickly from there if the need arose in the course of the fighting . He believed it was more effective to use them in order to create operational density (which is to say, I repeat, to increase the depth of the defenses). Here, they could play a dual role: both to hold their occupied line in the event of an enemy breakthrough to their positions, and at the same time, they could be quickly sent to other sectors. After all, this was the Front's second strategic echelon, the troops of which, following regulations, should be held out of combat until a need for them arose.

The motivations of the General of the Army's proposals become more understandable if you consider an important detail; at the moment when this alternative of using the reserves was under consideration, Moscow still had not decided whether it would attack or defend in the course of the summer campaign. Up until the end of April, in addition to the 69th Army and the 35th Guards Rifle Corps, N.F. Vatutin had under his command only two mobile formations, the 2nd Guards and 5th Guards Tank Corps. They might be useful only for launching flank attacks, and nothing more than that. Then Vatutin received a more serious reinforcement – the 1st Tank Army. However, the *Stavka* immediately banned the use of it on the defensive; in an extreme case, the Voronezh Front command might use it only for launching counterattacks in the event the enemy achieved a deep breakthrough, since this tank army was intended for the offensive into Ukraine. It was only in the latter half of May, when Moscow finally settled on a plan for the summer campaign, and the mobile reserves, including the 1st Tank Army, would be included in the defensive plan for participating in counterattacks, as well as for conducting defensive combat actions on a specific line for them.[135] Therefore, if N.F. Vatutin had assembled the 69th Army and 35th Guards Rifle Corps in the first echelon in order to create tactical density on vulnerable directions, as K.K. Rokossovsky did (having transferred his reserve 18th Guards Rifle Corps to the 13th Army), he simply would have been deprived of the bulk of his reserves – a commander's primary lever of influence on an operational situation. On the eve of the upcoming operation, this meant knowingly condemning oneself to a defeat. This would be especially so if the enemy launched not one, but two powerful attacks against the Voronezh Front's defenses, which N.F. Vatutin was anticipating.

Relying on the conception of a system of defense outlined above, N.F. Vatutin proposed the following plan of actions for his troops, but one with alternatives. In his opinion, when working out this document, it was necessary to pay attention to two key questions. First, how to prevent the enemy from making a deep penetration into the Front's defenses in the first several days of the enemy's offensive and to contain his panzer divisions within the tactical zone? Second, how to reduce the breaching power of the German assault groups not only by means of effective fire from the tanks, self-propelled guns, and the infantry of the first and second echelons, but also to

---

135 TsAMO RF, F.203, Op.2863, D.426, l. 65.

force the enemy command to disperse the strength of the panzer wedges across the entire front, and prevent the enemy from concentrating them at the spearhead of the main attack?

When addressing these questions, N.F. Vatutin primarily counted upon relying on his important "ally" – the terrain. The successful exploitation of this key factor, both when preparing for the Battle of Kursk and throughout the summer fighting, was one of the characteristic features of his generalship. The only case when he was compelled to ignore the terrain conditions, the counterattack at Prokhorovka, led to a tragic outcome. The highlight of Vatutin's plan was the idea to split Army Group South's attacking forces that were directed toward Kursk by means of creating powerful center of resistance on the joint flanks of Army Group South's two shock groupings (the Fourth Panzer Army and Army Detachment Kempf). N.F. Vatutin was anticipating that von Manstein's main grouping would form up in the Borisovka – Belgorod area and its main forces would launch an attack (to create the inner front of encirclement) to the north, in the direction of Oboian', or to the northeast – toward Prokhorovka (the Fourth Panzer Army), while the screening forces for the main grouping (the outer front of encirclement) would attack out of Belgorod to the east (Army Detachment Kempf) in the direction of Korocha. However, in order to be successful, it was extremely for the assault wedge remain intact. A breakthrough along the Oboian' highway was the most direct route to Kursk, but at the same time it gave the defenders the best possibility of derailing the offensive, if proper use was made of the terrain, particularly the basins of the Vorskla, Pena, Donets and Psel Rivers, as natural anti-tank obstacles.

However, no one could be certain that Erich von Manstein would in fact advance his main forces toward Oboian'. K.S. Moskalenko recalled that N.F. Vatutin told him that "One characteristic of von Manstein when using armored forces consists in the fact that he is always searching for a weaknesses in the defenses, usually a flank."[136] In order to provoke the enemy to launch the main attack precisely along the Oboian' highway and to lure his main grouping into the midst of the Front's defenses where it would be most advantageous for the Soviet side (since a breakthrough in the first days was practically unavoidable), N.F. Vatutin used a military stratagem, which to a civilian might seem very cynical. The Voronezh Front Commander-in-Chief proposed to arrange the defenses of the 6th Guards Army, that were holding the Oboian' direction (the 67th Guards, 52nd Guards and 375th Rifle Divisions) in a single echelon, while the divisions of the 40th and 7th Guards Army on the flanks of the 6th Guards Army were arrayed in two echelons, in order to create a greater tactical density of forces on the 6th Guards Army's flanks than in the sector of Chistiakov's army, including at the Oboian' highway. Considering that the Pena River, although narrow, but with a swampy basin, was located behind the 67th Guards Rifle Division, while good ground for tanks – the Oboian' corridor – lay behind the 52nd Guards Rifle Division and partially the 375th Rifle Division, Vatutin anticipated that the main events of the first day or two of the offensive should develop in the sector of the 52nd Guards Rifle Division. In addition, Vatutin planned to give the 40th and 7th Guards Army serious reinforcements. The former would receive almost as many forces and means as the 6th Guards Army, while the defenses of the latter already had a strong natural asset – the Severskii Donets River, but in addition, Vatutin planned to direct significant mobile and anti-tank reserves of the Front to its sector.

---

136 Parot'kin (ed.), *Kurskaia bitva*, p. 106.

Thus, Vatutin strove simultaneously to indicate to the German intelligence that the Oboian' direction (and the Oboian' highway) were objectively the most suitable place for the main attack toward Kursk: the shortest route to their objective, while the operational density of the Soviet forces here was not so high here, while ensuring that I.M. Chistiakov's neighbors had strong anti-tank defenses, in the event that the adversary struck with its main forces not toward Oboian', but toward Korocha (through the sector held by the 7th Guards Army) or toward Sudzha (through the sector held by the 40th Army). It should be noted that the military historians G.A. Koltunov and B.G. Solov'ev in their book *Kurskaia bitva* were the first to point out the unusual system of defense adopted by the Voronezh Front – the relatively low tactical density of troops on the most likely axis of the enemy's main attack and the rather high density at the 40th and 7th Guards Armies' boundaries with the 6th Guards Army. However, they did not explain the reasons for this, and only observed that this decision "corresponded to the existing situation."[137]

Accordingly, from the beginning N.F. Vatutin was sacrificing at a minimum two rifle divisions, which were deployed on the Oboian' direction (the 52nd Guards Rifle Division and 375th Rifle Division), by subjecting them to the attack of significantly superior enemy forces. He could not help but realize that even if they weren't in fact completely destroyed on the first day of the offensive, their losses would prove to be very high. However, this approach is one of the most widely used in the arsenal of military commanders. Moreover, he would seek to do all he could on his part to create an elaborate system of defenses here as well, and would bolster these divisions with anti-tank means, in order to keep their losses in the first 24 hours of the fighting at a minimum.

However, to "lure" von Manstein to the Oboian' direction was only half of the matter; the main thing was to make sure that his assault grouping became bogged down in this area and unable to make further progress to the north. An analysis of declassified documents in the TsAMO RF shows that the principle scheme to contain the main forces of Army Group South looked as follows. In order to advance successfully toward Kursk, it was important for both halves of von Manstein's shock grouping, which would be penetrating Vatutin's defenses in order to create the inner (Fourth Panzer Army) and outer (Army Detachment Kempf) ring of encirclement, to advance at the same pace and to stay in contact with each other. This would ensure the efficient use of the force, by keeping them concentrated in an attacking spearhead, and complicate the enemy's maneuvering with forces and means, thereby creating the conditions to penetrate the line of the 6th and 7th Guards Armies quickly and to expand the breakthrough corridor, which was extremely important in the offensive's first days. Accordingly, it was necessary hold the Fourth Panzer Army on the left, having enmeshed it in the fortifications and obstacles of the main defensive belt of Chistiakov's army, and to contain it within them for as long as possible, while knocking out German armor by every possible means.

In order to achieve this, Vatutin planned first to assign the 6th Guards Army the largest quantity of artillery and other anti-tank means, and to lace its sector (especially the main defensive belt) with mines and artificial obstacles, thereby creating a model of contemporary field fortifications, utilizing both combat experience and the latest designs and testing. This would enable its troops to hold the enemy as long as possible while inflicting casualties and

---

137 Koltunov and Solov'ev, *Kurskaia bitva*, p. 55.

material losses and allow the possibility of bringing up operational reserves. On 21 April 1943, the Commander-in-Chief of the Voronezh Front wrote Stalin:

> I'm especially reporting on the measures adopted to repulse large-scale attacks by tanks. I've decided to achieve this goal with all means of struggle:
> a. To arm all the units and formations with anti-tank rifles and anti-tank artillery in accordance with their establishment tables, and to equip sapper and engineer units with anti-tank rifles above their authorized strength.
> b. By April 1943, to man and equip all of the anti-tank artillery brigades and regiments fully, having attached them to the armies on the following basis: 38th and 40th Armies – one anti-tank artillery brigade and three anti-tank artillery regiments each; 21st Army [6th Guards Army] – six anti-tank and self-propelled artillery regiments, and two anti-tank artillery brigades; 64th Army [7th Guards Army] – six anti-tank and self-propelled artillery regiments and one anti-tank artillery brigade; and 69th Army – one anti-tank artillery brigade. In addition, on 25 April 1943, six anti-tank artillery regiments and three regiments of light artillery will be placed in the reserve of the Front.
> c. By 25 April 1943, to form and equip three battalions of anti-tank rifles each in the 38th and 40th Armies; five battalions of anti-tank rifles each in the 21st and 64th Armies, and five battalions of anti-tank rifles in the Front reserve. In addition, three battalions will be arriving from the *Stavka* reserve. Thus, altogether there will be 28 anti-tank rifle battalions.
> d. The order has been issued to deploy 150,000 anti-tank mines in the course of April.
> e. To implement practical measures in accordance with coded message No. 52 from 12 April 1943, a copy of which has been sent to the Chief of the Red Army's General Staff.[138]

Second, considering that the opening attack would be the strongest, while Chistiakov's divisions would be spread out into a single line, it was assumed that they would be able to hold their positions for approximately 24 hours. Therefore, Vatutin decided that already on the second day, or at most on the third day of the operation to move up the main forces of Lieutenant General M.E. Katukov's 1st Tank Army into the 6th Guards Army's second belt of defenses, where they would become a quasi-third echelon of Chistiakov's army. An a small number of its tanks (from the 3rd Mechanized Corps) would be deployed in the vicinity of Iakovlevo (on the Oboian' highway) already in June 1943. With its three tank and mechanized corps, the 1st Tank Army would strengthen the defenses in the bend of the Pena River (behind the 67th Guards Rifle Division) and serve as an armored shield to block the primary tank-vulnerable "corridor" (behind the 52nd Guards Rifle Division) between the Pena and Lipovyi Donets Rivers (along the Syrtsevo – Izotovo woods – Iakovlevo – Bol'shie Maiachki line), along which the Germans, it was assumed, would move out from Belgorod to the north (toward Oboian'), and possibly to the northeast as well (toward Prokhorovka). Accordingly, there was no real

---

138 Glantz and House, *Kurskaia bitva: Reshaiushchii povorotnyi punkt*, p. 392.

weakening of the 6th Guards Army. The Front was not planning for any other army a third, and moreover armored echelon on both likely directions of the German advance – the Oboian' and Prokhorovka directions (given the need, both the 1st Tank Army's 31st Tank Corps and the 5th Guards "Stalingrad" Tank Corps would move out to this area).

On top of all this, the commander of the 40th Army Lieutenant General K.S. Moskalenko was instructed to plan to make strong counterattacks on its left flank in the direction of the 6th Guards Army's sector. Its troops should carry out two primary tasks that flowed from their proximity to the deployment area of Army Group South's main grouping and the likely axis of its main attack. First, they were to screen securely the Sudzha direction. Second, they were to serve as Vatutin's reserve, from which, if the situation demanded, he could draw upon forces for holding the main direction. At the same time, they should loom over the left flank of the German main grouping that was launching the attack toward Kursk, and as soon as the enemy forces broke through on the Oboian' direction, strike at its left flank, at the base of the Fourth Panzer Army's penetration. For this purpose, the 40th Army's commander was given significant amounts of artillery and infantry support tanks; according to their number, by the beginning of July 1943, the 40th Army would stand in third place among the Voronezh Front's six armies.

According to how the situation developed, Lieutenant General V.D. Kriuchenkin's 69th Army was also preparing to launch counterattacks (from out of the Front's second echelon) against the right flank of an enemy grouping that was advancing toward Oboian'. Thus, N.F. Vatutin was planning that on approximately the second or third day of the fighting, Army Group South's assault wedge on the Oboian' direction would run into the armored shield of the 1st Tank Army, and its flanking divisions, boxed in by the Vorskla and Donets Rivers, would get caught in the powerful pincers created by the 40th and 69th Armies. Meanwhile, the adversary would be forced to continue to be engaged in hard fighting with the 6th Guards Army's forces.

The Soviet command did not have accurate information on the forces that Army Group South would draw upon for launching the main attack, and therefore the danger that they would even overcome the "corridor of fire" of the four defending armies still existed. In order to reduce this danger, and in the event of a breakthrough of the 6th Guards Army's second echelon, so that the Germans wouldn't be able to develop this tactical success into operational space, it was vital to block securely their auxiliary grouping as well, which according to N.F. Vatutin's calculations, would strike the 7th Guards Army east of Belgorod toward Korocha. Given the failure of its offensive, even von Manstein's significant forces on the Oboian' direction wouldn't be able to reach operational space within a relatively short period of time. Two primary factors would affect their progress: the losses in the course of breaking through the defenses of the 6th Guards Army while repulsing the counterattacks of the 40th and 69th Armies, and the simultaneous need to divert substantial forces in order to screen the flanks, which would grow longer as the Germans advanced.

However, all of this was possible only in case that the enemy could not commit extremely large reserves into the fighting immediately upon breaching the 6th Guards Army's defenses. So, this possibility received thorough consideration, and the leadership of the Voronezh Front and the *Stavka* also prepared substantial reserves for this possible development. Even so, if Army Detachment Kempf was not stopped by the 7th Guards Army just as Army Group South committed reserves to exploit the success, then naturally the Soviet operational, and possibly even the strategic reserves would begin to disintegrate. In this case the defensive operation might proceed according to the worst scenario with disastrous consequences. Therefore, the Voronezh Front absolutely had to prevent the consolidation of both of the enemy's groupings (the Fourth Panzer Army and Army Detachment Kempf) into a unified striking "fist", and force them to diverge from each other already in the first days of the offensive, in order to force the Germans to divert strength to screen not just two flanks (in the event that they were able to advance side-by-side), but four.

N.F. Vatutin planned to handle this task in the following manner. First, by reinforcing the line of the 7th Guards Army across its entire front, in order to prevent Army Detachment Kempf from advancing through its sector at the same pace as the Fourth Panzer Army if it broke through toward Oboian', if Hoth's troops proved able to overcome the 6th Guards Army's main defensive belt. Second, by setting up an impregnable obstacle at the boundary between 6th Guards and 7th Guards Armies and to repulse Army Detachment Kempf's attack not only with the forces of the 7th Guards Army, but also of the 69th Army (or with the Front's reserves from its positions).

A strike at the boundary between two units or formations is the most widely adopted and effective approach for a breakthrough when attacking. N.F. Vatutin decided to counter this with his defensive set-up. He made sure that a virtually impassable swampy terrain – the confluence of the Severskii and Lipovyi Donets Rivers – lay behind the forward edge of the first-line divisions of the 6th Guards Army and 7th Guards Army. Therefore, it was here that he drew the boundary between the two armies, and then planned to strengthen this sector (Erik – Chernaia Poliana – Staryi Gorod – forced labor colony) substantially. As already noted, he positioned divisions into two echelons here and assembled a significant amount of artillery to back them up. By the end of June 1943, a density of 19-23 guns per kilometer had been created at the adjacent flanks of the 6th Guards and 7th Guards Armies (between the 81st Guards Rifle Division and 375th Rifle Division).[139] No other sector of the Voronezh Front had such a high indicator. In addition, just as the General Staff demanded, their commands were given impressive forces – tank, artillery and engineer units – especially for covering the boundary between these two armies. They were to work out in a short period of time plans for counterattacks and cooperation between themselves in the event of an enemy penetration at their boundary. How thoroughly the covering of the adjacent flanks of the 6th Guards and 7th Guards Armies was pondered is shown by a document I found in the TsAMO – an act regarding the final strengthening of the forces and the division of responsibilities in this sector, which was signed on 12 May 1943 by highly-posted officers and generals of both armies.

However, the reinforcement of this sector did not end with these measures. N.F. Vatutin also planned to assemble the 69th Army between the bottomlands of the two rivers in order to cover this very same boundary between the 6th Guards and 7th Guards Armies. As a result of the natural obstacle – the interfluvial area between the Severskii and Lipovyi Donets Rivers, which formed a narrow wedge that extended toward the front, was to be converted into an arrow-headed, fortified knot of resistance through the efforts of Kriuchenkin's subordinate troops. Rifle regiments and the sizable artillery grouping of the 81st Guards Rifle Division and 375th Rifle Division together with attached assets were being readied to deploy in two echelons in front of this spearhead. The Voronezh Front Commander-in-Chief assumed that if

---

139 Zamulin, V.N., *Zabytoe srazhenie Ognennoi dugi* [*Forgotten battle of the Bulge of Fire*] (Moscow: Iauza, 2009), p. 24. This book has been translated by Stuart Britton and published by Helion Press in 2018 under the title *The Forgotten Battle of the Kursk Salient: 7th Guards Army's Stand against Army Detachment Kempf*.

the forces of Manstein's assault wedge were unable to penetrate the boundary between the 6th Guards and 7th Guards Armies, they would be forced to try to bypass it, which would mean the unified front of Army Group South's offensive would cleave into two separate groupings, with no close contact between each other. If the adversary in this case nevertheless attempted to break through into the depth of the 6th and 7th Guards Army's defenses, the right flank of the Fourth Panzer Army and the left flank of Army Detachment Kempf would be exposed to counterattacks by the 69th Army and the Front's mobile reserves.

Initially (in April), it was anticipated that only two separate tank corps (the 2nd Guards and 5th Guards Tank Corps) that N.F. Vatutin possessed at that time would be available for counterattacks together with Kriuchenkin's army. However, as already mentioned above, at the end of May the *Stavka* would make the decision to use tank armies as well directly in the defense at Kursk. For this purpose, Katukov's 1st Tank Army would be transferred to the Voronezh Front, and N.F. Vatutin would issue an order to the army commander to work out alternative counterattacks in close cooperation with the separate corps within the framework of his plan. This step would become an important additional element, which would give the Soviet side confidence in "Vatutin's plan" (on the main directions), and would unquestionably increase the sturdiness of the Front's defense as a whole.

It was further being assumed that after the Fourth Panzer Army would be stopped, the 6th Guards Army and 1st Tank Army with the support of the 69th and 40th Armies would cut up its grouping, while the Front reserves in cooperation with the 7th Guards Army would at the same time launch an attack against Army Detachment Kempf. After eliminating both parts of Manstein's grouping, the Voronezh Front together with the *Stavka*'s strategic reserves (the Steppe Military District) that had been brought up by this time would launch a decisive counteroffensive through Belgorod and Tomarovka toward Ukraine.

Considering that the 7th Guards Army was defending the likely axis of the enemy's auxiliary attack, as well as the fact that the Severskii Donets River was fronting its line, N.F. Vatutin allocated noticeably fewer artillery means to M.S. Shumilov than he did to I.M. Chistiakov, but at the same time transferred to the 7th Guards Army more infantry support tanks (the equivalent of more than a tank corps), and also directed into its sector a portion of his mobile (the 2nd Guards Tank Corps) and anti-tank reserve. On the whole, this army received an impressive amount of assets in order to carry out its assignments.

The forward edge of the 69th Army, which already at the beginning of April was deployed behind the boundary between Chistiakov's and Shumilov's armies, ran along the Bogorodetskoe – Vypolzovka – Alekseevka – Nechaevka – Belyi Kolodez', Bol'shoe Troitskoe, Belianka, Efremovka line. It had three main tasks.[140] First, in the event of a breakthrough of the 6th Guards Army and 7th Guards Army sectors, or the withdrawal of their flank divisions, in cooperation with their troops and the Front's reserves it was to destroy the enemy that had broken through. Second, given the successful repulse of the adversary's attack by the armies standing in front of it, the 69th Army was to be ready for an offensive and to exploit a success in three directions: Tomarovka – Graivoron – Akhtyrka; Belgorod – Khar'kov; and Volchansk – Khar'kov. However, there was a problem; from the outset, Kriuchenkin's 69th Army was the weakest in the Voronezh Front. Even with the start of the Battle of Kursk, it had not fully

---

140 TsAMO RF, F.426, Op.10753, D.410, l. 17, 18.

completed the process of reforming and replenishing its divisions. N.F. Vatutin was anticipating this and already at the end of April ordered Lieutenant General S.G. Goriachev, the commander of the 35th Guards Rifle Corps, to establish cooperation with its headquarters, so at any moment it could efficiently be included in the army. Goriachev's corps was positioned 15-25 km behind the line of the 69th Army and was virtually its second defensive echelon. Goriachev's corps had three rifle divisions, which had been formed up only in April 1943, but by the start of the battle, they had been practically brought up to their authorized strength. In addition, already in the course of the defensive fighting, it was anticipated that the 69th Army would also be reinforced with forces from out of the Front's reserve. Thus, N.F. Vatutin was doing everything within his power to strengthen Kriuchenkin's army and was therefore considering that the 6th Guards and 7th Guards Armies, having received the enemy's opening attacks, would in cooperation with the 1st Tank Army inflict serious losses on the Germans, so the 69th Army should be encountering enemy divisions that had already been battered and worn down in the fighting. Therefore, it seemed fully capable of carrying out its orders to become a barrier on the boundary between the 6th Guards and 7th Guards Armies, and a flanking threat in the event in the event the Germans neglected to screen their flanks. However, this piece of the plan proved to be most weakly elaborated. The reliance on the tenacity of Kriuchenkin's and Goriachev's troops proved to be too much, for subjective reasons as well. The command staff of their divisions, which had been appointed to their posts in the spring of 1943, would show themselves unready not only to carry out combat assignments, but in a number of cases even to do their elementary duties.

"Vatutin's plan" in the form that it has been presented above, was not known to historians prior writing this book. The possibility to grasp the Voronezh Front Commander-in-Chief's scheme appeared only after I had analyzed a recently declassified large block of documentary sources in the TsAMO RF at the *front-* and army-level. The mistaken assertion of several domestic historians, who purported that the presence of large forces and means in the 40th Army before the Battle of Kursk confirmed the inability of the Front's leadership to determine the direction of Army Group South's main axis of attack, is also connected with this circumstance. Therefore, it supposedly spread its forces across all the possible tank-vulnerable directions.[141] This assertion directly echoes the debatable thesis advanced by K.K. Rokossovsky in the early 1960s. In fact, according to their manpower and number of weapons, the 40th and 6th Guards Army were practically equivalent, but this does not contradict Vatutin's scheme. I will remind the reader that the letter from the Front's Military Council from 21 April 1943 expressed the opinion that the Germans wouldn't likely be launching their main attack in 40th Army's sector, but only a secondary attack, and with that consideration, N.F. Vatutin gave K.S. Moskalenko one more problematic assignment: to draw a portion of the enemy forces away from the 6th Guards Army's sector, so the substantial reinforcement of his army was fully justified. K.S. Moskalenko even wrote about this in his memoirs:

> When estimating the possible direction of the enemy's main attack, the Voronezh Front command finally came to the conclusion that the shortest and most convenient route to Kursk, toward which the enemy would be striving, lay along the highway through Oboian'. So, it was this axis that received the most cover. However, could the

---

141 Isaev, *1943: Ot Khar'kov do Kurska* [*1943: From Khar'kov to Kursk*] (Moscow: Veche, 2008), p. 193.

Front Commander-in-Chief limit himself with this? Was he correct in thinking that the German-fascist command would choose the shortest direction, even though it was doubtlessly aware of the preparation of the strongest defenses here? The answer to this question can only be negative. Especially since the fascist armored groupings, having encountered stubborn resistance, often rejected frontal attacks and sought bypassing routes of advance ...

That is why the Voronezh Front command did not limit itself with the creation of a particularly sturdy defense in the sector of the 6th Guards Army alone and the assembly here of powerful means of reinforcement, as well as the entire 1st Tank Army in the second echelon. Alongside this he took the necessary steps as dictated by the situation to organize the repulse of possible enemy attempts to break through the defenses to the right or left of the shortest direction, which is to say, in the sectors of the 40th Army and 7th Guards Army.

It mustn't be forgotten that the massing of the greatest forces and means in the sector of the 6th Guards Army immediately confirms the accuracy of the Front command's assessment of precisely where the German main attack would land. As concerns the 40th Army, the assembly of troops and assets here was intended not only for a defense in the event of an enemy's bypassing maneuver, but also for launching counterattacks in the southwestern direction. Such a counterattack already received attention from us when readying the defense. It was foreseen that it would be launched after the enemy went on the offensive against the 6th Guards Army. Directed toward Cherkasskoe, which is to say at the base of the anticipated penetration, it might play role in defeating the attacking hostile grouping. Our plan was approved by N.F. Vatutin and we thoroughly planned for its implementation.[142]

The Oboian' direction was always viewed by N.F. Vatutin as the most dangerous one, where Army Group South would most likely commit its main forces. Moreover, this assessment did not remain only on paper. A point in Vatutin's plan regarding the setting in motion of all of the Front's mobile reserves – the 1st Tank Army, the 5th Guards Tank Corps, the 2nd Guards Tank Corps. as well as the 14th Separate Destroyer Anti-Tank Artillery Brigade from the Front's anti-tank reserves – to this axis from the start of the fighting shows this. At an order from the Front's chief of staff Lieutenant General S.P. Ivanov at the end of May, their command staff began reconnoitering the routes of movement and nighttime marches of the brigades to the sector of Chistiakov's army. A forward observation post for Lieutenant General M.E. Katukov was set up in the sector of the 6th Guards Army's 52nd Guards Rifle Division, while the full 1st Guards Tank Brigade was dug into the ground in the second belt of defenses in the Iakovlevo area as the forward detachment of the 1st Tank Army's 3rd Mechanized Corps. Nothing like this was done in the sector of the 40th Army.

From the outset, Moskalenko's 40th Army had a primary assignment: together with defending its own lines (the probable direction of an auxiliary enemy attack), to contribute to keeping the enemy grouping that was attacking the 6th Guards Army contained within the army-level

---

142 Moskalenko, K.S., *Na iugo-zapadnom napravlenii* [*On the southwestern direction*] (Moscow: Voenizdat, 1979), pp. 62-63.

defensive belts through counterattacks launched by its own forces, and given the need, to send units and even divisions to its neighbor on the left in order to reinforce the Oboian' direction. As is known, in the first four days, the Voronezh Front command would conduct the defensive operation strictly in accordance with the previously devised plan that had been confirmed by Moscow. N.F. Vatutin would begin to improvise only on the evening of 9 July, when in the name of the Front's Military Council, he would petition the *Stavka* to authorize a counterattack with the use of the strategic reserves of the Steppe Military District. Therefore, skipping somewhat ahead in the events, I will note that already on the second day of the operation, N.F. Vatutin's pragmatic decisions would justify the 40th Army's assignments as outlined above. Between 5 and 15 July 1943, he would shift only five units and formations from the 38th Army to the 6th Guards Army's sector, including one rifle division and two tank brigades, but in contrast would remove 16 units and formations from the 40th Army, including three rifle and one anti-aircraft division and eight tank and destroyer anti-tank artillery brigades, and send them to the 6th Guards Army's sector.[143] Moreover, Vatutin would take the majority of these forces from the 40th Army and send them to the 6th Guards Army's sector prior to 9 July inclusively. In addition, even weakened, the 40th Army would nevertheless take part in the counterattack on 8 July 1943, but instead of a full counterattack, it conducted only demonstrative attacks against the left wing of the Fourth Panzer Army according to the plan that had been readied that spring. Incidentally, the account of its headquarters about the fighting on 8 July 1943 mentioned the plan for an attack into the flank of the enemy's Oboian' grouping (in the direction of Tomarovka) that had been confirmed by the Front's leadership before the start of the Battle of Kursk, with the aim of diverting enemy forces from the sector of the 6th Guards Army – and gave reasons why it was unable to carry it out: "The previously settled question about the shock grouping of troops of the 40th Army's left flank going on an offensive toward Tomarovka, after the removal of almost all of its assets and one rifle division[144], was changed at a directive from the Front headquarters on 8 July 1943 into limited attacks in this direction with two divisions. At the order of the army commander, Major General Comrade Perkhorovich's 52nd Rifle Corps was charged with conducting this operation … from 1000 on 8 July 1943."[145]

Finally, when analyzing the N.F. Vatutin's decisions (and incidentally, those of K.K. Rokossovsky as well) regarding the key considerations in the preparations for the Battle of Kursk, in my view two important aspects should always be kept in mind. They will help avoid making mistakes when assessing their activities.

First, the commander-in-chief of any *front* was operating with those forces and means that were given to him by the *Stavka*, depending on its own view of the situation, which unfortunately was not always correct. The "gap" between the two concepts ("forces required for meeting the objective" and "those available to a *front*") had to be filled by the talent of the commander when organizing and conducting combat work, as well as by increasing the pressure on the troops. However, frequently the deficit of strength because of this invisible influence was significantly larger than what commander-in-chief had in mind for an operation, and the subordinate troops were already at the limit of their physical possibilities. Before the Battle of Kursk, K.K.

---

143 Parot'kin, *Kurskaia bitva*, p. 315.
144 The 40th Army lost these forces on 6 and 7 July 1943, when they were taken away to reinforce the 6th Guards Tank Army and 1st Tank Army on the Oboian' direction.
145 TsAMO RF, F.203, Op.2843, D.520, l. 220.

Rokossovsky virtually had no such gap; he was given everything necessary for a defense, which cannot be said about N.F. Vatutin. Because of Moscow's miscalculation in determining where the enemy's main attack would take place around the Kursk bulge[146], Rokossovsky would be given over-the-top support, beyond all reasonable calculations. General of the Army Vatutin and his subordinates just did not have the abilities to cover this deficit. It was for precisely this reason that already on the second day of the German offensive, Moscow would be forced to send entire corps and armies hastily to the south, and not because of the fact that N.F. Vatutin was a short-sighted commander and the troops of his Front were less tenacious than their neighbors to the north.

Second, between 15 and 20 skilled, for the standards of those times, professionals of high rank took part in the planning of the Kursk defensive operation. The Front headquarters prepared the documentation and worked out the plan in detail with the *Stavka* representatives Marshals of the Soviet Union A.M. Vasilevsky and G.K. Zhukov, who spent more time among the troops around Kursk than they did in Moscow. Then the plan was meticulously gone over and analyzed in the General Staff. Only after this did it come under discussion in the Kremlin. Unquestionably, no one was immune to mistakes, but in such a "processing chain", the mistakes could only be very large, which is to say, of a strategic nature. At the very least, the drafters of the plan were splendidly aware of the fact that in the sector of the 6th Guards Army, which was defending the likely axis of the enemy's main attack, Chistiakov's operational density of troops was lower than that of its adjacent neighbors, while the 40th Army had more tanks than the 6th Guards Army. After all, the planning of any defense begins with the availability and distribution of forces and means. If their allocation was decided in such a fashion, it means that one should first search for a motive, and not simply accuse the military commanders of incompetence as a statement of fact and stop with that.

Thus, Vatutin's plan was entirely directed first at dispersing the strength of the German groupings, and second, neutralizing their qualitative superiority over our troops in armored fighting vehicles, by resting primarily on the challenging terrain and the coordinated actions of all of the armies of the Voronezh Front's left flank and center. I will emphasize that the reliance of the Voronezh Front's Commander-in-Chief on fully exploiting the terrain was a correct decision not only when laying out and building the armies' defensive belts, but also in order to cleave Manstein's assault groupings along two diverging axes of advance. Even though Vatutin was unsuccessful in fully realizing his plan due to the mistake made by the *Stavka* when determining where the main German attack would land, the General of the Army's foresight and calculations would play a key role in the successful repulse of the enemy's offensive.

Now let us return to the northern face of the Kursk bulge, to the Central Front's sector, and take a look at how the work was going here to prepare for the summer campaign. This Front began to form up hastily on the basis of the Don Front's field command according to *Stavka* Directive No. 46056 from 5 February 1943.[147] Its process of forming up was to be completed within 10 days, on 15 February. Recalled K.K. Rokossovsky:

---

146 Zhukov, *Vospominaniia i razmyshleniia*, Vol. 3, p. 37.
147 *Russkii arkhiv. Velikaia Otechestvennaia voina: Stavka Verkhovnogo Glavnokomandovaniia. Dokumenty i materialy 1943*, p. 70.

The forces of the new *front* were to deploy between the Briansk and Voronezh Fronts, which at the time were continuing to attack toward Kursk and in the direction of Khar'kov, and working in concert with the Briansk Front, to launch a deep enveloping attack in the overall direction of Gomel' and Smolensk, into the flank and rear of the enemy's Orel grouping. The start of this exquisitely designed operation was set to begin on 15 February. However, before it could begin, it was necessary first of all to assemble the forces ... My arguments that this deadline was not realistic failed to convince the *Stavka*.[148]

Therefore, in the aforementioned directive, a very complicated and large task was placed before the General Staff: in the shortest period of time, between 12 and 23 February, to gather all the forces included under the new *front* at Kursk. Rokossovsky's Central Front received them from three sources: the former Don Front, which had been sent by railroad from Stalingrad and consisted of the 21st Army, 65th Army and 16th Air Army; the 2nd Tank Army, which Rokossovsky received from the Briansk Front; and the newly-formed 70th Army from out of the *Stavka* Reserve. The assembly of the forces did not go smoothly at all, including because of departmental squabbles; the former First Deputy Chief of the Red Army's Department of Military Communications at that time testified:

> The *Stavka* decided to send the freed-up armies to Kursk in order to continue the offensive. The task was urgent. Approximately 900 trains would be needed to carry it out. The People's Commissar of Railroads assured that empty boxcars were already standing in place on the Stalingrad – Povorino line in a loading area north of Stalingrad. However, the chief of the Front's Military Transport Department General I.V. Dmitriev was reporting from there that not a single train had arrived to embark the troops. I called A.V. Khrulev [the USSR People's Commissar of Railroads and the Chief of the Red Army's Rear Services] and he answered: "That's the report that you have, but I have a different one. They've reported to me that trains have been brought up, but that there are no troops at the points of embarkation."
>
> Odd, wouldn't you say? This after all was not at the front, where sometimes you cannot make heads or tails out of a situation. This was the deep rear. I trusted Dmitriev unconditionally. For a long time I knew him to be a punctual and honest comrade. I got in touch with him: "Go, take a look into the situation." He replied, "I'm heading to all the embarkation points." While he was driving around, looking for the boxcars at all six stations, I became convinced that he wouldn't find any; the time had lapsed. I called Khrulev, and once again it was a waste of time. I told him, "There are no boxcars." He told me, "There are boxcars." I had to seek out the Front Commander-in-Chief K.K. Rokossovsky over the telephone. He told me that together with Dmitriev, they had divided up the embarkation points and literally went through them with a fine-toothed comb. There were no boxcars. Instead, railcars were standing here and there loaded with military supplies that had not been used in the recent operation.

---

148 Rokossovsky, K.K., *Soldatskii dolg* [*Soldier's duty*] (Moscow: Voenizdat, 1997), p. 242.

However, even so there were few of them. Moreover, platform cars were needed for loading artillery and tanks.

The fruitless discussions and conversations delayed the transport of the Central Front's troops for several days. I was forced to report to Stalin. "Fine!" he said, and then hung up the phone. An hour later Beria called me and said, "Listen, come see me, we'll figure things out." I went to the Lubianka. Khrulev, his deputy at the People's Commissariat of Railroads, German Kovalev, and other comrades were already seated in Beria's office. Beria called upon Khrulev to speak. Andrei Vasil'evich began to rebuke our service with false information. Then I asked Beria to connect us with the Front Commander-in-Chief Rokossovsky. He quickly got in touch with him, and Rokossovsky, followed by Dmitriev from a different switching office, repeated that there were no trains; Khrulev was referring to just loaded cars that had not been adapted for transporting troops. It was February outside, and there were no heating stoves in the cars, the walls of which had numerous gaps and loopholes. The soldiers would freeze. However, Khrulev became stubborn and refused to budge. Then Beria said, "Listen, let us go out into the adjacent room." What they said there to each other, I don't know, but Andrei Vasil'evich returned pale and he silently departed. I drove off to the People's Commissariat of Railroads together with the chief of the Main Department of Transport G.V. Kovalev and did not leave until they had brought up boxcars for Rokossovsky's troops, and the men began to embark.[149]

For the sake of justice, it should be noted that in the future, the railroad workers, particularly in the area of the Kursk bulge, did a large amount of work to keep the forces supplied with everything necessary. Here is just one, clear example: Pursuant to the State Defense Committee's Decree No. 3160 from 10 April 1943, they quickly increased the trafficability of the Elets – Kastornoe railroad to 36 train-pairs, the Kastornoe – Kursk railroad to 24 train-pairs, the Kastornoe – Valuiki railroad to 18 train-pairs, and the Valuiki – Kupiansk railroad to 18 train-pairs per day.[150] If in March 1943 a train ran along the Kastornoe – Shshigry railroad sector at a rate of 15 km/hour and the Shshigry – Kursk sector at a rate of 20 km/hour, then in June the operating speed rose to up 30 km/hour and 45 km/hour respectively. Between April and July 1943, the workers of the Kursk railroad hub were able to ensure the arrival of 2,513 military trains and the departure of 2,732 military trains.[151]

However, let us return to the events of February. As is known, the *Stavka* plan to destroy the German Orel grouping went awry. Combat operations on the Briansk and Sevsk directions, which got underway in February – March, were substantially hampered by the incomplete assembly of Rokossovsky's forces, the difficult conditions of a harsh (snowy and frigid) winter, the stubborn German resistance, and the successful advance of German forces in the Khar'kov area and Donbas.

In fact, given the assembly of a strategic formation at a new location, as was the case with the Central Front, and given the stabilization of combat operations after large offensive or defensive

---

149 Kumanev, G., *Govoriat Stalinskie narkomy* [*Stalin's People's Commissars speak*] (Smolensk: Rusich, 2005), pp. 323-324.
150 RGASPI, F.644, Op.1, D.102, l. 136, 137.
151 GAPI, KO, F.P-1, Op. 1, D.3068, l. 33.

battles (for example, the situation of the Voronezh Front in March 1943), the first order of business for its command was the matter of determining the area for the deployment of its forces and the timetable for their movement into these areas. The primary requirements for determining locations were the convenience they offered for directing the troops (the proximity of the area to them) and a relatively high degree of protection (camouflage or cover) from the enemy's ground and aerial reconnaissance. In the course of an offensive, given the large dynamics of the fighting, the requirements for camouflaging are naturally lesser.

As a rule, the main departments of a headquarters (the operations department, intelligence department, etc.) were accommodated in intact buildings of small villages (in schools, hospitals, or in the extreme case, spacious detached houses) that were 25-30 km behind the front. However, once a situation began to stabilize, the command sought to relocate the command posts at every level, and first of all those of a *front*, to new areas closer to the front, and its departments had to be housed not in settlements, where there was a danger of their destruction, but in bunkers and dugouts, set up in overgrown balkas or wooded areas. The vegetation itself and the size of the wooded area (a patch of woods, a forest, etc.) were the primary means of camouflage and were widely used for concealing points of command. At the same time, as a rule, inhabited dugouts were not to be located in places where the majority of the staff bunkers were located. Even the accommodation of the senior and higher command staff in nearby villages apart from the deployment area of the main departments and offices was considered acceptable. According to the security requirements of those times, it took about a month to relocate a first-echelon *front* headquarters. If a headquarters tarried in one place any longer than that, it was believed that the likelihood of its detection and destruction by the enemy rose exponentially. In the acting army everyone was aware of this, but nevertheless this rule was broken not infrequently, which at times led to hazardous consequences. There were many such examples, including with both Rokossovsky's and Vatutin's command posts prior to the Battle of Kursk, when both commanders survived only thanks to chance.

The forward echelon of the Voronezh Front's headquarters back in the course of the Khar'kov defensive operation had moved from Novyi Oskol closer to the front, to Bobryshovo (17 km east of Oboian'). At first it was located in the village itself, and in fact, the Front's new commander-in-chief General of the Army N.F. Vatutin had arrived here on 25 March 1943. In April it moved into a nearby birch grove. As soon as the dirt roads began to dry out, the question arose about choosing a new location for the Front headquarters and moving the headquarters of the 2nd Air Army from Novyi Oskol. On 9 April, the chief of engineers and the chief of communications received an order about preparing a new command post by 5 May 1943.[152] After the reconnoitering of the area was finished, the Military Council decided to set up the new command post in a forested area that lay 10 km north of the Rzhava railroad station[153],

---

152 TsAMO RF, F.203, Op.2843, D.301, l. 195.
153 Rzhava was a station southeast (today south) of the railroad, located 31 km east of Oboian'. It was founded in 1869. Up until 1898 it carried the name Mar'ino, and until 1915 it was then called Kleimikhelovo. It received its final name in honor of a river that flows just 1.5 km away. In 1882 the narrow-gauge Rzhava – Oboian' railway was commissioned, which was continuing to function in the years of the Great Patriotic War as well.

which was located in the Kursk – Belgorod sector (in the village of Mar'ino[154], 78 km southeast of Kursk), while the headquarters of the 2nd Air Army by 30 April had moved to Chernovets (northeast of Mar'ino). Both of these villages were located between the rear army-level defensive belt and the first front-level line. The fixed attention of the Front's leadership to the location of the 2nd Air Army's headquarters was connected not only with the fact that the main components of the command over the troops, including those of the combined-arms armies, were already located in new places by this time (prior to the Battle of Kursk, only the 5th Guards Tank Corps would shift the location of its headquarters on 7 June). The point was that the expenditure of resources when readying its headquarters was no less than what the Front's command post required, because it was necessary to lay out communication cables to not only the headquarters of the aviation corps and divisions, but also to the armies, as well as to each airfield location, of which there were many.

Initially the command post in the Rzhava area was viewed as a reserve post. However, already in the course of its construction, the decision was made in response to the arriving intelligence that significant enemy forces were assembling in the Khar'kov area to prepare an alternate headquarters behind the first front-level defensive line in the village of Manturovo. Therefore, from May 1943 the Front command post in the Rzhava area officially became the main one, while the command post in Manturovo became the alternate; meanwhile the former command post in Bobryshovo became only a reserve signals hub to handle communications with Moscow and was camouflaged by the SMERSH counter-intelligence organs to appear as a major headquarters, though in certain documents it is called a reserve command post. However, no other auxiliary command posts on the Voronezh Front were planned or built. A large number of log and dirt bunkers were prepared in the areas of the above-listed command posts, primarily in wooded locations, and prefab cottages for the work and rest of the command staffs. In addition, main command and service facilities, utility bunkers, dugouts for telegraph posts and long-distance telephone switchboards, and facilities for high-frequency stations were set up deep underground. For concealment purposes, all of the lines of communication out to 2-3 km from the command post were buried underground. To set up these command posts required a lot of extremely labor-intensive and hard work, which as a rule was done at night.

However, according to the recollections of General V.V. Zvenigorodsky, who at that time was the Front's first deputy chief of communications, the alternate command post in Manturovo was the largest in size and had the most communication means. It took two months to set it up, being initially commissioned only on 30 May, but only the main work was completed before the Battle of Kursk. Skipping somewhat ahead in the events, I will note that the alternate command post in Manturovo would be called upon only once, on 11 July 1943, and at that only partially. On this day the enemy was nearing Prokhorovka Station, which was located 26 km from Rzhava, and I.V. Stalin issued an order over the telephone to N.F. Vatutin to move to Manturovo. However, the Front Commander-in-Chief sent only an operational communications group there, while he himself remained in the command post in Rzhava.

As was in fact planned, the main command post was completely ready by the beginning of May. In addition, 6 km away in the village of Mar'ino, the construction of a mess hall for the

---

154 Between 1934 and 1959, the village of Mar'ino was a district center of Kursk Oblast; in 1959 it was renamed Pristep', the center of a district of Kursk Oblast that bears the same name.

officers and generals of the entire command staff was completed, as well as facilities for the work and rest of the personnel of the Front's Political Department, the headquarters for the different arms of service, a field post office, and an airfield for liaison aircraft. However, the movement into it could not be executed right away, because the security guard for it had not yet formed up, nor had the last major active concealment step been conducted – the compulsory evacuation of all the residents from Rzhava and the nearby state farm under the pretext of the need to quarantine them in the wards of a hospital for infectious diseases.[155] At the decision of the Front's Military Council, the evacuation of the civilian population was to be completed by the end of 8 May, but the process continued until the latter half of the month. In addition, the special company to guard the command post from the 234th Reserve Regiment also arrived with a delay, not until after 13 May. Largely due to this delay, at the end of May something happened that forced N.F. Vatutin to wrap up the Bobryshovo command post and to depart in response to an alarm in the course of one single night. Recalled V.V. Zvenigorodsky:

> On the evening of 23 May, a German reconnaissance aircraft was shot down over Bobyrshovo – the pilot bailed out successfully, was captured, and delivered to the command post in Bobryshovo. Under interrogation, the pilot indicated that he was making the final reconnaissance flight over the location of a major Soviet headquarters in Bobryshovo, and that on the next day, on 25 May, Bobryshovo would be subjected to an air strike. At a meeting held afterward, General of the Army N.F. Vatutin made the decision to move the Front's command post to the alternate command post over the night of 23-24 May, which is to say, to a wooded ravine lying immediately to the west of the village of Rzhava. In fact, at sunrise on 25 May, Bobryshovo came under a destructive bombing raid, but the Front headquarters was no longer there.[156]

At 2400 on 23 May, the deputy chief of staff Major General S.I. Teteshkin sent Combat Directive No. 00102 to the troops:

> The Front Commander-in-Chief has ordered:
> 1. 25 May 1943, the field command headquarters of the Voronezh Front is to redeploy to the Solntsevo area [as was written in the documents in order to conceal the real location of the command post]. The communications center is on the southern outskirts of Zuevka.
> 2. It is forbidden to give anyone information on the location of the command posts and departments. Only the commandant of the headquarters is to provide the information after the corresponding inspection of papers.
> 3. The chiefs of staffs of the commands and the chiefs of departments are to receive the schedule of movement and the rules for corresponding with higher-standing and subordinate headquarters and departments personally from the deputy chief of staff Major General Comrade Bensky.[157]

---

155 TsAMO RF, F.203, Op.2843, D.301, l. 216.
156 Author's personal archive.
157 TsAMO RF, F.203, Op.2843, D.301, l. 220.

From this moment on up to the start of the counteroffensive into the Ukraine, the leadership of the Voronezh Front was implemented from this unnoticed ravine just several kilometers away from the tiny railroad station of Rzhava, which was swallowed up by the vast expanses of the Central Black Earth region.

The situation with the deployment of the Central Front's headquarters during the preparatory period for the Battle of Kursk was similar to that which occurred on the Voronezh Front, but in certain respects was even more precarious. If N.F. Vatutin, to a large extent only by chance, avoided coming under a concentrated strike by German bombers, then K.K. Rokossovsky managed to survive a fatally dangerous incident that resulted from the negligent implementation of basic security measures, including by Rokossovsky himself. He arrived at Kursk from Stalingrad with an operational command group in early February 1943, and initially set up the Front's command post in Elets. At this moment this was justifiable and convenient, because it was here that a significant number of troop trains were arriving, so staff officers had the opportunity to meet them and efficiently direct them to their designated areas. Rokossovsky recalled:

> From April, the forces of both sides in the area of the Kursk area began to intensify the preparations for the summer campaign. Our command post was located in Elets. This major railroad hub attracted the enemy's attention and was subjected to frequent bombings. Therefore, the location was no longer suitable. In the new situation, the need appeared to shift the command post closer to the front. So, we moved to the village of Svoboda, north of Kursk. By this time, through the labors of our headquarters staff, the new command post was fully ready and was linked with all of the armies and corps, as well as with the neighboring *fronts* on the right and left.[158]

The book's manuscript was written in the 1960s, so it probably slipped the Marshal's mind that his command post had actually moved to Svoboda (25 km north of Kursk) on 23 February 1943 and did not move again from this moment on prior to the Battle of Kursk. The Front's first echelon of the command staff traveled to the new area, where the main commands, departments and services were already gathering. Their schedule was confirmed by a special directive of the General Staff;[159] the remaining staff remained in the second echelon. The total staff strength of a *front* command post exceeded 1,000 men (varying between 1,200 and 1,500 soldiers and officers, depending on the size of the subordinate forces). On 21 May 1943, there were 22 subsidiary elements in the first echelon of the Central Front's command post, which had 611 men on their rosters, including 301 generals and officers, 219 enlisted men, and 91 civilian personnel.[160] The services of the command post's second echelon were scattered throughout a number of villages out to 30-40 km from Svoboda. It included the department of the SMERSH counter-intelligence service, the engineer headquarters, the chemical and topographical departments, and a number of others. For the arriving representatives of various departments from Moscow (other than the General Staff), including journalists and senior officers of the Military Council's

---

158 Rokossovsky, *Soldatskii dolg*, p. 231.
159 The Red Army General Staff also regulated the size of the army headquarters' first echelon. Prior to the Battle of Kursk, the resolution of this question was being governed by its Directive No. 155920 from 29 June 1942 (TsAMO RF, F.326, Op.321, D.6, l. 149).
160 TsAMO RF, F.326, Op.321, D.6, l. 362, 263.

reserve, quarters were prepared in the hamlet of the Postoialye Hostels, which also came under the direction of the Front's headquarters commandant Colonel Iakimovich.

In the combat documents, Svoboda is referred to as an "out of the way place", which is to say, a small hamlet. In fact, this was the grounds of a monastery that had been closed before the war, situated on the banks of the Tuskar' River, where several wooden administrative structures and cottages remained, in which the Commander-in-Chief, members of the Military Council and the Front's chief of staff lived, in violation of regulatory guidelines. Before the Battle of Kursk, this negligence almost cost K.K. Rokossovsky his life. The Marshal recalled:

> We noticed that reconnaissance aircraft appeared above the village where our command post was located. We were staying in farmhouses. Therefore, just in case, slit trenches were dug into the earth around each hut for protection from fragments and bullets. The fact that we forgot about building bunkers was, of course, our big oversight. The residence in which I was staying stood opposite the gates leading into the grounds of the monastery. Not far away rose two large poplars. In one word, this was noticeable. However, we paid attention to this only when German aircraft began to appear frequently overhead. We decided to move the command post's location, but no one had time for this. Usually late into the evening I would peruse coded messages, then head over to the Military Council's mess hall that was located in a neighboring building to have a late dinner. However, once for some reason I did not wait for the cipher clerk to arrive, and having called him, asked him to bring the messages straight to the mess hall. Soon, Kazakov, Malinin, Telegin and several other staff officers arrived. Right at 2300 the cipher clerk brought in the dispatches. At this same moment, a German aircraft flew overhead, dropped an illumination flare, and then we caught the sound of another aircraft followed by the whistle of the bombs it had released. I just had time to give the order "Drop!" Everyone dropped flat on the floor, and then there was a deafening explosion … The room became filled with the dust of crumbling plaster. Shattered glass flew from the windows with a tinkling sound. After this explosion there was a second, but now more distant. Not a single one of us was injured. However, there was nothing left of the residence where I'd been staying – it had been blown to pieces by the second bomb. Only sheer coincidence, or possibly some intuition, saved me. In war, anything can happen.
>
> Even so, we did not escape without casualties. A sentry who'd been posted not far from my quarters was killed by a bomb fragment, and a second sentry and a junior adjutant, who'd had time to leap into a slit trench, were wounded. General G.N. Orel arrived. Shrugging his shoulders in perplexity, he said, "That's a fine how do you do!" It turns out that having seen the "chandelier" dropped by the German pilot, he took cover in a slit trench, but then could not tolerate it and went back to his quarters. Just then the bomb exploded. It had landed squarely in the slit trench in which the general had just been crouched. Yes, in war, much depends on chance.
>
> Someone asked, "Just how did you figure out that it was time to leave the trench?"
>
> Grigorii Nikolaevich burst out laughing: "You know, it was very cramped and cold there, as if I had just fallen into a grave that had been dug just for you. I gave up and climbed out: If it was time to die, better to do so in my quarters, where it was warm …"
>
> We all laughed and joked about this, but we did not have the right to take any more chances. The complicated situation did not give us the possibility to move the

command post. So, we decided to dig into the earth here. Through the efforts of the Front's Chief of Staff Malinin and the Chief of Engineers Proshliakov, fine bunkers were soon ready on the grounds of the former monastery, into which we then moved.[161]

Now let us return to the combat composition of the Central Front. In the spring of 1943, due to the rapidly changing operational situation, in order to optimize the command over the troops and the execution of existing missions, the Briansk, Central and Voronezh Fronts exchanged not only separate divisions with each other several times, but also entire armies. There was a short period of time when the Briansk Front was abolished, but then reconstituted again, and a similar situation occurred with the Orel Front, which existed for just several days. Therefore, the composition of the Central Front with which it started the summer campaign was not formed immediately after its full deployment at Kursk. The "shakedown" continued from March until the first ten days of May 1943. On 12 March, in addition to the already available 65th Army, 2nd Tank Army and 16th Air Army, K.K. Rokossovsky received from the Briansk Front the main forces of the 3rd, 48th and 13th Armies; the 28th Rifle Corps; the 19th Tank Corps; the 19th Guards Cavalry Corps; and means of reinforcement. The last major re-subordination took place on 27 March: the 3rd Army went back to the Briansk Front, and in return the Voronezh Front transferred its 60th Army to the Central Front. Subsequently, Rokossovsky received additional corps and divisions under his command from Moscow, as well as newly formed formations within the Front itself; his armies were also exchanging major formations, while a substantial portion of his armored and cavalry forces were withdrawn into the *Stavka* Reserve. However, it was precisely 27 March that can be considered as the date of the formation of the backbone of Rokossovsky's Central Front, with which it would enter the Battle of Kursk.

Just what was it? This is important to know first of all in order to understand the amount of work done by its command staff when preparing for the defensive operation. let us turn to documentary sources, which only quite recently became available to scholars. So, by the start of April, the Central Front included five combined-arms armies (the 13th, 48th, 60th, 65th and 70th Armies), the 2nd Tank Army, and the 16th Air Army, as well as a reserve that was directly subordinate to the Front headquarters (the 24th Rifle Corps with its 112th Rifle Division, 42nd Rifle Brigade and 29th Ski Brigade; the 6th, 70th and 75th Guards Rifle Divisions; the 2nd Destroyer [Anti-Tank Artillery] Division (with the 3rd and 4th Destroyer Anti-Tank Artillery Brigade); and the 19th Cavalry Corps (with the 8th and 51st Cavalry Divisions). Altogether, they combined: two rifle corps, 35 rifle divisions, four rifle brigades and three ski brigades; four tank corps, five separate tank brigades and 14 separate tank regiments; two cavalry corps and five cavalry divisions; three artillery divisions, one destroyer anti-tank artillery division, one separate destroyer anti-tank artillery brigade, two separate artillery regiments, 12 destroyer anti-tank artillery regiments, 15 separate mortar regiments, eight regiments of rocket launchers; four anti-aircraft divisions and six anti-aircraft regiments; one bomber division, two ground-attack aircraft divisions, three fighter divisions, one night bomber division and two separate aviation regiments; and four engineer brigades and 12 engineer battalions.

According to clarified information, after the transfer of the 3rd Army, on 27 March 1943 the Central Front was sharing a boundary line with the Briansk Front's 3rd Army on the right

161 Rokossovsky, *Soldatskii dolg*, p. 242-243.

– Efremov, Mikhailovskoe, Verkhov'e, Nikol'skoe, Stish' (all except Stish' exclusively for the Central Front) and a boundary line with the Voronezh Front's 38th Army on the left – Staryi Oskol, Dezhovka, Verkhnii Reutets, Lokinskaia Station, Kornevo Station, Bruski (all except for Staryi Oskol inclusively for the Central Front). His armies were holding the following sectors:

Lieutenant General P.L. Romanenko's 48th Army – Gorodishche – Panskaia, which extended for 36 km;
Lieutenant General N.P. Pukhov's 13th Army – (excl.) Panskaia – (excl.) Gremiach'e, which extended for 58 km;
Major General G.F. Tarasov's 70th Army – Gremiach'e – (excl.) Asmon', which extended for 36 km;
Lieutenant General P.I. Batov's 65th Army – Asmon' – Selino, which extended for 88 km;
Lieutenant General I.D. Cherniakhovsky's 60th Army – (excl.) Selino – Sheptukhovka Station, which extended for 94 km.

The Front's reserve, Lieutenant General A.G. Rodin's 2nd Tank Army (16th and 11th Tank Corps and the 11th Guards Tank Brigade) was assembled in the Verkhnii Liubazh – Putchina – Miroliubovo – Khmelevoe area, with its headquarters in Miroliubovo. It also had the 9th Tank Corps, 6th Guards Rifle Division, 2nd Artillery Division, 24th Anti-Aircraft Division; nine mortar, destroyer anti-tank artillery and anti-aircraft regiments; and three armored train battalions.[162]

The Front's line of defense in total amounted to 312 km. Later it was adjusted to 306 km, which also led to changes in the armies' sectors.

Just like in the case of its neighbor to the south, in the headquarters of the Central Front, the first drafts of the plan for the future defensive operation were completed prior to 12 April, but the main work to revise it was done after the conference in the Kremlin. Indeed, the first version of the plan in its final form was submitted to Moscow in the latter half of the month, and on 28 April, it underwent discussion in the *Stavka*. K.K. Rokossovsky's starting point was the Soviet High Command's supposition that the main events in the nearest future would unfold in the area of the Kursk bulge, and his forces would play one of the key roles here. The enemy's optimal plan suggested itself: not to split the salient with an attack from the west toward Kursk, but to encircle the Soviet forces with two concentric attacks. Within the sectors being held by his Front, there weren't many directions (significantly fewer than on the Voronezh Front), where Army Group Center might launch a main attack while using its primary breakthrough instrument – the panzer divisions. Therefore, he believed not without justification that all of the command's attention should focus on the right wing. He later recalled:

> We saw the greatest danger … at the base of the Orel bulge, which loomed over our right flank. Therefore, it was decided to create here the densest force grouping … Such a decision flowed from of the following observations. The Orel – Kursk axis was the most advantageous for the enemy's offensive, and the main attack (to the south or southeast)

---

162 TsAMO RF, F.62, Op.321, D.4, l. 107.

should be expected here. A German-fascist offensive in any other direction wouldn't create a threat, because the Front's forces and assets that were positioned opposite the base of the Orel salient could at any moment be directed to reinforce a threatened sector. It the worst case this offensive might lead only to driving our defending forces out of the Kursk salient, and not to their encirclement and destruction. ... Opposite the enemy's Orel grouping, the divisions of the 48th, 13th and 70th Armies were defending on a front from Gorodishche to Briantsevo, which extended for 132 kilometers. To the left, on a 174-km front from Briantsevo to Kornevo, the troops of the 65th and 60th Armies were occupying a defense.[163]

Based on this assessment, three directions were determined where the enemy's main attack should be expected. They ran in a sector of approximately 95 km, which is to say, they occupied 31 percent of the Front's entire frontage:

1. Zmievka – Fedorovka – Droskovo – Livny (at the boundary between the 13th and 48th Armies);
2. Gremiach'e – Ponyri Station – Zolotukhino Station – Kursk (along the Orel – Kursk railroad;
3. Kromy – Trostna – Fatezh – Kursk, (at the boundary between the 13th and 70th Armies.

K.K. Rokossovsky and his staff considered the second option to be the most likely.

Accordingly, already when first planning the defensive operation, the leadership of the Central Front relied on an accurate understanding of the enemy's overall plan in the nearest future. However, it made a mistake when determining the point where the enemy's main attack would land. As already noted, Model settled upon an axis west of the Orel – Kursk railroad, which is to say, at a point between the second and third anticipated directions of attack. Nevertheless, even given this erroneous conclusion, the 13th Army's sector was correctly determined as the most important one, since given any alternative development of the operational situation, it would become the "core" of the Front's defense. It the combat operations went according to the first option, Malinin's staff believed that its right flank would become the area of deployment of the Front's counterattack group, directed against the right flank of the enemy's assault wedge. The second and third alternatives presumed a German offensive in the center and at the army's left wing, and in this case the main forces and the Front's reserves foreseen for the operation would be concentrated in the 13th Army's sector.

In his memoirs, Rokossovsky mentioned the miscalculation made when determining the location of the main German attack, but only in passing and without offering any explanations for it. Unfortunately, I've not succeeded in finding any documents in the TsAMO RF that might in some way help to solve this "riddle". Russian historians have made no comment on this error by Rokossovsky and his staff and have not subjected it to analysis. Only G.A. Koltunov and B.G. Solov'ev, although superficially so, made an attempt to explain it: "Considering the assembly of the main Nazi force grouping in the Glazunovka – Tagino area, as well as the direction of

---

163 Rokossovsky, *Soldatskii dolg*, p. 256-257.

the Kursk – Orel highway and railroad, the Front command came to the conclusion that the direction of the attack would most likely run through Ponyri toward Kursk."[164] However, these arguments provide little in the way of understanding the logic of the Front's headquarters staff. Actually, Glazunovka is a railroad station on a section of the Orel – Kursk railroad, which ran through the center of the 13th Army's defenses. However, there are two villages of Tagino, an upper and a lower (Verkhnee and Nizhnee), which are located opposite the boundary between the 13th Army and 70th Army. It is not clear why the Front command decided that the enemy panzer grouping deployed in the Tagino – Glazunovka area had to launch the attack precisely in the direction of Ponyri, and not in the direction of Fatezh. After all, there is a significantly more suitable corridor for the breakthrough of a panzer grouping toward Kursk at the boundary between Pukhov's and Galanin's armies, the Kromy – Kursk highway.

The 13th Army's sector, according to the rules for conducting offensive and defensive fighting, can be split into three sections. The area to the east of the Polevaia Snova River, in the Maloarkhangel'sk – Livy direction (the boundary with the 48th Army), which is situated within the basins of the Such'ia, Dubovik and Sosna Rivers, is the most difficult for conducting an attack from the north, where the Ninth Army was positioned. It is cut by deep balkas and ravines and divided by a dense network of shallow rivers (no deeper than 0.3 to 0.6 meters) and streams, with sandy bottoms and muddy basins that were impassable for tanks. The heights here consisted of extended, sloping hills, which allowed the defender to bring up forces in concealment. However, because of them, the defending side also had serious difficulties with observation, since they obstructed the line of vision and created many "dead" zones. Therefore, the sharply cut terrain at the boundary between the 13th Army and 48th Army that had a large number of natural water obstacles substantially hampered the use of the offensive's main instrument – the panzer divisions. This factor became decisive for the Ninth Army command when it opted not to launch the main attack here. For this reason, the given direction was the first to be rejected by the Germans. Unquestionably, an attack to the southeast had alluring prospects; it was from here that a path opened to Shshigry, which was located on the only railroad trunk line that linked the Central Front with the country's economic and military centers. Indeed, in the event of cutting this artery, Rokossovsky's forces would be deprived of their main channel of supplies. However, the execution of this scheme of attack would require too much strength, which Model did not have. Yet the Soviet side did not take the factor of enemy strength into its calculations, and believed this direction was the most suitable for the Germans, since having attacked toward Livny, they would deeply envelop the entire grouping that was defending the Kursk salient.[165]

The second section, along the Orel – Kursk railroad (the center of the 13th Army's defenses), was located between the basins of the Polevaia Snova and Snova Rivers, and was most suitable for active offensive operations with large mechanized formations. The ground here was significantly less cut by ravines and was fully passable for armored vehicles, particularly between the rivers, although they did substantially constrict the maneuvering of forces. After the rivers, the primary obstacles here were Ponyri Station and the village of Ponyri-1, which essentially blocked the only passable corridor between the river basins for the movement of armor to the south, toward

---

164 Koltunov and Solov'ev, *Kurskaia bitva*, p. 48.
165 Judging from available information, Soviet intelligence was unable to provide Moscow with the necessary information for understanding the Wehrmacht's given problem.

Kursk, along which ran the railroad. They were essentially unique gates blocking the entryway of this path and it was extremely difficult to bypass them. With a well-planned system of defense, they could virtually become an impenetrable obstacle. On this same railroad branch, south of Ponyri, were the two railroad stations of Vozy and Zolotukhino, which could also be converted into sturdy strongpoints on this axis of advance. The final feature that favored the defenders on this axis was the confluence of the Snova and Polevaia Snova Rivers, which substantially strengthened the defensive possibilities in this sector. Along the rivers, a continuous chain of villages and hamlets stretched, which were convenient for creating and concealing an elaborate system of defense. In addition, the terrain here had more hills that offered a field of view out to 10-15 km, and this was a substantial benefit for the defenders.

Even so, the opposing sides assessed the characteristics of this (second) section differently. It is not clear why, but the Central Front command believed that the adversary would commit his main shock forces – the panzer divisions – precisely through this bottleneck of terrain, even though almost right beside it was a more suitable place for their use: the Fatezh direction. It is possible that Rokossovsky was assuming that the decisive factor for the enemy when striving to meet such an ambitious objective as the simultaneous encirclement of two *fronts* within the Kursk bulge was time, and this route to Kursk was the shortest. If so, then the supposition of the Soviet side might be considered fully reasonable, although still debatable. Relying on this conclusion, the Front command and the 13th Army's headquarters nevertheless chose to create the most powerful center of defense here: to combine Ponyri Station and the adjacent villages into the so-called "Ponyri enclosure". In addition to constructing the usual network of entrenchments, points of fire, anti-tank emplacements and obstacles, an increased laying of mines on the approaches to the enclosure and within the enclosure itself was planned. Meanwhile, Army Group Center was assessing this direction more soberly, and considering the defensive possibilities outlined above, marked it only for an auxiliary attack.

The third section, located to the west of the Snova River (from the village of Ol'khovatka and further on to the west), was most suitable for the employment of the enemy's panzer divisions. Relative to the other areas, the ground here was level with a small number of balkas and hills, and not very saturated with water obstacles (first of all, large ones) right down to Kursk itself. Moreover, the boundary between the 70th and 13th Armies lay here, which increased its attractiveness for an attack even more. An attack by main forces here allowed the German forces not only to take advantage of favorable terrain for the rapid drive of the panzer divisions to Kursk, but also already during the course of the breakthrough to the city, would seriously complicate keeping three armies of the Central Front supplied all at once. In the event of the complete breaching of the 70th Army's lines, the enemy would then be able to destroy its supply bases and rear facilities that were positioned along the Kromy – Kursk thoroughfare – the primary line of communications in this area, and with a subsequent advance to the south, cut the sole Ryl'sk – Kursk railroad that kept the 65th Army and 60th Army's supplied (through L'vov Station and Ryl'sk Station respectively). All of this made the Fatezh direction most advantageous for the enemy. Therefore, it was chosen by the Ninth Army command as the point for the main attack, whereas Rokossovsky for some reason known only to him, believed it was the most unsuitable of the three possible, alternative sections for a German attack.

The impression forms that when anticipating an attack toward Livny, the Central Front's Commander-in-Chief and staff were exaggerating its likelihood without having reliable information on the enemy's potential. In their prognosis, they did not take into account one of the Germans' chief characteristics: They always planned the use of armor thoroughly and directed an attack not only over passable ground, but ground that afforded the possibility of wide maneuvering. It is difficult to recall any offensive operation, when the command of German forces drove major mobile formations into a bottleneck, which cannot be said about the Soviet side, where such cases were not few, even in the summer of 1943. Even so, it should be emphasized that the major significance that the enemy gave to roads when planning the breakthrough of a defense was unquestionably known by the leadership of the Central Front at this moment; Directive No.032/op from its artillery commander from 21 April 1943, which will be discussed below, testifies to this. Relying first of all on the combat experience on the Eastern Front in 1941, the former commander of Panzergruppe 3, General H. Guderian, wrote in his memoirs:

> A tank must choose such ground over which it can rapidly travel. Only on favorable ground for the tank can the power of its long-range gun and the possibility of fire support be employed fully. … A tank is of little use for fighting in populated places, and completely unsuitable for street fighting in large cities. In these conditions their maneuverability, as well as their vision is too constricted. The enemy, equipped with means of close combat, can find cover everywhere, in which it is not easy to spot him. Wherever it is possible, therefore, it is sensible to bypass populated places.[166]

I will remind the reader that in the first months of the war, Major General K.K. Rokossovsky was commanding the 9th Mechanized Corps, and his right-hand man M.S. Malinin was heading the 7th Mechanized Corps' headquarters. Accordingly, they could not help but be aware of these important characteristics of German panzer tactics, and that not only on paper, but in reality, the Germans always sought to bypass villages and defiles if there was even a little chance to avoid them or to encircle their defending troops. Historians, however, teach that people, including historical figures, often deliberately disregard their own, particularly negative experiences. More precisely, they are unable to handle their emotions, or possibly their ambitions (or grievances), and process their experiences in their own way to use them in the future. I suppose that subconsciously or not, the Commander-in-Chief of the Central Front was also sometimes guilty of this. As an example, I will cite an episode that Colonel V.V. Zhdanov, the son of Colonel General V.T. Vol'sky, related to me. In the first months of the war, Colonel General Vol'sky was the assistant commander of the Southwestern Front's armored and mechanized forces:

> In September 1941, at an order from the USSR Deputy People's Commissar of Defense Lieutenant General of Armored Forces Comrade Fedorenko, V.T. Vol'sky prepared a report about the combat operations of the Southwestern Front's motorized and mechanized forces for the period between 22 June and 1 August 1941.[167] As Zhdanov related, it contained the following criticisms:

---

166 Hoth, H; Guderian, H., *Tankovye operatsii/Tanki "vpered!* [*Panzer operations/Panzer Leader*] (Smolensk: Rusich, 1999), p. 236, 375. This is a Russian edition that combined Hoth's memoirs with Guderian's memoirs.
167 TsAMO RF, F.229, Op.157, D.8 (Doklady avtobronetankovomu upravleniiu fronta, GABTU KA, Voennomu sovetu fronta ob opyte primeneniia i o sostoiannii tankovykh voisk) [Reports to the Front's

There were a lot of mistakes made directly by the commanders of the mechanized units and formations:

> The command staff of the mechanized corps, tank divisions and tank regiments still did not have the proper operational or tactical skills; they were unable to draw the correct conclusions or to fully understand the intents of the army and *front* commanders;
>
> The command staff does not have sufficient initiative;
>
> The command staff did not use all of the means of mobility that the mechanized units possess;
>
> There was no maneuvering – there was slackness and tardiness in carrying out assignments;
>
> The actions as a rule were of the nature of frontal assaults, which led to the needless loss of materiel and manpower, and this was because commanders at every level ignore reconnaissance;
>
> There was the clumsy organization of a corps' combat formations on directions to block the path of movement to the enemy, while the latter primarily advances along roads;
>
> Obstacles were not used, and cooperation with the engineers was completely lacking;
>
> There was no striving to prevent the enemy of bringing up fuel and ammunition;
>
> Ambushes weren't employed on the main directions of the enemy's actions;
>
> The enemy's operations against the flanks led to the fear of being encircled, at a time when tank units had nothing to fear of encirclement.

Vol'sky concluded that the headquarters were poorly prepared, and as a rule staffed with commanders from different branches of service, who did not have the experience of working in armored forces [Rokossovsky himself arrived in the mechanized corps in November 1940 from the cavalry]. Some of the commanders proved to be not up to scratch and were completely unable to handle the command of a corps. He wrapped up with the statement that the report was compiled on the basis of a large amount of statistical material … as well as his personal time among the troops, which yielded a detailed picture of the activity of the command staff of armored forces and identified the primary shortcomings in the combat application and exploitation of tanks. Vol'sky then proposed ways to eliminate the main shortcomings.

The report eventually wound up at the Southwestern Front's Military Council, and all of the commanders of the mechanized corps became familiar with it. In the report, General Vol'sky did not identify the commanders by name, with rare exceptions. Having rich experience in dealing with various oversight organs, he knew full well that in 1941 this might jeopardize the lives of identified men, who were conscientiously striving to do their duties and were simply making mistakes due to their complete inexperience. However, despite its relatively neutral tone, one mechanized corps

Directorate of Armored Forces, the Chief of the Red Army's Armored and Mechanized Forces and the Front's Military Council about the experience of using tank forces and their condition], pp. 217-229.

commander with whom V.T. Vol'sky was unable to forge a good relationship right up to 1945 disliked the report. His name was K.K. Rokossovsky.[168]

Once again, I will stress that this is only my speculation, which is based not only on the above, tale but also on a number of other pieces of evidence.

In order to understand the expression "unable to forge a good relationship", I will say that in 1945 Colonel General V.T. Vol'sky was commanding the 5th Guards Tank Army, which had been transferred to Rokossovsky's Front and distinguished itself in the course of the East Prussia operation, but back then the Marshal of the Soviet Union "forgot" to recommend the tank army commander for a well-deserved honor, which is to say V.T. Vol'sky received no honor or decoration at all for this operation. Marshal of the Soviet Union A.M. Vasilevsky corrected this injustice by recommending him for the Order of Kutuzov 1st Class and the rank of Marshal of Armored Forces, but V.T. Vol'sky did not live to receive these awards, having unexpectedly died in February 1946 from a chronic illness.

Unquestionably, the error in determining the location where the main German attack would fall negatively influenced the course of Central Front's defensive operation. Because of it, the 70th Army was not reinforced in the proper manner prior to the Battle of Kursk. The Front command failed to pay the necessary attention to strengthen its sector, which resulted in a number of unfortunate oversights by General Malinin's subordinates, who "forgot" even to make plans for potential operations of the 19th Tank Corps on the 70th Army's right flank. However, the most negative consequence of this became the 13th Army command's error made when allocating artillery to the different directions. Looming over N.P. Pukhov, the commander of the 13th Army, was the opinion of the Front Commander-in-Chief that in addition to the army's center, it was primarily necessary to strengthen the army's right flank (since the enemy would most likely launch if not the main attack here, then an auxiliary attack), which compelled Pukhov to create the greatest density of artillery on the Maloarkhangel'sk (Livy) axis. This substantially reduced the amount of artillery on 13th Army's left flank, where in July 1943 the enemy actually struck. This problem will receive more detailed analysis below.

Stemming from the three possible directions of the adversary's attacks, the Front headquarters worked out three options for the actions of its subordinate forces. According to the second, most likely option, his armies received the following assignments.

On the first day of the enemy's offensive, the 13th Army in the event of a penetration by the assaulting German forces, the divisions of its first echelon were to hold the Nizhniaia Gnilusha – Maloarkhangel'sk – Dobrovka – Ponyri – Saborovka line strongly, while the second-echelon 17th and 18th Guards Rifle Corps were respectively to occupy a defense along the Hill 256.9 – Bitiug – Kashara line and to deploy on the Mamoshin – Orlianka – Prilepy line.

On the second day, the 13th Army was to go over to a decisive counteroffensive with all its forces, launching the main attack against the penetrating enemy in the Ponyri – Ladyrevo – Koshelovo direction.

The 48th Army, simultaneously with the 13th Army, was to launch an attack in the Panskaia – Shamshin – Borisoglebskoe – Zmievka direction with its left wing. The 70th Army with its

---

168 Author's personal archive.

right flank, simultaneously with the 13th and 48th Armies, was to go on the counterattack in the Probuzhdenie – Gorchakovo – Zinov'evka – Kromy direction.

The 2nd Tank Army on the night following the first day of the German offensive was to move its main forces up to the following lines: 3rd Tank Corps, to the area of Hill 264.2, the Ponyri settlements, and the patch of woods east of Hill 252.2; the 16th Tank Corps, to the Derlovka, Hill 210.2, Kutyrki line; and the 11th Guards Separate Tank Brigade, to the Leninskii – Hill 224.3 line. From the morning of the second or third day of the operation, they were to attack in the direction of Rzhavets and Koshelovo with the assignment to cooperate with the 13th Army and 16th Air Army in the destruction of the German forces in the Protasorvo, Arkhangel'skoe, Ponyri-1 area.

On the night before the 13th Army and 2nd Tank Army went on the counterattack, the 16th Air Army was to destroy command posts and communication centers through night bombing attacks, thereby disrupting the German command and control of its troops. After sunrise, its bombers and ground attack aircraft were to support the 18th Guards Rifle Corps and 3rd Tank Corps, by preventing the approach of enemy reserves from the Glazunovka – Koshelovo – Bogorodetskoe direction. Meanwhile, its fighter aviation corps was to cover the main grouping of the 13th Army and 2nd Tank Army.[169]

The account of the headquarters of the Front's armored and mechanized forces notes:

> The second option anticipated that the enemy would need 2-3 days to overcome the resistance of our units in the main belt and fight his way through the intermediate lines before reaching the second belt of defenses. However, the calculations with respect to the time needed to move up the reserves – just one day – were wrong and badly underestimated the time required. This seriously affected the entire course of the defensive battle, since it became necessary already on the morning of the operation's second day to commit the reserves in order to stop the enemy, which had created an unprecedented density of forces and means in a narrow sector of the front and was striving at any cost to break through the defenses in order to emerge in operational space.[170]

Thus, in addition to the mistake made when determining the direction of the enemy's main attack, the headquarters of the Central Front miscalculated also when planning the actions of its main forces in the first days of the defensive operation.

The Front Commander-in-Chief's mobile reserve was considered his main lever of influence on a situation. It had been formed out of the 2nd Tank Army and two tank corps: Major General S.I. Bogdanov's 9th Tank Corps and Major General I.V. Vasil'ev's 19th Tank Corps. On 4 July 1943, they totaled a number of 939 combat machines, which amounted to 49.7 percent of all of the Central Front's tanks and self-propelled guns. For comparison's sake, N.F. Vatutin had more armored vehicles, a total of 1,073 tanks and self-propelled guns (57.9 percent) in his mobile reserve. This advantage was largely due to the composition of its 1st Tank Army, which

---

169 TsAMO RF, F.62, Op.343, D.29, l. 13, 14.
170 Ibid., l. 14.

had three subordinate corps, while the 2nd Tank Army had only two corps, plus a separate tank brigade.

K.K. Rokossovsky planned to use the mobile reserve not only against the German assault grouping, which would be attacking according to one of three possible options (against the 48th, 13th or 70th Armies). He also strove to take into account other possible dangers. Therefore, he positioned his mobile forces to the north and south of Kursk (in essence, behind the Front's center). In doing so, he was ensuring the possibility of maneuvering them to the north, west or south for counterattacks not only against the most likely direction of advance of the Ninth Army's shock grouping, but also to either of the Front's flanks. In addition, such a placement of the mobile reserves insured him against unpleasant surprise from out of the sector of his left-hand neighbor, the Voronezh Front.

The assembly areas for the mobile reserves were determined by three main factors. First was the desire to minimize the distance they would have to cover to allow them to maneuver rapidly to sectors of any of the three armies and to both of the Front's flanks. Second, was the presence and condition of the unsurfaced roads, as well as the close proximity to a railroad. Finally, was the presence of natural cover in order to conceal the significant number of armored vehicles and trucks, and to hide the dispositions of the men. Due credit should be payed, including to the command of the Front's armored and mechanized forces; through an intensive search, such places were found. So, by the start of the battle, the 2nd Tank Army for example would be able to move out quickly from its assembly areas to its jumping-off areas. According to any of the three options, it would require 5-6 hours, and 8-10 hours for the operational deployment of the entire army after receiving a combat order.[171]

The Front command was placing its main hopes on the 2nd Tank Army; it comprised the 54 percent of its armored reserve. At the end of April 1943, it was assembled in the Kondrika – Brekhovo – Kochetki area (behind the boundary between the 13th Army and 48th Army), and in early summer it would be directed to assist either the 70th Army, the 48th Army or the 13th Army. In the meantime, it, just like the Voronezh Front's 1st Tank Army, was bringing itself back to order, taking in tanks and replacement personnel, and preparing only for a counteroffensive. The plan for the 2nd Tank Army's actions in the first phase of the Battle of Kursk, which is to say during the repulse of the enemy's Citadel offensive, would be fleshed out only in the beginning of June.

The 9th Tank Corps at this time was positioned significantly more distant from the front than the 2nd Tank Army, in the Tsvetovo – Mokva – Maslovo – Sukhodolovka area (15 km southwest of Kursk and had a wider array of combat assignments. In addition to its other tasks, it was to screen the Front's left flank against a possible attack out of the Belgorod area. The corps received the order to prepare to operate:

    a.   In the Orel direction, with the arrival of its main forces in its jumping-off areas:
           Kosorzha – Belyi Kolodets – within 8-10 hours after receiving the order;
           North of Zolotukhino Station – within 8 hours after receiving the order;
           Fatezh area – within 12 hours after receiving the order;

---

171 Ibid., l. 30.

b. In the L'vov – Ryl'sk direction – with an arrival in the Fatezh, Gustomoi, Iznoskovo, Artakovka area within 6 to 8 hours;
c. In the Belgorod direction – with an arrival in the Ivnia, Kruglik, Vladimirovka, Kurasovka area within 10 hours.

A special role was given to the 19th Tank Corps; the assignments it received notably differed from those that the formations of the 2nd Tank Army and 9th Tank Corps received. The Front's intelligence had detected a large German panzer grouping on the Kromy axis, and in the opinion of its headquarters, the struggle with it would likely take place in the depth of its own defenses. Therefore, Rokossovsky decided to play it safe. He deployed Vasil'ev's tank corps behind the right wing of the 70th Army in the Verkhnii Liubazh, Putchino, Troitskoe area (directly behind the third army-level defensive belt). In the event of an enemy penetration at the adjoining flanks of the 70th and 13th Armies, the tank corps would thus be able (in cooperation with the 70th Army's reserves) to deplete the enemy's strength with short, sharp counterattacks in the tactical depth, and protect the deployment of the Front's reserves for a more powerful counterblow.

The first two days of the Battle of Kursk already fully confirmed the correct selection of the 2nd Tank Army's and 9th Tank Corps' assembly areas, as well as the accuracy of the tasks given to them. In the case of the 19th Tank Corps, however, the Front headquarters made serious errors regarding the options of using it together with the forces of the 70th Army. Noted the headquarters of the 2nd Tank Army, "The actions of the 19th Tank Corps anticipated only the third option, according to which it was to take up a defense along the Svapa River between the western outskirts of Molotychi and Iasensk."[172] The corps command therefore had no clear indications of what it should do in the event the enemy undertook an offensive according to the first two options (which in fact happened).

The troops of the Central Front initiated work on the field defenses in the latter half of March, when active combat operations were still continuing, but it had already become clear that the Soviet offensive was running out of steam. On 16 March 1943 a number of important decisions were made, which came to light in two directives from the Military Council. The first was "On the construction of the Front's defensive belts", which set the task of creating a system of defenses on the Plavsk – Livny line while fortifying the largest administrative and industrial center in the Front's sector – the city of Kursk.

The second directive was addressed to the Soviet and Communist Party leadership in the Kursk, Orel and Tula Oblasts and demanded the mobilization of the local population to support the Supreme High Command's 34th Bureau of Defensive Construction, which was to oversee the fortification work on all of these front lines. On this same day, 16 March 1943, the Kursk Committee of Defense was established, at the head of which sat the First Secretary of the Oblast Committee Major General P.I. Doronin, who had just returned from the Southern Front.

However, while all these measures were agreed upon with the General Staff, they still had no direct connection with preparations for the Battle of Kursk. This was the ordinary work assigned to the troops to lay out and construct a Front's sector upon reaching a new line, which naturally comported with the defensive lines of the neighbors and the acting army as a whole. Even so, it

172 TsAMO RF, F.307, Op.4148, D.145, l. 3.

played an important role, because after Moscow's decision to create a deeply-echeloned defense, the work to construct it did not have to start from scratch. K.K. Rokossovsky wrote:

> I want to say straight away that this was an ordinary defense at the time, to which we went over with the aim of gaining time to prepare the troops for the summer offensive. However, when it became known that the foe was preparing an attack in the area of the Kursk bulge, the defense now took on a specific, premeditated character. It received an uncommonly powerful development with the use of engineers, especially after mid-April.[173]

On 21 March 1943 the Central Front's offensive essentially came to an end (officially, the Dmitrov – Sevsk operation ended, although the combat for Sevsk continued until 27 March). From this day on through the following 15 days, its headquarters prepared guiding documents and issued them to the troops, which lay at the basis of the preparation for the future Battle of Kursk. They touched upon three main points: the composition of the Front's forces; their main tasks up until 1 May (the initial date of the expected start of the German offensive); and the development of the system of defense. General of the Army N.F. Vatutin, who on 22 March assumed command of the Voronezh Front, was focused on the same things. The order about his Front's adoption of a defensive posture and the construction of the lines was signed by him on 27 March. Thus, the system of the deeply-echeloned defenses of the Kursk salient, which later entered all the books about the history of the Great Patriotic War, began to form in fact over the several weeks before the conference in the Kremlin on 12 April, which determined the essence of the summer campaign, its stages, and the main directions for preparing for it.

Rokossovsky's Order No.00123/op about creating a sturdy defense along the Gorodishche – Maloarkhangel'sk – Trosna – Liutezh – Korenevo line and artillery commander Major General V.I. Kazakov's[174] Directive No. 032/op about organizing the anti-tank defenses, which were signed on 21 March 1943, became the first of a series of the most important orders issued to the

---

173 Parot'kin (ed.), *Kurskaia bitva*, p. 88.
174 Kazakov, Vasilii Ivanovich (1898-1968), Marshal of Artillery (1955), Hero of the Soviet Union (1945). Before the Great Patriotic War, he was the commander of the 7th Mechanized Corps' artillery, then of the artillery of the Western Front's 16th Army. He showed himself well in the heavy defensive fighting in the first phase of the war. In order to counter the German tanks, he proposed the idea of combined anti-tank strongpoints, which mutually supported each other with the fire of anti-tank guns and heavy artillery, as well as rifle and machine-gun fire against the enemy infantry. Subsequently, the creation of such strongpoints (which the Germans called Pak fronts), became an obligatory requirement when organizing a defense throughout the acting Red Army. All of these ideas of V.I. Kazakov found the support of the commander-in-chief of the 16th Army General K.K. Rokossovsky. They not only worked together, but also became close comrades; Kazakov served as the artillery commander under Rokossovsky almost to the very end of the war: from July 1942 on the Briansk Front; from October 1942 on the Stalingrad Front, and then the Don Front; from February 1943 on the Central Front. In the course of repulsing the Ninth Army's offensive in July 1943, Kazakov skillfully organized the control of the artillery fire on the directions of the main and auxiliary attack, and personally directed its use in combat. For his outstanding performance in the Battle of Kursk he was decorated with the Order of the Red Banner. After the war, he worked in a variety of command posts. He retired in 1965 and wrote about the readying of the Central Front's artillery for the Battle of Kursk and his participation in it in his memoirs, *Artilleriia, ogon'!* [*Artillery, fire!*].

troops of the Central Front. They laid down the principles of construction that system of defense, against which the assault wedge of Model's army would crash in the summer, and virtually set the mechanism in motion for building it. The planning of it began several days before the appearance of these documents that determined the density of strength necessary to carry out the primary task – the repulse of any enemy attack. As the artillery chief of staff General G.S. Nadysev recalled, at this time the Front command staff, relying on intelligence and combat experience, believed that the Germans might deploy up to 50 tanks per kilometer of frontage in order to break through to Kursk. By early April, the Central Front's sector extended for more than 300 km.[175] The artillery headquarters started from the assumption that one gun, prior to the moment of its destruction, would be able to destroy two combat machines; accordingly, in order to hold a panzer grouping consisting of 1,500 armored vehicles within the tactical zone, not less than 25 tubes per kilometer of the defensive front had to be assembled. For those times, this was a large figure. K.K. Rokossovsky's order set the following tasks:

> To create deep army defenses, for which you are to begin the reconnoitering and construction of the army's rear lines and the strengthening of the forward lines according to the plan attached to this order. In order to conduct the reconnoitering, create army reconnoitering teams made up of experienced commanders. When laying out the lines and strongpoints, you are to be guided by the following:
> a) Battalion centers of defense at points that encompass the primary directions are the main defense. The intervals between them that are accessible to the enemy must be occupied by small rifle elements and full of obstacles.
> b) Set up the battalion centers of defense and company areas of defense that are positioned on ground accessible for tanks as anti-tank strongpoints and areas.
> c) All of the anti-tank obstacles must be subject to active anti-tank, mortar and machine-gun fire. Make primary use of natural obstacles, and where there aren't any – create minefields, abatis, anti-tank traps, etc.
> d) First and foremost, do the work to ensure observation and command and control: build anti-tank obstacles; main and alternate firing positions; and shelters against artillery and aircraft fire with the mandatory camouflaging of them.
> e) Convert populated places that are part of the battalion centers of defense, and the system of defensive fortifications and artificial obstacles on the approaches into a fortress, capable of stopping the enemy's advance and able to struggle independently for a lengthy period of time even in encirclement.
> f) Construct the immediate defense of large villages and towns according to the principle of the defense of fortified areas, which is to say, prepare ahead of time several strongpoints and centers of resistance that cover the approaches to them.
> g) Obstruct all the roads not being used by the troops by means of setting up obstacles to the movement of infantry and tanks. Prepare the roads left for the movement of troops for destruction.[176]

---

175 Nadysev, G.S., *Na sluzhbe shtabnoi* [*In staff service*] (Moscow: Voenizdat, 1976), p. 110.
176 TsAMO RF, F.62, Op.321, D.5, l. 81, 82.

Two important dates were established in the document. First, before 27 March all of the armies were to complete the reconnoitering and submit updated schemes for their defensive belts to the Military Council. Second, the order gave the forces 40 days to do the main fortification work, but first to complete the work on the main directions by 10 April, and the entire system of defenses by 1 May. Alongside the rebuilding of the forces, the Central Front Commander-in-Chief considered this task to be the most vital, and therefore took it under his personal control. All of the army commanders were to report to him on the work done every five days through the deputy chief of engineers Major General A.M. Proshliakov, with the submission of maps that depicted the completed sites and indicated the amount of completed work. Thus, the planning and creation of the army's defensive belts in the area of the Kursk salient got underway precisely one month before the receipt of *Stavka* Directive No. 30103 about creating it.

However, the document presented above from the outset was not directed at building a deeply-echeloned defense; at this moment no one was even thinking about one, though for all practical purposes what the *fronts* did before receiving *Stavka* Directive No. 30103 became the foundation for it on both *fronts*, since Vatutin in fact signed an order similar to Rokossovsky's at the same time.

The construction of the field defenses on both the Central and Voronezh Front's went through three stages. The first (at the order of their Military Councils) lasted from the end of March to the latter half of April. This was the time for planning, regroupings, and for laying out and building a temporary or the initial system of defenses. The second stage, the main one, lasted approximately one and half months and in effect ended on the first day of summer, since according to a directive from G.K. Zhukov, from 1 June 1943 the combat formations had to shift their main attention to combat training and preparations.[177] It was in this period of time that in fact the main work to raise a deeply-echeloned system of defenses at Kursk was done (including on the front lines). Its result would be the complete readiness of the main belt of defenses around the entire Kursk bulge, approximately 50-60 percent of the planned work on the second defensive belt, and less than half of the planned work on the third (or final) army-level belt of defenses. The third, concluding stage took place in June. In the course of this month, the fortification work on all of the defensive belts would continue, albeit with substantial interruptions, but their results would prove to be significantly more modest. Skipping somewhat ahead of the events, I will note that despite all of the enormous efforts exerted by the troops and local population to complete the plan for three defensive belts that was unveiled back in April, neither Rokossovsky's Central Front or Vatutin's Voronezh Front were able to finish it completely.

V.I. Kozakov in his Directive No. 032/op required the following from the artillery commanders of the armies and corps.[178] First, the anti-tank defenses should be based around the principle of strongpoints that were echeloned in depth. They should be tightly be tied in with artificial and natural obstacles, as well as the fire of the rifle units. In turn, at all of the strongpoints, the fire of anti-tank rifles had to be strictly tied in with the fire of the anti-tank guns. The tight coordination of fire had to be laid down in the anti-tank rifle groups, and with regards for the anti-tank rifle's relatively ineffective fire, it was particularly necessary that they

---

177 TsAMO RF, F.403, Op.9657, D.87, l. 111.
178 TsAMO RF, F.226, Op.20991ss, D.4, l. 47, 48.

be arrayed in compact groups of not less than 3-4 teams in each, so that the junior commander had the possibility of directing their fire by voice.

Second, in addition to the anti-tank artillery, all of the available cannon batteries should be positioned near roads, since it was presumed that with the onset of spring, all of the enemy's main forces of mobile divisions would be concentrated on them. The directive also specified that cannon batteries be deployed on directions vulnerable to tanks for the possible creation of a strongpoint. Given the rifle divisions' absence of necessary anti-tank means at the forward edge, the directive authorized a portion of the cannon batteries of the divisional artillery regiments and regiments of the Supreme High Command to be moved up to the first line of defenses and to be used for creating strongpoints.

Third, the artillery commanders of the corps and armies were obligated to form a mobile anti-tank reserve in the shortest period of time. For them, positions were to be readied on the directions of greatest risk, routes of movement scouted, and roads and bridges be prepared.

Fourth, all of the artillery positions should be set up by engineers, gun pits should be dug in the jumping-off positions, and in those places where this was impossible, defensive palisades prepared in order to protect the guns and crews by digging in three to four rows of logs and filling the spaces between each row with earth. In each frontline division, positions were to be prepared for the divisional artillery to fire over open sights: six for the 76mm guns and four for the 122mm howitzers.

Finally, in order to camouflage the positions and to confuse the enemy regarding the system of defense, it was necessary for each division to prepare prior to 5 April six dummy positions for four-gun batteries and 18 dummy anti-tank gun positions. Before the end of March, artillery commanders were to prepare a timetable for the actions of shoot-and-scoot guns for April and implement it actively. Not less than one or two roving guns were to operate in each division, and by fire and movement they should seek to imitate four-gun batteries.

In preceding years, the spring thaw arrived in the European part of the USSR in the first week of April and lasted for approximately a month. During this period, active combat operations, as a rule, shut down. Therefore, the Soviet command issued the tasks to the troops in the first ten days of April and set the deadline for them to be completed by the beginning of May. The spring of 1943 began differently; the roads became virtually impassable already in the last ten days of March, approximately two weeks earlier than usual, yet even so, intense fighting continued in the southern and central portions of the Soviet-German front. Moscow therefore was alarmed by the possibility of a fresh attack by a strong grouping out of Khar'kov to the north and the assembly of the Ninth Army in the Orel salient. So, the Soviet General Staff issued Directive No.11916 from 2 April 1943 regarding the adoption of a general defense and the tasks for the spring with no consideration of the weather conditions, as was typical before, but with regard for the operational situation and the probable threats, which is to say, approximately a week after the front finally became stabilized in the area of the Kursk bulge.

The relatively late appearance of Order No.00180 about the tasks of the Central Front during the muddy season was connected with this circumstance; it was signed only on 4 April. This document became the program of actions for Rokossovsky's troops when preparing for the summer campaign. In it, the Commander-in-Chief of the Central Front wrote:

> The main tasks … of the Front for the spring muddy season, tentatively between 10 April and 10 May 1943, are as follows:

a. To create a strong defense and to strengthen both the main and intermediary lines, especially on tank-vulnerable directions;
b. To train the troops to conduct defensive and offensive fighting in strict accordance with the requirements of the Red Army's service regulations, paying particular attention to organizing the cooperation of the infantry with the artillery, and the air force with the tanks on the battlefield;
c. To amass supplies of all types and by the end of April to have no less than two combat loads of ammunition, no less than three refills of fuel, and enough food, grains and forage for five or six days;
d. To make repairs to the combat machines and weapons, and to get them ready for normal combat.[179]

When working on the lines, the troops and officers were to follow the guidelines contained in previously mentioned orders from 21 March 1943. The commanders at every level paid particular regard to the depth of the defenses. The battalion centers of resistance had to be echeloned in depth and prepared to repulse primarily panzer attacks; standard entrenchments for the rifle units and emplacements for the mortar and anti-tank rifle units had to be dug, while earth and timber bunkers were to be built for the heavy machine guns. In addition, all of the firing positions, fortifications and emplacements had to be linked by communication trenches with a depth of not less than one to one and a half meters.

Considering that the question as to whether the troops would be attacking or defending in the nearest months had yet to be answered, the principle of the equal significance was applied to the training: from 10 to 25 April, the training focused on defensive combat, and between 25 April to 10 May, it switched to lessons in offensive fighting. In addition, Rokossovsky insisted that no chalkboard teaching be tolerated; all the training was to be conducted in the field, with the use of combat weapons. Exceptions were to be allowed only for the armored forces. When forging the teamwork of crews, platoons and companies, it was requisite to conduct all of the tactical exercises in the field with dismounted tank crews, which is to say without the tanks, so as to imitate the crews' activities during combat in depth. In order to meet the timetable for strengthening the lines, training in defensive fighting drills were to be connected with the work on the fortifications, which was to proceed for 14 hours each day.

After 25 April the general amount of labor was not supposed to decrease, but with consideration of the operational situation, the training of the men and their work on the defensive positions were separately scheduled for seven hours each per day. To ensure all the men received the proper amount of training, Rokossovsky required the rotation of units between the first and second echelons every seven to ten days. Accordingly, with consideration of the remaining duties, which no one ever removed from a Red Army soldier, given such a regimen he could rest in the best case for five or six hours each day.

In addition, on the Central Front as well as the Voronezh Front, the rear areas were in the stage of being organized, and in a few of the divisions, there was a lack of food products, and even cases of the death of military personnel due to malnutrition and starvation. The overall condition of the men in the combat units can therefore be assessed as extremely poor. The

---

179 TsAMO RF, F.62, Op.321, D.5, l. 120.

former commander of a submachine gun company of the Voronezh Front's 375th Rifle Division P.G. Zolotukhin offered the following recollection of the service conditions of the frontline soldiers at this time:

> Toward the end of April, warm days returned again. The snow no longer offered shelter. It was necessary to dig deeper into the ground. The snow was disappearing from the earth in its distinctive way. Under the snow, water therefore appeared. In the trenches, the conditions were wet and muddy. All of this noticeably told on the health of the men. The battalion occupied the defenses in such conditions until the month of May. For the machine gunners, things were particularly hard because the machine gun belts of ammunition, which were made out of cloth, were rotting. It was impossible to load them with cartridges. The belts were sent back to a village, where they were dried out, and there they did the task of loading them with cartridges.[180]

Taking all of the above into consideration, it should be acknowledged that even one month of the work as planned by the Front command was colossal in scale.

However, for its success not only the already mentioned problems had to be solved, but also another, extremely important one. The point is that the Fronts' command staff at the tactical level was still not up to the task of organizing, controlling and executing everything that had been planned. At this moment, the commanders of platoons, companies and even of many battalions weren't properly ready for this. Back at the end of February 1943, one of the more far-sighted and energetic commanders of the Central Front's armies, Lieutenant General N.P. Pukhov, recognizing the complexity and at the same time great importance of the work to raise the professional level of this category of commanders, wrote:

> During the preceding fighting, the command staff suffered significant losses. The commanders at the levels of the platoon, company and battalion have almost been completely replaced by new, inadequately prepared commanders, while the leadership of them on the part of senior chiefs (the commanders of regiments and divisions) remains unchanged. They are giving general orders, assuming that the subordinate commanders are able to orient themselves in a complex situation, to draw the correct conclusions and to implement the necessary measures. Meanwhile this new command staff to a significant extent has no combat experience. I demand from the commanders of the divisions and regiments more concrete leadership of subordinate commanders, with detailed explanations to them, in the event they have any doubts about how they need to act. Exert particularly firm control over the proper execution of orders and the instructions of senior chiefs.[181]

However, it was impossible to solve this problem only through strict supervision. The senior command staff had also suffered debilitating casualties, especially in the course of such lengthy offensives as the one over the winter of 1942-43. It was because of a shortage of regiment

---

180 Author's personal archive.
181 TsAMO RF, F.361, Op.6099, D.59, l. 65 obr.

commanders that even hastily retrained commissars had begun to be assigned to these posts since the autumn of 1942. Another fact testifies to the low level of the professional training and the substantial shortage of rifle regiment commanders, for example in the Voronezh Front. In April 1943, when transforming the 7th Rifle Corps that had fought heroically at Stalingrad into the 35th Guards Rifle Corps, battalion commanders with the rank of captain were assigned to take command of regiments, and they remained as such even after the conclusion of the Battle of Kursk. Indeed, this was no longer 1941, but now the middle of the war! At the same time, some of the regiment commanders who had shown themselves well in the preceding fighting were promoted to higher posts. In the spring of 1943, in the *fronts* that were operating in the area of the Kursk salient, cases were encountered when the complete replacement of all the regiment commanders took place in a division. Such details should also receive consideration. First, it was not every officer who had combat experience, but not in prolonged defensive fighting, who could quickly and properly furnish his unit with a defensive plan, bind the system of fire with the artificial obstacles, and so forth. Second, not each man could teach another, even one who mastered things pretty rapidly. At first glance this seems to be not so important, but this is the case only if the discussion is about imparting personal experience regarding individual matters. When, however, the task becomes the arrangement of a system of training for hundreds and thousands of men, the given factor plays an important role. The problem of increasing the professional skill of commanders at the divisional level was also particularly acute.

Several important documents that had been adopted just several months before were supposed to guide the training of the personnel and the construction of the occupied positions: The Field Manual of the Red Army (1943) [FM-43]; the Red Army's Combat Manual – Infantry (1942) [CMI – 42], Parts 1 and 2; People's Commissar of Defense Order No. 306 from 8 October 1942 "On improving the tactics of offensive combat and the combat formations of elements, units and formations", and Order No. 325 from 16 October 1942 "On the combat use of tank and mechanized units and formations". Unfortunately, even the senior command staff had not yet studied them thoroughly. On the Voronezh Front this problem was resolved rather simply. For example, the commander of the 21st Army Lieutenant General I.M. Chistiakov summoned his regiment commanders and gave them several hours of nighttime to study FM-43, and then the next morning tested their knowledge of it. Hardly anyone passed it; their qualification level was not very high, and the army commander himself did not have a professional education. Those whose memories "slipped a bit" naturally had an unpleasant time in front of the general, but no one was removed from his post, since they had other important qualities that were valued in the war first and foremost – combat experience and organizational capabilities. Those who did not score well at all operated according to the "iron" principle of the front – "fight as best you can, and if you blunder, the war will write it off".

The aforementioned manuals and orders contained the accumulated the experience of almost two years of war, which had been gained at a high cost of blood and had brought about major changes: new principles regarding shaping a battle and conducting combat had been formulated; and new methods of command and control of the troops and ways of arraying their combat formations had been introduced. Indeed, in the period of the spring lull in operations and during the Battle of Kursk itself, these newly introduced ideas were tested for the first time on the scale of several *fronts*. The FM-43 viewed contemporary warfare "first of all as the combat of combined branches of service, in which various combat weapons take part on a massed scale: artillery of all types, mortars, tanks and aircraft."[182] It assigned the main role to the infantry. The manual determined offensive combat as the main type of combat operations, though it recognized the need for a defense and even a retrograde movement "as an independent maneuver, when the situation requires a withdrawal of the troops out from under the attack of superior enemy forces."[183]

For our subject most interesting are the articles that regulated the layout and construction of a defensive line and the use of the troops holding it. A defense was divided into two possible types in CMI-42, depending on the existing assignment, the available forces and the nature of the terrain: a positional or a maneuvering defense.[184] In order to conduct it, the armies, corps, divisions and brigades were given zones or belts of a defense; regiments – sectors; and battalions and companies – areas. It is impossible to present a historiography of the Battle of Kursk without describing our defensive lines. It is obligatory for authors to name the armies' defensive zones, but they don't always explain why they were called so. let us turn to CMI-42 – the original source of these labels. According to the points in the new regulations, a defense of an all-arms army should be built in two echelons and consist of:

- forward defensive positions or a security zone, the forward edge of which lay 1 to 1.5 kilometers out in front of the main defensive belt;
- the main belt, with a depth of 5-6 km;
- a second belt, which was positioned 10-12 km behind the forward line of the main belt;
- a third or rear army-level belt, which ran 10-15 km behind the forward edge of the second belt.[185]

The forward defensive positions had to be screened by mines, and they represented the place for organizing combat security; given the presence of buildings or even a village that was not occupied by the enemy, a forward detachment would be moved up to it with the aim of screening the main defensive belt from unexpected attacks by large reconnaissance forces or the enemy's assault groups. On the Central Front it was impossible to advance forward detachments, because of the close proximity of the combat lines of the two opposing sides, but on the Voronezh Front, the situation was different. The forward detachment of the 67th Guards Rifle Division deployed in the village of Butovo (in the 6th Guards Army's zone); it had a strength of a rifle battalion and on the eve of the Battle of Kursk, it played an important role in defending the division's lines.

The main and subsequent belts were to consist of battalion-sized areas of defense, each of which occupied 2 km of frontage and had a depth of 1.5 to 2 km. The company-sized areas represented terrain sectors that extended up to 700 meters in length and depth, which were to be occupied by platoon-sized strongpoints. At the beginning of April, the Voronezh and Central Front's system of defenses began to be raised according to this scheme. They subsequently did not change fundamentally, but work went on to improve them and develop them in depth.

182 Field Manual of the Red Army (Moscow: Voenizdat, 1945), p. 5.
183 Ibid., p. 8.
184 Combat Manual Infantry of the Red Army, Part 2 (Moscow: Voenizdat, 1942), p. 204.
185 Field Manual of the Red Army, pp. 228-230.

Despite the strict deadlines established in K.K. Rokossovsky's order from 21 March, the fortification strengthening of his Central Front's defensive belts, with rare exception, did not get underway until approximately the last ten days of April. The troops were experiencing an acute deficit of explosives and did not receive a necessary amount of them until mid-May. Second, the muddy season had started, and the majority of the roads and bridges were impassable, so it was impossible to bring up engineering gear (mines, barbed wire, tools and construction materials) or do any earth work. In addition, a significant number of the horses – the troops' primary logistics means – had come out of the winter in poor condition because of the lack of fodder and were infested with mites. Third, the forces had not yet fully assembled, and major force regroupings and the rebuilding of units were both in process. Fourth, there was no clear plan of actions for the immediate future: it was not clear whether to prepare primarily for an offensive or a defense. Finally, it was necessary to evacuate the civilian population from the deployment areas of the combat formations.

According to *Stavka* Directive No. 170663 from 15 October 1942, immediately after a front became stabilized, a frontline zone had to be determined, from which all of the civilian population had to be evacuated promptly.[186] The need to protect them explained this, but also the desire to thwart the activity of German agents. On the Central Front, the plan was to complete this process by 10 April, and over the following 48 hours after the order was issued, the NKVD organs were busy with removing the residents who were refusing resettlement, and there were always more than a few such people.[187] However, because of the widespread circulation of typhus, first at the decision of the Front's Military Council from 30 March, the evacuation zone was temporarily reduced from 25 km to 3 km from the forward edge, and on 30 April K.K. Rokossovsky was forced for the same reasons to appeal to I.V. Stalin to decrease the frontline zone for his forces from 25 km to at least 15 km, which was in fact done. The diary of Lieutenant Suris, a translator with the 258th Rifle Division of the Southern Front's 5th Shock Army, where at the same time such measures were being implemented, notes:

> 24 March 1943. The civilian population is being evacuated from Dmitrievka. The measure is harsh, but necessary. Very hard scenes are playing out. An old man and woman are hauling a cart with their worldly belongings. An axle is broken, and no one is stopping to help them or to give them a lift ... Vehicles are passing by indifferently. The old woman is wailing pitifully; the cart is emitting a playful squeak as it bucks along. A woman with two sick children asked to spend the night in our hut. She is

---

186 A frontline zone was the ground adjacent to the front lines, within which the units, formations, and the armies' and *fronts*' rear services were to deploy. Within it, a special regime for the civilian population was established. In a number of cases when preparing for an operation, the population could be partially or fully evacuated. The depth of the frontal zone depended on the details of the theater of combat operations, the operational assembly of the forces, the employed means of combat, and other factors, and could extend from 20 to 50 km in depth. Directive No. 170663 prescribed establishing a frontline zone with a depth of 25 km and the corresponding regime, to alter its tracing in accordance with the changes in the front lines, to create not less than three belts of defenses within it, and to prepare all villages, collective farms and towns in it for an all-round defense.
187 TsAMO RF, F.62, Op.321, D.6, l. 132.

crying, "The Germans did not touch us, but now we are being forced to move." She was perhaps even cursing us ... Everything was hard, so hard!'[188]

In March and April 1943, typhus was rife everywhere, even though an intense struggle against it underway. The difficult sanitary conditions in the liberated villages and hamlets; the infrastructure devastation; and the extreme fatigue and physical depletion of the civilians and service personnel were all contributing to the spread of the illness. A military doctor of the 140th Rifle Division's sanitary battalion L.M. Zhdanov (Garkavenko) wrote in a daily journal:

> I passed through villages where our units were standing. I went from home to home, forcing people to wash themselves and to heat their undergarments thoroughly in stoves. There were a lot of sick among the civilian population. The entire medical-sanitation battalion was sick with typhus, including its chief, Beloborodov. The Germans left behind hotspots of typhus in each village and home. In the units there were only a few cases, but I think we prevented the outbreak of an epidemic in the division.[189]

Therefore, as well as because of the muddy season, despite the strict instructions from the *front* commands, the defenses of even the frontline forces at this time were plainly weak. There could be no talk of extensive minefields and a continuous network of trenches with main reserve and dummy positions. Primarily it consisted of temporary field works, foxholes and a few minefields and booby trap obstacles thrown up by the troops back in the latter half of March. For example, in the 70th Army's entire 40-km sector of defense in mid-April, there were only nine minefields containing a total number of up to 800 mines. Here is how the 10-km line of the 13th Army's 81st Rifle Division (Novyi Khutor – Hill 257.3 – Probuzhdenie (excl.) – Bobrik) looked on 20 April, when it was withdrawn into the second echelon and handed over its positions to the 15th Rifle Division of the same army:

> The following fortifications have been turned over and taken up:
> 1. Rifle trenches for squads – 155;
> 2. Firing positions for 50mm and 82mm mortars – 72;
> 3. Trenches for anti-tank rifles – 92;
> 4. Sites for heavy machine guns – 84;
> 5. Observation posts – 30;
> 6. Communication trenches – 7,260 meters;
> 7. Dugouts – 233;
> 8. Earth and timber bunkers – 68;
> 9. Firing positions for 45mm guns – 15;
> 10. Firing for 76mm guns – 11;
> 11. Sites for 120mm mortars – 12;
> 12. Three-meter cheval de frise – 2,000 meters;
> 13. Double apron wire fencing – 1,065 meters;

---

188 Suris, B., *Frontovyi dnevnik: dnevnik, rasskazy* [*Frontline diaries: A diary and tales*] (Moscow: Tsentrpoligraf, 2010), p. 109.
189 *Chelovecheskie dokumenty voiny* [*Human documents of the war*] (Kursk, 1998), p. 245.

14. The division's communication means and trench shelters for quarters have been fully set up.

    When assuming the positions, the following flaws were spotted: the artificial obstacles and the trench and earthworks along the forward edge in certain places are arrayed in a single row; the rifle trenches are unfinished (they are eroding and not adapted to for moving out on the attack; the camouflaging of them is haphazard).[190]

This was for an entire division that numbered several thousand men! The process of turning over a sector included a summary of the minefield locations. In this case, they only blocked tank-vulnerable locations in several places, but there could be no talk of any sort of an anti-tank system of defense with ditches, escarpments, electrified obstacles, or so forth, which wouldn't appear here until the end of May 1943.

A similar situation existed along the entire central and southern portions of the Soviet-German front. Again, turning to the diary of Lieutenant B. Suris, a translator with the Southern Front's 258th Rifle Division:

> 20 March. What kind of defense is this? Here's what: three men sitting on a line of 3 km. There are no shells, few mines, and not enough bullets. There's no grub for the men. The terrain consists of reeds and tall weeds, in which the German cannot see us, but also hinders us from seeing him; mud, from the thaw; canals, streams, and a branch of the Mius River – and out in front are high hills, along which the German defense runs. They have trenches with bunkers, a few mortars and pieces of artillery linked by trenches, and snipers; out in front of the forward edge are barbed wire obstacles. They have a lot of machine guns. ... We have very, very few firing means and abominable command and control (the battalion has no telephone contact with the regiment and no one knows where the regiment headquarters is located!) On the other hand, a multitude of "representatives from above" and "coordinators" are snooping around. The soldiers are cursing: they'll give away our positions! All of this is stupid and terrible from beginning to end. ... Schmoozing is flourishing ... there are a lot of people who are not working conscientiously, but out of fear. The battalion command post, the Devil knows why, has been brought up to almost the frontline itself. The guys, losing no time, set up the command post: They positioned machine guns at embrasures and laid out a bundle of 30 grenades on the breastwork. A coded message has just come in with a warning that enemy active operations are possible at sunrise. I'm afraid of this: just one strong blow – and everything will go to hell in a handbasket.[191]

On the Voronezh Front, the creation of a system of defenses began with clearing the territory of the Front, the area of which by this time amounted to 18,600 square kilometers and putting in order the main lines of transport communications and infrastructure in order to create normal conditions for the activity of the troops and the living arrangement of the local population. A

---

190 TsAMO RF, F.804, Op.290935s, D.1, l. 11.
191 Suris, *Frontovyi dnevnik*, pp. 105-106.

coded message from the Deputy Chief of the General Staff General A.I. Antonov from 10 April 1943 to the Chief of Staff of the Voronezh Front gives a picture of what the ground looked like after the winter fighting and the started muddy season:

> According to the information from the General Staff, the armies' and *fronts*' roads in the Novyi Oskol – Korocha – Oboian' and Staryi Oskol – Tim – Kursk sectors and others are difficult for movement, and certain of them are almost totally impassable. In the area of Staryi Oskol and Tim there are a lot of uncollected remains of humans and horses, which might become sources of infection and the spread of epidemic illnesses. In these same areas there is a large number of destroyed tanks and vehicles, and shells and mines.
>
> I request that you check and take urgent measures to eliminate the indicated facts. Report upon your execution of this order.[192]

In order to clean up the ground, burial teams were organized, while assembly points for broken-down machines were set up and mobile repair bases and engineers moved out to the indicated areas.

The strengthening of the defensive zones of the Voronezh Front's first echelon immediately after the front became stabilized near Belgorod began as usual with the deployment of mines. This was the simplest, quickest and most effective means both to counter enemy armor and in general to hold the lines. By the evening of 29 March, the 21st Army, which was holding the most threatened sector of the Voronezh Front, had laid a total of 2,500 anti-tank mines. However, in order to cover the forward edge, it still lacked at least 13,000 anti-tank mines. The army had no anti-personnel mines at all, yet it needed a minimum of 8,000 of these.[193] On 8 April, N.F. Vatutin informed I.M. Chistiakov that 12,000 anti-tank mines, 18,000 anti-personnel mines, 6,500 shovels and 8,000 entrenching tools were on the way to him via railroad.[194] In the meantime, he proposed sending to Chistiakov's army the 27th Dog Tank-Hunting Battalion as an anti-tank reserve.[195] The army commander immediately agreed without hesitation; the situation was forcing him to be ready to accept even these crumbs. The promised mines and tools arrived only in the latter half of April, when the muddy season had brought traffic to a stop. So, the thorough mining of all three army-level defensive belts and the serious strengthening of the directions that were vulnerable to armor did not begin until closer to May.

N.F. Vatutin had signed Order No.0087/op about setting up the defensive belts with engineer support on 27 March, when spring was already in full bloom and the entire Soviet-German front virtually dissolved into impassable mud. Thus, the fortification work was divided into two

---

192 *Russkii arkhiv: Velikaia Otechestvennaia voina*, No. 23 (12-3) (Moscow: TERRA, 1999), p. 106.
193 TsAMO RF, F.203, Op.2846, D.469, l. 30.
194 Ibid., l. 44.
195 The 27th Separate Battalion of mine-seeking and tank hunting dogs consisted of three platoons. The 1st Platoon had 31 men, 23 dogs, four anti-tank rifles and two light machine guns; the 2nd Platoon had 34 men, 23 dogs, four anti-tank rifles and two light machine guns; 3rd Platoon had 31 men and 21 dogs, and was armed with four anti-tank rifles and two light machine guns. During the Battle of Kursk it was parceled out by platoons to the 6th Guards Army's 67th Guards and 51st Guards Rifle Divisions and participated effectively in the fighting. (TsAMO RF, F.203, Op.2843, D.241, l. 207.)

parts – a first and second phase. The construction of everything most necessary to repulse enemy attacks went on in the first phase:

a. The mining of the main tank-vulnerable directions and the preparation of bridges for demolition throughout the entire depth of the defenses with the maximum use of captured mines, explosives, artillery shells and aerial bombs;
b. the construction of trenches with main and alternate firing rifle and machine-gun positions and anti-tank rifle positions with the clearing of fields of observation and fire;
c. the setting up of main and alternative positions for artillery and mortars with the simplest shelters for the crews and materiel;
d. the construction of anti-infantry obstacles in front of the forward edge;
e. the establishment of command posts;
f. the construction of earth and timber bunkers on the forward edge for the main weapons;
g. the preparation of cross-country tracks and treadway roads that ensure the delivery of supplies to the troops during the muddy season.

The order contained strict deadlines for the execution of this work; the extremely complex operational situation required this. It was necessary to complete the work on the main defensive belt by 5 April; on the second defensive belt on the main directions by 5 April and the entire line by 15 April; on the intermediary lines by 5 April; on the rear defensive belt and switch positions by 15 April; on the first *front*-level line on the main directions by 15 April, and on the entire line by 25 April.[196]

The second phase included setting up dummy positions and areas; digging trench shelters, bunkers and dugouts; building supplementary positions for all the weapons; developing communication trenches to the depth and across the front; improving trenches, weapons pits and firing positions for the artillery and mortars by adding embrasures, niches, water drainage lines and revetments; deploying anti-infantry obstacles in the depth of the defenses and on the flanks of the battalion areas and strongpoints; and constructing earth and timber bunkers for main weapons in the depth of the defenses.[197]

The responsibility for laying out and preparing the main and second defensive belts was placed upon the first-echelon armies within their own respective boundaries. They were also to build the rear defensive line, with the exception of the 7th Guards Army, which from the beginning was supposed to be withdrawn into the Front reserve in order to get ready for an offensive toward Khar'kov. Responsibility for the rear defensive belt was allocated in the following manner: the 38th Army was supposed to construct it from Malaia Loknia to Korocha (excl.); the 40th Army from Korocha to Uslanets; the 21st Army (of the 6th Guards Army) from Uslanets (excl.) to Vasil'evka. The 1st Tank Army was instructed to build the intermediary Kartamysheva – Ivnia – Kurasovka – Ship' line, even though at that time it was not formally under the command of the Voronezh Front.

---

196 TsAMO RF, F.203, Op.2843, D.323, l. 13-14.
197 Ibid., l. 15.

One rather important detail: The document expressly stated that major anti-tank obstacles like ditches, escarpments, tank traps and so forth should not be created. First, they required a lot of manpower and would divert significant personnel resources from elements of the defensive belts that were no less important but would require less effort. Second, as of yet Moscow still had not finally set upon a plan for the summer campaign. Prior to the decision about whether the acting army would go over to a defense or prepare for an offensive, the main thing was to strengthen the forward edge, in order to create the conditions to repulse any local attacks. The Soviet command believed for understandable reasons that the Germans wouldn't conduct any large-scale operation in the month of April. Thus, major obstacles on the main belt of defenses began to be thrown up only in May, when the essential defenses would already be in place, and the plan for summer had been adopted. Even so, it is impossible not to note the foresight of the Voronezh Front's headquarters, which in the order from 27 March had directed to prepare anti-tank minefield obstacles first and foremost, relying on the terrain conditions: "When reconnoitering and choosing places to plant the mines, particularly take account of overflowing rivers and flooded lowlands, having determined the boundaries of flooded sectors. Identify sectors suitable for flooding and anticipate the erection of the simple dams on them with the aim of holding back snowmelt and floodwaters."[198] The troops of the Central Front would also employ artificially-created mires and inundated places as a means of obstructing suitable directions of advance for German armor formations, but later.

The schedule for completing the work in the second phase was extremely tight: on the main defensive belt by 5 April; on the second belt of defenses no later than 25 April; on the intermediary and switch lines – by 15 April; on the army rear defensive belt by 25 April; and on the first *front*-level line at the most important directions by 25 April. The order emphasized that after the completion of this work, the troops were to start work on improving their combat positions.

The *Stavka* and the General Staff attached great significance not only to strengthening the entire Kursk salient, but particularly on the planned and systematic nature of this process. In order to unify the work, they created a single set of instructions for the troops when erecting the field defenses. Both Fronts at Kursk had very similar documents regarding the steady implementation of the fortification work and deadlines for completing it.

Unquestionably, there was the potential threat of an unexpected attack and even the breakthrough of the defenses of both *fronts* at this time. However, in reality, as the intelligence organs were reporting, the troops of Army Groups Center and South were also exhausted after the winter fighting, the ranks of their divisions had noticeably thinned, and their roads and bridges, just like those on our side, were virtually impassable due to the spring thaw. Therefore, from the beginning of April 1943, each of the opposing sides concentrated on rebuilding the forces, bringing them back to order and deploying them in their assembly areas.

There were also several more reasons why our defenses in the area of the Kursk salient remained plainly weak until the end of April. These were the inertia of thought and the inability of the command staff, first of all at the tactical level, to assess a situation accurately and to use their own combat experience. In Soviet historiography, just as in contemporary Russian history books, the authors set these matters aside. Possibly, at first glance they seem too minor,

---

198 TsAMO RF, F.203, Op.2843, D.323, l. 16.

even though the veterans of these events wrote openly about them back in the early 1970s and believed they were substantial. let us turn to the memoirs of the operations chief of the Briansk Front's 63rd Army, who at that time was a colonel, V.A. Beliavsky. Here is how he described a visit by the army's chief of staff, Major General Iu.L. Gorodinsky, to the 41st Rifle Division, which had just become part of the 63rd Army, and the condition of its defensive sector:

> The company [commander] plainly lacked the efficiency and bearing of a regular officer, or the crisp and concise military language when reporting. However, judging from all else, he knew war; this was not his first year of fighting, and he plainly fought pretty well, even though he did not have sufficiently deep and proper understanding of certain questions regarding the organization of a defense.
>
> The company's entrenchment was shallow, and here and there when moving along it you had to crouch. In one place I stopped at a heavy machine gun. The machine gunner, having tugged me by the arm, promptly pulled me to the earth, telling me, "German snipers are at work here, keep your head down …".
>
> Visiting the entrenchments, Major General Iu.L. Gorodinsky pointed out to the company commander their inadequacy.
>
> "The fieldworks are poor," he said. "They aren't deep enough to offer protection against fire. There are no communication trenches. How can this be?"
>
> The company commander replied to the General, "They say that when having no trench contact with other companies or communication trenches, a company will never abandon them under enemy attack."
>
> "I'm surprised at you, Senior Lieutenant. How can you seriously say such things? Get busy, give better support to your company with engineers," Gorodinsky sharply stated.
>
> Back at the division headquarters, Major General Iu.L. Gorodinsky ordered Colonel A.I. Surchenko to get busy quickly with improving the defenses.
>
> "Why aren't you developing and deepening the system of trenches?" he asked the division commander. Why don't you have any communication trenches leading to your frontline companies?"
>
> A.I. Surchenko tried to explain: "There's the opinion, Comrade General, that we won't be here for very long."
>
> "But you've been sitting here for more than a year already," Iu.L. Gorodinsky angrily observed. "Get to serious work on the defenses. Calculate how much time you need for this and report back to me. Meanwhile, you, Comrade Beliavsky," the General turned to me; "Tell the army's chief engineer that he should check on the condition of the fieldworks in the sector of the 41st Division."[199]

From the latter half of April 1943, Moscow became more confident that Berlin was nevertheless preparing a major offensive in the area of the Kursk bulge, though the possibility of strong diversionary attacks in other sectors as well was not excluded. In connection with this, on 21

---

199 Beliavsky, V.A., *Strely skrestilis' na Shpree* [*The arrows intersected at the Spree*] (Moscow: Voenizdat, 1973), pp. 78-79.

April 1943 the *Stavka* of the Soviet High Command sent a directive to the Commander-in-Chief of the Central Front, in which it demanded to put the tactical zone into proper order and to activate work to strengthen the defenses:

> As a result of our forces' advance during the winter operations of 1942/1943, the requirements of the *Stavka* Directive No.170663 from 15 October 1942 about the establishment of a frontal zone to a depth of 25 kilometers, which banned the civilian population's movement access to it, proved to be violated in a number of *fronts*.
>
> Not all of the *front* commanders took timely steps to create a new frontal zone that corresponded to the front's changed situation.
>
> The *Stavka* of the Supreme High Command orders:
>
> 1. To establish a frontal zone according to the requirements of the *Stavka* Directive No.170663 and by 10 May complete the expulsion of the entire civilian population within the 25-kilometer boundary of the Front's occupied line to the rear.
>
>   Establish the rear boundary of the frontal zone for the Central Front along the Griaznoe, Viazovatoe, Vas'kovo, Voinovo, Topki, Khmelevaia, Lukovets, Goriainovo, Nizhnee Smorodnoe, Gorki, Khlynino, Mikhailovka, Krupets, Kuznetsovka, Arbuzovo, Shustovo, Sherekino, Ekaterinovka, Pogrebki line – all points inclusive for the frontal zone.
>
> 2. Immediately set to work constructing two or three army-level defensive lines in the frontal zone, one behind the other, and to adapting all of the towns and villages in this zone for a defense.
>
>   Convert all of the cities and major populated places in the zone, from which all of the civilian population must be expelled, into bastions independently of their distance from the front line, being guided by the instructions laid out in *Stavka* Directive No.170663.
>
> 3. Get to work immediately to carrying out the given directive. Report on the implemented steps and on the designated lines for the fieldworks by 25 April 1943.[200]

This document was important for accelerating the preparations of the Central Front for the Battle of Kursk. First, it became the first major step in implementing the decision reached at the conference in the Kremlin on 12 April and gave substantial impetus to the large-scale roll out of fortification work on the lines of Rokossovsky's forces. In essence it was precisely this moment that can be counted as the creation of a deeply-echeloned defense in the northern portion of the Kursk bulge. Even so, as mentioned above, for already a month the Front's leadership had done a large amount of preparatory work for its creation. In addition, the document once again demonstrated to the command of the acting army that Moscow was inclined to confirm at last the tentative decision to go over to the defense and was making preparations for it mandatory.

Second, the directive plainly showed that the *Stavka* was concerned first and foremost with the Moscow direction, so it was the first in a series of similar documents addressed personally

---

200 *Russkii arkhiv. Velikaia Otechestvennaia voina: Kurskaia bitva; Dokumenty i materialy 27 marta – 23 avgusta 1943* [*Russian archive. Great Patriotic War: The Battle of Kursk; Documents and materials 27 March to 23 August 1943*] Vol. 15 (4-4) (Moscow: TERRA, 1997), p. 19.

to the Commander-in-Chief of the Central Front, where the main events were expected, and from whence the greatest possible threat to the capital might arise. Three days later, on 24 April a directive similar in content regarding the main task went out to the commanders-in-chief of all 10 *fronts* deployed from Lake Ladoga near Leningrad down to the Black Sea. It required to build-up strength and to initiate work on the construction of two field defensive lines each, with the *front*-level defensive belt to be completed by 15 June, and a State-level defensive belt – by 25 June. With regard for the decision made on 12 April, Moscow as the first order of business directed resources to the construction of a *front* line at Plavsk, Kursk, Alekseevka and Voronezh. Quickly, more than half of the Defense Construction commands available in the *Stavka* Reserve (the 22nd, 23rd, 27th, 28th, 35th, 36th and 38th Defense Construction Commands), in which there was a total of 31 military field construction corps staffed with trained and experienced cadres were quickly sent here. A portion of them became directly subordinate to K.K. Rokossovsky and N.F. Vatutin. This was a substantial amount of labor force. For example, the 27th and 38th Defense Construction Commands had on their rosters 16,000 skilled workers and 6,000 mobilized civilians, and 11,000 skilled workers and 7,000 mobilized civilians respectively.[201]

The entire 38th Defense Construction Command remained on the Voronezh Front right up to the end of the Battle of Kursk, doing fortification work on the Front's line. The 27th Defense Construction Command in early April received the assignment to prepare first the 107-km Koritskoe – Alekseevka – Chuprinin sector of the Front's line, and then in order to screen the Front's left flank on the Kursk axis, to fortify the Okuni – Kazatskoe switch line and to create a powerful knot of defense in Staryi Oskol, having built an encircling line around it that extended for a total of 141 km. However, already at the end of the month, according to Directive No.125931 from the Chief of the Main Command of Defense Construction from 30 April, the bulk of the 27th Defense Construction Command began to be shifted to the Don River. Here along the left bank the construction of a State-level line of defense was underway, which the *Stavka*, together with the forces of the Steppe Military District, viewed as the main means to block the path to German forces into the country's interior (beyond the Don River) in the event of a deep penetration of the positions of the Voronezh or Central Fronts. It was therefore no coincidence that the leadership of the Steppe Military District was given the responsibility for strengthening the Don State Line of Defense. The planned work here was very large: the 27th Defense Construction Command alone received the assignment to fortify a sector that extended for 232 km, which also included ground on the right bank of the river (to strengthen bridgeheads). It was to create 82 battalion areas, and 36 company-sized and 19 platoon-sized strongpoints.

The Central Front also received a large force of military construction workers and sappers: the 34th Defense Construction Command under the leadership of Colonel T.I. Ponimash and 245 sapper companies. They in fact became the main creators of the bulk of its forces' field system of defense. Rokossovsky and his Military Council distributed them in the following manner:

---

201 Maliarov, V.N. *Stroitel'nyi front v gody Velikoi Otechestvennoi voiny. Sozdanie strategicheskikh rubezhei i platsdarmov dlia obespecheniia oboronitel'nykh operatsii vooruzhenykh sil v 1941-1945 gg.* [*The construction front in the years of the Great Patriotic War. The creation of strategic lines and staging areas for supporting defensive operations of the armed forces in the years 1941-1945*] (St Petersburg: Voenno-inzhenernyi universitet, 2000), p. 179.

- 100 companies were assigned to build the main defensive belt, and they worked according to the plans of the regimental, divisional and corps engineer services;
- 70 companies were directed to build the second belt of defenses, and they were subordinate to the armies' engineer chiefs;
- 30 companies and the local population were to prepare the rear army-level defensive belt; the work here was done under the direction of the engineer chiefs of both the armies and the Front;
- the remaining 45 sapper companies and a portion of the 34th Defense Construction Command were directed to build the *front*-level defensive lines (a main and rear one) and to fortify Kursk, where it was also planned to draw upon the labor of the local population.

The 34th Defense Construction Command consisted of four headquarters of military field construction, which received the assignment:

a. The 15th Headquarters of Army Military Field Construction (led by Colonel S.I. Gavrili, then by Engineer-Captain A.A. Poletaev) was to do the fortification work immediately in the Kursk area;
b. The 125th Headquarters of Military Field Construction (led by Engineer-Lieutenant Colonel I.V. Kosynkin) was to strengthen the sector of the *front*-level line in the rear of the 13th Army;
c. The 126th Headquarters of Military Field Construction was to prepare positions on the *front*-level line behind the forces of the 70th Army;
d. The 127th Headquarters of Military Field Construction (headed by Engineer-Lieutenant Colonel V. Goriunov) together with mobilized civilians were to build the Voronezh Front's defenses at Oboian' and to the southwest of there.

As already mentioned, it was planned to split the *front*-level line of defenses behind Rokossovsky's forces into two separate, independent positions, a main one and a rear one. Two fortified regions were to deploy on the main line; their presence was one of the most noticeable distinctions between the Central Front's system of defenses and that of its neighbor, the Voronezh Front. Given a penetration of the army-level defensive belts by the German Ninth Army, the fortified areas were to block the approaches to Kursk – the largest city within the Kursk bulge. This was one of the consequences of the *Stavka*'s mistaken calculation that the enemy was going to launch the main attack against the Central Front. From K.K. Rokossovsky's Order No.00125 from 7 April 1943:

> On the basis of *Stavka* Order No.0061 from 31 March 1943, the 119th and 161st Fortified Regions that have arrived from the Moscow Fortified District are to come under the Central Front's control. They consist of the 552nd and 243rd Separate Signals Companies; the 168th and 104th Flamethrower-Trench Companies, and the 16th, 356th, 370th, 399th, 401st, 415th, 13th, 383rd, 384th, 405th, 406th, 407th and 408th Separate Machine Gun – Artillery Battalions.
> I am ordering:
> 1. The 161st Fortified Region consisting of seven separate machine gun – artillery battalions to remain in the Front's reserve and to take up a position at the

alphabetical designation "O" on the *front*-level line with the task to fortify and defend within the boundaries: on the right – Drovosechnoe (excl.), Rogatyi, Maloarkhangel'sk; on the left – Svoboda, Fatezh. Cover the a) Maloarkhangel'sk; b) Ponyri axis particularly strongly. Command post: Nikolaevka.

2. The 119th Fortified Region consisting of six separate machine gun – artillery battalions is to be held in the Front's reserve and to be positioned on the outer ring of fortifications around Kursk, with the task to defend the approaches to Kursk from the north, northwest, and the L'gov – Oboian' direction. Strongly cover the a) Fatezh; b) L'gov and c) Oboian' directions within the boundaries: on the left – Ryshkovo (excl.), Paniki (excl.). Command post of the 119th Fortified Region – northwestern outskirts of Kursk.

Readiness of the system of fire and the sapper works of first priority on the lines occupied by the Fortified Regions – 18 April 1943.[202]

The rear positions began to take shape on the basis of the Front's Military Council Decree No.00142/op from 27 March. They were to be erected along the Zabrevo – Bol'shoe Ol'khovatka – Budakovka – Verkhniaia Medveditsa line especially for covering the Front's main and only Kursk – Kastornoe railroad trunk line from the north. It was supposed to be linked with Kursk's outer ring of fortifications. The responsibility for organizing and conducting the reconnoitering work was placed on a headquarters department of the Front's Fortified Regions. The task was to strengthen as the first order of business the directions Orel – Kursk, Maloarkhangel'sk – Shshigry, and Kolpnia – Marmyzhi directions to a regimental depth. The document noted:

4. Responsibility for the construction of the line is to be placed on the 126th Headquarters of Military Field Construction's 34th Headquarters of Defense Construction, which is to be removed from work on the front-level line that is located in the zones of the 61st and 3rd Armies. In the future, before their acceptance by units of the Orel Front, hand over the completed fortifications to local authorities.
5. The chief of the 34th Defense Construction Command is to assemble the 126th Headquarters of Military Field Construction at the work site on 5 April 1943 and to initiate the construction work simultaneously with the reconnoitering of the lines. The deadline for completing the first-order works is 10 May 1943.
6. The Kursk Oblast Executive Committee is to mobilize additionally 5,000 people and 200 horses at this line.[203]

Civilians took active part in creating the earthworks throughout the entire period of preparations for the battle, but their use was regulated by the season of the year and weather conditions. Until the start of their work in the fields, which is to say, from the latter half of March to approximately mid-April, as far as they could they helped the troops in creating fortification works, but then the majority of them were busy with the planting season. In addition, a significant portion of

---

202 TsAMO RF, F.62, Op.321, D.5, l. 128-129.
203 Ibid., l. 99.

the civilian population were drawn upon to work on the army-level defensive belts at the end of May and in June, before the start of the harvest drive. The first official document, on the basis of which the residents of the Kursk Oblast were directed to building the Central Front's field defenses was its Military Council's Decree No.0041/op from 26 March, which stated:

> With the aims of greater efficiency and the most rapid fulfillment of the Military Council's tasks regarding defensive construction in the Central Front's zone, both at the present moment and in the future, the Military Council has decreed:
> 1. To oblige the Kursk Executive Committee to form four columns of workers – each of 1,000 people from among the called-up senior ages [at the decision of the Kursk Executive Committee from 20 March 1943] – and to hand them over to the 34th Defense Construction Command no later than 4 April 1943.
> 2. The Kursk Executive Committee at the expense of the Oblast's funds is to ensure the organization of the feeding of all four columns via the Oblast's Consumers Union and Village Cooperative Stores according to the norms set by the People's Commissar of Trade, as well as to provide housing for them until 25 April 1943, after which the members of the columns will pass to the 34th Defense Construction Command for the provisioning of all types of allowances.
> 3. The chief of the 34th Defense Construction Command is to assist the Kursk Executive Committee during the period of formation and in the future to post members of the command staff over the columns.[204]

The number of civilians working on the army's positions continued to increase. For example, in April 1943 105,000 dwellers of Kursk Oblast were working on the lines of the Central and Voronezh Fronts, but by May now almost 300,000. In addition, more than 10,000 residents of Kursk were assisting the troops of the Steppe District and Southwestern Front, while more than 82,000 residents of the Orel Oblast were assisting the Central Front and Steppe District. Residents of Voronezh Oblast and Khar'kov Oblast made their own contributions to the general cause. Even though the chief part of Khar'kov Oblast just as before remained under German occupation, even so, 32,000 residents of Ukraine, who'd been liberated in the winter of 1943, were drawn into working on the fortifications in the area of the Kursk salient. The civilian laborers and population were concentrated only on the rear army-level defensive belt and the *front*-level and State-level lines not by coincidence. As already mentioned above, all of the civilian residents were to be evacuated beyond the second army-level defensive belt, so it was authorized to use them only in the rear.

In connection with this I want to stop at a question that I believe is important and to express my own point of view, relying on the information stored in the archives. More than once I've happened to hear from scholars, museum colleagues and foreign historians the assertion that the Soviet side made active use of not only the troops of the acting army and civilians when constructing the defenses around the Kursk bulge, but also prisoners of war and even convicts. As evidence they cite the fact that supposedly authorities especially established two prison camps in order to fortify the rear army-level line (or the first *front*-level line) of the Central

---

204 Ibid., l. 97-98.

Front, and it was these prisoners, not the civilian population of the Kursk Oblast, who dug the entrenchments, communication trenches and dugouts. In fact, at this time in the Soviet Union, the labor of convicts and prisoners of war were widely employed, including in providing work to the military industry or the construction of military sites. Thus, their employment here was also possible. However, I've happened to work on the subject of the Battle of Kursk for a long time in various archives, and thus far I've not come across any documents that would directly or indirectly confirm these speculations. On the contrary, uncovered documents show that the Soviet command staff at the army and Front level demanded not to draw upon prisoners of war for the construction of the army-level defensive belts, in particular those of the Voronezh Front, and did not even use them as an auxiliary labor force, as was widely practiced in the Wehrmacht (the so-called Hiwis). I will cite as an example an excerpt from the commander of the 7th Guards Army from 19 April 1943:

> On this date at 0800, a foreign truck belonging to the 662nd Aerial Observation, Warning and Communications Company, driven by a captured German prisoner of war, as a result of a malfunction rolled in reverse down a hill in the vicinity of my bunker[205] and ran into a prisoner of war and a sergeant of the security company, injuring the latter. The senior officer in the machine was the company's assistant commander for armaments Senior Lieutenant Borisov. A similar case might have occurred due to the exceptional lack of discipline in the company because passage to the command post area is banned. A trip to the units, where the requirements regarding vehicular use are observed, is also not allowed in a machine needing repairs. Moreover, keeping a captured driver – a German at that – and allowing him to work is a crude violation of my order, since all prisoners are to be sent off immediately to prisoner of war camps. This violation of my order at the same time shows the complete absence of vigilance in the 622nd Aerial Observation, Warning and Communications Company. I am ordering:
> 1. All combat formations and units, in which there still might be any prisoners of war, are to send them off under armed escort to a prisoner of war camp and are to warn that they are not to be held in the units or called upon to work.[206]

Further on in the order, a formal rebuke was given to the deputy commander of anti-aircraft artillery Lieutenant Colonel Sergeev, while the commander of the 662nd Aerial Observation, Warning and Communications Company Captain Khomenko, the company's deputy political commander Lieutenant Amusov, and the company assistant commander Senior Lieutenant were ordered to be arrested and held for 5 days and be deprived of 50 percent of their pay for this period of detention. The order was to be announced to the entire command staff right up to the company commander himself, and was plainly intended for internal circulation, since it was

---

205 From March to mid-April, the army's headquarters was located in the village of Protopopovka, and then, after 15 April, it moved into bunkers that had been prepared in a wooded area between the settlements of Krasnaia Zaria and Ternovaia (*Na Belgorodskom napravlenii. Vospominaniia uchastnikov boev*) [*On the Belgorod axis. Recollections of combat veterans*] (Belgorod: Belgorodskoe knizhnoe izdatel'stvo, 1963), p. 95.
206 TsAMO RF, F.290 mp., Op.20928s. D.4, l. 199.

distributed for use in the troops (the cited example was found in the files for the 290th Mortar Regiment). Thus, there is no justification to doubt in the sincerity of the army commander, who required the immediate dispatch of prisoners of war to a prisoner of war camp.

The *Stavka* also directed for all of the cities, major villages and stations in the Kursk salient to be readied for an all-round defense. This work made widespread use of the positive experience gleaned from the defense of Leningrad. Throughout 1942, a special commission of the General Staff repeatedly inspected the isolated city's defenses. The collected information was compiled in a *Stavka* directive from 14 October 1942, in which it was stated that major populated places that have been adapted in advance for conducting an all-round defense, are able to stop the advance of major enemy forces, while the troops that are holding them can fight on in encirclement for a long time. On the basis of this document, in early May 1943 an inspection of Kursk's fortifications was conducted by a special commission. It found that the system that had been created according to the principle of field lines was not suitable for holding it. Therefore, the General Staff directed to employ the experience acquired when defending the Neva River's citadel, and to convert Kursk into a fortress city, which is to say to create the necessary conditions for conducting prolonged and stubborn combat operations within the city itself, even when completely surrounded.

On 13 May the Central Front's Military Council confirmed the layout of the forward edge, the grouping of the battalion strongpoints of defense, and the system of fire on the field lines in the Kursk area (the outer ring of fortifications) and within the city itself.[207] In addition to the outer ring of fortifications that had already been constructed around it (its most important sector ran along the Detdom – northern outskirts of Kazatskaia Sloboda – Hill 255.2 – Mokva-1 – Seim River – southern outskirts of Kursk line), the city was divided into 16 combat districts, which consisted of company-sized strongpoints. The combat districts were to be divided by anti-tank ditches, while hidden communication trenches were to be prepared for maintaining contact between them. All of the streets were to be blocked by barricades, reinforced with anti-tank hedgehogs, while the corner buildings were converted into pillboxes. Artesian wells were to be drilled in 12 of the combat districts (in the event the city's water supply system failed), and the plan was to build 900 earth and timber bunkers and 130 artillery pillboxes. In order to do such a large amount of work, eight columns of workers from the 34th Defense Construction Command headed to Kursk, and the plan was to recruit 15,000 to 20,000 residents of the city for the work as well. Skipping somewhat ahead in the events, I'll note that this plan was essentially realized before the middle of July (including with some corrections).

The measures to regroup the forces, realign the sectors of defense and to establish final boundary lines in Galinin's, Pukhov's and Romanenko's armies were primarily completed by the end of April. So, their troops then started upon the second main stage of fortification work on their lines, which continued to the beginning of June.

In the Red Army, the moment when the commander of a combat formation received an order to go over to a defense triggered the process of organizing it. This included a number of steps, such as clarifying the order from higher command; the commander's acceptance of the decision to take up a defense; the issuing of tasks to his subordinate formations and units, as well as any attached assets; the organization of command and control and establishing cooperation;

---

207 TsAMO RF, F.62, Op.321, D.6, l. 260.

fortifying the ground occupied by the troops; arraying a system of fire; and doing political-education work among the troops. In parallel, a number of steps were taken in order to control the execution of the commander's decision (through orders and directives) and to assist the subordinates in implementing it. The system of control was an inseparable and important part of the concept of "organizing a defense".

A commander's first steps after the end of a battle (or the cessation of fighting) were to consolidate their hold on the captured territory and to issue immediate tasks to the troops. Only then, after receiving and clarifying an order for a defense, did he start work to implement it. Therefore, in all the armies of both the Central and Voronezh Fronts, the main construction work on the defensive lines started with the exhaustive study of the terrain and the issuing of assignments. Immediately after Moscow made the decision to adopt a pre-designated defense around the entire Kursk bulge temporarily, their Military Councils issued the primary task to the troops: Once the enemy launched the attack, to grind down his forces using prepared defensive positions, and to prevent a penetration through both army-level defensive belts, especially at the flanks.

A key moment when organizing a system of defenses was when the army commander himself made the decision regarding the adoption of a defensive posture. At its basis was a scheme of actions that determined: the pattern of fire against the enemy with available weapons on the directions where the adversary would most likely go on the offensive; the areas (sectors) of terrain which directly affected the strength of the entire system of defense; the construction of a line of defense with regard for the lay of the ground; and any potential maneuvers with forces.

According to the new Infantry Combat Manual adopted in 1942, the strength of a defense and the length of the troops' resistance in set positions depended first of all on how well the critical (trafficable) sectors of ground, the populated places in them and even the isolated building or structure (dwellings, hangars, rail sidings, etc.) were fortified. The document remarked that only by having converted them into powerful strongpoints and centers of resistance, reinforced with minefields, was it possible to count upon a success. The control over these sectors and strongpoints enabled the defenders to block the enemy's path of advance into the depth of the unit's or formation's position, and in the event of a penetration, to deprive the enemy of the possibility of maneuvering, while simultaneously enabling the command of the defending troops, through the retention of them, to regain a lost position with fire and counterattacks (or counterblows). If there was not enough strength for active operations, these strongpoints and centers of resistance would block the adversary's further expansion into the depth of the combat positions. In order to reinforce the sectors that were considered key, commanders were to allocate the main forces of manpower, weapons and engineers to them. The commanders of the regiments, divisions, corps and even the army commanders themselves should personally engage in determining the relative significance of these areas and sectors. Only after the thorough analysis of the terrain on a map, the commander's reconnoitering of a sector, and the confirmation of the higher command's decisions did large-scale fortification work begin. Such an approach helped reduce the possibility of a mistake to a minimum and enabled the more rational use of the units' and elements' energy when doing heavy earth work. Even so, of course, in practice, there were not rarely diversions from this scheme in the troops, which led first of all to blunders in determining the locations of permanent firing positions and when arranging the system of fire.

The 70th Army, from the moment of going over to a defense, occupied the central position in the Central Front (with the 60th and 65th Armies to its left and the 13th and 48th Armies on its right right), covering the important Kromy – Kursk operational direction. After determining the most likely place where the enemy would launch the main attack, as his first step K.K. Rokossovsky redrew the boundary between the 13th and 70th Armies and increased the sector of defense held by the latter by shortening its neighbor's sector of responsibility. By 25 April, it had received this sector and the main forces it would have in the course of the Battle of Kursk. The Commander-in-Chief of the Central Front issued his Combat Directive No.00166/op to the 70th Army at 2300 on 20 April, which in part stated:

> From 2400 on 20 April 1943, the 28th Rifle Corps consisting of the 211th Rifle Division, 280th Rifle Division and 132nd Rifle Division, together with its combat sector and assignments will pass from the 13th Army to the 70th Army. From this point in time, establish the boundary line between the 13th Army and the 70th Army as follows: as far as the village of Vozy – as before; further on – Samodurovka, Gnilets, Voronets, Zarech'e, Oka River to the mouth of the Itska River. Include all the points, except for Vozy Station, Samodurovka and Gnilets, for the 70th Army. I am placing responsibility for protecting the boundary between the 13th and 70th Armies on the commander of the 13th Army.
>
> The commander of the 70th Army by 25 April 1943 is to rearrange the army's combat formation, having four rifle divisions in the first echelon along with the main armor and artillery assets. Keep four rifle divisions in the second echelon; position three of the rifle divisions behind the army's right flank in the Krasovka, Nikol'skoe, Chernomoshnoe, Kal'chevskii Iasenok, Petroselki area and one division in the Korovki, Gremiach'e, Possernovo, Mokhovoe area.
>
> On 25 April 1943, shift the main command post to the Redogon' area, and the auxiliary command post to Kubartkino area.[208]

Together with this order, the 70th Army's command also received an adjusted combat task. It was now to hold a line with a forward edge that ran along the line: Hill 204.1 – northern fringe of woods north of Bolotnyi – Rudovo – Kotomki -- Shepelevka – Verkhnoe Grankino – Il'insko-Nagornyi – Chern' – Zolotoe dno – patch of woods east of Novaia Ialta – ravine southeast of Hill 260.2 – Khal'zevo – Hill 258.4 – Trofimovka – Ferezevo – Briantsevo (excl.). The army's boundary on the right with the 13th Army: Vozy Station (excl.) – Samodurovka (excl.), Gnilets (excl.), Voronets, Zarech'e, Oka River to the mouth of the Itska River. The boundary on its left with the 65th Army passed through Shmarnoe, Nizhniaia Zhdanovka, Mikhailovka, Razvet'e, Briantsevo, Lukinino, with all except Shmarnoe belonging to the 65th Army.

The reason for the regrouping was as follows: having decided that the Germans would launch their main attack against the 13th Army, the Front's leadership was concerned primarily with strengthening it, and also with the creation of a strong defense of all major directions that offered favorable ground for armor operations in the sector of all three armies, including, naturally, in the sector of Galanin's 70th Army. In the opinion of K.K. Rokossovsky, the order cited above simultaneously resolved two main problems: it reduced the sector held by Pukhin's 13th Army by almost half, and seriously reinforced Galanin's 70th Army. In reality, the important

---

208 TsAMO RF, F.62, Op.321, D.5, l. 132-133.

significance of this order for the 13th Army, obviously as far as the 70th Army was concerned, played a positive role for both armies. A large-scale inspection conducted in early April showed that the combat capabilities of all of the 70th Army's divisions, putting it gently, weren't very high, and its headquarters had no experience at all in conducting a major defensive operation. K.K. Rokossovsky therefore decided to reinforce Galanin's army, having transferred to his command on 20 April three seasoned divisions, the 132nd, 211th and 280th Rifle Divisions, all under the command of the 28th Rifle Corps. They were occupying a defense on the right flank, covering the main sector that was vulnerable to tanks – the area of the Orel – Kromy – Kursk highway. N.V. Galanin also took steps to reinforce his right wing with his inherent forces. The sector to the east of the Belyi Nemed' River, which extended for 24 km was now being held simultaneously by five rifle, one artillery and one anti-aircraft artillery division, as well as by two tank regiments.[209]

As is known, the boundary lines within and between armies are always the weakest sector when arranging the defenses of any army. The opposing sides therefore always paid great attention to them and sought in the first place to determine as accurately as possible the enemy's boundary lines, and secondly, to strengthen their own boundaries and in the process keep them concealed from the foe. However, with respect to Galanin's 70th Army, from the outset the Front command made a number of mistakes. For example, the boundary lines of the 70th Army with its neighbors, and the boundary lines within it between the divisions, were not chosen well. The boundary with the 13th Army ran across Hill 218.3 and further to the north along the Oka River. In this area, the enemy's side of the line featured natural masking terrain – the large cultivated area at Verkhne Tagino (the Sadovod State Farm), as well as a lot of ravines that were overgrown with trees, which the Germans could use (and did use) to mask the assembly of significant forces, including armored vehicles as well. The boundary between the 28th Rifle Corps' 280th and 211th Rifle Divisions ran just 1 km away from the Orel – Kursk highway. On both sides of this boundary, the Germans were holding commanding heights, Hill 257.0 and Hill 254.5, and between them was a patch of woods and an overgrown ravine. Thus, the hills ensured splendid observation and shellfire of the army's defenses, while the wooded patch and ravine offered concealment for the bringing up of enemy forces from Sokovinki. These same miscalculations were made on the 70th Army's left wing. Large patches of woods on the enemy-occupied territory were located at the boundary with the 65th Army and at the boundaries of its 106th and 102nd Rifle Divisions (in the area of the villages of Shcherpod'e and Lavrovo). Meanwhile, the junction between the 106th and 211th Rifle Divisions ran along a natural boundary, the Belyi Nemed' River, which allowed the Germans to determine the boundary between these two divisions without any particular difficulty.

The determination of boundary lines is a prerogative of the Front command. Why its headquarters and staff, which had a relatively large amount of experience with conducting defensive operations, did not pay much attention to this matter still is not clear, even though judging from the army's account, this problem was obvious to its command. Skipping ahead of the events somewhat, I will note that when planning the defense of Galanin's 70th Army, Lieutenant General M.S. Malinin's subordinates also made a number of substantive errors,

---

209 On 5 May 1943, through its acceptance of the Hill 218.3 (excl.), Hill 232.0, patch of woods east of Probuzhdeniia line from the 13th Army, this sector increased to 30 km. The 70th Army's sector over the course of April to June 1943 increased twice through the reduction of the 13th Army's line.

likely because of blindly following in the footsteps of the Central Front Military Council's mistaken decision regarding the most likely axis of the German main attack in the sectors of the 13th Army and 48th Army. In connection with this, it is appropriate here to mention how strikingly different was the approach of the Voronezh Front's leadership to resolving such problems. N.F. Vatutin worked over these questions very meticulously and thoroughly. When personally drawing the boundaries between the armies of the first echelon, he not only simply considered all the details of the terrain, but also made masterful use of natural obstacles to strengthen the armies' boundaries. The boundary between the 6th Guards and 7th Guards Armies can serve as a clear example of this. It ran across ground that offered extremely difficult going at the confluence of the Lipovyi Donets and Severskii Donets Rivers. Even though this was in the area of Army Group South's main attack, its forces were in fact forced to bypass it to either side. Only on the fifth day of the offensive, due to the threat of enemy encirclement, would the units of the 6th Guards Army's 375th Rifle Division and 7th Guards Army's 81st Guards Rifle Division be compelled to withdraw from this area. As we will see below, the situation on the first day of the Battle of Kursk went tragically at the boundary between the 70th Army and 13th Army. To no small extent, the unsuccessful drawing of the army sectors would contribute to this. According to the defensive plan, the line of the 70th Army would consist of:

a) a main defensive belt, the depth of which would vary between 3 and 6 km;
b) a second defensive belt, running at a distance of 6-11 km from the forward edge of the main belt;
c) a rear army-level belt of defenses, located 13-19 km from forward edge of the second defensive belt;
d) a tête-de-pont (or bridgehead) which was erected at a distance of 37-39 km from the forward edge of the main defensive belt in the Fatezh area.

By the start of the Battle of Kursk, the main belt of defenses ran along the line: Hill 218.0, patch of woods east of Probuzhdeniia, Rudovo, Kotomki, Shepelevka, Verkhne Grankino, Novyi svet, nameless elevation 800 meters west of Hill 256.5, Khal'zevo, Trofimovka, Ferezevo, Briantsevo (excl.). It consisted of 43 battalion areas of defense and 12 company-sized strongpoints, which were being occupied by the 132nd, 280th, 211th, 106th and 102nd Rifle Divisions.

The second defensive belt lay along the line: Hill 228.9, Hill 250.2, Hill 246.8, Hill 228.4, Chernomoshnoe, Iuzhnye Tur'i, Studenok, Gorodnoe, Korovino, Volkovo, Ivanovskii, Opeka, Gorki. It consisted of 32 battalion areas of defense, which were being occupied by units of the 175th, 140th and 162nd Rifle Divisions (in the army's second echelon).

The rear army-level defensive belt was formed out of 14 battalion areas of defense along the southern bank of the Svapa River. It was not occupied by troops.

There was hardly any no-man's-land between the opposing forces; the entrenchments of the divisions of 70th Army's first echelon were located at a minimal distance from the enemy. Only on certain sectors was the forward edge screened by combat outposts. The plan foresaw the creation of sectors of obstacles in front of the main belt of defenses, within it, at the boundaries, and in front of the second defensive belt. The plan was to create the maximal possible density of them on the right flank, from the highway to the east as far as the junction with the 13th Army. It was proposed to cover the positions west of the Belyi Nemed' River more lightly.

As noted above, already in the latter half of April the General Staff was demanding that the entire defense at Kursk be built primarily as an anti-tank defense, organized to the entire depth of the armies, and particularly strongly in the system of the main belt of defenses. The fire of artillery and tanks; obstacles both artificial and natural (linked to the system of fire); the timely maneuver of anti-tank artillery and tank reserves and mobile blocking detachments; and a system of observation and reporting should comprise its basis. The defensive belts in all of the armies consisted of battalion areas of defense, each of which in turn was divided into three company-sized strongpoints. In addition, the battalion areas of defense featured anti-tank strongpoints, which were to strengthen the defense in sectors of terrain offering good ground for the operation of tanks. According to the calculations of the 70th Army's command staff, in order to conduct successful defensive combat, each battalion area of defense had to be equipped at a minimum with 10 artillery positions; 10 mortar positions; 24 entrenchments for the anti-tank rifle teams; 24 machine-gun nests; 36 infantry fighting positions; four observation and command posts; 18 shelters and dugouts; 2 km of anti-tank obstacles of all types; 3 km of anti-personnel obstacles of all types; and 4 km of communication trenches.

The foundation of the artificial obstacles was comprised of mines and booby traps that were closely tied into natural obstacles and the system of fire of all types. However, from the end of March and through almost the entire month of April, the 70th Army and its attached sapper units were forced to be busy with earth works, and at that for only very limited amounts of time. Fighting positions, trenches, dugouts and various anti-tank and anti-personnel obstacles were made ready, depending on the weather and soil conditions. Mining of sectors was done, but in small amounts, only at the divisional boundaries and on the army's right flank, in the vicinity of the highway. Large-scale work to deploy minefield obstacles in the army's entire sector got underway only in mid-May, with dense mining in the main defensive belt, and only after 20 May in the second and rear defensive belts. Incidentally, German intelligence, failing to fully understand the problems of the Soviet side, regarded the absence of deep minefields up to that time in the armies of the Central Front as one of the important indicators that they were preparing not for a defense, but for an offensive.

Nevertheless, despite such a substantial delay, the plan of fortifications in Galanin's 70th Army was almost completely implemented before the start of the Battle of Kursk. This required a colossal amount of work; almost 3.5 million cubic meters of earth alone were excavated. Considering that there were no substantial natural obstacles in front of the main defensive belt, a number of artificial obstacles had to be erected, and the dense planting of mines had to be conducted in front of the first line of trenches. In total, 178 anti-tank and 119 anti-personnel minefields were laid (in several rows), which extended for 77,100 and 81,195 meters respectively and contained 89,143 various mine and explosive devices.

The account of the 70th Army headquarters observed:

> Efforts were focused not only along the front line, but also in the depth on these directions. For this purpose, the work created a sufficient number of lines, from the forward edge into the depth ... In our defenses, the plan foresaw areas where the enemy was to be held and where he would be given an all-out battle (Verkhne Tagino and the Kursk – Orel highway). Here the defenses were calculated so that it would be possible to build up our forces and to offset the enemy's numerical superiority, which he would have at the initial moment of combat. The planning of the defense emphasized that the fighting for the initial positions be prolonged, with the goal to neutralize the enemy's advantage in a surprise attack and to force the Germans to commit their reserve forces in areas foreseen by the plan.

Minefields, not without justification, are considered a most important element of a system of defense. By the start of the Battle of Kursk, especially many of them would be laid in the sectors of the Voronezh Front's 6th Guards Army and Central Front's 13th Army. In order to do the engineer and mine-laying work, the *Stavka* assigned the *fronts* at Kursk two sapper brigades, including one of special designation; Colonel I.F. Ioffe's 1st Guards Separate Engineer Brigade of Special Designation was directed to K.K. Rokossovsky, while N.F. Vatutin received Colonel V.P. Krasnov's 42nd Separate Engineer Brigade. They both had large experience with such work and the latest specialized equipment. Ioffe's brigade had particularly distinguished itself in the Battle of Stalingrad, while Krasnov's subordinates had demonstrated a high degree of skill in the course of Khar'kov's defense in February and March 1943.

The ground from the forward edge of the 70th Army's second defensive belt back to the forward edge of the rear defensive belt was especially marked for reinforced mine-laying by elements of the 1st Guards Separate Engineer Brigade of Special Designation, which from the latter half of May was split between the 13th and 70th Armies. N.P. Pukhov received three battalions, while I.V. Galinin received two. They were to reconnoiter the terrain; determine the types, system and number of obstacles; and mark the primary routes for the activities of the mobile blocking detachments in the event that fighting started. After concluding this work, they were to turn immediately to fortifying the terrain:

> The 6th Guards Engineer Battalion within the boundaries of the Krasnaia Zaria, Tureika, Rudovo, Raznovil'e front; boundary on the right: Krasnaia Zaria, Podolian' (excl.), Bobrik (excl.), Samodurovka; on the left: Raznovil'e (excl.), Chernomoshchnoe (excl.) as far as the Svapa River. The main direction for the activity of the mobile blocking detachments – the Orel – Kursk highway and the boundary between the armies.
>
> The 4th Guards Engineer Battalion within the boundaries of the Lepelevo, Nizhniaia Grankina, Chern', Ploskoe, Opoikovo, Briantsevo; boundary on the right: boundary with the 6th Guards Engineer Battalion; boundary on the left – Briantsevo (excl.), Razvet'e (excl.).

Two other battalions of this brigade – the 3rd and 7th Guards Engineer Battalions – were directed to the *front*-level line. They received the mission to create the Central Front's zone of obstacles in the operational depth and simultaneously became the brigade commander's reserve. Meanwhile, the remaining 8th Guards Battalion, which handled specialized mine-laying tasks, was assigned for actions in the sector of the entire Front.

V.K. Kharchenko, who at the time was a lieutenant colonel and the deputy commander of the 1st Guards Separate Engineer Brigade, recalled in his memoirs:

> Soon after arriving at the new destination, the brigade commander and I were summoned to the village of Svoboda, in the environs of Kursk, to the Central Front's chief of engineers General Proshliakov. Aleksei Ivanovich unfolded a topographical map marked up with various-colored pencils and pointed out:
> "The adversary's main attack is being expected in the sectors of defense of the 13th and 70th Armies. The brigade is being made responsible for creating a system of minefields in this sector, as well as in the *front*-level zone. The plans call for the installation of electrified obstacles and the laying of mines by means of specialized

equipment at the most important locations. Prepare your proposals and report to me within two days."

It happened that Mikhail Fedeevich and I had to drive with the report to General A.I. Proshliakov with heavy colds. Over the two days we had prepared maps showing the obstacles, and our calculations and tables. In my view, all of these documents were rather convincing.

Having spread the documents out on a table, I reported the plan of the brigade's operations to set up the obstacles. Proshliakov, as always, listened attentively without interrupting me. When I finished, he inquired: "Is that all you have?"

I could tell by the tone of the question that the General was dissatisfied with the report. He asked to indicate on the map the locations of the intended minefields, then asked by what means and from where the mines would be delivered. Aleksei Ivanovich called for me to give the names of the individuals responsible for this operation and to describe their backgrounds. The questions regarding who and by what means the order to set up the minefields should be given, and in which direction the sappers should withdraw in the event of an enemy breakthrough, were troubling Proshliakov.

Already through the questions he asked it became clear to me that we would have to revise the plan and have to consider literally all of these so-called trifles, the neglect of which in a frontline situation might cost us dearly. I also realized something else: The General was making known the plan's shortcomings in the most proper manner.

"Have the operational groups been readied?" Proshliakov inquired.

I replied affirmatively. At the end of our discussion, Aleksei Ivanovich once again reminded us, "For the successful actions of the mobile blocking detachments, thoroughly and completely reconnoiter the ground, mark the lines to be mined, the movement routes to them, and set up stockpiles of mines ahead of time."[210]

It should be noted that the brigade carried out the plan quickly and precisely. As a result of the efficiently conducted reconnoitering of the terrain, a scheme was compiled showing the locations of the obstacles in the sector of both armies and on the *front*-level line as well, which also was agreed upon with the commandants of the fortified districts that were positioned on *front*-level sectors and with the leadership of the 34th Defense Construction Command. In this document, the following tasks were set before the brigade:

1. To block tank-vulnerable directions with obstacles, starting from the second army-level belt back to and including the third army-level belt, as well as to create intermediate mined lines between the two defensive belts. In the process, naturally, it was to take consideration of the overall arrangement of the fortifications, anti-tank obstacles and system of fire.
2. To mine the main directions vulnerable to tanks: the Orel – Kursk highway, the ground along the Orel – Kursk highway, and all the vulnerable corridors in the

---

210 Kharchenko, V.K., ... *Spetsial'nogo naznacheniia* [... *of Special designation*] (Moscow: Voenizdat, 1973), pp. 89-90.

Maloarkhangel'sk – Zolotukhino – Kosorzha, Droskovo – Kolpnia, and Droskovo – Livny directions.
3. To create bridgehead fortifications in front of Fatezh (a tête-de-pont).
5. To set up knots of resistance around the commanding heights in no-man's land.
6. To mine the bridges and wire the dams with explosives.
7. To mine wooded areas.
8. To wire roads, bridges and sites (particularly infrastructure) with delayed-action mines.

Brigade commander M.F. Ioffe decided to execute the order in two phases. First, to set up command-detonated explosives and delayed-action mines, and to mine bridges to the second level of readiness (placement of the explosives without their fuses). Next, he planned to sow the selected fields with mines to the third level of readiness (which is to say, without backfilling the cavity containing the emplaced mine). This mine-laying was done only in the defensive depth; fields were marked off, holes were dug and camouflaged, log sheets were filled out, but the explosive charges (the mines and fougasse) and firing devices were stacked nearby. It took a squad of minelayers about an hour to make such a field (with a length of 60 to 100 meters) ready.

After the completion of these two stages, the brigade's command staff was supposed to study the routes of movement for the mobile blocking detachments and the locations for stockpiles of mines for them.[211] In step with the completion of documentation, detailed study of the ground in the sector of both armies progressed, and upon its completion, the brigade's headquarters was forced to adjust its decision somewhat and to direct its main efforts toward:

a. strengthening the entire forward edge of defenses with continuous anti-tank and anti-personnel minefields;
b. preparing minefield to the second or third level of readiness on main tank-vulnerable directions, and around likely objectives and structures, while keeping teams of minelayers and the necessary materiel at them;
c. seeding wooded areas with mines in the sector of the 70th Army and its boundary with the 13th Army;
d. timely preparing the Orel – Kursk highway from Hill 248.3 to Hill 212.5 with command-detonated explosive devices, seeding man-made structures with mines, and to lay delayed-action mines at them to a second level of readiness;
e. thoroughly studying the terrain that offered good ground for the operations of armor, in order to determine locations for mines and explosive devices, and the organization of field stockpiles for carrying out mine-laying given an enemy breakthrough into the army's depth, and immediately for the mobile blocking detachments in the course of the fighting.

The 3rd and 7th Engineer Battalions received the assignment to reconnoiter the terrain for laying out the Front's second and third belts of obstacles in the operational depth, and in no-man's land

---

211 TsAMO RF, F.30300, Op.1, D.20, l. 4obr.

to a depth of 15 km and in front of the forward edge of the lines to a depth of 5 km within the boundaries:

a) Line "O" – on the right: Ol'khovatka – Krasnyi Oktiabr'; on the left: Buzets Station – Fatezh;
b) Line "A" – on the right: Droskovo – Nizhnyi Zhernovets; on the left: Kanaeva – Sluzhnia;
c) Line "L" – on the right: Peresukha – Znamenskaia – Evlanovo; on the left: Svoboda – Nikol'skoe – Novye Savintsy.[212]

The highest density of mines and explosive devices emplaced by the brigade and its sappers was on the right flank of the 70th Army. Here, within a 30-km sector held by the 28th Rifle Corps, they prepared 87 anti-tank minefields, 54 anti-personnel minefields and 10 combined minefields that held a total of 48,875 anti-tank and anti-personnel mines. As a result, each kilometer of frontage contained on average respectively 806 and 823 mines. This was a very high indicator for those times.

Moreover, when preparing the army's defenses for the battle, its command staff paid substantial attention to other types of artificial obstacles as well, especially on the right flank. According to the documents of the headquarters, by the start of July, 30,741 meters of anti-tank obstacles and 22,935 meters of anti-infantry obstacles had been prepared in its sector, as well as six weirs, with the help of which a total amount of 2,400 square meters of ground could be flooded. This defensive method had been first used by the Red Army on a significant scale back in the autumn of 1941 near Moscow. Back then, a large volume of water had been released from the Ivankovo Reservoir (known informally as the Moscow Sea), as a result of which the German panzers were unable to cross the Zavidovo swamp at Konakovo.[213] However, in the future this means, because of its specific nature, did not receive widespread application in the acting army. There was recollection of it only in the spring of 1943, when the General Staff prior to the Battle of Kursk summarized the entire successful experience of constructing a field defense over the first two years of the war. In order to complicate the breakthrough of the lines by German armor, hydraulic facilities were also under consideration for use on the Voronezh Front. In particular, recently declassified documents stored in the TsAMO RF show that in order to create ground inaccessible to tanks, the flooding of areas in the sectors of its flanking 38th and 7th Guards Army's received consideration. However, there has been no success in determining how fully this scheme was implemented or the effect that it had. On the main direction, where the 6th Guards Army was occupying the defense, there was no possibility to take such a step. However, as the combat operations on 5 July 1943 in the area of Cherkasskoe would show, the 67th Guards Rifle Division was able to hold in check even a very powerful panzer grouping (the main forces of the *Grossdeutschland* Panzer Grenadier Division and its attached brigade of Panthers) for almost an entire 24 hours by taking advantage of one small, swampy balka,

---

212 Ibid., l. 4.
213 Korshunov, E.L. and Rupasov, A.I., "Pri stroitel'stve protivotankovykh prepiatstvii uchityvat' melkie vodnye pregrady ..." ["When constructing anti-tank obstacles, consider small water barriers ..."] *Voenno-istoricheskii zhurnal*, No. 9 (2013), p. 3.

covered by mines, explosive devices and firing means, and thereby disrupted the enemy's plan for a rapid thrust into the depth of the 6th Guards Army's defenses.

In the course of the springtime pause in operations along the entire front of the Kursk salient, not only were portions of the divisions of the first echelon pulled back into the rear for training and rest; there was also a complete rotation of the frontline units. Therefore, practically all of the divisions took part in turn in preparing the main and second belts of defenses. In the process, other than the muddy season, specific factors in each army affected the speed and quality of the constructed defenses. In particular, in the 70th Army, such a factor was the ground upon which it was deployed. The account of its headquarters notes:

> The main base of our entire grouping [*front*] was Kursk Station. This situation constrained the normal organization of the arrangement of the operational rear services of the armies positioned in the Kursk bulge, which of course, affected the 70th Army's lines of communication. The sole artery feeding the army was the Kromy – Kursk highway. The remaining roads in the springtime muddy season were unsuitable for movement. This required equipping supply units and in general all of the army's mobile means with all-terrain vehicles. Therefore, the rear facilities had to be positioned along the highway. The close proximity of the base to the highway and the sharply marked suitability of the highway for transportation was the reason for the German air forces constant attacks on it.[214]

Even so, by early July, the 70th Army had constructed a powerful, contemporary system of field defenses, with its right flank conspicuous by its particular strength; here, there were 1,016 meters of anti-tank obstacles and 764 meters of anti-personnel obstacles of all types per each linear kilometer. The left flank was considerably weaker in terms of fortifications, although the 106th and 102nd Rifle Divisions also did a large amount of work while exhibiting creativity and high professional skill in the process. Their defenses had on average 383 anti-tank mines and 580 anti-personnel mines per linear kilometer, and in total they constructed 1,008 meters of anti-infantry obstacles and 848 meters of anti-tank obstacles. Nevertheless, this proved insufficient to offset their lack of authorized explosives, so these divisions made significantly more use of captured German artillery ammunition than their neighbors and prepared various types of surprises and booby traps; they also employed trip-wire activated R-2-400F grenades to strengthen the obstacles with explosives. Cheval-de-frise crafted from branches of timber found widespread use in their units as anti-infantry obstacles. For example, in the 102nd Rifle Division alone, 7,750 trip-wire activated grenades and 6,370 chevaux-de-frise were emplaced.

The command of the German Ninth Army intently tracked the preparations of the Soviet side. Around the clock, observers on the forward edge studied everything that was happening in the dispositions of the opposing side, and at every opportunity called down intense artillery fire on aggregations of Soviet troops or vehicles, or on an area where the construction of fieldworks were underway. Therefore, laying mines in the frontline battalions was done exclusively during

---

214 *Kursk kraevedcheskii muzei. Fond "Museia Kurskoi bitvy". Korobka No. 5 "Otchet shtaba 70A o boevykh deistviiakh v Kurskoi bitve"* [Kursk District Museum. Archive of the *"Museum of the Battle of Kursk". Container No. 5 "Account of the headquarters of the 70th Army about the combat operations in the Battle of Kursk"*], p. 25.

nighttime hours. This was complex and extremely fatiguing work. There was always the danger of an explosion because one's own mistake or the poor quality of the explosives, and at night this hazard rose exponentially.

As stealthily as possible, the Soviet troops, sappers and mobilized civilians sought to initiate their digging on the forward edge in the twilight hours, and at the same time tried to ensure that everything that had been completed be camouflaged before sunrise. However, this was not always observed scrupulously in all of the units. In addition, the turf removed when laying mines and roadside bombs dried out, and because of this the mine-strewn sectors began to stand out against the general background. The adversary took notice of this and tried to use such locations in order to create secure "corridors" for their patrols, but not rarely committed an oversight, which now the Soviet side exploited. For example, in early June in one of the sectors of the 102nd Rifle Division, a group of enemy sappers discovered a minefield, but when withdrawing left behind a probe and several items of gear. The division's combat outposts noted the arrival of the "guests" and assumed that the Germans would return the following night to lift some mines and retrieve their forgotten items. In order to prepare a worthy meeting, the division command quickly dispatched a platoon of the 10th Sapper Battalion, which set up several rows of trip-wire booby traps in this area. The calculation proved to be correct, and in the morning two German sappers and an officer were blown up on the "surprises" that had been left behind.[215] This is only one of dozens of examples of not only a responsible attitude toward service, but also the ingenuity and skill of the 70th Army's troops, which filled those days. Yet it should be acknowledged that at the same time, quite a few errors, mistakes and simply open bungling were committed by Galanin's first-echelon troops as well. Here is just one example from Directive No.12456 from the Chief of Staff of the Red Army Marshal of the Soviet Union A.M. Vasilevsky from 25 May 1943: "In the 106th Rifle Division … entire units are leaving the front to head to the rear for breakfast, lunch and dinner, leaving behind only observers, and sometimes even abandoning the trenches altogether. As a result, on 13 May 1943, a group of Germans penetrated the defense unhampered, seized two machine guns, and made their way back unpunished."[216]

The anti-tank defenses of Galanin's 70th Army were echeloned in depth. The main aim was to prevent a deep breakthrough by German armor along the Orel – Kursk highway, as well as to deprive them of maneuvering space in the event of a penetration in this area. In addition to this highway, there were other directions accessible to armor in the army's sector as well, for example, the Voronets – Nikol'skoe, Shchernod'e, Verkhnee Grankino and Zhiriatino – Chern' directions, but they weren't viewed as dangerous, so all of I.V. Galanin's attention was focused on strengthening his right flank in the sector held by the 28th Rifle Corps.

By the start of the Battle of Kursk, the 70th Army had the following means to counter the German panzers: the organic guns of 24 rifle regiments; the inherent eight anti-tank battalions of the rifle divisions; the 378th Destroyer Anti-Tank Artillery Regiment; a destroyer brigade of the 2nd Destroyer Division; three tank regiments; 204 anti-tank minefields concealing a total of 49,973 mines; 95,643 anti-tank obstacles; and also artificial barriers in the three of the army's sectors. In total his army possessed 204 45mm anti-tank guns and 46 76mm guns of

---

215 Ibid., p. 18.
216 TsAMO RF, F.426, Op.10753, D.84, l. 97.

the divisional artillery, of which 165 and 24 respectively were positioned in the first echelon. Despite these impressive numbers, given the 69 km of frontage occupied by the 70th Army, the density of anti-tank means in the first echelon turned out to be extremely low: three guns, 567 anti-tank mines and 834 anti-tank obstacles per kilometer. The total density of anti-tank guns for the army, including those of the second-echelon troops, was also modest and amounted to 3.8 per linear kilometer.

However, Rokossovsky positioned significantly more anti-tank guns on his right flank. The 28th Rifle Corps (the 280th and 132nd Rifle Divisions was holding a sector of 19 km, had in total 213 45mm and 76mm anti-tank guns. As a result, here there were 10 guns per kilometer of front in the first echelon, and 16 per kilometer in the second. For sake of comparison, in the sector of the 106th Rifle Division these figures were almost two times lower – six and nine respectively.

All of the anti-tank means were supposed to be brought together into anti-tank strongpoints, which were to block corridors offering good ground for tanks and strengthen the defenses of the rifle battalions to which they belonged. Depending on the terrain, each anti-tank strongpoint had a varying number of heavy weapons. On average, each one had four to five 45mm anti-tank guns, one or two 76mm anti-tank guns, and 8-10 anti-tank rifle teams. All of the roads in its sector of responsibility were sown with mines, and any bridges were wired for demolition. Moreover, the Soviets worked out a clear plan in advance: Who was responsible for blowing the bridge, and under what circumstances it should be destroyed. All of the anti-tank strongpoints were connected by the general system of artificial obstacles and overlapping fields of fire, so in combat they were in a position to cooperate closely with each other. In addition, while preparing for the battle, the artillery command made sure that the fire of their units (right down to each tube) was rigidly bound to the infantry fire, and the artillery located outside the anti-tank strongpoint in reverse slope positions (the howitzer regiments) each had a designated sector or direction of responsibility, and each artillery commander clearly knew them.

Under the circumstances of a deficit of anti-tank guns, the 70th Army commander I.V. Galanin strove to bolster the anti-tank strongpoints on the most vulnerable sectors to tanks, including with non-establishment means, like for example, with Katiusha rocket launchers. Ramps were set up at a shallow angle, so that their crews, given the need, had the possibility to fire directly at enemy armor.

As already observed, from the beginning K.K. Rokossovsky thought that Model might strike the 70th Army but viewed this option as much less likely than the Ponyri and particularly the Maloarkhangel'sk directions. I.V. Galanin therefore was given relatively few of the deficit mines and artillery. The Front Commander-in-Chief thought instead, given the need, that it would be fully adequate to reinforce the 70th Army with the Front's reserve 19th Tank Corps. This was one more of Rokossovsky's vexing mistakes, which would have to be hastily corrected already in the first days of the Battle of Kursk. Moreover, his headquarters even treated the use of this tank corps in the sector of the 70th Army rather lackadaisically.

In April and May 1943, with respect to the changing situation, several optional plans of actions were devised in the event that the Germans went on the offensive first, and the headquarters of the armies and Front worked jointly on the document. The final plan was adopted by the Central Front's Military Council on 25 May 1943 and foresaw five possible courses of the events.

The first was a breakthrough by a panzer grouping at the boundary with the 13th Army and a subsequent advance in the Podolian' – Soborovka direction. This is precisely how the combat operations would unfold from 5 July 1943 on, but no consideration was made regarding the possibility of using the 19th Tank Corps to counter the enemy on this axis. The account of the 70th Army notes:

> In order to repulse an enemy attack in the event of a breakthrough of our defenses, the 19th Tank Corps would go under the 70th Army's command, but at the start of the fighting it was not subordinate to the army. The army headquarters compiled a table of cooperation with it, which foresaw only two variants of combat operations.
>
> The first – in the event of an enemy breakthrough along the Kromy – Kursk highway, a subsequent advance in the direction of Hill 228.4 and Hill 238.6.
>
> The second – in the event of a breakthrough at the boundary between the 106th and 102nd Rifle Divisions, a subsequent advance in the Ploskoe – Volkovo, Gremiach'e direction.
>
> Experience demonstrated that it was necessary to foresee a third alternative, which considered the possibility of an enemy breakthrough at the boundary between the 70th and 13th Armies.[217]

That boundaries are the weakest place in the defenses of combat formations is axiomatic for any commander. It is not clear therefore why the 70th Army's command staff did not include such a powerful reinforcement as the 19th Tank Corps in the plan of defense for this axis. Possibly, it was assumed that the tank corps would be operating according to a special plan as the Front's reserve, but even so, its coordination with the 70th Army was extremely necessary under any version of a plan. After all, the 19th Tank Corps was not supposed to operate independently, but within the army's system of defenses. Particularly surprising is the marked inattention of the Front headquarters in securing the boundary between the 13th Army and 70th Army, which is to say, the axis which it determined as one of the three most vulnerable to tanks.

When analyzing those few mistakes already mentioned above (with the allocation of sectors and the 19th Tank Corps), the feeling arises that Central Front's chief of staff General M.S. Malinin and his subordinate staff officers were taking K.K. Rokossovsky's presumption too literally. So, the preparation of the forces and defenses according to a third option (an attack at the boundary between the 13th Army and 70th Army) was not done as thoroughly and thoughtfully as were the other two alternatives. It is hard to explain this number of crude blunders in any other way. Even individual commanders of the rifle divisions that were defending the 70th Army's right flank had a similar careless attitude toward protecting the boundary with the neighboring 13th Army at this time, which prompted the nervousness of others. On 3 July 1943, the chief of staff of the 140th Rifle Division Colonel P.O. Bauman wrote the following in his personal diary:

> The day before yesterday and yesterday, we received a warning, the Fritzes are preparing an offensive, to make sure we were ready. We should expect it between 3 and 6 July … In my mind I went through all the prepared alternatives. <u>Options in the direction of our right flank haven't been worked out, but the enemy might test the boundary with the 13th Army</u>[!]. Tomorrow morning just in case I will drive out in the direction of

---

217 Kursk Kraevedcheskii Muzei. Fond "Muzeia Kurskoi bitvy", Korobka No. 5, l. 17.

Samodurovka. I have a certain conviction that the Fritzes must attack in a narrow sector and it will have to be in the direction of the Fatezh highway. I spoke with Kiselev [the division commander], but he believes they will attack on a broad front.[218]

This miscalculation with the 19th Tank Corps would have a substantially negative influence on the course of the combat operations in the first few days of the battle, since it would reinforce a number of other mistakes in the system of defense at the boundary between the 13th Army and 70th Army. The commander of the 28th Rifle Corps Major General A.N. Nechaev was responsible for protecting the boundary with the 13th Army. In turn, he made the commander of the 132nd Rifle Division Major General Shkrylev responsible for the boundary between the adjacent flanks of the divisions of the first echelon – the 13th Army's 15th Rifle Division and the 28th Rifle Corps' 132nd Rifle Division – and between the 15th Rifle Division's 47th Rifle Regiment and the 132nd Rifle Division's 712th Rifle Regiment to the commander of the latter, Lieutenant G.M. Movchan. At the boundary between the two armies, the defenses were echeloned in depth and fully occupied by troops. This was implemented in the following manner: the combat formations of the units of the 132nd Rifle Division were arrayed in two echelons, and the 712th Rifle Regiment was in the first, holding a sector that ran for 5.5 km with all of its battalions in the front line. In the second echelon were the 498th and 605th Rifle Regiments in an intermediate line behind the 712th Rifle Regiment. In addition, the combat formations of the 498th Rifle Regiment were deployed in three echelons. Moreover, a penal company that was attached to the division was dug in along a line that ran from 1 km east of Krasnyi Ugolok through the eastern slopes of Hill 244.9 to Hill 194.2, between the first and second echelons of the 132nd Rifle Division. It was being calculated that such a high density of forces would be able to withstand a powerful enemy attack. As the 70th Army headquarters' account notes: "Every 1 to 1.5 kilometers, the enemy would run into new, perfectly set up defensive lines occupied in advance by troops. In addition, this would allow the possibility of removing units (say, a battalion) for launching a counterblow in any direction without disrupting the overall system of fire at the boundary.[219]

However, this combat formation also had its negative aspects. Up to a certain moment, the units of the second and third echelons wouldn't be able to employ small arms weapons, while in the process they themselves would suffer losses from enemy artillery and air strikes. In addition, the headquarters of the 70th Army made a substantial oversight when setting up the artificial obstacles in this area by not planning switch positions to screen the flank in the event the enemy broke through into the depth of the 13th Army's defenses at the boundary. This would in fact happen on the very first day of the German offensive, even though in the main belt of defenses, all the entrenchments and communication trenches at the boundary with the 13th Army were built in such a way as to give the possibility of conducting counterattacks into the sector of its 15th Rifle Division in the direction of Iasnaia Poliana. Nevertheless, the absence of switch positions substantially complicated the conducting of combat operations on the army's right flank throughout the entire period of the defensive operation.

---

218 *Kurskaia bitva: vzgliad iz XXI veka. Voenno-istoricheskie i publitsistecheskie ocherki* [*Battle of Kursk: View from the XXI Century. Military-historical and socio-political essays*] (Moscow: Russkii Renessans, 2008), p. 26. Author's emphasis.
219 Kursk Kraevedcheskii Muzei. Fond "Muzeia Kurskoi bitvy", Korobka 5, l. 20.

Galanin's 70th Army also received little of its own tanks and self-propelled guns, just three tank regiments of direct infantry support, though it should be emphasized that their use was planned completely rationally. In the first stage of the fighting, when the enemy had not yet deeply penetrated into the positions, the tank regiments were to be used to offer support to the infantry with their fire and as armored anti-tank firing positions dug into the ground. The 240th and 259th Tank Regiments were assembled in the wooded area east of the villages of Mogilevskii and Chermoshnoe, while the 251st Tank Regiment was in the woods west of Lapukhino. They were prepared to conduct concentrated fire from fixed positions simultaneously with all of their companies. In order to repulse a possible attack by enemy armor along the Orel – Kursk highway, on the northeastern fringe of the woods 1.5 km northeast of Chermoshnoe, the dug-in positions especially for the 259th Tank Regiment's tanks had exit ramps. In the event of the enemy's subsequent advance, the regiment was to be activated for short, sharp counterattacks into the flanks of the German kampfgruppen. In the spring, all of the tank crews had thoroughly studied the probable areas of combat actions and the routes leading to them. More than once, they moved out on foot along them during dismounted tank training sessions, while the sapper elements did work to improve the trafficability of the roads and to reinforce the bridges in this area.

When preparing for the Battle of Kursk, the Soviet side sought to expand the possibility of the commanders of units and formations to have an effect on the operational situation, especially when struggling against groups of German panzers, by creating strong, mobile anti-tank reserves. The leadership of the Central and Voronezh Fronts when determining their allocation strictly connected it to the overall plan of defense and the likely directions of the enemy's attacks. For example, N.F. Vatutin, assuming that Army Group South's main attack would fall upon the 6th Guards Army, and its auxiliary attack would strike the 7th Guards Army, transferred to the reserve of their first-echelon division commanders substantial forces of not only artillery and sappers, but also infantry support tank regiments.

K.K. Rokossovsky followed the same path. However, Galanin's 70th Army was still playing a tertiary role behind the 13th Army and 48th Army, so its divisional commanders received very modest reserves; on average, each received up to a company of anti-tank rifles, a battery of anti-tank guns, and a platoon of sappers, while their regiment commanders received a section of an engineer battalion. The army's anti-tank reserve was also modest, with only the 3rd Destroyer Brigade, the 378th Destroyer Anti-tank Artillery Regiment, one company each from the 371st and 368th Engineer Battalions, and a company of the 7th Engineer Battalion. The army commander deployed both his anti-tank reserve and main forces of artillery on the extreme right flank (to the right of the Orel highway) in the following areas: 378th Destroyer Anti-tank Artillery Regiment – in the Nikol'skoe – Berezovka – Sergeevka – Petroselki area, and the 3rd Destroyer Brigade – in the Point 241.0 – Svapa – Sergeevka – Novoselki – Vetrenka area. Several options were devised for its use, but all of the anti-tank artillery was aimed at the highway. In addition, the assembly areas for the units and formations of the reserves had been planned, so that in accordance with the selected option, they could take up positions within 30-40 minutes after receiving the signal to move out. Nevertheless, I will emphasize once again that the lack of a strong artillery reserve in the hands of the artillery commanders of the divisions and corps had a large and negative influence on the results of the 70th Army's combat work, particularly in the first 2-3 days of trying to repulse the German offensive. In addition, it would be impossible to correct this shortcoming with anything other than increasing the army artillery grouping with forces and means.

Already when issuing the troops their initial tasks regarding the anti-tank defense immediately after the front became stabilized, the commanders at every level received an order to instruct and train the men as closely as possible to the realities of war. The artillery rehearsed cooperation with fire using real shells, while the drivers of prime movers and vehicles several times each day and night drove out along the very same routes that they might have to use in combat conditions. As the events of July 1943 would reveal, this was a most important factor in enhancing the maneuverability and effectiveness of the troops. Only the tank crews were an exception to this: they studied their jumping-off positions and routes of movement only on foot (in the interests of economizing on fuel and keeping the training concealed). The positions on all the likely directions were fully ready: for the guns (main and alternative positions with shelters for ammunition); for the crews (slit trenches and pits); and protected areas for prime movers and horse teams).

The 13th Army was occupying the Central Front's most important sector based on K.K. Rokossovsky's calculations. It went over to a defense 60 km south of Orel in the beginning of March 1943 following its unsuccessful offensive in the Briansk direction. After ceasing combat operations, in this same month, and then even later, its sector would be adjusted repeatedly, and on 5 July 1943 it would run along the woods southwest of Hill 250.7, Veselyi Berezhok, highway 2 km west of Krasnaia Zaria line and stretched for 33 km.

On 30 March, the army was the Central Front's strongest; it had nine rifle divisions and three tank brigades, and was covering three of the most critical directions:

1. Maloarkhangel'sk – Kolpnia – Livny;
2. Along the Orel – Kursk railroad;
3. The sector west of the railroad leading to Ol'khovatka.

The terrain upon which its main forces deployed was fully suitable for conducting a successful defense. The front lines between the Soviet and German forces ran from west to east along a ridge of hills, which divided the basins of the Volga, Dnepr and Don Rivers. To the north, on the territory occupied by Model's forces, flowed the Neruch' and Oka Rivers, which belonged to the Volga River's basin, and to the south, where the 13th Army was located, were the Snova, Polevaia Snova and Svapa Rivers, which belonged to the Dnepr River's basin. Because of a large number of balkas and ravines that obstructed movement, as well as the dense network of streams and creeks, the 13th Army's right flank presented much greater difficulty for conducting an offensive from the north with panzer formations than its left flank, where Model's panzers could effectively exploit their main qualities: speed, armor and firepower. In the center, there was a corridor in the interfluvial area between the Snova and Polevaia Snova Rivers, along which it might be possible to reach Zolotukhino Station and to emerge further on toward Kursk. However, this corridor was very narrow and at its opening (in the north), it was being screened by Ponyri Station, which presented a suitable place for constructing a powerful knot of resistance. One interesting detail: the position of this railroad station was very similar to the location of the village of Miasoedovo on the southern side of the Kursk salient between the Razumnaia and Severskii Donets Rivers. The Germans would choose both of these bottlenecks as the place for launching their auxiliary attacks: Model – for the XXXXI Panzer Corps; von Manstein – for Army Detachment Kempf's 3rd Panzer Corps, although their motivations for doing so differed.

Moreover, the entire sector of the 13th Army had two more important characteristics for the Soviet forces. On the positive side was the abundance of small and medium-sized populated places, which merged into a continuous chain of buildings and structures that stretched primarily along the rivers and deep ravines for dozens of kilometers. This was particularly seen in the center, in the basin of the Svapa River and the villages of Shirokoe Boloto, Ponyri and so on. For the defenders, this eased the tasks of masking the fortification of the terrain and the process of bringing up forces, while for the attackers, this substantially complicated a rapid breakthrough, since panzer divisions weren't intended for conducting combat in built-up areas.

A negative aspect was the fact that the vegetation growth here was sparse: primarily a few orchards in the populated places and in the field, rare patches of woods and ravines overgrown with oak trees, and isolated willows and cottonwoods in bottomlands. However, this factor, which was unsuitable for a defense, was countered to a certain degree by another, which was useful for the Soviet forces. By the start of July there was mature rye, the most widely sown type of grain in the Kursk area at this time; in these fields, as staff officers of the 13th Army asserted, the grain was as tall as an average man.[220] Photographs taken by Soviet war correspondents who were working in the summer of the Central Front in the summer of 1943 also show this. The rye substantially eased the concealed movement of manpower and masked the minefields, which had been emplaced in the fields immediately after they were sown. By early July, the grain completely covered the emplaced mines and thereby created a virtually impassable belt of mines that were hard to detect prior to a detonation, as well as after one.

Just like that of its neighbor the 70th Army, the 13th Army's plan of defense was essentially ready by mid-April but finishing touches to it continued until the end of the month. The reason for this was not only the weather conditions, but also the transfer of its left-flank 28th Rifle Corps to the 70th Army and the planned regrouping of its remaining forces, since following the transfer K.K. Rokossovsky placed the responsibility for the boundary with the 70th Army on N.P. Pukhov.

With regard for the available significant forces and those promised to him by the Front, the commander of the 13th Army decided to build his defenses in three echelons. In the first (the army's first defensive belt), he planned to deploy four reinforced rifle divisions (on 5 July 1943, they would be the 15th, 81st, 148th and 8th Rifle Divisions); in the second echelon (the army's second belt of defenses) – three rifle divisions (the 6th Guards, 307th and 74th Rifle Divisions); and in the third echelon (the army's rear line of defenses) – five rifle divisions (the 18th Guards Rifle Corps' 2nd Guards, 3rd Guards and 4th Guards Airborne Divisions and the 17th Guards Rifle Corps' 70th Guards and 75th Guards Rifle Divisions). He planned to deploy the army's mobile reserve (the 129th Separate Tank Brigade; the 27th Guards, 30th Guards, 43rd Tank and 237th Separate Tank Regiments; the 1442nd Self-propelled Artillery Regiment and 1541st Heavy Self-propelled Artillery Regiment; and the 49th Separate Battalion of Armored Trains). As a result, all three defensive belts were to be occupied by rifle divisions, which would be girded to its entire depth by infantry support tanks, self-propelled guns and the brigades of the Soviet High Command Reserve's 4th Breakthrough Artillery Corps. The total depth of the army's offenses amounted to 35 km.[221]

---

220 TsAMO RF, F.13A, Op.6079, D.223, l. 8.
221 TsAMO RF, F.361, Op.6079, D.222, l. 95.

In its account, the 13th Army's headquarters noted:

> The following main requirements constituted the basis of the defense's planning:
> 1. The defense was built as an anti-tank defense to its core, calculated to withstand a head-on enemy tank attack.
> 2. The defense also emphasized anti-artillery fire, calculated not only to protect the manpower and weapons from concentrated enemy artillery fire, but also to suppress and destroy the enemy's artillery before the start of the offensive by means of a counter-artillery preparation.
> 3. The defense was constructed around anti-aircraft fire, which was supposed to counter the enemy's massed use of attacks by aircraft.
> 4. The defenses should be built in such a way that the entire system of defensive lines (including intermediary and switch positions, etc.) would enable the timely localization of particular enemy successes in any sector of our defense and to ensure the timely maneuvering of all of the army's reserves.
> 5. The system of defenses should be built so that given any situation, it would prevent the enemy in the event of a breakthrough of our defenses the possibility to expand the breach in one of the sectors by means of rolling up our combat positions.
> 6. In the event of an enemy penetration into our defenses, our entire system of defenses was to ensure the creation of a powerful fist for launching a counterblow, the destruction of the penetrating enemy, and the restoration of the position.[222]

After thorough reconnoitering by his headquarters' staff, which at that time was headed by Major General A.V. Petrushevsky, three army-level belts of defenses were marked out. The main (forward edge) defensive belt was to run along the woods southwest of Hill 256.7, Veselyi Berezhok, highway 2 km west of Krasnaia Zaria line, which extended for 33 km and had a depth of 5 to 6 kilometers. The second defensive belt was to stretch from Kamenka (excl.) through Ponyri Station to Soborovka, with its forward edge running 10-12 km behind the forward edge of the main defensive belt. The army's third (or rear) defensive belt was to run along the Arkharovo, Gubkino-1, Poselka Gorianovo, Ol'khovatka line at a distance 12-15 km behind the forward edge of the second belt of defenses.

It was planned to construct switch positions at the most critical directions, which as a rule were to link the main and second belts of defenses. In the event of an enemy breakthrough, they were to serve as a connecting link that created a single line of defense and would parry a possible enemy attack into the rear of the defending forces on the flanks of the breach. In addition, the plan proposed preparing divisional intermediary lines in the main belt of defenses.

Considering that the main events in the sector of the 13th Army in the course of the Kursk defensive operation would take place in the second defensive belt, I will cite its general characteristics from a report of an officer of the General Staff with the 13th Army headquarters Colonel Busurman from 15 July 1943:

---

222 TsAMO RF, F.13A, Op.6079, D.223, l. 36.

The army's second defensive belt was located 8-12 km behind the forward edge of the main defensive belt and extended for 44 km. It was split into four divisional sectors with the presence of 12 km of natural anti-tank obstacles. It was linked with the main defensive belt by switch positions and anti-tank areas, with the aim of halting tanks and other enemy units in the event of a breakthrough of the main defensive belt and to ensure a jumping-off line for our forces for counterattacks from out of the depth.

The first divisional sector had a width of 10 km and a depth of up to 6 km. The forward edge ran: Dvubratniki, southern outskirts of Kamenki, Nizhniaia Gnilusha, along the western outskirts of Onegino; it was prepared with two, three and four lines, but was not occupied by troops. It would be occupied by the 74th Rifle Division, as foreseen by plan, if the situation required this.

The second divisional sector, held by the 8th Rifle Division, had a frontage of 10 km and a depth of 6 km. The forward edge ran along the Hill 244.5, Hill 249.4, Maloarkhangel'sk, Teniakovskii State Farm line. It's layout in a tactical respect was correct, deviating from the 1943 Field Manual – the distancing of the forward edge of the second defensive belt from the main line of defense by 8 km was prompted by the fact that Maloarkhangel'sk, as a major city and strongly fortified center of resistance, was included in the system of defenses of the second army-level defensive belt. The rifle regiments of the 8th Rifle Division were arrayed in a single line and comprised company-level and battalion-level centers of resistance.

The third divisional sector, occupied first by the 81st Rifle Division, then by the 307th Rifle Division (by the start of July), had a frontage of 9 km and a depth of up to 6 km. The forward edge ran along the Hill 257.1 – Ponyri Station – Hill 248.9 line. in a tactical sense, its layout was proper. The division's regiments were arrayed in a single line. The nearness of the second defensive belt's forward edge in the Ponyri area was explained by the inclusion of the facilities of Ponyri Station, which offered tactical advantages to a defender.

The fourth divisional sector – that of the 6th Guards Rifle Division (which was part of the 17th Guards Rifle Corps) stretched for 11 km and had a depth of 6 km. The forward edge ran along the Hill 248.6, Hill 244.2, Point 214.7, Point 223.6, Point 238.5 line. The division positioned two rifle regiments in the first echelon and kept one rifle regiment in the second.[223]

The fortification of the army's positions began in March, as usual with the laying of mines on the roads and in the tank-vulnerable ground in front of the forward edge. The forward edge of the main defensive belt was screened by artificial obstacles and minefields back to the depth of the rifle divisions' first echelons. The depth and density of the obstacles varied, and notably increased on the larger (wider) corridors offering good ground for tanks: along the Orel – Kursk railroad and in the direction of Ol'khovatka.

The largest populated places in the 13th Army's sector – the city of Maloarkhangel'sk on the right and Ponyri Station in the center – were prepared as powerful, independent centers of resistance, capable of an all-round defense. It was proposed to prepare an elaborate network of

---

223 TsAMO RF, F.361, Op. 6099, D.52, l. 358.

trenches around and in them, but also anti-tank ditches, escarps, and an increased density of minefields with the use of powerful, radio-triggered mines. The plan was to devise a scheme for embedding the Ponyri area (especially the railroad station and along the the Ponyri – Kursk railroad) with a particularly complex and diverse array of means, because of its key location. The first to arrive for work here already in April were units of the 6th Engineer-Sapper Brigade of the Soviet High Command Reserve, which had been operating as part of the army since winter. N.M. Lapotyshkin recalled:

> The brigade was occupying a defense west of Ponyri Station on the Krasnaia Slobodka – Glazunovka – Verkhnee Tagino – Tureika line … With its main forces it was working on the line of the 13th Army, but a portion of it was also setting up defenses on the line of the 48th Army to the northeast of Maloarkhangel'sk, as well as positions of the 60th Army between the cities of Dmitrovsk-L'govskii and Fatezh.
>
> Captain Menshikov's battalion in the area northeast of Maloarkhangel'sk excavated 7 km of anti-tank ditches (of which 3 km were dummy) … In June Captain Safonov's battalion completed the construction of defensive fortifications along the Lipova River. A dam was built in the area of Odintsovka, which flooded a large area covering the boundary between the 13th Army and 48th Army, making it inaccessible to tanks. The dam was 180 meters long, 40 meters wide at its base, 4 meters wide at its top, and stood 7 meters tall. On the dam itself, the sappers laid the words "Onward to the west" in stone letters that were a meter-high.
>
> However, the brigade's primary activity consisted in creating power minefield obstacles in the sector of the 13th Army. The sappers of the 112th Engineer Battalion had removed several thousand German mines from the line of defense of the preceding winter, and transferred them to the new location. Previously, these mines had been blocking the path to us, but now they were facing the Germans.
>
> Ponyri was converted into a powerful defensive strongpoint. The sappers of the 112th Engineer Battalion riddled the area with explosives. This zone entered history as the "Ponyri enclosure". Dense minefields guarded the station. Among them were roadside bombs from captured German stockpiles; each bomb weighed 55 to 250 kg that could be remotely detonated. Wires stretched back from the mines to the trenches, where the sappers were. The calculation was that if a German tank was passing by a mine, all a sapper had to do was to give a tug to the wire in order to trigger a 250 kg charge and destroy it. How much courage, steady nerves and valor a soldier had to have in order to control these mines on the field of battle, under a storm of gunfire and with enemy tanks so near!
>
> We were emplacing a wide variety of mines: the Soviet IAM-5 [anti-tank box mines], TM-35 [metal-cased anti-tank mines], POMZ-2 [a stake-mounted anti-personnel fragmentation mine], OZM [a bouncing type of anti-personnel mine]; and German S-mines [also known as "Bouncing Betties"] and T-35 Teller anti-tank mines. Yet when there weren't enough mines available, the initiative and resourcefulness of the sappers helped out. POMZ-2 mines were crafted out of German artillery shells, and fragmentation anti-personnel mines out of aerial bombs. They made anti-tank mines out standard blocks of trotyl explosives, and pressure-activated anti-personnel mines out of small-caliber artillery shells. Crafting and laying mines became a passion of the brigade's officers and enlisted men, who widely employed creativity and innovation

in the process. Corporal Malukha, Senior Lieutenant Kulakov and Lieutenant Mishchenko created a unique device for controlling minefields. The previous means for setting up and wiring minefields were unsatisfactory. A jumper cable could only be used in the depth of the defenses. The sappers were planting mines not where the sappers wanted, but in places that a cable could reach. Lieutenant Brodsky proposed an original elliptical cable, with the help of which mines could be set up by a single man crawling along on his belly.[224]

As in the case of the 70th Army, the fortification of the terrain from the forward edge of the second defensive belt back to the third defensive belt was being done in the 13th Army by the 1st, 2nd and 5th Guards Battalions for creating artificial obstacles and the 6th Guards Electrical-Technical Battalion of the 1st Guards Engineer-Sapper Brigade of Special Designation. By 18 May 1943, they were assembled in the Karataeva, Legostaevo-1, Nizhnyi Laimin area, having become subordinate to the army's chief of engineers. After reconnoitering the terrain, they were to immediately get to work setting up obstacles.

The 1st Guards Engineer Battalion was responsible for the Hill 248.5, Hill 244.2, Hill 223.6, Hill 235.9, Saborovka, Point 204.6, Hill 234.0, Brusovets Creek [excl.], Nizhnee Smorodnoe, Vozy Station, Hill 246.2, southeastern outskirts of Brusovoe sector. The main routes for the actions of the mobile blocking detachments were determined as: a) Podsoborovka – Snova; b) Podsoborovka – Kutyrki.

The 2nd Guards Engineer Battalion was responsible for the Ponyri-1, Ponyri settlements, Berezovets Creeek (excl.), southeastern outskirts of Brusovoe, Hill 242.6, Hill 244.4, Malaia Plotka, Dobroe Nachalo, Such'ia Creek (excl.), Tiniakovskii State Farm (excl.), Fedorovka, Ponyri Station sector. The main routes for its mobile blocking detachments were: a) Ponyri State Farm – Iudinka; b) First of May, Hill 248.5, and along the Orel – Kursk railroad.

The 5th Guards Engineer Battalion worked in the Verkniaia Gnilusha, Zelenaia Roshcha, Maloarkhangel'sk, Salovka, Tiniakovskii State Farm, Such'ia River, Koshelevka sector, with the boundary on the right running through Aleksandrovka, Fedorovka, Perevedenovka as far as the Sosna River. The main routes for the activities of its mobile blocking detachment were: a) Maloarkhangel'sk, Iudinka, Verkhniaia Sosna; b) Rep'evka, Mamoshina, Kashelevka; c) Maloarkhangel'sk, Rep'evka, Orlianka.

The 6th Guards Electrical-Technical Battalion received the assignment to set up electrified obstacles along the forward edge of the army's defenses from Hill 254.6 to Nikol'skoe-1 (including to block the Orel – Kursk railroad); and from Novyi Khutor to Budarin Creek. It was also to reconnoiter a second reserve line in the areas of Zelenaia Roshcha, Iudinka, Fedorovka, northern outskirts of Ponyri (District Executive Committee) and Druzhovetskii, Podsoborovka, Samodurovka.

Electrified barriers were part of the Red Army's arsenal even before the Great Patriotic War. They were then actively used in the fighting in front of Moscow, on the Leningrad front, and in the Battle of Stalingrad. Incidentally, Major A.T. Rozhdestvensky's 6th Guards Electrical-Technical Battalion distinguished itself in the battle on the Volga, where it operated as part of

---

224 Kurskii Kraevedcheskii Muzei. Rukopis' vospominaniii polkovnika N. Lapotyshkin "Na Kurskoi duge" [Kursk District Museum. Manuscript of the recollections of Colonel N. Lapotyshkin entitled "On the Kursk bulge"]. Edinitsa khraneniia 456.

the Don Front. Mobile AE-2 electrical generators equipped the battalion. They generated a high voltage current through a network of cables to specialized wire obstacles. The battalion was able to set up approximately 6 km of such obstacles across a front. As a rule, the approaches to them from the enemy's direction were covered by remote-controlled anti-tank mines. All of the electrical circuits were constantly kept at combat readiness, and if in the course of the fighting or an air raid they were interrupted, the soldiers were supposed to restore the current quickly. In the period of the preparations for the Battle of Kursk, these specialized means were proposed to be used only in the Central Front; they became one of the particularities of its system of defenses, but they were only deployed in the sector of the 13th Army. From the outset, there was no plan to use electrified barriers on the southern face of the Kursk bulge.

During the course of the next two months, the three engineer battalions of Ioffe's brigade did an enormous amount of work. In order to increase the effectiveness of the minefields, the majority of them contained a mixture of mine types. For example, in one field a mixture of three or four types of mines, such as the IAM-5, the PTM-5 and captured German mines would be emplaced by the sappers. The Soviet anti-tank mines, which at the front were often called "tank-disabling mines", had little explosive power. Their charge was sufficient only to break a tank's tracks or to blow off an idler sprocket or roller wheel. Therefore, the sappers used captured shells and bombs to reinforce the anti-tank minefields; large stockpiles of them had been captured in the winter of 1943 on the territory of Kursk Oblast, including at the Kursk railroad station. For example, according to the documents of the headquarters of the 1st Guards Separate Engineer Brigade of Special Designation, the strongpoint of Ponyri Station from the north and northwest was screened by minefields reinforced with German aerial bombs, most of which could be triggered by the application of pressure.[225]

Simultaneously with the main forces of Ioffe's brigade, its 8th Guards Battalion of Specialized Mining was working along the forward edge of the 13th and 70th Armies in the Krasnaia Slobodka, Verkhee Tagino, Briantsevov sector. Here, approximately 200 remotely-triggered anti-tank mines and 82 remotely-triggered fragmentation anti-personnel mines were deployed by the sappers. Recalled V.K. Kharchenko:

> In the course of May and June, the 8th Guards Battalion of specialized mining set up a large number of radio-controlled roadside bombs. They were especially numerous in the area of Ponyri Station and the cities of Kursk, L'gov, Fatezh, Dmitriev-L'govskii, as well as along the Maloarkhangel'sk – Livny and Orel – Fatezh – Kursk highways and on the Briansk – Kursk railroad (in the sector between Dmitriev-L'govsk and L'gov). All of the radio-controlled devices were setup without wiring them to the power supply source. This final step was to be done at a needed moment through an order from the Central Front's chief of engineers. A group of experienced specialists and vehicles were assigned to execute this task.
>
> At the same time, the 3rd and 7th Guards Engineer Battalions after reconnoitering the second and third belts of the Front's active obstacles started work to set up minefields in no-man's land in front of the Front's defensive line to a depth of 15 km. By 5 July 1943 both battalions had planted more than 30,000 anti-tank and anti-personnel

---

225 TsAMO RF, F.62, Op.321, D.96, l. 144obr.

mines, 1,500 remotely-controlled fragmentation anti-personnel mines and anti-tank roadside bombs to the second level of readiness; emplaced 109 delayed-action mines; and prepared 16 bridges for demolition.[226]

As of 4 July 1943, in the sector of the 13th Army sappers had established 254 anti-tank minefields with a total number of 50,755 mines and 23 composite minefields, which contained 30,650 mines in the main defensive belt and 20,100 in the second defensive belt.[227] Minelaying was hard, extremely laborious and in every respect very dangerous work. A.B. Nemchinsky, a lieutenant in command of a sapper company with the 210th Engineer Battalion of the 42nd Separate Engineer-Sapper Brigade of Special Designation recalled a combat line's daily routines ne on the Voronezh Front:

> In the sector of the 67th and 52nd Guards Rifle Divisions, our company emplaced around 5,000 mines. Each fold of ground and each clump of bushes on the forward edge of defense north of Tomarovka received careful study. Is it really possible to forget the personal tension that was always connected with spending time between our own and the enemy's positions? Is it possible to forget that sometimes our own infantry soldiers crouched in the trenches spotted our minelayers as they were crawling back from the enemy's direction and opened fire? Not everyone's nerves could endure this. Indeed, each in his own way experienced an encounter with danger.
>
> Our emotional memory preserves the sensations that a man experiences when he leaves his own troops' position and heads out on an assignment in the direction of the enemy. However, it is not so easy to talk about this. In each case, my comrades showed their tension in a different way. Some seemed to be completely calm, others could not hide the anxiety that had seized them, and a third group showed only a light trembling of the hands …
>
> Some soldiers before heading out into no-man's land would ask, "Comrade Lieutenant, if something happens, write back to my home …" Indeed, this request always seemed to me to be fully logical; after all, if a man is confident that his close ones will find out after his death that he did his duty, then it is easier for him to face a mortal danger and overcome it.
>
> Independently from their individual ways of facing danger, the men of the company always did their duty. Volodia Nazarov was right when he said that courage in fact consists of overcoming the sense of danger and in doing your duty at any cost.[228]

The mobile blocking detachments had great significance in the struggle against the enemy's armored forces. As the fighting showed, this was an effective and mobile means of the division commander for quickly blocking a breakthrough. In the hardest conditions, when an enemy kampfgruppe had already penetrated the forward edge of defense, they were to give time to the division commander to bring up reserves in order to localize the breach that had been made. In the rifle divisions, the mobile blocking detachments were formed out of elements of their

---

226 Kharchenko, … *Spetsial'nogo naznacheniia*, p. 90.
227 TsAMO RF, F.62, Op.321, D.96, l. 143obr.
228 Nemchinsky, A.B., *Ostorozhno, miny!* [*Warning, mines!*] (Moscow: Voenizdat, 1973), pp. 73-74.

engineer battalions; commonly, this was a platoon of minelayers in one or two vehicles or drawn by a team of horses. Just like the other army commanders, N.I. Pukhov also had in his reserve several mobile blocking detachments, which were formed on the basis of the army's sapper battalion and Ioffe's brigade. By the start of the Battle of Kursk, they numbered five and were to operate in the following sectors:

- 1st – on the Maloarkhangel'sk direction, in close cooperation with the 15th Rifle Division;
- 2nd – on the Ponyri direction, together with the 81st and 307th Rifle Divisions;
- 3rd – on the Ol'khovatka direction, together with the 15th Rifle Division and 17th Guards Rifle Corps;
- 4th and 5th – constituted the reserve of the 13th Army's chief of engineers Major General Z.P. Kolesnikov.

All of the army's mobile blocking detachments were equipped with ZiS-5 trucks and an array of anti-tank mines and given the need they could replenish it from stockpiles (ammunition shelters) that were scattered throughout the entire depth of the defense.[229]

However, the Soviet command was placing its main hope in the struggle against the German panzer formations on its artillery, including anti-tank artillery. H.Guderian shared his rich experience of fighting on the Eastern Front:

> Of all the obstacles, a tank's most dangerous adversary were mines, although in the conditions of maneuvering warfare, they were significant only as a delaying factor. For a tank the main danger is, however, not so much mines as the anti-tank gun firing from positions behind the minefields. The explosion of a mine would damage a track, the tank would come to a stop and be deprived of its greatest advantage – mobility.[230]

So, in connection with the question "Mine or weapon?" with which the Soviet troops would have to paralyze the striking power of the Wehrmacht's main instrument of the offensive – the panzer formations – the artillery means should step forward as the leader.

Having determined the likely axis of the main attack, the Central Front command began to strengthen the 13th Army intensively with artillery. As a result, by the start of the battle, no other single combined-arms army, not only of both Fronts in the Kursk salient, but over the entire years of the war, had as much artillery as Pukhov's army received before the start of the German offensive toward Kursk. On the morning of 5 July 1943, it had 1,523 guns, of which 801 or 53.6 percent were located in the system of its line's anti-tank defenses, which amounted to an average of 25 guns per kilometer of frontage. At this time, neither of its neighbors possessed even half as much artillery. For example, the 70th Army received 513 anti-tank guns, which amounted to 8.3 guns per kilometer of frontage, while the 48th Army received 473, or 12.4 per kilometer.

---

229 TsAMO RF, F.62, Op.321, D.96, l. 144.
230 Hoth and Guderian, *Tankovye operatsii / "Tanki – vpered!"*, p. 391.

"It would be better if we grind down the enemy on our defenses ..." 409

Such significant artillery strength allowed the army commander to give each of the divisions of the first echelon between five and seven artillery and mortar regiments, out of which together with their organic artillery they formed artillery groups to reinforce the rifle regiments of the first and second echelons. For each division of Major General I.I. Liudnikov's 15th Rifle Corps (plus the 15th and 81st Rifle Divisions, which were under the general leadership of General Pukhov himself) that were located in the army's first echelon, groups of heavy artillery were created that comprised five artillery regiments, which were directed by the artillery commanders of the rifle divisions. Moreover, two heavy cannon brigades were assigned to support the 307th and 74th Rifle Divisions, which were located in the second belt of defenses, while the 5th Guards Mortar Division and 86th Mortar Regiment, which comprised the personal reserve of the 13th Army commander General Pukhov, were deployed behind the third army-level belt of defenses. The 100th and 104th Heavy Howitzer Artillery Brigades, the Front Commander-in-Chief's reserve, were located here.[231]

In addition, when constructing the army's lines, great significance was given to anti-tank defenses. By the start of June 1943, 138 anti-tank strongpoints combined into 37 areas, which were also echeloned in depth, had been organized.[232] In the main defensive belt there were 13 anti-tank areas, which consisted of 44 anti-tank strongpoints (204 guns); in the second – nine and 34 respectively (160 guns); and in the third – 15 and 60 (342 guns). The 13th Army's anti-tank reserve, the 874th Destroyer Anti-tank Artillery Regiment, was positioned in the area of the Ponyri settlements and was ready to operate across the entire front of the army's defense.[233]

The troops that were positioned in the three army-level belts of defenses, and especially the artillery grouping, were covered by the fire of two anti-aircraft divisions. In addition, these divisions, just like the crews of the howitzer and cannon regiments, received the order to be ready in their positions to fire at enemy armored vehicles.[234]

Thus, the 13th Army's artillery grouping was not only very powerful (and numerous), but also deeply echeloned, which in the opinion of the Front's leadership allowed it to cover reliably virtually all of the more dangerous directions, while enabling the implementation of rapid maneuver with fire and wheels. The distribution of the artillery in the 13th Army's defenses on 28 June 1943 is depicted in Table 14:

231 TsAMO RF, F.361, Op.3007, D.19, ll. 174-176.
232 TsAMO RF, F.361, Op.34379, D.4, l. 92.
233 TsAMO RF, F.361, Op.8007, D.19, l. 171.
234 Ibid.

Table 14a: The 13th Army's artillery grouping and its density as of 28 June 1943

Division	Width of sector	Number of artillery and mortar batteries	Total 45mm, 50mm A-T Guns	Total Artillery	Total Mortars	Total Tubes of Artillery and Mortars	Total Rocket launchers	Density of tubes per kilometer
8th Rifle Division								
Organic	6.5 km	54	29	140	125	294	22	
Attached[235]		15	36	62	46	133	-	
Total:		**69**	**65**	**202**	**169**	**407**	**22**	**62.7**
148th Rifle Division								
Organic	6.5 km	43	33	134	202	369	20	
Attached[236]		31	8	104	15	127	-	
Total:		**74**	**41**	**238**	**217**	**496**	**20**	**76.3**
81st Rifle Division								
Organic	10 km	48	27	148	199	374	24	
Attached[237]		29	5	117	36	158	-	
Total:		**77**	**32**	**265**	**235**	**532**	**24**	**53.2**
15th Rifle Division								

235 Attachments: From the 16th Rifle Division, 3rd Battalion of the 224th Artillery Regiment, 2nd Battalion of the 652nd Artillery Regiment and a mortar battery from the 167th Rifle Regiment.
236 Attachments: From the 8th Rifle Division, 3rd Battalion of the 62nd Artillery Regiment, 1st Battalion of the 467th Mortar Regiment; and the 468th Howitzer Artillery Regiment and 786th Light Artillery Regiment. From the 81st Rifle Division, 2nd Battalion of the 346th Artillery Regiment, plus the 540th and 697th Mortar Regiments.
237 Attachments: From the 148th Rifle Division, the 2nd and 3rd Battalions of the 326th Artillery Regiment, and the 872nd, 539th and 232nd Mortar Regiments; from the 15th Rifle Division, the 1st Battalion of the 203rd Artillery Regiment; and the 876th Howitzer Artillery Regiment.

"It would be better if we grind down the enemy on our defenses …"   411

Organic		40	32	138	123	293	19	—
Attached[238]	8 km	26	5	101	36	142	—	—
Total:		66	37	239	159	435	19	54.4
Total in the first echelon	31 km	286	121	944	780	1,809	85	58.4
74th Rifle Division								
Organic		11	32	38	90	160	—	—
Attached								
Total:		11	32	38	90	160	—	—
307th Rifle Division								
Organic		27	26	72	91	189	—	—
Attached								
Total:		27	26	72	91	189	—	—
Total for the 18th GRC[239]		73	126	218	350	694	218	—
Total for the 17th GRC[240]		33	140	129	308	577	129	—
Total in second echelon		150	324	192	839	1,355	480	—
Total for the army[241]		317	445	1,040	1,488	2,973	432	—

238 From the 81st Rifle Division, the 3rd Battalion of the 346th Artillery Regiment, the 293rd and 208th Howitzer Artillery Regiments, and the 106th Mortar Regiment. From the 132nd Rifle Division, the 425th Artillery Regiment and the 203rd Howitzer Artillery Regiment.
239 Including artillery, mortars and rocket launchers directly subordinate to 18th Guards Rifle Corps' headquarters
240 Including artillery, mortars and rocket launchers directly subordinate to 17th Guards Rifle Corps' headquarters
241 Including artillery, mortars and rocket launchers directly subordinate to 13th Army headquarters.

Table 14b: Allocation of men and weapons to the 13th Army's defensive belts as of the morning of 5 July 1943[242]

Defensive belt	Active bayonets	Field guns	Anti-tank guns	Mortars, not including 50mm	Rocket launchers	Heavy machine guns	PPSh and PPD submachine guns	Tanks
First	10,600	520	115	442	132	271	2,500	-
Second	8,500	216	101	268	467	253	4,600	147
Third (rear)	14,300	315	218	480	-	729	11,500	52
Total:	**33,400**	**1,051**	**434**	**1,390**	**599**	**1,253**	**18,600**	**199**

From this it follows that 44.1 percent of the army's entire artillery was in the main defensive belt, of which all of the 45mm anti-tank guns, 76mm regimental guns, and 31.8 percent (70 of 220) 76mm divisional guns could be used to counter enemy tanks. The second defensive belt had 12.3 percent of the army's artillery, including 85.3 percent of the 45mm anti-tank guns, 82.8 percent of the 76mm regimental guns and 66.7 percent of the 76mm divisional guns could be used in the struggle with tanks. In the third defensive belt, these figures were respectively 43.5 percent, 100 percent of the 45mm anti-tank guns and 76mm regimental guns, and 54.7 percent of the 76mm divisional guns.

The clear relative weakness of the second defensive belt with respect to guns and accordingly anti-tank artillery was connected with the fact that the Front leadership was viewing it essentially as an intermediate line, in which troops falling back from the first defensive belt under enemy pressure could regroup and consolidate. Accordingly, it was thought that the density of manpower and weapons here would substantially rise with the addition of the first-echelon units. In addition, it was planned that the defending forces would hold the first belt of defenses for at least two days, and already on the second day of the German offensive, the plan was for the 2nd Tank Army and two reserve tank corps would come up and launch counterattacks. In an anti-tank respect, therefore, even with the losses of the first two days of fighting, the second defensive belt should be substantially reinforced in the course of the battle and at a minimum equal the strength of the first and third defensive belts.

The army commander did not distribute the available artillery evenly across the 13th Army's entire 33-km defensive frontage. Relying on the not quite accurate supposition of K.K. Rokossovsky about where the enemy's main attack would likely land, he moved out more than half of the artillery, 53.5 percent, to the right flank (the Maloarkhangel'sk) direction, where in a sector of 13 km (the line held by the 8th and 148th Rifle Divisions) 695 pieces of artillery were deployed. Second in size was the artillery grouping in the army's central sector – 371 guns (37.1 percent), which were concentrated in a 10-km sector along the railroad in the area of Ponyri Station. At the boundary with the 70th Army to the left (the Sadovod State Farm – Ol'khovatka sector held by the 15th Rifle Division, which stretched for 8 km), which is to say where Model was planning to launch his main attack, were the remaining 280 guns (35.2

242 Source: TsAMO RF, F.13a, Op.6079, D.271, l. 161.

percent). Table 14a shows the detailed distribution of the 13th Army's artillery across the directions on 28 June 1943.

This misalignment would in fact become the main reason why already on the first day of the Battle of Kursk, the Germans would breach the main defensive belt to its entire depth and make a penetration into the second belt of defenses on the Ol'khovatka axis, thereby substantially disrupting the overall plan of the defensive operation. Nevertheless, it was precisely the presence of a large amount of artillery immediately among the combat formations of the rifle divisions of Pukhov's 13th Army in all three of its defensive belts (something that N.F. Vatutin and especially I.M. Chistiakov could only dream about), and the lack of German infantry which would become the key factors that fundamentally brought about the failure of the Ninth Army's offensive.

However, certain miscalculations should be noted as well when deploying the units and formations of the 4th Breakthrough Artillery Corps across the line of the 13th Army. One of the most substantive errors was the failure to screen the Corps' Guards mortar units, which were positioned approximately 1.5 to 2 km from the forward edge, with strong and numerous anti-tank artillery. It is not clear why this happened, since it is hard to believe that the 13th Army command seriously counted on stopping an enemy penetration into the main belt of defenses before it could reach the positions of the rocket launchers. Probably, this was a system-related blunder connected with lack of the staff artillery officers' experience with planning an operation with the use of such major forces. Simultaneous with this, the 4th Breakthrough Artillery Corps' sole anti-tank means – two regiments of light artillery (the 1007th and 1214th Light Artillery Regiments) – were withdrawn from direct subordination to the Corps, and at the same time the units of the 5th Guards Mortar Division were decentralized; they had simply been distributed piecemeal to the rifle divisions.[243] All of this taken together already on 5 July 1943 would greatly hamper the direction of the fire and lead to unjustified losses of personnel and materiel in the Guards mortar regiments.

By the beginning of July, all three defensive belts of the 13th Army were ready for a defense, and something just as important, were fully occupied by troops. The distribution of personnel and means is shown in Table 14b. As is clear from the presented data, the first defensive belt was not the densest with forces, except for the artillery, which was supposed to knock out German panzers and self-propelled guns on the first day of the offensive. It had 30 percent of the active bayonets, 50 percent of the field artillery and mortars, less than 33 percent of the rocket launchers, and no armored vehicles at all. As a result, each kilometer of frontage had an average of 321 men, 19.2 guns of all types (including 15.8 field guns and 3.5 anti-tank guns), 13.4 mortars (not including the 50mm mortars), four rocket launchers, 8.2 heavy machine guns and 75.8 submachine guns. From the outset, the third or rear army-level belt was most densely packed with forces and means, as insurance in the event of a German breakthrough of the first and second defensive belts, as was the typical experience in 1941 and 1942, and a precaution against the failure of the defensive operation as a whole. In the third belt of defenses, with the exception of artillery, the amount of forces and means was from the outset larger than in the first defensive belt, and with the withdrawal of the units of the first and second echelons factored in, the density of forces in it would increase substantially. Thus, in pace with the advance of the

---

243 TsAMO RF, F.4akp, Op.1, D.14, l. 9.

Ninth Army's assault wedge, the degree of resistance it encountered in the lines of the Central Front would increase. This was the essential idea behind an echeloned defense.

So, it was anticipated by the Soviet command that given an unfavorable development of the defensive operation (in the event of a deep penetration) in the first two or three, or possibly four days of fighting, the most powerful line would form in the rear defensive belt, and with the approach of the Front's reserves, in the opinion of the Soviet side, it would present an insurmountable obstacle for the enemy.

The command staff of both the Central Front and the 13th Army took the guarding of its boundary with the 48th Army very seriously. In order to ensure this, the maximum possible number of weapons would be positioned here, supported by plans for counterattacks with all types of reserves. In fact, this was done on time and within a short period of time. On 19 April Rokossovsky approved a plan for securing the boundary between the two armies, even though prior to this decision work was already in full motion to strengthen it. See below for excerpts from this document:

1. Approaches from the enemy's direction: At the boundary between the 13th Army and 48th Army, and in the Nikitovka – Shcherbatovo sector, the likely approaches from the enemy's direction might be:
   a) Out of the Sandrovka, Goliatikha area in the direction of Nikitovka and Kamenka;
   b) Out of the Pesochnyi, Iasnaia Poliana area toward Panskaia and Verkhniaia Gnilusha;
   c) Out of the Glazunovkii forestry area and Zelenaia Roshcha toward Krasnaia Slobodka and Verkhniaia Gnilusha, and toward Pokhval'naia, Elizavetino and Maloarkhangel'sk;
   d) Out of the area of the Parashino Agricultural College and along the branch of the Stanovaia River toward Maloarkhangel'sk.

These same directions are also the most likely axes of the actions of the enemy tanks.

II. The assigned forces and means for protecting the boundary between the armies:
1. From the 48th Army: The 399th Rifle Division's 1348th Rifle Regiment is defending on the Panskaia (excl.) – alley 300 meters southwest of Kamenolomnia front and in the depth as far as the "Rectangular" woods and Point 248.0.

   From out of the depth of the defenses, the 16th Guards Rifle Division together with the 43rd Tank Regiment and the 73rd Rifle Division have been designated for counterattacks.

   For the immediate protection of the boundary with the 74th Rifle Division, the commander of the 399th Rifle Division is to assign not less than three heavy machine guns, four 45mm guns and two 76mm guns, and four anti-tank rifles (the anti-tank artillery and anti-tank rifles compose anti-tank strongpoints).

   Artillery: A group of artillery supports the infantry of the 1348th Rifle Regiment – the 3rd Battalion of the 1046th Artillery Regiment, the 232nd Mortar Regiment, a battery of 120mm mortars of the 1348th Rifle Regiment, and a battery of 45mm guns of the 436th Destroyer Anti-Tank Artillery Battalion.

The group of the 399th Rifle Division's artillery commander consists of the 786th Light Artillery Regiment (six batteries).

The army's artillery commander's group consists of the 2nd Battalion of the 155th Cannon Artillery Regiment and the 1st Battalion of the 221st Guards Mortar Regiment.

2. From the 13th Army: On the front extending from the alley (300 meters southwest of Kamenolomnia to the Stanovaia River and in the depth as far as Livadii, the 74th Rifle Division is defending, having a shared boundary with the 399th Rifle Division's 360th Rifle Regiment. In the division's second echelon on the line from Point 247.3 (excl.) to Hill 260, the 3rd Battalion of the 78th Rifle Regiment is defending, and in the area of Livadii – the training battalion.

The 148th Rifle Division and two rifle regiments of the 15th Rifle Division are designated for counterattacks from out of the depth of the defenses.

For the immediate protection of the boundary with the 399th Rifle Division, the commander of the 74th Rifle Division assigns not less than three heavy machine guns, four 45mm guns, two 76mm regimental guns, and four anti-tank rifles (the anti-tank artillery comprises anti-tank strongpoints).

Artillery: the group of artillery support for of the 360th Rifle Regiment's infantry is the 876th Howitzer Artillery Regiment; the group of artillery support for the 76th Rifle Regiment's infantry is the 6th Artillery Regiment.

The army's artillery commander's group consists of two battalions of the 642nd Cannon Artillery Regiment.

In addition, the 60th Battalion of the 6th Guards Mortar Regiment prepares for fire in the Krasnaia Slobodka, Neskuchnaia sector.

...

IV. Engineer support at the boundary:
1) Approaches from the enemy's direction in the Panskaia, Krasnaia Slobodka, spring east of Neskuchnaia are to be blocked by a belt of anti-tank and anti-personnel minefields and barbed wire entanglements. The deadline for implementation of this order is no later than 20 April 1943.
2) Switch positions are to be constructed for the 399th Rifle Division in the sectors:
   a) "Rectangular" woods, cemetery, Nikol'skoe (facing the south and southwest);
   b) Zheludki, Point 246.0 and woods to the south (facing the southwest).

   For the 74th Rifle Division in the Nizhniaia Gnilusha, Point 204.8, Livadiia sector (facing the north and northwest). Deadline for execution of this order is no later than 20 April 1943.[244]

As we can see, here even switch positions were not forgotten, in contrast to the case on the 13th Army's left flank, and not a single division was overlooked when planning the counterattacks.

244 TsAMO RF, F.361, Op.8007s, D.14, ll. 31-33.

In the works of the Soviet historians, the descriptions of the preparations for the Battle of Kursk, including the construction of the field defenses by Rokossovsky's and Vatutin's troops are overflowing with heroic rhetoric and a multitude of both real and fictitious examples of the labor achievement of the Red Army soldiers and area civilians. However, there is not even a mention in a single book about those associated costs paid by the population of Kursk Oblast. This concerns not only the fate of the evacuated residents of the villages and hamlets that fell within the 25-kilometer zone. Although primarily women, children and senior citizens were evacuated from the zone, no one bothered to build any special accommodations for them or to organize a reception of them. On their own, they had to seek "good people" or relatives, if there were any such in the nearest circle, to house them as long as the war continued in their area. Yet tens of thousands of people were forcibly removed! For example, in the area of the 48th Army alone, by 10 June 1943 they emptied 118 villages and hamlets, from which 21,886 people were expelled (or 88.7 percent of the population).[245] It does not do to condemn the Soviet military authorities for these harsh measures. The evacuation was unquestionably done for a proper purpose – to save the people, but I also consider it amoral not to mention those poor souls who were left in an empty field with no roof over their heads and small children in their arms. I am writing these lines just for that purpose, so that even today readers will pause to reflect on their sufferings.

There were also other, no less important problems which are often encountered in the documents of both Soviet *fronts*, and they are connected with the callous attitude of the troops to the modest property that was located there, even wherever their rear units were deployed. The matter of protecting household property, store rooms and other valuables located on liberated territory was prominent in front of the military and government authorities of the Soviet Union already in the first year of the war. In 1942, therefore, Order No.0169 was signed by the People's Commissar of Defense, which required commanders at every level to take good care of everything that remained after the expulsion of the occupants and to prevent plundering and destruction. However, this problem remained urgent even a year later. In the spring and summer of 1943, the destruction of planted areas, agricultural buildings and the remaining residences from which the people had been expelled occurred not only, and not so much for the purpose of erecting defenses or the troop preparations for a defense, but because of the elementary callous attitude of the command staff. This was happening on both *fronts*, and the scale of the manifestations was so large that commanders of divisions and even of the armies had to intervene personally. Here are just two examples. Order No.16 from the deputy commander of the 70th Army's 280th Rifle Division from 5 June 1943 read:

> Cases are being noted of the demolition of buildings and the removal of doors and windows in the rural settlements of the evacuated zone. Cases are also being noted of the destruction of sown areas. The commandants who've been assigned to protect the buildings and sown areas don't have precise instructions regarding their rights and responsibilities. By a directive of the army's Military Council, among the duties of a commandant of a settlement is making a list of all the structures and fields and keeping

---

245 TsAMO RF, F.403, Op.9657, D.87, l. 114.

track of their security. The execution of the given task is an extremely important assignment that has large government significance.[246]

See below for Order No.49 from the commander of the 13th Army on 20 June 1943:

Over recent times, a large number of complaints addressed to the Military Council are coming in from local organs of power regarding the fact that in the frontal zone of evacuation, there are cases of a barbaric attitude toward government, collective farm and personal property. Residences belonging to collective farmers, as well as government facilities, are being taken apart by combat units and being destroyed for fuel. For example, in May 1943 in the village of Novo-Slabodka-1, the quartered units there of the 6th Engineer-Sapper Brigade, the 3rd Airborne Division and the 161st Fortified District have ransacked private apartments of tables, chairs and beds, and destroyed the doors, windows and entire inventory of a school for fuel. In the village of Ostrov, one building has been completely destroyed. In the village of Orlianka, a new school has been completely destroyed, and all the ceiling beams, floor joists, etc. of a destroyed church there have been burned.

Local organs of authority without the assistance of the command staff of units are unable to prevent the looting and destruction of buildings and civilian property, since arrested servicemen refuse to provide their unit's identity and threaten authorities with a weapon, so guilty parties aren't identified and remain unpunished (the engineer battalion of the 1007th Artillery Regiment of the 12th Artillery Division and the 3rd Battalion of the 8th Rifle Division's 229th Rifle Regiment).

Despite the categorical demands of representatives of rural councils in front of the command staff of units about revealing the guilty parties and bringing the latter to responsibility, and putting a stop to illegal activities, no real steps have been taken and the guilty parties remain concealed. From this it is clear that certain garrison chiefs and commanders of combat units and installations are not carrying out Order No.0169, Order No.69 to the troops of the 13th Army from 3 May 1943 or the Directive No.0010 of the Front's Military Council from 4 April 1943. They are not taking up questions of the protection of socialist property and are not demanding this of their subordinates.

I am ordering:

1. The division commands to demand of the commanders of subordinate units and elements to carry out strictly People's Commissar of Defense Order No.0169 from 1942, Directive No.0010 of the Front's Military Council from 4 April 1943 and the order from the 13th Army; bring those guilty of plundering and the destruction of socialist property to the strictest responsibility according to martial law.
2. All commandants of the garrisons of populated places and the commanders of units and elements are to take every measure to protect government, collective farm and personal property, for which in necessary cases they are to set up watches and conduct patrolling.

246 TsAMO RF, F.18 gv.sk., Op.1, D.50, l. 108.

3. Unit commanders as well as the garrison commandants upon the receipt of a complaint from representatives of local authority or individual citizens regarding cases of the plundering and destruction of residential buildings, inventory, etc. are to take immediate steps to investigate, identify the guilty parties, and bring them to responsibility.
   I am warning all unit commanders that they will bear personal responsibility for failing to take steps to protect government, collective farm or personal property.
4. Announce the order to the entire command staff down to the platoon commander inclusively.[247]

The problem of the destruction of sites in the defensive belts that were already prepared for use, primarily in the army's rear belt of defenses and the *front*-level line, but not only those, was also acute. Moreover, its scope was significantly larger than the looting of the housing stock in abandoned populated places, so not even army commanders, but the Front leaderships were dealing with this problem. Here is an excerpt from the Military Council of the Voronezh Front's Decree No.0062 on 5 June 1943:

> In the defensive lines of the Voronezh Front, there are cases involving the destruction of fortification works by the local population and separate combat units for fuel and other daily needs.
> The Military Council has decreed:
> 1. Ban the destruction of fortification works in the defensive lines by the local population and combat units.
> 2. Bring the violators to the strictest responsibility all the way up to trial before a military tribunal.
> 3. The army commanders, the commanders of separate Front formations and the chiefs of the Voronezh Front's Department of Defense Construction, who are working to build the defensive lines are to organize security of the defensive lines that are under work and of the individual fortification sites, and in the places where this is not possible, keep them under the watch of the district or oblast executive committees. Complete the organization of security at the defensive works that are under construction and repair the damaged fortification works by 15 June 1943.[248]

This order appeared after the May 1943 inspection conducted by staff officers of the Voronezh Front regarding how the construction of the defensive works was going and the condition of the army-level defensive belts, in the course of which they revealed, even in the second army-level belt of defenses, a number of ransacked bunkers and trench shelters for the personnel. Unquestionably, it is impossible to justify the destruction of the labor-intensive defensive works intended to protect the lives of the soldiers and commanders who were preparing to face the attack of a powerful enemy grouping, and according to martial law, this act was considered a serious crime. However, it is important to understand the perpetrators motives as well, and

247 TsAMO RF, F.361, Op.6099, D. 59, l. 375, 375obr.
248 TsAMO RF, F.341, Op.5312, D.12, l. 104.

they turned out to be completely diverse. The local population was prompted to act by hopeless impoverishment, but the combat units' criminal behavior was due to the irresponsibility and foot dragging of their commanders, since the problems and possibilities of a combat unit and those of an ordinary man, who had been deprived in a short period of time of all his belongings by the war, were not comparable. As became clear, the village residents were taking the logs removed from firing positions back to their farms, where they were building dugouts next to their devastated homes in order to survive the winter. Pieces of boards, with which the embrasures were framed, were being used as firewood in order to prepare food. The combat units, in contrast, were taking the excavated construction material back to the rear, in order to build dugouts for the staff officers and bunkers for the men, which by the Front's orders in May 1943 were to be moved out of towns and villages into the fields, and partially as fuel for the field kitchens. Now let us return to the south of the Kursk salient and take a look at how the building of the field defenses was going here.

On 25 March 1943, when the situation in the area of Belgorod finally became stabilized, the Voronezh Front was holding a sector of 264 km.[249] In April, sectors were drawn for the armies and approximately 19 km of frontage was turned over to its neighboring Southwestern Front on the left. As a result, the overall width of the Voronezh Front's sector shrank to 245 km, which was being held by four armies that were occupying a defense in the first echelon.

The 38th Army under the command of Lieutenant General N.E. Chibisov on the right flank was holding the Sheputovka Station – Ugroedy sector, which in April extended for 75 km of frontage (in March it had been 80 km). It consisted of six rifle divisions, one rifle brigade and composite brigades formed from the training battalions. Lieutenant General K.S. Moskalenko's 40th Army was occupying a sector that stretched for 52 km (in March it had been 50 km) from Ugroedy (excl.) to Sumy Station. He had under his command seven rifle divisions. Lieutenant General I.M. Chistiakov's 21st Army was holding the sector from Sumy Station (excl.) to Melekhovo, which ran for 65 km (in March, 64 km), but 58 km as the crow flies. Chistiakov had seven rifle divisions (four of which – the 71st Guards, 67th Guards, 52nd Guards Rifle Divisions and the 375th Rifle Division were in the first echelon), and the 27th and 28th Separate Destroyer Anti-Tank Artillery Brigades. Lieutenant General Shumilov's 64th Army anchored the left. Its sector stretched from Melekhovo (excl.) to Khotomlia for 53 km (its sector had been 70-km wide in March). Shumilov had a total of seven rifle divisions and one destroyer anti-tank artillery brigade. Finally, Voronezh Front had in reserve Lieutenant General V.D. Kriuchenkin's 64th Army in the Novyi Oskol, Nikitovka, Gotov'e area, as well as the 2nd and 5th Guards Tank Corps in the second echelon.[250]

In addition, Lieutenant General M.E. Katukov's 1st Tank Army was assembled near Oboian'. It would be directed into the Front's sector, but in the mean time it was serving as the Deputy Supreme Commander-in-Chief G.K. Zhukov's personal reserve.

Thus, of the 35 Guards and regular rifle divisions, which the Voronezh Front possessed by the beginning of July 1943, it placed 17 rifle divisions in the first echelon, in the main defensive belt, while holding 18 in the second and rear army-level lines, as well as the reserve. The average tactical density amounted to 14.5 km of frontage for each division. Considering

---

249 TsAMO RF, F.203, Op. 2843, D.365, l. 75.
250 Ibid.

the characteristics of the terrain, on directions that offered good ground for tanks, the sectors of certain divisions fell to 12-13 km, but on secondary directions they increased to 16-20 km.

On 27 March 1943 the Front's Military Council issued Order No.0087 regarding the organization of the defense. In the expectation of a future major enemy offensive, the order foresaw the creation of a complex, echeloned defense relying on an elaborate system of lines and the broad use of artificial obstacles. The anticipation was to have not less than five defensive belts on all directions, echeloned in depth to not less than 100 km.

As in the north, the main elements of Vatutin's system of defenses was to become three army-level belts with a depth of 30 to 50 km:

1. The main belt had its forward edge on the line that had been achieved. Subsequently it would become the first army-level line and had stretched for 245 km along the layout of the forward edge.
2. The second defensive belt (or second army-level line) had a forward edge running through Liubimovka, Basovka, Oleshnia, Tarasovka, Velikaia Rybitsa, Strelki, Ugrody, Rep'iakhovka, Semeinaia, Rakitnoe, Vasil'evka, Alekseevka, Dmitrievka, (excl.) Petrovskii, Sazhnoe, Shlaikhovoe, Miasoedovo, Shebekino, and Poklonnoe. Its total extent was 216 km.
3. The rear belt stretched from Malaia Loknia through Sudzha, Ulanok, Kamyshnoe, Presechnoe, Korochka, Oboian', Ship', Bogorodetskoe (excl.), Teterevino, Zhimolostnoe, Novoselovka, Vypolzovka, Mazikino, Sorokovka, Prudki, Osnovka, Belianka, Rybalka and Efimovka to Nechaevka.[251]

In addition, work was supposed to start on three *front*-level defensive lines at a depth of 180-200 kilometers.

In the event of a penetration or the breaching of the main belt of defenses, intermediate positions and switch positions (with a total extent of 134 km) were planned, as well an intermediate line, being occupied by the 35th Guards Rifle Corps (the sector of which stretched for 86 km) and a *front*-level switch line that ran for 125 km. According to the calculations of the Front command, these defensive belts would screen all the possible direction of enemy attack and enable its troops to succeed in holding their lines.

I will note right away and point out that the construction plan for the defensive belts contained no prepared switch lines in the 7th Guards and 69th Armies' sectors of defense to the south of Prokhorovka Station. The command of Army Group South would not fail to exploit this. After breaking through the 7th Guards Army's main defensive belt on the Korocha direction, it would pivot the main forces of Army Detachment Kempf to the north, and begin rolling up the defenses of the Soviet forces.

It should be particularly noted that in all the stages of the planning of the defensive operation, and then in the process of building the system of lines, one can trace the large amount of work done personally by the Front commander-in-chief General of the Army N.F. Vatutin. Incidentally, back when studying in the Military Academy of the General Staff, in 1938 he defended his dissertation on the subject "The role of fortified areas in a contemporary war". The

---

251 TsAMO RF, F.203, Op.2843, D.227, l. 1-2.

knowledge he acquired while writing his dissertation was unquestionably in high demand and assisted him in the spring and early summer of 1943.

As noted in a number of documents of the Voronezh Front headquarters, from the moment of receiving the Military Council's directive, work went slowly virtually until the end of April 1941, especially in the first two weeks. Therefore, the planned amount of defensive work for the most part was not completed. This was because of a number of objective factors. First, the muddy season did not fully come to an end until 10-12 April, so prior to this moment it was difficult to dig trenches or build positions. Second, right up to the beginning of May, the Front did not have the necessary number of mines. At the end of March and throughout the month of April, because of the poor supply with mines and explosives, minelaying was basically done by the troops with the authorized mines that were removed from old defensive lines (like the Don River line) and captured artillery shells, which the sappers converted into pressure-activated mines. Third, the engineer units subordinate to the divisions and armies were under establishment strength in personnel, which reduced their capabilities. In addition, the sappers were diverted to clearing ground and building the rear infrastructure, as well as by establishing command posts, observation posts and access routes (roads and bridges) to the forward edge. The men of the rifle divisions were doing what they could to build defensive works, but their numbers were small after the winter fighting and replacements had not yet arrived, so it is impossible to speak of any significant planned amount of work. Meanwhile, the local population was busy with the spring plantings, and it was impossible to divert them totally from this work, since the harvest was not only a source of subsistence for the physically-depleted women, children and senior citizens who'd just been freed from German occupation, but it was also a necessary source of supply for the Front.

There were also a number of subjective reasons that substantially affected the course of building the lines. The command staff of the Front's armies slowly and with large oscillations was preparing the plans for strengthening their sectors with the use of engineers. Because of foot dragging and in a number of cases the irresponsibility and inactivity of high-ranked commanders, the troops did not have everything necessary in order to start to work. There was a noticeable shortage of tools: shovels, picks, saws and axes, and the headquarters staff was not exerting proper control over the proper layout of the positions selected by the commanders at the tactical level or the positioning of important artificial obstacles. Prior to the latter half of April, it became clear from the trips to the front made by the Front leadership and specially-selected commanders that if the situation did not change fundamentally, it would be impossible to create the planned system of defenses.

On 20 April, the Voronezh Front Commander-in-Chief signed an order, which disclosed the revealed shortcomings and issued the task to eliminate them quickly and to get the massive amount of needed work going seriously. On 25 April, by a decision of the *Stavka*, a 25-kilometer tactical zone was determined for the Voronezh Front, from which the entire civilian population was to be evacuated. Primarily, this was to allow the conducting of active combat operations to the entire depth of the tactical zone, so in order to keep them safe, the residents of the villages in the zone were to be moved temporarily to other populated places outside the zone. Secondly, the *Stavka* wanted to establish complete control over the area by military officials in order to thwart the enemy's intelligence and sabotage activities and to shut off the flow of information about the condition of the defensive belts. This circumstance to a great extent determined that the Front's own troops had to build the first two defensive belts.

Across the entire front sector there was no success in preparing the ground in front of the defenses. In the course of the winter fighting, the situation on the Voronezh Front was complicated by the fact that nearly all of its troops were in direct contact with the enemy; only those of the 38th Army and 6th Guards Army were an exception. In their sectors, there was a gap between the forward edge of the German forces and the frontlines of these armies – up to 6-7 kilometers between the two frontline trenches. In these places that featured a broader no-man's land, the army commanders decided to deploy forward detachments, reinforced rifle battalions (numbering 420-472 men each for the 6th Guards Army's 52nd Guards Rifle Division), which set up defensive outposts at a distance of 2-3 km from the forward edge of the main defensive line. In essence, these were reinforced combat outposts that created a dummy forward edge.

The forward detachments primarily occupied a line of small villages in the neutral zone and screened their forward edge with anti-personnel and anti-tank artificial obstacles. In the 6th Guards Army, for example, such villages were Butovo (67th Guards Rifle Division), Dragunskoe (67th Guards Rifle Division), and Streletskoe and Iakhontovo (52nd Guards Rifle Division). In the sector held by the 375th Rifle Division, there were no forward detachments.

The weakness of the forward detachments was the fact that they were set up on a broad front and had no direct contact or overlapping fields of fire with each other, other than the security outposts of the first-echelon divisions that were positioned at a distance of 1-2 km behind the forward detachments. However, in a number of places, such as Gertsovka (71st Guards Rifle Division), Butovo (67th Guards Rifle Division) and Dragunskoe (67th Guards Rifle Division), this was not the case, and the security outposts were beyond the range to support the forward detachments with their fire.

With the capture of the positions of the 6th Guards Army's forward detachments on 4 July 1943, the forces of the Fourth Panzer Army would proceed with the execution of Citadel's plan. The enemy would be aware of not only the location of the forward detachment's positions, but also their system of defenses. Therefore, although their men would in fact inflict painful losses to the German assault groups, the forward detachments could not present a serious obstacle for them. The reinforced battalions would hold their positions for five to seven hours, and then under the pressure of superior forces fall back to the first line of trenches. Only one of the forward detachments, the one in Butovo, would become encircled on 4 July 1943 and almost be completely wiped out.

Almost all of the armies, except for the 7th Guards Army, would deploy a screen of security outposts. Commonly, they consisted of one to three platoons, the positions of which were 1-2 km out in front of the main defensive belt. They were made up of strong points, occupying an all-round defense, the approaches to which were partially or completely girded by anti-personnel minefields. In the 6th Guards Army their number consisted of 7-8 outposts per division with a total strength of 240 to 400 soldiers and commanders. The strength of a single outpost varied between 21 and 96 men according to its location in the 52nd Guards Rifle Division, and from 15 to 50 men in the 375th Rifle Division. As a reinforcement, each was given one or two Maksim heavy machine guns, two to 11 light DP-27 machine guns and one or two 50mm mortars. In rare cases, their assets might include two to four 45mm anti-tank guns and even field artillery or 82mm mortars. A senior officer of the General Staff with the Voronezh Front on 9 June 1943 reported:

> The gaps between the platoon strongpoints of the combat outposts in the majority of cases were left unguarded by anyone, as a result of which on 18 May in the sector of

the 71st Guards Rifle Division, the enemy infiltrated through one of these gaps, cut the combat outpost's line of communication with the battalion, destroyed most of the combat outpost and took seven men prisoner. Patrolling out in front of the combat outposts and in the intervals between them and with the main defensive belt hasn't been organized.

Earth and timber bunkers in the security outposts' strongpoints don't protect the personnel from injury. Narrow slit trenches and bomb shelters in order to protect the men in the trenches are absent, as a result of which a direct hit by one shell on 23 May killed five men of a combat outpost of the 71st Guards Rifle Division's 210th Guards Rifle Regiment. The gaps between the platoon combat outposts haven't been mined, wire entanglements and booby traps are absent in the intervals, and not all of the outposts are protected from the front by anti-tank and anti-infantry artificial obstacles and minefields.[252]

In addition to these defects, there was a number of others. Reserve positions weren't created everywhere, and the men who'd been assigned to a combat outpost did not always receive precise and clear instructions about paths of retreat. Each outpost also did not receive much ammunition (just 100-150 bullets per rifle, three to six drums per machine gun, and enough mortar shells for 30 minutes of combat). All this might lead, and in a number of cases did in fact lead to the partial or complete elimination of the men holding a combat outpost by enemy artillery fire, and on the bootheels of the retreating outpost, the enemy broke into the main belt of defenses. However, a number of the aforementioned comments by the General Staff officer were addressed before the start of the German offensive, and in general the combat outposts across the entire front fully handled the tasks they'd received.

An important role in this was played by the system of artillery fire that supported the forward detachments and combat outposts. Up to two artillery battalions received the mission to support a forward detachment, and on average four to six artillery batteries supported the combat outposts. The artillery firing positions were just 1-2 kilometers from the forward edge of the main defensive belt, well within range of the forward detachments and combat outposts, and in addition alternate firing positions were prepared directly on the forward edge for guns and even Katiusha rocket launchers. Nevertheless, in the sake of justice it should be noted that the command of the artillery units did not quickly work out the firing data and failed to open timely fire at the enemy when the men of the forward detachments and combat outposts were still in need of the support fire, or before the strongpoint or outposts had been destroyed.

The first two belts of defenses comprised the tactical zone of defense, and the basis of it was the first (main) line, to which the majority of forces and means of the divisions (and corps) of the first-echelon armies were assigned. It had the most elaborate system of fighting trenches, communication trenches, firing positions and other fortifications. For the first time in the war, the depth of the tactical zone of defense amounted to 15 to 20 kilometers. Reported Colonel Kostin, "Depending on the terrain and its tactical evaluation, the forward edge of the main belt of defenses was properly selected, with the exception of several sectors. The convolution of the

---

252 TsAMO RF, F.203, Op.2843, D.365, l. 73.

line, along which the forward edge runs, creates natural killing grounds and offers favorable conditions for creating oblique angles of flanking fire and crossfire.[253]

The 6th Guards Army's main defensive belt consisted of battalion areas of defense (2 to 3.5 km wide and from 800 meters to 1 km in depth), which in turn were made up of company areas, and the positions of the battalion's reserve and attached assets. Two or three such areas, positioned in one or two echelons, formed the regimental sectors (4 to 7 km of frontage and 3-4 km in depth) with positions for the regimental reserve: a rifle company, a submachine gun company, an anti-tank rifle platoon and sapper units. The three sectors of the rifle regiments composed a division's sector of defense.

The rifle divisions together with their attached assets in the main defensive belt had an average depth of defense of 6-7 km, which corresponded to the requirements of the combat manuals of that time. A training battalion and specialized elements comprised the division commander's general reserve, and they were deployed in prepared positions at a distance of 3-4 km from the forward edge on the most likely directions of the enemy's attack. On the directions most favorable for panzer operations, which the Front command believed to be in the sector of the 6th Guards Army, the commanders of a number of divisions, including the 67th Guards Rifle Division and 52nd Guards Rifle Division received special reserves: destroyer anti-tank artillery regiments and regiments of infantry support tanks, as well as self-propelled artillery regiments, battalions of heavy howitzers, anti-aircraft regiments and even battalions of rocket launchers.

The weak aspect of the defenses of the main belt was the fact that the divisions that were dug into it, including those on the direction of the Fourth Panzer Army's main attack, were arranged in a single echelon, which is to say the positions of all three of their subordinate rifle regiments were stretched out in a single row. Given such an arrangement, it was virtually impossible to contain the enemy for a lengthy amount of time, especially the panzer formations. This decision was made by the majority of the division commanders and supported by the command staffs of the armies and Front. It was prompted by the fact that the sectors drawn for the divisions were longer than called for by the 1942 combat manual (14-15 km instead of the appropriate 12 km), because of the Voronezh Front's lack of adequate forces. The rifle regiments on average were each defending sector of 3-6 kilometers across the front.

As a rule, the first line of trenches was occupied by submachine gunners and tank hunters. The main firing positions were anti-fragmentation nests for the infantry and earth and timber firing positions for the machine guns, which were usually positioned in the second line. In the sector of the 52nd Guards Rifle Division of the 6th Guards Army's 23rd Guards Rifle Corps, which had three and, in some cases, only two lines of defense, outlying firing positions for heavy machine guns, that were positioned on average 100 to 150 meters in front of the first line of trenches, were widespread. These firing positions represented open machine-gun emplacements that were well-camouflaged against enemy aerial and ground surveillance and had slit trenches or bunkers to provide cover for the men. They did not open fire until the start of the enemy's attack so as not to reveal themselves, having the task to open surprise fire and restore the system of fire after the enemy worked over our forward edge with airstrikes and artillery and went on the attack.[254]

253 Ibid., l. 71.
254 TsAMO RF, F.203, Op.2843, D.227, ll. 3-5, 8, 9.

By the start of the offensive, on average six to seven light earth-and-timber bunkers or of a reinforced type had been built for each kilometer of the main defensive belt's front. These bunkers typically consisted of timber blocks measuring 2 x 2 meters, which were almost completely buried into the ground and covered by several layers of logs with a diameter of 12 to 15 centimeters, with packed earth between each layer. Depending on the number of layers, the bunkers were divided into light and reinforced types. The forward wall, which contained the embrasure, was doubled, with earth packed between the two walls of timber. Typically, such firing positions were set up on elevations that were difficult to approach or in folds of ground, and contained heavy (more rarely, light) machine guns for covering a certain sector of the defense with fire, or to reinforce the fire of the rifle elements positioned in the forward trenches. In the main belt, all of the structures in the villages and hamlets were fortified, as well as in the separately standing field camps[255] and machine-tractor stations, which were typically located outside populated places or on the outskirts of them. Not only the buildings themselves and their garrets used, but also the cellars of brick ruins. The defenders sought to adapt all of the built-up places for an all-round defense.

However, it is necessary to acknowledge that the situation with the system of defense prior to the start of the Battle of Kursk was not the same in all of the 6th Guards Army's divisions and did not correspond to the demands of the General Staff's April instructions. Even on the eve of the battle, not all of the divisions managed to ensure the accurate implementation of orders regarding the fortification of their sectors. I will cite an excerpt from a report following the joint inspection of the lines of the 6th Guards Army's 52nd Guards Rifle Division and 375th Rifle Division, to which the reserve battalions of the 51st Guards Rifle Division had been committed, made on 22 June 1943. The commanders of all three divisions took part in the commission:

> **52nd Guards Rifle Division**: Earth and timber bunkers have been set up in sufficient number, but the majority of them represent anti-fragmentation nests, designed primarily for conducting frontal fire. The roofs of the bunkers consist of one to four layers of logs with a thickness of 10-13 cm each. Many of the bunkers' sectors of fire are overgrown with rye (151st, 155th Guards Rifle Regiment), and the embrasures have been camouflaged up to 70 percent . Each heavy machine gun has only one alternative firing position. The light machine guns have thin overhead cover (2/155th Guards Rifle Regiment) consisting of a single layer of logs with a thickness of 10-15 cm. There are no reserve positions. The anti-tank rifles have only one position. The dugouts are covered for the most part by one thin layer and haven't been adapted to provide shelter against gas attacks, and there are no specialized shelters for this purpose. The trenches are narrow, just 60-80 cm wide; foxholes are absent, and there are few weapon pits. There is no camouflage for the weaponry of the 6th Rifle Company of 2/155th Guards Rifle Regiment, and in the remaining companies 76 percent of the camouflage needs renewal.
>
> **375th Rifle Division**: The digging of the first trench line is incomplete (1/1245th Rifle Regiment); in places its depth reaches only 0.7 m, there are few weapon pits, the sumps

---

255 Ed. note: These were typically wooden structures out in the fields to support the collective farmers as they worked. They typically contained storage sheds and meal canteens, where the farmers could get their meals.

have collapsed, and there are no foxholes; all the communication trenches haven't been dug to the depth of the defenses, and the available ones have a depth of 50-70 cm (1/1245th and 3/1243 Rifle Regiments). A sector of observation and fire is completely lacking (3/1243rd Rifle Regiment); the ground excavated from the anti-tank ditch, which hasn't been leveled and concealed, hampers observation and fire. In addition, unharvested rye obstructs the line of sight and in certain places only the ground out to 40-70 m is within view.

Earth and timber bunkers are few and their overhead cover is weak – one layer of logs and an added layer of earth, with a thickness of 20-30 cm. The field of vision is poor (3/1243rd, 1/1245th Rifle Regiments). Embrasures haven't been fitted and the mounts for the heavy machine guns are weak. Concealed firing positions are lacking, there are no alternate or dummy bunkers, and camouflage is absent. The earth and timber bunkers have no niches. There are no dugouts, but there is a parody of trench shelters with poor overhead cover; the soldiers have no plank beds and sleep on the floor, and the command staff have no separate dugouts. There are no shelters at all against gas attacks. The company commanders and battalion commander of 3/1243rd Rifle Regiment have no observation posts. In certain places, the wire entanglements aren't covered by fire. Regiment commanders haven't issued an order regarding the defense to battalion commanders.[256]

Theoretically, in divisions on the main axis, a density of 9-10 bullets per running meter could be achieved within one minute; secondary divisions could reach 6-7 bullets. However, considering that the battalion, regimental and divisional reserves were located in the depth of the defenses, in practice a density of 4-6 bullets was created in each zone of 300-400 meters on the forward edge of the main axis, and 3-4 bullets on a secondary direction.

Considering that in the course of defensive fighting, the maneuver of firing means played an important role, it was vitally important to create the conditions for this – to devise a plan, make it known to the personnel, and to rehearse it in practice. Unfortunately, this was left undone even in units in the main belt of defenses. During an inspection of a number of divisions, it became clear that "… plans for the maneuver of fire haven't been devised in the companies, battalions and regiments; even the simplest signal means for summoning infantry fire are absent in the majority of units, and where such exist, then they haven't introduced to the operators."[257]

The Soviet defenses employed a widely developed system of artificial obstacles in order to repulse the attacks of tanks and motorized infantry: anti-tank ditches, escarpments, three rows of staked barbed wire, abatis, and both ordinary and remotely-controlled minefields. Mines and explosive devices that were closely tied in with the system of fire of all types, natural obstacles and other artificial obstacles comprised the basis of the obstacles laid out by engineers when setting up the defenses. They paid particular attention to them. The Soviet command believed this was the simplest and most effective means of disrupting the enemy attacks and first of all containing the enemy tanks within the system of the divisions' defensive positions. In combination with artillery fire, this was the optimal method to eliminate them. Active work

---

256 TsAMO RF, F.335, Op.5113, D.219, l. 241.
257 TsAMO RF, F.203, Op.2843, D.365, l. 74.

went on therefore not only to create extensive fields of regular anti-personnel and anti-tank mines in front of the main defensive belt's forward edge and to obstruct directions offering good ground for tanks in the depth of the defenses, but in addition various types of specialized mines were devised and emplaced. I will stress: continuous belts of mines were planted only in the first two defensive belts; the rear defensive belt featured only the partial emplacement of mines on the directions of the enemy's most likely advance, while a portion of the territory was prepared for setting up minefield obstacles.

The experience of the war had demonstrated that minefield in the depth of the defenses were more effective that those fronting the forward edge of the first and second defensive lines. Whereas on the forward edge it took 350-400 emplaced anti-tank mines to knock out a single tank, then in the depth this statistic decreased to 120-150 anti-tank mines. The difference is explained by the fact that the emplacement of mines in the depth of the defenses occurred on already revealed directions of the enemy's offensive. On directions vulnerable to enemy armor, for the first time in the war the density of mined ground reached 1,400 to 1,600 mines per kilometer of front.

It is interesting that in addition to the establishment mines, the defenses made wide use of incendiary fougasse mines. In distinction from ordinary mines, they struck the enemy not only with a blast wave and fragments, but also flames that resulted from the explosion. Minefields consisting of incendiary fougasse mines, given good camouflage, were difficult to detect and clear. The flames rose to 30-40 meters in height before collapsing and spreading out onto the heads of soldiers. These fougasse mines made a horrifying impression on the German soldiers and shook their morale.

At the disposal of each commander, from the regimental level up to the Front command, were mobile blocking detachments of mixed composition, the task of which was to mine routes used by enemy tanks and to blow up sections of roads and bridges. One document stated:

> Mobile blocking detachments were subordinate to the army's chief of engineers and the engineer officers of the divisions (divisional mobile blocking detachments) and collaborated with the rifle divisions and the artillery, mortar and tank units. Each detachment was given its own sector of operations. The commanders of the engineer battalions maintained constant contact with the troops.[258]

The Front's anti-tank reserve included one engineer-obstacle battalion and three engineer-sapper battalions. The 209th Engineer-Obstacle Battalion was positioned in the village of Orlovka and was responsible for the Oboian' direction. The battalion had 3,000 anti-tank mines, three vehicles and 10 horse-drawn wagons. The 109th Engineer-Sapper Battalion was based in Prokhorovka Station and was covering the Prokhorovka direction. It possessed 3,500 anti-tank mines, 500 anti-personnel mines, 300 kg of explosives, five vehicles and 10 horse-drawn wagons. The 47th Engineer-Sapper Battalion was located in the city of Korocha and had the order to screen the Korocha direction. In order to carry out this assignment, the battalion received 4,700 anti-tank mines, 500 kg of explosives, three vehicles and 10 wagons. The 105th Engineer-Sapper Battalion was deployed in the vicinity of Rzhava Station and busy with setting

---

258 TsAMO RF, F.203, Op.2845, D.227, l. 19.

up the command post of the Voronezh Front. It stood in readiness to reinforce the actions of the other battalions or to operate on unforeseen directions. The 105th Engineer-Support Battalion had 2,000 anti-tank mines, 500 kg. of explosives, five vehicles and 10 wagons.[259]

Work to screen the forward edge with minefields proceeded at a particularly high rate from the end of May, once the Front began to receive mines in large numbers. This work was fully completed on the main defensive belt prior to the initiation of Operation Citadel. Table 15 shows the number of emplaced mines and fougasse mines for the armies as of 5 July 1943.

Table 15: Quantity of emplaced mines in the armies of Voronezh Front's first echelon as of 5 July 1943

Army	Anti-tank mines	Anti-personnel mines	Artillery shells (fougasse)
38th Army	56,723	68,992	11,446
40th Army	59,032	70,994	6,377
6th Guards Army	89,888	63,843	9,162
7th Guards Army	66,746	85,140	3,441
69th Army	19,542	17,146	-
Total for the Front:	**291,930**	**306,115**	**20,426**

Considering the significance that the Voronezh Front command was giving to strengthening the front of the 6th Guards Army, the work was proceeding on a particularly large scale in its divisions. Moreover, assuming that the enemy would commit a significantly large number of tanks simultaneously in order to break through the defenses, emphasis was placed on anti-tank means of struggle, and first of all, on mines. They were relatively cheap and simple to use. Given the breaching of a line by the enemy, expansive fields strewn with "silent death", as the German panzer crews labeled the mines, would give the defenders vitally important time to regroup forces and bring up tactical reserves. By the number of emplaced anti-tank mines and booby traps, the 6th Guards Army's sector noticeably stood out in comparison with other sectors of the Voronezh Front's armies. S. Gabov, a Red Army sapper with the 6th Guards Army, recalled:

> The army's engineer units in April and May were primarily occupied with the construction, repair and reinforcement of bridges; keeping the roads trafficable; building command and observation posts for the army's command staff and the commanders at the corps level; assisting the division's organic sappers in mining the main belt of defenses; and carrying out service as a mobile anti-tank reserve, having in each battalion an engineer company equipped with trucks and 600 mines. With the end of the muddy season, they increased their aid to the troops in emplacing explosive obstacles.

259 Ibid.

The engineer units of the Supreme High Command Reserve were carrying out analogous tasks in the operational depth, and were primarily employed building roads and bridges, conducting preliminary work to create a network of obstacles in the operational depth, and mining and guarding bridges, while a portion of their engineers were helping the combat sappers lay mines. One company of each battalion was being held in a mobile anti-tank reserve.[260]

The system of obstacles in the 6th Guards Army's main belt of defenses alone had embedded special radio-controlled mine fields and fougasse explosives. This work was done by the Supreme High Command's 42nd Engineer Brigade of Special Designation under the command of Colonel V.P. Krasnov, which was attached to the army.[261] For two months, in April and May, each night its battalions emplaced fragmentation blocking mines (the OMZ-152) in the sectors of the 52nd and 67th Guards Rifle Divisions, which could be triggered by electrical wire, as well as captured heavy German artillery shells that were converted into pressure-activated mines. A large stockpile of these shells had been captured by forces of the 40th Army in the course of the winter offensive. In the account of the Front's engineer forces, there is the note:

> On the forward edge of the 6th Guards Army's main belt of defenses, units equipped with radio-controlled fougasse mines were activated. They were the first in the world at the time of their first appearance in the Red Army back in 1932 and given the acronym TOS [*Tekhnika Osoboi Sekretnosti*, or "top secret equipment"] The engineers set up the devices on the most important directions of likely enemy advances in combination with other explosive obstacles.
>
> Altogether, radio-controlled 31 FTD [*fugas takticheskogo deistviia*, or fougasse of tactical action] devices were emplaced, the detonation of which would in turn trigger 135 OZM-152 and 107 fougasse mines packed with 50 kg to 250 kg of explosives.
>
> The TOS units were deployed in five areas:
> 1. Village of Cherkasskoe: three radio-controlled minefields, which screened good terrain for armor in the Butovo – Zavidovka, Butovo – Belgorod-Kursk highway directions. Altogether in this area, eight FTD devices were deployed, which activated 20 fougasse mines and 46 OZM-152.
> 2. The village of Trirechnoe: four minefields, which blocked the advantageous ground for armor between the Lapin Ravine and the ravines northwest of Hill 233.6 on the Dragunskoe – Ol'khovka direction. A total of eight FTD radio-controlled devices were emplaced here, which activated in turn 25 fougasse mines and 19 OZM-152.
> 3. Hill 228.6: one minefield on the northern slopes of the hill which girded the trenches, bunkers, and bomb shelters on the Tomarovka – Bykovka direction. A total of two FTD devices were deployed here which activated 40 fougasse mines and 21 OZM-152.

---

260 Gabov, S., *Sapery ognennoi dugi* [*Sappers of the bulge of fire*] (Voronezh: Tsentral'no-Chernozemnoe izdatel'stvo, 1987), p. 64.
261 Prior to this, the brigade had distinguished itself in the fighting around Khar'kov, and then, in the latter half of March 1943, it screened the withdrawal of Soviet forces in the Korocha direction.

4. The village of Kamennyi Log: three minefields, which screened ground vulnerable to tanks between the Kamennyi Ravine and the wooded patch southeast of Kammenyi Log on the Tomarovka – Bykovka direction. This area had eight FTD devices that in turn activated 19 fougasse mines and 47 OZM-152.
5. The villages of Shishino and Belomestnaia: three bridges on the Shishino – Belomostnaia Station road were mined, one of which crossed the Severskii Donets River.

  Each area was served by a special team consisting of 31 men. The team crew consisted of four telephone operators, five radio operators, three observers, 18 sapper-radio operators and a chief.[262]

The work of the sappers was not only physically demanding, even exhausting, but also very dangerous. The minelaying had to be done in no-man's land right under the enemy's noses with no illumination, while observing professional precision and silence. Over a single night, on average a sapper company could emplace 100 to 150 mines, sometimes as many as 250. However, there were also nights when the Germans prevented any work at all. Then it was necessary to wait.

The weakness of all the mines was their poor survivability. They could be detonated during an artillery barrage or by the fall of a bomb in its immediate area. Soviet observers watched as the Germans cleared corridors through the minefields with the assistance of dive bombers on the first two days of the offensive, particularly in the sector of the Fourth Panzer Army. However, the Germans subsequently ceased using this practice. In the first place, by this time they had already passed through the main belt of defenses and were operating in the second belt, where there was no dense mining. Second, this practice diverted the Stukas from striking more important and well-fortified strongpoints in our defenses, which were more difficult to destroy without the use of airstrikes. Finally, in order to detonate all the mines required the use of a significant amount of munitions.

In addition, the Soviet anti-tank mines, such as the IaM-5, had a serious defect – they had very little explosive power. Their detonation would only damage a tank's running gear, and at that, only lightly, while the bulk of the combat machine remained unharmed. Given the enemy's well-tuned system of recovery and repair, these combat machines were quickly back in service. Knowing this characteristic, in certain key sectors of the main defensive belt, the sappers would place two mines simultaneously in a single hole or reinforce the mine's effects with a large-caliber shell. This would increase the blast effects of the mine by two or three times. However, this practice saw use only in small sectors and only in the main belt of defenses, since it was impossible to create "doubled" minefields everywhere. Therefore, the Front command already in the first days of the summer fighting, having assessed the situation, demanded that the troops keep firing at enemy tanks until they brewed up. A significant number of the German panzers were equipped with smoke candles, and at the outset of the offensive nearly all of the crews had them, so that if a panzer became immobilized in the course of an attack, the German tankers would quickly toss a smoke candle onto the motor compartment hatch or drop one from a

262 TsAMO RF, F.203, Op.2845, D.227, ll. 13-14.

bottom hatch, and our anti-tank gunners would initially be thrown into confusion. Incidentally, our tankers also made wide use of this practice, but primarily when under attack by German dive bombers and tank-busting aircraft.

In addition to the extensive mining, three rows of staked barbed wire stretched out across the entire sector of the forward edge of our main defensive belt. It was used, of course, to hamper infantry, but also as a primitive, but no less effective warning system, especially during the nighttime hours. The troops would hang various metallic objects in various places on the barbed wire: tin cans filled with pebbles, punctured mess kits, parts of shell casing, etc. During any attempt to remove or pass through the wire, these "little bells" would emit a sound, alerting the machine gunners who were posted around the clock to the enemy's intentions.

Artificial anti-tank obstacles – escarpments and anti-tank ditches – played an important role in the system of defenses of all the lines, and first of all of the main defensive belt. Considering that the enemy was relying on armor to "steamroll" through the deeply-echeloned Soviet defenses, these obstacles given proper positioning and careful preparation could play a very large role in keeping the enemy in check.

There were two types of anti-tank ditches: the first, to obstruct the path of advance to light tanks and halftracks; and the second, to obstruct medium and heavy machines. They differed in their respective depth and width, but in any case, they had to be not less than 6-meters wide. As a rule, when excavating them, the engineers linked them with natural obstacles – deep balkas, ravines, swampy branches, thereby to create a total obstruction in a sector, giving the enemy no way of getting around it. It was mandatory to mine the approaches to the ditch, and to ensure it was covered by both light infantry weapons and artillery. The ditch in the sector of the 67th Guards Rifle Division south of Cherkasskoe can serve as an example of the proper placement of an anti-tank ditch. Owing to the fact that it was linked with the swampy arm of a balka, and the approaches to it were clearly observable and kept under artillery fire, on 5 July the enemy was able to surmount it only late in the day, with enormous difficulty and serious losses.

In contrast, the anti-tank ditches in front of the 52nd Guards Rifle Division weren't fully excavated and prepared. By the start of the Battle of Kursk, they had not been completed in front of the boundary between the 151st Guards and 155th Guards Rifle Regiments; they were shallow and passable for heavy tanks, so despite the heavy artillery fire, a kampfgruppe of SS Panzer Grenadier Division *Leibstandarte Adolf Hitler* was able to cross them rather rapidly.

As in the case of the Central Front, Vatutin's entire system of defenses stressed anti-tank combat. Anti-tank defenses were organized to the entire depth of the armies, but primarily concentrated in the main defensive belt. At the same time, the artillery would be given a particularly prominent role in the future battle.

By the start of the Battle of Kursk, according to the information from Voronezh Front's artillery headquarters, the average density of artillery per kilometer of frontage amounted to 8.8 guns of 76mm to 203mm caliber, and 17 82mm and 120mm mortars. The total density therefore amounted to 25-26 tubes per kilometer, and an average density of anti-tank artillery amounted to 5.8 guns. Table 16 provides the total number of guns and mortars in the armies of the Voronezh Front on 4 July 1943 according to the account of its artillery headquarters.

Table 16: Quantity of artillery tubes, mortars and anti-tank weapons on the Voronezh Front as of 4 July 1943[263]

Army or corps	Guns and howitzers							Mortars			Anti-tank rifles
	45mm anti-tank	76mm regimental	76mm divisional	122mm	152mm	203mm	50mm	82mm	120mm		
38th Army	98	61	139	37	18	–	360	419	132	216
40th Army	309	84	231	86	54	–	164	598	271	216
Total:	**407**	**146**	**370**	**123**	**72**	–	**524**	**1,117**	**403**	**432**
6th Guards Army	335	83	324	81	72	–	392	547	232	360
7th Guards Army	356	79	234	69	52	36	283	481	172	360
69th Army	221	88	107	48	–	–	288	443	147	1,783
1st Tank Army	20	–	24	–	–	–	–	154	95	–
2nd Gds Tank Corps	20	–	24	–	–	–	–	55	42	–
35th Gds Rifle Corps	144	40	76	36	–	–	–	290	72	–
Front Reserve (including the 5th Gds Tank Corps)	40	–	104	–	–	24	–	–	180	576
Total:	**1,136**	**281**	**937**	**234**	**124**	**60**	**963**	**1,970**	**940**	**3,079**
Total for the Front:	**1,543**	**426**	**1,307**	**357**	**196**	**60**	**1,487**	**2,987**	**1,343**	**3,511**
			3,889					5,817		3,511

263 Source: TsAMO RF, F.203, Op.2843, D.421, l. 4.

Anti-tank strongpoints comprised the basis of the system of anti-tank defenses. On the Voronezh Front, as a rule they were positioned in the company and battalion defensive areas. Normally, the commander of a destroyer anti-tank artillery regiment commanded the strongpoint. Practice showed this decision was not justified. The rifle regiment commander was responsible for the sector of defense, but he had no direct influence on the commander of its anti-tank strongpoint. In turn, the commander of the anti-tank strongpoint did not always know the situation in the sector of the rifle units, and could make a decision only on the basis of his visual assessment of a situation. The Central Front addressed this matter more successfully. There, the anti-tank strongpoints were located in the sectors of the rifle regiments, and were amalgamated into anti-tank areas. The commander of the rifle regiment was designated as the commandant of the anti-tank areas, and the commander of the artillery regiment served as his deputy.

An anti-tank strongpoint represented well-camouflaged firing positions for six to 12 guns with a broad sector of fire and had a similar number of anti-tank rifles. They were protected from the fire of German panzer grenadiers by up to a platoon of submachine gunners. On the directions that were more vulnerable to armor, the number of guns in these anti-tank strongpoints increased up to 30, and the anti-tank rifles – up to 32. The German panzer crews referred to these strongpoints as "PaK fronts".

In the 6th Guards Army's main defensive belt, 20 anti-tank strongpoints were created, including three (Nos. 15-17) in the sector of the 375th Rifle Division; four (Nos. 11-14) in the sector of the 52nd Guards Rifle Division; four (Nos. 7-10) in the sector of the 67th Guards Rifle Division; and six (Nos. 1-6) in the sector of the 71st Guards Rifle Division. The second belt of defenses had 11 prepared anti-tank strongpoints. Anti-tank areas of defense were also organized in the vicinities of Vasil'evka, Korovino, Cherkasskoe, Kamennyi Log, Koz'ma-Dem'ianovka, Shopino, Khokhlovo, and Dal'niaia Igumenka, which were made subordinate to the division commanders.

In the rear defensive belt, 19 anti-tank strongpoints were set up in the sector of the 69th Army. There were seven such strongpoints in the sector of the 183rd Rifle Division; eight in the sector of the 305th Rifle Division; and four in the sector of the 107th Rifle Division.

The fire of the anti-tank strongpoints was enhanced by the howitzer regiments and battalions firing from defilade positions. On the direction affording good ground for armor, they conducted both shifting and fixed blocking fire. Such fire not only disrupted the attackers' combat formations, but also primarily separated the panzers from the accompanying panzer grenadiers and inflicted serious casualties to the latter. In addition, this slowed the enemy's overall rate of advance. Deprived of infantry support, the panzer crews usually ceased their attack or withdrew their panzers to a safe distance. Then, using the capabilities of their guns and sights, they would begin to fire at the anti-tank gun positions methodically from a range of 1,000 to 1,200 meters. In addition, the Soviet side prepared lines and positions for all of the howitzer and cannon artillery to conduct direct fire at the German tanks.

It should be mentioned that all of the anti-tank strongpoint positions, including the main, the alternate and dummy positions, were built only by the crewmen of the artillery batteries. Accordingly, it was the fate of the artillerymen, like their fellow infantry soldiers, to excavate with shovels more than a tonn of their native soil when preparing for this grandiose battle. Moreover, the most important requirement for doing the fortification work on both fronts was the concealment and camouflaging of the constructed lines. All of the large-scale work on the first and second defensive belts therefore had to be done, as a rule, at night. From the memoirs of V.A. Ul'ianov, a former artilleryman with a battery of the 92nd Guards Rifle Division's anti-tank battalion. This division served in the Voronezh Front's 35th Guards Rifle Corps:

> In April 1943 we were shifted to the Korocha area. We were quartered in a small wooded area. Firing positions were marked out and set up on the fringe of the woods. Several days later an order arrived – to make crowbars, pickaxes and shovels, and to wash out our flasks and fill them with fresh water. On the next day our platoon, leaving behind four sentries, set off to the place of work. We moved out in darkness. We had been warned not to smoke or to speak in loud voices. After some amount of time had passed (no one had a watch), an officer met us and directed us to follow him. When we arrived at the worksite, he pointed out stakes and the layout and said, "This is a concealed firing position for a 45mm gun. You must finish this work before sunrise. Camouflage the position and wait. Someone will come for you."
>
> How were positions set up for a 45mm gun? We dug out a circle with a diameter of about 3 meters and a depth of 40-50 centimeters; the excavated dirt formed a parapet around it. In the front of the position we prepared a niche for the gun, covered with logs, into which the gun could be manhandled in the event of an artillery barrage or aerial bombing. To the left of the gun we dug out a slit trench for the gun commander, and a bit behind it an underground storage area for the cases of shells. To the right of the gun we dug a pit to shelter the gun crew.
>
> The work was hard. We'd break up the ground with the pickaxes (we had two of them), then shovel away the dirt. We were given no rest breaks: we only traded places with each other, in order to give the relieved man a bit of rest. We managed to get done before sunrise, and when an officer arrived, we were already under our waterproof capes, having a smoke. He examined everything we had done, said "You are real troopers!", and then showed us the way we should go. At the indicated assembly place, we were inspected, and then we headed back to our quarters. We arrived just as the sun was coming up. We received breakfast and then slept until lunch. With the onset of darkness, we headed out again. That was our routine: we prepared firing positions for anti-tank artillery and dug entrenchments. Once we grew accustomed to the work, we would see columns of men moving in single-file or two abreast marching out and back along parallel routes. Shovels being held in the "shoulder arms" position glittered in the moonlight. It turned out that there were plenty of earthmovers like us. We were preparing the second belt of defenses.
>
> Upon completion of the work, we made ourselves ready: We rehearsed actions to prepare our guns for battle and zeroed-in our guns. For gunnery practice we went to deep balkas a little bit in our rear. Our targets were mock-ups of German tanks and self-propelled guns. In addition, we studied colored pamphlets depicting the vulnerable locations of German armor. We trained well.[264]

---

[264] Drabkin, A., *My dralis' s "tigrami": "Glavnoe – vybit' u nikh tanki!"* [*We fought with Tigers: "The most important thing – to knock out their tanks!"*] (Moscow: Iauza, 2015), pp. 39-41.

A senior officer of the General Staff with the headquarters of the Voronezh Front, Colonel Kostin, reported to Moscow on 9 June 1943 about the status of the artillery support for the main defensive belt:

> The majority of the artillery positions have been selected well and allow the possibility of rapid maneuver with fire and wheels. The disposition of the artillery positions is deeply echeloned; on the forward edge, 45mm guns, 76mm regimental artillery and some of the 76mm divisional artillery are located in anti-tank strongpoints, as a rule, in open positions. Behind the anti-tank strongpoints is the divisional artillery and attached artillery assets, having alternate firing positions for forward and reverse movement. Behind the divisional artillery is the long-range, heavy artillery. The total depth of the artillery's echeloning reaches 15 km.
>
> The artillery has well-built and camouflaged firing positions, bunkers and slit trenches for the men. The artillery firing positions have cover, consisting of rifle units and submachine gunners, as well as cover by the anti-tank rifle teams, but are inadequately protected by artificial anti-tank and anti-personnel obstacles.
>
> As a rule, the rifle divisions have roving batteries, which conduct fire according to the previously prepared plan. There are 10-15 dummy firing positions in the sector of each division, from some of which harassing fire is being conducted that prompt enemy return fire. The fire, ranging marks and lines of the artillery have been pre-registered, and there are schemes of fire and tables for summoning fire.
>
> On 1 June 1943, the number of guns, mortars and anti-tank rifles in the first-echelon armies was as follows:
>
> **38th Army**: 339 guns, 380 mortars, 924 anti-tank rifles. Frontage: 75 km.
>
> Density of anti-tank guns per km of front is equal to 3.1 guns and 12.3 anti-tank rifles.
>
> Density of guns and mortars per km of front amounts to 9.6 tubes.
>
> **40th Army**: 209 guns, 955 mortars, 1,931 anti-tank rifles. Frontage: 52 km.
>
> Density of anti-tank guns per km of front is equal to 10 guns and 37 anti-tank rifles.
>
> Density of guns and mortars per km of front amounts to 28.8 tubes.
>
> **6th Guards Army**: 686 guns, 538 mortars, 2,805 anti-tank rifles. Frontage: 65 km.
>
> Density of anti-tank guns per km of front is equal to 8.2 guns and 43.3 anti-tank rifles.
>
> Density of guns and mortars per km of front amounts to 18.8 tubes.
>
> **7th Guards Army**: 658 guns, 721 mortars and 2,048 anti-tank rifles. Frontage: 53 km.
>
> Density of anti-tank guns per km of front is equal to 10.2 guns and 38.5 anti-tank rifles.
>
> Density of guns and mortars per km of front amounts to 26 tubes.
>
> The average operational density of artillery firing means of the armies of the first echelon of defense amounts to: 7.3 anti-tank guns per km of front and 30.6 anti-tank rifles; guns and mortars per km of front – 19.4 tubes.

From the presented figures, it is clear that the 7th Guards and 6th Guards Armies, which are positioned on the enemy's most likely direction of advance, have the greatest saturation of firing means.[265]

By the start of the fighting, the density of the saturation with artillery means per running km of the front, including all of the attached artillery but minus the 50mm mortars and Katiusha rocket launchers, amounted to the following in the 6th Guards Army's first-echelon divisions:

71st Guards Rifle Division – 14-15 guns, 13 anti-tank rifles;
67th Guards Rifle Division – 12-13 guns, 15 anti-tank rifles;
52nd Guards Rifle Division – 15-16 guns, 13 anti-tank rifles;
375th Rifle Division – 20-21 guns, 22 anti-tank rifles.[266]

Considering that it would fall to these four divisions on the first day of the offensive to take on the enemy's main attack with two panzer corps simultaneously, having more than 1,000 operational tanks and self-propelled guns, then the cited figures don't seem to be all that significant. In addition, some of the artillery was being held in the reserve, several kilometers from the forward edge, so the real density of artillery fire that the enemy encountered proved to be even lower, and that of the anti-tank guns – significantly less.

One important detail: of the 407 45mm, 76mm regimental and divisional guns and those of the attached regiments, including the nine SU-76 of the 1440th Self-propelled Artillery Regiment, which were located in the four divisions presented above, 68.7 percent consisted of 76mm guns. However, considering that the actual layout of the forward edge of the defenses extended for a total of 65 km, the density of anti-tank guns amounts to 6.2 guns per km. Even if you include in the total sum the mobile divisional special reserve (the 230th and 245th Separate Tank Regiments and the 96th Separate Tank Brigade) that consisted of 133 operational tanks, then the density does not exceed 8.2 guns per km.

This circumstance in combination with the arrangement of the Voronezh Front's four divisions in a single line predetermined the relatively rapid breakthrough of the main defensive belt even despite its significant fortification and artificial obstacles. Nevertheless, in the course of Citadel it was in the cards for the Soviet artillery to play a key role. I will cite the conclusion made by military specialists already after the war, when aggregating the experience of the fighting around the Kursk bulge: "In the successful struggle with attacking tanks, artillery played a very important role. It is sufficient to show that of the total number of knocked-out and destroyed enemy tanks and self-propelled guns in the defensive period of the fighting, 63 percent were destroyed by artillery fire.[267]

The second defensive belt in all of the Voronezh Front's armies ran approximately 10-15 km from the forward edge of the main belt (depending on the tracing of the forward edge). Its total length amounted to 216 km, including 54 km for the 38th Army, 46 km for the 40th Army, 60 km for the 6th Guards Army (according to the tracing of the forward edge), and 46 km for the

---

265 TsAMO RF, F.203, Op.2843, D.365, l. 75.
266 TsAMO RF, F.335, Op.5113, D.235, l. 12.
267 I.V. Porod'ko [ed.], *Kurskaia bitva* [*Battle of Kursk*] (Moscow: Nauka, 1970), pp. 233-234. [Ed. note: The Soviet concept of "artillery" includes tank guns and anti-tank guns.

7th Guards Army. In all of the armies, there were forces in the second echelon, but their strength varied: in the 38th Army, it was the 37th Rifle Brigade and a brigade of training battalions (on the right flank, the Viktorovka – Makhnovka line); in the 40th Army – two rifle divisions and one destroyer anti-tank artillery brigade, which were covering the most tank-vulnerable Graivoron – Beloe direction; in the 6th Guards Army – the 90th Guards, 51st Guards and 89th Guards Rifle Divisions, the 27th and 28th Separate Destroyer Anti-Tank Artillery Brigades, as well as the 227th Rifle Regiment of the 69th Army's 183rd Rifle Division (the Volovuevka – Sazhnoe – (excl.) Krivtsovo – Kleimenovo sector); and in the 7th Guards Army – three rifle divisions and one separate anti-tank artillery brigade. Each of the second-echelon divisions held a front that ran for 15 to 25 km, depending on the importance of the sector and the terrain. The greatest density of force was created in the 7th Guards and 6th Guards Armies; their fronts ran for 14-23 km and had a depth of 5-6 km.

In Chistiakov's 6th Guards Army, each division commander of the first echelon had a reserve – two rifle battalions each, which were taken from the three divisions deployed in the second echelon. In addition, these second-echelon divisions – the 51st Guards, 89th Guards and 90th Guards Rifle Divisions – had no assets whatsoever. Thus, it is impossible to call the 6th Guards Army's second echelon robust. The Front command realized this, but believed that they would be bolstered in the course of the fighting, when the 1st Tank Army, positioned in the rear in the Oboian' area, reached the second defensive belt, while some of the 6th Guards Army's first echelon would fall back from the main defensive belt. The account of the Front's engineers observed:

> The forward edge [of the second defensive belt] for the most part runs along a natural line in the 6th Guards Army, having in front of it swampy or dry ravines with wide bottom lands, with the exceptions of separate sectors of the 7th Guards Army and the right flank of the 38th Army, where the forward edge runs across level ground. The fields of vision and fire are comparable with the forward edge of the main defensive belt. The disposition of the troops of the second defensive belt (in the 6th Guards, 7th Guards and 40th Armies) is such that is like that of the main defensive belt, with the only exception being that the divisions had no forward detachments or contact with the enemy. They had a great opportunity to improve the defenses, so the network of trenches, emplacements and other fortifications are more highly developed. Here there are outlying emplacements for rifle machine-gun squads, as well as platoon-sized, company-sized and even battalion-sized areas of defense, which assume a more pronounced character with the presence of strongpoints and centers of resistance (90th Guards and 51st Guards Rifle Divisions).[268]

Only the 40th Army and 6th Guards Army had their own third, rear belt of defenses. In the sector of the 7th Guards Army and on the left wing of the 6th Guards Army, it was being occupied by the troops of the 69th Army. In the 40th Army, the third belt stretched from the Psel River along the Peny – Vyshnie Peny line, and with its left flank approached the 6th Guards Army's second defensive belt in the sector of Vengerovka, thereby creating a quasi-switch line

---

268 TsAMO RF, F.203, Op.2843, D.365, l. 80.

for the 6th Guards Army. The entire third belt in the 40th Army was being occupied by its 184th Rifle Division.

When tracing and positioning the defensive belts, the Voronezh Front command first of all took account of the natural barriers that were inaccessible for armored vehicles (the basins of small rivers, ravines, etc.), which in combination with the artificial obstacles and the anti-tank fire might stop or at least slow down the advance of the German armored wedges. The desire to take advantage of the right bank of the Psel River as a natural barrier led the decision to pull the rear defensive belt of the 6th Guards Army back to a depth of 20 km from the forward edge of the second defensive belt and to arrange it along the right bank of the river. This in turn required the creation of an intermediate line stretching from Kartamyshevka through Ivnia and Kurasovka to Ship' (subsequently, its tracing would be altered somewhat).

The right bank of the Psel River was higher, so the sector of defense here commanded all of the ground in front of it. It offered splendid fields of view, not only over the ground approaching the opposite bank of the river, but also out to a significant portion of the second defensive belt. The river was 35 to 45 meters wide and had a depth of 2 to 2.5 meters, with a steep right bank and a swampy basin, which presented a rather substantial obstacle to the enemy's motorized units, which had not been calculated to force water barriers. From the account written by Lieutenant Colonel Shamov, a General Staff officer with the 6th Guards Army headquarters: "The third army-level defensive line, which consisted of 36 battalion areas, was raised by the engineer battalions and local population in full accordance with the 1942 Combat Field Manual. In addition, between the army's second and third defensive belts, an army-level intermediate line and a number of switch positions were created; the work that was being done to set them up was 77 percent complete by the start of the operation."[269]

Shumilov's 7th Guards Army began to deploy near Belgorod not on vacant terrain. For example, at the moment that the 7th Guards Army divisions took over the sectors from the 69th Army that had been positioned here, the initial steps to fortify the ground were already complete. This concerns the defenses that ran directly along the Severskii Donets River, though by early April 1943 even the network of trenches, weapon pits and dugouts were partially ready in the second echelon. In particular, the 69th Army's 183rd Rifle Division (at Solomino and Dorogobuzheno) was actively engaged in this, but not for very long, before it turned over its sector to the 213th Rifle Division. Even so, in various sectors the quality of this work was uneven. So approximately up until 15-20 April, all of the efforts of the army's command staff were focused on strengthening the first and at that moment the main defensive belt, as well as creating a minimal logistics infrastructure. The preparation of the ground by the frontline battalions with the assistance of engineers, not only near Belgorod, but around the entire Kursk salient, was done under exceptionally difficult conditions, in direct contact with the adversary. The Germans (and primarily their artillery) always took advantage of any opportunity to impede the work.

It should be also noted that one of the particularities of the operational situation that was unfolding in the sector of the 7th Guards Army was the unsettled situation on its right flank right up until the last ten days of April. The Front command was persistently demanding that Shumilov drive the Germans out of Mikhailovka, and thereby deprive the enemy of this

---

269 TsAMO RF, F.335, Op.5113, D.235, l. 9.

important bridgehead. In order to try to carry out this order, several unsuccessful attempts to storm it were undertaken. The final one came on 16 April 1943 with the forces of two regiments of the 73rd Guards Rifle Division, but it also failed; the enemy managed to retain possession of this village.[270] Therefore the construction of the system of defenses according to the same plans for the entire army got underway in this area only in the latter half of April.

The main distinguishing characteristic of the 7th Guards Army's combat sector consisted in the fact that, as already mentioned, its forward edge ran along the left [eastern] bank of the Severskii Donets River. Only in one place – in the village of Mikhailovka, did the adversary manage at the end of April to grab and hold a small bridgehead. The presence of the river was a substantial advantage for Shumilov's forces. General of the Army V. Pliaskin, the 7th Guards Army's chief of engineers, recalled:

> Emerging on the line of the Severskii Donets River, the divisions of the 64th Army were forced first of all to eliminate the small bridgeheads that and been seized and were being held by the enemy directly near Belgorod (the Mikhailovka bridgehead), as well as opposite the village of Pushkarnoe, Dal'nie Peski, Solomino, Karnaukhovki, Bezliudovka and Maslova Pristan'. Thanks to the heroism of the units of the Guards divisions, all of the bridgeheads, with the exception of the one at Mikhailovka, were eliminated. In this fighting, the engineer units played a large role.
>
> Wet, sullen weather with subfreezing temperatures at night settled over the area. Worn out in the preceding fighting, the enemy did not have time to consolidate strongly in the bridgeheads they had captured. Our sappers decided to take advantage of this. A group of sappers of the 329th Engineer-Sapper Battalion under the command of Lieutenant Vasil'ev, using the darkness of night and the poor vigilance of the German sentries, on 26 March stealthily made their way to the bridge in the village of Karnaukhovki, wired it with explosives, and blew it up. Simultaneously with the sudden explosion, our infantry attacked the stunned enemy. Some of the Germans were killed, while the rest fled in panic to the western bank.
>
> On the night of 27-28 March, with the same success two bridges in the Dorogobuzheno area were destroyed. Groups of sappers led by Lieutenants Berezovsky and Kadyrov conducted these operations.
>
> The assignment to destroy the bridges in the Solomino and Pushkarnoe areas that had been taken by the enemy took place in exceptionally difficult conditions. Sappers under the command of Lieutenant Golovkin, who was a well-known miner and scout in the army, managed to make their way past the German security posts without being noticed, and to blow up a bridge right under the enemy's nose, while suffering no losses.[271]

Moving ahead of events, I will note that the river became one of the main reasons why the army was able to hold its positions in the initial days of Army Detachment Kempf's offensive and to inflict considerable damage to the enemy forces, which thereby disrupted the plan of Army

---

270 TsAMO RF, F.211 gv. sp., Op.145061, D.3, l. 21.
271 *Na belgorodskom napravlenii. Vospominaniia uchastnikav boev* [*On the Belgorod axis. Recollections of combat veterans*] (Belgorod: Belgorodskoe knizhnoe izdatel'stvo, 1963), p. 96.

Group South's command regarding the screening of the right wing of the Fourth Panzer Army by the Army Detachment's divisions. In the Front's remaining armies, the distance between the frontline Soviet and German trenches was approximately 900 to 1,400 meters.

On 4 April 1943, the 7th Guards Army's Military Council sent Order No.00147 to the subordinate corps, which laid out the primary principles for constructing a solid defense and an array of steps regarding the development of the fortifications. The document demanded that the division commanders, before 7 April, conduct a detailed reconnoitering of the terrain together with the command staff of the units, to check the correctness of the sectors that had been drawn for each of its rifle regiments, and to assess the decisions of their commands regarding the organization of the system of fire and the protection of the boundaries.

According to the Front's plan of defense, Shumilov's army was given the duty to prepare the main and second army-level defensive belts, while the 69th Army was supposed to construct the third army-level line, which would become the main defensive belt for it. Moreover, only the forces of the 7th Guards Army were to occupy the first two defensive belts.

As in the case of the other armies, the main element of all three defensive belts on the Korocha direction were to be battalion areas of defense, anti-tank strongpoints and areas, and a complex system of artificial obstacles. Relying on the requirements and recommendations of the Front command and its headquarters departments, the leadership of the 7th Guards Army worked out two schemes of defense separately for the divisions of the first and second echelons. They were similar and adjusted according to the specific terrain on which each division had deployed. The main characteristics of the system of defenses of the main belt were:

- The echeloning of the units of the rifle divisions, unlike in the case of the 6th Guards Army, which is to say that in the divisions, the rifle regiments were not positioned in a single line, like the neighbor's disposition, but in two ranks, with two regiments in the first echelon and the third in the second echelon, behind the boundary shared by the first two regiments. The battalions were arranged in the same manner. This decision strengthened the defense substantially, by giving it more resilience and greater elasticity.
- The greater fortification of the forward edge of the main defensive belt (relative to the second defensive belt) with artificial obstacles (minefields, ditches, chevaux de frise and so forth).
- The availability in each division of not less than two (as a rule, three) positions along two lines of trenches (in each) and the mining of all accessible directions for armor in the depth of the main defensive belt.
- The mandatory reinforcement by the army of the regiments of the first echelon with infantry and anti-tank reserves (and even their battalions located on particularly important directions) through penal companies (in the 7th Guards Army, there were five such companies), anti-tank rifle battalions, artillery, mortars and even infantry support tank units made operationally subordinate to them. The strengthening of the fortifications in all of the divisional sectors was essentially the same, so the transfer of these units and elements from the army commander's reserve was the main, and essentially only lever of influence (if you don't include the planned actions of the army's mobile reserve and anti-tank artillery reserves) by which he could genuinely strengthen threatened sectors. This showed more clearly when preparing the lines of the divisions that were holding the army's flanks.

The divisions of the second echelon (by the start of the fighting, these were the 15th Guards, 73rd Guards and 213th Rifle Divisions) were considered the reserve (of the army commander and both corps commanders); their main task consisted in preparing counterattacks in previously determined directions. Even so, they also worked to prepare their positions in the second echelon. The difference only was that their regiments weren't echeloned into two ranks, but were positioned in a single line, and the ground in front of their forward edges was not as heavily mined.

On 1 July 1943, the total frontage of the main defensive belt amounted to 53 km, or 21.6 percent of the Voronezh Front's entire 245-km sector according to the tracing of the forward edge. The divisions of its first echelon were arrayed as follows:

81st Guards Rifle Division (on the army's right flank) occupied an 8-km sector: Patch of woods 1 km east of Chernaia Poliana – Staryi Gorod – corrective labor colony – Iastrebovo – Andreevskie;
78th Guards Rifle Division – a 10-km sector: (Excl.) corrective labor colony – Dorogobuzheno – Nizhnii Ol'shanets – Krutoi Log – Generalovka;
72nd Guards Rifle Division – A 15-km sector: (excl.) Nizhnii Ol'shanets – Maslova Pristan' – (excl.) Point 104.2 – western edge of the Dacha Shebekinskaia woods;
36th Guards Rifle Division (on the army's left flank) – A 20-km sector: Point 104.2 – Gatishche-1 and -2 – (excl.) Sovetskoe-1 – western portion of Volchansk – Timovka.

The army's second echelon extended for 46 km, or 21.3 percent of the length of the Front's entire second defensive belt (216 km). Three rifle divisions occupied it: two, each serving as a reserve for one of the corps commanders, and one serving as the army commander's reserve. The second-echelon divisions were arrayed as follows:

73rd Guards Rifle Division (reserve of the 25th Guards Rifle Corps): (Excl.) Sheino – Miasoedovo – Solov'ev Collective Farm – Korenskaia Dacha woods – (excl.) Nikol'skoe;
213th Rifle Division (reserve of the 24th Guards Rifle Corps): Gremiachii [Gremiachee] – Poliana State Farm – Shebekino – Nezhigol' – Churaevo;
15th Guards Rifle Division (M.S. Shumilov's reserve): The 23.5 km sector Shebetkinsky State Farm – Plebenevka [?] State Farm – Gerlegovka – Zavody-2 – Volchanskie Khutora – Point 156.2.

The divisions of the 7th Guards Army's first echelon did not send out a reinforced combat security in the form of forward detachments, as was the case in the 6th Guards Army; the river fronting it did not make this possible. In addition, reinforced combat security outposts weren't organized either. In order to guard the forward edge and the minefields, instead each forward company sent out patrols at night. The company commanders determined the size and weaponry of the patrols. For example, in 1/224th Guards Rifle Regiment of the 72nd Guards Rifle Division, each company assigned three men (equipped with a light machine gun, two PPSh submachine guns and six grenades). Because of the fact that the forward edge was located on the edge of a swampy river basin, the patrols did not advance far from the forward edge, only about 100 meters. This did not allow them to carry out the security mission in full measure. A relatively large distance remained to the river channel, approximately 350-400 meters, and this enabled the German assault groups to cross the river stealthily at night, and concealed by the swamp's overgrowth, having accumulated their strength, they destroyed the thin screen of outposts in a single lunge and broke into the first line of trenches. The Soviet side recognized the imminent peril and attempted to take steps to set up secret listening posts close to the riverbank in order to keep watch over the surface of the river and to thwart German attempts to cross it undetected. For example, the 72nd Guards Rifle Division's command issued an order to embed barrels, one atop the other, to serve as an outpost position; the design resembled a rifle pit, but this brainstorm was unsuccessful.

The forward edge of the 7th Guards Army's main defensive belt was strengthened in the same way as in the other armies: First anti-tank mines were emplaced, then anti-personnel mines; then chevaux de frise were fashioned out of tree branches and set out in a single line (in order to delay the infantry). This was followed by concertina wire and trip wires, staked barbed wire in three rows (the span between the wires was 60-70 cm). All of these obstacles were covered by the fire of infantry weapons and mortars. In certain divisions, before the forward edge of the second-echelon regiment, fields of Molotov cocktails containing chemicals that would ignite upon contact with air were created along with the minefields [in the hope that their ignition would set ablaze a tank that passed over them]. Such an obstacle, for example, blanketed the entire forward edge of 1/233rd Guards Rifle Regiment of the 81st Guards Rifle Division, and covered the entire 2-km of ground between the road running from Hill 153.2 to the railroad and from Hill 156.6 to Staryi Gorod. General Plaskin recalled:

> During the preparation of the defenses around the Kursk bulge, several hundred thousand anti-tank, anti-personnel and fougasse mines were emplaced by the engineers. A large number of bridges and other important sites were readied for demolition. Near Belgorod, each kilometer of front contained more than 2,000 anti-tank mines and more than 2,600 anti-personnel mines. In connection with this, I want to mention the heroism and self-sacrifice with which this system of obstacles was created. In the period of the spring thaw, several boxcars of anti-personnel and anti-tank mines were delivered to the Belyi Kolodez' train station by order of the Front. This train station was located in the sector of an adjacent army of the Southwestern Front. How and by what means could this precious cargo be moved to the 7th Guards Army? I had to take a large risk. We asked the station commandant and the locomotive driver to deliver the railcars to Volchansk Station, where the 15th Guards Rifle Division was defending. The town and rail station of Volchansk were being shelled by enemy artillery. It was necessary to act swiftly and boldly. Having explained the situation, the station commandant ordered the locomotive drivers (it is a pity that my memory hasn't retained their family names), exploiting the nighttime darkness, to take the train to Volchansk, where a battalion of infantry and Major D. Ushakov's 48th Engineer-Sapper Battalion were waiting for it. Deftly and quickly, observing complete silence, under the cover of the night the soldiers unloaded the deadly cargo from the railcars, and the locomotive drivers headed back in their train. Among the boxcars with the mines, we discovered one loaded with Molotov cocktails! They came in handy when repulsing tank attacks. Soon, the mines were transported in wagons to the divisions. Everything went successfully. After all,

it was sufficient for just one shell to hit a boxcar, and nothing would be left of them or around them. However, we had no other alternative.[272]

By the start of the Battle of Kursk, the defensive belts of Shumilov's 7th Guards Army consisted of three lines in the main defensive belt and two lines in the second belt of defenses. In the main belt, the lines were positioned one behind the other at a distance of 1,200 to 2,000 meters (depending on the terrain). The basis of the fortification of the belts consisted of standard trenches and communication trenches. Each position had two or three lines of entrenchments, or between six and nine in the main defensive belt and four to six in the second defensive belt. As was later calculated by military historians, for each running kilometer of the front, up to 8 km of continuous standard entrenchments and communication trenches were excavated. When constructing the main defensive belt of the Central Front's 13th Army, this figure went up to 10 km.[273] Former chief of engineers of the Steppe Front General A.D. Tsirlin wrote:

> Up until the end of 1942, our views toward fortifying field sectors and positions were determined by the theory and practice of preparing fortified areas. Battalion centers of resistance in the engineer respect were set up with a system of separate earth and timber firing positions of the casemate type, tied together with the system of fire. The units and formations at that time did not always have the necessary of weapons to ensure the effectiveness of the system of fire in such a battalion center of resistance. Communication trenches were absent between the earth and timber bunkers, as a result of which the elements could not stealthily maneuver their means of fire within the strongpoint in the course of the fighting. A system of trenches, the adoption of which began in a number of *fronts* at the initiative of the troops back in 1942, and everywhere – on the basis of the General Staff directives from the spring of 1943 – in combination with powerful obstacles imparted new qualities to our defenses.
>
> The use of trenches eliminated the well-known constraints of a system of fire, which as already noted was based on immobile firing positions with limited sectors of fire. The trenches facilitated the activity of the infantry, which received the possibility of maneuvering widely in concealment from the enemy on the battlefield ... The enemy was deprived of the possibility of targeted fire at the elements positioned in the trenches and other shelters.[274]

In addition, the network of entrenchments included heavy artillery positions, as well as tanks and self-propelled guns that were dug into the ground to serve as immobile, armored firing positions. Altogether, this should have enhanced the defense's resilience, activity and maneuverability. In order to break through such a system, the enemy would require significantly more means of fire, equipment and ammunition. This novelty, in contrast to the construction of individual casemates, accelerated the fortification works in the divisions, eased the strengthening of a line, and also reduced the number of man-hours needed to build hardened (which also meant costly) firing positions. The freed-up labor force was directed instead to building a large number of

272 Ibid., pp. 100-101.
273 TsAMO RF, F.240, Op.2779, D.453, l. 118.
274 Parot'kin [ed.], *Kurskaia bitva*, p. 242.

simplified (anti-fragmentation) shelters for the infantry, which together with concealment and dummy positions reduced the casualty rate, which in turn meant the retention of the elements' effective combat strength.

The German command at the same time also came to the conclusion that a network of trenches was more effective and reliable means for conserving manpower. Moreover, they reached this conclusion on the basis of their observation of the Soviet forces. I will cite a captured document of the OKH from 11 March 1943, which was entitled "Combat Experience No. 3". This was an informational leaflet (in essence, instruction), which was sent to the troops on the Eastern Front for guidance when preparing positions for the impending spring:

> Before the large offensive this winter, the Russians were intensively digging into their assembly areas, in order to avoid needless losses from artillery fire and airstrikes. Particular significance in this was given to deception and camouflage ... In the process [of their offensive], the enemy managed to crush our positions, which were poorly set up mostly with dug-in emplacements and isolated earth and timber bunkers, and also our guns of all types.
>
> In order to avoid unnecessary losses from artillery fire, narrow and deep entrenchments and dug outs made by explosive mines [the explosion of a deeply-embedded charge] have been particularly justifying themselves. Only during a heavy barrage were there isolated cases of a direct hit on such entrenchments. Enemy tanks also have trouble identifying such fighting positions, so it is easier to knock them out from such burrows and slit trenches. It was necessary that the entrenchment, at the very least, had a dog leg every 10-15 meters. The shortcoming of such entrenchments is the excessive number of communication trenches. They complicate the orientation of our soldiers, and it is easier for the enemy thereby to consolidate in our former positions and this later requires large forces for a counterattack. At the same time, it is necessary when evacuating the wounded to take into attention the negative aspects of a narrow trench. There, wherever the soil and water table allow it, it is necessary to demand the construction of shelters to protect the men using explosive charges, as well as sumps in the walls of the entrenchment that face the enemy, in order to shelter weapons and ammunition. These shelters [entrenchments and dugouts] should be narrow, as far as possible with sheer walls, and well camouflaged, so that they aren't destroyed in advance by artillery fire or as the result of directly placed fire from individual tanks. In order to deceive the enemy, dummy entrenchments should be occupied occasionally.[275]

The most widespread shelters for machine gunners were bunkers with embrasures and tables for mounting the machine guns. Anti-fragmentation shelters were prepared for the riflemen, and command, observation and often combined command and observation posts for the commanders of the elements and units. All of these fortifications were similar and constructed out of two primary materials – wooden logs and earth. The earth and timber emplacements were built in the form of timber blockhouses (usually 2.2 x 2.2 meters), which stood 2 meters high and were almost completely dug into the ground. The roof was made out of two layers of logs, with 50-60

---

275 TsAMO RF, F.500, Op.1248, D.15, l. 66.

cm of soil packed between them. In the direction of the enemy, one embrasure (typically) with a width of up to 60 cm was cut out of the wood, and inside it something resembling a table would be crafted in order to mount the machine guns. The machine-gun "nests" (bunkers) were as a rule positioned in a checkerboard fashion, in order to cover the flanks of neighbors. The ideal shelter for a firing position was a brick structure (better a cellar), but there was very few of these in the sector of the 7th Guards Army; primarily they were located in Staryi Gorod (the sector of the 81st Guards Rifle Division) in the buildings of the railroad depot. The majority of the villages and hamlets in the main and second defensive belts had been seriously damaged in the course of previous fighting, so even only a few wooden buildings and outbuildings remained standing in them.

The anti-fragmentation shelters were timber blockhouses with four (rarely three) walls, made out of logs with a thickness of 18-20 cm, which rose above the soil level. Its walls were usually masked with turf and loose soil, and in order to strengthen it on steep slopes, a wattle of vines and branches were applied to them. They were roofed with two layers of logs, but the logs used were less thick than, for example, those on the earth and timber bunkers or dug outs. The troops would make one or two embrasures in the shelter's walls.

In order to direct the units and fire, two observation posts or command-observation posts were built for each commander of a rifle company (and higher). They were built like ordinary bunkers, but with several embrasures for observation (and for mounting observation devices), no less than two entries (a main one and alternate one), and three lines of communication (a main, alternate and reserve). The observation posts and command-observation posts of the commanders at various levels were distinguished only by the number of log layers covering them – the company commander normally had two, but a regiment commander had three or even more.

Already at the end of March, all of the villages in the tactical zone of the 7th Guards Army began to be adapted for a defense, and on 30 April, Special Directive No.00914 was signed by the Front's Military Council, which demanded:

> All of the populated places in the combat, rear and army defensive belts are to be utilized as strongpoints and anti-tank areas, assigning their defensive works to Group B. In addition, prepare the following populated places, assigning them to Group A:
> 6th Guards Army – Ol'khovka, Gostishchevo, Dal'niaia Igumenka, Shakhovo, Shliakhovoe, Sheino, Lomovo and Oboian';
> 7th Guards Army – Miasoedovo, Shebekino, Volchansk, Zovody-1 and -2, Nezhigol' and Voznesenovka;
> 69th Army – Aleksandrovskii [Prokhorovka Station], Alekseevka, Korocha, Bol'she-Troitskoe.
> Construct field defensive perimeters around the points of Group A, according to the scheme for fortified areas, and create in the built-up areas themselves a system of fortifications and obstacles.
> Set to work immediately to fortify the places indicated in the given directive.
> The deadline for the preliminary readiness of the populated places for a defense is 25 May 1943. The deadline for the complete readiness of the fortifications ... 10 June 1943.

> Report through the Chief of Fortified Areas every five days on the course of the work according to the given directive with an indication of the number of buildings and embrasures prepared by type of weapon for each populated place.[276]

So that the reader might more clearly picture the difference between Group A and Group B, I will dwell on this question in a little more detail. In the system of field defensive perimeters, the following were included: a continuous, elaborate line of standard trenches with fortified firing positions and prepared positions for artillery and mortars; the mining of the forward edge; three lines of staked barbed wire and the construction of such major artificial obstacles to obstruct tank-vulnerable directions as anti-tank ditches, escarpments and counterscarps. In parallel with this, in the built-up area itself a network of trenches was prepared, all of the buildings (cellars) were converted into hardened firing positions with all-round fields of fire; communication trenches were dug, and ramps were excavated for dug-in tanks, which were to be used to help defend the village (for example, in the village of Miasoedovo, the tank crews of the 167th Separate Tank Regiment prepared the positions for their tanks).

The decision about fortifying populated places substantially increased the burden on both the troops and on the local population but proved to be far-sighted. By early July 1943, the demands of the directive were for the most part implemented. Indeed, as subsequent events would show, all of the anti-tank strongpoints, including the anti-tank strongpoints located in the villages of the tactical zone played an important role in containing or slowing the enemy kampfgruppen in the course of the German offensive toward Kursk. The defensive strongpoints in the villages of Krutoi Log, Razumnoe and Maslova Pristan' were organized particularly successfully. Of the 15 populated places in the sector of the 6th Guards and 7th Guards Armies that were prepared according to the scheme of fortified areas, seven were taken by the enemy, but the storming of them required one to three days, with the engagement of significant forces not only of panzer grenadiers, but also armored vehicles. Moreover, the enemy suffered substantial losses in this fighting.

Correctly assuming that in the course of the defensive operation the main problem would be the enemy's panzer groups, the 7th Guards Army command staff from the first days of organizing the defenses attached primary significance to strengthening them in an anti-tank respect. However, the fulfillment of this task was complicated by the terrain conditions. The territory where its troops had dug in proved difficult for the employment of anti-tank artillery as the main element of the defense. The eastern bank of the Severskii Donets River, held by our forces, was lower than the western bank, which rose above the water by 1 to 1.5 meters. All of the commanding heights in the surroundings were in the possession of Kempf's troops; therefore, as noted in the documents of its artillery headquarters, from their ground observation posts the Germans could survey the 7th Guards Army's defenses out to a depth of 5 to 8 km. However, as the commander of the 7th Panzer Division Major General H. von Funck complained, not all of the hills could be used for observation posts, since they were low in height and forested.

The Guardsmen, on the other hand, from an observation post on the eastern bank could observe enemy positions only out to a distance of 1 to 3 km; only in certain sectors did this

---

276 TsAMO RF, F.203, Op.2843, D.301, ll. 200-201.

extend out to 5 or 6 km. At the same time, the majority of the balkas on the eastern bank ran perpendicular to the channel of the river, so it was impossible to set up concealed, defilade firing positions for the artillery in them. Only in the single Rzhavets – Titovka area were there dense woods that approached almost right up to the eastern bank of the Severskii Donets River, which allowed the concealed regrouping of units. In addition, a serious problem arose with the sandy soil, which predominated in the 7th Guards Army's sector, since it could not ensure the necessary solidity of the fortifications and required their constant upkeep. The sectors between the Severskii Donets and Razumnaia Rivers, as well as along the eastern bank of the latter, which covered 5 to 8 km, was chiefly open ground, which given an enemy breakthrough might permit the launching of an attack by panzer groups to the northeast. The III Panzer Corps successfully exploited this corridor in the course of Citadel.

At the same time, a number of natural obstacles favored the Soviet side and gave it substantial advantages when organizing an anti-tank defense. The main one, of course, was the Severskii Donets River. Although it in fact fell into the category of shallow rivers, it had a rather wide and swampy basin (out to 200 meters from the channel on the eastern and western banks). In addition, the Koren' and Korocha Rivers that flowed from north to south and the presence of dense wooded areas around them reduced the possibility of a maneuver by enemy armor through the right flank and center of the 7th Guards Army in an eastern direction. Based on a detailed analysis of the area of defense, the army headquarters determined six directions in its sector that were vulnerable to panzer operations, of which three were the most dangerous, including two in the sector of the 25th Guards Rifle Corps and one in the sector of the 24th Guards Rifle Corps:

> First (main) direction – out of the Mikhailovka bridgehead (sector of the 81st Guards Rifle Division);
> > Second – toward Korocha (81st Guards and 78th Guards Rifle Divisions);
> > Third – Volchansk – Volokonovka (36th Guards Rifle Division.

Taking this into account, along the forward edge of the main defensive belt, 12 divisional anti-tank strongpoints were established, and 15 army anti-tank areas in the second belt of defenses. For sake of comparison, the 6th Guards Army had a total of 28 anti-tank strongpoints, including 18 in the main defensive belt and 10 in the second belt of defenses. According to the thinking of the Front's artillery command, with the aim of achieving the anti-tank strongpoints' maximum effectiveness, they should be self-sufficient as far as possible. Although the basis of their strength was the fire of the anti-tank rifles and anti-tank guns, the plan was to screen the centers of resistance mandatorily with rifle units and to reinforce them with mortars and a mobile blocking detachment. This was necessary so that its garrison could on its own thwart attempts by enemy sappers to clear passages through the minefields; separate the escorting infantry from the tanks, eliminate submachine gunners as they attempted to infiltrate the firing positions, and block attempts by the German panzer groups to bypass the strongpoints around their flanks (by moving out groups of sappers to the probable breakthrough directions).

The command of the 7th Guards Army not only supported this proposal, but also persistently worked to enforce it when preparing its defenses. The artillery commander Lieutenant General A.N. Petrov each day drove out to the troops to explain its positive aspects, and on the spot resolved arising questions of cooperation with each artillery commander of the divisions and corps. Commandants were put in command of the strongpoints – an artillery officer, and each gun had telephone communications and a messenger. Signals for summoning artillery fire by the rifle units in the event of the appearance of German tanks were established and rehearsed. In order not to disclose the location of the firing points prematurely, specific guns and crews were determined, which had the order to open fire at small groups of armor and infantry. On the right flank of the army, heavy KV tanks from the 262nd Heavy Tank Regiment were dug into the strongpoints to serve as immobile firing positions. In addition, all of the concealed positions of the howitzer artillery (of the divisional and regimental assets) were ready to fire directly at enemy armor, and if this was not possible, nearby alternative emplacements were set up.

Despite the obvious advantages of the new scheme for reinforcing the anti-tank strongpoints, it prompted a lot of arguments, lack of understanding, and even opposition on the part of infantry commanders, and not only them. The staff officers of the Voronezh Front's artillery headquarters wrote in its account:

> It is necessary, however, to note that when implementing this scheme in practice, quite a few difficulties were encountered. The main one was the lack of understanding, even among artillery officers, of the need to bind all of the measures together to ensure a reliable, unyielding anti-tank defense. The incomprehension was connected with the fact that the fire of the guns comprises the basis of an anti-tank defense, and because of this it was the artillery chief who should resolve the questions about the need of supplementing the artillery fire with other measures. By itself it stands to reason that when organizing an anti-tank defense, each artillery chief started from the overall plan of defense adopted by the combined-arms chiefs who were responsible for the defense of the given sector. A lot had to be worked out … it was required to dispatch several directives from the Front's Military Council and artillery headquarters.[277]

If to digress from the "optimists" and the rather vague declarations from the account of General S.S. Varentsov's artillery headquarters, and to express the essence of the problem concisely, it all boiled down to the narrow-mindedness and professional illiteracy of a significant portion of the officers. A large number of both the infantry and artillery commanders were satisfied to fight "in the old style" and placed their own petty interests above their service duties. However, I will start everything from the beginning. Prior to this moment, the senior chief who was responsible for holding a sector was the commander of the infantry battalion, but now the responsibility for the anti-tank strongpoint and the fortification of the positions was being placed on the artillerymen. Jealousy appeared among the infantry officers (arguments began over who was in charge), and their arguments were as follows: The "cannoneers" know their business, but their "points of view" were too narrow; we were the first to meet the Fritzes and to decide the main questions of a defense (what to mine, where to dig trenches and escarpments, and so on and so forth), while they were standing behind our backs. The novelty also was not to the taste of the artillerymen – the responsibility was too much, and all the fuss and bother was being multiplied. However, all of these squabbles, without which not a single new idea can get by, abated as soon as the fighting began, and the well-organized, and I will say directly, sensible system of anti-tank strongpoints demonstrated their durability and effectiveness.

277 TsAMO RF, F.203, Op.2843, D.421, l. 15.

For the sake of justice, it should be noted that in the course of constructing the system of anti-tank strongpoints, more than a few serious problems also arose in the Central Front when bringing all of its components together to cooperate with each other. In fact, at the end of May this question became so acute that V.I. Kazakov was forced to prepare a special directive regarding the organization of the anti-tank defenses, which was confirmed by the Military Council and issued to all of the armies on 1 June 1943. In particular, this document stated:

> An inspection of the organization of the system of anti-tank defenses in the units of the Front's armies revealed that there is no single opinion among the infantry, artillery and other commanders about how to construct anti-tank defenses, and no sense of responsibility for its organization and execution.
> The commanders responsible for the anti-tank defense (see p. 132 of the 1943 Field Manual) have become accustomed to believe that the anti-tank defense consists only of organizing the anti-tank strongpoints, and fail to take into account the organization of anti-tank blocking fire, a system of observation, artificial and natural obstacles, the availability of divisional artillery, the heavy artillery of the Supreme High Command Reserve and anti-tank reserves.
> From this it is clear that no cooperation among the separate elements of an anti-tank defense have been planned, and accordingly not implemented either. The anti-tank defenses of the 70th Army can serve as an example of this. The army's artillery headquarters hasn't issued any concrete directives to its subordinate artillery units. The organization of the anti-tank defense consisted only in demanding schemes for it from subordinates, and no analysis of these schemes was done. Separate anti-tank strongpoints were set up that had no connection between each other. Sectors of 2-3 km remained without anti-tank protection. The firing positions of the divisional artillery, as a rule, haven't been adapted for an anti-tank role, and no anti-tank blocking fire has been prepared.
> The equipping and arming of separate anti-tank strongpoints also have a number of substantial shortcomings – poor communications between separate firing positions, inadequate camouflage, the lack of an all-round field of fire, and the impermissibly small number of anti-tank weapons in individual anti-tank strongpoints (just one gun).
> The prepared positions have no mobile anti-tank reserve. Approach routes from the reserve's lines of departure haven't been measured or prepared.
> The anti-tank defense plan completely ignores the inclusion of the divisional artillery and heavy artillery of the Supreme High Command Reserve in the struggle against enemy armor given their penetration into the defensive belts and does not anticipate the maneuver of firing means from neighboring sectors.
> The same situation exists with anti-tank defenses in other armies as well.[278]

The 7th Guards Army command staff gave great importance to strengthening the Belgorod – Titovka railroad bed.[279] This branch ran across almost the 7th Guards Army's entire sector of

---

278 TsAMO RF, F.361, Op.6099, D.59, l. 382.
279 This railroad branch links the two district centers of Belgorod and Volchansk, so it would be logical to label it the Belgorod – Volchansk railroad. However, in the combat documents of the opposing sides,

defense, from the left-flank 36th Guards Rifle Division to the Kreida switchyards on left-flank of the 81st Guards Rifle Division on the right, and lay almost parallel to the forward edge. It connected such villages, which had been converted into anti-tank strongpoints, as Gatishche-1, Bezliudovka, Maslova Pristan' and Razumnoe. In places, swampy ground flanked the railway embankment, which made the defense of these sectors even stronger. In essence, the embankment to a significant extent was already a prepared artificial obstacle, so it was necessary only to incorporate it properly within the overall system of defenses, which the Guardsmen worked on throughout the entire spring and did rather successfully. As a result, over the first two days of the Battle of Kursk, the railroad bank, which was densely mined and laced with booby traps and firing positions played an important role in the ability of the first-echelon divisions of both Soviet corps to hold their positions. It became a unique buffer, which neither the infantry of Korps Raus nor the kampfgruppen of III Panzerkorps were able to overcome from the march.

Now let us take a more detailed look at how the construction of the defenses directly within the frontline rifle divisions went. Considering the entire array of complex tasks that stood before the armies, and especially the main one – to prevent the enemy's auxiliary grouping from linking up with the main forces, the leadership of the 7th Guards Army strove to set up a balanced defense with its available forces.

At the suggestion of G.K. Zhukov, who in March and April 1943 often visited the Voronezh Front and reconnoitered the terrain in the sector of the 7th Guards Army together with N.F. Vatutin, the forward edge of the main belt on the right flank of the 25th Guards Rifle Corps (the sector of the 81st Guards Rifle Division) and the left flank of the 24th Guards Rifle Corps (the sector of the 36th Guards Rifle Division) were most heavily fortified. At the suggestion of M.S. Shumilov, the third division of each corps was to occupy a line in the second echelon behind the boundary between the two divisions of the first echelon. However, the Marshal of the Soviet Union demanded the echeloning of the forces on the flanks and to position the third division of each Guards rifle corps to bolster the boundary with the neighboring corps. At the same time the commanders of the second-echelon divisions received an order to prepare positions throughout the entire second defensive belt and to work out plans for counterattacks in the event of an enemy breakthrough both at the boundary between their respective corps and at the boundary between the two first-echelon divisions within the corps themselves. By the start of the Battle of Kursk, the 73rd Guards Rifle Division was positioned behind the right-flank 81st Guards Rifle Division, and the 15th Guards Rifle Division was located behind the left-flank 36th Guards Rifle Division. The 213th Rifle Division, which by this time had passed into M.S. Shumilov's reserve, was directed toward the boundary between the two corps. The army commander also ordered to prepare routes for the maneuvering of the second-echelon forces of the two corps, both to the area of the boundary between them, and into the sectors of their flanking divisions. In addition, the divisions of the army's first line holding an outer flank (the 81st Guards and 36th Guards Rifle Divisions) were supposed to receive the bulk of the reserve artillery and tanks, which had been assigned by the Front to reinforce the 7th Guards Army. G.K. Zhukov's demand regarding the substantial strengthening of the armies'

---

it is frequently called the Belgorod – Titovka railroad. Likely this is because Volchansk was located behind the 7th Guards Army's sector of defense and outside Army Detachment Kempf's main sector of operations. So I will stick to the Belgorod – Titovka railroad in the present research.

and Front's flanks was dictated by the sad experience of the summer fighting in 1942, including in this very same area, when the Germans split the Soviet forces with powerful panzer attacks precisely at the boundaries between major formations and armies.

The 81st Guards Rifle Division arrived in the Voronezh Front back in the first half of March. Having unloaded at the Printsevka Station and having conducted a 100-km march, from 15 March it occupied a defense near Belgorod in the second echelon and set to work on fortifying its sector. However, already a month later, on the night of 4-5 May, a planned rotation was conducted on the army's right flank, and Morozov's 81st Guards Rifle Division took over the positions of Colonel S.A. Kozak's 73rd Guards Rifle Division in the first echelon. This was done not only for the purpose of giving the men of the 73rd Guards Rifle Division the opportunity to rest and conduct combat training. The point was that the 73rd Guards Rifle Division was covering the promising northeastern direction for the enemy and at the same time was the only division that had direct contact with the enemy: opposite the center of its combat formation was the main "sore point" on the eastern bank, the village of Mikhailovka that was held by the Germans. The bridgehead was a small one; including the river basin, only around 15 square kilometers (and around 9 square kilometers of firm ground). Nevertheless, it was possible for the Germans to stage a strong attacking force within it of up to 40 panzers, which greatly concerned the Soviet side. Kozak's division, like all of the army's divisions, had arrived from Stalingrad in a weakened condition, and throughout the month of April was engaged in heavy fighting for Mikhailovka. Therefore, by the beginning of May it was the weakest division in the 7th Guards Army (on 5 May 1943 it had only a total of 6,824 men).[280] Having received the first intelligence warning about a possible German attack prior to 10 May, the Front command therefore moved a stronger division into this important sector.

When transferring its lines, the 73rd Guards Rifle Division left behind all of its assets in their positions. In addition, in the month of June the 81st Guards Rifle Division was given additional assets, while the fortification work in its positions already from May had begun to be prepared with more thoroughness. By the start of the Battle of Kursk, Morozov's division had fully prepared two positions in the main defensive belt: a first consisting of three lines of trenches, and a second (reserve) with two lines, which ran along a line from the woods near Belovskoe through Sevriukovo to a hill 300 meters north of Sevriukovo. The Guardsmen set up five anti-tank strongpoints: Staryi Gorod on the right flank, the Kreida switchyard on the left flank, the corrective labor colony on the boundary with the 78th Guards Rifle Division, and in the depth of the defenses: the villages of Blizhniaia Igumenka and Belovskoe. In addition, M.S. Shumilov focused the 73rd Guards Rifle Division and the right-hand tank group of his mobile reserve toward the northeast axis, which offered good ground for armor.

Major G.T. Skirut's 235th Guards Rifle Regiment and Major T.F. Kriuchikhin's 238th Guards Rifle Regiment together with attached assets were fully positioned in the 81st Guards Rifle Division's first echelon. G.T. Skirut had the responsibility for the boundary between the two regiments. Considering that boundary ran directly opposite Mikhailovka, the division command made the 65th Separate Army Penal Company subordinate to him, which the regiment commander shifted to the left flank of his 1st Rifle Battalion. Major S.I. Titarenko's 233rd Guards Rifle Regiment together with its attached assets was located in the depth

---

280 TsAMO RF, F.203, Op.2843, D.426, l. without number; army summary for 5 May 1943.

of the main belt of defenses (behind the boundary between the two forward regiments) in the Blizhniaia Igumenka – hamlet of the Machine Tractor Station – (excl.) Day of Harvest Collective Farm sector.

The 81st Guards Rifle Division's system of defenses relative to that of the other two divisions had a number of distinctive features. First, its sector was the smallest, a total of just 8 km (according to the tracing of the forward edge, 9 km) in width and 6 km in depth. Thus, each frontline regiment received a sector (on average) of 4 to 4.5 km, just as the 1942 Combat Field Manual specified. However, considering details of the terrain and the importance of separate directions, Major General I.K. Morozov decreased the frontage of the 238th Guards Rifle Regiment's sector relative to that of the 235th Guards Rifle Regiment. In addition, conjecturing that the Germans would launch their main attack with armor out of Mikhailovka against the left-flanking 238th Guards Rifle Regiment, he ordered its battalions to be echeloned in depth, with two battalions in the first trench line and one battalion in the second, while the 235th Guards Rifle Regiment was to move up all of its battalions into the first line of trenches, which is to say, to deploy into a single line.

Second, in the rear position of the regiments of the first echelon (the third line of trenches), the division's third regiment, the 233rd Guards Rifle Regiment was to deploy, and it was on this line that anti-tank strongpoints had been set up. Here also was the division commander's reserve – Major Medvedev's separate training rifle battalion. In addition, each battalion of Titarenko's regiment fortified its sector according to the same scheme as in the forward regiments. Such a significant density of force in the 81st Guards Rifle Division's sector in the main defensive belt to a great extent pre-determined its high degree of strength and resilence in the course of Citadel, even given the lengthy systematic attacks of the German panzer formations.

Third, several regiments of the army's artillery were made operationally subordinate to I.K. Morozov; they had a total of 34 152mm cannons and howitzers, 36 120mm mortars, 20 76mm ZiS-3 anti-tank guns, 48 BM-13 rocket launchers and 71 anti-tank rifles. Thus, by 5 July 1943, the division had received an artillery grouping that was unrivalled by any other division of the 7th Guards Army in terms of its number and firepower. In total, including the 81st Guards Rifle Division's organic artillery, it had 57 122mm and 152mm howitzers, 65 76mm ZiS-3 anti-tank guns, 12 76mm regimental guns, 41 45mm anti-tank guns, 87 82mm mortars, 60 120mm mortars, 48 BM-13 rocket launchers and 348 anti-tank rifles. Such a significant number of heavy weapons allowed the division commander to strengthen substantially not only the first, but also the second echelon with both anti-tank weapons (the 76mm batteries of the 114th Guards Destroyer Anti-Tank Artillery Regiment) and field guns of medium and large caliber. In its sector, in addition a second divisional artillery regiment – the 153rd Guards Artillery Regiment from the 73rd Guards Rifle Division – was deployed. From its own and the attached units, Morozov formed several artillery groups: a heavy artillery group (the 161st Guards Cannon Artillery Regiment), an artillery group of infantry support (five battalions), and an anti-tank reserve (a separate destroyer anti-tank artillery battalion and a company of tank hunters). Finally, a subgroup of the army's artillery group (the 265th Cannon Artillery Regiment and the 290th Mortar Regiment) was positioned in the division's sector.

As the commander of the 81st Guards Rifle Division wrote in his memoirs, in his division even the Katiusha rocket launchers were adapted for use to conduct fire at close ranges. The crews of two battalions of the 97th Guards Mortar Regiment excavated special shelters in the railroad embankment of the Belgorod – Titovka railway, so that they could wedge their

BM-13 rocket launchers into them and conduct direct fire at the attacking enemy out of the Mikhailovka bridgehead.

In addition to the artillery, M.S. Shumilov moved the 262nd Heavy Breakthrough Tank Regiment, which was armed with 24 KV tanks, out of his reserve into the sector of the 81st Guards Rifle Division and made it subordinate to Morozov as a tank reserve. For the purpose of being able to react quickly to a developing situation, one command-observation post was prepared for the division commander and tank regiment commander. A portion of his heavy tanks were dug into the system of defenses of the 235th Guards and 238th Guards Rifle Regiments in order to serve as immobile armored firing positions in the first stage of the operation. The 1st Tank Company (four KV tanks) took up position in the area of the Kreida switchyard; the 2nd Tank Company (four KV tanks) deployed in the woods south of Mikhailovka; the 4th Tank Company (two KV tanks) was dug into the southeastern outskirts of Staryi Gorod; the remaining tanks: five KV of the 3rd Tank Company, one KV of the 2nd Tank Company, three KV of the 4th Tank Company, two reserve machines and the company's command tank were located in the tank regiment commander's reserve in woods 1 km west of Belovskoe.

As a result, the average density per kilometer of the division's front (if you consider a sector of 8 km) amounted to 23.1 tubes of artillery and tanks; 24.3 tubes with a caliber of 45mm to 152mm (not including the 14 reserve KV tanks of the 262nd Heavy Tank Regiment), rocket launchers and mortars with a caliber of 82mm to 120mm; and 34.8 anti-tank rifles.

Even this was not all. Within the 81st Guards Rifle Division, just as in other divisions, a mobile blocking detachment was formed out of sapper units. However, assuming that the main events would unfold on the right flank of his corps, Major General G.B. Safiulin also assembled his own corps blocking detachment in the sector of Morozov's Guards division. This proved to be a very prudent decision, and in the course of repulsing the III Panzerkorps' attacks, this detachment would render great assistance to the Guardsmen.

I.K. Morozov assigned primary significance to the rifle units' system of fire. The most important requirements for it were its density, sweep, and ability to cover the firing positions of the heavy weapons securely. With this aim, the battalions located on most threatened directions received narrower sectors of defense than those in secondary sectors. The frontline regiments set up firing positions on the forward edge for all of the light and heavy machine guns. In particular, the 1st and 3rd Battalions of the 235th Guards Rifle Regiment, which were defending opposite the eastern and northeastern outskirts of Mikhailovka, had respectively sectors of 1.1 and 1.5 km of frontage, while the 2nd Battalion held a sector of 2.5 km. As a result, by the start of the fighting the 81st Guards Rifle Division could create a zone of dense fire out to 400 meters. The average density for the division was 8.8 bullets per running meter, and in critical sectors up to 11 bullets per running meter (1/235th Guards Rifle Regiment); this was the highest indicator in comparison not only with the army's other divisions, but also of the entire Voronezh Front.

According to an order from the division commander, in each battalion in addition to the planned machine-gun nests, no less than four heavy earth and timber bunkers should be built, with a layer of six to eight logs for the roof and using logs with a diameter of 20-25 cm for the construction. A significant portion of the machine-gun positions were set up in the brick buildings in Staryi Gorod, in the structures of the railroad facilities and in two semi-destroyed grain elevators at the Kreida switchyard. They were more heavily fortified than earth and timber bunkers, and much more like pillboxes.

The following information testifies to the impressive scale of the fortification works done by Morozov's division. By 20 June 1943, 39 km of standard trenches and communication trenches had been excavated, which connected the first three trench lines, the reserve position, and the observation posts from the level of the company commander up to the division commander; 222 emplacements for infantry, 486 for machine guns, 148 for mortars, 136 for the anti-tank rifles and 143 for the anti-tank guns had been dug; 16 tanks had been dug into the ground; 56 brick buildings had been converted into firing positions; 48 earth and timber bunkers had been constructed; 228 shelters for the men had been built; and 35 km of terrain had been mined, especially densely on the directions offering good ground for armor, including 13.5 km blocked anti-tank mines; in addition, 24,789 anti-personnel mines had been emplaced.[281] Moreover, these indicators would increase over the two weeks before the start of the Battle of Kursk on 5 July 1943.

It should be noted that all of the steps listed above to strengthen the positions of the right-flank division of the 7th Guards Army were connected primarily with inspections by the Front's command staff, which took place at the end of April. They revealed a number of substantial omissions when strengthening the boundaries of the formations and armies along the entire front. At the personal order of N.F. Vatutin, special commissions were created to eliminate them. For example, a commission formed that included Major General P.F. Lagutin, the deputy commander of the 6th Guards Army; Major General D.I. Turbin, the artillery commander of the 6th Guards Army; Colonel A.A. Funtikov, the chief of staff of the 7th Guards Army's 25th Guards Rifle Corps; Colonel S.A. Kozak, the commander of the 73rd Guards Rifle Division; Colonel P.D. Govorunenko; the artillery commanders of the 6th Guards Army's 23rd Guards Rifle Corps and the 7th Guards Army's 25th Guards Rifle Corps; the divisional engineers of the 81st Guards Rifle Division and 375th Rifle Division; and a number of other important officers. This commission was responsible for analyzing the terrain and developing the optimal steps to strengthen the boundaries of the 6th Guards and 7th Guards Armies. The commission reported:

> According to a decision of this commission, the following formations of the 6th Guards Army were earmarked in order to secure the boundaries: the 93rd Cannon Artillery Regiment, the 493rd Destroyer Anti-tank Artillery Regiment, the 375th Rifle Division's 932nd Artillery Regiment, the 16th Guards Mortar Regiment, and the 265th Mortar Regiment; of the 7th Guards Army: the 173rd Guards Artillery Regiment of the 81st Guards Rifle Division, the 114th Guards Destroyer Anti-tank Artillery Regiment, the 161st Guards Cannon Artillery Regiment and 1/290th Mortar Regiment. In addition, all of the firing means positioned in the following anti-tank strongpoints are to be involved in this: Shishino, Dal'niaia Igumenka, Blizhniaia Igumenka, Postnikov and Staryi Gorod.
>
> The commission also worked out all the measures to employ the second echelon. For example, in the event of a breakthrough by enemy infantry and tanks at the armies' boundary the 73rd Guards Rifle and 375th Rifle Divisions should with fire and counterattacks contain the enemy on the Petropavlovka, Dal'niaia Igumenka, Miasoedovo, Iastrebovo, Razumnoe line, and the 6th Guards Army's 89th Guards Rifle Division (with two regiments) and the 96th Separate Tank Brigade after assembling

281 TsAMO RF, F.477, Op.188378, D.2, ll. 22-59.

in the Khokhlovo, Dal'niaia Igumenka area should counterattack in the direction of Staryi Gorod. The 16th Guards Mortar Regiment and two artillery regiments should support the [Guards Rifle] division.

The 81st Guards Rifle Division, after assembling in the vicinity of the Batratskaia Dacha State Farm, in the event of an enemy breakthrough at the armies' boundary has the task to counterattack the Germans in the Staryi Gorod, Batratskaia Dacha State Farm, Razumnoe direction. The 167th Separate Tank Regiment, the 30th Separate Destroyer Anti-tank Artillery Brigade, the 265th Guards Cannon Artillery Regiment and the 1438th Self-propelled Artillery Regiment are to support the division. Thus, the concentric attacks by the 89th Guards and 81st Guards Rifle Divisions with the attached assets should in cooperation with the units of the first echelon encircle and destroy the enemy that has penetrated at the boundary and restore the position on the armies' adjacent flanks.

The engineer units have been given the assignment to organize the mining of the approaches to Dal'niaia Igumenka, the southern outskirts of Melikhovo, the western outskirts of Sheino, the highway in the Staryi Gorod sector and the woods to the north, the ravine northwest of Hill 212.1 and the road north of there. For cooperation between the armies, communications have been established by radio, telephone and through liaison officers.

It should be stated that the entire work to secure the boundaries dates back to the first half of May 1943. Subsequently certain adjustments have been made: a number of divisions that were occupying a sector in the main defensive belt (for example, the 73rd Guards and 15th Guards Rifle Divisions) have been replaced by fresh divisions. By early July, certain changes also took place in the artillery grouping on the boundaries. However, despite these and other changes, the intent of the Voronezh Front command and that of the armies to secure the boundaries has remained unchanged at every level of command. The Front Commander-in-Chief and the army commanders have personally made repeated visits to the troops and have inspected the organization of the defensive works at the boundaries.[282]

To the above I will add that the Front command staff also took part in ensuring the boundary between the 6th Guards and 7th Guards Armies. In the rear army-level belt of defenses on the axis of the boundary between these armies, in May 1943 two rifle divisions of the 69th Army (the 305th and 107th Rifle Divisions) deployed, and in their rear on the first *front*-level line – the 92nd Guards Rifle Division.

In addition to the objective need to reinforce the armies' boundaries and the boundary between the Voronezh and Southwestern Fronts (always the most vulnerable point in any defense), N.F. Vatutin had other weighty reasons to pay particular attention to this matter in the case of the 7th Guards Army. As already noted above, the Staryi Gorod area was playing a special role in his plan to split von Manstein's two assault groupings. Thus, the General of the Army, having received information from an inspection that both army commanders were paying inadequate

---

282 *Sbornik po obobshcheniiu opyta voiny* [Handbook on the aggregation of the war's experience], No. 11 (Moscow: Voenizdat, 1944), pp. 105-106.

attention to their boundaries, demanded not only to create the commission discussed above, but also between May and the start of the fighting more than once personally visited this area, and not only checked on the execution of decisions and the quality of work done to fortify the sectors (he even visited the frontline regiments), but also provided valuable advice. For example, in the middle of June he once again inspected the 81st Guards Rifle Division together with a member of the Military Council Lieutenant General N.S. Khrushchev, and during this visit suggested to the division commander a unique means of employing the heavy machine guns in the river's flood plain. I.K. Morozov recalled:

> The Germans might force a crossing of the Donets River; its banks were high, 1.5 to 2 meters, which mean the surface of the river was not exposed to fire and remained a large dead zone. [He recommended:] Set the machine guns up lower; make wells and mounts inside them, then cut out embrasures just above the water line by 16-20 centimeters and push away the soil covering the barrel of the machine-gun once it will be necessary. Bring communication trenches to the wells from the rear and make emplacements for the machine guns positioned like "whiskers", in order to place fire on defiladed approaches. Do the work at night, and camouflage it by sunrise. In this fashion, the number of raking machine guns that cover the surface of the Donets had to be increased.[283]

On 15 June 1943, the division command sent a scheme of the division's improved defenses to the headquarters of the 7th Guards Army, with an explanatory note that laid out the organization of fire across the river's surface in the two regiments of the first line in particular detail:

> 1. In the sector of the 235th Guards Rifle Regiment, the 2nd and 3rd Rifle Battalions are occupying the defense behind the Severskii Donets River. In order to cover the river's surface with fire, earth and timber bunkers have been set up for the heavy and light machine guns. In the 2nd Rifle Battalion, there are 10 such bunkers for the heavy machine guns, two of which have been set up in buildings. The other eight have been newly constructed and are covered with 3-4 layers of logs. For the light machine guns, earth and timber bunkers of a light type have been set up covered by a single layer of logs.
> In the 3/235th Guards Rifle Regiment, three bunkers have been set up for heavy machine guns to cover the water's surface, two of which have been established in cellars and one of which is covered by logs; five light earth and timber bunkers have been built for light machine guns, covered by a single layer of logs.
> The direct line that links the bunkers with the river varies between 150 and 750 meters. In the majority of cases, the bank of the Severskii Donets is screened from the bunkers by bushes and reeds. Two observation posts have been set forth in order to keep watch on the surface of the river.

---

283 Morozov, I.K., *Polki srazhalis' po-Gvardeiski* [*Regiments fought like Guardsmen*] (Volgograd, 1962), p. 135.

2. In the sector of the 238th Rifle Regiment, the 3rd Rifle Battalion is occupying a defense behind the Severskii Donets River. Three firing groups have been created in order to cover the river's surface with fire:

First group – consists of three earth and timber bunkers with heavy machine guns;

Second group – one bunker with a heavy machine gun and a light machine gun on a mount, and one rifle entrenchment;

Third group – one bunker with a heavy machine gun, a mount for a light machine gun, and a rifle entrenchment.

All the bunkers have three layers of logs covering them with a diameter of 20-30 centimeters. At a distance of 250 to 500 meters as the crow flies to the river, the entire surface of the water is not exposed to fire, since the river's flood plain out to 200 to 1,000 meters is overgrown with tall grass, reeds and bushes. The constructed system of fire covers the entire basin of the Severskii Donets River on its eastern and western side with fire.

Communication trenches from the regiment commander to the battalion commanders have been completely dug. Communication trenches from the battalion commanders to the company commanders aren't finished. In the 233 Guards Rifle Regiment, a communication trench has been dug from the regiment command post to the division command post but has not been finished in the other regiments.[284]

G.K. Zhukov also traveled to the 7th Guards Army more than once to inspect its defenses. In June, he returned once again, and gave both M.S. Shumilov and N.F. Vatutin a directive: together with the commands of the 57th Army and the Southwestern Front, to reinforce the defenses at the boundary between the two *fronts*. The Marshal of the Soviet Union, like the commander-in-chief of the Southwestern Front Colonel General R.Ia. Malinovsky, believed that there was a large possibility that the Germans would strike precisely at the boundary between the Voronezh Front and Southwestern Front. Indeed, in June I.V. Stalin almost became convinced in this, and he allowed Malinovsky to conduct a partial regrouping of his forces to his right flank, and an order followed to N.F. Vatutin to echelon his forces on his left flank deeply. In order to implement this, a special commission was also created, but its participants had significantly higher ranks. In addition to both army commanders, their artillery commanders, their chiefs of engineers, the commanders of the armored and mechanized forces and so forth, it also included the Voronezh Front's deputy chief of staff. I will dwell on its decisions in more detail below.

In the 24th Guards Rifle Corps, the system of defenses in the period of preparation for the Battle of Kursk also changed substantially and improved relative to the initial scheme, especially on its left flank, and acquired its final form only after 20 June. The reason for this was the fact that the Soviet side had no practical experience in raising such powerful and deep defensive belts. In addition, contradictory intelligence kept arriving periodically. The leadership of the Voronezh Front and of the armies sensed the large responsibility that lay on their shoulders, so again and again they studied the state of affairs in the troops, especially those that were holding

---

284 TsAMO RF, F.25 gv. sk., Op.1, D.12, ll. 56-57.

directions most vulnerable to tanks, and the flanks of the armies, and strove to reinforce them based on the capabilities they had at that moment.

In the sector of Vasil'ev's 24th Guards Rifle Corps, eight likely directions of enemy armored attacks were determined:

1. Maslova Pristan' – Poliana State Farm – Churaevo;
2. Maslova Pristan' – Ustitnka;
3. Titovka – Shebekino;
4. Novaia Tavolzhanka – Shebekino Station – Logovoe;
5. Novaia Tavolzhanka – Pletenevka State Farm and further on toward Voznesenovka or Volchanskie Khutory;
6. Ogurtsovo – Gatishche-2 – northern outskirts of Volchansk;
7. Staritsa – Volchansk – Rubezhnoe;
8. Pervoe Krasnoarmeiskoe – Volchansk.

In order to block the favorable directions for armored attacks, his forces set up 14 anti-tank areas and strongpoints: Karnaukhovka, Maslova Pristan', the Kar'ernaia switchyards, Bezliudovka, Novaia Tavolzhanka, Gatishche-1, Gatishche-2, Prilipy, southwestern outskirts of Volchansk, Sinel'nikovo, Oktiabr'skoe, Pletenevka State Farm, and Hills 167.3 and 162.3.

Of the above listed directions, five ran through the left wing of the 24th Guards Rifle Corps, so strengthening the Nezhigol' River – Prilipy sector received special attention. Until the end of May, the 15th Guards Rifle Division was positioned on the left flank of the 24th Guards Rifle Corps' main defensive belt. Of all four divisions of the army's first line, it had the lengthiest sector – 20 km – while at the same time having only modest assets: the 115th Guards Destroyer Anti-tank Artillery Regiment, 1 and 2/109th Guards Cannon Artillery Regiment, and the 5th Anti-tank Rifle Battalion. In June, according to G.K. Zhukov's directions (with respect to the fact that the left flank of the 7th Guards Army was adjacent to the boundary with the Southwestern Front), large fortification work began to unfold here. At the decision of the joint commission, N.F. Vatutin was supposed to allocate the main forces in order to secure the boundary between the Voronezh and Southwestern Fronts more reliably. M.S. Shumilov received an order to direct the 36th and 15th Guards Rifle Divisions, the 27th Guards Tank Brigade, four artillery regiments, and the 34th Separate Armored Train Battalion to this flank, as well as a mobile anti-tank reserve (the 148th Separate Tank Regiment, the 1670th Destroyer Anti-tank Artillery Regiment and a company of engineers). On its part, the Front command positioned the 270th Rifle Division in the rear belt and also directed it's attention toward the boundary between the 7th Guards and 57th Armies.

Between 29 and 31 May, Major General M.I. Denisenko's 36th Guards Rifle Division was moved up into the army's first echelon to the Nezhigol' – Gatishche-1—Prilipy – northern outskirts of Volchansk line. At the same time, all of the assets held by the previous first-echelon division were left behind for the 36th Guards Rifle Division. After the rotation, striving to firm up the 24th Guards Rifle Corps' left wing and increase the firepower on the forward edge of this division, at the authorization of the Front, M.S. Shumilov first transferred the 15th Guards Rifle Division's 43rd Guards Artillery Regiment to the 36th Guards Rifle Division, and secondly, used the 15th Guards Rifle Division's 44th Guards Rifle Regiment to substitute for a portion of the 36th Guards Rifle Division that had remained in the second echelon (in the western section of Volchansk, Oktiabr'skoe, Point 133.6 area), and moved those troops up into the first echelon. Even so, the density of artillery tubes with a caliber between 45mm and 152mm (not including the guns of the 34th Separate Armored Train Battalion) remained relatively low in Denisenko's division – 8 per kilometer of front.

The army commander had only one means left to address the problem by transferring a portion of his mobile reserve to the division, which he in fact did. In early June, the commander of the 36th Guards Rifle Division received under his operational control the 148th Separate Tank Regiment (33 T-34, 13 T-70 and one T-60). This allowed him to bring up the density of artillery guns to 10.5 per kilometer. M.I. Denisenko then quickly shifted the main forces of the Volchanskie Khutora anti-tank area to the division's left flank. Three companies of the tank regiment assembled in the vicinity of Industrial Plant No. 2 in Volchansk, while one company of T-34 tanks was sent to his right flank (the boundary with the 72nd Guards Rifle Division) to the machine tractor station 1.5 km southeast of Titovka and received the task to prepare counterattacks with the units that were holding the flanks.

Between 31 May and 1 June 1942, the 1529th Heavy Self-propelled Artillery Regiment arrived in the 7th Guards Army and received the order to set up its main positions west of Hill 171.8, which was located in the center behind the 36th Guards Rifle Division's combat positions. In addition, the command of the army's armored and mechanized forces worked out a plan for a possible counterattack with a portion of the left group of the army commander's tank reserve (the 201st Separate Tank Brigade and the 1529th Heavy Self-propelled Artillery Regiment) out of the Bochkovo area toward either flank or the center of the 36th Guards Rifle Division's sector. The forces assigned to defend the boundary received the following assignments:

1. 15th Guards Rifle Division:
   a. Prevent an aggregation of enemy forces on the western bank of the Severskii Donets River at the crossing sites opposite Sovetskoe-1 and Pisarevka with the fire of not less than two battalions;
   b. Destroy the enemy's tanks and infantry with the fire of artillery and mortars as they attempt to cross the Severskii Donets River in the Sovetskoe-1 – Pisarevka sector;
   c. Prepare the place the fire of two battalions on Sovetskoe-1 and Krasnoarmeiskoe-1 and the fire of two battalions on the northern outskirts of Sherstirivka and Petrovka;
   d. Support the counterattack of the second echelon (36th Guards Rifle Division) and tanks toward Ukrainskoe with the fire of two heavy artillery battalions;
   e. Move up two rifle battalions, reinforced with anti-tank guns and anti-tank rifles, in order to defend the southwestern and southern approaches to Volchansk (in the 57th Army's sector of defense);
   f. Ready one reinforced rifle battalion for the defense of the Sinel'nikovo, Oktiabr'skoe, Point 147.6 anti-tank region;
   g. Take up the anti-tank defense of the Point 137.2, Point +6, Point 133.6 with one reinforced rifle battalion, excluding the bridge across the Vol'chia River.
2. The 36th Guards Rifle Division and 148th Separate Tank Regiment:
   a. Prepare a counterattack in two directions: Kim State Farm – Ukrainskoe, and Volchanskie Khutora – Belyi Kolodez'.
   b. Prepare the fire of the division's artillery regiment on the northern exits out of Zemlianoi Iar and the northern slopes of Hills 182.7 and 189.7;

3. 27th Guards Tank Brigade: Prepare for counterattacks in the Volchanskie Khutora – Ukrainskoe and Pokalianoe – Belyi Kolodez' directions.[285]

The heavy reinforcement of the 7th Guards Army's left flank went on for more than a month, but in spite of this, the desired result was not achieved, even though the situation here continued to trouble the Soviet command. Indeed, this is understandable; the sector had only slightly been strengthened in an anti-tank respect – there was still relatively little artillery and the operational density of the rifle units was low. However, by mid-June, Shumilov's army had exhausted all of its own possibilities to strengthen the defense. At this time N.F. Vatutin was sick and bed-ridden, but despite this he continued to ponder this problem. Having analyzed it once again, on the evening of 19 June he summoned the chief of staff of the 7th Guards Army Lieutenant General S.P. Ivanov and directed him to pass a decision to his commander over the telephone:

> Ivanov. Comrade Nikolaev [Vatutin's code name] believes that your steps to strengthen the defense are too little, and has ordered you to do the following:
> 1. It is necessary to strengthen and thicken the combat positions of the 36th Guards Rifle Division, thereby to create a greater density of fire and a strong defense on the forward edge. For this purpose, place one regiment of the 15th Guards Rifle Division in the front line; you decide for yourself the most suitable place for it. In order to fill the created gap and not to weaken the defense of the second echelon, position a regiment of the 213th Rifle Division in place of the 15th Guards Rifle Division's regiment.
> 2. Anticipate the following measures and work them out most meticulously: We are thinking to move Kriuchenkin's 10th Destroyer Brigade[286] to the right flank of your army, and to shift the 8th Destroyer Brigade[287] to the left flank of your army. Equip and form these brigades with a calculation of constant readiness for combat. Send the towing means we are giving you to the two regiments, then finish forming up the others. You are to be ready to regroup the brigades, but are to conduct it only with our authorization according to the situation.
> 3. The 148th Mortar Regiment will arrive for you on the left flank no later than the end of day of 21 June.
> 4. Conduct the regrouping of the rifle regiments and the strengthening of the 36th Guards Rifle Division by the morning of 21 June. That is all.
> Stepnoi.[288] I request that you report to Comrade Nikolaev to confirm the following:
> To have the 36th Guards Rifle Division in a single echelon, and in place of the regiment of the 36th Guards Rifle Division's second echelon to move up a regiment

---

285 Sbornik po obobshcheniiu opyta voiny, No. 11, pp. 105-106.
286 This was the 31st Separate Destroyer Anti-tank Artillery Brigade from the mobile reserve of the Front commander-in-chief, which at this time was still forming up in Korocha.
287 The 30th Separate Destroyer Anti-tank Artillery Brigade, which at this moment was located in the center of the army's defensive position.
288 The code name of M.S. Shumilov.

of the 15th Guards Rifle Division from the army's second echelon, without shifting the regiment of the 213th Rifle Division. The rest I understand. Over.

S.P. Ivanov. As far as I understand you, you do not want the regiment of the 15th Guards Rifle Division to move up to the forward edge. Is that so?

Stepnoi. I presently have the 36th Guards Rifle Division occupying a defense with two regiments in the first echelon and one regiment in the second echelon. I request in order to flesh out the combat positions and to increase the density of fire to array the defense of the 36th Guards Rifle Division in a single echelon, and in place of the 36th Guards Rifle Division's second-echelon regiment, to move up a regiment out of the 15th Guards Rifle Division's second echelon, without touching the units of the 213th Rifle Division. The 15th Guards Rifle Division, in this fashion, will be left without a second echelon. Over.

S.P. Ivanov. No; Comrade Nikolaev does not agree. Given your option, in the event of the slightest breakthrough by the enemy of the 36th Guards Rifle Division's front, the commander of this division will now be in no condition to resist the enemy; he'll have nothing with which to maneuver. To subordinate to him a regiment of a different division means to split up the 15th Guards Rifle Division, and to do this makes no sense. It is better to give a piece of the terrain with a view to one regiment of the 15th Guards Rifle Division, which will subsequently strongly defend it. Consider as well that you have no right to weaken the boundary with the neighbor on the left, and to beggar Comrade Iur'ev[289] hasn't been confirmed. Yet given such an option, if you have a firm opinion about the senselessness of moving up a regiment of the 213th Rifle Division, it will be possible to agree with this. After you sort things out and come to a decision, in accordance with the instructions you've received, report by 1200 on 20 June 1943.[290]

I have specially cited an entire excerpt from this transcript, which touches upon this matter. First, the document presents a clear image of the process of making decisions when constructing the Voronezh Front's lines. Second, it demonstrates the thoroughness with which N.F. Vatutin arranged the Front's system of defenses. Third, it shows at what a high level the question was resolved about positioning even an individual regiment. To this I can add that when working with the files of the 6th Guards Army in the TsAMO RF, I came across documents in which N.F. Vatutin issued an order to shift even separate rifle battalions within the system of the main defenses. Possibly, it is not the job of a Front Commander-in-Chief to engage in such matters, but the reality was such, and we must recognize it in order to understand and really grasp the problems in the history of the Battle of Kursk. Indeed, in conclusion, relying on the transcript, it is possible to picture the rigid frameworks in which (not only) the army commander was located when reaching such decisions that resulted in even insignificant changes in the system of defenses. A similar process of decision-making continued already during the Kursk defensive operation, although at this time the army commander (and the corps commander as well) had more freedom in their decisions due to the demands of the battle's dynamics. In this connection, I want to make an appeal to scholars of the Battle of Kursk: Before hurling accusations at Red

289 The code name for G.K. Zhukov.
290 TsAMO RF, F.203, Op.28423, D.461, l. 91.

Army commanders at all levels in miscalculations and blunders, first picture their place in the system of command and try first to grasp the motivations that directed them when making one or another decision. After all even generals, who obviously enjoyed great authority and control, were still only the executives of the will of higher-ranking commanders and were located within rigid boundaries – both formal and real. Of course, there is no need to say that N.F. Vatutin himself was under such control and pressure, just like other Front commanders.

However, now let us return to the events in the 7th Guards Army at the end of June 1943. After conducting the regrouping, by the start of the Battle of Kursk, the 36th Guards Rifle Division was occupying a defense in the sector: mouth of the Nezhigol' River, (excl.) Sovetskoe-1, Nezhigol' railroad station. As a result, seven rifle battalions arrayed in a single line had been assembled in the first echelon of the main defensive belt, and two more rifle battalions were in the second echelon on the left flank. The army had not yet received the 148th Mortar Regiment, but the decision to transfer Lieutenant Colonel S.V. Shmanov's 31st Separate Anti-tank Artillery Brigade to it proved to be far-sighted. Already on the second day of the German offensive, the brigade would be committed into the fighting in the sector of the 7th Guards Army and would play a key role in the struggle against the III Panzer Corps assault grouping, which had broken through from Razumnoe to the Iastrebovo – Solov'ev Collective Farm area. As is known from history, the enemy did not launch an attack against the 36th Guards Rifle Division as was expected by the Soviet side. In the course of Operation Citadel, the enemy wouldn't conduct any active combat operations in the division's sector (other than a reconnaissance probe on 5 July). Therefore, Shumilov would be forced to shift a significant portion of the assets from it on the very first day of the German offensive in order to parry the penetrations made in the line of the neighboring 72nd Guards Rifle Division, which by mid-day on 5 July had been carved apart into several pieces.

Further to this, it is impossible to anticipate everything in war; despite their high posts, neither G.K. Zhukov nor N.F. Vatutin nor M.S. Shumilov were prophets in the given situation; they simply sought to carry out orders conscientiously, based not only on the needs of the troops, but also the Voronezh Front's capabilities, which weren't so large. In the situation with the 72nd Guards Rifle Division, judging from available records, the Front command was relying to a significant extent on the difficult terrain (the river and its swampy flood plain) and the fortification of the army's belts, even though when planning the defense of the 7th Guards Army, an attack against the boundary between the 25th and 24th Guards Rifle Corps was viewed at every level of command as one of the enemy's most likely options. So, despite the fact that the forward edge of the 72nd Guards Rifle Division was swampy, it was not assigned a lengthy sector – one of just 15 km – while its neighboring 78th Guards Rifle Division was given one even smaller (just 10 km of frontage). Regardless, the 25th Guards Rifle Corps' commander Safiulin had been ordered to work out a maneuver and a pivot of the facing of the 81st Guards Rifle Division's artillery assets (given the need) toward the sector of the left-flank 78th Guards Rifle Division (the neighbor of the 72nd Guards Rifle Division). The combat formation of the 72nd Guards and 78th Guards Rifle Divisions had been arranged in two echelons, and by the quantity of received artillery assets, the 72nd Guards Rifle Division stood in third place in the army. In addition to three artillery battalions (28 76mm to 152mm guns) and the army's 101st Anti-tank Rifle Battalion (59 anti-tank rifles and 262 men), the division commander received subordinate the 1st Company of the army's 175th Guards Engineer Battalion (70 men), 66th Penal Company (234 men) and the 185th Blocking Detachment (185 men). However, it must be recognized that this was not very substantial aid in a struggle against tanks. The figures are unforgiving – the center of the 7th Guards Army's defenses was the weakest in terms of assets. In Losev's and Skvortsov's divisions, which Army Detachment Kempf's III Panzer Corps would strike on 5 July, had the lowest average density of artillery with a caliber between 45mm and 152mm per kilometer of front: in the 78th Guards Rifle Division, nine artillery tubes per kilometer, and in the 72nd Guards Rifle Division even less, only eight artillery tubes per kilometer. However, this does not mean that the Soviet side made an obvious mistake here.

Considering that the 78th Guards Rifle Division was fated to take on Army Detachment Kemp's main attack, let us dwell in more detail on its combat formation. By the start of the Battle of Kursk, Skvortsov's Guards rifle division was the weakest of all of the army's division in terms of manpower. It had 8,346 men on its roster, including 849 officers, 2,317 non-commissioned officers and 5,180 enlisted men.[291] It received the assignment to defend a sector running from a point 1 km southwest of the labor correctional colony through Dal'nie Peski to Nizhnii Ol'shanets. The terrain here had a number of characteristics which substantially hindered the construction of a strong defense. Major General A.V. Skvortsov reported:

> The steep slopes on the western bank of the Severskii Donets River, the system of heights that were covered by woods to a depth of 2-3 km from the forward edge, and the settlements running along the western bank gave an advantage to the enemy to arrange his forces stealthily, while the availability of graded dirt roads leading to the front and parallel to it enabled the enemy to assemble forces and means smoothly for an offensive in any direction and to conduct concealed maneuvers with reserves opposite the division. The ground on the eastern bank is a lowland, which gradually rises to the east and is deprived of natural cover. The open terrain is observable from the enemy's side to the entire depth of defense and created difficulties when masking the disposition of our forces, the maneuvering of reserves, and complicated the actions of counterattacking units. The absence of commanding heights made the organization of observation posts difficult and did not allow the observation of the enemy's combat positions. The lack of highways and improved roads in the division's sector and the 100 km distance to the Volokolovka supply base prevented the complete and timely provisioning of the personnel with the materiel for conducting combat.[292]

The division's sector of defense was organized like that for the entire army; it consisted of a main and a secondary defensive belt, the former with three lines of trenches and the latter, which ran along the Belgorod-Titovka railroad, with two lines of trenches. The regiments were arranged in two echelons, with Major General I.A. Khitsov's 228th Guards Rifle Regiment and Major D.S. Khorolenko's 225th Guards Rifle Regiment in the first echelon, and Major S.A. Arshinov's 223rd Guards Rifle Regiment in the second. Their assigned sectors were unequal. The right-flank 228th Guards Rifle Regiment (reinforced with two companies of the 4th Anti-tank Rifle Battalion and two batteries of a separate destroyer anti-tank artillery battalion – eight 45mm anti-tank guns) was deployed on a line running from a point 1 km southwest of the labor correctional colony to Dorogobuzheno, which extended for around 5 km. The regiment was first

---

291 Ibid., page not numbered.
292 TsAMO RF, F.1225, Op.1, D.11, l. 108.

of all to prevent a penetration through its left flank to the Razumnoe and Generalovka villages. I.A. Khitsov, like his neighbors, received one artillery battalion (2/158th Guards Artillery Regiment) as an asset, which had set up its main firing positions 1 km northeast of Razumnoe. This village was located on the boundary between the 228th Guards and 225th Guards Rifle Regiments, and the strongpoint here was supposed to serve as a firebreak in the event of an enemy attempt to split their common defense.

The left-flank 225th Guards Rifle Regiment (with one company of the 4th Anti-tank Rifle Battalion) was defending a 7-km sector from (excl.) Dorogobuzheno to Nizhnii Ol'shanets. The 1/158th Guards Artillery Regiment, which had deployed together with the 3/158th Guards Rifle Regiment in the anti-tank strongpoint of Krutoi Log (which was located behind the secondary positions of the 225th Guards Rifle Regiment) were prepared to support it. In addition, to the left of Krutoi Log, but still within the sector of the 225th Guards Rifle Regiment, the 3rd Battalion of the 213th Rifle Division's 671st Artillery Regiment dug in; it had been transferred to the 78th Guards Rifle Division commander as his personal reserve.

The 223rd Guards Rifle Regiment (minus one battalion) was defending the Generalovka – Krutoi Log – Hill 164.7 sector. It had the task to hold its line along the Razumnaia River, and in the event of a breakthrough of the division's first echelon by the enemy, it was to eliminate the penetrating enemy with a counterattack together with the division's combined-arms reserve (1/223rd Guards Rifle Regiment and a battery of the 80th Separate Destroyer Anti-tank Artillery Battalion).

Already when allocating the sectors, and then when organizing the 225th Guards Rifle Regiment's combat formation, two important factors became embedded in the process, which reduced the staying power of its line even relative to that of its neighbor on the right. First, its forward battalions were holding a line of 3.5 km, while at the same time the neighboring 228th Guards Rifle Regiment was holding a sector of just 2 to 2.5 km. Second, even though the battalions of both regiments were echeloned in depth, in the 228th Guards Rifle Regiment the third battalion was positioned compactly behind the boundary between the two forward battalions, while the 3/225th Guards Rifle Regiment had been dispersed by company. For example, the 7th Rifle Company was defending the Razumnoe switchyards, located in the second defensive belt, while the 8th and 9th Companies were somewhat to the east, in the Krutoi Log anti-tank strongpoint. Certain specialized publications published back in the Soviet era also pay attention to the low density of forces on the 78th Guards Rifle Division's left flank. For example, in the book *Taktika v boevykh primerakh: Divisiia* [*Tactics in combat examples: The division*] under the general editorship of General of the Army A.I. Radzievsky, there is the observation:

> The terrain conditions did not allow the enemy to launch the main attack along the Razumnaia River. The presence of settlements within the boundaries of the sector and on its forward edge, which had been prepared for a defense, and the unsuitable ground for the operations of attacking forces contributed to the creation of a strong defense even with fewer forces. That way it would have been more sensible to organize a significant density of firing means on the division's left flank.[293]

---

293 *Taktika v boevykh primerakh: Diviziia* [*Tactics in combat examples: The division*] (Moscow: Voenizdat, 1976), p. 202.

Ideally, in fact it would have made more sense to use some of the assets attached to the 228th Guards Rifle Regiment to reinforce the 225th Guards Rifle Regiment instead. Even without this, the conditions for creating an insurmountable line of defense were almost ideal: the boundary between the regiments ran along the swampy basin of the Razumnaia River; the village of Razumnoe itself had been turned into an anti-tank strongpoint; on the forward edge (which extended for less than 5 km) there were two villages arranged in a line; and the remaining ground was partially swampy and in part covered with orchards. However, for division commander Skvortsov, theoretical calculations weren't paramount when laying out the position for the 228th Guards Rifle Regiment. Judging from archival documents, when allocating the sectors to the regiments, not only the division commander and corps commander checked them (as was stipulated by regulations), but even M.S. Shumilov and N.F. Vatutin in person. The reason for such fixed attention was the special arrangement of the Voronezh Front's defenses to split von Manstein's assault groupings that has already been mentioned above (the "Vatutin Plan"). The 228th Guards Rifle Regiment was deliberately strengthened to a certain excess (based on the available forces), in order to guarantee, as far as possible, the shielding of the 81st Guards Rifle Division's left flank. Remember, together with the 375th Rifle Division, the 81st Guards Rifle Division occupied a special place in the system of the main belt of defenses. This was the reason for both the narrow sector and the larger amount of artillery given to the 228th Guards Rifle Regiment relative to its neighbor, the 225th Guards Rifle Regiment, as well as the preparation for the shifting the fire of 2/290th Mortar Regiment from the sector of the 81st Guards Rifle to the sector of the 228th Guards Rifle Regiment.

In connection with this, the following question is appropriate: "Wasn't the Front command being distracted by reinforcing the 81st Guards Rifle Division and creating an impenetrable fortress in the Staryi Gorod area, and thereby overlooking the weaknesses in other, less significant sectors?" In fact, if N.F. Vatutin and M.S. Shumilov understood that the situation on the left flank of the 78th Guards Rifle Division was fraught with serious consequences, then why did not they react to this, as was the case in the 6th Guards Army? In the latter army, the regiments of all the divisions that were holding the main defensive belt were organized into a line, even though it was apparent that the 67th Guards and 52nd Guards Rifle Divisions had insufficient strength to cover certain vulnerable sectors. So, with the agreement of the Front's Military Council, I.M. Chistiakov made several artillery battalions each operationally subordinate to their commanders from the divisions of the second echelon (the 90th Guards and 51st Guards Rifle Divisions), as well as two rifle battalions each. In the 7th Guards Army, only the 36th Guards Rifle Division was reinforced in a similar manner at the expense of the 15th Guards Rifle Division. The impression forms that the Front command either underestimated the danger to the center of the army's defenses, or were acting deliberately.

Certain scholars express the opinion that N.F. Vatutin, realizing that the initial German attack would be very powerful and that a penetration of the forward edge was unavoidable, deliberately left weakly covered sectors in the lines of each army of the first echelon (or at least in two of them) on the likely directions of the enemy's main attack. According to this conjecture, it was in these places that the defense would first begin to crack, and where the enemy would persistently attempt to introduce fresh forces into these breaches. However, the path forward would lead to a dead end, since directly beyond this gap, a snare would lay in wait for the Germans, which had been set by the Soviet forces – difficult terrain, with a multitude of unpleasant "surprises" prepared by the Soviet engineers, or a powerful flanking attack (or all taken together). However, if this was Vatutin's ploy, supposedly it did not work in full. As an example, one can cite the case of the 6th Guards Army's 52nd Guards Rifle Division.[294] Despite that it was covering the critical direction – the Belgorod - Oboian' highway, its defenses were unable to withstand the strong German attack already on the first day of the battle, and after 17 hours of combat, the II SS Panzer Corps was able to overcome them. At first glance this seems to be very similar to the case of the 7th Guards Army's 78th Guards Rifle Division.

In fact, in the war years when conducting major operations there were cases when the Soviet side resorted to cunning ploys of various types in order to confuse the enemy: diversionary attacks, feigned attempts to force a crossing of a river in places where the main forces were not to be committed, etc. A whole number of examples confirm this even with respect to the plans to use such methods when defending the Kursk bulge. It is possible that the Voronezh Front command considered such options when discussing the future operation. However, to date not all of the transcripts of N.F. Vatutin's discussions with the General Staff and the *Stavka* have been de-classified, so it is premature to come to any final conclusions. Today, however, on the basis of documents that are accessible to scholars it is possible to state with confidence that there is still no indisputable evidence that confirms whether such a plan ever existed or implemented. In addition, the nervous atmosphere that reigned in the General Staff and on the fronts in June 1943 speaks against this argument, since the heavy memories of the failure in Ukraine in February-March 1943 were still fresh, just like the German recollections of Stalingrad were to enemy. Of course, these catastrophes are not on par with each other, but their emotional impacts were similar. However, Stalingrad did not teach Hitler anything, but only prompted him to the new adventure at Kursk. In contrast, the Soviet side by this time had lost even more battles and engagements, so when preparing for the summer campaign of 1943, their approach to decision-making was more prudent; for example, despite the enormous reserves it had accumulated, the decision was that it was better to wait and adopt a deliberate defense. Like no one else, Vatutin understood full well the weaknesses of the Front's troops: the poor training of the soldiers, the poor preparation of the command staff up to the corps level inclusively, the problems with mobility, etc. In this situation he was not up to toying with the Nazis, and Moscow was strictly demanding just one thing – to create a strong defense out of the available forces and means, which would guarantee against the failures and setbacks of 1942. Therefore, he was relying first of all on elaborate and strong defensive belts and counterattacks in the depth. As for the miscalculations that became evident already in the course of the fighting, well, no one is insured against them, and at the time the General of the Army did not have the power to prepare for every contingency.

By the start of the Battle of Kursk, not without justification the Front command believed that the line of the 81st Guards Rifle Division had been sufficiently fortified. Therefore, the second-echelon 73rd Guards Rifle Division was directed toward regaining a position (in the event of a German penetration) and assisting the 78th Guards Rifle Division in holding its sector of defense. The shifting of Kozak's division by the end of 2 July 1943 to the Hill 205.5, Hill 191.8, Solov'ev Collective Farm, Batratskaia Dacha State Farm, Hill 210.4 line behind the 78th Guards Rifle Division on the left flank of the 25th Guards Rifle Corps testifies to this. By 2300 the division without its artillery regiment had reassembled in the woods 4 km east of Iastrebovo and began

---

294 Lopukhovsky, L., *Prokhorovka bez grifa sekretnosti* [*Prokhorovka without the seal of secrecy*] (Moscow: Iauza, Eksmo, 2012), p. 156.

to take up its indicated position. However, on 3 July a directive arrived from the headquarters of the 25th Guards Rifle Corps: "Be ready to move to the northeast", which is to say, nearer to the positions of the 78th Guards Rifle Division's second-echelon regiment. Accordingly, at the final moment, the Soviet side had fully figured out the enemy's plan and created the greatest density of forces and means opposite the spearhead of Army Detachment Kempf's attack. The 81st Guards Rifle Division had the largest possible number of assets and density of artillery per kilometer of frontage, higher than anywhere else across the entire front (not to mention the extremely high preparations of its defensive lines), while an entire division was deployed in the second echelon behind the 78th Guards Rifle Division! After this, it is hard to agree with authors of works on the Battle of Kursk, even with such authorities as Marshal of the Soviet Union K.K. Rokossovsky, who accuse N.F. Vatutin of miscalculations and errors when preparing his system of defenses and arranging his Front's forces before the start of the battle.[295]

As is known, the basis of a successful, long-term defense is the commander's availability of full-strength reserve formations and armies, especially artillery and mobile (armored) reserves. Thanks to them, the defending rifle units have the possibility to neutralize quickly the enemy's superiority at the points where he launches his strongest attacks. In the course of preparing for the Battle of Kursk, for the first time in the war, the Soviet side was able to create operational mobile reserves and reserves of anti-tank guns not only in armies and corps, but also in divisions and even rifle regiments. In the 7th Guards Army, relative to its neighbor on the right (the 6th Guards Army), these reserves were rather modest. Nevertheless, the divisions that were holding its main defensive belt also received additional cannon, mortar and even tank regiments.

By the start of the battle, Shumilov had an impressive amount of artillery, but it was inadequate for holding a 53-km sector of front. No replenishments were anticipated, so the army commander, based on tactical assessment of the terrain and the approximate enemy strength, decided to use his assets primarily to reinforce the right flank, since the Mikhailovka bridgehead and the boundary with the 6th Guards Army were located here. He concentrated the bulk of his artillery assets – two cannon artillery regiments (34 152mm howitzers) and a heavy mortar regiment (36 120mm mortars) in the sector of the 81st Guards Rifle Division. The third cannon artillery regiment was shared between the two other forward divisions; two of its battalions (12 152mm howitzers) went to the 36th Guards Rifle Division on his left flank, and the third – to the 72nd Guards Rifle Division.

Even so, as already mentioned, in order to increase the density of artillery fire on the main defensive belt, the army commander was forced to subordinate anywhere from two artillery battalions up to a full artillery regiment to the commanders of the frontline divisions from the divisions of the second echelon. In addition, in order to counter the heavy German Tiger tanks, which the Front's troops had already encountered in the course of the February and March 1943 fighting for Khar'kov, Shumilov, with the authorization of the Front's Military Council, directed to deploy 12 122mm howitzers in the positions of the 72nd Guards Rifle Division and to prepare firing positions for the heavy 152mm howitzers in order to fire directly at the German tanks. I will remind the reader that at this time, howitzers represented a highly valuable weapon, and it was categorically banned to use them directly at the front. In the event that this order

---

295 See Rokossovsky, K.K., *Soldatskii dolg* [*Soldier's duty*] (Moscow: Veche, 2013), p. 251. For a full discussion of this argument between Rokossovsky, Vatutin, and their adherents, see Zamulin, *Battle of Kursk: Neglected and Controversial Aspects* [Solihull: Helion and Company, 2017].

was violated and the howitzers were lost, its commander would face a trial in front of a military tribunal. Only at a critical moment of the Battle of Kursk, on 9 July 1943, was the leadership of the Voronezh Front forced to give permission to bring up the howitzer regiments into direct firing positions in the sector of the 6th Guards Army as well. Thus, by the start of the fighting, the divisions of the 7th Guards Army's first echelon had the following unit assets:

1. 81st Guards Rifle Division: 161st Cannon Artillery Regiment, 153rd Guards Artillery Regiment (from the 73rd Guards Rifle Division), the 290th Mortar Regiment, the 114th Guards Destroyer Anti-tank Artillery Regiment, the 97th Guards and 315th Guards Mortar Regiments, and the 2nd Anti-tank Rifle Battalion.'
2. 78th Guards Rifle Division: 3/671st Artillery Regiment (from the 213th Rifle Division) and the 4th Anti-tank Rifle Battalion;
3. 72nd Guards Rifle Division: 3/109th Guards Army Cannon Artillery Regiment, 1 and 2/671st Artillery Regiment (from the 213th Rifle Division) and the 1st Anti-tank Rifle Battalion;
4. 36th Guards Rifle Division: 43rd Guards Artillery Regiment (from 15th Rifle Division), 1 and 2/109th Guards Army Cannon Artillery Regiment, the 115th Guards Destroyer Anti-tank Artillery Regiment, the 5th and 6th Anti-tank Rifle Battalions, the 148th Separate Tank Regiment and the 34th Separate Armored Train Battalion.

In case the calculations proved to be not quite accurate and the enemy launched the main attack at a place where it was not expected, or conducted a breakthrough in a less protected sector, the artillery headquarters of the 7th Guards Army foresaw a maneuver of the attached cannon and mortar units, as well as organic divisional artillery regiments, and the shifting of their fire into adjacent sectors when organizing the plan of fire. For example:

a. The 161st Cannon Artillery Regiment planned to shift its fire to the north (by 90^0) into the sector of the 6th Guards Army's 375th Rifle Division on its right, or to pivot it around in the event of a penetration of the 78th Guards Rifle Division's lines, and a maneuver to support the 73rd Guards Rifle Division when it launched its counterattack in the direction of Sabynino;
b. The 265th Guards Cannon Artillery Regiment planned to pivot its fire by 90^0 to the south into the sector of the 78th Guards Rifle Division;
c. The 2/290th Mortar Regiment was designated for shifting its fire by 90^0 to the south into the sector of the 78th Guards Rifle Division, and for a maneuver to the area of Nizhnii Ol'shanets;
d. The 1st and 2nd Artillery Battalions of the 109th Cannon Artillery Regiment planned to shift their fire to the south by 90^0 or to maneuver to support its neighbor on the left, the 57th Army's 19th Rifle Division.
e. The 97th Guards Mortar Regiment was to maneuver its rocket launchers across the entire front in order to support all of the frontline divisions.

The army commander's own anti-tank reserve included the 30th Separate Destroyer Anti-tank Artillery Brigade with two of its regiments deployed on the Starikovo – Kupino – Krasnaia

Poliana line (its third regiment did not have any guns); the 1669th Army Destroyer Anti-tank Artillery Regiment in firing positions in the areas of Hill 133.6, the Arbuzovsky switch yards and the southern outskirts of Volchanskie Khutora (two of its batteries were on the southern outskirts of Volchansk). He also had at his disposal the 1670th Destroyer Anti-tank Artillery Regiment, although it had only four serviceable anti-tank guns and was not ready for combat.

The anti-tank artillery brigade was positioned in the center of the army's second belt of defenses, but in the event of a German armored breakthrough on the flanks, it was to be ready to move out to the threatened sectors. For this purpose, firing positions were ready for it on directions that offered good ground for armored operations – gun emplacements, foxholes for the crews, stowage pits for the shells, and access ramps for the vehicles. Analogous work was also done in the 1669th Destroyer Anti-tank Artillery Regiment, which was planned for use both for active operations on the left flank (including in order to support the adjacent 57th Army as well) and in the center of the army's sector. In addition, N.F. Vatutin when devising the plan for employing his own mobile anti-tank reserves foresaw maneuvering them from the Korocha area (where they were assembled before the battle) to the right flank or center of Shumilov's 7th Guards Army.

Back in May, the commanders of all the artillery regiments reconnoitered the routes of movement for maneuvers together with the rifle unit commanders, and prepared auxiliary positions and observation posts for shifting fire into adjacent sectors. Unfortunately, the plans for switching fire, especially that of the 81st Guards Rifle Division's artillery assets, to the sector of the 78th Guards Rifle Division did not pan out in the first two days of the defensive operation, with the exception of the 2nd Mortar Battalion of the 290th Mortar Regiment. The artillery regiments and rocket-launching regiments were deployed too distant from the forward edge of the 78th Guards Rifle Division and were unable to place effective fire on the enemy's crossing sites and bridgeheads. So, for example, the command of the 25th Guards Rifle Corps already on the morning of 5 July was forced to make a decision to shift guns from a number of regiments out of the 81st Guards Rifle Division's sector to the corps' left flank.

Commanders at every level are skittish about their flanks, so M.S. Shumilov back in April ordered for the artillery commanders of the divisions and corps to reconnoiter their flanks before planning the system of covering them; to determine the necessary forces and means to secure them; as well as to select personally the combat positions for the artillery units. In addition, the army commander wanted to make sure that direct telephone communications existed between all of the division commanders. For this purpose, the artillery headquarters of the 7th Guards Army established telephone and radio communications with the command of both the Southwestern Front's 57th Army and the 93rd Cannon Artillery Regiment of the 6th Guards Army's 27th Heavy Cannon Artillery Brigade (which was assigned to cover the boundary with the 7th Guards Army on the part of the 6th Guards Tank Army) and laid down a direct telephone line between the 93rd Cannon Artillery Regiment and the 81st Guards Rifle Division's 161st Guards Cannon Artillery Regiment. Shared observation posts were also set up for the latter two artillery regiments. The 36th Guards Rifle Division on the left also had shared observation posts with the 57th Army's right-flanking 15th Rifle Division.

The 69th Army was occupying a defense with a frontage of 120 km that stretched from Prokhorovka Station down to the Voronezh Front's left-hand boundary in the Efremovka area. Five divisions were defending this sector and arranged in a single echelon. Thus, on average each division was holding a front of 22-28 km, depending on the significance of its sector. This was approximately twice larger than that dictated by regulations.

As on the Central Front, the first two defensive belts were erected exclusively by the personnel of the rifle divisions and specialized engineer units, while civilians took significant part in construction of the rear line of defenses. Table 17 presents the number of Kursk civilians (today, Belgorod) Oblast that were mobilized for fortification work.

Table 17: The civilian population of Kursk (present-day Belgorod) Oblast, who were mobilized for fortification labor in the sector of the Voronezh Front as of 1 July 1943[296]

District	Existing number of collective farm workers capable of laboring	Mobilized for work			
		On lines	On airfields	On roads	Total
Belenikhino	5,480	2,000	600	150	2,750
Prokhorovka	10,360	2,900	1,900	700	5,500
Ivniansk	11,545	2,500	200	700	3,400
Korocha	11,757	1,700	1,500	700	3,900
Babrovo-Dvorsky	7,005	3,000	1,500	-	4,500
Bol'she-Troitsky	6,200	3,000	300	300	3,600
Valuiky	7,497	4,000	400	70	4,470
Veliko-Mikhailovka	66,800	2,000	300	25	2,825
Volokonovka	9,440	5,500	300	75	5,875
Chernianka	9,800	2,500	300	40	2,840
Novyi Oskol	13,906	4,500	300	40	4,840
Skorodniansk	7,432	2,500	1,500	700	4,700
Staryi Oskol	14,787	3,500	1,500	75	5,075
Urazovo	5,800	2,500	400	50	2,950
Total:	**127,809**	**42,100**	**11,000**	**3,725**	**57,225**[297]

The Prokhorovka railroad station, near to which the culminating engagement of the Kursk defensive operation in the south took place, was situated on the edge of the rear defensive belt. Its forward edge on the Prokhorovka direction ran along the line: (excl.) Bogoroditskoe, Teterevino, Zhimolostnoe, Novoselovka, Vypolzovka, Mazikino. From Prokhorovka Station,

---

296 Vo imia Pobedy (Belgorodchina v Velikoi Otechestvennoi Voine 1941-1945). Po dokumentam i materialam oblastnogo arkhiva [In the name of Victory (the Belgorod area in the Great Patriotic War 1941-1945. According to documents and materials of the Oblast archive)] (Belgorod, 2000), s. 132.
297 The existing number of labor-capable workers have been taken from information regarding the number who signed up for war bonds. The actual number of collective farmers, which could be mobilized for labor on the defensive works was less than 30-40% of the total population of collective farmers, since the total population includes women who had young children and by law were not subject to mobilization.

the Bogoroditskoe – Teterevino sector ran for 12 km, the Zhimolostnoe – Novoselovka sector – for 9 km, and from Vypolzovka to Mazikino – 18 km.

At a point 3.5 km southwest of Prokhorovka's outskirts lay the final major anti-tank obstacle before reaching the village: an anti-tank ditch that blocked the Prokhorovka – Iakovlevo road and the kilometer of terrain passable by tanks to the north of the road. The ditch was supposed to be excavated by the local population and the men of the 14th Separate Destroyer Anti-tank Artillery Brigade, which comprised the Front Commander-in-Chief's anti-tank artillery reserve. By the beginning of July 1943, the ditch was not finished, but the approaches to it had been mined.

Throughout the entire period of preparations to repulse the enemy's offensive, which on the Voronezh Front officially ran from 27 March to 3 July 1943, the work to create the defensive lines, fortify the terrain, emplace artificial obstacles and build infrastructure went with great intensity on the part of all of the Front's men and the civilians who resided in this area. At the same time, because of both objective factors and subjective reasons, large problems arose which affected the pace of the construction, as well as its quality. N.F. Vatutin was personally monitoring the defensive works as they went up, and most attentively followed the preparation of the lines, striving as much as possible to hasten and improve their readiness until the moment the Germans finally went on the offensive. For this purpose, he repeatedly drove out to the troops and dispatched large control commissions, which together with the commands of the formations checked both the implementation of the work and the quality of the completed sites. They discussed shortcomings, put together decrees that set specific deadlines for eliminating the revealed defects and met with the Front's Military Council. Then the commissions would return without fail to the problem locations and inspect them again, as the work was being done to fix them.

Indeed, indisputably the army commander played the key role in organizing this important and mission-critical measure, but each of them regarded this work differently, and far from always with the appropriate level of responsibility and zeal. The majority of them spent days and nights at the front, but there were also those who neglected their duties, and they had to be reminded several times, even by the General Staff. I will cite just one document, General A.I. Antonov's letter to the Chief of Staff of the Voronezh Front from 1 May 1943:

> An inspection conducted at a directive of the *Stavka* and the Front by General Staff officers in units of the 40th Army established:
> a. The defensive work to create a strong defense, particularly an anti-tank defense, is being done slowly and unsatisfactorily, without the due control on the part of the command staff and headquarters.
> b. The forward edge in a number of places has been laid down poorly in a tactical sense and offers limited fields of fire or observation.
> c. Strongpoints and centers of resistance have not been adapted for an all-round defense.
> d. Boundaries are poorly secured.
> e. Anti-tank reserves haven't been allocated and all the means are distributed evenly across the front.
> f. Vigilance and combat readiness in the units and elements are on a low level.
> g. The civilian population is continuing to reside even at the front, cultivating their kitchen gardens.

h. An entire number of intolerable manifestations have been revealed in the everyday services to the soldiers (undergarments haven't been changed in months, men are walking around in winter uniforms, the rations are unsatisfactory, etc.)

The aforementioned problems are known to Comrade Moskalenko from numerous written reports of officers, but plainly, no suitable efforts have been undertaken in order to eliminate them.

Report by 5 May on the concrete steps that have been taken by the Front command to eliminate these shortcomings in the units of the 40th Army.[298]

It was at the end of May that an emergency situation arose, which not only affected the pace of the defensive works on the main defensive belt, but also forced the commanders at every level to plan and approach the work with more diligence. The Front leadership realized that it had been unsuccessful in concealing such large-scale works from the enemy. The German intelligence was making extensive efforts to gather intelligence about the Russians' intentions. For this purpose, they were maintaining around the clock observation of the forward edge, prisoners were regularly being taken, and in particular the Germans succeeded in probing the combat outposts of the first-echelon divisions. Intelligence agents were being dropped by parachute into the rear areas, and Red Army men who'd been taken prisoner in the winter and spring of 1943 were recruited and dispatched under the guise of returning to their divisions. Such a case was revealed, in particular, in the 51st Guards Rifle Division. The adversary was not above using even adolescents from occupied territory to obtain information. However, aerial reconnaissance flights proved to be the most effective. Reconnaissance aircraft were systematically photographing the forward edge of the Front's first-echelon armies. After developing the film, the photographs arrived at the headquarters of the Fourth Panzer Army and Army Group South. Comparing the acquired images with those taken just a week or two before, their staff officers could clearly see how the ground opposite their front was changing. Thus, for the enemy, the plan of the Soviet command to meet the offensive with a deeply-echeloned defense was no secret.

In this situation, the primary task for the Fourth Panzer Army's command was to analyze the system of anti-tank defenses and to determine precisely the concentrations of artillery and tanks in the sectors that had been selected for the breakthrough. Indeed, it must be said that German intelligence service was quite successful in this. At the end of May, on the left flank of the 6th Guards Army, a German aircraft was shot down (over the sector of the 375th Rifle Division); its pilot survived and was captured. He was found to have a map of the forward edge of the 67th Guards, 52nd Guards and 375th Rifle Divisions. When this map was spread out in the Operations Department of the Voronezh Front's headquarters, it was found to have the scheme of these division's defenses depicted on it. The map proved to be very similar to the Soviet map, and in certain places the combat positions and firing positions, particularly of the artillery and tanks, had seemingly been copied from the authentic Soviet map. For example, all of the dug-in shelters for the tanks of the 245th Separate Tank Regiment, which was attached to the 67th Guards Rifle Division, were indicated on the captured map. For the Soviet side, the capture of this information was both a major success and a large headache. It should be noted that the

---

298 Russkii arkhiv. Velikaia Otechestvennaia voina, No. 23 [12 (3)] (Moscow: Terra, 1999), p. 128.

capture of such a valuable document in the sector of the 6th Guards Army was the sole case of such a type in the period of preparing for the Battle of Kursk.

After becoming familiar with the captured materials, the Front leadership quickly worked out a plan to neutralize the information gained by the enemy. In the process, it addressed not only that which was shown on the map, but also on any other possible map that the enemy might have had for the other armies of the first echelon, and this meant the digging of hundreds of new firing positions and kilometers of communication trenches, which would entail the excavation of tons of soil. Combat Order No. 0059 from the chief of staff of the 6th Guards Army's 67th Guards Rifle Division Colonel A.A. Dokolin on 1 June 1943 read:

> To the commanders of the 196th Guards, 199th Guards, 201st Guards Rifle Regiments and of the 245th Mortar Regiment.
> To the artillery commander:
> 1. Throughout the entire period of defense, the enemy has been conducting and continues to conduct thorough close-range overflights by aircraft over the combat positions of our units, the areas of the artillery and mortar firing positions, tanks, and obstacles, both on the forward edge and in the depth of the defenses.
>   A captured map of a German pilot, whose He-126 was shot down on 28 May 1943 by the fire of infantry weapons in the vicinity of the Home of Invalids shows that the enemy has managed to disclose a number of firing positions of our artillery and tanks, as well as observation posts and command posts.
>   The division commander has ordered:
> 1. Conduct a replacement of firing positions for the artillery, tanks and mortars and the observation posts and command posts that have been revealed by enemy aircraft, as shown and which in fact coincide with the map I've sent.
> 2. Conduct the exchange at night after preparing dummy guns and tanks, in order to position them in the revealed positions while observing thorough concealment.
> 3. Thoroughly camouflage the areas of the firing positions for the artillery and tanks, as well as the observation posts and command posts, and forbid superfluous movement during overflights by enemy reconnaissance aircraft.
> 4. Report the results of the implemented work by 12.00 on 2 June 1943.[299]

According to the demands of the Front headquarters, each division of the 6th Guards Army devised its own plan to increase the camouflaging of the positions, equipment and heavy weapons. Here, for example, here are the planned steps contained in the document prepared by the 52nd Rifle Division's Operations Department:

> 1. <u>Materiel of the artillery, tanks, tractors and vehicles</u>. Mask the firing positions from aerial and ground observation:
>   a. Prepare ground-level camouflage from improvised and authorized means;

---

299 TsAMO RF, F.1119, Op.1, D.30, l. 93.

    b. Construct and emplace dummy batteries and tanks in the amount of 25-30 percent of the actual number of combat batteries and tanks;
    c. Conceal and completely camouflage all the roads leading to the firing positions of the artillery and tanks out to a distance of at least 500 meters;
    d. Construct shelters with canopies for the guns and deep apertures with steps and platforms for conducting fire at tanks at the necessary moment;
    e. Distort the outline of the entrenchments with the use of camouflage.
2. <u>Defensive installations, anti-tank obstacles, trenches and bunkers</u>. Camouflage them by means of:
    a. Concealing completely and partially with turf; camouflaging and masking with authorized camouflage netting and nets crafted from rope, grass, sticks, wire, etc.
    b. Dressing the ground with soil; for example, if yellowish soil lays against a black background, in this case cover it with black earth.
    c. Constructing dummy earth and timber bunkers and entrenchments [numbering five false firing positions per company, with 4-5 foxholes and dummy soldiers per company]
    d. Concealing anti-tank ditches with branches and hiding the excavated soil against the backdrop of the surrounding terrain.
3. <u>The command posts and observation posts of the regiments and units</u>. Camouflage the shelters, dugouts, and slit trenches at the command posts and observation posts, as well as the defensive positions. All of the roads and paths leading to the command posts and observation posts must be concealed out to at least 500 meters. The approaches to command posts and observation posts must be covered, running along a ravine, trenches, through clumps of bushes and so forth. Telephone lines running to the command posts and observation posts must be unrolled along the ground, and in no case allow overhead telephone lines.
4. <u>Minefields</u>. Emplace fake minefields marked with signs saying "Mines!", numbering 40-50 percent of the real minefields, and thoroughly camouflage the mines against the backdrop of the terrain with turf and so forth.[300]

This plan and number of supplementary measures as determined by Combat Order No. 042 from the divisional headquarters were to be implemented by 12.00 on 4 June 1943.[301]

    Recognizing the consequences of the information obtained by the Germans on the resulting fighting, the troops seriously approached the fulfillment of the Front command's plan to neutralize it. For example, the chief of staff of the 38th Army Major General A.P. Pilipenko in addition to replacing the positions and setting up dummy positions, ordered the headquarters' aviation department to conduct overflights of the army's combat positions in a U-2 aircraft, in order to check how meticulously the camouflaging was done.[302] It is difficult to say how effectively the work was done in early June to enhance the concealment, but unquestionably it was useful to a considerable extent. As future events would show, the enemy was not only unable

---

300 TsAMO RF, F.119, Op.1, D.32, ll. 82, 82obr.
301 Ibid., p. 81.
302 TsAMO RF, F.375, Op.9027, D.45, l. 282.

to disclose the system of defenses of the first echelon, but also did not even know where the main army-level defensive belt ran.

A key decision when creating the Soviet defenses in the area of the Kursk salient was the use of not only infantry support tank units to help hold the lines, but also major tank formations and even tank armies. According to the *Stavka*'s plan, each of the defending *fronts* received one tank army and two separate tank corps. On the Voronezh Front, separate tank regiments, brigades and self-propelled artillery regiments were positioned in the first echelon of the armored forces; they were subordinate to the deputy commander for armored and mechanized forces of the combined-arms armies. In certain cases, there were transferred as a mobile reserve to the commanders of the first-echelon divisions (in the main defensive belt), and simultaneously they coudld be employed as anti-tank strongpoints. The 7th Guards Army possessed the greatest number of them: three regiments (one heavy), two brigades, and two self-propelled artillery regiments (one heavy). It was being assumed that on the army's front, even though the enemy would be launching a secondary attack, substantial armored forces would be needed in order to contain it. So, the 2nd Guards Tatsinskaia Tank Corps was also directed into the 7th Guards Army's sector. The sector of the 6th Guards Army, as already noted, was from the outset being prepared to repulse the main attack, so two separate tank regiments (the 230th and 245th Separate Tank Regiments), one brigade (the 96th Separate Tank Brigade) and one self-propelled artillery regiment (the 1440th) were transferred to it. This was reinforcement only to ensure the holding of the main defensive belt for one or two days of combat. The plan was for the entire 1st Tank Army to move up to support the 6th Guards Army, and in the event of need, to maneuver the 5th Guards Stalingrad Tank Corps into its sector as well.

The 2nd and 5th Guards Tank Corps and the 1st Tank Army comprised the second echelon of the armored forces. They were positioned at a distance of 32-50 km from the forward edge of the main defensive belt and were located directly subordinate to the Front Commander-in-Chief, comprising the Front's shock force for launching counterattacks and exploiting successes.

For the Soviet side, early May became the first serious test of its restraint. With the ground drying up and becoming firm, and in connection with incoming information about the likely start of the German offensive in the next several days, Moscow undertook a number of important steps at that time.

First, on 30 April, the *Stavka* issued a directive about increasing the number of fighters in the *fronts*' air forces in the area of the Kursk bulge. The following fighter formations were made operationally subordinate:

1. The Central Front's 16th Air Army received the 6th Fighter Aviation Corps, and by 12 May it was to restage to the Kursk, Shshigry, Tim area;
2. The Briansk Front's 15th Air Army received subordinate to it the 1st Guards Fighter Aviation Corps; according to plans, it was to redeploy to the triangular Plavsk – Tula – Stalinogorsk area by 8 May;
3. The Steppe Military District's 5th Air Army received the 234th Fighter Aviation Division (minus one regiment); it was to assemble by 8 May in the Riazhsk area.

Second, within the framework of previously taken decisions to weaken the Luftwaffe formations, on 4 May the command of the Red Army's Air Force issued an assignment to its subordinate forces to conduct large-scale operations between 6 and 16 May with the aim of destroying enemy aircraft on their airfields and to disrupt the German vehicular and railroad shipments in the area of the Kursk salient. The air forces of the Briansk, Central, Voronezh and Southwestern Fronts were called upon to implement this. The 15th Air Army was directed to strike targets in the Orel bulge – in Bolkhov, Karachev, Navlia, Dmitrovsk-Orel and Orel (it was authorized to conduct a total of up to 650 individual aircraft sorties of ground attack aircraft, night bombers and fighters).[303] The 16th Army received orders to strike the airfields of Dmitrovsk-Orel, Trubchesk, Shostka, Konotop and Vorozhba as well as the roads and railroads east of the Trubchesk – Konotop line and the Mikhailovskii – Konotop rail line toward Vorozhba (with up to 1,050 individual sorties).[304] The 2nd Air Army was to attack airfields and base complexes in Belopol'e, Romny, Poltava, Novaia Vodolaga and Merfer, as well as the railroad infrastructure in Poltava and Khar'kov (with up to 1,990 sorties), while the 17th Air Army was to work over the areas of Zmiev, Krasnograd, Dnepropetrovsk, Chaplino, Krasnoarmeiskoe and Slaviansk (with up to 2,300 sorties).[305]

Third, at 1615 on 5 May the commands of the Briansk, Central, Voronezh and Southwestern Fronts over the signatures of A.M. Vasilevsky and A.I. Antonov received the first warning about possible "active enemy operations" at the Kursk salient in the next few days.[306] Such a conclusion was based on the significant movement of enemy troops and transport vehicles in the areas of Orel, Belgorod and Khar'kov that had been noted recently. The document directed to carry out the full plan for utilizing the *fronts*' air armies to destroy enemy aircraft and disrupt German railroad traffic (" … in these days, everything must be squeezed out of the air force in order to fulfill this mission, and thereby foil the enemy's preparations for an offensive"); to pay maximum attention to all types of intelligence gathering with the aim of revealing the enemy's assault groupings; to inspect the condition of the defenses and troops; to use each hour to strengthen the lines; and with only responsible staff officers, check on how this was being done.[307]

However, on the evening of 8 May, they received an even more alarming fresh directive signed by I.V. Stalin, which stated:

> According to certain intelligence, the enemy might launch an offensive between 10 and 12 May in the Orel-Kursk or Belgorod-Oboian directions, or both simultaneously. The *Stavka* of the Supreme High Command is ordering by the morning of 10 May to have both the frontline forces and the reserves at full combat readiness to meet the possible enemy attack. Pay main attention to the readiness of our air forces, so that in the event of an enemy offensive, they can not only repulse attacks by his aircraft, but also so as to gain superiority in the air from the very first moment of his active operations.[308]

The headquarters of the Steppe Military District also received a document that was similar in content before midnight. From its command, Moscow was demanding "… to accelerate the build-up of the district's forces in every possible way and by 10 May have all of the available

---

303 TsAMO RF, F.48a, Op.3409, D.8, l. 95.
304 Ibid., ll. 97-98.
305 Ibid., ll. 99-102.
306 TsAMO RF, F.48a, Op. 3409, D.14, ll. 303-304.
307 Ibid., l. 303.
308 TsAMO RF, F.48a, Op.3409, D.8, l. 184.

troops at full combat readiness, both for a defense and for active operations at the *Stavka*'s orders."[309]

Fourth, on 8 May the *Stavka* took the decision to move up its strategic reserve, the Steppe Military District, to cover the Kursk axis directly, in the rear of Rokossovsky's and Vatutin's forces. Its commander received the order:

a. To move the 27th Army to the Elets, Izmalkovo, Livny, Dolgorukovo area and to give it the task to prepare a defense approximately along the Izmalkovo, Livny, Kshen' River line and counterattacks out of the Livny area to assist the Central Front – in the direction toward Maloarkhangel'sk and Shshigry;

b. The 53rd Army was to cover the Kastornoe railroad hub and the sector of the railroad between (excl.) Dolgorukovo and Gorshechnoe and to prepare a defense along the Kshen' River; in addition, the army was to prepare a counterattack out of the Kastornoe area toward Kursk and Oboian', which is to say, simultaneously into the sectors of both the Central and Voronezh Fronts;

c. The 5th Guards Army was to move up to the Staryi Oskol, Iastrebovka, Bol'shaia Khopen', Chernianka area to screen the Gorshechnoe – Staryi Oskol – Cherniaka sector of the railroad and to prepare a defense along the Iastrebovka – Istobnoe – Belyi Kolodets line; it was also to be ready to assist the Voronezh Front by launching counterattacks out of the Staryi Oskol area in the direction of Oboian' and Belgorod.

The regrouping had to conducted between 9 and 15 May, and at the same time the 27th Army was to receive a tank brigade and tank regiment as a reinforcement, while the 53rd Army was to receive two tank regiments.[310]

The above-listed steps were timely; they stemmed from those key decisions that had been reached earlier and had their own logic and symbiotic relationship. Even so, it must be recognized that not all of them at that moment received effective implementation or yielded a desired result. The simplest in terms of the expended time and resources was the reinforcement of the aerial attacks and bringing the forces up to combat readiness. They were already positioned on their lines and in their staging locations anyway; scrambles in response to an alarm and the taking up of positions had been repeatedly rehearsed; and the operation to destroy the German air force in the area of the Kursk bulge was already well under way. For example, K.K. Rokossovsky already on 10 May reported to the Supreme Commander:

In execution of the *Stavka* directive from 8 May 1943 No.30123, I am reporting:

1. With the receipt of the *Stavka* directive, an order has been issued to all the armies and separate corps of the Central Front about bringing up the troops to combat readiness by the morning of 10 May 1943.
2. In the course of 9 and 10 May, the following has been done:

---

309 Ibid., l. 183.
310 Ibid., ll. 123-125.

a) The troops have been briefed about possible enemy offensive actions in the nearest future;
b) The units of the first and second echelons, as well as the reserve have been brought up to full combat readiness. The headquarters and command staff are inspecting the troops' readiness in place;
c) In the armies' sectors, particularly on the Oboian' direction, combat reconnaissance and fire have intensified against the enemy. In the first-echelon divisions, the coordination of fire has been checked in practice. Units of the second echelons and the reserve are once again reconnoitering the directions of possible actions and clarifying matters of cooperation with the units of the first combat echelon. Ammunition stockpiles are being replenished in the firing positions. Obstacles have been strengthened, particularly on directions vulnerable to tanks. The depth of the defensive belts is being mined. Communication devices been checked – they are operating without interruption.

3. The 16th Air Army has activated aerial reconnaissance and is conducting rigorous surveillance over the enemy in the Glazunovka, Orel, Kromy, Komarchi area. The army's aviation corps and units have been brought up to full readiness in order to repulse enemy air attacks and disrupt his offensive operations.
4. In order to thwart the enemy's possible offensive on the Orel – Kursk axis, a counter-preparation has been prepared, which will involve all of the artillery of the 13th Army and aircraft of the 16th Air Army.[311]

The massed airstrikes against enemy airfields in the frontal zone were the most ambiguous according to the results, or more accurately, to the assessments of those results. In Soviet historiography, they were considered very successful. According to the information of G.A. Koltunov and B.G. Solov'ev, more than 500 aircraft were destroyed on the 17 airfields that were subjected to attack.[312] Accordingly, relying on this data, over three days of operations, the German IV and VI Luftflötten were virtually drained of aircraft, if not to say more. Of course, the Germans continued to contest the skies over the Kursk bulge and conduct airstrike missions throughout the Battle of Kursk.

Today, however, publications have appeared, such as for example the book *Chernaia smert* [*Black death*] by D. Degtev and D. Zubov, in which the authors, relying on German records, refute this enormous figure of Luftwaffe losses. They maintain that not only were all the efforts in vain, but on the contrary, it was the Soviet air formations that suffered the highest and most senseless losses, particularly in *Shturmovik* ground attack aircraft. The authors of *Chernaia smert* observed:

> Altogether over the course of three days, between 6 and 8 May 1943, the Soviet air force conducted 1,392 aircraft sorties, of which 325 were flown by Il-2 ground attack aircraft. According to official Soviet records, 501 German aircraft were destroyed

---

311 TsAMO RF, F.62, Op.329, D.33, ll. 69-70.
312 Koltunov and Solov'ev, *Kurskaia bitva*, p. 38.

on the ground! If to trust this triumphant information, then it turns out that entire Luftwaffe squadrons perished on the airfields and the Germans lost all their aircraft. It is even possible to say that over these three days of May, an entire German air fleet must have been destroyed. For the Third Reich, in general this would have been a defeat comparable in scale to the consequences of the capitulations of the German Sixth Army at Stalingrad and Army Group Africa in Tunisia.

However, not the slightest indication of this was seen in Germany at the time. It was as if the enemy did not even notice all these attacks. This is not surprising, since in fact the Germans lost only five aircraft on the ground: three He 111 bombers, one Ju 88-D, and one Bf 109-G. Another 20 aircraft suffered various degrees of damage but were able to be repaired. These misery losses, naturally, did not have any noticeable effect on the course of the air war even on any single local sector.

Here it must be said that the definite exaggeration of their own successes and the corresponding enemy losses has always existed in every army. Such is the essence of human nature. If to examine the official results of the May airstrikes on the German airfields, then this exaggeration reaches literally a fantastic hundredfold scale! Such an enormous difference between the announced results and reality never existed anywhere else over the entire war. Here it is appropriate to recall an excerpt from the secret Order No.3323s to the Red Army's Air Force on 20 June 1942: "The lack of veracity is so large that at times it borders on implausibility."

At the same time, the total losses of the attackers amounted to 134 aircraft. Among them were 77 Il-2, of which 45 were shot down by German fighters, and the rest – by anti-aircraft artillery. The ground attack regiments were deprived of 52 pilots and 41 rear gunners. In essence, the Germans over these three days destroyed an entire ground attack aviation division.[313]

The cited figure for the loss of Soviet aircraft in this operation is unquestionably high, and at first glance might prompt disbelief. However, turning to a message from the commander of the 15th Air Army Lieutenant General N.F. Naumenko regarding the results of a June 1943 raid on enemy airfields, then the May figures don't seem so unrealistic:

> I am reporting: the 15th Air Army on 8 June 1943 at an order from the Commander-in-Chief of the Red Army Air Force contained in Coded Telegram No.1364 from 8 August conducted an attack on enemy airfields with bombers and *Shturmoviki*. …
>
> As a result of the activities of *Shturmoviki* and fighters, eight aircraft were left burning on the ground at the civilian airport in Orel. In the two group dogfights that took place, four FW-190 were shot down by the covering fighters. With the ground attack actions of the blockading groups on the Mezenka airfield, five bombers were destroyed – noted as left burning – and in the conducted five group dogfights, six enemy aircraft (1 Me-109 and 5 FW-190) were shot down. Altogether, 23 enemy

---

313 Degtev, D.M., Zubov, D.V., *Chernaia smert': Pravda i mif o boevom primenenii shturmovika Il-2, 1941-1945* [*Black death: Truth and myth about the combat use of the IL-2 Shturmovik,, 1941-1945*] (Moscow: ZAO "Tsentrpoligraf", 2013), p. 144.

aircraft were destroyed, of which 13 were on airfields and noted as burning, and 10 were shot down in aerial combats.

Our losses: One Il-2 was downed by the fire of enemy anti-aircraft artillery and fell burning 15-20 km south of Mtsensk. One La-5 suffered a catastrophe when making a forced landing on the unfamiliar airfield at Vypolzovo after flying a mission; presumably the pilot had been wounded in a dogfight. One Iak-7 was damaged and made a forced landing in the area of Beloe Krytsyno; upon landing the aircraft was destroyed and the pilot was injured. The following aircraft also failed to return from the mission: 11 Il-2 of the 225th Ground Attack Aviation Division, 3 La-5 of the 315th Fighter Aviation Division, 2 La-5 and 6 Iak-7 of the 1st Guards Fighter Aviation Corps. According to information, eight Il-2 were seen flying across the front lines, but their location hasn't been established.

The heavy losses are explained by the fact that the inexperienced pilots were caught in a zone of intense anti-aircraft fire, lost combat formation and scattered, which allowed the enemy to attack our fighters and Shturmoviki one by one and in small groups by superior forces.[314]

Accordingly, the results of the attack were 23 destroyed German aircraft and 25 destroyed Soviet aircraft.

A weakness of the book *Chernaia smert'* is the authors' inadequate attention to documenting the numbers they give. There are extremely few references to statistical material, which as a rule are recent, so their conclusions stand against the backdrop of Russian society's image of those events, which makes them seem radical, but also unfounded. However, a significant portion of the scholars, who work with the combat documents of the Soviet forces from the war period, to which I might assign myself, don't consider them to be so.

It is unquestionably hard not to agree with the two noted problems with the book by D. Degtev and D. Zubov. In the first place, if in fact their book is based on the works on the Battle of Kursk, published only over the past decade, then the scale of the lies, silence and distortion of facts of its history, as written by us in the Soviet period, breaks all records. Moreover, if you accept the authors' conclusions and compare them, for example, with the more enduring myth about Prokhorovka, which also arises from the combat documents of combat headquarters, then unquestionably the lie about the air force's May operation seems even larger and without conscience, though once again I will repeat that so far these conclusions haven't been suitably based on documentary sources.

Second, in fact the Luftwaffe did not sustain such enormous damage as written by our historians. If in fact it had, then the Soviet side simply wouldn't have had to conduct a repeated air operation against the German airfields in the first days of June 1943.

However, to assert that the Germans did not even notice the large May raids by Soviet aircraft on their airfields and communication lines is also inaccurate, particularly with respect to the latter. From the German Ninth Army's journal of combat operations:

---

314 TsAMO RF, F.202, Op.5, D.1159, l. 21, 21obr.

6 May. Over the preceding 24 hours, the enemy displayed high activity in the air. In the morning, 200 aircraft-sorties were recorded. The main target of the enemy aircraft were the airfields and [railroad] stations in the Orel area. More than 50 enemy aircraft were shot down by German fighters or Flak gunners. The precise number of hostile aircraft that fell in our territory is being ascertained ...
9 May. Today raids by enemy aircraft resumed, the intensity of which has temporarily weakened. At the same time, the general intensity of the enemy raids grew to never before seen dimensions. Since in the past year a major enemy attack in daylight hours, frustrated by our fighters and Flak artillery, cost the enemy heavy losses, he has shifted his active operations to nighttime hours. This step of the Russian air force has been successful. Bombings and strafing attacks have inflicted substantial losses on us (!). On the whole, a factor that was previously only unique to the German air force, such as the unexpectedly large concentration of [tactical] aviation forces in an individual sector, has begun to extend to the operations of the Red air force.[315]

In documents of this nature, German officers, even though they did mention their own losses, for understandable reasons did not describe them in bright colors, while they spent more time on the damage done to the enemy, even if it was known only in general outlines. Thus, it is not worth paying attention to the modest depiction of the combat work of the Soviet air force in this document; if it was written that the losses were substantial, then that was actually the case. I've had to encounter such a treatment more than once over the more than fifteen years of professional work with captured German wartime sources. Therefore, I consider it impossible to assert that the Soviet aerial operations in the month of May were completely senseless. One thing is inarguable: the objectives given by the *Stavka* to the air forces to weaken the Luftwaffe significantly in the area of the Kursk salient and to disrupt the Wehrmacht's preparations for the offensive were not achieved. Yet in the process, a significant number of pilots and aircraft were lost, and a lot of precious, even deficit fuel was expended for the operation.

The reasons for the failure were several. First was the excellent protection offered by the anti-aircraft fire and the relatively high saturation of the enemy airfields with the technical means to control the air space. Second was the poor organization of the operation on the division and regiment level, and the low professional skills of the command staff that prepared it, and of the pilots themselves. As the Doctor of History D.B. Khazanov observed:

> The Luftwaffe as before was substantially superior to the Soviet VVS [air forces] in the average level of training of the pilots. The Soviet high command had devised and was demanding the unswerving fulfillment of the timetable to send replacements to the front; it did not take into consideration any objections. A particularly large number of young pilots, almost always half-trained, arrived at the front in May 1943; a number of aviation divisions were staffed up to 70-75 percent with novices. As the commander of the 288th Fighter Aviation Division Colonel B.A. Smirnov recalled, the young men were eager to go to the front and many were striving to take a place in the cockpit of a

---

315 NARA US, T.312, R.317, F.7886082, 7886085.

fighter as soon as possible and to destroy the hated enemy. It was just that their level of training left much to be desired.

The Germans were also committing green replacements into the fighting; however, they had received lengthy and intensive training. The percentage of inexperienced pilots was small. The documents of II/JG 3 present a picture of what a German Jagdgruppe [Fighter group] looked like in the East. According to records for 22 May 1943, of the 55 pilots on its staff, 29 could be fully considered to be experienced aces; the group commander and the commander of one of its squadrons had hundreds of combat sorties and more than 100 aerial victories under their belts.[316]

Third, the Soviet VVS still was not ready to conduct such major operations, even though the *Stavka* was placing exaggerated expectations (demands) on the VVS command. It was striving to meet them, despite the fact that those serious problems in the combat units and formations were unquestionably known to it.

Incidentally, at the same time the Luftwaffe was also applying quite a bit of effort to disrupt the military shipments to the Central and Voronezh Fronts, executing systematic raids on the lines of communication and on the major transportation hubs of Kursk, Marmyzhi, Kastornoe, Elets, Staryi Oskol and Valuiki. Between March and July 1943, more than 5,700 individual sorties were flown against the railroad sectors in the Kursk bulge, and more than 12,000 bombs were dropped.[317] Between April and July 1943, 29 air raids were launched against the Kursk railroad hub, in which a total of 1,247 German aircraft took part.[318]

In addition to the above-mentioned reasons, the Germans themselves at that particular moment were expecting our own offensive, and this also had a serious influence on the low effectiveness of our aviators' performance. For example, according to the information from observers, agent networks and deserters, the German command, and in particular the leadership of the Ninth Army, had formed a firm conviction that the movements in the operational rear and tactical zone of the Central Front that had been recorded in the first days of May meant nothing other than the preparation of a major attack. The substantially rising activity and the scale of the reconnaissance activity and probes by assault teams in its sector were also prompting this thought – they were a plain sign of the preparation for an offensive.

In reality, the Central Front headquarters, by initiating the activity of the reconnaissance units, wanted only to confirm or refute its suppositions regarding the enemy's intentions. Thus, it undertook unusual steps – in addition to taking prisoners, strengthening surveillance and bringing forces up to combat readiness, on 7 May it conducted an unexpectedly strong reconnaissance-in-force in the Khitrovo area with several rifle battalions of the 48th Army supported by tanks. Its purpose was not only to gather information about the German troops that

---

316 Khazanov, D.B., "70 let vozdushnoi bitve pod Kurskom" [70th Anniversary of the air struggle over Kursk] in *Kurskaia bitva: vzgliad iz XXI veka. Sbornik materialov mezhdunarodnoi nauchno-prakticheskoi konferentsii, sostoiavsheisia 2 iulia 2013 v Tsentral'nom muzee Velikoi Otechestvennoi voiny* [*Battle of Kursk: View from the XXI Century. Collection of materials from the international academic workshop that took place on 2 July 2013 in the Central Museum of the Great Patriotic War*] (Moscow, 2014), p. 75.
317 Kumanev, G.A., *Sovetskie zheleznodorozhniki v gody Velikoi Otechestvennoi voiny 1941-1945* [*Soviet railroad workers in the years of the Great Patriotic War, 1941-1945*] (Moscow, 1963), p. 180.
318 *Voennye soobshcheniia v bitve pod Kurskom* [*Military announcements during the Battle of Kursk*] (Moscow, 1951), pp. 72-73.

were defending the likely axis of the enemy's main attack, but also to determine their intentions, the depth of their defenses, their ability to bring up reserves quickly, and their approximate strength. Despite the expectations that the Russians were going to attack, this reconnaissance-in-force proved to be a surprise to the command of the XXIII Corps. The main attack struck the boundary between the 86th Infantry Division and 78th Sturm Division, and the attackers not only made a rapid penetration, they also swiftly took even Glazunovka Station and the village of Vasil'evka. The fighting continued for almost 48 hours and subsided only on the afternoon of 8 May with the withdrawal of our forces back to their jumping-off positions. Model was extremely dissatisfied with how the penetration was first localized, and then eliminated. In his opinion, "The direction of the troops on the part of the XXIII Corps' command was not at the suitable level."[319] All this taken together naturally could not help but lead the enemy command to the thought about possible preemptive actions on the part of the Russians and the desire to prepare better for them.

Expectations of a Red Army offensive were also being nurtured by the circumstance that the Ninth Army at that moment still had not completed its regrouping and process of replenishment. Its leadership believed that the danger of an enemy attack while some of forces were still not in position was sufficiently high. From the Ninth Army's combat journal:

> 6 May. Recently a change in the enemy behavior has been noted. <u>Information is gradually accumulating that the positional calm in the course of the recent weeks is approaching an end.</u> The enemy has replaced the units that have been in positions for a long time with fresh reserves. In the process, here and there he has achieved a substantial assembly of fresh forces. He has concentrated the bulk of his artillery in the Maloarkhangel'sk area. In so doing, the majority of the batteries are located in the tactical depth …. According to the testimonies of numerous deserters that have been interrogated in the XXXXI Panzer Corps, an enemy offensive has been planned for tomorrow. However, other than the unusual concentration of enemy forces, no other direct signs for an offensive is being observed.
>
> <u>The army commander, on the basis of personal observations he made when flying over the positions of the XXXI, XXXXVII and XXXXVI Panzer Corps, has passed along the impression that it is necessary to strengthen the defenses quickly. In connection with this, the corps have been given a categorical order: In the event of a Russian offensive, to concentrate the corps' main forces and take up a defensive stance.</u> The following point in the order placed emphasis on a focal center in the defense. As a reserve for counterattacks, it was proposed to set aside the 78th Sturm Division, the 18th, 20th and 12th Panzer Divisions and the 7th Infantry Division. It is necessary to free up the bulk of the organic artillery and to prepare for conducing blocking fire. Strengthen the anti-tank defense. Conduct reconnaissance of the enemy with the attacks of combat groups in several sectors. All of the tanks must be dug in and thoroughly camouflaged (with netting).
>
> 7 May. <u>The attack on the front of the all the corps that was expected yesterday is still possible today! … The army commander has issued a coded order that by 10 May,</u>

---

319   NARA US, T.312, R.317, F.7886084.

<u>it is necessary to achieve the maximal defensive readiness in order to repulse a large Russian offensive</u> [Emphasis the author's].[320]

The headquarters of Model's Ninth Army remained under such tension right up until the middle of the month. That was why the German forces in the area of the Kursk bulge, including its Luftwaffe formations, from the beginning of May had been brought up to combat readiness and were expecting air raids on its bases and lines of communication. Naturally, in such a situation it was hard to hope for high results, even from massed air strikes, but the Soviet command was unaware of this.

More effective for improving the system of defenses and preparing the troops for battle were the large-scale inspections of the fronts by Rokossovsky and Vatutin. They were conducted at three levels at this time.

First, they were implemented by General Staff officers and the headquarters of the *fronts* themselves with the aim of checking the status and the level of readiness of sectors of the defense. Their results on the Central Front showed that in the 13th and 70th Armies, the fortification work by 1 May had primarily gone according to plan, although a number of problems were spotted, which could be and should be quickly resolved by the armies themselves. However, a number of substantial shortcomings were found in the actions of the command of the 48th Army and its divisions. The General Staff representative Colonel L.I. Busurman issued the following report:

> On 1 May 1943, all of the divisional units, other than the 16th Guards Lithuanian Rifle Division, have excavated and set up entrenchments, emplacements for machine guns and anti-tank rifles, and firing positions for all types of artillery and mortars. However, the volume of work to create complete defenses for the authorized number of weapons and men of the divisions remains large and requires enormous efforts from the troops and a high tempo in producing obstacles and other works.[321]
>
> According to tentative data of the army's Department of Engineers, the defensive works have been completed to the following extent in the main indicators as of 1 May 1943:
>
> As a result of the on location officers inspection of the Red Army General Staff and familiarization with the materials of the army headquarters' inspection, I find that the defensive works in the army's sector are proceeding slowly and in their majority are of substandard quality. Commanders are often tolerating departures from the established requirements and in the build-up of the defenses, primarily in artificial obstacles, despite the repeated admonitions in the course of the inspections. Individual commanders aren't taking seriously the fulfillment of combat tasks for the defense and are ignoring the demands of the army's Military Council. I ascribe the following facts to the basic abnormalities:
> 1. Up to the present time, there are no fully considered and objectively calculated plans for the defensive works in the majority of the army's units (73rd Guards,

---

320 NARA USA, T.312, R.317, F.7886082, 7886083.
321 TsAMO RF, F.403, Op.9657, D.87, ll. 63-64.

16th Guards Lithuanian and 399th Rifle Divisions). A general plan of works for the army with an account of the number of destroyed emplacements and timetables for carrying out the work in priority order hasn't been put together. The works are being done in an orderly manner, with no consideration of a sequence to satisfy the most urgent demands of a positional defense.

2. Control over the course and quality of the fortification works on the part of the army's Department of Engineers and the divisional and regimental engineers is weak (with the exception of the 143rd Rifle Division).
3. Adaptation of built-up places for a defense hasn't even started (with very few exceptions).
4. Trenches in a number of places have not been brought up to standard and don't even link with each other even within the boundaries of the company defensive areas (the sector of defense of the 137th Rifle Division, now the 73rd Guards Rifle Division). In the main defensive belt, on average only up to 20 percent of the needed communication trenches have been dug, but in the sector of the 137th Rifle Division, the digging of communication trenches started only recently.
5. The earth and timber bunkers, dugouts and observation posts haven't been completely set up, with covers of one to two layers of top logs; in places they are half-rotten and have not even been fastened together with brackets. In the sector of defense of the 137th Rifle Division, up until 27 April 1943 not a single dugout or slit trench had been built to shelter the infantry.
6. The concealment of the bunkers, entrenchments and other installations is lacking everywhere, allowing the enemy a fine view of the defenses from the air.
7. The anti-tank and anti-personnel obstacles are being emplaced slowly in front of the forward edge of defense. The exception is the 143rd Rifle Division, in the sector of which on average 90 percent of this work has been completed. In the sector of the 147th Rifle Division, only 20 percent of the needed mines and barbed wire obstacles have been emplaced within its boundaries.
8. The pre-registration of fire hasn't been completed in the 73rd Rifle Division's sector of defense. Targeting schemes haven't been compiled. The calling for artillery fire hasn't been agreed upon and virtually hasn't been checked (with rare exception). The preparation of the artillery, mortar and infantry guns for night-time fire hasn't been done in the majority of units.
9. There were no bottles filled with an incendiary mixture in the forward units up until 3 May 1943. The acquisition of these bottles from the army's stockpiles is going slowly.
10. The depth of the defenses is not being maintained. There are no entrenchments in the depth of the defenses. In the 143rd Rifle Division and 399th Rifle Division, the depth of the company and battalion areas is being created setting up earth and timber bunkers and machine-gun emplacements in the depth (with no consideration of the artillery), but they are far from fully supplied with materiel. In the sector of the 137th Rifle Division, the defense has been set up only in one line. The emplacement of mines and barbed wire entanglements hasn't even started in the depth of the defenses. The maneuvering of firing means in the depth of the defenses is limited by the absence of alternate firing positions, earth and timber bunkers and machine-gun nests.

11. The anti-tank areas have been created, but their internal organization does not ensure success in the struggle with enemy tanks. The commandants of the anti-tank areas and sectors don't know their responsibilities well and haven't been instructed to a sufficient degree. The question of the coordination of fire both within the anti-tank areas and between the anti-tank areas has been poorly elaborated.
12. The protection of the boundaries is satisfactory and this matter has been given adequate attention, but in the 73rd Rifle Division an intolerable carelessness was allowed to happen: Over three days of its occupation of the defense after replacing the 137th Rifle Division (from 26 April to 30 April 1943), not a single commander of the division's units bothered to check the security of the boundaries, took a look at them on the spot, or visited with neighbors regarding this concern …
15. The density of manpower and fire per kilometer of front does not correspond with the information of the army headquarters in reality. The difference is as follows:

Thus, for over the almost three months of his time at the head of the 48th Army, Lieutenant General P.L. Romanenko had not in fact been able to reverse the negative tendencies in its leadership. Inertia, negligence of the command staff, inactivity and whitewashing continued to flourish both in the army headquarters and in the divisions subordinate to it. These subjective problems added to the serious objective factors connected with the diversion of the Central Front's leadership to constructing first and foremost the system of defenses of the adjacent 13th Army and the acute lack in both the 48th Army and the Front of the basic anti-tank means – anti-tank guns. All of this taken together led to the fact that the line of the 48th Army by early May was the most vulnerable in the event of an enemy attack. Even G.K. Zhukov would point to this problem in his report, after personally inspecting the 48th Army in the latter half of May.

Second, according to the instructions issued after the conferences in the Kremlin on 26 and 28 April, the military councils of the Voronezh and Central Fronts were supposed to give a summary regarding the full readiness of their troops to conduct a defensive operation between 10 and 12 May. These reports primarily required them to shed light on the level of the divisions' staffing with personnel and equipment, and also the steps taken to repulse a possible enemy attack. N.F Vatutin issued his report regarding the fulfillment of this order to the *Stavka* on the evening of 11 May. In his opinion, the Germans still weren't ready for an offensive, and he assumed that it might be expected at some point after 15 May. Nevertheless, the document he signed contained a proposal regarding an ambitious, tentative plan for a regrouping and the use of strategic reserves in order to repel a possible attack (by bringing the armies of the first strategic echelon up in succession to the most threatened directions – the Oboian' – Prokhorovka and Korocha directions). Vatutin wrote:

> The troops of the Voronezh Front are ready to carry out the defensive task. All of the rifle divisions of the 38th, 40th, 6th Guards and 7th Guards Armies, with very few exceptions, have more than 8,000 men. The 69th Army has divisions that number between 6,000 and 7,000 men. The divisions of the 35th Guards Rifle Corps [Vatutin's combined-arms reserve] are fully manned up to authorized strength.
>
> Of the assets that have been assigned to the Front, the following have not yet arrived: three regiments of self-propelled guns, two destroyer anti-tank artillery regiments, two mortar regiments, five anti-aircraft artillery regiments and one cannon artillery brigade. In addition, the towing vehicles (the Studebaker trucks and Willys

jeeps) that have been additionally assigned to the Front haven't arrived. The divisions of the 69th Army will also be brought up to a strength of not less than 8,000 men each by 20 May 1943. The tank units and formations are almost fully replenished up to establishment strength. There are no tank reserves. In terms of fortifications, the lines of defense are not badly prepared.

3. Considering everything laid out above, the approach of the 5th Guards Army, as well as the plan to destroy the enemy, without permitting a breakthrough of our defenses by him in any event, I've decided to conduct the following regrouping of the Front's reserves by the morning of 15 May 1943:

a) To shift the 5th Guards Tank Corps from the Mar'ino area to the Beloe, Mokrusheno, Bobrovo area and to prepare counterattacks in the northwestern, southern, southeastern and eastern directions;

b) To move the 1st Tank Army primarily to the southern bank of the Psel River in the Ivnia, Kruglik, Ol'khovka, Oboian', Peschanoe area, where prepared lines are available, and from there it will be possible to launch strong counterattacks in the southern and southeastern directions;

I will gradually shift the 35th Guards Rifle Corps as well to this same area, which will effectively cooperate with the 1st Tank Army. In the process, a division of the 35th Guards Rifle Corps will be able to reach this area by the morning of 17 May, and the other two – by the morning of 20 May 1943;

c) To shift the 2nd Guards Tank Corps from the Korocha area to the Prokhorovka (40 km northeast of Korocha), Komsomolets State Farm, Pravorot' area, from where it will prepare for a counterattack in the western, southwestern, southern and southeastern directions;

d) In accordance with the situation, I intend by 20 May 1943 to replace Shumilov's 7th Guards Army with units of the 69th Army (the 183rd, 305th, 107th, 111th, 270th and 213th Rifle Divisions), and after its replacement, to withdraw four of the 7th Guards Army's divisions to the line now occupied by the 69th Army, and two of its divisions to the Korotnoe (10 km northeast of Koracha's location), Zhigailovka, Vorovka (20 km southwest of Novyi Oskol) line. From this position, the 7th Guards Army can swiftly assemble for an attack [which is to say, to prepare for the option when the Front might launch an offensive first].

Such an arrangement of the reserves ensures their cooperation and a more rapid shift to a counteroffensive. I request that you confirm the decision laid out above to regroup the Front's reserves.[322]

Practically right after the arrival of this report in Moscow, G.K. Zhukov arrived at the Voronezh Front for an inspection, which rated the condition of its defenses highly, but at this moment a fresh intelligence warning arrived about a possible German offensive. In these conditions, the *Stavka* opted not to conduct a major regrouping and refused to confirm N.F. Vatutin's proposal, but also did not reject it, since they were closely tied to the Front's overall plan for an offensive

---

322 TsAMO RF, F.203, Op.2777, D.75, l. 171.

operation. That is precisely why at the end of June, when the question again arose about the Red Army to be first to take the offensive, the *Stavka* allowed N.F. Vatutin to begin to implement his array of steps. In particular, several days before the start of the Battle of Kursk, the 69th Army began to move its divisions up into the 7th Guards Army's rear area in order to replace it on the line of the Severskii Donets River. Fortunately, however, this process did not get very far, and both armies would meet the adversary virtually in full combat readiness, although the initiated regrouping would give the commander of the 69th Army quite a few problems with restoring command and control over his forces.

Thus far, the report from the leadership of the Central Front about its readiness to repulse an attack still hasn't been found. However, relying on other archival sources, it is highly likely that N.F. Vatutin was feeling more confident at this time. The situation of Rokossovsky's forces was noticeably inferior both according to the degree of replenishing its already available divisions with personnel and equipment, and also those that had been promised, but had not yet arrived. At the very least, it is known that his Front lagged behind its neighbor in terms of the manpower strength of its divisions by 800 to 1,000 men each, was in need of anti-tank artillery, and was also experiencing serious problems with the delivery of new armored vehicles.

Third and most important was the inspection at the third level, which at the behest of I.V. Stalin was conducted by G.K. Zhukov personally. It began in mid-May and was the first exhaustive inspection done after the deadline passed for the Voronezh and Central Fronts to be ready for a defense, though naturally it was prompted primarily by the intelligence reports of a possible German attack. I will remind the reader that the Kursk defensive operation had been worked out in common for both *fronts* that were defending the salient, so all of the inspections on the two *fronts* employed the same set of criteria. I will immediately note that for N.F. Vatutin, the results of the inspections proved to be more positive. On 16 May, the first account of I.V. Stalin's first deputy regarding the state of affairs in the southern portion of the Kursk bulge lay on his desk. It came to the following conclusions:

> Judging from the rather small amount of infantry in the first echelon, the absence of infantry and artillery groupings in the depth of the enemy's defenses, and the enemy's activities and behavior, I believe that the enemy in the Belgorod area still is not prepared for a large offensive operation, and plainly will not be able to attack before the end of May.
>
> The operational-tactical disposition of the units of the Voronezh Front and the grouping of forces and means across the armies and directions don't cause me any concerns. I believe that the operational decisions of the Front's Military Council correspond to the situation and the enemy's possibilities.[323]

The document itself was rather voluminous, and it described the condition of both our troops and the enemy's troops, the possible alternatives of events, and so forth in detail. However, the key information was concentrated in the cited excerpt. First, the Marshal of the Soviet Union accurately assessed the Germans' intentions, and still unaware of the second intelligence warning regarding a possible looming German offensive, which came out a bit later, he waved off any

323 Ibid., l. 192.

conjectures about a possible enemy offensive in the nearest future. Zhukov also confirmed his full agreement with "Vatutin's Plan", which by this time had already been realized in the combat dispositions of his forces and gave it his high rating. Zhukov also believed that the adversary would launch his main attack out of the Orel area toward Kursk, and the Voronezh Front was now completely capable of withstanding the attack of the auxiliary grouping, which would likely come out of the Belgorod area. This was apparent because the Marshal in his account did not request any additional combat units for N.F. Vatutin (as he would do in his report about the situation of affairs on Rokossovsky's Central Front), other than transport means, of which there was a catastrophic deficit on the Voronezh Front, in order to bring it up at least close to establishment strength. Observed G.K. Zhukov:

> It is bad that Krivoshein's mechanized corps of Katukov's army lacks more than 600 transport vehicles, and therefore will be forced to be used as foot infantry. If it is possible, I ask you to order to supply 600 vehicles to Katukov. In addition, there is also a large shortage of motorized transport in the other forces of the Voronezh Front, as a result of which the 69th Army and many of the 38th and 40th Armies' infantry divisions are almost immobile and unable to bring up ammunition supplies and food. The shortage of motorized vehicles in the Front amounts to 4,546. I request that you order the dispatch to the Voronezh Front at least 250 vehicles for the 69th Army, 150 vehicles for the 38th Army, and 250 vehicles for the 40th Army, so altogether with Katukov, I ask you to give the Voronezh Front 1,250 machines.[324]

On 19 May, G.K. Zhukov traveled to the Central Front, where he learned that the *Stavka* had again, for the second time, warned the *fronts* about the possible start of a German offensive, now between 19 and 26 May.[325] However, following his personal visit to the troops of the 13th Army's first echelon, his discussion with the army commanders and divisional commanders, and his analysis of the latest intelligence information, the Marshal came to the same conclusion that he offered in his account regarding the Voronezh Front: " ... The enemy on the forward edge has no immediate readiness for an offensive. Perhaps I am mistaken; the enemy is very artfully masking his preparations, but when analyzing the dispositions of his tank units, the inadequate density of the infantry divisions, the absence of heavy artillery groupings, and the wide dispersion of the reserves, I believe the enemy cannot go on the offensive before the end of May."[326]

However, determining the enemy's intentions was only the Marshal's first task. In addition, he had to assess the overall condition of the Central Front's system of defenses and to specify its needs in order to ensure I.V. Stalin's prompt personal intervention. The problems of K.K. Rokossovsky, which could only be resolved on that level, turned out to be noticeably greater than his neighbor's, both with respect to the system of defenses (once again the 48th Army cropped up) and the means of reinforcement, especially considering the *Stavka*'s concerns that the Germans might be aiming for Moscow through his sector of the front. On the night of 21-22 May, the Marshal reported:

---

324 Ibid., l. 193.
325 TsAMO RF, F.148 a., Op. 3763, D.143, l. 152.
326 Zhukov, *Vospominaniia i razmyshleniia*, Vol. 3 (Novosti, 1990), pp. 34-35.

2. The defenses of the 13th and 70th Armies are organized properly and are deeply echeloned. The defense of the 48th army presently lacks depth and is very weak in artillery; if the enemy attacks Romanenko's army and plans to bypass [Malo-]Arkhangel'sk from the east with the intention of enveloping Kostin's main grouping [the code name for K.K. Rokossovsky in discussions and correspondence], then Romanenko will not be able to withstand the enemy's attack. The Front's reserves are primarily positioned behind Pukhov's and Galanin's armies and will not be able to go to the assistance of Romanenko in time.

I consider that Romanenko must be reinforced with two rifle divisions, three T-34 tank regiments, two destroyer anti-tank artillery regiments and two mortar regiments or artillery regiments from the *Stavka* Reserve. If these will be given to Romanenko, then he will be able to organize a good defense, and if it is necessary, might be able to launch a counteroffensive with a compact grouping.

In the defenses of Pukhov's, Galanin's and the other armies of the Front, the main shortcomings consist in the lack of destroyer anti-tank artillery regiments. The Front at the present day has a total of four destroyer anti-tank artillery regiments; those that lack towing means are located in the Front's rear.

In view of the large shortage of 45mm guns in the battalions and regiments, the anti-tank defense of the forward echelons and the forward edge has been weakly organized.

I believe that Kostin needs to be given four regiments of anti-tank artillery as quickly as possible (with Romanenko – 6), and three regiments of self-propelled 152mm artillery …

4. Pukhov now has 12 divisions, six of which are consolidated in two corps, while Pukhov himself is commanding the other six divisions. As a beneficial matter, I request that you urgently order to form and send to Pukhov two corps headquarters, and to form and send one corps headquarters for Galanin, who now has five separate divisions in addition to a rifle corps.[327]

Accordingly, the command of the Central Front had put the question of defending the Livy direction (the sector of the 48th Army) on the back burner, even though it, together with the two other army sectors, was still considered to be the most likely area where the Ninth Army would launch its main attack. Yet as Rokossovsky had decided, his headquarters had focused only on the sector of the 13th Army. G.K. Zhukov, who also believed that Pukhov's 13th Army was holding the key sector of the line, nevertheless did not approve of such an approach. The Marshal had accurately prognosed the Germans' most probable actions with respect to the Maloarkhangel'sk direction. I will remind the reader that back on 22 April 1943, the chief of staff of Army Group Center General H. Krebs, following a conference with Elverfeldt's staff, had sent Model an update for the Citadel plan, in which he had requested "to shift the boundary between the XXXXI Panzer Corps and XXIII Corps by 2 km to the west, with the aim of ensuring for the XXIII Corps the best possibility of enveloping the enemy fortifications in the

---

327 Ibid., p. 35.

Maloarkhangel'sk area."[328] At the same time, the Marshal understood that the Front's available forces weren't elastic. Therefore, he did not target Rokossovsky with any comments, but in front of the Supreme Commander, as a matter of priority, he placed the question about strengthening Romanenko's army.

Nevertheless, judging from the report, G.K. Zhukov did fully share K.K. Rokossovsky's point of view that the main attack would come in the direction of Ponyri, because he approved all of Rokossovsky's decisions regarding this sector. Therefore, not only the Front leadership must bear significant responsibility for this miscalculation, but also the Deputy Supreme Commander, who was supervising the Central Front in the *Stavka*'s name. The Marshal not only took part in working out the plan for this sector's defense (in April 1943), but also over the following two months more than once inspected the course of its implementation on site and personally drove out to both the Ponyri and Ol'khovatka directions, so he could not help but know the characteristics of the terrain in both areas.

It is not understandable why the entire higher command staff of the Central Front and the Red Army's key figures, who were drawn into the preparation of the defense and who more than once visited its lines, had no doubt that they were correct about the likely direction of the enemy's main attack. Why did they all believe that the bottleneck between the Snova and Polevaia Snova Rivers would be the most suitable place for the deployment of the Germans' main shock grouping of mobile formations? One can only speculate that it is possible they were working according to the principle of collegiality: one man might be mistaken, but not collective thought.

Incidentally, German generals in similar situations demonstrated greater flexibility and independent thought. In May, the questions of where to deliver the main attack were also reviewed by the command of both army groups at the Kursk salient, even though formally the process of planning Citadel had seemingly already ended. The leadership of both shock armies stepped forward as the initiators of fresh discussions regarding the decisions that had been reached. I will remind the reader that despite that fact, during the conference of 10-11 May Hoth had managed somehow to persuade E. von Manstein to alter the direction of the main attack of his forces and to redraw the boundaries for his Fourth Panzer Army and the adjacent Army Detachment Kempf. The reason was all one and the same – the extremely difficult terrain for employing armor, which was at the same time convenient for creating a strong defense by the Russians. Judging from recently disclosed captured German documents, the same question was taken up in the headquarters of the Ninth Army almost simultaneously. The catalyst of this was intelligence information. No matter how paradoxical it may sound, it was precisely the Soviet side with its high, but poorly concealed activity to fortify the Ponyri and Maloarkhangel'sk areas that was prodding the Germans to operate with its main forces against the weakly covered Ol'khovatka direction. Here is how the Ninth Army leadership went about forming its assessment of the strength of the entire sector of defense of the 70th, 13th and 48th Armies:

> **26 April** ... On the enemy side, the intensive movement of artillery, including Katiusha rocket launchers has been recently observed along the Trosna – Fatezh highway <u>to the east, from the western flank closer to the center of the 13th Army. Apparently, this</u>

---

328 NARA US, T.312, R.317, F.7886053.

shows the strengthening of the defense on the sector of front between the Trosna – Fatezh highway and the Orel – Kursk rail line.
30 April … The regrouping of forces in the sector of the Russian 13th Army is continuing … By all odds, it is possible to assume that the enemy has assembled very strong forces in the defensive positions in the sector between the Trosna – Fatezh highway and the Orel – Kursk railroad. Our aerial reconnaissance has paid particular attention to photographing this area. The analysis of the obtained photographs over a certain period, when superimposed on a map, has revealed the main principles guiding the enemy when preparing the defensive positions.
1 May … Regarding the enemy situation and the assessment of his plans, then significant changes are observable here. In particular, the appearance of the 7th Artillery Division, the 65th Guards Mortar Regiment, and one more unidentified Guards mortar regiment in the Ponyri area (20 km southwest of Maloarkhangel'sk) calls attention to itself. In aggregation it is possible to assess this as the very substantial reinforcement of enemy artillery in this sector … On the whole one can draw the conclusion that the enemy is strengthening his defensive capabilities in the Belyi Nemed' – Maloarkhangel'sk sector [the left flank of the 70th Army and right flank of the 13th Army].
3 May … Surveillance of the enemy compels one to assume … that he is concentrating his main forces along both sides of the forming German offensive wedge [which is to say, strengthening the area of Ponyri and Maloarkhangel'sk and the right flank of the 70th Army].

Reconnaissance flights have observed the intensive movement of motorized transport in the area of the boundary between the Russians' 13th and 70th Armies. In this same area, the approach of forces to the front has been observed.
4 May … Aerial reconnaissance in recent days has repeatedly identified signs of the assembly of enemy tank reserves in the Maloarkhangel'sk area. One tank regiment each has been identified in the Gnilushi area [6 km north of Maloarkhangel'sk], in Maloarkhangel'sk itself, and north of Ponyri.
5 May …. As concerns the enemy's reinforcement of the adjacent flanks between the 13th and 48th Armies that has been observed recently, it has received additional confirmation. There are no doubts that the enemy has forces here that are larger than the needs of a defense. On the basis of this, one can come to the conclusion that the capture of the Maloarkhangel'sk area might have great significance for the success of the offensive, since this area is a key sector in the enemy's defenses.
20 May … The enemy is actively throwing up field fortifications opposite the sector of the XXXXI Panzer Corps [the Ponyri direction], from which it is possible to conclude that the enemy is expecting the main German attack at this place. Given this consideration, it makes no sense to launch the main attack here.[329]

The absence of any active German operations following the two warnings from the *Stavka*, and also unquestionably the high degree of readiness of the Front's forces were prodding N.F. Vatutin to the thought that it made sense for the Red Army to go on the offensive first. The

---

329 NARA US, T.312, R.317, F.7886069, 7886074, 7886082, 7886095. All emphases are the author's.

Stavka over all this time was also experiencing a lack of confidence that its decision to adopt an intentional defense was correct – the cost of a mistake was too high. A.M. Vasilevsky wrote, "After the first warning, when it was not confirmed, the Voronezh Front's Military Council took a look at this hesitation, and perhaps even the adversary's rejection of the idea to launch an offensive and asked the Supreme Commander to decide whether or not it made sense to launch a preemptive attack. I.V. Stalin took a serious interest in this proposal, and it cost us – Zhukov, Antonov and me – certain exertions to persuade him not to do this."[330]

G.K. Zhukov recalled, "I.V. Stalin was concerned that our defense might not be able to withstand an attack of the German forces, as had happened more than once in 1941 and 1942. At the same time, he had no confidence that we would be able to defeat the enemy with our own offensive actions. This vacillation continued, as I recall, almost up to the middle of May."[331] Indeed, although his suggestion did not convince the *Stavka*, N.F. Vatutin clung to this position and still believed that he should act first. He took up this matter again a month later, in the latter half of June.

In the historiography on the battle, especially Western works on the subject, there exists the opinion that the repeated postponement of the start date for Operation Citadel in May and June 1943 to a great extent caused the German defeat in the Battle of Kursk. I will remind that it was first postponed on 20 April for fully objective reasons: The Ninth Army was not ready for an offensive (its forces had not even had time to assemble fully for an attack). In principle, everyone agreed with this decision, including Hitler, the OKH and the leadership of both army groups. Yet its further postponement to 12 June, which was brought up first by Hitler as a topic for discussion at the conference on 4 May and was subsequently confirmed by him in his order from 6 May, prompted stormy debates among the generals involved in the preparations for Citadel. This Führer decision was based on the fact that the main trump card for the summer campaign – the Tiger and Panther tanks – still weren't ready. However, this postponement did not prove to be the last one. Neither in May 1943 nor in the first 10 days of June was the German industry able to meet the planned output of this armor, so Hitler once again postponed the offensive.

A number of German military commanders were the first to express the point of view about the catastrophic consequences of this decision immediately after the war. For example, Field Marshal E. von Kleist in 1951, when being questioned by Soviet officers, asserted that "the Germans were late by four weeks with the battle around Kursk; such was our opinion before the start of the fighting."[332] E. von Manstein, who was already free by this time, also expressed a similar opinion. In his memoirs, which were published in Germany in 1955, he wrote that Citadel might have been successful, had it gotten underway no later than the end of May or the beginning of June.[333] He argued that before this time, the Russians still had not been able to recover from the winter fighting and their troops had low combat capabilities, but the pause in June allowed Moscow to bring them back up to strength.

---

330 Vasilevsky, *Delo vsei zhizni*, Book 2, p. 24.
331 Zhukov, *Vospominaniia i razmyshleniia*, Vol. 3 (Moscow: Novosti, 1990), p. 31.
332 Khristoforov, V., Makarov, V. and Khavkin, B., "Fel'dmarshal fon Kleist na Lubianke" ["Field Marshal von Kleist in the Lubianka"] *Rodina*, No. 6 (2010), p. 94.
333 Manstein, *Uteriannye pobedy*, p. 543.

Among the scholars, it was the American historian S. Newton in his book, *Battle of Kursk: The German view*, who most extensively developed this position on the basis of Model's example.[334] However, the figures he cites, in particular regarding the manning levels of the Soviet divisions and armies, are not always accurate, so his conclusions do raise doubts. We will try to take a deeper look into this matter, using recently declassified combat documents of the Red Army of this period stored in the TsAMO RF.

There were several reasons for the success of the Soviet forces in the Battle of Kursk, but primarily three. First was the high degree of readiness of the forces that were defending the Kursk salient. Second was the *Stavka*'s seemingly unending flow of reserves. Third was the extremely powerful field defenses constructed in April to June 1943 in this area. The assertion made by the German military commanders and of the Western scholars that share the opinion that the Soviet forces in the Kursk salient weren't ready for battle in May 1943 is based on ignorance of the details of the *Stavka*'s plan for the summer campaign and the scale of the work done in the period of the spring thaw. For example, I will remind you that on 12 April 1943 at a conference in the Kremlin, the participants reached the conclusion that the Wehrmacht would quickly launch an offensive with the objective of eliminating the Kursk bulge once the ground dried (somewhere around the beginning of May). Thus, the conference attendees made the tentative decision to adopt a strategic defensive posture. The plan was essentially to rebuild the forces of the Central and Voronezh Fronts before the end of this same month, and at the same time for their Military Councils to devise plans for the defensive operation in close cooperation with the General Staff. On 25 and 28 April, the command of both *fronts* reported that both processes had primarily been completed. The *Stavka* confirmed the general plan for the Kursk strategic defensive operation that had been submitted by them and issued an order: to prepare the troops fully to repulse the adversary's attack by 10 May, and also set 1 June 1943 as the latest date when they might go on the offensive.[335]

It was thanks to the fulfillment of the far-reaching decisions of 12 April 1943 that the Soviet side was primarily ready to conduct successful defensive operations at Kursk against those forces that the Wehrmacht possessed in this area at that time already by the end of the first ten days of May. By the end of June, the numerical strength of the Central and Voronezh Fronts reached the indicators that they would have in July, before the Battle of Kursk. The fact that this was the case, and that the *Stavka*'s orders were actually fulfilled on time, is apparent from the following figures.

For example, on 30 March 1943, Central Front had a combat strength of 304,464 man, but by 5 May, it had now increased by 61,167 men to 365,641, which amounted to 78 percent of its strength by the start of the Battle of Kursk (for more detail, see Table 18).[336]

At the same time, the strength of its 13th Army under the command of Lieutenant General N.P. Pukhov, which was to take on the main attack by Model's Ninth Army, grew by 42,552 men to 114,456, which was 86 percent of the manpower it would have on 5 July (for more detail, see Table 19).

The increase primarily resulted from the transfer of three rifle divisions to it, although the average manpower strength of its own divisions also rose perceptibly – by 18 percent (from 6,378

---

334 Newton, *Kurskaia bitva: Nemetskii vzgliad*, pp. 463-476.
335 TsAMO RF, F.16-A, Op. 321, D. 138, l. unnumbered.
336 TsAMO RF, F. 62, Op.1720, D.14, l. 23.

to 7,527). For Pukhov's army, April was the period when it received its largest replenishment with men over the entire time of the preparations for the summer fighting. By 29 May another 14,701 replacements arrived at its disposal, and thereupon its strength increased up to 129,157 commanders and enlisted men, or 97 percent of those it would have available on 5 July. Meanwhile, the total manpower strength of the Central Front by the end of May amounted to 451,179 men, or 97 percent of its total strength by the start of Operation Citadel.[337]

Table 18: Rate of increase in the effective combat strength of the Central and Voronezh Fronts during the 1943 spring and summer operational pause

	Central Front[338]		Voronezh Front[339]		
Date	Number of men	Increase in manpower and percentage growth relative to 30 March	Date	Number of men	Increase in manpower and percentage growth relative to 30 March
30 March	304,464	–/100			
10 April	322,535	18,071/6%	5 April	211,340	–/100
15 April	331,703	27,239/9%	15 April	273,687	62,347/29.5%
25 April	356,612	52,148/17%	25 April	?	?
30 April	334,978	30,514/10%	30 April	341,909	130,569/61.8%
5 May	365,641	64,833/21.3%	5 May	351,459	140,119/66.3%
10 May	382,322	77,858/25.6%	10 May	373,518	162,178/76.6%
15 May	412,856	108,392/35.6%	15 May	389,778	178,438/84.4%
20 May	434,874	130,410/42.3%	20 May	401,178	189,838/89.8%
25 May	443,883	139,419/45.8%	25 May	406,936	195,596/92.5%
30 May	451,179	146,715/48.2%	30 May	409,785	198,445/93.9%
5 June	458,861	154,397/50.7%	5 June	408,512	197,172/93.3%
10 June	461,180	156,716/51.5%	10 June	409,781	198,441/95.8%
15 June	461,141	156,677/51.5%	15 June	413,745	202,404/95.8%
25 June	?	?	25 June	423,137	211,797/100%
30 June	462,404	157,940/51.9%	30 June	427,783	216,443/102%
5 July	467,179	162,715/53.4%	5 July	417,451	206,111/97.5%

337 TsAMO RF, F.16-A, Op.321, D.138, l. unnumbered.
338 TsAMO RF, F.62, Op.321, D.138
339 TsAMO RF, F.203, Op.2843, D.?, ll. 425-426.

Table 19: Rate of manpower increase in the rifle divisions of certain first-echelon armies of the Voronezh and Central Fronts, between April and June 1943

Date	Total number of men	Establishment number of rifle divisions	Average number of men per division	Rate of increase
6th Guards Army				
5 April 1943	42,574	6	5,982	-
5 May 1943	72,836	7	7,666	28%
5 June 1943	79,937	7	8,182	37%
5 July 1943	79,653	7	8,505	42%
7th Guards Army				
5 April 1943	57,824	7	5,965	-
5 May 1943	67,231	7	7,600	27%
5 June 1943	71,332	7	7,625	28%
5 July 1943	76,831	7	8,643	45%
13th Army				
5 April 1943	71,904	9	6,378	-
5 May 1943	114,456	12	7,527	18%
5 June 1943	129,517	12	7,770	22%
5 July 1943 1943	133,715	12	7,883	23%
70th Army				
30 March 1943	42,795	5	7,000	-
5 May 1943	66,086	8	?	?
29 May 1943	73,106	8	7,667	1%
5 July 1943	73,113	8	7,392	0.6%

The rebuilding of the Voronezh Front's combat capabilities went at the same high tempo. On 5 April it had 208,391 servicemen, and on 5 May – 351,459, an increase of 143,068.[340] This was 84 percent of the number achieved by 5 July. Over this time, 30,262 more men were sent to the 6th Guards Army (which was defending the most likely direction of the attack by Army Group South's main forces), and its manpower rose to 72,836, which led to the average increase in the strength of its rifle divisions of 28 percent, from 5,982 to 7,666); meanwhile, the 7th Guards Army (which was defending the area where the possible auxiliary attack might strike) received

---

340 TsAMO RF, F.203, Op.2843, D.425, l. 425.

another 9,407 men, as a result of which its strength amounted to 67,231 (the average increase in manpower of its divisions rose by 27 percent, from 5,965 to 7,600). By 30 May, the combat strength of Vatutin's Voronezh Front grew to 409,785 men (98 percent of that it would have by 5 July), while Chistiakov's and Shumilov's armies grew respectively 79,937 and 71,332 by 5 June, which was respectively 100 percent and 93 percent of the strength it would have a month later.

The situation was similar with the artillery. By 6 May, both the Central Front and the 13th Army had received 80 percent of the guns and mortars (not including the rocket launchers) of the number they would have on 5 July 1943, and on 29 May, the Front had a total of 4,544 field and anti-tank guns and 7,161 mortar tubes, which corresponded respectively to 87 percent and 89 percent it would have by 5 July; the 70th Army, which was defending to the left of the 13th Army and would also be taking on a powerful enemy attack, had respectively 796 field and anti-tank guns and 1,280 mortar tubes, or 93 percent and 98 percent of the total it would have on 5 July.

The replenishment of Rokossovsky's Central Front and Vatutin's Voronezh Front with tanks did not go as swiftly or evenly. (For the pace of the increase in the number of serviceable armored vehicles of the Central Front during the spring operational pause, see Table 20).

Table 20: Rate of growth in serviceable armored fighting vehicles of the Central Front during the spring operational pause of 1943[341]

Day, month and hour	Total number of serviceable tanks	Domestically-produced tanks		Lend-Lease tanks obtained from abroad	Percentage increase over the month relative to 29 March	Number of domestically-produced self-propelled guns	Percentage increase in self-propelled guns over the month	Total percentage increase in tanks and self-propelled guns over the month relative to 29 March
		Total	Including T-34/KV					
29 March, 22.00	543	420	171/61	123	–	0	–	–
3 May, 22.00	674	637	329/86	37	24%/24%	38	100%	31%/31%
5 June, 22.00	1,216	1,176	754/86	148	180%/224%	43	13%	83%/121%
4 July, 22.00	1,688[342]	1,487	955/99	150	139%/310%	96	123%	48%/229%

341 TsAMO RF, F.62, Op.321, D.16, l.36, 37, 125; F.38, Op.11360, D.192, l.52.
342 On 1 June 1943, there were 1,906 on the list of tanks, of which 212 were undergoing repairs.

On 3 May the Central Front had 674 tanks (plus 38 self-propelled guns), or 40 percent of those it would have available on 5 July.[343] Its 13th Army had 137 tanks, or 64 percent of the number it had by the start of the fighting.[344]

The situation with armored vehicles on the southern sector of the Kursk bulge by this time was noticeably better. There were two reasons for this. First, at the beginning of spring, there were substantial interruptions in the delivery of tanks and self-propelled guns from the factories to the acting Red Army. According to Memorandum No. 1149518s from the Commander of the Red Army's Armored and Mechanized Forces to the Deputy Chairman of the State Defense Committee V.M. Molotov on 11 March 1943, over the first ten days of March, all five of the country's tank factories had fulfilled only 18.4 percent of the plan, which meant that instead of 1,935 T-70, T-34, KV-1s and KV-8 tanks, the troops had received only 357.[345] Second, the mobile formations that took part in the winter and spring fighting on the Voronezh and Southwestern Fronts had suffered very heavy losses. In some of the corps, the total number of tanks did not that of a full-strength tank battalion.

Because of this, already at the end of March, the *Stavka* decided to replenish the Voronezh Front's armored vehicles as the first order of business.[346] Throughout the month of April, the bulk of the tanks and self-propelled guns coming out of the factories were sent to these tank and mechanized corps. Thus, the rebuilding of Vatutin's armored forces went in quantum leaps. For example, over the two weeks from 1 April to 15 April, they received 219 new combat machines and 6,432 men for the tank corps and tank brigades.[347] As a result, if on 9 April the Voronezh Front had 276 serviceable combat machines, then on 21 April in now had 540 operational tanks and self-propelled guns. In parallel with the arriving new armored vehicles, the Front's repair services actively worked to put disabled machines back into service.

Finally, on 28 April the *Stavka* formally transferred the 1st Tank Army to N.V. Vatutin's Voronezh Front, which had arrived from the Northwestern Front to the Kursk area back in March, as well as several separate tank corps and brigades. By 5 May, Katukov's 1st Tank Army was equipped with 72.9 percent of the armored fighting vehicles it would have on 5 July, and had 481 tanks; on 1 June it had 581 tanks, 88 percent of that which it would have on 5 July;[348] on 5 July it would have a total of 660 tanks, including 638 that were operational.[349] In addition, by early June the 1st Tank Army, 5th Guards Stalingrad Tank Corps and 2nd Tatsinskaia Tank Corps were supplied with 3 standard combat loads of ammunition for the tanks; between 1.5

---

343 TsAMO RF, F.62, Op.321, D.16, l. 86 obr.
344 Ibid., l. 86.
345 *Ogennaia duga. Strategiia Pobedy (k 70-letiiu Kurskoi bitvy). Katalog istoriko-dokumental'nyoi vystavki* [*Bulge of fire. Strategy of victory (on the 70th anniversary of the Battle of Kursk)*]. Catalog of historical-documentary exhibits] (Moscow: Rossisskoi gosudarstvennyi arkhiv ekonomiki, 2013), p. 15.
346 *Stavka* Directives No. 46090 from 30 March 1943 about replenishing the 23rd and 2nd Tank Corps and the 1st Guards Mechanized Corps; No. 46091 from 30 March about replenishing the 2nd Guards and 5th Guards Tank Corps; No. 46093 from 31 March about replenishing the 3rd Guards Tank Corps; and No. 46093 from 31 March about replenishing the 1st Guards "Don", 12th, 15th and 18th Tank Corps.
347 Zamulin, V., *Kurskii izlom: Reshaiushchaia bitva Velikoi Otechestvennoi* [*Kursk turning point: Decisive battle of the Great Patriotic War*] (Moscow: Iauza, EKSMO, 2008), pp. 101-102.
348 TsAMO RF, F.203, Op.2843, D.365, l. 83.
349 TsAMO RF, F.203, Op.2843, D.341, l. 210.

and 3 standard combat loads for the other types of troops; 5-7 refills of fuel for the combat machines and 1.5-3 refills for the motorized transport; and 15 days' worth of "untouchable" reserves.[350]

The Central Front therefore at the beginning of May was substantially inferior to its neighbor in terms of armored fighting vehicles: on 15 May the Voronezh Front had 1,380 operational tanks and self-propelled guns, or 76 percent of the total number that it would receive by the start of the Battle of Kursk, while the Central Front had only half as many. However, already by the end of this month the situation began to change, and 1 June K.K. Rokossovsky had a total number of 1,216 serviceable combat machines (72 percent of the number it would have on 5 July), including 171 in the 13th Army (88 percent of the number it would have on 5 July).[351]

I want to bring the reader's attention to one very substantial detail. A decision taken by Moscow in early 1943 played a major role in quickly rebuilding the armored forces after the 1942-1943 winter campaign in all the *fronts*, but in particular in Rokossovsky's and Vatutin's forces. The situation with the repair of disabled tanks, which were increasing in the acting army with each passing month, noticeably began to become acute already in the latter half of 1942. Therefore, in February 1943, the State Defense Committee obliged the Red Army's Headquarters for Armored and Mechanized Forces to initiate active work to increase the troops' recovery and repair capabilities substantially by forming recovery and repair battalions and repair bases. After this resolution, the situation began gradually to change for the better, but there was no success in implementing a rapid, and most importantly, uninterrupted process of bringing knocked-out tanks back into service. Now the main problem became the lack of the possibility to repair key components of tanks quickly at the front, without resorting to sending them back to factories for overhaul and repair. In May 1943 the State Defense Committee returned to this matter and demanded the formation of two mobile assembly-repair factories. As a result of these steps, a wide network of repair units was created in the Red Army, which in the second quarter of 1943 enabled the return of a total of more than 10,000 tanks to service across all the *fronts*.[352]

I will mention that an axiom exists in the theory of military arts: for the success of an offensive operation on the strategic level, the attacking side must have an advantage in strength over the defending side, at a minimal correlation of 3:1.[353] However, as is known, there is no rule without its exceptions; for example, the German General Heinrici, the former commander of the Fourth Army, which performed successfully as part of Army Group Center, told the British historian Lidell Hart after the war, "I would say that, for success the attacker needs six to one or seven to one against a well-knit defence that has a reasonable frontage to cover. There were times when my troops held their own against odds of 12 to 1 or even 18 to 1."[354]

Considering that Hitler was giving primary significant to the armored forces in order to meet Citadel's objectives, I will share certain figures on their number in the period under examination. In May 1943, Army Group Center, which included the Ninth Army, had on its

---

350 TsAMO, RF.203, Op.2843, D.365, l. 83.
351 TsAMO RF, F.62, Op.321, D.16, l. 127, 127 obr.
352 *Voennye kadry sovetskogo gosudarstva v Velikoi Otechestvennoi voine 1941-1945* [*Military cadres of the Soviet state in the Great Patriotic War 1941-1945*] (Moscow: Voenizdat, 1963), p. 111.
353 Glantz and House, *Kurskaia bitva: Reshaiushchii povorotnyi punkt Vtoroi Mirovoi voiny* (Moscow: AST, 2006), p. 80.
354 Lidell Hart, B.H., *Po druguiu storony kholma* [*On the other side of the hill*] (Moscow: AST, 2014), p. 329.

list a total of 442 panzers (Pz.Kpfw. III, Pz.Kpfw. IV and not a single Pz.Kpfw. VI Tiger), of which 71 percent (or 314) were operational; in contrast Army Group South had 1,087 panzers, of which 728 (71 percent) were serviceable.[355] Thus, already in May, the correlation of forces in this important type of arms corresponded to 1.5:1 in favor of the Soviet side on the northern portion of the Kursk bulge, and 1.3:1 in the south. Yet by the beginning of the first month of summer, the gap in these indicators grew even larger. For example, in the six panzer divisions and one separate heavy panzer battalion of Tiger tanks of the Ninth Army on 3 June 1943, there was a total of 352 panzer in service.[356] In the opposing Central Front on this same day, there was a total of 1,257 tanks and self-propelled guns, or 3.5 times as many.[357] A serious shortage of armored vehicles would be observable in the German combat units even in mid-June. According to the status on 16 June 1943, the four panzer divisions of the Ninth Army's shock XXXXVII Panzer Corps would have respectively: 59 panzers in the 2nd Panzer Division, 91 in the 4th Panzer Division, 33 in 9th Panzer Division, and 61 in the 12th Panzer Division (of which 18 would have short barreled guns).[358] For a general offensive, these were just crumbs, especially if you consider that in May and in the first half of June, Model's grouping received only a portion of its Tigers, and none of its promised Ferdinand or Brummbär self-propelled guns, which the Germans would activate in order to breach the main, most heavily fortified belt of defenses. They would arrive only in the latter half of June and early July.

In addition, the German forces on the northern side of the Kursk salient even in June would be experiencing an acute shortage of ammunition; the Ninth Army's stockpiles were half-empty. On 5 June the Operations Department of Army Group Center through Telegram No. 3398/43 would inform the Ninth Army command that "… the situation with shells for the light field howitzers (105mm) designated for Operation Citadel has worsened, and the creation of the necessary supplies of shells remains under question. In addition, complications with the delivery of machine-gun rounds is being observed, the expenditure of which has exceeded the planned indicators in view of the enemy's high activity."[359]

Approximately the same situation with armored vehicles was evident in von Manstein's grouping as well. For example, the difference in the number of operational panzers in his main Fourth Panzer Army between 1 June and 4 July amounted to 353 (respectively 467 and 820), an increase of 76.2 percent (for more detail see Tables 21 – 21e). Moreover, over the entire month of June and first four days of July, one of the two assault formations of Hoth's panzer army that were designated for the breakthrough to Kursk, the XXXXVIII Panzer Corps, was supposed to receive a most impressive amount of armor fighting vehicles – 303, or an increase of 347 percent ! It is therefore impossible not to agree with the commander of Army Group South's 6th Panzer

---

355 Arkhiv IVI, F.191, Op.233, D.108; *Doklady generala-inspektora tankovykh voisk Guderiana – Gitleru s 3.5.1943 po 1.6.1944* (perevod s nemetskogo), Chast. 1 [*Arkhiv of the Institute of Military History. Reports of Guderian, the General-Inspector of Panzer Troops to Hitler from 3 May 1943 to 1 June 1944*] (translated from the German), Part 1 (Moscow: Voenno-istoricheskoe upravleniie Genshtaba VS SSSR, 1947), pp. 6-7.
356 NARA US, T.312, R.320, F.7889449.
357 TsAMO RF, F.62, Op.321, D.16, l. 125.
358 NARA US, T.314, R.1128, F.000410-000572. By 5 July 1943, this panzer corps would have a different roster of divisions.
359 NARA US, T.312, R.317, F.7886113.

Division Generalleutnant von Hünersdorff, who at a meeting on 22 May called Operation Citadel "idiotic" and asserted that the entire operation violated the ground rules of leadership.[360]

I cannot but pause for a moment on Steven Newton's assertion about Model's supposed fundamental mistake that he made due to faulty intelligence in a report to Hitler regarding the calculation of the correlation of forces between his Ninth Army and Rokossovsky's Central Front in early May. The American scholar writes:

> Contrary to German intelligence estimates, the Soviet Central Front had deployed only about 1,000 tanks and assault guns in late April-early May, rather than 1,500. This was a critical misinterpretation that explains much about Model's insistence on delaying the offensive. With 800 AFVs facing 1,500, the army commander had a legitimate case for arguing that additional panzers, especially Panthers and Tigers, were absolutely necessary for the assault. Had Model realized that Russian armored superiority was only about 200 vehicles, he would have been far more willing to proceed. By waiting, Ninth Army augmented its AFV holdings by about 25 percent, but the Soviets nearly doubled theirs.[361]

First, the figures and correlations indicated by S. Newton are inaccurate. As the evidence presented above show, in early May W. Model did not possess 800 armored fighting vehicles. The entire Army Group Center had almost half as much of them, while Rokossovsky's Central Front was superior to the Germans in the number of tanks by more than 1.5 times, 442 against 674.

Second, if to rely on the memoirs of Field Marshal von Monstein and Colonel General Guderian, who participated in the meeting in Munich on 4 May, where Hitler read Model's letter aloud and the participants settled the question about postponing the start of the operation from May to June, the requirement regarding the delivery of tanks, which the commander of the Ninth Army raised in his letter, was not the main consideration. From the outset, Model did not possess large armored forces; they were in the south, in von Manstein's army group, and no one had promised Model to deliver large amounts of armored vehicles to him. Therefore, in order to break through the Soviet defenses, back in April he had placed his reliance on infantry, reinforced with artillery, assault guns and sappers, unlike von Manstein. This approach remained unchanged right up to the start of the Battle of Kursk. Therefore, in step with the strengthening of the Central Front's lines, the main question that troubled Model, just as it did the commander of the Fourth Panzer Army Colonel General Hoth in the south, was whether the troops of the first echelon be capable of breaching the main and second defensive belts of the Soviet forces, so that the panzers could emerge in operational space. By May, Model already possessed the minimum number of panzers in order to develop a success into the depth after overcoming the most heavily fortified sector of defense. However, in order to ensure the rupturing of the Central Front's lines, he believed that it was extremely necessary to provide the forward troops with heavy panzers (well-armored, with powerful main guns), which in the first stage of the offensive would clear a path for the infantry by destroying fixed enemy firing

---

360 Cross, *Operatsiia Tsitadel'* [*Operation Citadel*] (Smolensk: Rusich, 2006), p. 133.
361 Newton, S., *Kurskaia bitva: nemetskii vzgliad* [*Battle of Kursk: The German view*] (Moscow: Iauza, EKSMO, 2006), p. 475.

positions and enemy armor in the event of counterattacks. On 3 May, he did not possess a single tank of that type. So, Walter Model was not simply demanding an increase in armored fighting vehicles because the Russians had 1.5 times more than he did, but instead persistently calling for heavy machines of the Tiger and Panther types, as well as Ferdinand self-propelled heavy tank destroyers.

In addition, as captured documents testify, as I've discovered in the US National Archives, the commander of the Ninth Army was also wrestling with the major problem of bringing the infantry divisions back up to establishment levels, since at that time they were in a seriously battered shape.[362] The situation with manpower replacements was so difficult and at the same time critical, that it was because of the inability to resolve it that the OKH for the first time on 20 April 1943 decided to push back the date for the start of the offensive toward Kursk.[363] Therefore the Colonel General had attached an aerial reconnaissance photograph to his letter, which plainly revealed the scale of the fortification of the Soviet side's forward edge, and thereby demanded that Hitler either cancel the offensive or come quickly to an operational decision regarding the problem with the lack of heavy armor and men.

Considering the above, it is hard to agree with the assertion that if Model had known the true number of tanks in the Central Front, he already in May would have been ready to take part in an offensive toward Kursk. Model was an opponent of Citadel. He was one of the few who not only understood its lack of prospects, but also something very important, was not afraid to speak openly to Hitler about this while clearly arguing his position.

It would be inaccurate to state that the situation with the restoration of the combat capabilities of the Central and Voronezh Fronts was proceeding smoothly and without hitches in the first half of May 1943. All of the information from the reports of their headquarters presented above should not be taken literally. If it was written that men and armored vehicles had arrived in the Front, this does not mean that that they had already been passed on to the units and elements. A certain number of weapons and equipment marked as having been received by the *fronts* were either still located in their stockpiles or were nearing their stations of unloading. For example, N.F. Vatutin on 11 May reported to *Stavka*:

> The main lots of armaments have arrived by railroad in the most recent days. Thus, the bulk of the weapons will be allocated to the troops by the end of 14 May. Nine more trains with armaments are on their way, and they will be received by the troops in the period between 18 and 20 May. After this, the troops will have 100 percent of their establishment strength in mortars, anti-tank rifles, PPSh submachine guns and regimental artillery; 74 percent of the rifles; 57 percent of the light machine guns; 65 percent of the Maksim machine guns; 71 percent of the 45mm anti-tank guns; 80 percent of the 76mm divisional artillery; and 70 percent of the 122mm howitzers.[364]

Even so, already by the middle of the month of May, the forces of the Voronezh Front had been brought up to a high level of readiness, and its command was so confident in its own strength (and not without justification) that it even proposed to the *Stavka* to go on the offensive first. It

---

362 NARA US, T.312, R.317, F.7886042, 7886046.
363 NARA US, T.312, R.317, F.7886050.
364 TsAMO RF, F.203, Op.2777, D.75, l. 171.

is hard to imagine that N.F. Vatutin would have shown such initiative while realizing that his armies still weren't ready for combat, at a time when the *Stavka* was not insisting on this and even to the contrary, believed such a step to be premature.

Concluding our examination of the question of the Soviet forces' combat readiness at Kursk in early June 1943, I believe it is important once again to emphasize that having reached the decision on 12 April to adopt the strategic defensive, and having determined the enemy's likely axis of the main attack, the Soviet High Command in the course of a month had primarily brought the *fronts* that were defending the Kursk bulge back up to strength, as well as the their armies that were covering the important directions. As had been planned, by 10 May the strength of Rokossovsky's and Vatutin's groupings according to the two most important indicators for conducting a defense – manpower and artillery means – exceeded 80 percent of those they would have on 5 July (and respectively 40 percent and 74 percent of the tanks). By 5 June, the total strength in personnel of the Central and Voronezh Fronts exceeded 98 percent of the data for 5 July 1943, while the strength in artillery approached 90 percent and the number of tanks varied between 72 percent and 76 percent.

Thus, both strategic *fronts* were virtually fully ready for the Battle of Kursk by early May. At the same time, for example, the Ninth Army's grouping had yet to receive even the minimum of that which had been promised to it before Citadel by the beginning of May. Its infantry and panzer divisions still had not been completely rebuilt and would prove unable to meet the objectives set for the summer campaign. Meanwhile the Soviet side by that time was already able to repulse an attack launched by the enemy's available forces Thus, E. von Manstein's assertion that the Red Army's forces opposite Army Group Center and Army Group South in the Kursk area were supposedly not fully combat ready in May proves to be at odds with the historical truth.[365]

The Soviet strategic reserves – the Steppe Military District – would play a substantial role both in the successful conclusion of the Kursk defensive operation and in the victory at Kursk as a whole. Three of its five ground armies – the 5th Guards Tank Army and the 5th Guards and 53rd Armies – took an active part in repulsing Army Group South's offensive in the sector of the Voronezh Front. Thus, for a complete analysis of the subject, it is exceptionally important to understand the condition of these forces in the examined period of time. The *Stavka* initiated the formation of its reserves back in February 1943. However, because of setbacks and difficulties in the course of the early 1943 offensive in Ukraine, the conclusion of this process, which is to say unifying these forces into a military district, took place only after the front became stabilized on the southwestern direction.

On 4 April 1943, the Deputy Chief of the General Staff Lieutenant General A.I. Antonov sent an order from the People's Commissar of Defense to the commander of the 41st Army: to form the Reserve Front headquarters (from 15 April 1943, the Steppe Military District) on the basis of the army headquarters prior to 15 April.[366] Two days later, on 6 April, I.V. Stalin signed a document addressed to the deputy commander of the Southwestern Front Lieutenant General M.M. Popov, with a classification that was rare even for those times: "Completely secret. Only personally. In your own hands". It stated:

---

365 Manstein, *Uteriannye pobedy*, p. 543.
366 TsAMO RF, F.240, Op.2779, D.6, l. 57.

The *Stavka* of the High Command is ordering:

1. To form the Reserve Front by 30 April 1943. Location of the Reserve Front's field headquarters: the Voronezh area.
2. To appoint as commander-in-chief of the Reserve Front Lieutenant General Comrade M.M. Popov, having freed him from the duties of deputy commander of the Southwestern Front. To authorize Major General F.P. Ozerov to carry out the duties of the Reserve Front's chief of staff.
3. Include as part of the Reserve Front:
   a. The field headquarters of the Reserve Front, having deployed it on the basis of the field headquarters of the 41st Army as authorized by No.02/240;
   b. the 2nd Reserve Army;
   c. the 24th, 53rd, 47th and 46th Armies;
   d. the 1st, 3rd and 4th Guards Tank Corps and the 3rd, 10th and 18th Tank Corps;
   e. the 1st and 5th Mechanized Corps;
4. Report on the execution of this order.[367]

The first stage of the Front's (or District's) formation presented two main tasks to its command: the assembly of the armies in the areas set for them by the end of April; and to begin the process of bringing them back up to strength. Moscow was placing high hopes on its reserves in the forthcoming summer campaign. Thus, their equipping and manning became a matter of primary importance. For this purpose, a special overseer from the State Defense Committee was appointed, Politburo member M.I. Mikoyan, who not only had sweeping authorities, but also possessed great organizational skills. By the indicated deadline, all of the district's forces were located in the places designated for them, and some of them had even initiated combat preparations. After resolving the initial tasks to assemble, the *Stavka* demanded to bring the strength of the reserves up to authorized levels in the course of May and to begin fostering teamwork among the combat elements and units, so that by 1 June the district would be completely ready to conduct combat operations, both when on the defensive and when on the offensive. Between 1 and 15 May, training went on at the platoon, company, and reinforced battalion levels, and between 16 and 31 May at the level of the rifle regiment.

In addition, in the last month of spring, the plan was to alter the district's combat roster of armies and corps substantially. By the end of May, it was to possess five combined-arms armies (the 4th and 5th Guards and the 27th, 47th and 53rd Armies), one tank army (the 5th Guards Tank Army) and one air army (the 5th Air Army), as well as three tank (3rd and 4th Guards and 10th), three mechanized (2nd and 3rd Guards and 1st), and three cavalry (3rd, 5th and 7th Guards) corps. It was with this grouping that it would enter the Battle of Kursk. All of the aforementioned tasks were primarily resolved within the indicated deadlines.

Thus far, unfortunately, information on the strength of the Steppe Military District by the beginning of May hasn't been found. According to A.I. Mikoyan, all of its armies were to be "fully equipped, armed and supplied with all types of rations within the following deadlines:

---

367 TsAMO RF, F.240, Op.2779, D.285, ll. 35-36.

2nd Reserve (63rd) and 24th (4th Guards) – by 15 April; 66th (5th Guards) by 20 April; 46th and 53rd – by 30 April; and 47th – by 10 May."[368] As already mentioned above, provisioning the *Stavka*'s reserves was the primary order of business, so their requests were met even before the claims of the Central Front and Voronezh Front commands. As of 1 June 1943, the difference in the manning and equipping levels between the forces deployed within the Kursk salient and the *Stavka*'s reserves varied between10 to 15 percent . Thus, it is possible to speculate that the timetables given by A.I. Mikoyan for equipping the reserves with all types of armaments and personnel were kept. If by 5 May the strength of Rokossovsky's and Vatutin's groupings according to the two most important indicators for a defense – in manpower and artillery means – exceeded 80 percent of the indicators for 5 July, these figures in Popov's forces ranged between 90 percent and 95 percent . Substantial problems in the district might have arisen only with armored fighting vehicles, since the losses of them in the acting army by the start of the muddy season had been very high. In his memoirs, Mikoyan indicates that by 25 April, all ten of the district's tank corps on average had been brought up to 60 percent of their authorized manpower, 38 percent of their armaments, and 60 percent of their gear.[369] So I presume that if by 10 May the number of tanks in the Central and Voronezh Fronts were respectively 40 percent and 74 percent of their 5 July number, then in the Steppe Military District, this figure was probably somewhere between 65 percent and 70 percent .

Extensive data not only for the district as a whole, but also for all of its armies has been found for the beginning of June 1943. According to a report from M.M. Popov to I.V. Stalin on 1 July 1943, the Steppe Military District was short only 6,000 men to bring the troops up to the establishment figure, of which 2,000 were to go to the rifle divisions, and 4,000 – to the tank and mechanized formations.[370] Accordingly, if to consider that by the start of the fighting the manpower strength of the Steppe Military District was 573,295 men, and the strength in the combat units was 449,130, then according to manpower levels it was staffed virtually at 100 percent of establishment levels.

The situation with artillery was also normal. Most of its units had been brought up to full strength and had accumulated 30 45mm anti-tank guns (eight more were on their way), 37 76mm regimental guns (with 47 more on the way), 17 122mm howitzers (with eight more on the way) and 71 37mm anti-aircraft guns (with 18 more on the way). There was a considerable reserve of certain kinds of artillery and mortars above and beyond table strength. For example, for 76mm M1942 divisional guns, the establishment strength was 1,595, but the District had 1,616 available and 20 more on their way; for 50mm mortars, the respective numbers were 2,359, 2487 and 80; for 82mm mortars, 4,460, 4,596 and 98; for 120mm mortars, 1,820, 1,894 and 79.[371]

More significant, but far from critical problems existed with armored vehicles, as well with combat assets, service and supply units and reserve units. By 3 June, the Steppe Military District still had not received 433 tanks and self-propelled guns (including 233 T-34 and 196 T-70),

368 Mikoyan, A.I., *Tak byli. Razmyshlenie o minuvshem* [*As it was. Thoughts about the past*] (Moscow: Tsentrpoligraf, 2014), p. 490.
369 Ibid., p. 494.
370 TsAMO RF, F.240, Op.2779, D.285, ll. 49-50.
371 Ibid., l. 20.

which amounted to 25.6 percent of the authorized strength.[372] In separate tank and mechanized corps, the following elements still had not arrived:

a. 10th Tank Corps – the medical-sanitation platoon and tank reserve;
b. 18th Separate Tank Corps – the tank reserve;
c. 3rd Guards Tank Corps – the tank reserve;
d. 4th Guards Tank Corps – the field bakery and tank reserve;
e. 1st Mechanized Corps – the self-propelled artillery regiment, anti-aircraft regiment and tank reserve;
f. 2nd Guards Mechanized Corps – the self-propelled artillery regiment, anti-aircraft regiment, mortar regiment, signals battalion and tank reserve;
g. 3rd Guards Mechanized Corps – the self-propelled artillery regiment, anti-aircraft regiment, mortar regiment, destroyer anti-tank artillery regiment and tank reserve.[373]

However, all of these problems did not have a large effect on the combat capabilities of those three armies, which in July 1943 would be fated to take part in the struggle to defeat Operation Citadel. For example, according to the TO&E for rifle divisions, the rifle divisions in the 53rd Army and 5th Guards Army should have had 56,000 soldiers and commanders. By 1 June, they respectively had 55,796 (with another 1,449 already earmarked for the army) and 53,303 (with a train carrying another 2,500 replacements on the way).[374]

The 5th Guards Tank Army was also virtually at full strength, although it had certain problems. I will mention that between mid-March and 5 July 1943, it had only two corps: the 29th Tank Corps and 5th Guards Mechanized Corps, even though Moscow had promised to return to Rotmistrov his "own" 3rd Guards "Kotel'nikovo" Tank Corps but had not followed through with it. On 6 July, before setting out on the march to the Voronezh Front, instead the 5th Guards Tank Army was given the 18th Separate Tank Corps. So, when analyzing the tank army's condition, presented below, information for this separate tank corps will be used, as well as that for the 10th Tank Corps from the 5th Guards Army, which already on 7 July 1943 would be sent to the southern portion of the Kursk bulge (to Prokhorovka).

By TO&E, the 5th Guards Tank Army should have had 37,231 servicemen, but on 1 July it had 35,302, a shortage of 1,929 men or 5 percent of table strength. For separate types of guns (the 76mm divisional artillery and 122mm howitzers) and mortars (50mm and 82mm), between 4 and 13 pieces still had not been received by its troops (although all of this materiel was already on the way), but according to other types (120mm mortars and 45mm anti-tank guns), its troops were 4 to 10 tubes above table strength.[375]

The shortage of armored fighting vehicles was more significant, though not in Rotmistrov's tank army itself, but in individual corps of the District, which would operate together with it on the Voronezh Front. On 3 July 1943, the shortage of tanks and self-propelled artillery amounted to 4 T-34 and 19 BTR MZA-1 (small-caliber armored motorized anti-aircraft artillery) in the

---

372 Ibid., l. 13.
373 Ibid., l. 18.
374 Ibid., l. 43.
375 Ibid., l. 75.

29th Tank Corps; 2 T-34 and 3 BTR MZA-1 in the 5th Guards Mechanized Corps; 3 T-70 in other combat units of the army; 35 T-34, 7 T-70 and 14 BTR MZA-1 in the 18th Separate Tank Corps; and 32 T-34, 7 T-70 and 8 BTR MZA-1 in the 10th Tank Corps.[376]

Accordingly, if before entering combat on 12 July 1943, the commander of the 5th Guards Tank Army had in his three corps (18th Separate Tank, 29th Tank and 5th Guards Mechanized Corps) and separate reserve motorcycle and tank regiments a total of 690 combat machines (not including the self-propelled guns), then the 48 tanks of this number that were absent on 3 June in the 18th Separate and 29th Tank Corps and 5th Guards Mechanized Corps amounted to only 0.07 percent . Meanwhile, the SS Panzer Corps on 1 June 1943 relative to 4 July still had not received 21 percent of its tanks.

In conclusion I will note that in M.M. Popov's letter, the lack of a large number of horses, 28,000, including 26,000 for the cavalry corps and the rest for the rifle divisions, was named among the number of more substantial problems. However, considering that the cavalry corps did not take part in repulsing the German attack toward Kursk, this problem does not have any connection with the subject under discussion.

Thus, the entire Steppe Military District and its separate armies, which would play an important role in the defensive phase of the Battle of Kursk, by 1 June 1943 were virtually fully ready for combat, and possessed approximately the same number of primary weapons and personnel as they would have on 5 July. Judging from the statements of a number of German military commanders and the leadership of the Third Reich, they did not even suspect this. At the same time, it must be recognized that over the final month of June before the battle, the level of training of the District's men unquestionably increased, and those problems mentioned above in staffing and equipping were also settleed. In addition, if to judge from the memoirs of the former commander-in-chief of the Steppe Military District Colonel General I.S. Konev[377]

---

376 Ibid., l. 13.
377 Konev, Ivan Stepanovich (1897-1973), Marshal of the Soviet Union (1944), twice Hero of the Soviet Union (1944, 1945). A veteran of the First World War and Russian Civil War. In the Red Army from 1918. In January 1941, he was appointed in command of the North Caucasus Military District. With the start of the Great Patriotic War, he assumed command of the Western Front's 19th Army. From September 1941 he served as the commander-in-chief of the Western, and then the Kalinin Front from October of the same year. On 26 August 1942 Konev returned to the post of commander-in-chief of the Western Front, but on 27 February 1943 he was removed from this post and sent to command the less important Northwestern Front. On 23 June 1943 Konev was appointed as commander-in-chief of the Steppe Military District, which became the Steppe Front on 9 July 1943. His forces entered the Battle of Kursk on 18 July 1943 south of Prokhorovka Station, and up until 23 July 1943 it fought in close cooperation with the Voronezh Front, forcing Army Group South back to the line from which its divisions had started Operation Citadel. In Operation "Polkovodets Rumiantsev", Konev's Steppe Front would play a primary role. His troops liberated Belgorod on 5 August 1943, followed by Khar'kov on 23 August. For the successes in the fighting near Kursk, Konev was deemed worthy of the commander's Order, the Order of Suvorov 1st Class. In October 1943, the Steppe Front was renamed as the 2nd Ukrainian Front, and I.S. Konev continued to command it. For encircling the enemy grouping at Korsun'-Shevchenkovsky, Konev acquired the title Marshal of the Soviet Union. From May 1944 and until the end of the war, Konev commanded the 1st Ukrainian Front. For his stellar combat record in the struggle on the fronts of the Great Patriotic War, Konev was awarded the highest commander's order, the Order of Victory (No. 4). After the war, he served in a variety of command posts. Konev retired in 1961. He described his part in the Battle of Kursk in his book *Zapiski komanduiushchego frontom* [*Notes of a Front commander*].

and certain archival documents, it was at the end of June that specific cooperative measures were put in place between the District command and the leadership of the Voronezh Front, where its forces were due to operate. I.S. Konev recollected:

> I.V. Stalin recommended that I visit the Voronezh Front, in order to be brought up to date on the situation and to learn the directions of possible enemy attacks. So, I repeatedly drove out to General N.F. Vatutin's headquarters. Several times I was in Kursk, on the Oboian' direction or at the boundary with the Southwestern Front. The situation on the Voronezh and Central Fronts, and all of the efforts that the Fronts were undertaking to strengthen the defenses, were clear to me.[378]

Notably, not only the readiness of the Soviet forces brought about the failure of Citadel, but also the skillfully arranged, deeply-echeloned defenses. However, the German generals and Western scholars almost never point to this factor as decisive in the Wehrmacht's lack of success. Nevertheless, I consider it important to dwell briefly on its condition in this period. If to analyze in depth the main efforts of both N.F. Vatutin and K.K. Rokossovsky in May and June 1943, they were focused on improving the lines and training the men to make effective use of them. In fact, there were serious objective reasons for this. For example, the inspections done in the first half of May by General Staff officers show that on the Voronezh Front's main army-level belt, all of the work of first and second priority had been completed, but regarding the second and third defensive belts, here substantial, though not critical, shortcomings had been revealed in fortifying the positions (insufficient mining of the ground between the belts, shallow trenches, poor camouflage, etc.), which already by the beginning of June had been corrected to a significant extent. For example, up until 5 May, the 6th Guards Army had managed to emplace only 17 percent of the 90,000 anti-tank mines that had been planned, and only 16 percent of the 64,000 anti-personnel mines that had been planned to be in place by 5 July. In the 7th Guards Army, the given indicators were also extremely low, even by 16 May, although they were higher than the neighbor's: in anti-tank mines, approximately 22.4 percent of the 65,000 anti-tank mines that had been planned, and 16.9 percent of the 84,000 anti-personnel mines.[379]

It should be emphasized that the insignificant number of emplaced mines does not indicate that the directions offering good ground for tanks on the lines of the Voronezh and Central Fronts were open for enemy armored vehicles. By 5 May, the plans for mining the ground in front of the main defensive belt and within its system of defenses had been implemented. The problems with laying mines remained in the zones between the defensive belts, and within the second and third defensive belts. The problems with mine-laying were first of all in the muddy season, which complicated the work and the transportation of supplies and sappers. Secondly, there was a lack of the necessary quantities of mines and explosives. From the end of April, Moscow was late in allocating them, so the Front commands were actively seeking internal reserves; mainly, they relied on captured means – German mines and artillery shells which were converted into improvised explosive devises. However, even here more than a few difficulties

---

378 Konev, I.S., *Zapiski komanduiuschego frontom* [*Notes of a Front commander*] (Moscow: Tsentrpoligraf, 2014), p. 104.
379 TsAMO RF, F.375, Op.9022, D.5, l. 21.

arose, and not rarely due to subjective factors. From Order No. 49 from the Red Army's Chief of Engineers Lieutenant General M.P. Vorob'ev from 18 June 1943:

> On 23 May in the area of Voronezh, a temporary stockpile of anti-tank mines belonging to the Voronezh Front exploded. In the stockpile, there were 2,700 anti-tank mines that had been transported by representatives of the Voronezh Front Captain Naugol'nikov and Senior Lieutenant Kolibr. The German T-35 mines were being trucked without their detonators but with open apertures in their covers and with blasting caps still inside. The explosion happened due to incautious handling of the mines when unloading them. The work crews had not been instructed and did not understand explosive mines or the precautionary measures when handling them. The command staff failed to organize the work and was not overseeing it. The explosion destroyed 2,700 mines, two trucks, and killed seven service personnel and 15 to 20 civilians, who were located in the vicinity of the stockpile, because the location for the stockpile had been chosen in direct proximity of a thoroughfare with heavy traffic.
> ... The country, experiencing the greatest exertion of efforts and resources, is giving everything to the front and sacrificing everything for victory over the foe. Soviet people in the rear have a single slogan – "More mines and shells, explosives and ammunition for the front!" but a group of slackers, having lost all semblance of a commander and sensing no responsibility for an assignment, instead of handling each gram of valuable property with care, through their negligence and slackness allowed the destruction of dozens of tons of precious materiel, the lives of Soviet people, and tens of thousands of hard-earned rubles.[380]

Even so, the defenses at Kursk on the whole by the start of the fighting should notbe idealized, as the authors of the books published in the Soviet period often indulged in doing. As a rule, they described them in superlative expressions, stressing their excellence; although they never as a rule bothered to analyze them in detail, they always emphasized that the defenses were uniquely strong, on the verge of perfection. However, if we turn even to "dusty" account documents, then this flight of fancy immediately vanishes. On the Central Front, the final rotation of first-echelon divisions before the battle took place in the 13th Army between 26 and 28 June. Here is what the 81st Rifle Division's headquarters said upon taking over the sector of defense from the 307th Rifle Division:

> 27 June 1943. The 81st Rifle Division replaced units of the 307th Rifle Division on the line: Hill 254.6, Hill 257.5, Nikol'skaia-1, Veselyi Berezhok, having adopted a combat formation with two regiments in line and a third regiment in reserve, occupying the Hill 251.9, Shirokoe Boloto, (excl.) Point 248.1 line. The accepted area of defense has been poorly prepared with respect to fortifications. The forward edge was screened in places by minefields, barbed wire entanglements and electrified grids … There was a system of entrenchments and communication trenches, and command and observation

380 TsAMO RF, F.426, Op.10751, D.11, ll. 37-38.

posts. The forward edge ran along the commanding heights of Hills 254.6, 257.3, 257.5 and was advantageous for our troops.

Amongst the shortcomings of the defense, the following should be assigned: the absence of clearly delineated system of defensive strongpoints; no trenches spanning the front; excessively narrow communication trenches at the forward edge (particularly in the area of Hill. 254.6 and Hill 257.5); the almost complete absence of bunkers, and those that have been built don't in anyway meet the requirements applicable for such a type of structure (speaking only about the forward edge). The lack of the necessary number of earth-and-timber bunkers in the course of the fighting resulted in the rapid loss of a significant number of heavy and light machine guns of the first line.[381]

See below for one more example from Order No. 0019 from the commander of the 13th Army on 26 June 1943:

Inspections conducted by the army headquarters have established cases of the reduced quality of carrying out service at the forward edge and in combat outposts, as well as the inadequate cover of the forward edge with artificial obstacles up to the present day, which allows enemy patrols to reach our forward edge and individual traitors to cross over to the enemy's side undetected.

The following characteristic shortcomings have been noted:
a) Many of the established minefields do not have sufficient density per kilometer of front; they've been planted sparsely and do not prevent the crossing of them freely;
b) The passages left in the minefields are frequently known to a wide circle of individuals;
c) The minelaying is frequently done by junior commanders, who don't have sufficient practical experience and poorly orient themselves in the field, so the compiled schemes of the minefields suffer from large inaccuracies, and instead of a continuous minefield, in reality gaps result.
d) The regimental and divisional engineers don't check the location of the minefields in person systematically and don't know how in reality the forward edge is covered, where there are passages, and who or how they are guarded, while the overall commanders don't monitor the system of minefields and other obstacles.[382]

Nevertheless, by the beginning of summer, the readiness of the system of defenses of both *fronts* was at a sufficiently high level. On 1 June 1943, the preparation of the first and second army-level belts of Vatutin's forces reached 80 percent and 65 percent respectively, and in the third, 40-45 percent of the top-priority sites.[383] From the report of a senior officer of the General Staff with the headquarters of the Voronezh Front, Colonel M.N. Kostin, about the condition of its lines on 5 June 1943:

381 TsAMO RF, F.29 sk., Op.1, D.6, l. 2 obr.
382 TsAMO RF, F.361, Op.6099, D.59, l. 372.
383 TsAMO RF, F.203, Op.2843, D.365, l. 82.

1. The organization of the Front's main grouping in the center and on the left flank responds to the alternative possible enemy actions with due regard for his groupings, the configuration of the frontlines and assessments of the terrain.
2. The disposition of the Front's troops in the defenses fully ensures an adequate operational depth, both for operations of the Front's reserves when launching counterattacks and for the flexibility of the defenses when regrouping the Front's forces, as well as for organizing the delivery of meals and construction material and the supply with everything necessary.
3. The absence of a no-man's land in many of the armies given the circumstances when taking up a defense during meeting engagements and withdrawal marches is a fully possible and normal manifestation. The presence of forward detachments, given the absence of a zone of no-man's land in places with a large separation from the enemy ensures the execution of a necessary and timely maneuver in the main belt of defenses at the moment the forward detachments enter combat, but given their removal from the forward edge of the main defensive belt, [there is a need for] strongly developed fortifications, anti-tank and anti-personnel obstacles, and also well-organized oblique, crossing and frontal fire of all types – particularly anti-tank fire.
4. The large width of the armies' defensive belts on ground that is not accessible for the enemy everywhere does not provide a normal front even for divisions positioned on the main direction. A division's broad front requires the construction of defenses out of centers of resistance with an intensively developed system of damaging fire from all types of weapons, anti-tank and anti-infantry fortifications, and the creation of beaten zones of fire. All this taken together requires the Front's troops to exert maximal energy and efforts to improve and further develop the defenses. Create a defensive sector that is impenetrable for the foe and yet suitable for our Front's troops to go on the offensive.
5. The artillery saturation of the Front's defenses ensures the sturdiness of the defense. The echeloned depth of the artillery firing positions ensures the conducting of combat both in front of the forward edge and in the defense's depth.

    The artillery's lack of mechanized tow, primarily prime movers like Studebakers and tractors, does not provide for the maneuver of the artillery with fire and wheels, and also complicates keeping the artillery supplied with ammunition, fuel and food, which might create difficult conditions at a critical moment of the fighting.

    The density of the anti-tank means, both on the main and secondary directions is insufficient, but given the careful organization of cooperation between the armies' anti-tank artillery and the Front's reserves and the use of natural and artificial anti-tank obstacles, as well as the anti-personnel means of the infantry and the skillful maneuvering of the fire, a sufficiently strong anti-tank defense results, capable of resisting the attack of major tank formations.
7. The absence of deeply-echeloned, artificial anti-tank obstacles makes it harder for the Front's troops to conduct stubborn fighting successfully in the depth of the defenses.

    …

10. The troops occupying the main defensive belt and the defensive sector of the 69th Army have elaborate defenses, but the ground of the second defensive belt and the defensive sector of the 69th Army hasn't been prepared to receive withdrawing forces from the main defensive belt.

    The cooperation between the troops of the main belt of defenses with the troops of the armies' second defensive belt hasn't been orchestrated and no special training exercises are being done on these matters.
11. The availability of the Front's tank, motorized and mechanized formations and units of reinforcements, positioned on the most likely directions of the enemy's attacks, fully ensures the tenacity and flexibility of the Front's defenses.
12. The organization of command and control of the troops at the army level down to the regiments ensures direction of the fighting, given the preliminary settling of a few individual questions, but command and control at the battalion level down to the squad level needs a large amount of work and thoughtful organization given the necessary conditions of eliminating all of the shortcomings that are present.[384]

The report is of a summary nature, prepared on the basis of information supplied not by the command of the Front's units and formations, which might be suspected of sugar coating the situation of affairs, but by independent General Staff officers that were subordinate only to Moscow. So, it would seem there is no basis to doubt in the conclusions.

However, this is not quite so. In the books and publications on the Battle of Kursk from the Soviet period, the description of the system of defenses at the beginning of July does not correspond to the way things stood in reality. Putting it more precisely, in their works the Soviet historians passed off the *plans* of the Red Army's command to construct the system of defenses as the *actual results* achieved by the start of the combat operations. Everything that had been planned from the outset to construct was fully completed only for the main defensive belt; the second army-level belt and rear belt of defenses by the start of Operation Citadel were not yet ready in the form in which they had been put down on paper. A portion of the planned works had been started, but was not completely finished (the trenches and anti-tank trenches were shallow, etc.), but the construction of other fortifications had not even started, and primarily this relates to the rear army-level belt of defenses. The actual works were particularly lagging from the plans on both *fronts* with respect to the rear defensive belt. In his report on the condition of the army's defenses dated 10 June 1943, the General Staff officer Lieutenant Colonel A.A. Rogoznik, who was with the 48th Army, observed:

> The second defensive belt hasn't been fully set up and requires additional work to complete it by the troops that are occupying it. ... The number of battalion areas ready for a defense range between 36 percent and 90 percent.
>
> The third belt ... is in the stage of construction and work to set it up in accordance with the demands of the Central Front and hasn't been completed. ... On the rear line, there is a total of 17 battalion areas, of which 9 have been set up by the 161st Fortified District, which is subordinate to the Front, and all of the information about the works

---

384 Ibid., l. 85.

is being passed on directly to the front. Eight battalion areas must be set up by the army's efforts, but at the present time no work is being done on them.[385]

This document about the unreadiness of the second and third defensive belts for a defense was reported by its author in the latter half of June.[386] However, for the sake of justice, it must be emphasized that in the course of preparing for the summer fighting, Romanenko's 48th Army never stood out in one of the key aspects of preparing for the summer campaign. As a rule, the situation in it fell behind that of its neighbor, the 13th Army, in consideration, as well as that of the Voronezh Front. However, substantive problems remained in all of the armies that were located within the Kursk salient in bringing up the second and third defensive belts to at least the planned indicators by the beginning of July.

An analysis of the reports of inspections regarding the Voronezh Front, which were done in mid-June, shows that the system of the army-level defensive belts (primarily the main and secondary ones) showed a particularly large number of serious shortcomings in the units' organization of fire and fortification of positions. Certain division commanders were ignoring a number of orders from the army headquarters and Front, sometimes because of inexperience, but more often because of negligence and complacency; the battalion sectors were poorly fortified, the fire had been organized incompetently, and in certain places the Germans had stealthily removed some of the minefields right under the noses of lackadaisical commanders, and they were even unaware of this. Even though the elimination of shortcomings and open disgraces proceeded at a feverish pace, this task was not completely finished even by the end of June.

In the 7th Guards Army, the greatest number of problems were identified in the 72nd Guards Rifle Division. Between 18 and 20 June, an inspection of its 224th Guards Rifle Regiment took place. As a result, a document that was festooned with unsightly facts in the regiment, which was positioned in the main belt of defenses, went up to the Front's leadership and the army's Military Council. See below for one excerpt:

Organization and securing of the main belt of defenses:
All of the 2nd Company's weapons have been advanced to the forward edge. According to a report from the 1st Guards Battalion commander Captain Ragulin, the density of rifle and machine-gun fire in the zone out to 400 meters from the forward edge amounts to 4 bullets per meter in front of each company. The distance from the forward edge to the river is more than 500 meters. Approaches to the forward edge of defense are protected by oblique and flanking fire. The river's surface cannot be swept with fire. Weapons haven't been adapted to fire at night. Shooting documentation is absent in the platoons and squads. ... A combat plan has been devised in the regiment, but the battalion and company commanders don't know it well.

Artificial fortifications:
1. The available communication trenches do not support the maneuvering of elements. In the 1st and 2nd Companies, there are no linking entrenchments, so

---

385 TsAMO RF, F.403, Op.9657, D.87, l. 111, 111 obr.
386 Ibid., l. 113 obr.

in order to reach the 1st Company from the 2nd Company, it is necessary to cross a sector of not less than 400 meters that is exposed to enemy fire. All of the firing positions (even the machine-gun nests) are not linked by trenches. The existing trenches are shallow and narrow, and also don't provide for the maneuvering of elements. The walls of the entrenchments and communication trenches have a low gradient, which leads in the majority of them to collapsing walls (the soil is sandy). The communication trenches for the most part haven't been not adapted for external defense.

2. So far there are no earth-and-timber bunkers in all of the battalions. In the 2nd Company, there are incompetently constructed anti-fragmentation nests. The primary shortcomings of the anti-fragmentation nests:
    a) Large apertures of the embrasure ports from the inside;
    b) In individual firing positions, excessively large mounting platforms for the machine guns have been installed (2/2nd Rifle Battalion);
    c) Low ceilings, which hinder the conducting of fire (1/2nd Rifle Battalion – in Junior Sergeant Krylov's squad, a light machine gun is totally unable to fire from within the bunker);
    d) Embrasures are absent in many firing positions;
    e) Many of the gun ports have been placed too high, which leads to large dead zones;
3. For the majority of the machine guns and anti-tank rifles, there are no alternate sites.
4. There are no compact fighting positions for organizing resistance with the fire of infantry weapons (the positions consist of separate foxholes, scattered at a distance of 80 meters from one another within the system of communication trenches).
5. The personnel have been fully provided with dugouts, but there are entrances to them from the enemy's direction and vestibules are lacking.

Condition of communications:
The primary means of communication is wire telephony, which is duplicated by mobile means. The radios don't work to transmit, but only to receive; the checking of radio contact is done through signals. The survivability of wire communications is inadequate – the scheme is underdeveloped and there are no alternate lines. It is necessary to have a minimum two-way contact. Lateral communications within the battalion are absent.

The laying of lines in the area of command posts and observation posts, as well as input terminals, is unsatisfactory (a jumble of cables that haven't been buried underground).[387]

It is possible that the given excerpt is too lengthy, but it clearly shows the state of affairs in a division that two weeks later would take on the main attack of Army Detachment Kempf's kampfgruppen. In fact, all of the shortcomings indicted above, which were tolerated, including

---

387 TsAMO RF, F.203, Op.2843, D.365, ll. 56-57.

because of the negligence and inertia at the command level, would place the division in a difficult situation. It would virtually fall apart into several pieces; command and control would become lost; and in the course of 12 hours the division commander Losev would be unable to establish the location of his regiments or learn of their condition.

In order to repulse an enemy offensive successfully, not only the presence of a developed system of field defenses on all the directions and sectors without exception is of great significance. It is also important that the enemy cannot make heads or tails of it before the start of the offensive and is unable to grasp its logic, and for this purpose camouflage and deception (decoy positions, dummy minefields, etc.) have primary significance. When preparing for the fighting at Kursk, the Soviet troops demonstrated that they had fully mastered this art, particularly on the Voronezh Front. Not only the command of the Red Army noted this, but the enemy also recognized it. Wrote the chief of staff of the Fourth Panzer Army's XXXXVIII Panzer Corps Major General F.W. von Mellenthin:

> Aerial photos were available for every square yard of the Kursk salient. But though these photographs showed the depth and size of the Russian positions, they did not reveal details or give any indication of the strength of their forces, for the Russians are the masters in the art of camouflage. Inevitably their strength was considerably underestimated.[388]

Thus, throughout the month of June, the layout and construction of the army-level defensive belts continued on both *fronts*; however, because of the intensified combat training of the troops that began on 1 June, this work went slowly. Therefore, by 5 July (relative to the beginning of June), neither individual sectors nor the entire system of defenses changed fundamentally. The formations and units that were arriving in these areas wouldn't have time to complete the work hastily, while doing this under fire and bombs already in the course of the fighting under way.

For a "pure experiment", it would have been useful to compare other indicators as well, such as the Soviet troops' availability of ammunition, fuel and lubricants, and so forth. This is a task for future research. However, all of the information presented above, taken together, allows the confident assertion that after 1 June 1943, a further delay with the start of Operation Citadel had no fundamental significance for the Red Army, as was just the case back at the beginning of May. Neither of the German shock groupings at the base of the Kursk salient was able to surpass the Central or Voronezh Fronts in numerical strength, which I repeat, according to military theory is a necessary condition for the success of an offensive, or even to approach their strength in manpower, armored fighting vehicles and artillery. Of course, this consideration does not even include the major *Stavka* reserves that were combined into the Steppe Military District, which already in May took position behind Rokossovsky's and Vatutin's forces. Unquestionably, there is justification to suppose that if the German offensive had started in early June, the problems with bringing up the field defenses to their planned level in the Kursk bulge might have led to increased casualties and losses among the defending Soviet troops but would not have in any way led to their defeat.

---

388 Mellenthin, F.W., *Bronirovannyi kulak vermakhta* [*Armored fist of the Wehrmacht*] (Smolensk: Rusich, 1999), p. 325.

Therefore, under no circumstance could the Germans count upon a victory at Kursk, neither in May nor in June 1943, and the postwar assertions of the German military commanders and their supporters about the possible success of Citadel, had the attack been launched in the beginning of the summer of 1943, was only putting a brave face on a sorry business. Arguments in favor of this point of view, which are encountered in Western books on the Battle of Kursk, including those that cite Field Marshal von Manstein, given detailed analysis of documentary sources, aren't confirmed. The Field Marshal himself acknowledged that the Wehrmacht command was mistaken in the question of assessing the level of combat readiness of the Soviet troops at Kursk, and after the war he gave a high rating to the work done by the USSR's political and military leadership on the eve of the 1943 summer fighting, including in preparation for the Battle of Kursk. In his memoirs he wrote: "We, of course, did not expect from the Soviet side such great organizational capabilities, which it displayed in this matter, as well as in the expansion of its military industry. We encountered a genuine Hydra, which in place of one cut-off head grew two new ones."[389]

The third phase of planning and preparations for the Soviet side for the Battle of Kursk and the summer campaign as a whole commenced in mid-May. It was at this time that Moscow finally came to the conclusion that in order to make the most effective use of the accumulated forces and to resolve the task of liberating the country by the end of the year, the tentative decision that had been reached about going over to the strategic defensive was the correct one, and from this moment on it became final. Even so, just as before the thought existed that if it became clear that Berlin was rejecting active operations, the Red Army should be fully ready to launch quickly a powerful blow against both of the enemy groupings in the area of the Kursk bulge. Recalled G.K. Zhukov: "After multiple discussions with the Supreme Commander, the decision was finally made to meet the German offensive with fire of all types of a deeply-echeloned defense, with powerful airstrikes and counterattacks by operational and strategic reserves. Then, having worn down the enemy and bled him white, to finish him off with a powerful counteroffensive in the Belgorod-Khar'kov and Orel directions, after which to conduct deep offensive operations on all the important directions."[390]

In order to achieve this goal, several tasks came to the fore, the key ones of which were the following:

a) To conclude the work-up of plans for the offensive operations of Colonel General A.D. Sokolovsky's Western Front, Colonel General M.A. Reiter's Briansk Front, and Colonel General R.Ia. Malinovsky's Southwestern Front, in order to use them in the event that the Germans were first to go on the offensive at Kursk, so they might divert German forces from the sectors of the Central and Voronezh Fronts, and in order to pursue independent objectives: the liquidation of the Orel salient and the liberation of the Donbass.

b) Regarding the growing evidence about the enemy and the proposals that were discussed in the course of the second stage of preparations, to make improvements to the plan of using the forces on the defensive (first of all, the major armored

---

389 Manstein, *Uteriannye pobedy*, p. 546.
390 Zhukov, *Vospominaniia i razymyshleniia*, Vol. 3, p. 31.

formations and artillery) in order to repulse the enemy offensive in the sectors of the Central and Voronezh Fronts.
c) To develop and improve the defensive belts in the depth of the forces that were holding the Kursk salient and to create a genuinely deeply echeloned field defense as far as the Don River.
d) To bring the combat strength of the forces up to the maximal planned indicators and to increase their level of training, having intensified their combat preparations.

As already noted above, the process of planning the summer campaign proceeded in parallel with the planning and preparations for the Battle of Kursk, which would be its initial phase. According to the *Stavka*'s plan, which acquired its final form in early May, the summer campaign would unfold in two stages. The first would be the repulse of the German armies' offensive toward Kursk, and to bleed white its panzer formations, in order to deprive the German command of its most important instrument to counter the Red Army's counteroffensive in Belorussia and Ukraine in the second stage.

Assuming that the Wehrmacht would gather an extremely powerful force for the attack in the area of the Kursk bulge, the Soviet side prepared to repulse this attack not only with the forces of the Central and Voronezh Fronts in their defensive lines, but also to draw upon the Western, Briansk and Southwestern Fronts for this purpose. With this aim in mind, their commands already in the latter half of April began preparing for an offensive operation "of dual purpose".

Moscow was assuming that the enemy would operate against K.K. Rokossovsky in successive waves and would activate his main forces once the Ninth Army penetrated the Central Front's defenses. At that point, the divisions of the second and third echelons would enter the breach. In order to prevent this, the Soviet command planned to conduct a strong pinning operation, which in the future might develop into a larger operation (or snowball into its second stage) to destroy the entire Orel salient. Here is how the commander-in-chief of the Briansk Front Colonel General M.A. Reiter described the overall plan to his chief of staff Lieutenant General L.M. Sandalov, after Reiter had attended a conference in General Staff in the latter half of April:

> As soon as the German forces thrust into the defenses of the Central Front and have become enmeshed in it, the Western and Briansk Fronts will launch the Orel offensive operation. The *Stavka* intends to destroy the enemy's Orel grouping and to eliminate the Orel salient with concentric attacks of the Western, Briansk and Central Fronts. However, the attacks in the Orel operation will have to be launched with only the three armies of our Front and the left-flank army of the Western Front. The Central Front will be firmly engaged by the enemy grouping's offensive, and for a time will at least have to withstand its onslaught. Of course, the significance of the Central Front should be high, but it will only be able to take part in the offensive operation given its successful development. Then the forces of the Central Front's right wing will attack in the direction of Kromy.[391]

---

391 Sandalov, L.M., *1941: Na moskovskom napravlenii* [*1941: On the Moscow direction*] (Moscow: Veche, 2010), pp. 339-340.

This operation received the code name "Kutuzov". The Briansk Front's 61st, 63rd and 3rd Armies, and the Western Front's 11th Guards Army would play the main role in it.

The Southwestern Front was to devise an operation with similar aims (first to aid the Voronezh Front – given a need – and then to clear the enemy from the Donbass). However, here the planning had its own specifics. The *Stavka* was pre-supposing that the Germans would not be employing their main forces against N.F. Vatutin. Therefore, a task was set for R.Ia. Malinovsky: first to defend stubbornly his own lines, and then to conduct an offensive operation now in the second stage of the summer campaign, in the course of the counteroffensive, in cooperation with the Steppe Military District and the Voronezh Front. Marshal of the Soviet Union V.I. Chuikov, the former commander of the 8th Guards Army, which at that time was on the left flank of the 57th Army that was positioned on the boundary with the neighboring Voronezh Front, recalled:

> Malinovsky brought me a map, and on it was a line drawn by operational staff members of the Front's headquarters. We were to prepare defensive lines along it, and dig firmly and deeply into the ground. The line ran along the Oskol River in the Dvurechnaia, Kupiansk, Sen'kovo, Gorokhvatka sector with a front facing the west and southwest. Ordering us to deploy the army for the defense of a comparatively narrow sector, R.Ia. Malinovsky also demanded that we be ready, if the enemy went on the offensive, to launch a strong counterblow in the Kupiansk – Volchansk direction and Kupiansk – Chuguev direction, along the right bank of the Oskol River toward the city of Izium, and if possible to cross the Severskii Donets River.[392]

As we can see, in this decision, a consideration that the enemy might attack the boundary between the Voronezh and Southwestern Fronts is not discernable in any way. Unquestionably, this was only a plan, and in the event of a marked deterioration of the situation in the sector of Vatutin's Voronezh Front, Malinovsky's Southwestern Front was to go to its assistance. However, this should be prepared in advance. For a lengthy amount of time, both the *Stavka* and its staff did not pay any particular attention to this matter. On 24 June, G.K. Zhukov and A.M. Vasilevsky in the name of the *Stavka* issued Directive No. 30141, which demanded the detailing of a plan to repulse a possible enemy attack at the boundary between the two *fronts*. In particular, the document stated:

> Your operational directives, which foresee actions of the Front's reserves in the event of an enemy breakthrough in the Volchansk, Izium and Voroshilovgrad directions, have a number of shortcomings, of which the main ones are as follows:
> 1. Troop operations given an enemy offensive at the boundary with the Voronezh Front and a simultaneous attack in the direction of Izium and Kolchansk, or given a simultaneous enemy offensive at the boundary with the Voronezh or

---

392 Chuikov, V.I., *Ot Stalingrada do Berlina* [*From Stalingrad to Berlin*] (Moscow: Sovetskaia Rossiia, 1985), p. 354.

Southern Fronts aren't foreseen, yet this option is the most likely direction of enemy operations.[393]

By the start of July, this order had been fully implemented. The reason for Moscow's fixed attention to R.Ia. Malinovsky's decisions was connected not only with the desire to correct uncovered flaws, but first of all with the effort to ensure the support of the Voronezh Front with everything necessary as much as possible, which in any case would be expected to take on one of the enemy's main attacks. It was G.K. Zhukov who most actively and persistently argued the point of view throughout the entire period of planning that the Germans would most likely attack the boundary between Vatutin's and Malinovsky's *fronts*. It was he who insisted that the Southwestern Front be made responsible for the boundary with the Voronezh Front, in particular its 57th Army, and who in early June supported R.Ia. Malinovsky's proposal to direct his 12th Army toward the boundary. As the events of early July 1943 would show, the reinforcement of the boundary between the Voronezh and Southwestern Fronts was a matter of playing it safe by the Soviet side. At the same time, it plainly shows how meticulously the *Stavka* was working an all the important questions of the defensive phase of the Battle of Kursk.

After the attack toward Kursk had been repulsed, the second stage of the summer campaign was to begin – the Soviet counteroffensive. In the course of it, it was anticipated that three *fronts*, A.D. Sokolovsky's Western Front, M.A. Reiter's Briansk Front and K.K. Rokossovsky's Central Front would completely eliminate the Orel salient and continue the offensive to the west, while the Voronezh, Steppe (brought up from the depth) and Southwestern Fronts would destroy the enemy's Khar'kov and Donbass groupings and reach the Dnepr River. The Voronezh and Steppe Fronts' offensive received the code name "Polkovodets Rumiantsev", and had the single primary objective of crushing Army Group South's left flank in order to break through to the Dnepr.

After the issuing of the main tasks to the *fronts* to devise their own operations, in the latter half of April the General Staff in parallel was busy until approximately the beginning of May with resolving theoretical matters connected with problems of an operational nature concerning the upcoming fighting, which arose immediately after making the decision regarding a deliberate defense first, followed by a counteroffensive. As S.M. Shtemenko recalled:

> There was a multitude of them: How to guarantee the success of such a defense, and was it acceptable to implement it with fewer forces than the enemy? Was it necessary to have a previously created superiority of force? At what level should this superiority exist – at the tactical or operational, at the army level or *front* level? Possibly, was it best of all to concentrate reserves in the *Stavka*'s hands, and with their help at a suitable moment to create a decisive advantage in force when going on the counteroffensive? When and at what point in the operation was it best to launch the counterstroke? It was impermissible to allow the enemy to inflict great damage to our defending forces. However, it was also impermissible to hurry, to step off prematurely, without having first weakened the enemy …

---

393 Russkii arkhiv. Velikaia Otechestvennaia. General'nyi shtab v gody Velikoi Otechestvennoi voiny: Dokumenty I materialy, 1943 (Moscow: TERRA, 1999), p. 183.

When the Supreme Commander was asked about the moment of launching the counteroffensive, he gave the following sort of reply:

> "Let the *fronts* decide this themselves, depending on the existing situation. The General Staff is obligated only to make sure their cooperation is not disrupted, and so that there won't be any large pause, during which the enemy might consolidate on his achieved lines. It is very important also to commit the *Stavka* reserves at the right moment."[394]

When the question arose in the latter half of April about working out plans for the counteroffensive, Moscow still did not have full awareness about the intentions of the German command, but it did envision the large amount of work that would have to be done to rebuild the forces, and first of all those of the Central and Voronezh Fronts. So not only K.K. Rokossovsky and N.F. Vatutin, but also the remaining *fronts* were given a date to be ready to go on the counteroffensive – 1 June. The headquarters of the Western, Briansk and Southwestern Fronts timely worked up the documentation for the operations, and at the end of April submitted them to the *Stavka* for its approval. According to regulations, after receiving this approval, inspections began by members of the General Staff, and *Stavka* representatives traveled to the *fronts* in order to assess the troops' condition and needs on the spot, and to check that the plans for the operation corresponded to the objectives set by Moscow. From 10 May G.K. Zhukov was visiting the Central and Voronezh Fronts, while A.M Vasilevsky was inspecting the Western and Briansk Fronts.

There were enough serious problems in all the *fronts*, but M.A. Reiter's Briansk Front was in the most difficult situation, although everything did not go smoothly for A.M. Vasilevsky either. From Vasilevsky's report to I.V. Stalin:

1. In the course of 19 and 20 May, together with Comrades Sokolovsky and Bulganin [a member of the Western Front's Military Council], I checked the preparations of Comrade Bagramian's 11th Guards Army for the operation. In comparison with the Briansk Front, here a large amount of work has been done, both for the preparation of the command staff and the troops as a whole; there only remains to work out isolated aspects and to receive the directive to move the troops up into their jumping-off positions. It is weak with tanks and aircraft. The available two breakthrough tank regiments and four separate tank brigades have been allocated to Bagramian by the Front command. Only a total of 100 tanks has been received to refit the 1st and 5th Tank Corps. It would be extremely desirable before the start of the operation to strengthen them with two additional breakthrough tank regiments. With respect to aviation, Comrade Novikov reported that at the *Stavka* decision, the latter is being reinforced, but unfortunately, only by 15 June, which apparently means after the start of the operation.
2. On the evening of 20 May, a return to Belov [the commander of the 61st Army]. Here, as well as with Kolpachki [the 63rd Army], the working out of tasks and cooperation is proceeding on the spot with the regiment and battalion

---

394 Shtemenko, *General'nyi shtab v gody voiny*, pp. 154-155.

commanders. The readiness of the Front's forces is being held up by the paltry supply of ammunition and the 7th Artillery Corps, which still hasn't arrived for Belov.
3. I believe that the troops on the whole will be ready to occupy the jumping-off positions by 28 May. Up to five days will be needed to move into the jumping-off positions and to deploy the artillery.
4. Simultaneously with the preparation of the operation, special attention should be given to the readiness of our defenses, and particularly on the Spas-Demiansk, Zhizdrensk and Belov directions.[395]

Even according to the rather timid account of the Chief of the General Staff it is clear that the pace of work in the Briansk Front did not match the complexity of the situation. Moscow saw the reason for this in poor leadership. So already at the beginning of June, I.V. Stalin replaced its commander: M.A. Reiter assumed command of the Steppe Military District, and in his place a more energetic and better prepared M.M. Popov arrived. However, M.A. Reiter did not remain long in command of the *Stavka*'s strategic reserves. Moscow thought poorly of his command capabilities, so just two months later he was appointed to a new post as commander of the Southern Urals Military District. In January 1946, however, and totally due to poor health, he left active work in the army and was appointed as the Chief of the "Shot" Higher Tactical Courses. The Colonel General himself believed that his career as a commander was written off only due to the efforts of detractors, who exploited certain facts in his background. L.M. Sandalov recalled:

> In parting, Maks Andreevich with tears in his eyes said, "Again someone has recalled that I was a Tsarist colonel and spent some time in a prisoner of war camp in Germany. He gave no thought to the fact that I became a prisoner while sick with typhoid fever, that I was a member of the Party for more than 20 years, or that I'd been wounded four times and once concussed while fighting for Soviet power."[396]

It is not difficult to understand the man's grievance; in February 1943, for the successfully completed Voronezh – Kastornoe operation, he'd been awarded the Order of Suvorov, but in June, without any obvious reasons he was dismissed from his post. However, it is hard to agree with his allegation. A political motive was not used in 1943 in order to remove a Front commander-in-chief from his post. The circle of generals and marshals who found themselves in this situation was extremely few in number, and they had been checked out for dozens of years in various high posts. Therefore, in the first months after reaching a decision, an assessment in the occupant of such a high post went only according to professional and volitional qualities of character. If in fact the general was actually talented or had unquestionable capabilities to command a strategic formation, then he was forgiven many real shortcomings of character, especially service in the Tsarist Army that had passed into oblivion. As an example, it is possible to recall the command biography of his replacement, General M.M. Popov.

---

395 Vasilevsky, *Delo vsei zhizni*, p. 21.
396 *General Sandalov. Sbornik dokumentov i materialov* [*General Sandalov. Compilation of documents and materials*] (Moscow, 2011), p. 276.

Many contemporary eyewitnesses remarked that having entrusted a man with a high post, I.V. Stalin did not rush to draw conclusions about his effectiveness, and allowed him the possibility to reveal his capabilities in the position, if of course he had any. Therefore, not only A.M. Vasilevsky's inspection trip influenced the decision to replace M.A. Reiter, but also a number of other factors, including a sharp argument that arose between the commander of the 11th Guards Army Lieutenant General I.Kh. Bagramian[397] on one side, and the General Staff and commanders-in-chief of the Western and Briansk Fronts on the other. It was in fact M.A. Reiter who most actively contradicted the army commander. The essence of the divergence of views consisted in the fact that I.Kh. Bagramian not without basis had doubts about the Central Front's capabilities. It was supposed to strike the southern flank of the enemy's Orel grouping (to eventually link-up with his 11th Guards Army) once the defensive fighting concluded, and then promptly initiate an offensive operation: to advance over 120 km and to link up with the 11th Guards Army in the Khotynets area, in order to close the ring of encirclement around Army Group Center's main forces in the Orel bulge. In the opinion of the army commander, this "gung-ho" plan was born under the impression of the Stalingrad successes, but in the given case the situation was different: the terrain presented hard-going for an offensive, the enemy had been preparing the defenses for two years, and only modest forces were assigned to the operation. Therefore, Bagramian proposed to resolve the operation's tasks in piecemeal fashion. Initially, the main task was to tie down the German forces, in order to prevent them from being committed against the Central Front. For this purpose, the initial offensive should only be directed against the German Bolkhov grouping alone, and to destroy it with the combined forces of his army and the Briansk Front. As a result, a large breach would form, the enemy's defenses would lose their operational resilience, and only then would it be possible to address

---

397 Bagramian, Ivan Khristoforovich (1897-1982), Marshal of the Soviet Union (1955), twice Hero of the Soviet Union (1944, 1978). A veteran of the First World War and Russian Civil War. In the Red Army from 1918. From November 1940, Bagramian was the operations chief and the deputy chief of staff of the Kiev Special Military District. With the outbreak of the Great Patriotic War, the Southwestern Front was deployed on the basis of the district, and I.Kh. Bagramian remained in his post. In September 1941, the Southwestern Front became encircled and a significant portion of its men were either killed or captured. Major General I.Kh. Bagramian managed to escape the pocket and to bring out around 20,000 men together with him. On 28 December 1941 he became the chief of staff of the Southwestern Direction, but on 1 April 1942 he was transferred to take the same post with the Southwestern Front. On 26 June 1942 Bagramian became the chief of staff of the 28th Army, but already on 7 July 1942 he became the deputy commander of the Western Front's 61st Army. On 13 July 1942 Bagramian assumed his first command post when he became the commander of the same Front's 16th Army, which was operated successfully in the central sector of the Soviet-German front. On 9 April 1943 he was one of the first in the Red Army to be deemed worthy of the command order, the Order of Kutuzov 1st Class, and his army was transformed into the 11th Guards Army. In the spring of 1943, the *Stavka* was working out the plan for the Orel strategic operation, Operation "Kutuzov", which contained a number of important ideas offered by I.Kh. Bagramian. For his participation in the Battle of Kursk, on 27 August 1943 he was awarded the Order of Suvorov 1st Class. On 19 November 1943, Bagramian became the commander-in-chief of the 1st Baltic Front. On 24 February 1944 in connection with the abolishment of the 1st Baltic Front, he was first appointed as the deputy commander, and then on 26 April as the commander-in-chief of the 3rd Belorussian Front. After the war he commanded the forces of a district, and became eventually the USSR Deputy Minister of Defense. Bagramian retired in 1968. He described his role in the preparation and conducting of the Battle of Kursk in his memoirs, *Tak my shli k pobede* [*That's how we marched to victory*]

the entire Orel salient. In the contrary case, he kept insisting, his army required substantial reinforcements.

The first serious clash between I.Kh. Bagramian and M.A. Reiter[398] took place at the end of April when discussing the plan for the Orel operation in the General Staff. The army commander was upset by the result; he saw no correlation between the given tasks and the forces he'd be given for resolving them and openly pointed this out, but the Front Commander-in-Chief "went with the tide", conforming to the general opinion of the leadership. M.A. Reiter admonished Bagramian: "Well, who are you, Ivan Khristoforovich, to be digging in your heels? After all, everything has already been agreed upon and everything is clear."[399] Then everyone other than Bagramian took the side of the Front Commander-in-Chief, including A.I. Antonov, who was conducting the meeting. However, the army commander, as he subsequently recalled, "was defeated, but not convinced". In May, the operation's plan was now being discussed in the *Stavka*. When the blueprint, against which I.Kh. Bagramian spoke up against, had virtually been confirmed, and those that had gathered began rolling up their maps, something unexpected happened. Ivan Khristoforovich recalled:

> The Supreme Leader asked: "Is everyone in agreement with this decision? Possibly, someone has a differing opinion?" This was my last opportunity. I asked permission to speak. Stalin looked at me, not without surprise, but at the same time sympathetically: "Go ahead."
>
> Again, maps were unrolled. Striving to restrain my agitation, I laid out my point of view. Having finished, I glanced at everyone, sensing that now the "Big Troika" – two Front commanders-in-chief and the Deputy Chief of the General Staff – would pounce upon me. Silence reigned for one or two minutes. Then A.D. Sokolovsky spoke up, followed by M.A. Reiter. Both were trying to refute my arguments. Maks Andreevich spoke particularly heatedly. He ended his rebuttal with the words: "Comrade Stalin, Bagramian is stubbornly pressing for conditions that would make it easier for him to resolve his tasks. If you listen to him, then it turns out that it will not only be necessary to reinforce the 11th Guards Army's combat strength, but also to support the operations of this army with attacks by the neighbors."

---

398 Reiter, Maks Andreevich [real name: Martinysh] (1886-1950), Colonel General (1943). In the Russian Army from 1906, he took part in the First World War in the final rank of colonel. In the Red Army from 1919. Reiter took part in the Russian Civil War. In the inter-war period, he commanded first a rifle brigade and then a division. Reiter participated in the conflict over the Chinese-East Railroad. In the acting Red Army from August 1941, when he served as the logistics chief and deputy commander-in-chief of the Central and Briansk Fronts. Between March and September 1942, Reiter commanded the Central Front's 20th Army, and the Briansk Front between September 1942 and June 1943 (with a short interruption), the troops of which distinguished themselves in the course of the Voronezh – Kastornoe offensive operation. For his successful conducting of it, Reiter was awarded the Order of Suvorov 1st Class. In February and March 1943, the Briansk Front together with the Central Front took part in liberation of the Kursk and Orel oblasts, resulting in the formation of the Kursk salient. Between 5 and 22 June 1943, Reiter commanded the Steppe Military District. From August to September 1943, he served as the deputy commander-in-chief of the Voronezh Front. Between January 1946 and January 1950, Reiter served as the chief of the "Shot" Higher Tactical Courses.

399 Bagramian, *Tak my shli k pobede*, p. 386.

Stalin, who before this had been attentively studying a map, raised his head, removed the pipe from his mouth, and slowly stroked his mustache. Everyone fell silent. Reiter threw me an accusatory glance, as if he wanted to say, "We warned you to keep your mouth shut! You did not listen, and now you have only yourself to blame." Then suddenly the Supreme Leader very softly and calmly said, "Bagramian is making sense. Indeed, in my opinion it is necessary to agree with his suggestion. As concerns the army commander's anxiety about more favorable conditions for carrying out an assignment, then this is commendable. After all, in the event of failure, all of the responsibility rests on him …." Advocates for continuing the debate could not be found.[400]

The planning of the Voronezh Front's offensive did not go simply either. Its command and the General Staff also had diverging opinions over determining the axis of the main attack. According to the recollections of participants in those events, N.F. Vatutin's proposal to attack toward Khar'kov and further on toward Dnepropetrovsk, with the aim of creating a bridgehead on the Dnepr River with a subsequence emergence in the Kremenchug, Krivoi Rog, Kherson area (and if the offensive went successfully, on the Cherkassy – Nikolaev line) initially prompted interest. It offered a tantalizing possibility of smashing von Manstein's Army Group South and of reaching the borders of Germany's allies, Romania and Hungary. However, a political factor overruled this. The *Stavka* opted to operate along the Khar'kov – Poltava – Kiev axis with the main objective of liberating Ukraine's capital. In addition, it was assumed that out of the Kiev area, it would be possible to strike the right flank of Army Group Center and into the rear of Army Group South, which at that moment was the strongest Wehrmacht strategic grouping on the Soviet-German front.[401] The Voronezh Front command was compelled to agree with this approach.

At this same time, the process of planning K.K. Rokossovsky's offensive was in full swing; here, divergences arose on a number of fundamental questions. G.K. Zhukov reported to I.V. Stalin after the May 1943 inspection:

Kostin's [Rokossovsky's code name in the spring of 1943] preparations for an offensive aren't complete. Having worked through this problem on the spot with Kostin and Pukkhov, we came to the conclusion about the need to shift the breakthrough sector 2 or 3 kilometers to the west of the sector that had been set by Kostin; in other words, to shift it as far as Arkhangel'sk inclusively, and to put one reinforced corps and a tank corps in the first echelon west of the railroad.

With the planned artillery grouping, Kostin will be unable to make a breakthrough since the enemy has significantly strengthened and deeply echeloned his defenses on this direction. In order to make a breakthrough certain, Kostin needs to be sent an additional artillery corps.

---

400 Ibid., pp. 386-387.
401 Shtemenko, *General'nyi shtab v gody voiny*, pp. 160-161.

> On average, the Front has one and half standard combat loads of ammunition. I ask you to oblige Iakovlev within two weeks to deliver three combat loads of the main calibers to the Front.[402]

Nevertheless, Malinin's staff, just like those of the remaining *fronts*, finished the offensive planning on time, and by the beginning of June it had completed the main steps to prepare for it. The fact that process of working up the plan for the summer campaign was essentially finished by the beginning of June, but continued to be polished for another entire month, was an important factor in its success; it allowed the Soviet side to consider a number of important problems that it encountered in this process more thoroughly and deliberately. However, it should be recognized that this did not spare the *Stavka* of major mistakes, which we will discuss below. By the beginning of June on the Central Front, three problems stood most acutely: logistical support of the troops; wrapping up the redeployment of units; and increasing the quality of the training and combat preparation of the men.

The successful and essentially timely resolution of the tasks set at the 12 April 1943 conference to bring the troops at Kursk back into shape and to bring them up to a high state of readiness, both for the defense and an offense, enabled the *Stavka* at the end of May to adjust its view of the upcoming battles in this area. The lengthy period of preparing for a likely enemy offensive on the one hand, and the danger that our infantry still wouldn't be able to withstand the powerful attacks of the German panzer wedges, prompted the *Stavka* to an atypical idea for that time: to involve major armored formations (corps) and even tank armies directly in a positional defense. In the General Staff's opinion, they were to stiffen the rifle divisions and bolster their performance.

Initially, from the moment the situation stabilized at the end of March, both *fronts* within the Kursk bulge were arrayed in a single echelon, and K.K. Rokossovsky's 2nd Tank Army and N.F. Vatutin's 69th Army were viewed as their reserves. However, as the intentions of the German command became clearer and the Voronezh Front and Central Front became stronger, the views of the General Staff on how to conduct the Red Army's combat operations in this area gradually began to change. Within the framework of readying for the summer campaign, back on 28 April the *Stavka* had made the 1st Tank Army subordinate to the Voronezh Front. However, at that time both of the tank armies (1st and 2nd Tank Armies) were being viewed not as instruments of defense, but as means for exploiting a success in the event that the forces of the two *fronts* went on the offensive toward Ukraine first. However, this does not mean that during the course of the enemy's attempt to break through their lines toward Kursk, the tank armies would remain inactive; they simply weren't included in the general plan of the *front's* positional defense, and they continued to remain in reserve (in the role of a "fire brigade"). The decision to use the tank corps of the 1st and 2nd Tank Armies as an "armored belt" behind the first strategic echelons of the Central and Voronezh Fronts, and the work on their counterattack plans in the course of the Kursk defensive operation was reached only at the end of May. It was just at this time that the armies received their concrete tasks as part of this defensive operation. For the Soviet military arts, a step like this one was a novelty. In addition, the tank armies were to handle one more important task: to support the morale of the infantry, to strengthen their

---

402 Zhukov, *Vospominaniia i razhmyshleniia*, Vol.3, pp. 35-36.

martial spirits and resolve, because at that time the infantry was still weak and suffering from "tank fright", which was the scourge of many Soviet units and formations. The clear recognition of the fact that these negative tendencies were widely prevalent among the combined-arms formations and substantially affected their combat performance was one of the factors that prompted I.V. Stalin to make this decision. From a report submitted by the headquarters of 2nd Tank Army:

> On the basis of personal directives from the chief of staff Lieutenant General Malinin, issued to the army's chief of staff Major General Comrade Preisman in the headquarters of the 13th Army on 27 May 1943, a plan for the defensive operation has been devised by the headquarters of the 2nd Tank Army, consisting of three alternatives, which foresee the troops' actions in three likely directions of enemy operations.
> Option one: With the launching of the enemy's main attack in the Nizhniaia Sergeevka – Panskaia sector in the direction of Federovka and further on toward Livny;
> Option two: The enemy launches the main attack along the railroad to the south in the general direction of Ponyri and Zolotukhino;
> Option three: With the launching of the enemy's main attack out of the Kromy – Trosna area in the direction of Fatezh.[403]

Just five days later, the headquarters' staff finished the plan for the operations and its governing documents and issued it to the troops. On 2 June 1943, the tank army's headquarters broadcast Directive No. 00881/op to the commanders of the subordinate corps and of the 11th Guards Separate Tank Brigade, which determined:

a) the route of march and alternative routes;
b) the jumping-off areas;
c) the probable directions of attack;
d) with whom and how to cooperate;
e) the locations of the headquarters of the army, corps and 11th Separate Guards Tank Brigade;
f) the overall instructions to the command staff of the 3rd and 16th Tank Corps and the 11th Separate Guards Tank Brigade down to company commanders inclusively to study the routes of march; down to the platoon commanders inclusively – to determine the directions of attack and in the process identify the jumping-off areas, the locations for the command posts, observation posts and alternative observation posts, the firing lines for actions out of ambush positions, and the areas of assembly, while simultaneously establishing the amount of work necessary (preparation of bridges, descents and ascents).[404]

---

403 TsAMO RF, F.307, Op.4148, D.145, ll. 1-2.
404 Ibid., ll. 3-4.

Thus, in the first ten days of June, the plan for repulsing the enemy's attack at Kursk by the Central and Voronezh Fronts took on its final form. In addition to the detailed spelling out of the actions of the combined-arms armies, it also included one more important feature that had been worked out, which increased the resilience of our defenses – the operations of major armored formations directly in support of the positional defense.

So, June had arrived, and together with it, worry reigned in the Soviet headquarters just as it had in the beginning of May, because of the ambiguous enemy behavior. S.M. Shtemenko recalled:

> The entire month of May passed in stressful expectations. Information was coming in to the General Staff about the massed redeployments of enemy armor from west to east. However, other than the evidence of the concentration of forces, there were no other signs of German preparations to go on the offensive.
>
> The first month of summer began. The German-fascist command typically timed the most active operations of their forces with this period of short summer nights and fine summer weather. Would they repeat this practice in 1943? Were we mistaken in the assessment of the enemy's intentions? If we were mistaken, who knows what the consequences of this might be?
>
> I.V. Stalin was showing a certain nervousness. Indeed, if you will, it was because of this that tempests once again erupted in the *Stavka*. Information had arrived there about the dispatch of fighter aircraft with ineffective skin to the Kursk salient. Stalin then came to the conclusions that our entire fighter air force was not fit for combat .... Fortunately, the matter turned out to be not so serious and was settled rather quickly. There were also other days of great agitation.
>
> On 6 June, for example, the Operations Department when analyzing the situation pointed to the enemy's somewhat strange behavior. Doubt arose in us regarding the disposition of his panzer divisions. It became clear that the very same doubts were also gnawing at Antonov. We agreed to check the genuine locations of the enemy tanks through the headquarters of the *fronts*. On that same day a telegram went out over the signature of Antonov with the following contents: "It is exceptionally important now for us to know whether or not the enemy's grouping of panzer divisions remains the same or whether it has changed. Therefore, issue a task to all types of intelligence to determine the location of the enemy's armored divisions."
>
> A deadline of five days was set. At the end of it, the headquarters sent along soothing assurances – at the front, everything was as before; the grouping of enemy tanks had not changed. That meant everything was in order."[405]

In fact, the situation turned out to be not as "rosy" as Shtemenko described it, especially opposite the Central Front's sector. In its headquarters, the two key figures, M.S. Malinin and his deputy, who was also the intelligence chief, Colonel A.I. Kaminsky had diametrically opposing views both toward the question supplied by Moscow and whether or not the Germans

---

405 Shtemenko, *General'nyi shtab v gody voiny*, p. 167.

were intending to attack at all.[406] Meanwhile, the professional debate sparked by the message to the General Staff, which S.M. Shtemenko mentioned, and which later grew into a personal conflict that cost A.I. Kaminsky his post, did not come to an end. It continued throughout June and finally was resolved only in the early dawn hours of 5 July 1943, when the Germans initiated their artillery preparation.

During the latter half of June, both in the Wehrmacht and among the Red Army's high command staff, tension over the subject of the summer campaign rose substantially, particularly in the last ten days of the month, and one can see a sharp polarization of opinions about the German plans. The Commander-in-Chief of the Voronezh Front was the first to give way to the agonizing suspense. A.M. Vasilevsky recalled:

> In the mid-June, Zhukov, being the First Deputy of the People's Commissariat of Defense, again visited the troops within the Kursk bulge. As a result of the troops' constant and most diligent observation of the enemy, both on the Voronezh and Central Fronts, as well as the arriving information from all types of intelligence, it had already become clearly known to us that the fascists were completely ready for an offensive. However, for some reason they had not started the offensive, and this uncertainty considerably troubled us, and even shook the equanimity of some. The Commander-in-Chief of the Voronezh Front N.F. Vatutin began to demonstrate particular impatience.

406 Kaminsky, Aleksandr Il'ich, Major General (2 November 1944). Born on 30 July 1899 in the Vologda Oblast village of Pachevo into a family of workers. He completed a parochial school, and in 1914 a county vocational school. After graduation he worked as an apprentice carpenter in a Baltic shipbuilding factory. In the winter of 1918, Kaminsky voluntarily joined the Red Army. A participant in the Russian Civil War. In 1927 he completed a two-year course of study at the Kamenev Kiev Consolidated Military School, and in April 1931, the annual Courses to improve intelligence with the Intelligence Department of the Workers and Peasants Red Army's headquarters. Kaminsky subsequently served in the intelligence departments of the 8th and 6th Rifle Corps of the Kiev Military District. In 1938, Major A.I. Kaminsky was appointed chief of the Intelligence Department of F.A. Parusinov's Odessa Group of Armies. In this post he participated in the campaign into Bessarabia and Norther Bukovina in 1939. In October 1939, A.I. Kaminsky became the intelligence chief of the Kiev Special Military District's 12th Army. In June 1941, having completed two courses of study in the Frunze Military Academy, he was appointed as the deputy chief of intelligence of the Kiev Special Military District. Between June 1941 and January 1942, Kaminsky served as the Southwestern Front's chief of intelligence and then in the same post with the Southwestern Direction. When coming out of encirclement, he behaved courageously and skillfully. On 6 November 1941, he was awared the Order of the Red Banner. From December 1941 Kaminsky served as the intelligence chief of the Southwestern Front's Mobile Group (Group Kostenko), and between January and March 1942, as the chief of intelligence of the Southwestern Front. Between August 1942 and February 1943, Colonel A.I. Kaminsky served as the chief of intelligence with the Trans-Caucasus Front. For distinguishing himself in the battle for the Caucasus, on 13 December 1942 he was awarded the Order of the Red Star. From February 1943 to August 1943, Kaminsky served first as the deputy chief of staff for intelligence and the chief of intelligence of the Central Front., and from August 1943 to June 1945, as the chief of intelligence of the Central Asia Military District and then of the Turkmenistan Military District. Between 1946 and 1949, Kaminsky was the commandant of the Linz and Potsdam Districts (in Germany). In September 1949, Kaminsky became the military commissar of the Kiev Oblast Military Commission. He retired in September 1953 and passed away on 18 July 1992. He is buried in Kiev.

Nikolai Fedorovich repeatedly posed the question to me about the need to launch our own offensive.[407]

Vatutin viewed the Germans' repeated delays with starting the offensive as their lack of readiness for active operations and lack of confidence in success. However, this failed to convince the Chief of the General Staff. So, on 21 June N.F. Vatutin personally called I.V. Stalin with the suggestion to allow the Voronezh Front to go on the offensive first with the aim of encircling and crushing the Germans west of the Vorskla River. He then proposed to exploit the offensive in the direction of the Dnepr River to a depth of up to 300 km. The Supreme Leader was also troubled by the murky situation that had settled over the Kursk bulge and quickly got in touch with A.M. Vasilevsky.

Certain scholars assess this phone call to Stalin as at least evidence of the Vatutin's lack of foresight. It is hard to agree with this. In fact, further events would show that it was restraint and yet even more restraint that was needed by the Soviet side. At the same time, I want to call the reader's attention to the words of A.M. Vasilevsky that by the middle of June, the Soviet leadership were supposedly aware that the Germans were completely ready to make a lunge toward Kursk. This assertion plainly reveals that the Soviet intelligence had not supplied the Supreme Command in full measure with information that would allow it to judge the enemy's intentions objectively. How can there be any talk of readiness, if by that time not even all of Model's divisions that were designated to take part in Operation Citadel had yet emerged from the Briansk forests and made their way to their assembly areas?!

The reasons for the stress in both N.F. Vatutin and I.V. Stalin become more understandable, if we turn to the events that were happening around them at that time, and to the information that was arriving on their desks. First, the condition of the General of the Army's troops at this time were strikingly different from how they had stood back at the end of March, when he assumed command of the Voronezh Front. Back then, they had suffered heavy attrition in the fighting in Ukraine, and were poorly equipped, hungry and in a state of low morale because of the hard, unsuccessful operation. Now, they had been fully refitted, having received more than 1,800 tanks and self-propelled guns, and were well-trained and in high combat spirits, ready to take on any challenge.

Second, based on the arriving intelligence information, the *Stavka* had already issued a warning several times that the Wehrmacht stood poised for a grand offensive, but time had passed, and still a relative calm reigned at the front. Also, the second month of the relatively dry and warm period of the year was passing, when it was most convenient to conduct sweeping combat operations to liberate the country. During his long period of service both in the General Staff and in the acting Red Army, N.F. Vatutin had a direct contact with intelligence information on various levels. He therefore understood full well that ordinary men were serving in it, who might be mistaken, especially when such an experienced and well-trained adversary like the German Abwehr was operating against them. It had the capability of conducting a powerful disinformation campaign in every way. In addition, the General of the Army could not help but consider the circumstance as well that at this moment the Red Army's special services were still in the early days after a large-scale reorganization, which had started at the end of April. This,

---

407 Vasilevsky, *Delo vsei zhizni*, Vol. 2, p. 24.

naturally, still was not helping matters. Therefore, the conclusion arose on its own accord: It was necessary to strike the Germans while the weather allowed this, and sufficient forces had been gathered into a fist.

Problems on a different scale were weighing upon I.V. Stalin. On 4 June 1943, he had received a letter from the President of the United States, Franklin Delano Roosevelt, in which the Allies had officially informed him that they were postponing the landing in France now for the third time. Now it was being postponed from August 1943 to 1944, even though in January and February 1943, they had firmly promised to open a second front on the continent. In addition, in March 1943, they had ceased shipments of arms, equipment and materials along the northern sea route.[408] This meant that for the third year of the war, the semi-famished country, shedding its blood, would be continuing to fight alone on the continent, yet on the eve of a colossal battle, wouldn't receive the needed amount of Lend-Lease aid in order to continue this struggle. However, this in fact was not all; on 4 June 1943 and in the course of the next two weeks, the Luftwaffe would launch heavy attacks on all of the largest defense factories. They bombed out the main assembly line of the large automobile factory in Gor'kii, where trucks and light tanks were being assembled, and almost completely burned the Iaroslavl' Motor Factory and a number of factories of the rubber and elastics industry in Iaroslavl', which produced more than 40 percent of all the country's rubber output. These enterprises were the main suppliers of tires for the vehicles, airplanes, and artillery, and of rubber-coated roller wheels for tanks. The inflicted damage proved to be so substantial that the country, even after exerting maximum efforts, was only able to get the damaged and destroyed sites up and running again at the beginning of autumn.[409]

Against this backdrop, the ambiguous steps of the USSR's old "friend" Prime Minister Winston Churchill heightened Stalin's unease. In early February 1943, soon after the German defeat on the Volga, he had held personal discussions with the leadership of Turkey, which according to Soviet intelligence, stood ready to come out on Hitler's side during the Battle of Stalingrad. Even after this meeting, Turkey signed yet another economic agreement with Nazi Germany. It is not hard to imagine that a man, standing at the helm of a warring country and who was aware of all this wouldn't have suspicions that the Allies were secretly dealing with the Reich's leadership, and it was the fierce anti-Communist, the British Prime Minister, who was acting as the main inspirational force behind this. Thus, the soonest possible defeat of the Germans at Kursk would not only mean the destruction of a major enemy force grouping and a most important element of the summer 1943 campaign, but also an essential need, which would permit the Soviet Union to break up a possible extremely dangerous plan for the country of a separate pact between the Western countries and Hitler. Incidentally, during my conversations with former Wehrmacht soldiers and officers, veterans of the Battle of Kursk, they indicated that during the period of preparations for Citadel, their commanders tried to convince them that in the event of a German success, complete discord would erupt in the anti-Hitler coalition, and Germany might conclude a separate peace agreement with the Anglo-Saxons.

However, let us return to the conversation of the Supreme Leader with his Chief of the General Staff after N.F. Vatutin's phone call:

---

408 *Sovetsko-angliiskie otnosheniia vo vremia Velikoi Otechestvennoi voiny 1941-1945*, Tom 1 [*Soviet-British relationships during the Great Patriotic War 1941-1945*, Vol. 1] (Moscow: Politizdat, 1983), p. 393.
409 Kumanev, G., *Govoriat stalinskie narkomy* [*Stalin's commissars speak*] (Smolensk: Rusich, 2005), p. 434.

Stalin said that he considered this proposal merited the most serious attention, and that he had ordered Vatutin to prepare and report his ideas for the Voronezh Front to the *Stavka*. He gave me instructions, first, to help Vatutin, and second, to summon the Commander-in-Chief of the Southwestern Front R.Ia. Malinovsky, in order that he on his part worked out and submitted to the *Stavka* proposals for his Front. Stalin added that he was intending to speak with Zhukov about this matter with respect to K.K. Rokossovsky's Central Front. I replied that his instructions would be carried out and remarked that for us it would be much more propitious if the foe preempted us with his own offensive, which, according to all intelligence, should be expected in the nearest time. At the end of the discussion, Stalin said that I should appear in Moscow no later than 22 June. The next day I passed along the Supreme Leader's directive to R.Ia. Malinovsky and the Military Council member of the Southwestern Front A.S. Zheltov, who had arrived to see me. From a conversation with G.K. Zhukov that took place later, I found out that so far Stalin had not discussed this subject with him. We were both convinced that the enemy would launch his attack first in the course of the next few weeks. With such thoughts, I left the Voronezh Front on 22 June.[410]

Nevertheless, the entire apparatus of the General Staff and the *front* commands immediately set to work on an analysis of the situation and the elaboration of their own positions regarding the enemy's nearest plans and their own decisions on the basis of the most recent intelligence information. In the course of this work, the smoldering conflict in the headquarters of the Central Front between its chief of staff and his deputy for intelligence flared up with renewed intensity. The conflict arose at the time when a response was being prepared for Moscow to a coded telegram, sent by the General Staff on 6 June, which demanded the accurate determination of the enemy armored grouping's location opposite the *front*'s defenses within the next five days. Mikhail Sergeevich Malinin was a very complex, hard-bitten man. Possessing high professional qualities and organizational skills and enjoying the support of K.K. Rokossovsky, he allowed himself to ignore the opinion of subordinates, with whom he disagreed, without studying it properly, even those regarding serious questions. He simply forced his own authority and status on them. This, naturally, did not help matters, but ordinarily his subordinates abided his style, because the Front Commander-in-Chief constantly demonstrated his complete faith in Malinin. However, A.I. Kaminsky, who'd been appointed as the intelligence chief in February 1943, was a man of a different nature, who knew how to defend his position obstinately and argumentatively.

The chief of staff was still adhering to the view that he had laid out in his letter to the *Stavka* back in April 1943: that the Soviets should be first to go on the offensive, because the Germans weren't ready to attack. In the message sent to the General Staff before 10 June, he also informed it that the armored grouping in the enemy's operational rear had not changed, or had even become smaller, so the Germans had no intention to attack in the nearest future. However, A.I. Kaminsky disagreed with this conclusion, and the information collected by the second half of the month was only confirming his opinion. He recalled after the war:

410 Vasilevsky, *Delo vsei zhizni*, Vol. 2, p. 25.

A complex situation came together for us back then. My intelligence information was saying that the Nazis were on the verge of undertaking a counteroffensive in order to cut off the so-called Kursk salient. However, the removal of four divisions at that time in order to eliminate the partisans in the Briansk forests disoriented certain of our leaders somewhat, including the Front's chief of staff. They supposed that in such a case, no sort of counteroffensive was in view, and that my evidence – so they said, was just a crafty ploy by the fascists in order to confuse us. The matter reached the *Stavka*. It expressed dissatisfaction on the subject of our disagreements in coming up with further decisions for the Front's combat operations. Several days later, a *Stavka* commission was already working at our Central Front ... The decision was reached to capture a verification "tongue" [a prisoner willing or made to talk] ....[411]

Simultaneously, a task was issued: to conduct a simultaneous search in the sectors of several armies. The chief of staff personally attended to this matter along with the Intelligence Department. In the course of the following two weeks, reconnaissance probes and reconnaissance-in-force operations ensued on various sectors of the front. The groups had several tasks: first, to probe the strength of the German defenses and to scout the system of fire; second, to be sure to capture a prisoner for interrogation purposes; third, to attempt to grasp whether the enemy was really ready, by judging the enemy's reaction and speed in reacting, and if possible – to divert strength from the directions that were considered to be the most important. Each army commander had his own "sore spots" in the sector of defense, which is to say, limited sectors of terrain – hills and so forth – that it would be good to take from the enemy. Therefore, one task stood in front of the commanders who directly led the reconnaissance-in-force missions: to make tactical improvements to the line, while all the remaining tasks would be resolved in the course of combat by the scouts comprising the assault groups. Such a local operation was set for the end of June in the 48th Army by the forces of three penal companies (the 187th, 191st and 192nd Penal Companies) of the 143rd Rifle Division, and two rifle companies of the 16th Rifle Division's 156th Rifle Regiment with the support of artillery and self-propelled guns of the 1540th Self-propelled Artillery Regiment in the Khoroshevskiii-1 – (excl) Krest'ianka sector and toward Hill 235.0, which was being defended by units of the XXIII Corps' 383rd Infantry Division. It was also being used by the Front's intelligence officers in order to clarify the situation regarding the intentions of the Ninth Army's command; however, it brought no clarity.

Romanenko's army did not reveal any fresh divisions opposite its front; here, as before, the 299th and 383rd Infantry Divisions were defending in the first echelon, while the 216th Infantry Division and 18th Panzer Division were positioned in the second echelon. In addition, its headquarters reported: "A forceful attack on 25 June 1943 showed that the enemy possesses a developed system of defenses across the front and in the depth, with tactical and operational reserves in the depth of the defenses."[412] The stability of the forces on the forward edge and in the second echelon, the well-prepared system of defenses, which as observers repeatedly reported were being continuously strengthened with minefields and barbed wire entanglements,

---

411 Iarokhin, Iu.M., *Soldat Krasnoi Armii, general voennoi razvedki: Kaminsky, Aleksandr Il'ich* [*Soldier of the Red Army, general of military intelligene: Kaminsky, Aleksandr Il'ich*] (Kiev: Izdatel'skii Dom "Voennaia razvedka", 2012), p. 12.
412 TsAMO RF, F.403, Op.9657, D.90, l. 192 obr.

at first glance testified in favor of the point of view expressed by M.S. Malinin that the enemy had no intention to attack in the near future. However, on this same day, the intelligence staff of the 48th Army reported:

> At 1800 on 1 July, an aggregate of up to 200 tanks and 200 vehicles was noted at Kurakino Station. At 1600 on 1 July, the enemy placed a smokescreen in front of Nikitovka for 15 minutes, and at this same time, the sound of motors, presumably of tanks, was audible in the Nikitovka area. The sound of motors was also carrying from Kamenka area and the woods west of Stolbetsov, also presumably of tanks.[413]

If one is to believe this information, the Germans had shifted no less than a panzer division to this area. However, the question arose: "Why was the foe acting so demonstrably, by assembling so many armored vehicles in one place during daylight hours?" Indeed, such contradictory and puzzling reports were coming in from all the armies.

K.K. Rokossovsky wanted to believe A.I. Kaminsky's intelligence information; it was in accordance with his own desire for the enemy to strike first. Then, all of the Front's enormous work wouldn't be in vain, and the plans to destroy the enemy's most combat-capable divisions within the powerful and elaborate defenses would be realized. According to the recollections of A.I. Kaminsky, considering the importance of this question about the enemy's intentions, the Front Commander-in-Chief himself personally interrogated certain prisoners. However, M.S. Malinin's arguments also seemed not without foundation, so they could not simply be cast aside. A fresh and sharp turning point in the problem arose on 3-4 July, when the news came from the Voronezh Front headquarters that identified the active movement of lengthy enemy motorized columns from the areas of Belgorod and Khar'kov to the south during the nighttime hours. All of this taken together led to the thought that the Germans weren't planning to attack, and this naturally raised fresh anxieties on the Soviet side.

Using every possibility in terms of the analysis of more significant and diverse information than the *fronts* possessed, was well as their own personal influence and authority, G.K. Zhukov and A.V. Vasilevsky at the end of June managed to persuade I.V. Stalin to wait until mid-July. Only then, if the situation had not changed, would the Soviets strike first: initially against the Orel salient with Rokossovsky's forces and his neighboring *fronts* on the right, and five days later to advance into Ukraine with Vatutin's, Konev's and Malinovsky's forces. K.K. Rokossovsky also shared this opinion, considering the arguments of his Front's intelligence officer more convincing, but even so the dispute between M.S. Malinin and A.I. Kaminsky continued practically right up to the start of the Battle of Kursk.

Nevertheless, the leadership of the Voronezh Front continued to insist on its position that it was necessary to attack first. On 28 June, N.F. Vatutin and N.S. Khrushchev were received in the Kremlin. The latter recalled in his memoirs:

> An offensive operation had been prepared. The requisite forces and combat gear had been calculated for a breakthrough to Khar'kov through Belgorod, as had the necessary material resources. Afterward, Vatutin and I were asked to report to Stalin. Stalin

---

413 Ibid., l. 193.

said, "Come by air." Even before reporting to Stalin, our plans had been analyzed and corrected by the General Staff, and typically after our report they took on their final form. We briefed Stalin ... We were given a deadline – 20 July – and ordered to prepare for the launching of an offensive. The axis we had selected was endorsed. Next, we haggled over the main question: What replenishments might we receive in order to conduct this operation? As was always the case, the requests submitted by the commanders were never fully satisfied. We were given a lot, but it fell short of all we wanted. However, we were told: "These are your forces, go ahead and direct them, but behind you will be the reserve of the Supreme Command .... We left, very pleased with our conversation with Stalin and the results of our briefing.[414]

Just a week later, this entire matter would be filed away as events began to unfold at Kursk, which would enter history as the turning point in the war.

I want to emphasize that in the dispute between General M.S. Malinin and Colonel A.I. Kaminsky, who were two professionals in different "weight categories", the intelligence chief showed both a combative nature and a certain amount of courage. Owing to this, the large, difficult work of the Front's intelligence officers did not go in vain; it was not without reason that many of them had given up their lives when carrying out combat assignments in the enemy rear in order to collect crumbs of vital information about the enemy's intentions. For his high professionalism and effective work before the Battle of Kursk, on 9 August 1943 Colonel A.I. Kaminsky was honored with the Order of the Patriotic War 1st Class. His commendation, which was signed personally by Lieutenant General M.S. Malinin and approved by K.K. Rokossovsky, stated:

> Comrade Kaminsky is an exceptionally conscientious, studious and disciplined commander. In the period of the preparation of the defensive lines by the units of the Central Front, Comrade Kaminsky did a large amount of work to establish the actual enemy grouping, which helped the Front command to arrange its forces correctly in order to repulse the anticipated German attacks. In the July operations he capably organized the work of the department subordinate to him and kept the Front's Military Council timely informed about all the changes in the enemy forces, which contributed to the proper resolution of all the tasks regarding the launching of a major attack against the foe and the frustration of the German offensive.[415]

However, M.S. Malinin did not tolerate headstrong subordinates, even if they were highly capable professionals. Therefore, he did everything possible to remove his unpleasant deputy as far as possible from his eyesight. Already in the latter half of August 1943, Colonel A.I. Kaminsky would be transferred to the remote Central Asian Military District, which was distant from the war, and he would serve there until the end of the war.

Unfortunately, no light has been cast on A.I. Kaminsky's successful work in the post of Central Front's chief of intelligence in domestic military-historical literature. I haven't found

---

414 Khrushchev, N.S., *Vospominaniia*, Kn. 1 [*Recollections, Book 1*] (Moscow: Novosti, 1999), pp. 482-483.
415 TsAMO RF, F.33, Op.682526, Ed.khr. 1188.

any mention of him in memoirs either, including those of his direct superior K.K. Rokossovsky. Meanwhile, certain contemporary scholars, even those who specialize in the study of the history of the special services, have deliberately or unintentionally stricken his name from the history of the Battle of Kursk, maintaining that supposedly the Central Front's Intelligence Department at this time was headed by Major General P.N. Chekmazov.[416] Nevertheless, I hope the time has come when the contribution of this remarkable professional to the victory at Kursk will be worthily presented in our history of the battle.

Concluding this tale of the important phase in the planning and preparation of the Battle of Kursk and the problems that the Soviet side had to resolve, I believe it is important to stress that the Citadel plan was a gamble, taken under hopeless conditions for Germany. The attempt to encircle two Soviet *fronts* at Kursk was, in essence, a political act by the Reich's leadership, directed at restoring its prestige in the global arena and among its allies, and also at raising the troops' combat spirits and restoring the belief of the German people in inevitable victory, which had been shaken after the events on the Volga. The Wehrmacht was no longer able to conduct such a large-scale offensive while simultaneously maintaining the stability of the front along the entire line of contact with the Red Army, and the objectives that had been set for Army Group South and Army Group Center were unachievable because of their inadequate strength and the repeated interference of the political leadership in the process of planning. Nevertheless, it should be acknowledged that the command staff of Army Group South, under unfavorable conditions, thanks to the availability of larger resources that remained to it after the February and March 1943 fighting in Ukraine relative to those of Army Group Center, in fact succeeded in devising the optimal operational plan in the initial phase of Citadel and in securing the necessary forces for it. This enabled von Manstein's grouping to achieve to a considerable extent the objective of its first stage of the operation – by inflicting heavy losses on the Soviet operational and strategic reserves.

For its part, the decision by the Soviet Supreme Command and the political leadership about temporarily handing the initiative to the enemy was difficult, but also mature and far-sighted. In the process, this plan had a number of distinguishing features which had not been present in the process of planning such major operations in the preceding years.

First, it plainly showed both a deep faith in its own strength and a sober assessment of the level of the acting Red Army's combat capabilities (the insufficient training of the men of the infantry divisions and the inferior quality of certain types of armaments. This was a clear attempt to replace the "gung-ho" approach of the previous years with a deep pragmatism when conducting the war.

Second, the Red Army adopted a defense even though it had a numerical advantage over the enemy. It also retained the strategic initiative it had achieved in the winter of 1942-43.

Third, the plans of the operation to defend the Kursk salient and to launch a timely counteroffensive with the *fronts* in the area of the Orel salient and the Donbass were worked

---

416 See, for example, Pavlov, A.G., "Voennaia razvedka SSSR v 1941-1945" ["Soviet military intelligence in 1941-1945"] *Novaia i noveishaia istoriia*, No. 2 (1995), p. 36; Kolpakidi, A.I. and Prokhorov, D.P., *Imperiia GRU: Ocherki istorii rossiiskoi voennoi razvedki. Kn. 1* [*Empire of the Military Intelligence Service:* Essays of the history of Russian military intelligence. Book 1] (Moscow: OLMA-PRESS, 2001), p. 314; and Prokhorov, D.P., *Razvedka ot Stalina do Putina* [*Intelligence from Stalin to Putin*] (St Petersburg: Neva, 2005), p. 199.

out together; they were closely coordinated with respect to time, and they represented the key element of the entire strategic plan for the summer campaign of 1943. Moreover, the shift to active operations by the Western, Briansk, Southwestern and Southern Fronts were set in dependence of the results of the combat performance of Rokossovsky's and Vatutin's forces, and was simultaneously viewed as a most important element of influence on the success of their entire defensive operation. Thus, the desire of the *Stavka* to create beforehand the optimal conditions for the armies of the central sector of the Soviet-German front to launch a counteroffensive without a lengthy operational pause is clearly discernible. In addition, this counterblow would come after inflicting heavy damage to the enemy in the defensive fighting on prepared lines.

Fourth, for the first time in the practice of the Soviet Supreme Command, the bulk of the planning for a counteroffensive was done before the start of a defensive operation. The counterblow from out of the Kursk salient was supposed to transition into a general strategic offensive of the entire Red Army all across the Soviet-German front.

Fifth, the powerful system of defenses and the major strategic reserves that were deployed east of Kursk were to create conditions, under which the enemy would prove unable to encircle the Soviet forces (even if its mobile divisions reached the city of Kursk), nor to create a genuine threat to a most important economic (Voronezh direction) or key administrative and political centers (Moscow direction).

Sixth, a deliberate defense was justly seen as the primary means to neutralize the Wehrmacht's technical superiority, primarily in armored fighting vehicles. It would also offset the superior individual training of the men.

Finally, for the first time the Soviets planned the use of large tank armies and operational and tactical armored formations in order to hold a tactical sector of defense. The defense of the *fronts* in the area of the Kursk bulge was the first implementation of this idea.

Photo 2.01: Supreme Commander-in-Chief of the Red Army and Marshal of the Soviet Union I.V. Stalin, a 1943 photograph. (RGAKFD)

Photo 2.02: The Commander-in-Chief of the newly formed Central Front Colonel General K.K. Rokossovsky prepares to set off toward Kursk. The smiling officer leaning over his shoulder from the back seat is the Front's artillery commander Lieutenant General V.I. Kazakov, February 1943. (KOKM)

Photo 2.03: The bestowing of rifles to arriving replacements for one of the rifle regiments of the 48th Army's 16th Lithuanian Division of the Central Front, February 1943. (RGAKFD)

Photo 2.04: The crew of a 122mm M1931/1937 cannon of one of the 13th Army's formations prepares to fire another round at the enemy in the area of Malo-Arkhangel'sk, Central Front, February 1943. (RGAKFD)

Photo 2.05: Tankers of the 13th Army's 118th Tank Brigade of the Briansk Front meet happy civilians of the village of Ol'khovatka north of Kursk, which had just been liberated, February 1943. (RGAKFD)

Photo 2.06: Chief of the General Staff and Marshal of the Soviet Union A.M. Vasilevsky (front row, on the left) before the start of planning the Kursk defensive operation in the headquarters of the Central Front together with its commander. Next to him in the middle of the first row is Colonel General K.K. Rokossovsky, the Front Commander-in-Chief. On his left is Lieutenant General I.T. Peresypkin, the chief of the Red Army's Signals Department. Standing behind them, from left to right, are Lieutenant General S.I. Rudenko, the commander of the 16th Air Army, Major General K.F. Telegin, member of the Military Council, Major General G.N. Orel, commander of the Front's armored and mechanized forces and Lieutenant General V.I. Kazakov, the Central Front's artillery commander. (RGAKFD)

Photo 2.07: The commander of the 11th Guards Army Lieutenant General I.Kh. Bagramian (on the left) and the representative of the Presidium of the USSR Supreme Soviet M.I. Kalinin after the bestowal of the Order of Kutuzov 1st Class to Bagramian, April 1943. (RGAKFD)

Photo 2.08: The Commander-in-Chief of the Briansk Front M.A. Reiter (on the left) at work with his chief of staff Lieutenant General L.M. Sandalov while developing the plan for Operation Kutuzov, Briansk Front, May 1943. (Archive of E.V. Iurinaia)

Photo 2.09: Deputy Supreme Commander-in-Chief Marshal of the Soviet Union G.K. Zhukov takes a brief break from the preparations for the Kursk defensive operation, area of the Kursk bulge, May 1943. (RGAKFD)

Photo 2.10: One of the key participants in the preparations of the Red Army for the Battle of Kursk: Commander-in-Chief of the Voronezh Front General of the Army N.F. Vatutin during an inspection of the defenses' condition, April 1943. (RGAKFD)

Photo 2.11: A reconnaissance platoon commander Junior Lieutenant V.F. Epishev observes the enemy's lines through a stereo binocular, Central Front, April 1943. (RGAKFD)

Photo 2.12: The Central Front's chief of staff Lieutenant General M.S. Malinin during a moment of rest at the command post of the Front in the village of Svoboda, April 1943. (RGAKFD)

Photo 2.13: Artillerists bringing up cases of shells from a temporary field stockpile, Central Front, April 1943. (Author's personal archive)

Photo 2.14: A gun crew of Lieutenant Lieutenant Sh. Edvardas' anti-tank gun battery of the 48th Army's 16th Lithuanian Rifle Division rehearsing its movement when firing at targets on a training range, Central Front, June 1943. (A Levin photograph, RGAKFD)

Photo 2.15: The ground crew of one of the squadrons of the 820th Ground Attack Aviation Regiment of the 2nd Air Army's 292nd Ground Attack Aviation Division receives its orders before preparing an Il-2 aircraft for a sortie, May 1943. (RGAKFD)

Photo 2.16: The Commander-in-Chief of the Voronezh Front General of the Army N.F. Vatutin (second from the left) and Military Council member Lieutenant General N.S. Khrushchev (third from the left) study a proposal to improve the work of getting the armored vehicles in Major General A.L. Getman's 6th Tank Corps back in shape. Getman is standing in the foreground on the left, June 1943. (RGAKFD)

Photo 2.17: The command of a motorized rifle battalion in the 5th Guards Stalingrad Tank Corps conducting a tactical exercise together with elements of the Voronezh Front, May 1943. (RGAKFD)

Photo 2.18: Tactical training in a tank brigade of the 5th Guards Tank Corps to forge cooperation of the tank-riding companies with the tank units, Voronezh Front, May 1943. (RGAKFD)

Photo 2.19: Rifle units conduct an exercise on a training ground with the participation of a T-34 tank, Voronezh Front, May 1943. (RGAKFD)

Photo 2.20: A machine gunner takes a quick nap next to his Maksim heavy machine gun during a break from a gunnery exercise at a training range, Central Front, April 1943. (RGAKFD)

Photo 2.21: A crew of a PD-27 light machine gun of one of the divisions of the 13th Army's 15th Rifle Corps setting up a firing position, Central Front, April 1943. (RGAKFD)

Photo 2.22: A niche in the wall of a front-line trench of one of the units of the 48th Army for sheltering grenades and other ammunition, Central Front, May 1943. (TsAMO RF)

Photo 2.23: An aerial photograph of a sector of the 69th Army's 183rd Rifle Division's defenses in the vicinity of Prokhorovka Station, June 1943. (RGAKFD)

Photo 2.24: The commander of 1st Guards Separate Engineer-Sapper Brigade Colonel M.F. Ioffe reports to the commander-in-chief of the Central Front General of the Army K.K. Rokossovsky on the system of mine-laying in the Ponyri Station area, June 1943. (KOKM)

Photo 2.25: Team leader I.D. Kolesnikov and mechanic S.G. Galanov turn over a repaired tank to Senior Sergeant P.I. Baikov, Kursk, April 1943. (RGAKFD)

Photo 2.26: Collective farmer workers of the Kanashikhinskii rural council of Kursk Oblast dig trenches along the crest of a slope in the Central Front's sector of defense, 2 June 1943 (RGAKFD)

Photo 2.27: The chairman of the Kursk Committee of Defense Major General P.I. Doronin holds a conversation with military personnel on a Kursk street, June 1943. (RGAKFD)

Photo 2.28: The construction of the Staryi Oskol – Rzhava railroad, June 1943. (GA KO)

Photo 2.29: The repair of a gun at a battery of 76mm anti-tank guns of one of the brigades of the 5th Guards Tank Army of the Steppe Military District in the spring of 1943. (RGAKFD)

Photo 2.30: Men of one of the units of the Voronezh Front's 6th Guards Army take a break for a meal, May 1943. (RGAKFD)

Photo 2.31: A smiling baker of one of the mobile field kitchens prepares to distribute fresh bread to the men sent to collect it, Central Front, June 1943. (RGAKFD)

Photo 2.32: The commander of the 563rd Fighter Aviation Regiment of the 16th Air Army's 283rd Fighter Aviation Division Senior Lieutenant N.A. Naidenov poses next to his aircraft, in which he successfully made a forced landing after it was badly damaged in a dogfight in the Kursk area on 5 May 1943. (RGAKFD)

Photo 2.33: The commander of the 519th Fighter Aviation Regiment of the 16th Air Army's 283rd Fighter Aviation Division directs his engaged fighters by radio from an airfield in the Kursk area on 5 May 1943. (RGAKFD)

Photo 2.34: Kursk burns after a raid by German aircraft, 5 May 1943. (GA KO)

Photo 2.35: The commander of the 5th Guards Army's 95th Guards Rifle Division Major General N.S. Nikitchenko congratulates a senior officer upon his assignment to the post of regiment commander before an assembly of the division's command staff, Steppe Military District, April 1943. (AZV)

Photo 2.36: A tank element with riders aboard moves out onto a training ground. In the lower left corner, a front filmmaker records the scene, Steppe Military District, June 1943. (RGAKFD)

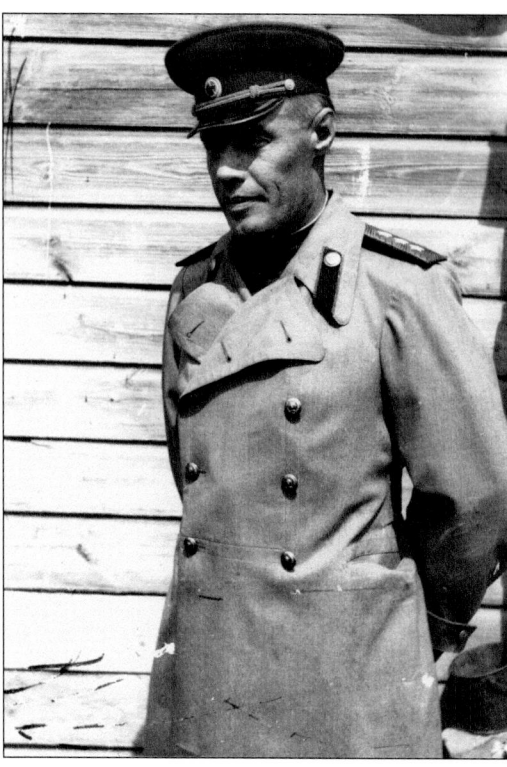

Photo 2.37: The commander-in-chief of the Steppe Military District Colonel General M.M. Popov, Voronezh, May 1943. (RGAKFD)

ПРИКАЗ № 13

Верховного командования Германской Армии

О военнослужащих Красной Армии, добровольно переходящих на сторону Германской Армии.

Благоразумные солдаты и офицеры Красной Армии не желают дальше бессмысленно жертвовать собой ради сохранения советского режима, о чем свидетельствует большое количество военнослужащих Красной Армии, переходящих добровольно на нашу сторону.

Всех офицеров и солдат Красной Армии добровольно переходящих к нам следует рассматривать, как противников советской власти и в соответствии с этим, с ними обращаться.

ПРИКАЗЫВАЮ:

I. Каждого военнослужащаго Красной Армии (офицера, политработника, бойца и др.) покинувшего свою часть и самостоятельно или в составе группы добровольно являющегося к нам, считать не военнопленным, а добровольно перешедшим на сторону Германской Армии.

II. Обращение с добровольно перешедшими:

а) В войсковых частях, дивизиях и корпусах:

1. Добровольно перешедших немедленно отделять от военнопленных и размещать, по возможности, в отдельных благоустроенных помещениях. Все личное имущество (деньги, ценные вещи, обмундирование, ордена, медали, знаки различия) оставлять неприкосновенным.
Добровольно перешедших обеспечить хорошим питанием.
Добровольно перешедших немедленно препровождать из зоны боевых действий в тыл, обеспечивая их, по мере возможности, средствами передвижения.
Больным и раненым оказывать немедленно медицинскую помощь.
2. Каждому добровольно перешедшему на основании имеющихся у него документов или нашего »пропуска« выдавать особое удостоверение.

б) На специальных сборных пунктах:

1. Добровольно перешедшим оказывать предпочтение при расквартировании (отопление, обеспечение постельными принадлежностями и. т. д.) Офицеров помещать отдельно и обеспечить им все необходимые удобства.
2. Добровольно перешедших обеспечивать довольствием наравне с добровольцами Русской Освободительной Армии и, по возможности, дополнительным снабжением (табаком и пр.)

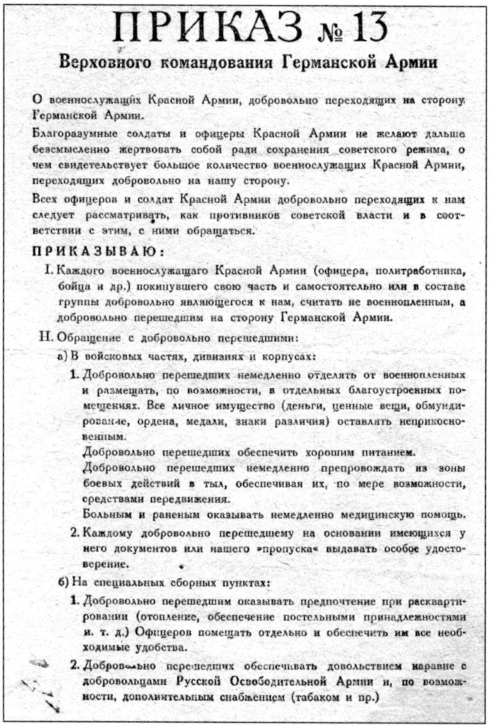

Photo 2.38: The first page of OKW Order No. 13 (Author's personal archive)

Photo 2.39: Senior Lieutenant E.I. Borovik (on the left) and radio operator Senior Sergeant I.T. Levechenko making a propaganda broadcast to soldiers of Infantry Regiment 676 of the Fourth Panzer Army's 322nd Infantry Division, June 1943. (RGAKFD)

Photo 2.40: The loading of German-language Soviet newspapers for Wehrmacht soldiers aboard aircraft of one of the Guards regiments in the Kursk salient for delivery to the troops, June 1943. (RGAKFD)

Photo 2.41: Voronezh Front Military Council member Lieutenant General N.S. Khrushchev, who was responsible for education and propaganda work among the troops, listens to a report while at work at his desk, Rzhava Station area, 11 June 1943 (Photograph by F. Kislova, RGAKFD)

Photo 2.42: The commander of the 1203rd Rifle Regiment of the 354th Rifle Division Lieutenant Colonel G.D. Vologdin studying the enemy's defenses from a concealed observation post. To his right on the wall is a map depicting the enemy's lines and firing positions, 65th Army, Central Front, June 1943 (Photograph by P. Troshkin, RGAKFD)

Index

A
Anti-infantry obstacles, 375, 393–94
Anti-partisan operations, 134, 138, 141, 143, 156, 198
Anti-personnel mines, 374, 393–94, 427–28, 442, 454, 509
Anti-tank area, 403, 409, 433, 445, 458, 486
Anti-tank artillery, 337, 352, 366, 389, 399, 408, 412–15, 431, 434, 488, 490
Anti-tank mines, 337, 374, 394, 396, 404, 408, 427–28, 442, 509–10
Anti-tank obstacles, 241, 364, 389, 391, 393–96, 474
Anti-tank rifles, 337, 365, 372, 374, 414–15, 433, 435–36, 447, 452–54, 459, 462
Anti-tank strongpoints, 364, 396, 409, 414–15, 433, 435, 440, 446–50, 452, 464–65, 475
Artillery Headquarters Operations Department, 99

B
Bagramian, Colonel I.K.h., 60, 292, 521, 523–25, 541
Belgorod, 47–49, 55–56, 68, 102, 121, 239–41, 286–87, 318–19, 327, 329–31, 337–38, 340, 348, 438–39, 449–52, 470, 476–77, 534
Belorussia, 83, 135, 288, 291, 294–95, 300, 518
Berlin, 12–15, 20–23, 33–34, 39, 41–42, 46–47, 54–55, 72–75, 85–86, 111–12, 158–59, 161–63, 173, 180–81, 188–89, 253–54, 306–7, 309–12
Bobryshovo, 347–49
Boguchar, 297, 305–6
Borisovka, 102, 329–30, 335
Breith, General H., 247–49, 251, 270
Briansk, 27, 62, 65, 90, 98, 127, 133–36, 142, 290–91, 313–14, 476
Briansk forest, 65, 137–38, 141, 155–56, 159, 161–62, 168, 310, 314, 530, 533
Briantsevo, 354, 386, 388, 390
Butovo, 102, 185, 239, 241, 311, 422, 429

C
Cannon Artillery Regiment, 415, 452, 454, 467–69
Chistiakov, General I.M., 240, 284, 322–23, 330–31, 340, 344, 369, 374, 413, 419, 437
Choltitz, General D. von, 7, 12, 33
Chuguev, 45–46, 49
Citadel, Operation
  cancellation, 74, 149
  conduct of, 75, 104–05, 149, 159, 177
  defeat of, 278, 296
  failure of, 37, 509
  idea of, 68, 113
  implementation of, 110, 173
  launch of, 52, 193
  master plan, 319
  objectives, 51, 237, 500
  opponents of, 114, 503
  preparation of, 90, 194
  staging of, 60, 237
  start of, 58, 64, 71, 91, 135, 145, 150, 220, 223–24, 242, 256
  success of, 187, 232

D
Dal'niaia Igumenka, 433, 445, 454–55
Defense Construction Command, 379–82, 384, 391
Dmitrovsk-Orel, 476
Don Basin, 23, 25, 53

E
Elverfeldt, Colonel H. von, 40–41, 55, 60–62, 67–68, 71–73, 77, 79–80, 82, 99, 144–45, 155, 157, 189, 191, 193
Engineer-Sapper Battalions, 427, 439, 442

F
Ferdinand (Elefant) heavy tank destroyer, 15, 34, 101–2, 104, 106, 113, 189, 191–93, 217, 219, 223

Flak guns, 94, 174, 215, 237, 251
Forward edge defense, 126, 239, 284, 331, 392, 407, 485, 514
Fougasse mine, 427–30, 442

G
Galanin, General I., 386–87, 389, 395–96, 399, 490
German Armed Forces (Wehrmacht), 7, 14, 113, 116, 118–19, 151–52, 186, 190, 204–5, 254, 256, 258
Goebbels, J., 19, 32, 110, 114, 116, 118
Goering, H., 19, 114, 237, 303–4
Goshawk, 44–47, 53, 68–69, 121
Gremiach'e, 353–54, 386
Guards Artillery, 452, 454, 458, 464, 468
Guards Cannon Artillery, 452, 454–55, 458, 468–69
Guards Destroyer Anti-Tank Artillery Regiments, 452, 454, 458, 468
Guards Engineers, 390, 405–6, 462
Guards Mortar Regiments, 331, 413, 415, 452, 454–55, 468, 492
Guards Rifle Regiments, 423, 425, 431, 441–42, 451–53, 456–58, 463–65, 473, 514

H
Headquarters Breitenbuch, 59, 141, 156, 189
Heavy Panzer Battalions, 51, 82, 101, 150, 156, 162, 192, 219–20, 223–24, 250
Heavy Panzerjäger Regiments, 166, 224
Heavy Self-propelled Artillery Regiments, 401, 459
Heinrici, General G., 86, 115, 120
Hitler, Adolf, 12–14, 16–17, 19–22, 24–30, 32–39, 45–47, 49–53, 74–76, 79, 86–87, 89, 97–98, 105–6, 110–20, 161–62, 178–79, 187–90, 196–98, 245–46, 254–56, 313, 500–503
Hoth, General H., 120, 122, 186, 276, 308
Howitzer Artillery Regiments, 410–11, 415

I
Ivanov, General S., 342, 460–61

K
Kaminsky Police Brigade, 528–29, 532–35
Kazakov, 351, 363, 449, 538, 540
Kempf, General W., 45, 111, 123, 198, 222, 240, 248, 250–52, 271
Khar'kov, 6–7, 10, 45–46, 73, 87, 102, 253–54, 278–79, 303–5, 311, 323, 340–41, 476, 525, 534
Khrushchev, N., 163, 287, 292, 325, 456, 534–35, 545, 558
Kleist, General P. von, 7, 260, 493
Kluge, General G. von, 27–29, 39, 42–44, 55, 68, 73–75, 77, 79, 86, 99–100, 105–10, 112, 115–16, 160–61, 164, 167, 178–81, 190, 192–94, 255
Krebs, General H., 40–41, 68, 71–73, 76, 78–81, 84, 99, 160–61, 167, 191–92, 194
Kupiansk, 44–45, 48, 121, 305, 519
Kursk bulge, 36–37, 63–65, 230–31, 281–83, 290–91, 301, 303–4, 306–7, 316, 327–28, 332–33, 344, 365–66, 377–78, 477–78, 516–18, 529–30
Kursk Oblast, 117, 163, 348, 382–83, 406, 416, 550
Kursk railway, 56, 63, 166, 232–33, 291, 346, 354–56, 400, 403–6, 492
Kursk salient, 32, 85, 87, 238–40, 283–84, 293, 295, 302–3, 321, 354–55, 376, 475–76, 494, 516, 536–37

M
Maloarkhangel'sk, 55–56, 60, 63–65, 91, 150, 153, 164–66, 233–34, 318–19, 359, 381, 403–6, 412, 414, 492
Manstein, Field Marshal E., 6, 22–23, 26–30, 34, 37–38, 46–47, 51–54, 68–70, 75–76, 105–7, 109, 111–12, 117–25, 179, 213–14, 220, 225, 232, 253–54, 293, 304, 335–36, 493, 525
Model, General W., 27, 35–41, 52–58, 64–68, 70–85, 89–90, 92–93, 97–103, 108–10, 112–13, 127–28, 131–32, 147–48, 150–52, 157, 159–67, 173, 189–96, 200–01, 216, 223–25, 228–30, 232–33, 235–37, 255–56, 400, 502–3, 530

O
Oboian, 122–23, 238–41, 284, 287, 329–31, 333, 335–39, 341–43, 347, 380–81, 419–20, 477–78, 486–87
OKH (Oberkommando des Heeres), 22–23, 29–30, 32–34, 46, 49–55, 66, 68–71, 73–79, 81–82, 87–88, 90, 103, 111–12, 119, 141, 160–61, 163–64, 178–81, 201–2, 253–55
OKW (Oberkommando der Wehrmacht), 29, 32–33, 38, 49, 52, 115–16, 177–79, 187–89, 253, 255, 303, 317
Operation Goshawk, 46–47
Operation Gypsy Baron, 136, 141, 143, 148, 156, 159–62, 195, 255, 310, 315
Operation Panther, 48, 68, 310
Operation Samara, 148–49, 191, 193
Orel, 13–14, 23–24, 27, 39–41, 43, 55–56, 63–64, 149–51, 178, 193, 232–33, 237, 313–15, 353–55, 387, 390–92, 399–400, 405–6, 476, 478–79
Oskol River, 45–46, 48, 519
OZM-152 (Anti-personnel mine), 429–30

P

Panzer (PzKpfw)
  I 219, 226-27, 244
  II 186, 219, 226-27, 244-45, 250
  III 52, 62, 81-82, 93-94, 112, 150, 162, 168-72, 192, 217, 219, 221-24, 226-27, 244-45, 247, 250, 501
  IV 52, 62, 77, 81-82, 93-94, 98, 112, 151, 162, 169-72, 191, 217, 219, 226, 244-45, 247, 250, 501
  V (Panther) 51, 93-94, 104, 108, 112-13, 117, 162, 221-22, 242, 244-47, 327
  VI (Tiger I) 15, 24, 51-52, 81-82, 93-94, 101-2, 104, 106, 112-13, 117, 150, 162, 192, 216-17, 219-224, 246-47, 250, 327, 501-2

Panzerjäger Battalions, 207–9, 212
Panzerjäger Regiments, 166, 223, 233
Partisans, 17, 24, 57, 61, 64–65, 74, 88, 92, 99, 127, 129–31, 133–34, 136–44, 148, 155, 161, 163, 229, 232, 255, 314
Prokhorovka, 122–25, 199–200, 238–41, 251, 258, 329–30, 335, 337, 466, 470–71, 480, 487

R

Razumnaia River, 447, 464–65
Rokossovsky, General K., 49, 284–85, 288–91, 298–99, 322, 326–28, 332–34, 343–47, 350–54, 356–59, 361–63, 365, 367, 379, 386–87, 396, 467, 477, 489–91, 497, 500, 502, 520, 532, 534–38

S

Schmidt, General G., 13–14, 27, 30, 43, 86, 254, 261
Separate Armored Train Battalions, 458–59, 468
Separate Destroyer Anti-Tank Artillery Brigades, 342, 352, 419, 437, 455, 460, 468, 471
Severskii Donets River, 45, 247–48, 253, 335, 340, 430, 438–39, 446–47, 456–57, 459, 463
Shtemenko, General S.M., 282–83, 286, 296, 312, 325, 520–21, 525, 528–29
Stalin, J., 277, 279–90, 292–97, 299–300, 315–16, 346, 348, 488–89, 493, 504, 506, 521–25, 527–28, 530–32, 534–36
Stavka, 277–84, 286–88, 290–91, 293–99, 303–4, 312–16, 320–22, 324–25, 333–34, 340, 343–45, 378–80, 384, 475–77, 481–82, 486–89, 492–94, 503–5, 518–26, 532–33
Stavka Directive, 284, 324–25, 344, 365, 371, 378, 499
Steppe Military District, 296–98, 340, 343, 379, 475–77, 504–6, 508, 516, 519, 522, 524, 552, 555
Sturmgeschütz (StuG) III, 217–18, 221–22, 244–45

Sudoplatov, General P.A., 18, 144–45, 301–2, 307–8

T

T-34 medium tank, 138, 280, 459, 547
Tomarovka, 69, 101–2, 184, 241, 311, 329–30, 340, 343, 407, 429–30

V

Vatutin, General N., 278, 284–87, 289–91, 298, 312, 322–44, 347–50, 374, 416, 454–55, 457–58, 460–62, 465–67, 477, 486, 488–89, 500, 503–4, 511, 526, 519–21, 529–30, 534, 537

Z

Zhukov, Marshal G., 277–78, 280, 282–93, 298–99, 313–14, 329–30, 344, 450, 461–62, 486–91, 493, 517, 519–21, 525–26, 532

Formations

German Army Groups & Armies

Army Detachment Kempf, 45, 47–48, 50, 123–24, 199–200, 222, 224, 238–40, 247–51, 253, 270–71, 335–36, 338–40
Army Group A, 10, 29, 38, 47, 88, 95, 119, 305
Army Group Center, 27–29, 33–35, 40–42, 50–55, 57–58, 65–66, 68, 70–71, 73–77, 79–83, 88–90, 92–94, 98–99, 103–4, 108–9, 134–36, 142–44, 160–61, 216–19, 500–502
Army Group Don, 6, 35
Army Group North, 10, 29, 152, 178
Army Group South, 9–10, 23–30, 34, 38, 40, 44, 46–48, 50–51, 53–54, 67–71, 105–6, 108–9, 111–12, 119–21, 228–29, 250–54, 318–19, 329–31, 338, 340–42

First Panzer Army, 45, 198, 232, 305, 309–10, 318
Second Army, 23, 27, 29, 39, 41–42, 51, 58, 63, 87, 98, 103, 127, 136, 143, 148, 184, 187, 200, 310
Fourth Panzer Army, 35–36, 43, 46–48, 57, 69–70, 79, 84, 93, 97, 100–2, 120, 122–25, 136, 181, 198, 232–33, 238–41, 247, 249–50, 269–70, 308–11, 335–36, 339–40, 500
Sixth Army, 8, 24, 31, 36, 47, 310, 318
Ninth Army, 27, 35–43, 53–66, 68–85, 91–93, 96–107, 112–13, 127–28, 131–32, 135–38, 140–43, 145–67, 187–94, 197–202, 213–22, 224–26, 229–30, 235–38, 255–57, 500–504
Seventeenth Army, 58, 70, 86–87, 305

German Groups & Corps

Group Esebeck, 191, 201, 206, 218–19, 226
Group Weiss, 58–59, 141, 147–48, 152, 180–82, 202, 237

II SS Panzer, 36, 51, 69, 117, 122-23, 184, 205, 225, 238–45, 247, 252, 270, 308, 311, 508
III Panzer, 69, 122, 238-39, 244, 247-50, 252, 326, 447, 462-63
XI, 251, 310
XX, 65, 72, 85, 148, 152, 155, 157, 160, 163, 193, 202, 206, 214, 236
XXIII, 59, 63, 74, 80, 85, 96, 151, 153, 164, 166, 193, 201-02, 223, 233-34, 236, 483, 490, 533
XXIV Panzer, 69
XXXV, 179, 193-94, 203
XXXXI Panzer, 42, 45, 63, 65, 80, 83, 85, 96–97, 100, 165–66, 223, 233–34, 236, 490, 492
XXXXVIII Panzer, 7, 45, 69, 123, 184, 220, 238–39, 241–44, 249, 252, 256
XXXXVI Panzer, 56, 59, 63–65, 96, 100, 164–65, 187, 189, 195, 197, 206, 208, 235–36
LII, 225, 240, 326

German Divisions

Infantry

4th 59
6th 41, 57, 66, 93, 100, 143, 160-61, 164-165, 167, 181, 201, 206, 210, 228, 230, 233-34
7th 41, 56, 59, 62, 65-66, 136, 138, 157, 165, 167, 187, 201, 206, 209, 228-29, 235, 483
18th 99
31st 160, 164-165, 167-68, 187, 195, 206, 209, 228, 235
36th 42, 57, 166, 181, 191-92, 201, 214, 228, 237
39th 240
40th 18
45th 41, 64, 148, 154-55, 201, 208
57th 185, 225, 240, 243
72nd 41, 62, 64, 72, 74, 81, 93, 201, 208
83rd 181
86th 41, 56, 63, 80-81, 166, 190, 201, 206, 212, 228, 233, 483
87th 42, 175
98th 57, 66, 138
102nd 41, 54, 61-62, 64, 66, 71, 93, 165, 206, 208, 219
106th 69, 225, 247
112th 181
137th 41, 64, 80, 154, 201-02, 207
161st 240
167th 225, 239, 242

168th 69, 204, 225, 247-48
181st 175
183rd 181
198th 225, 232
205th 175
206th 175
208th 100
216th 41, 56, 61, 63, 93, 201-02, 206, 213-14, 228, 234, 533
221st 136
241st 207
251st 41, 64, 80, 93, 154-155, 165, 201, 206, 209, 219, 229, 235
255th 224, 240, 243
258th 41, 56, 64, 154-155, 165, 201, 206, 209, 219, 229, 235
273rd 175
282nd 225, 240
291st 175
292nd 41, 56, 59, 65, 67, 74, 136, 166-67, 193, 201-202, 206, 212, 228, 233, 247
299th 61, 533
320th 69, 225
322nd 69, 240, 243
330th 175
383rd 41, 54, 56, 62-63, 155, 166, 189, 192-93, 201, 206, 213, 228, 234, 533
404th 59
407th 59
418th 59

Panzer

2nd 41, 44, 56, 63, 89, 93-94, 99, 112-113, 149-50, 155-56, 162, 164-65, 169, 201, 206, 210, 215, 218-20, 226, 228, 233, 501
3rd 42, 69, 95, 123-24, 185-87, 198, 225-26, 232, 242, 245-46, 308-09
4th 41, 56, 64, 76, 83, 93-94, 96, 99, 112, 136, 147, 151, 160, 162, 165, 167, 170, 206, 210, 218, 220, 226, 228, 230, 236-37, 313, 501
5th 42, 94, 181, 191, 218, 237
6th 95, 195, 225, 238-39, 244, 247-50, 308, 313, 501
7th 64, 95, 142, 225, 244, 247-48, 250, 308, 313
8th 42, 94, 112, 181, 191, 214, 218
9th 41, 56, 63, 89, 93, 99, 112, 150, 156, 162, 164-65, 171, 177-78, 193, 201, 206, 211, 218, 226, 228, 233, 308-09, 501
10th 211
11th 32, 69, 95, 185, 225, 238, 242, 244-46, 303, 313
12th 32, 41, 64-65, 93-94, 96, 112-13, 147, 156, 162, 164-65, 186-87, 191, 194, 201, 206, 213-15, 219, 226, 228, 236, 309, 483, 501

17th 69, 95
18th 41, 56, 93-94, 112, 132, 136, 138, 147, 162, 166, 198, 201, 206, 215, 219-20, 226, 228, 333, 483, 533
19th 69, 95, 225, 244, 247-48, 250
20th 41, 56, 63, 81, 93-94, 112, 151, 156, 160, 162, 165, 175, 195, 201, 205-06, 210, 218, 226, 228, 233, 483
23rd 95
25th 308-09
26th 309, 502
27th 308-09

10th *Panzergrenadier* 41, 44, 56, 63, 99, 113, 136, 147, 155-56, 160, 165, 167, 189, 191-92, 201, 206, 211, 228, 233, 265, 327

78th *Sturm* 62-63, 65-66, 72, 74, 81, 113, 166, 189, 201, 205-06, 212, 214-15, 228, 230, 234-35, 483

SS Leibstandarte 10, 69, 95, 225, 244-45, 269-70, 304, 313, 431
SS Das Reich 69, 95, 225, 244-45, 304, 313
SS Totenkopf 69, 95, 225, 244-45, 284, 304, 307, 313
SS Grossdeutschland 95, 123-24, 224, 242, 245-46, 313, 393
SS Wiking 308-09

3rd Mortar 242
12th Flak 100
21st *Fliegerdivision* 85, 103, 155

Soviet Fronts

Briansk Front, 27, 138, 281, 290–91, 295–96, 298, 345, 352, 518–19, 521–24, 540–41
Central Front, 66–67, 256–57, 290–91, 312–14, 321–23, 326, 332–34, 352–57, 359–60, 362–64, 366–68, 370–71, 378–80, 488–91, 494–501, 518, 523–24, 528–29, 539–40, 547–48
Reserve Front, 122, 281–82, 295–96, 504–5
Steppe Front, 45, 277, 292, 296–97, 443, 508, 520
Western Front, 35-36, 60, 109, 277, 290–91, 508, 517-20, 521, 523
Voronezh Front, 282–84, 286–87, 313–14, 325–29, 331–45, 347–50, 352–53, 367–70, 373–76, 418–19, 421–22, 431–36, 468–72, 486–89, 503–4, 506–11, 516–21, 524–26, 528–30

Soviet Armies

1st Air, 475-76, 479
1st Tank, 122, 184, 186, 237-39, 241-42, 325, 331, 333-34, 337-38, 340-43, 360-61, 375, 419, 432, 437, 475, 487, 499, 526
2nd Air, 163, 347-48, 476
2nd Tank, 257, 345, 352-53, 360-62, 412, 526-27
3rd, 352
5th Air, 296, 475, 505
6th Guards, 124, 237, 240-41, 253, 311-12, 325, 329-31, 333, 335-45, 370, 374-75, 388, 390, 393-94, 399, 422, 424-25, 428-29, 432-33, 435-38, 440-42, 445, 454, 461, 465-69, 472-73, 475, 496, 509
7th Guards, 248, 250, 253, 298, 325, 329-31, 335-40, 342, 375, 383, 388, 393, 399, 420, 422, 428, 432, 435, 437-52, 451-52, 454-60, 462-63, 465-69, 475, 487-88, 496, 509, 514
13th, 91-92, 153, 156-57, 166, 205-06, 214, 234, 257, 285, 332-34, 353-56, 359-61, 380, 386-90, 392, 396-415, 417, 443, 478, 486, 489-92, 494, 496-97, 499-500, 510-11, 514, 527
15th Air, 476, 479
16th Air, 137, 345, 352, 360, 475, 478
17th Air, 476
38th, 343, 353, 375, 419, 422, 428, 432, 435-37, 474, 489
40th, 284-85, 329, 333, 336, 338, 341-44, 375, 419, 428-29, 432, 435-38, 471-72, 489
48th, 91-92, 133, 153, 155, 166, 285, 353, 355, 359, 361, 399, 404, 408, 414, 416, 482, 484, 486, 489-90, 513-14, 533-34
60th, 154, 287, 352-53, 356, 404
61st, 521-23
63rd, 377, 521
65th, 65, 147-49, 153-54, 156, 285, 345, 352-53, 356, 386-87
69th, 324, 331, 333-34, 337-41, 428, 432-33, 437-38, 440, 445, 455, 469, 486-89, 513, 526
70th, 92, 154, 234-35, 285, 322, 345, 353, 355-56, 359, 361-62, 372, 380, 385-90, 392-99, 401, 405, 408, 412, 416, 449, 492, 496-97

RLA (Russian Liberation Army), 176–77

Soviet Corps

2nd Cavalry, 296
3rd Cavalry, 296
3rd Tank, 234, 257, 360
5th Cavalry, 290, 296
5th Guards Mechanized Corps, 122, 507-8
6th Cavalry, 296
6th Tank, 122

7th Cavalry, 296
9th Tank, 72, 353, 360-62
15th Rifle, 409
16th Tank, 257, 360, 527
17th Guards Rifle, 401, 403, 408, 411
18th Guards Rifle, 334, 359, 360, 401, 411
19th Guards Cavalry, 352
19th Tank, 257, 352, 359-60, 362
23rd Guards Rifle, 424, 454
24th Guards Rifle, 441, 447, 450, 457-58, 462
25th Guards Rifle, 441, 447, 450, 454, 462, 466-67, 469
28th Rifle, 395-96, 398, 401
35th Guards Rifle, 331, 333-34, 341, 369, 420, 434, 486-87
52nd, 343

Soviet Divisions

Airborne

3rd 417

Anti-Aircraft

24th 353

Artillery

5th 257
7th 492
12th 257

Cavalry

8th 252
51st 252

Destroyer (Anti-Tank Artillery)

2nd 352

Fighter Aviation

234th 475
283rd 553-54
288th 481
315th 480

Ground Attack Aviation

225th 480
290th 163
292nd 545

Guards Airborne

4th 401

Guards Rifle

6th 352-53, 401, 403, 425
7th 438, 487
15th 372, 398, 401, 408-10, 412, 414, 441-42, 455, 458-61, 465, 469
16th 484-85, 529, 533, 544
36th 441, 447, 450, 458-62, 467-68
51st 425, 437, 465, 372
52nd 284-85, 307, 335-37, 419, 422, 424-25, 429, 431, 433-36, 465-66, 473
67th 335, 337, 393, 419, 422, 429, 431, 433, 436, 472-73
71st 419, 423, 436
72nd 441-42, 459, 462-63, 467, 514
73rd 414, 439, 441, 450, 452, 454, 468, 485-86
75th 401
78th 441, 450, 462-68
81st 339, 372, 388, 401, 403, 408-10, 441-42, 445, 447, 452-56, 465-68, 510
89th 437
90th 437, 465
92nd 434, 455
95th 555
210th 423
375th 335, 339, 368, 388, 419, 422, 425, 431, 436, 454, 465, 468, 472

Rifle

8th 401, 403, 410, 412, 417
19th 468
41st 377
42nd 352
70th 352
74th 401, 403, 409, 411, 414-15
102nd 387-88, 394-95, 387
106th 387-88, 394-96
107th 409, 433, 455, 487
111th 487
112th 352
132nd 386-88, 396, 398
137th 485-86
140th 372, 388, 397
143rd 485, 533
147th 485
148th 401, 410, 412
160th 323
162nd 388
175th 388
211th 386-88

213th 438, 441, 450, 460-61, 464, 487
229th 417
258th 371, 373
270th 458, 487
280th 386-88, 396, 416
305th 433, 455, 487
307th 401, 403, 411, 510
354th 558
399th 414-15, 485